MICROCOMPUTERS

Business and Personal Applications

MICROCOMPUTERS

Business and Personal Applications

James R. Burns, TEXAS TECH UNIVERSITY

Darrell N. Eubanks, SINECURE SYSTEMS, INC.

WEST PUBLISHING COMPANY

St. Paul • New York • Los Angeles • San Francisco

Copyediting: Chris Thillen
Designer: Wendy Calmenson
Compositor: Graphic Typesetting Service
Cover photo: Don Carroll/The Image Bank

Library of Congress
Library of Congress Cataloging-in-Publication Data

Burns, James R.
Microcomputers : business and personal applications / James R. Burns, Darrell N. Eubanks.
p. cm.
Includes bibliographies and index.
ISBN 0-314-93159-7
1. Microcomputers. I. Eubanks, Darrell N. II. Title.
QA76.5.B84 1988
004.16--dc19 87-31027
CIP

Trademarks

Apple, Apple II LaserWriter, Lisa, MacDraw, Macintosh, MacWrite, and the Apple logo are registered trademarks of Apple Computer, Inc.
Bernoulli Box is a trademark of Iomega Corporation.
COMMODORE 64® and PET® are registered trademarks of Commodore Electronics Limited.
COMPAQ, COMPAQ DESKPRO 386, and COMPAQ PORTABLE 286 are trademarks of Compaq Computer Corporation.
CompuServe Information Service is a registered trademark of CompuServe, Inc.
CP/M and GEM are registered trademarks of Digital Research, Inc.
dBase III and dBase III Plus are registered trademarks of Ashton-Tate.
DEC and VAX are registered trademarks of Digital Equipment Corporation.
Dow-Jones News/Retrieval is a registered trademark of Dow-Jones & Company, Inc.
Hayes Smartmodem and Smartcom II are trademarks of Hayes Microcomputer Products, Inc.
IBM, IBM PC, IBM XT, IBM AT, IBM Personal System/2, and TopView are registered trademarks of International Business Machines Corporation.
Intel and Intel Above Board are registered trademarks of Intel Corporation.
Lotus, 1-2-3, Symphony, and Metro are registered trademarks of Lotus Development Corporation.
MC6800 is a trademark of Motorola, Inc.
MicroPro and WordStar are registered trademarks of MicroPro International Corporation.
Microsoft, MS-DOS, Microsoft Windows, Microsoft WORD, Multiplan, and Microsoft Excel are registered trademarks of Microsoft Corporation.
MindSight and IFPS are registered trademarks of Execucom, Inc.
Multimate and Multimate Advantage are registered trademarks of Multimate International, an Ashton-Tate company.
MultiSpeed and MultiSync are trademarks of NEC Home Electronics (USA) Inc.
PageMaker is a trademark of Aldus Corporation.
PC–Write is a trademark of Quicksoft.
PFS:File and PFS:Write are trademarks of Software Publishing Corporation.

(continued following index)

About the Authors

James R. Burns is a Professor of Management Science and Management Information Systems at Texas Tech University, where he has taught information systems courses since 1973. A native of Colorado, he earned his B.S. degree with honors from the University of Colorado. As a graduate student, he attended the University of Washington. As a graduate assistant, he taught courses at Purdue University. He received his M.S. and Ph.D. degrees from Purdue where he was an NSF fellow.

For several years Dr. Burns taught professional development seminars on microcomputers in ten of the largest cities in the southwestern United States. It was out of this experience that the present book developed.

Dr. Burns is an active scholar. He is coauthor of *Management Science: An Aid for Managerial Decision Making,* and *Management Science Models and the Microcomputer,* both published by Macmillan in 1985. A noted expert in methodologies for modeling and simulation, he has long been interested in methodological approaches for computer-related activities, be they writing, developing a worksheet model, or designing a specific relational data model. This book reflects his current thinking about these productivity methodologies. He has published over thirty-five different articles on topics as diverse as decision support systems and national energy modeling. These works are published in the following journals: *IEEE Transactions on Systems, Man, and Cybernetics; Management Science; Technological Forecasting and Social Change; Database; International Journal of Systems Science;* and *Socio-economic Planning Systems.*

Dr. Burns has consulted with Texas Instruments, Inc., White Sands Missile Range, Sandia Laboratories, and Los Alamos National Laboratories. His current interests include microcomputer applications, knowledge-based simulation, and mathematical programming.

Darrell Eubanks graduated *summa cum laude* from Eastern New Mexico University in 1978 with a dual major in psychology and religion. His master's work was in psychology, also at ENMU. He began the Ph.D. program in management information systems at Texas Tech University in 1982. In 1984–85 he held the graduate fellowship from the Business School's Center for Professional Development.

In 1983 Mr. Eubanks formed Sinecure Systems in order to pursue computer consulting work. Mr. Eubanks is the developer and chief programmer of two industry-leading oil and gas accounting and asset management programs marketed nationally under the RoyaltyWare label. Sinecure Systems is currently working on programs for income tracking and reporting for bank trust departments and for physical resource management for municipalities.

Mr. Eubanks' research interests include expert systems information collection, organizational change during automation, and automated tools for systems design.

To my beloved wife, Marilu, and my two children Marianne and Rebekah

JRB

To my beloved wife, Jan, and my two children Gail and Timothy

DNB

Contents

Preface xxi

PART I INTRODUCTION TO MICROCOMPUTERS 2

CHAPTER 1 THE WORLD OF MICROCOMPUTERS 4

Microcomputers Defined 5
History of Microcomputer Development 8
The Microcomputer and the Contemporary Office 11
Why Are Microcomputers Moving In? 11
Contemporary Uses of Microcomputers 12

Applications in Business and the Professions 14
Word Processing 15
Electronic Spreadsheets 15
Data Base Management Systems 16
Miscellaneous Applications 16
Integrated Applications 17
Accounting Applications 17

The Microcomputer and the Office of the Future 17
The Microcomputer and the Immediate Future 18
Possible Disbenefits from Microcomputer Use 19
Where to Get Additional Information 21
Summary 21; Key Terms 22; Self-Test 22; Exercises 22; References 23; Additional Reading 23

CHAPTER 2 **GETTING ACQUAINTED WITH MICROCOMPUTERS 26**

Components of Microcomputer Systems 27

Input Devices 27

Output Devices 27

Central Processing Unit 30

Secondary Storage 31

System Software 32

Applications Software 34

Classifying Microcomputers According to Form 34

Focus Feature *A Typical Computer Session: How It Goes* 38

User Interfaces 44

Directives: Commands and Menus and Icons 44

User Prompts, Default Settings, and Such 47

Care of Your Computer 47

Selecting a Site for the Computer 47

Other Considerations Relating to Care of Your Computer 48

Care of Floppy Disks and the Files Contained on Them 48

Making Backups 50

Summary 51; Key Terms 51; Self-Test 52; Exercises 52; Additional Reading 54

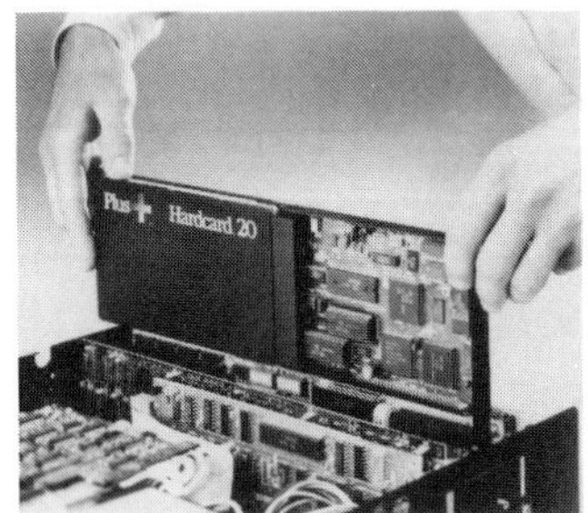

CHAPTER 3 **HARDWARE FOR MICROCOMPUTERS 55**

Printed Circuit Board and Printed Circuit Cards 56

Microprocessor 58

Primary Storage 59

Secondary Storage 61

Floppy Disks 61

Hard Disks 63

RAM Disks 65

Removable Magnetic Disk Storage 65

Optical Disk Storage 66

Focus Feature *Factors Affecting Processing Speed of the Microcomputer* 68

Cartridge Tape 70

Displays 71

Keyboards 74

Printers 76

Focus Feature *Printers: Up Close and Personal* 78

Other Devices for Input/Output 80

Ports and External Interfaces 82

Summary 82; Key Terms 83; Self-Test 84; Exercises 84; Cases 86; Additional Reading 86

CHAPTER 4 SYSTEM SOFTWARE AND OPERATING SYSTEMS 87

A Few Definitions 88

Operating Systems 89

The Console Command Processor 90

The Input/Output System 90

Focus Feature *Humble Beginnings. . . .* 91

Focus Feature *Operating System Compatibility Issues* 92

Single-user, Multiuser, and Multitasking Operating Systems 94

CP/M, MS-DOS, UNIX, UNIX Work-alikes, Macintosh, and Lisa Operating Systems 95

Focus Feature *The Evolution of DOS* 96

Applications Environments 101

Language Translators 102

Assembly Language 102

BASIC 103

Pascal and Modula-2 105

Focus Feature *What Is Structured Programming, and Why Is It Preferred?* 105

C 106

FORTH 108

Utility Programs 110

Focus Feature *Description of Utility Programs Available* 110

Advanced Features of Operating Systems 111

Summary 113; Key Terms 114; Self-Test 114; Exercises 115; Additional Reading 115

MS-DOS Tutorial 116

Exercises 123

Disk Exercises 124

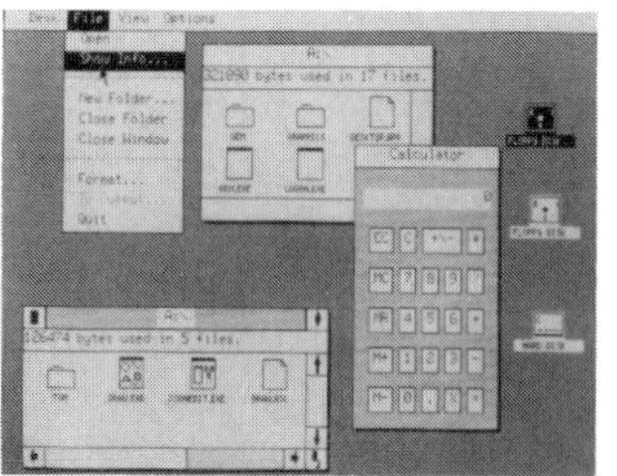

PART II PRODUCTIVITY TOOLS 126

CHAPTER 5 WORD PROCESSING CONCEPTS 128

A Bit of History 129

Business and Personal Uses for Word Processors 131

Word Processing for Business 131
Word Processing for Writers and Academics 132
Focus Feature *The Processed Word* 133
Word Processing for Students 133
Text Processing for Programmers 134

Software Concepts and Design Philosophies 134
Ease of Learning vs. Power 135
Other Word Processing Considerations 137
Word Processing Features 139
Focus Feature *Customizing a Word Processor* 140
Focus Feature *About Spelling, Grammar, and Style Checkers* 144
The Bottom Line 146

Using a Word Processor: An Overview 146
Focus Feature *Toward Better Writing and Composition* 148

Hardware and Software Requirements for Word Processing 150
Focus Feature *The Future of Word Processing?* 151
Summary 153; Key Terms 153; Self-Test 154; Exercises 154; Additional Reading 155

CHAPTER 6 WORD PROCESSING MECHANICS 157

The Screen Display 158
Split Screens and Windows 159

The Printed Page 159
Typing, Editing, and Revising Text 161
Document Navigation 162
Correcting Typos: Insertion vs. Type-over 162
Reforming Paragraphs 162
Block Manipulation 163
Writing and Reading Files 164
Block Column Move Operations 164
Using Find and Replace 165
Saving the Document 167
Of Libraries and Macros 167

Formatting and Printing Text 168
Default Format Settings 169
Focus Feature *Mechanics of Enhancers* 170
Saving Formats 172
Page Formats 172

Line and Paragraph Formats 174
Character Formats 175
Print Options 175
Background Printing 176
Print Queues 176
Printing to a Disk File 177
Printing in Columns 177
Merge Printing 177
Of Footnotes, Indexes and Tables of Contents 178
Focus Feature *Desktop Publishing* 180

Classifying and Characterizing Existing Word Processing Programs 182
Microsoft Word 184
WordPerfect 184
Multimate Advantage 185
PC Write 186
MacWrite 187
Summary 187; Key Terms 188; Self-Test 189; Exercises 189; Additional Reading 190
WordStar Tutorial 191
Exercises 199
Disk Exercises 200
WordPerfect Tutorial 202
Exercises 215
Disk Exercises 215

CHAPTER 7 SPREADSHEET CONCEPTS 216

Some Definitions 218
A Brief History of Spreadsheet Programs 219
Business and Personal Uses for Spreadsheet Programs 221
Software Concepts and Design Philosophies 224
A Spreadsheet's Internal Operations 225
Spreadsheet Speed 226
Focus Feature *Spreadsheet Size and Memory Management* 228

Using a Spreadsheet Program: An Overview 229
Focus Feature *Financial Modeling Programs* 230
Determine the Purpose 230
Synthesize a Well-Conceived Title 231
Specify Date and Authorship 232
Determine Independent and Dependent Variables 232

Layout the Worksheet on Scratch Paper 232
Enter Labels, Independent Variables, and Values 233
Enter Base Formulas 233
Copy Base Formulas 233
Focus Feature *A Few Spreadsheet Caveats* 234
Adjust Format [Global and Local] and Column Width 234
Verify and Validate the Worksheet 234
Document the Worksheet 235
Develop the Necessary Graphics 235
Perform "What-if" Analyses 236
Print the Required Outputs 236

Hardware and Software Requirements for Spreadsheet Programs 236

Summary 237; Key Terms 238; Self-Test 238; Exercises 238; Additional Reading 240

CHAPTER 8 SPREADSHEET MECHANICS 241

Typing, Editing, and Revising the Worksheet 242
Loading the Spreadsheet Program 242
The Worksheet Display 242
Cell and Range Specification 244
Worksheet Navigation and Entry 245
Command Entry 246
Entering Formulas and Functions 248
Copying and Moving Worksheet Information 248
Editing the Worksheet 253
Creating Windows 254

Formatting and Printing Worksheets 255
Format Settings 256
Adjusting Column Widths 257
Saving Formats 257
Print Options 257

Operators and Functions 259
Precedence Order of Operations 259
Functions 261

Building Worksheets for Use by Others 265
Templates 266
Hiding and Protecting Cells 266

Macros and Macro Languages 266
Creating Menus 267
Creating Forms 267

File Management and Operations 267
Saving and Retrieving Files 268
ASCII and Print Files 268
Merging (Importing) Files 269
Combining Files 269
File Interchanges with Other Programs 269

Classifying and Characterizing Existing Spreadsheet Programs 270
Microsoft Multiplan 270
Microsoft Excel 271
Javelin 272
SuperCalc4 274
Summary 274; Key Terms 275; Self-Test 276; Exercises 276; Additional Reading 277
Lotus 1-2-3 Tutorial 278
Exercises 308
Disk Exercises 309
Microsoft Excel Tutorial 312

CHAPTER 9 RECORD AND FILE MANAGEMENT SYSTEMS 319

Record and File Management Systems Defined 320
Organization of Data Files 320

The History of Record and File Management Systems 321
Focus Feature *Manual versus Computerized File Operations* 323

Business and Personal Uses for Record and File Management Systems 326

Software Concepts and Design Philosophies 329
File Management System Categories 329
The User Interface 329
File Management System Features 330
Focus Feature *Methods of Searching for Records Within Files* 332

Using a File Management System 333
Planning the Records 333
Creating the Records 335
Entering, Inserting or Appending Records 336

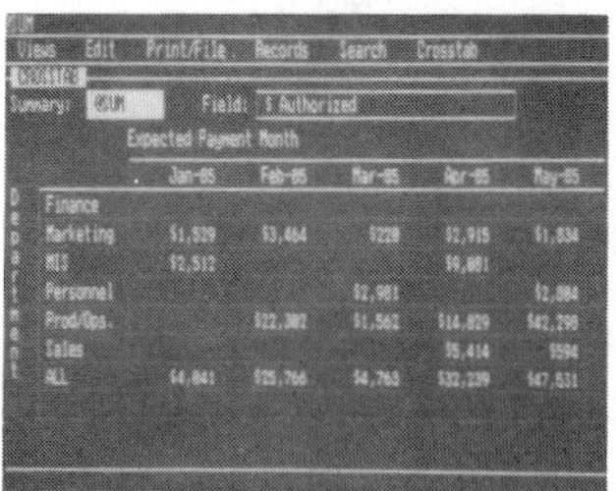

Searching for Particular Records 337
Editing and Deleting Records 338
Sorting and Indexing Records 338
Generating Reports 339
Focus Feature *Using a Spreadsheet like Lotus 1-2-3 as a Flatfile Manager* 340

Hardware and Software Requirements for File Management Systems 340

Summary 340; Key Terms 342; Self-Test 342; Exercises 342; References 342; Additional Reading 342

Lotus 1-2-3 File Management Tutorial 343
Exercises 348
Disk Exercises 348

CHAPTER 10 DATA BASE MANAGEMENT SYSTEMS 349

Data Base Management Systems Defined 350
The History of Data Base Management Systems 352
Business and Personal Uses for a Data Base Management System 353
Software Concepts and Design Philosophies 353
DBMS Categories 353
Focus Feature *Select, Project, and Join* 354
The User Interface 357
DBMS Features 359

Using a Data Base Management System 361
Focus Feature *AI Meets DB* 362
Planning the Data Base 362
Creating the Data Base 365
Adding or Appending Records 367
Editing Existing Records 367
Sorting and Indexing Files 367
Searching for Particular Records 367
Generating Reports 368

Hardware and Software Requirements for Data Base Management Systems 369

Summary 370; Key Terms 371; Self-Test 371; Exercises 371; References 372; Additional Reading 373; Publications 373

dBASE III and dBASE III Plus Tutorial 374
Exercises 390
Disk Exercises 390

CHAPTER 11 **GRAPHICS APPLICATIONS AND INTEGRATED SOFTWARE PACKAGES 391**

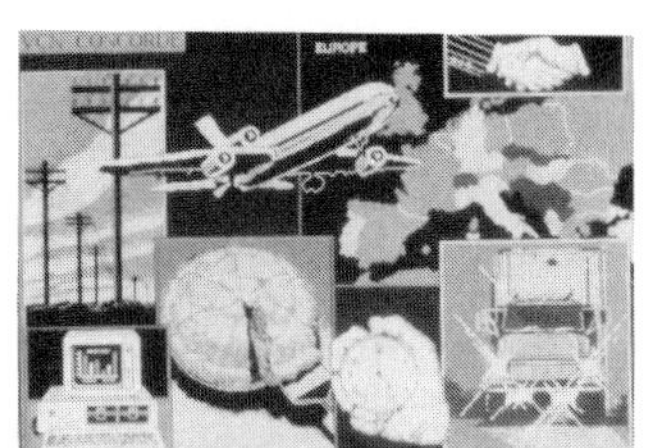

Graphics 392

Graphics Applications 392

Types of Charts and Graphs, and Their Uses 394

Analytic versus Presentation Graphics 394

Graphics Software 396

Hardware Required for Graphics 398

Integrated Software Packages 402

A Definition of Integrated Software 403

Why Integrated Software? 403

Goals of Integrated Software Packages 404

Features of Integrated Software 405

Software Concepts and Design Philosophies 406

Advantages/Disadvantages of Integrated Software 407

All-in-one Integrated Software Packages 408

Integrating Environment Packages 409

Hardware Required to Support Integrated Software 409

Summary 410; Key Terms 410; Self-Test 410; Exercises 410; References 410; Additional Reading 410

Lotus 1-2-3 Graphics Tutorial 412

Exercises 418

Disk Exercises 418

PART III ADDITIONAL CONCEPTS AND APPLICATIONS 420

CHAPTER 12 **OTHER POPULAR SOFTWARE FOR BUSINESS AND PERSONAL USE 422**

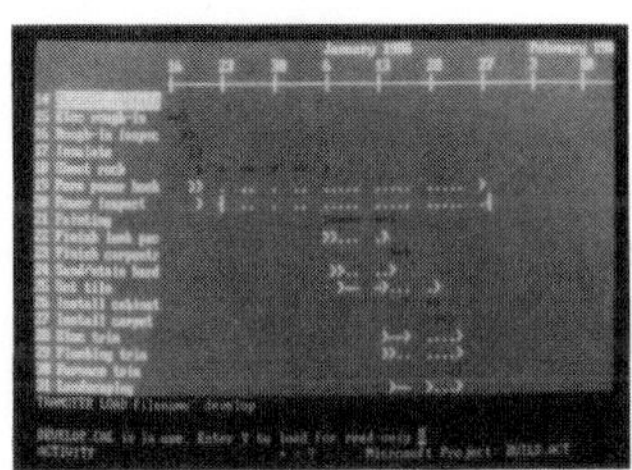

Desk Organizers 423

Background and Concepts of Desk Organizers 424

Desk Organizer Features 425

Other Desk Organizer Features 429

More on Memory-Resident Utilities 430

Project Management Software 431

Project Planning Definitions 433

Using Project Management Software 434

Entering Activity Information 435

Determining the Critical Path 435

Project Management Reports 437

Types and Features of Project Management Software 439

Expert Systems 440

History of Expert Systems 441

Expert Systems and Knowledge Bases 442

Structure of Expert Systems 443

Building Expert Systems 444

Displays Produced by Expert System Shells 445

Current Vendors of Expert System Shells 446

Decision Support Systems (DSS) 446

Anatomy of Decision Support System Generators 448

Software Features of Decision Support System Generators 449

Vendors of Decision Support System Generators 451

Summary 451; Key Terms 452; Self-Test 453; Exercises 453; References 454; Additional Reading 454

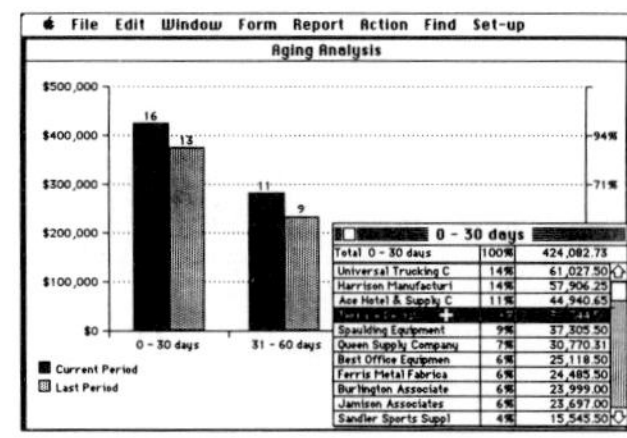

CHAPTER 13 INTEGRATED ACCOUNTING AND INVENTORY SYSTEMS 456

Accounting Systems Defined 457

A History of Accounting Systems 459

Business and Personal Uses of Accounting Systems 459

Software Concepts and Design Philosophies 460

Microcomputer Systems Accounting Software Vendors 460

General Ledger: The Heart of an Integrated Accounting System 461

Accounts Receivable Systems 467

Accounts Receivable System Objectives 469

Accounts Receivable Concepts and Design Philosophies 469

Focus Feature *Selecting and Installing an Accounting System* 470

Procedural and Structural Overview 472

Accounts Receivable Data Entry 473

Reports 474

Accounts Receivable Features 478

Accounts Payable Systems 479

Accounts Payable System Objectives 479

Procedural Overview 479

Focus Feature *Home Accounting Software Packages* 482

Data Entry Screens 482

Reports 482

Accounts Payable Features 484

Inventory Management Systems 486

Sales Inventory Systems 486

Inventory Systems for Manufacturers 487

Hardware and Software Requirements for Accounting 487

Summary 488; Key Terms 489; Self-Test 489; Exercises 489; References 490; Additional Reading 490

CHAPTER 14 DATA COMMUNICATIONS 492

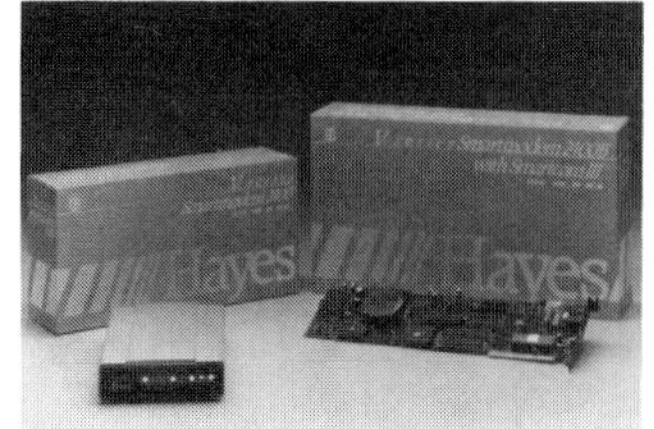

Why Communicate? 493

Types of Data Communication 493

Wide Area Networks 494

Focus Feature *Working for the Home Office* 494

Focus Feature *Are You Secure?* 496

Local Area Networks 497

Remote Processing Systems 497

Peripheral Communications 499

The Components of Data Communications 499

Ports and Interfaces 500

Communication Channels 502

The Data Communications Message 507

Communications Software 510

Information Utilities and Bulletin Board Systems 511

Summary 517; Key Terms 518; Self-Test 519; Exercises 519; Additional Reading 520

CHAPTER 15 LOCAL AREA NETWORKS 521

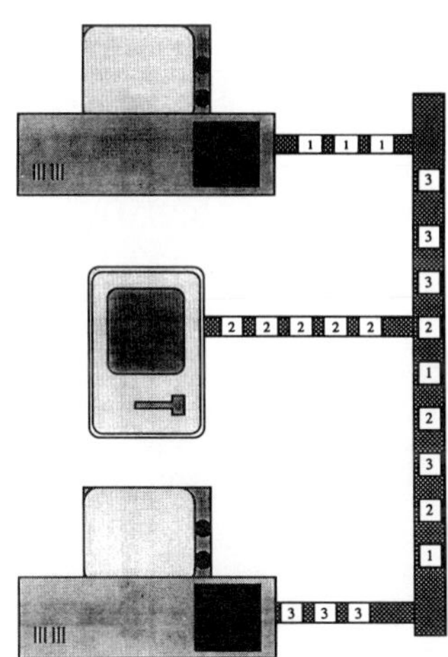

LANs Defined and Depicted 522

Advantages/Functions of Local Area Networks 522

Local Area Network Topologies 524

Local Area Network Media 526

Focus Feature *Multiuser Systems* 526

Local Area Network Architectures 528

The PBX Exchange 528

Broadband LANs 529

Baseband LANs 532

Specialized Nodes 535

Software Considerations 537

Summary 538; Key Terms 539; Self-Test 539; Exercises 539; Case 539; References 539; Additional Reading 539

CHAPTER 16 MICROCOMPUTER PURCHASE CONSIDERATIONS 542

Software Purchase Considerations 543

Make versus Buy Decisions 544

Focus Feature *About Custom Software Development Projects* 544

A Methodology for Selecting Software 546

Focus Feature *Of Vendor Support* 550

Of Protection and Piracy 554

System Purchase Considerations 555

Focus Feature *Capacity Requirements Planning* 556

Weight Determination 563

Grading Vendor Proposals 563

After-Tax, Net-Present-Value Analysis of Proposed Cost 564

Relating the After-Tax Present-Value Cost to the Grade 567

Summary 568; Key Terms 569; Self-Test 570; Exercises 570; References 573; Additional Reading 573

Checklist 575

Glossary 597

Index 607

Preface

In recent years, we have witnessed the proliferation of the microcomputer in virtually every sector of business and personal life. Hence, knowledge of microcomputer operations and applications has become essential to successfully using this new appliance.

A 1986 issue of *Fortune Magazine* suggested that although the corporate world has spent billions on microcomputer hardware and software, it has realized very little in the way of improved productivity. One explanation for this situation is the manifest need for training in the use of microcomputers. It was out of this need that this book was created. This book is not only for aspiring students of business and the professions; it is also for people who are interested in microcomputers for personal use. To serve both needs, this book provides a thorough, yet comprehensible treatment of the subject.

In the past few years, courses in microcomputer use have sprung up in colleges and universities throughout this country and in most of the Western world. This book has been written for use as a text in these varied courses. Students in microcomputer courses want lots of hands-on training and experience in the use of word processing, spreadsheet, and data base and file management programs. This text is intended to give that to them. At the same time, these students want broad coverage of each major microcomputer topical area, so they will know generally what to expect when approaching the use of microcomputer hardware and software. They want to be conceptually familiar with the software, so the microcomputer is not just a black box to them. And they want to know what features and facilities are generally available in microcomputer hardware and software. These are among the content goals toward which this book has been developed.

A MESSAGE TO THE INSTRUCTOR

This book is intended for use in the CIS-1 and CIS-2 courses in the established DBMA CURRICULUM '86. The text is, in general, appropriate for introductory courses on microcomputers.

In creating this text, several objectives were used to guide its design:

1. breadth (*and depth*) of coverage;
2. balanced presentation of concepts and mechanics, principles and practice;
3. opportunities for hands-on (*active*) learning of the best-selling and most widely used microcomputer software;
4. an effective pedagogical approach;
5. ease of comprehension; and
6. useful supplements.

Breadth and Depth of Coverage

This text covers a broad range of subjects. In addition to the usual topics (hardware, system software, word processing, spreadsheets, file and data base management, graphics, and communications), this text covers desk organizers, expert systems, decision support systems, project management systems, accounting systems, local area networks, and selection/implementation of hardware/software.

The reader will find that this text covers its subjects in depth as well. In-depth coverage usually appears in the form of special readings, or as they are called in the text, Focus Features. The following Focus Features are included:

A Typical Computer Session: How It Goes

Factors Affecting Processing Speed of the Microcomputer

Printers: Up Close and Personal

Humble Beginnings . . .

Operating System Compatibility Issues

The Evolution of DOS

What Is Structured Programming, and Why Is It Preferred?

Description of Utility Programs Available

The Processed Word

Customizing a Word Processor

About Spelling, Grammar, and Style Checkers

The Future of Word Processing

Toward Better Writing and Composition

Mechanics of Enhancers

Desktop Publishing

Spreadsheet Size and Memory Management

Financial Modeling Programs

A Few Spreadsheet Caveats

Manual versus Computerized File Operations

Methods of Searching for Records from Files

Using a Spreadsheet Like Lotus 1-2-3 as a Flatfile Manager

Select, Project, and Join

AI Meets DB

Selecting and Installing an Accounting System

Home Accounting Software Packages

Working for the Home Office

Are You Secure?

Multiuser Systems

About Custom Software Development Projects

Of Vendor Support

Capacity Requirements Planning

These articles expand on and deepen the students' understanding of the book's main text.

Balanced Emphasis on Concepts and Mechanics, Principles and Practice

The substance of this book is meant to give students a strong conceptual understanding of

what the functions of a hardware component or software application are; and

what features and facilities to expect in that hardware component or software application.

This kind of knowledge makes learning to use any specific hardware component or software application package far easier.

This text also describes how to use microcomputer hardware and software and their applications. The mechanics of use has an importance equal to that of concepts in this text. The text describes such mechanics in general, except in the tutorials. Students need to know generally how to load an application, how to open and read in a previously created file, how to edit or append work to the file, how to save the file at the end of the session, and how to print the file. The tutorials deal specifically with the mechanics of a popular software package.

We have endeavored to place equal importance on concepts and state-of-the-art mechanics. The concepts are the most enduring as the technology continually undergoes improvement and change, thereby changing the mechanics of interaction. Too much emphasis on the mechanics of any one software package can be undesirable because the package will eventually become technologically obsolete. Nevertheless, the mechanics reinforce the concepts. Both are needed. The approach of this book is to teach concepts first, to reinforce concepts with mechanics, and to solidify concepts and mechanics with hands-on tutorials. Without the tutorials, the learning experience would be devoid of reality—like taking a driver-education class that provided no hands-on driving experience. Before the hands-on experience can be had, however, there must be a fundamental understanding of concepts and mechanics. All three are needed to create a total learning experience.

Balancing MS-DOS (PC-DOS) with the Macintosh. Because so many of the texts implicitly emphasize MS-DOS with their coverage of hardware and software, this text endeavors to strike a balance between the two major systems. Many of the screens and illustrations are taken from Macintosh software. Both user interfaces are described and delineated in detail.

Opportunities for Hands-on (*Active*) Learning

In order to meet the demands of the goal of hands-on, active learning, seven extensive tutorials have been included:

MS-DOS

WordStar

WordPerfect

1-2-3 spreadsheet

1-2-3 file and record management

1-2-3 graphics

Excel

These tutorials give students a hands-on learning experience of state-of-the-art software packages. Many exercises have been written into the tutorials, including disk exercises. Disk exercises are a unique feature described under "Pedagogical Approach to Each Chapter."

Pedagogical Approach to Each Chapter

Each chapter begins with an outline and stated objectives. Each chapter concludes with a summary, key terms, self-test questions, exercises, references, and, in some cases, additional reading. Some chapters are followed by a tutorial on a leading applications software package such as WordStar, WordPerfect, Lotus' 1-2-3, or dBASE III Plus. The tutorials are followed by exercises and disk exercises. Each component has an important role in the students' learning process. For example, the outline gives students a visual picture of the entire contents of the chapter, so they can grasp its structure without having to leaf through each page of the chapter. The stated objectives describe what is to be learned. The summary restates and reinforces important concepts within the chapter. The key terms enable students to ascertain if they comprehend important terms (and hence, concepts). The self-test questions help students ascertain if they have achieved the stated objectives of the chapter. The exercises are intended as homework, and require a deeper inspection of the material in the chapter and its subsequent interpretation and application. The additional reading suggests to students some books and articles containing material relevant to the chapter. Thus the pedagogical format of each chapter is as follows:

Brief chapter outline

Chapter objectives

{Main body of the chapter}

Chapter summary

Definitions

Self-test

Exercises

References

Additional Reading

Tutorial
Tutorial exercises
Disk exercises

The tutorials are followed by ordinary exercises and disk exercises. Ordinary exercises involve the use of the application package in some way—perhaps to enter and edit some text, or to formulate a spreadsheet model or a data base. The disk exercises involve the use of data files contained on the work disk that comes with this text. To perform these exercises, the application software must be accessible.

Ease of Comprehension

Over a period of two years, the material in this text was tested in classrooms at Texas Tech University for comprehensibility and readability. Technically difficult concepts have been carefully articulated and illustrated for the utmost in reader usability.

Superior Supplements

Several other features distinguish this book as unique.

Detailed Checklists. At the end of the text is a section containing extensive checklists for every major hardware component and software application. Students can use the checklist to discriminately evaluate specific hardware components and software systems. These checklists used together with the methodology discussed in Chapter 16, provide students with a complete package for selecting and implementing hardware and software.

Ancillaries. No textbook is complete in itself. So it is with this book, which is accompanied by an extensive instuctor's manual consisting of the following for each chapter:

Chapter objectives
Key terms and concepts
Detailed chapter outline
Answers to all exercises at the end of each chapter
A test bank of multiple-choice and essay questions

Transparency masters are also available as an additional supplement.

ORGANIZATION OF THE TEXT

This text is organized into three parts:

Part I: Introduction to Microcomputers
Part II: Productivity Tools
Part III: Additional Concepts and Applications

Part I. Part I is concerned first with the world of microcomputers, as discussed in Chapter 1. The world of microcomputers is the real world of today and tomorrow. Microcomputers are pervasive now and will be even more so in the future.

That discussion is followed by a description of the most tangible component: the hardware of microcomputers, carried in Chapters 2 and 3 of the text. Chapter 2 is really an introduction to the microcomputer *system,* since the chapter presents an overview of the hardware *and software* of microcomputers.

The system software of microcomputers is described in Chapter 4, which also touches upon computer languages used by microcomputers. Chapter 4 is followed by an extensive tutorial on MS-DOS.

Part II. Part II describes the managerial productivity tools: word processing, spreadsheets, file and data base management, and graphics. These topics are presented in Chapters 5 through 11, together with accompanying tutorials and appendixes. Most of the content of this part is concerned with software in one form or another.

Chapters 5 and 6 are specifically concerned with the word processing software. Chapter 5 deals specifically with word processing concepts. Chapter 6 is concerned with the mechanics of word processor usage. Following Chapter 6 are tutorials on WordStar and WordPerfect.

Chapters 7 and 8 take a thorough look at electronic spreadsheets. As was the case for the word processing chapters, Chapter 7 deals with concepts while Chapter 8 describes the mechanics of spreadsheets. Chapter 8 is followed by spreadsheet tutorials on Lotus 1-2-3 and Microsoft Excel.

Chapters 9 and 10 discuss file and data base management systems and their uses. Chapter 9 is followed by a tutorial depicting the file management capabilities of Lotus 1-2-3.

Chapter 11 discusses graphics and integrated productivity software packages. Chapter 11 is followed by a tutorial that illustrates the graphics capabilities of Lotus 1-2-3.

Part III. Part III presents additional applications and concepts in Chapters 12 through 16.

Chapter 12 covers desk organizers (such as electronic calendars, electronic appointment books, electronic calculators, and other articles that cover a typical desktop), project management software, expert systems, and decision support systems (software systems to support decision making and advise decision makers).

Chapter 13 is specifically concerned with accounting and inventory packages, two very commonplace applications of microcomputers in small businesses.

Two chapters (Chapters 14 and 15) deal with data communications and networks. The final chapter (Chapter 16) presents methods for purchasing additional hardware and software.

A MESSAGE TO THE STUDENT

To the user of this text, expect a fascinating and delightful learning experience in your studies of the material in this book. This book was designed to serve your needs as both a student and a professional. Upon completion of the course for which this book is a text, please think of this book as a reference book, a repository of knowledge to which you can refer again and again. Having used the book as a text, you will find it becomes even more valuable because you know where to go to look up forgotten information. Upon completion of your study of this text, you should be able to

- understand the jargon, acronyms, and terms used in conjunction with microcomputers; you will be able to distinguish RAM from ROM, ROM from RFP; and you will be able to define CPU, CRT, and CP/M;
- use some of today's most popular information-related productivity tools;
- understand and be aware of what features are generally available in the major productivity applications of microcomputers; and
- select the significant hardware and software components that will effectively enable you to meet the information challenges of today and tomorrow.

We wish you the very best in all your endeavors. We believe that this book will significantly contribute to your understanding of microcomputer hardware and software. It will also develop your microcomputer-related skills in ways that will contribute significantly to your information-processing productivity throughout your life.

ACKNOWLEDGMENTS

The writing of any textbook is an exercise of tremendous magnitude, an undertaking of considerable proportions. It doesn't happen without the efforts of many more people than just two. We wish to take this opportunity to thank all who have labored with us through the several years this project was under way. We are especially indebted to the following reviewers for their forthright comments, concerns, and caveats:

Harvey Blessing, *Essex Community College*
Warren Boe, *University of Iowa*
George Bohlen, *University of Dayton*
Stephen Brown, *Gannon University*
James Cox, *Lane Community College*
Elaine Daly, *Oakton Community College*
Eileen Bechtold Dlugoss, *Cuyahoga Community College*
Irvin Englander, *Bentley College*
F. Robert Jacobs, *Indiana University*
Dana Johnson, *North Dakota State University*
Ed Keefe, *Des Moines Area Community College*
Rose Laird, *Northern Virginia Community College*
Marty Murray, *Portland Community College*
Jim Potter, *Cal State—Hayward*
Leonard Presby, *William Paterson State College*
Leona Roen, *Oakton Community College*

John Schrage, *Southern Illinois University—Edwardsville*

Neil Sheflin, *Rutgers University*

Arthur Strunk, *Queensborough Community College*

Karen Watterson, *Shoreline Community College*

Michael Williams, *Kirkwood Community College*

We wish to thank our acquisitions editor, Mary Schiller, whose comments were always enlightened and positive. Her substantive suggestions regarding content and style have significantly improved the structure of the book.

We are also indebted to Jit Fu Lim, who rendered much of the art that appears in the book. Mr. Lim's exceptional talent for visual appeal, and his skills in translating rough sketches and raw ideas into professional works of art, have contributed immeasurably to the book.

To the production editor, Pam Barnard, we are especially indebted for her help with the photo program and her participation in the design and production of the book. We also thank Barbara Fuller for completing the production process. To the copy editor and typesetters, we remain impressed, even allured, with your capacity to turn our manuscript into a beautiful text.

To all of you we owe a great debt of gratitude. It is, however, our duty to assume full responsibility for whatever shortcomings exist in the text.

James R. Burns
Darrell N. Eubanks

MICROCOMPUTERS

Business and Personal Applications

PART I

INTRODUCTION TO MICROCOMPUTERS

Think of this book as an adventure in discovery. What follows is material which describes the beginnings of one of the most important inventions known to humankind—the microcomputer. The world of microcomputers is a most fascinating one, but the reason there is interest in it is because it promises to augment and enhance the cognitive and information processing capabilities of its users in ways never before possible. Chances are, the reader has already had a taste of the power and convenience of the microcomputer. Term papers are easier to prepare, for example, and the resulting product is more professional. Calculations are easier to perform and data is more easily stored and manipulated. This book will take both uninitiated and initiated readers more deeply into the concepts and capabilities of microcomputers. Along the way the reader will develop skills that should greatly increase information and cognitive processing abilities.

Part I, covering Chapters 1 through 4 of this book is concerned with the environment and organization of microcomputers. It describes the world in which microcomputers operate and in that sense it describes their environment. It describes the organization of microcomputers by delineating their hardware and software components. It also explains those details which most strongly influence the behavior and personality of the microcomputer.

The goal of this part is to provide an introduction to the microcomputer—specifically, the environment, the hardware and system software.

CHAPTER

1

The World of Microcomputers

CHAPTER OUTLINE

Microcomputers Defined 5

History of Microcomputer Development 8

The Microcomputer and the Contemporary Office 11

Applications in Business and the Professions 14

The Microcomputer and the Office of the Future 17

The Microcomputer and the Immediate Future 18

Possible Disbenefits from Microcomputer Use 19

Where to Get Additional Information 21

CHAPTER OBJECTIVES

In this chapter you will learn

1 how the various computer sizes are differentiated
2 how the microcomputer got its start
3 what the major applications of microcomputers are
4 how the microcomputer can improve your personal productivity
5 how microcomputers are changing the workplace
6 caveats regarding use of the microcomputer
7 where to go for additional information

Have you stopped to think about the information content of your day recently? Perhaps you begin your day by absorbing information about the news and local weather from morning television programs. As you eat breakfast you read the newspaper for information on sporting events, employment opportunities, grocery bargains, or apartment housing. As you walk or drive to school you hear the latest news bulletins and perhaps a weather update. Once you arrive you begin studying your course notes in preparation for some occasion when you will use this information in your courses. Then you attend your morning classes, receiving information needed to pass the exams. At lunch you compare your opinions with those of your cohorts and receive new insights and information from them. In the evening you start reading a new textbook on microcomputers (this one, no doubt) to obtain additional information pertinent to their use.

Information is the substance from which all decisions are made and all problems solved. It is becoming increasingly important in an age characterized by some as the "information era." By 1990 over 70 percent of the jobs in the United States will be information related. In the private sector, industries like banking and insurance are information-intensive. In the public sector, practically every endeavor—from education to defense and from legislation to administration—depends on information in some way.

This book is about machines for processing information. Such machines are conventionally called computers. More specifically, this book is concerned with microcomputers as used in both business and personal applications. Like large computers, these smaller machines translate raw data into information—facts with implications for action. We call all such translations **data processing.**

Another basic function to which computers can be put is the manipulation of textual or manuscript materials. This is called **word processing.** It has been estimated that nearly 50 percent of microcomputer usage is in word processing—a very important application indeed.

In this chapter we hope to achieve several objectives, which are essential to an understanding of more important topics to follow. First, we want to introduce you to some of the history and uses of microcomputers. Some literacy in this area is necessary to converse intelligently with computer salespeople and to read the burgeoning literature on microcomputers. In addition we want to suggest where the microcomputer revolution is going, and where we must go to keep up with it. We've already described how "data processing" is distinct from "word processing," and we've hinted at the goals of both: the production of information. The term *information* itself should take on a sharper, more focused meaning for you.

Finally, we will attempt to convey some of the excitement and dynamism regarding the most tranquil revolution going on in our contemporary society. This will be accomplished by comparing the present with the recent past, by presenting some forecasts, and by taking a crystal-ball look into the future.

MICROCOMPUTERS DEFINED

Before proceeding further, let us define precisely what we mean by a microcomputer. A **microcomputer** is any computer suitable for use in an office environment without requiring special wiring, air conditioning, or support staff. This, of course, encompasses computers sufficiently small to fit on the manager's desk or credenza, but also includes a computer that is supported by its own stand, desk, or cabinet and is able to provide computing support for a small office staff.

Microcomputers are computers whose processor is entirely contained on one chip or integrated circuit, called a **microprocessor**. Our use of the term *microcomputer* is synonymous with *small computer.* When the microcomputer is used by an individual, it becomes his or her *personal computer.* Other appellations used for microcomputers include *work station, desktop computer,* and *home computer.* All of these computers are certainly microcomputers in the sense of our definition for microcomputers.

For our purposes, we prefer to use the term *microcomputer* as a generic term that includes and is synonymous with all of these computer names. Typical of such computer systems are those depicted in Figure 1–1. This definition also includes word processors. **Word processors** are machines whose primary function is to facilitate the entering, editing, formatting, and printing of documents. In recent years we have seen dedicated word processors become more versatile in that many such machines can do data processing as well, but the ultimate fate of dedicated word processors is extinction.

Microcomputers are priced from the hundreds of dollars all the way up to $40,000 in multiuser configurations. Desktop personal computers intended for professional use by a single user are priced from $450 to $8,500. Microcomputers are one of four categories of computers available today; the other three are minicomputers, mainframe computers, and supercomputers, in order of increasing power and size. Brief descriptions of these follow.

Minicomputers are usually priced in the $40,000 to $200,000 range. They have good price/performance ratios and they do not require special air conditioning or wiring. They do not require a data processing staff, because existing employees can be trained. They are modular and can expand as computer requirements increase. Figure 1–2 depicts the best-selling minicomputer of the early 1980s. The first minicomputer was introduced in 1965 by Digital Equipment Corporation, about ten years before the first microcomputer was introduced. Digital Equipment Corporation (DEC) has retained its lead in the minicomputer field for the past twenty years. Minicomputers were the first to support terminal-based computer access for many users at one time.

(a)

(b)

FIGURE 1–1

Some Typical Microcomputer Systems
(a) The Macintosh Plus. *(Courtesy of Apple Computer, Inc.)* (b) The IBM Personal System/2 Model 50. *(Courtesy of International Business Machines Corporation.)*

FIGURE 1–2

A Digital Equipment Corporation Vax 11-780 Minicomputer *(Courtesy of Commodore Electronics, Ltd. and Digital Equipment Corporation.)*

Some jobs are too big for the minicomputer to handle. For these jobs we need a mainframe computer. **Mainframe computers** have been used since the early days of computing in the late forties and fifties. With the exception of supercomputers, mainframe computers are the fastest in instructions processed per second, and they have the most storage and the best support. They are able to connect many users into the same source of information and data. They are also the most expensive, costing in excess of $200,000, and they require special wiring, air conditioning, and a data processing staff. Figure 1–3 exhibits a commonplace main-

FIGURE 1–3

An IBM 3090 Mainframe Computer *(Courtesy of International Business Machines Corporation.)*

FIGURE 1–4

A CRAY II Supercomputer System, one of the fastest computer systems in the world, is able to process nearly one billion instructions in one second. *(Courtesy of Cray Research, Inc.)*

frame computer. International Business Machines, or IBM, continues to maintain its position as the leading manufacturer of mainframe computers.

Supercomputers are used for scientific data processing and are able to accommodate large models of the weather and of resources like water or oil and so forth. These largest of computers are capable of processing more than one billion instructions in a single second. The computing capabilities of microcomputers are much less, on the order of a half million instructions per second up to three or four million instructions per second. Shown in Figure 1–4 is a supercomputer. We will not be concerned with minis, mainframes, or "monster" computers again in this book.

Microcomputer systems, like all other computer systems, consist of two basic artifacts: hardware and software. The **hardware** is the physical equipment, as depicted in Figures 1–1 through 1–4. The **software** is the programmed instructions necessary to drive the hardware in those tasks we as users want done.

HISTORY OF MICROCOMPUTER DEVELOPMENT

The microcomputer was developed by entrepreneurs and inventors in the early to mid-1970s. It was spawned by the microprocessor—an entire processor (or "brain") on a single chip. The first microprocessors appeared in the early 1970s and were used in calculators, microwave ovens, and industrial process control.

One of the most successful early microcomputers was the Apple, developed by Steve Wozniak and Steve Jobs in the mid-1970s. Versions of this machine are still selling as of this writing. As the story goes, both Wozniak and Jobs approached their prospective employers about development and production of the Apple and were turned down. They then decided to develop and build the machine themselves. Their first computer, the Apple I, was sold in kit form. They received an order for about one hundred of the units from the Byte Shop in southern California, with payment on delivery. They purchased the necessary parts with terms that would give them thirty days to pay the respective vendors. In thirty days, the first Apples were fabricated, literally in the inventors' garages, and delivered in time to receive payment and to pay off the vendors—and cash flow was created. Several hundred were sold when Wozniak and Jobs decided that a preassembled computer would be more widely received. This thought gave birth to the Apple II, versions of which are still in production.

Early versions of the Radio Shack TRS-80 Model 1 (shown in Figure 1–5) were also based on designs developed in the garages of the inventors. When Radio Shack made its decision to distribute the product through its stores, there was no way of knowing if the product would sell. Surprisingly, the little computer sold very well.

Still another early and important entry into the microcomputer marketplace was the Commodore Pet (and later, the Super Pet). The Commodore Pet (shown in Figure 1–6) was developed under the direction of Jack Tramiel. Following the introduction of the Pet and Super Pet, Commodore introduced the VIC 20 and

FIGURE 1–5

The Model I TRS-80 Computer System *(Courtesy of Radio Shack.)*

FIGURE 1–6

The Commodore Pet

(Photograph reprinted with permission of Commodore Business Machines, Inc.)

Commodore 64, both highly successful home computers. In 1984, there were more Commodore computers in the world than practically all of the other types of microcomputers combined.

A significant development occurred when IBM entered the microcomputer scene in August of 1981. In effect this legitimized the microcomputer marketplace and caused it to grow much more rapidly. IBM's influence in the marketplace caused sweeping changes to take place in this infant industry. The presence of IBM has helped to stabilize the industry and create standards.

Ten years have passed since the introduction of the first commercial microcomputer (the MITS Altair was developed by Ed Roberts, who is considered the father of the small computer). It is now possible, in retrospect, to perceive more clearly what the ramifications of this modern marvel have been and will be.

First, it is apparent that the microcomputer has the potential for enhancing the productivity of the white-collar worker like no other technology in the last century. While it has not been possible for managers and professionals to resort to twenty-eight-hour workweeks, the enhanced productivity has cut the cost of services and increased output. According to UCLA economist Daniel Freedman, the microcomputer should boost the gross national product, and thus our total wealth, as labor costs are pushed lower.

Moreover, new electronic services and technologies have grown out of the increased ubiquity of the microcomputer; services like home banking (carrying out banking transactions from the convenience of the home), on-line information utilities (mainframe computers with large amounts of consumer information), and telecommuting (working in the comfort of one's own home and sending one's output to the office electronically) have been available for some time. It is worth mentioning that these technologies are made possible by use of the telephone in addition to the microcomputer. The role of the telephone and other transport media in transporting information electronically from one place to another will be an important topic to be discussed later in this text.

THE MICROCOMPUTER AND THE CONTEMPORARY OFFICE

Why Are Microcomputers Moving In?

Microcomputers are permeating the offices of small and large firms alike. The reasons relate to the ever-increasing processing power and speed and the ever-decreasing costs of microcomputers. The cost of equivalent computing power is halved every two years.

Consider Table 1–1, which compares one of the early computers (the ENIAC—Electronic Numerical Integrator and Calculator) with the "typical" microcomputer available today. As the table suggests, the remarkable advances in improvement, if applied to the auto industry, would enable automobiles to be purchased for roughly $20.00 today.

There is no end in sight for this remarkable growth in computer technology. By the year 2000 we should be able to purchase a hand-held computer for about $40.00 and expect it to provide all the power of the mainframe computers of the 1960s.

As a result, a revolution is in the making. A recent study estimates that over five million computers were in use in 1983; by 1990, eight times as many will be in existence. The collective electronic brainpower capacity of computers doubles every two years. The annual worldwide investment in computers was running over $200 billion in 1987 and is expected to grow to nearly one trillion by 1990. It is no

TABLE 1–1

Comparison of ENIAC with the Microcomputers Available Today

1946 ENIAC	CONTEMPORARY MICROCOMPUTER	IMPROVEMENT RATIO
Weight		
30 tons	30 lbs.	2000:1
Power consumption		
150 kilowatts	150 watts	1000:1
Performance		
25,000 instr./sec.	500,000 instr./sec.	20:1
Components		
18,000 vacuum tubes	600,000 transistors within integrated circuits	33:1
Storage		
20 numbers of 10 digits each	Access to millions of 10-digit numbers	1,000,000:1
Cost in 1984 dollars		
$2,000,000.00	$2,000.00	1000:1

Conclusion
If the auto industry had advanced technologically at the same rate as the computer industry, cars would cost roughly $20.00, get 20,000 miles to the gallon, and be able to do a standing quarter mile in one second.

surprise to learn that the microcomputer industry is the fastest-growing industry in America today, with projected annual sales approaching $30 billion by 1990.

At the same time, all computers are getting smaller. Every fourteen months the amount of information that can be stored in a fixed volume of memory is doubled. By 1990 it should be possible to store the entire contents of the Library of Congress in one cubic meter of memory, whereas just thirty years ago the same cubic meter would accommodate less than twenty pages of typewritten material.

The mere fact that hardware costs are going down while equivalent computing power is going up does not alone account for the ever-increasing ubiquity of microcomputers. White-collar workers have the potential of greatly increasing their efficiency and effectiveness through the microcomputer's word-processing, spreadsheet calculator, and data management capabilities—subjects about which we will have much to say in forthcoming chapters. Moreover, microcomputers are able to provide quicker, more reliable information because of their vast memory and processing abilities, thereby increasing managerial control. An on-line inventory system can, upon request, provide an immediate status report on any one of 50,000 different inventory items. The status of a company's payables and receivables can be known immediately, and cash flow requirements can be projected.

In addition, computers are great at putting out paper. Today, everyone wants paper. The government wants reports on income and employee salaries. Corporate vice-presidents want reports on sales, production, and inventory. The production staff needs detailed schedules describing exactly what will be produced and when. Marketing management wants a detailed marketing plan for the next quarter. Corporate finance wants detailed cost data on each product produced. And so it goes. While computers are getting cheaper, labor is getting more expensive. Anytime paper-shuffling and information-handling activities can be off-loaded from people to computers, management should be saving money. Table 1–2 lists some of the benefits that can accrue from the use of microcomputers.

Contemporary Uses of Microcomputers

This section takes a realistic look at the processes and activities of the business office and other environments where microcomputers are being used. It will then suggest how software has developed to aid each of these activities. Every day, the base of software for the microcomputer matures and expands. And, almost daily, new categories of software are being invented. We provide here a brief synopsis of the material to follow in Chapters 4 through 16, also explaining what office procedure(s) motivated the development of the application in question.

Before moving into some of the applications of microcomputers in the contemporary office, it is appropriate to digress a moment to discuss the concept of office automation, about which much is written in the literature of microcomputers. **Office automation** is the term used to describe an office in which managerial access to information is more or less automated. A manager can easily retrieve information from a centralized source (called a **data base**) without having to ask a secretary to search for it in file cabinets. Similarly, managers can store or save information electronically in a centralized data base for later retrieval by others. Memos can be distributed from one manager to other managers through the use of **electronic mail**—the sending of messages from one work station to another electronically. The impetus for this important trend in the evolution of the office is the need for

TABLE 1–2

Benefits of Using Microcomputers for Business and Personal Use

What Can a Microcomputer System Do for Businesses?

- Improve management control
- Improve inventory control
- Improve cost control
- Improve quality control
- Increase productivity
- Improve the quality of decision-making
- Enable better servicing of aged accounts—old bills
- Automate payroll and payables
- Automate materials handling
- Automate accounting
- Improve communication with customers and clients

What can a Microcomputer System Do for You Personally?

- Improve your working and academic life
- Save you money
- Increase your productivity
- Improve your decision-making
- Enable you to provide marketable services
- Enhance your professional image
- Increase the accuracy, quality, and timeliness of your reports

timely access to information—a factor that is being perceived as absolutely essential to the success of the organization or firm.

Although the automated office of today has not yet reached the point of being paperless, where all work stations are neat and organized, the trend is in this direction. Each work station will consist of a system unit, keyboard, and display (a microcomputer, usually) networked to the other system units, keyboards, and displays of other work stations, as shown in Figure 1–7. The network that connects the various work stations together is an important component in the usage and functions of the microcomputer; Chapter 15 is devoted to microcomputer networks. Microcomputers coupled by means of a network and network software will permit access to and manipulation of shared data, shared software, and shared hardware. By sharing these resources, an organization can improve its productivity and cut costs.

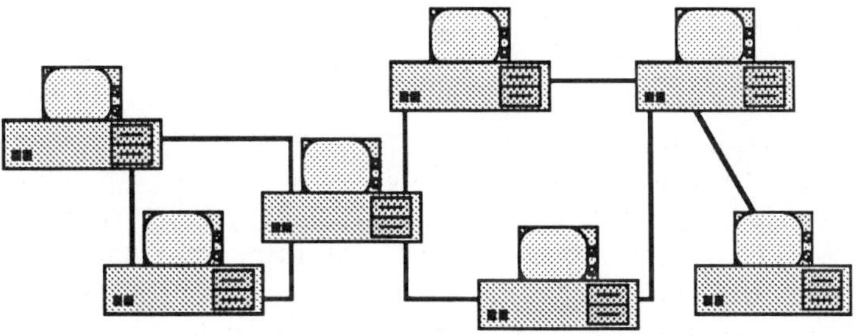

FIGURE 1–7

Work Stations Networked Together with Other Machines

APPLICATIONS IN BUSINESS AND THE PROFESSIONS

We find that business and professional people of every kind and type are making use of microcomputers. Salespeople use microcomputers to keep files on their clients, to send them letters of inquiry, and to promote products. Accountants use microcomputers to prepare income tax returns and to keep books for their clients. Attorneys use microcomputers to prepare legal documents. Architects use microcomputers to design landscapes and living areas, buildings and buttresses. Doctors use microcomputers to keep records on their patients, specifically medical histories and diagnoses. All of these people use microcomputers to invoice their clients and to track what is owed to them (their receivables) by their clients.

Certainly, microcomputers have become useful and ubiquitous in the sales and service-related professions: the small businesses. But what about manufacturing? What about large organizations such as government bureaucracies or multinational corporations? Manufacturing managers may use microcomputers to help monitor and control their inventories, to schedule their production, and to determine their labor requirements. Marketing managers use microcomputers to prepare marketing plans and proposals. Corporate vice-presidents will use microcomputers to develop long- and short-range business plans. Middle managers use microcomputers to prepare documents that, they hope, get read by upper-level managers. Budgets are monitored and controlled, schedules are prepared, plans are generated, information is stored and retrieved; all on microcomputers used within organizations.

Among the most important applications of microcomputers in business and professional contexts are the managerial productivity applications: word processing, spreadsheets, and data base management systems. This is readily perceived from the graphic in Figure 1–8. We will now briefly discuss the origins of these

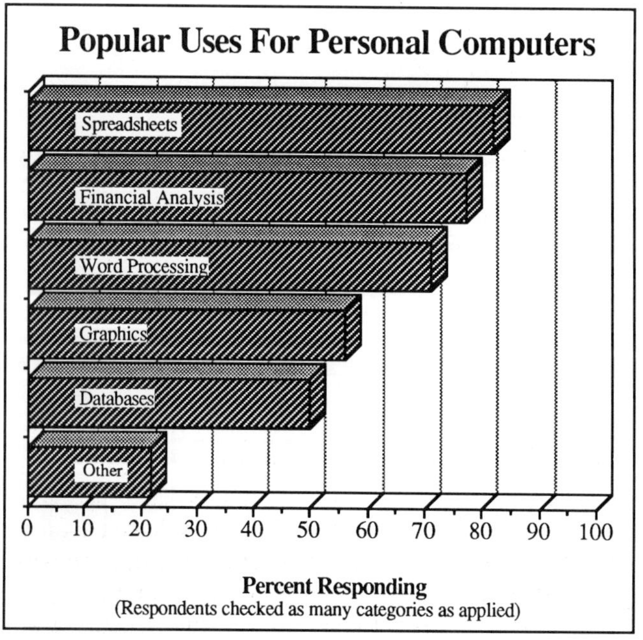

FIGURE 1–8

Popular Uses for Personal Computers *(Source: Infomatics Survey.)*

(a)

(b)

FIGURE 1–9

Examples of the New and Old Ways of Doing Word Processing (a) The "old" way of doing word processing via a dedicated word processor. The machines are expensive and operated by trained users only. (b) The "new" way of doing word processing via a microcomputer. The machines are inexpensive and can be operated by nearly everyone.

applications, along with other applications in accounting and inventory. A different software package is usually required to support each application of the microcomputer. Software devoted to supporting one or more applications is called *applications software*.

Word Processing

Figure 1–9 depicts the new and the old ways of doing word processing. Someday, word processing may be recognized as being as important to the continuing technological evolution of man as was Gutenberg's invention of the printing press. The need to prepare memos, letters, documents, manuals, books, and publications of every kind has motivated the development of word processing packages. The capability to permanently store text for later retrieval so that it can be edited and printed is a major improvement over previous approaches to manuscript preparation. Before word processing, if an error on a hard copy (sheet of paper) required correction, the error was whited out or erased and typed over. Occasionally, the entire page had to be retyped. With word processing, the text on the sheet of paper can be recalled from the memory banks of the computer and displayed on the screen so the correction can be made, after which the page of text is stored in the memory banks of the computer for later printing.

For the past few years, the trend is away from dedicated word processing systems and toward increased use of word processing packages on personal computers. At least one Fortune 500 company is doing away with many of its secretarial positions and placing the responsibility for manuscript preparation back in the hands of the manager or executive. The old adage, "Managers don't type," is no longer true. Managers and professionals should be typists if they are to use the microcomputer proficiently.

Electronic Spreadsheets

Two centuries ago, a classical mathematician stated that it is a waste of time for a scientist to engage in the drudgery of repetitive calculations. Today, this is true of business and professional people as well. Such is the motivation for electronic spreadsheets. Electronic spreadsheets got their start with a graduate business student, who tired of calculating and recalculating a manual spreadsheet he was working on. He subsequently asked his friend (who was also a programmer) to develop software to perform the calculations automatically for him. The package, known as VisiCalc (visible calculator), became an instant success and almost singlehandedly caused the microcomputer revolution. Applications burgeoned in accounting, finance, operations management, and anywhere tables of numbers had to be manipulated. It is believed that during the years 1979 to 1982, VisiCalc was responsible for the sale of a quarter million Apple II and II+ computers. During that time, it was fairly common to find a corporate executive in a large corporation doing calculations with an electronic spreadsheet on a microcomputer. Such a sight is even more common today, as usage of electronic spreadsheets has penetrated all levels of management in the public and private sectors.

Just what is an **electronic spreadsheet**? It is simply a two-dimensional table of numbers. The rows and columns of these tables can be labeled. Most of the numbers in the table are calculated from other numbers in the table using formulas. It is used to control budgets, to project balance sheets, to manage cash, to control credit, to develop plans and schedules of various types, and to manage portfolios.

Data Base Management Systems

Data base management has its beginnings in the office environment and dates from the time when managers found it useful to keep records and files on customers, clients, personnel, inventory, vendors, students, or product sales. What office would be complete without the usual complement of file cabinets? And, what secretary or stenographer would be considered sufficiently prepared without training in "filing"?

Suppose, for example, that an accounting clerk requires the names of all customers who purchased more than $20,000 of products in the last year. Manually, this job would require a clerk to search all the customer files in the cabinets, add up the invoices of each customer, and make note of those clients who spent more than $20,000. This could take some time. If this same information were contained in a microcomputer data base, it could be obtained in just a few seconds. Or suppose that a manager wanted a list of all employees who work in the accounts receivable department and speak Spanish. Manually, such a search could be quite time-consuming. Through the use of a computer it is almost instantaneous. Imagine the savings in labor cost alone; imagine the gains in accuracy and speed. It makes sense, therefore, that such computerized systems have contributed greatly to the improvement of productivity in the office.

If a manager wants clients to be listed alphabetically, and again by sales region, this is no problem for the computer. If a manager wants a list of all product items responsible for more than $10,000 in sales volume last year, his or her wish is the computer's command.

In short, with a **data base management system** (abbreviated DBMS), users can create their own data bases and store within those data bases any kind of information that they may subsequently want to retrieve.

Miscellaneous Applications

Literally hundreds of new categories of software now exist and are commonly used. For example, software for time management, appointment scheduling, notetaking, auto-dialing (of clients, say) have all become commonplace. Software that can assist with the design of products (everything from cars to cupcakes) is called computer-aided design (CAD) software, and is now commonplace. Software that can be used to train managers and decision makers in a managerial function will become increasingly widespread. Such software will incorporate the expertise of those well-versed in the managerial function for which the computerized training is being provided. For this reason, this software is called an **expert system.** Software that will assist with project planning is now also widely available.

Integrated Applications

Integrated software packages, which provide all of the applications mentioned so far and others as well, are becoming increasingly important in the world of microcomputers. Typical applications are data communications and graphics, in addition to word processing, spreadsheets, and data base management. These packages will possess a common set of user interface conventions, will allow for passing of files between the various applications, and will usually be less expensive than if the applications were purchased separately.

Accounting Applications

Accounting software has its origins in manually operated accounting and bookkeeping systems. The need to automate, speed up, and record the processing of business transactions has been perceived for some time. Small business accounting systems were first developed for the minicomputers of the 1970s. Large businesses (Fortune 1000 firms, banks, insurance companies, and thrift institutions) have done and will continue to do their accounting and bookkeeping on mainframe computers. It is the small firm with gross annual sales of $10 million or less that has benefited the most from using the microcomputer to do its own accounting work.

Accounting applications include general ledger, accounts receivable, accounts payable, payroll, customer invoicing/billing, and inventory.

THE MICROCOMPUTER AND THE OFFICE OF THE FUTURE

In the future, we can expect all computers to be microcomputers, or at least the size of microcomputers. As the switching time of computer circuitry becomes ever faster, the distance each signal can travel is decreased because the travel time must not exceed the switching time. Designers of the largest mainframe computers of today have learned that if the switching time is 1 **nanosecond** (10^{-9} second), then the length of any signal pathway in the processor must not exceed 30 centimeters.[1] Computers around the year 2010 will have switching times of about 6 **picoseconds** (6×10^{-12} second), restricting signal pathway lengths to about 0.15 centimeters. Therefore, if processing speeds are going to continue to go up, the physical size of the computing hardware must go down.

By just how much can we expect the processing speeds of microprocessor chips to increase? No one knows exactly, but it has been estimated that processors accommodating 64 zeros and ones (all data is stored in computers as zeros and ones) in each operation while running at 110 MHz (millions of cycles per second) are entirely possible within the next 50 years. Today's microprocessors are able to process 16 or 32 zeros and ones in each operation at clock rates of up to 20 MHz. There are physical limits to the processing speed and component density, but researchers should not reach those barriers in the next few years. The Department of Defense's Very High-Speed Integrated Circuits (VHSIC) Program is endeavoring to develop integrated circuits whose minimum clock speed exceeds 25 MHz.

We can expect processing speeds to continue to increase, but what advances are likely in other aspects of the microcomputing technology? Richard Grigonis[1,2] has furnished us with a very interesting look at what might be the work station of the future. According to Mr. Grigonis, the work station of the future may look similar to the one shown in Figure 1–10. Each work station might consist of a plastic enclosure with large, low-intensity, flat display screens surrounding a very comfortable chair. The environment is largely dust- and contaminant-free. Just sitting in the chair activates the work station, which uses a synthesized voice to talk to its user. It might also respond to voice commands and would most likely receive inputs from a keyboard, various devices for cursor control (Mr. Grigonis suggests a helmet that tracks eye movement and directs the cursor accordingly). The user identifies himself to the work station, possibly through voice recognition. Such identification is used to determine the user's security level of access to data in the computer's data bases.

THE MICROCOMPUTER AND THE IMMEDIATE FUTURE

Although advancements in the technology of microcomputers are expected to continue unabated through the year 2000, of more interest to us is the shorter term technological developments and the continued growth of the microcomputer industry. We can expect continued increases in the processing speed, storage capacity, and usefulness of microcomputers. Meanwhile, prices of existing and older technology machines will continue to go down. Consequently, we fully expect microcomputers to become more efficient as a result of increases in their processing capacity and speed, and more affordable as a result of decreases in cost.

We can expect computers of the late 1980s and beyond to be capable of doing several things at once, as opposed to just one thing at a time. Doing only one thing at a time may cause the user to wait on the computer to finish that one task, such as printing a document or calculating a spreadsheet, before the user can go on to the next task. Doing only one task at a time thus reduces the user's productivity.

The memory capacity of computers will continue to expand dramatically. By the time this book is in print, most new microcomputers being sold will have enough primary memory to accommodate nearly 300 pages of single-spaced text, up from less than 150 just two years before. Most computers of the late 1980s will have a disk storage capacity equivalent to nearly six thousand pages of single-spaced text, and by 1992 that capacity will have quadrupled to more than twenty thousand pages of single-spaced text.

While microcomputers are getting faster (so they can do several things at once), and their memory capacities are expanding, microcomputers will also get smaller (so they take up less space on the user's desktop), easier to use, and smarter.

FIGURE 1–10
Grigonis' Workstation of the Future.

By smarter we mean that computers will expect less sophistication on the part of the user. The user will be able to communicate with the computer through the use of a graphical interface that is able to interpret commands given in plain English. And, computer displays will contain far more detail and resolution. The future may also witness greater integration of the microcomputer with the telephone and communications systems. These are among the major changes to be expected in the near future. What changes can we expect in the microcomputer industry?

Figure 1–11 shows the growth forecast for the industry itself. The curves displayed there suggest that by the year 1990 microcomputers will be a $29-billion industry with sales of over 10 million units a year—up from 6 million units in 1985.

Figure 1–12 shows the percentage of desks that will have microcomputers on them and of users that will have access to microcomputers. Approximately 53% of all white-collar workers will have microcomputers on their own desks, and over 92 percent of white-collar workers will have access to a personal computer by the year 1989. It should be apparent that if employers are going to spend $25 to $30 billion a year to provide microcomputers for their employees, they are also going to expect their employees to be well trained in the use of these machines. To that end, let us proceed.

POSSIBLE DISBENEFITS FROM MICROCOMPUTER USE

To suggest that the introduction of this new technology called the microcomputer is entirely beneficial would be less than realistic and honest. As with any technology, there are effects that could be judged as detrimental. Some of these

FIGURE 1–11

Growth in Microcomputer Sales

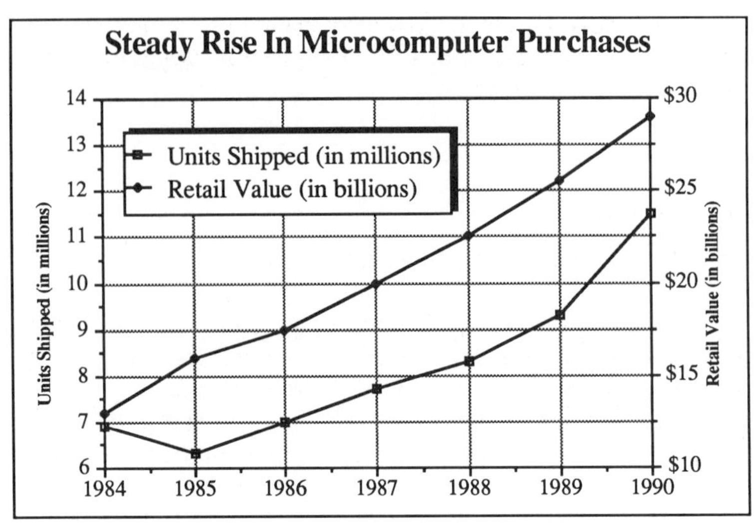

FIGURE 1–12

Percentage of Users Having Their Own Microcomputers

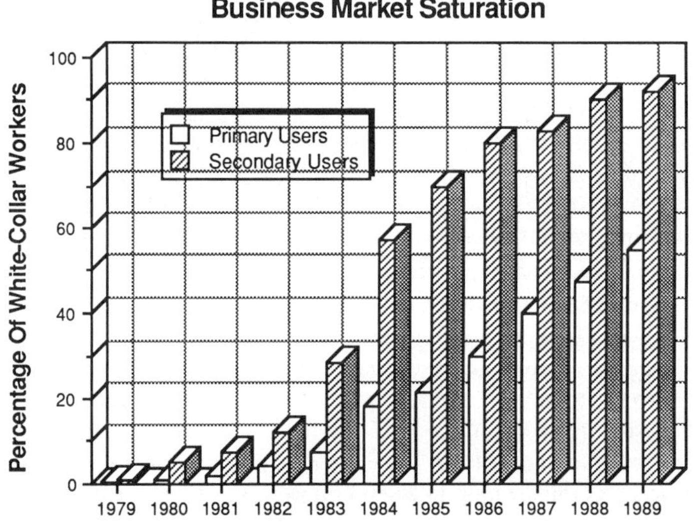

are due to the distributed nature of computing on microcomputers. Instead of sharing data, the data tends to become private and personalized. This makes access to it harder to control. Some who could benefit from access to it may be prevented from doing so. Another problem is just the opposite in the sense that others may obtain illicit and inappropriate access to this data. Protection of the confidentiality and security of the data is clearly more difficult. For example, one company reported that employees had downloaded lists of customers from their mainframes onto disks and sold this information to competitors.

The solution to this problem is one of training and technology. Managers must put into use technologies which will control access to data regardless of where it exists. Second, policies must be developed to protect against unauthorized access to data. Third, employees must be trained so that they fully understand the perils involved and how to avoid such catastrophes.

WHERE TO GET ADDITIONAL INFORMATION

Sources for additional information on hardware and software are many and varied. Books, periodicals, seminars, short courses, user groups, computer stores, and computer literacy courses on public television all serve this purpose. Periodicals dealing with microcomputers can be found on almost any book stand. Computer stores will provide books, periodicals, seminars, short courses, and consulting. At the end of this chapter is a selected bibliography of additional reading that can be helpful to the interested reader. Some discussion of the periodical literature follows.

To stay abreast of this fast-changing technology, it is necessary to subscribe to one or more of the periodicals. For readers without much background in computing, *Personal Computing, Desktop Computing,* or *PC World* is recommended. The latter magazine is, however, going to be specific to the IBM PC family of microcomputers and compatibles. These magazines are intended for users who are new to the field of microcomputing.

For users who are relatively literate in the field of microcomputers, periodicals like *Byte, Infoworld,* and *Small Business Computers* are recommended. For sophisticated readers interested in IBM PCs and compatibles, *PC Magazine* and *PC Tech Journal* are recommended. Numerous periodicals are produced for professionals in the industry, including *Computer Systems News, Computer Decisions, Datamation,* and others.

Some of the periodicals are specific to a particular brand name. You've probably already discovered that periodicals whose names begin with the letters PC are concerned with the IBM PC computers and compatible microcomputers. The periodical *80 Microcomputing* is concerned with Tandy products, and the periodical *MacWorld* is concerned with the Apple Macintosh.

For reviews of hardware and software, the following periodicals are recommended. First, *Infoworld* is famous for its reviews of both hardware and software. In the back of every *Infoworld* issue is a capsule summary (and overall grade) of every product that has been reviewed in a given year. Second, a section entitled "Reviews" always appears in *Byte.* Third, *PC Magazine* will have entire issues devoted to extensive testing of an entire category of products that are compatible with the IBM PC family, such as printers, word processing packages, spreadsheets, or data base management systems.

Summary

In this chapter we have introduced the world of microcomputers: devices that can be used in office environments, including desktop computers and dedicated word processors. All computers consist of hardware (the physical equipment) and software (the programmed instructions that direct the hardware in the necessary tasks). We will have more to say about these components in Chapter 2, where each hardware component is considered in some detail. We also learned some of the many applications to which the microcomputer can be put, and what the future is likely to hold for a society that is becoming increasingly computerized.

Key Terms

data base
data base management system
data processing
electronic mail
electronic spreadsheet
expert system
hardware
information
mainframe computer
microcomputer
microprocessor
minicomputer
nanosecond
office automation
picosecond
small computer
software
supercomputer
word processing

Self-Test

1. How are the various computer sizes differentiated?
2. How did the microcomputer get its start?
3. What are the major applications of microcomputers?
4. How can the microcomputer improve your personal productivity?
5. How are microcomputers changing the workplace?
6. List some caveats regarding use of the microcomputer.
7. Describe where to go to get additional information.

Exercises

1. List and describe the major uses to which microcomputers are currently being applied in the business and professional world.
2. Discuss the role that software plays in relation to the hardware.
3. Describe why microcomputers are playing an increasingly important role in large and small organizations alike.
4. Characterize the work station of the future.
5. What is meant by the following?

    electronic banking
    on-line information utilities
    telecommuting

    What component, in addition to the microcomputer, makes these services and technologies possible?
6. Describe why information has become so important in our contemporary society. What is the relationship of the microcomputer to information?
7. Compare the four classes of computers (supercomputers, mainframes, minicomputers, and microcomputers) with respect to price, physical characteristics, and performance features.
8. If you own a microcomputer, list and describe its characteristics as best you can. Explain why you bought it (what applications you use it for). Why did you choose it from among the myriad other microcomputers available for sale?

9. Research the literature to determine specifically how microcomputers are being used in the vocation corresponding to your major. For example, if your major is marketing, study the marketing literature to find out how microcomputers are being used in marketing. Write a brief report on your findings.
10. Match the applications on the left with the functions listed on the right; that is, which application is used to perform which function? The applications must be matched to more than one function, but each function will have associated with it exactly one application.

Application	*Function*
Word processing	budget control
Spreadsheets	balance sheet projection
Data base management	client searches
	document preparation
	generation of plans and schedules
	letter writing
	information retrieval

References

1. Richard Grigonis. "Fifth Generation Computers." *Dr. Dobb's Journal* 7, issue 12, no. 74 (December 1982).
2. Richard Grigonis. "And Still More Fifth Generation Computers." *Dr. Dobb's Journal* 8, issue 8, no. 82 (August 1983): 54–61.

Additional Reading

Books: General

Alberta-Hallam, Teresa; Stephen F. Hallam; and James Hallam. *Microcomputer Use: Word Processors, Spreadsheets, and Data Bases.* Orlando, Fla.: Academic Press, Inc., 1985.

Coburn, Edward J. *Microcomputers: Hardware, Software, and Programming.* Indianapolis: Bobbs-Merrill Educational Publishing, 1984.

Cohen, J. A., with C. S. Mckinney. *How to Computerize Your Small Business.* Englewood Cliffs, N.J.: Prentice-Hall, 1980.

Curtin, Dennis P. and Leslie R. Porter. *Microcomputers: Software and Applications.* Englewood Cliffs, N.J.: Prentice-Hall, 1986.

Datapro Research Corporation. *Datapro Reports on Minicomputers.* Delran, N.J.: updated annually.

Datapro Research Corporation. *Datapro Reports on Word Processors.* Delran, N.J.: updated annually.

Datapro Research Corporation. *Management of Small Computer Systems.* Delran, N.J.: updated annually.

Dologite, D. G. *Using Computers,* Englewood Cliffs, N.J.: Prentice-Hall, 1987.

———. *Using Small Business Computers.* Englewood Cliffs, N.J.: Prentice-Hall, 1984.

Goldstein, Larry Joel. *Microcomputer Applications: A Hands-on Approach to Problem Solving.* Reading, Mass.: Addison-Wesley Publishing Co., 1987.

Grauer, Robert T., and Paul K. Sugrue. *Microcomputer Applications.* New York: McGraw-Hill Book Company, 1987.

Heiser, Dick. *Real Managers Use Personal Computers.* Indianapolis: Que, 1983.

Isshiki, Koichiro R. *Small Business Computers: A Guide to Evaluation and Selection.* Englewood Cliffs, N.J.: Prentice-Hall, 1982.

Johnston, Randolph. *Microcomputers: Concepts and Applications.* Santa Cruz, Calif.: Mitchell Publishing Co. (a division of Random House, Inc.), 1987.

Leventhal, Lance A., and Irvin Stafford. *Why Do You Need A Personal Computer?* New York: John Wiley & Sons, 1981.

Madron, Thomas. *Microcomputers in Large Organizations.* Englewood Cliffs, N.J.: Prentice-Hall, 1983.

McGlynn, Daniel R. *Personal Computing: Home, Professional, and Small Business Applications.* New York: John Wiley & Sons, 1979, 1983.

McLeod, Raymond, Jr. *Decision Support Software for the IBM Personal Computer.* Chicago: Science Research Associates, Inc., 1985.

McNichols, Charles W., and Thomas D. Clark. *Microcomputer-based Information and Decision Support Systems for Small Businesses.* Reston, Va.: Reston Publishing Company, Inc., 1983.

McWilliams, Peter A. *The Personal Computer Book.* Los Angeles: Prelude Press, Distributed by Ballantine Books, 1982.

O'brien, James A. *Using Popular Software Packages: A Tutorial Introduction.* Homewood, Ill.: Richard D. Irwin, Inc., 1985.

Osborne, Adam, with Steven Cook. *Business System Buyer's Guide.* Berkeley, Calif.: Osborne/McGraw-Hill Book Company, 1981.

Segal, Hillel, and Jesse Berst. *How to Select Your Small Computer.* Englewood Cliffs, N.J.: Prentice-Hall, 1983.

Shaw, Donald R. *Your Small Business Computer: Evaluating, Selecting, Financing, Installing and Operating the Hardware and Software that Fits.* New York: Van Nostrand Reinhold Co., 1981.

Spence, J. Wayne, and John C. Windsor. *Using Microcomputers: Applications for Business.* St. Louis: Times Mirror/Mosby College Publishing, 1987.

Sullivan, David R.; Theodore G. Lewis; and Curtis R. Cook. *Computing Today: Microcomputer Concepts and Applications.* Boston: Houghton Mifflin Company, 1985.

Wolff, Terris B. *Microcomputer Applications: Using Small Systems Software.* Boston: Boyd & Fraser Publishing Company, 1985.

Books: Hardware

Alvernaz, Bil. *Expanding Your IBM PC.* Bowie, Md.: Brady Communications, 1984.

Coffron, James W. *The IBM PC Connection.* Berkeley, Calif.: Sybex, 1984.

Norton, Peter. *Inside the IBM PC: Access to Advanced Features and Programming.* Bowie, MD: Brady Communications, 1983.

Novogrodsky, Seth; Frederic E. Davis; and the editors of *PC World. The Complete IBM Personal Computer: The Authoritative Guide to Hardware for Expanding the IBM PC, XT, AT and Compatibles.* New York: Simon & Schuster, 1985.

Sargent, Murray III, and Richard L. Shoemaker. *The IBM Personal Computer from the Inside Out.* Reading, Mass.: Addison-Wesley, 1983.

Books: High-Level Languages

Brown, Jerald R., and LeRoy Finkel. *IBM PC Data File Programming.* New York: John Wiley & Sons, 1984.

Norton, Peter. *The Peter Norton Programmer's Guide to the IBM PC,* Bellevue, Wash.: Microsoft Press, 1985.

Pollack, Lawrence, and Bryan Cummings. *Programming in C on the IBM/PC.* Englewood Cliffs, N.J.: Prentice-Hall, 1984.

Purdom, Jack. *C Programming Guide.* Indianapolis: Que Corporation, 1983.

Sondak, Norman E., and Richard A. Hatch. *Using Basic on the IBM Personal Computer.* Chicago: Science Research Associates, Inc., 1985.

Sordillo, Donald A. *The Personal Computer Basic(s) Reference Manual, Book One.* Englewood Cliffs, N.J.: Prentice-Hall, 1983.

———. *The Personal Computer Basic(s) Reference Manual, Book Two.* Englewood Cliffs, N.J.: Prentice-Hall, 1985.

Stiegler, Mark, and Bob Hansen. *Programming Languages: Featuring the IBM PC and Compatibles.* New York: Baen Books, 1984.

Periodicals

The Automated Office
Byte
Business Software
Computer Decisions
Computer World
Datamation
Desktop Computing
80 Microcomputing
Infoworld
Interface Age
Mini-Micro Systems
PC Magazine
PC Tech Journal
PC Week
PC World
Personal Computer Age
Personal Computing
Popular Computing
Small Systems World
Software News
The Office
Today's Office

CHAPTER

2

Getting Acquainted with Microcomputers

CHAPTER OUTLINE

Components of Microcomputer Systems 27

Classifying Microcomputers According to Form 34

FOCUS FEATURE A Typical Computer Session: How It Goes 38

User Interfaces 44

Care of Your Computer 47

Care of Disks and the Files Contained on Them 48

CHAPTER OBJECTIVES

In this chapter you will learn

1. the components of microcomputer systems
2. the forms and sizes that microcomputers take
3. the essential information for your first computer session
4. how to save and retrieve text and data files
5. how to start and end a session with a microcomputer
6. what user interfaces are available
7. what is meant by user prompts
8. what default settings are and how these can be changed
9. how to use and care for disks
10. rules for naming files
11. the rudiments of MS-DOS and PC-DOS

In the previous chapter we described some of the contemporary uses to which microcomputers are being and will be put in business and personal contexts. Before presenting how to use the microcomputer in these application areas in some detail, it is necessary to briefly discuss the components and forms of microcomputer systems, and to describe how to begin and end a session with the microcomputer.

In addition, we will introduce in this chapter the configuration of microcomputer systems. These concepts will underlie and support much of the material in forthcoming chapters. We also present a classification of microcomputer types and sizes, to impart an understanding of the diversity of microcomputers available today. We conclude this chapter with discussion about how to care for your computer and your diskettes. In short, this chapter presents the rudimentary "get-acquainted" aspects of microcomputers.

COMPONENTS OF MICROCOMPUTER SYSTEMS

Microcomputers (like large computers) consist of four basic hardware components: **input devices, output devices, secondary storage,** and the **central processing unit (CPU),** as shown in Figure 2–1. In addition, microcomputers have two types of software components: **systems software** and **applications software.**

Depending on the configuration, hardware and software components may be placed in the same or separate boxes. Printers are almost always separate, for example. Keyboards are usually placed in detachable units as well. As shown in Figure 2–1, the system and applications software permanently reside in secondary storage and are brought into primary storage when needed. The *system unit* will generally consist of the CPU and secondary storage. In what follows, each major component is briefly described. Details are reserved for Chapter 3.

Input Devices

Whereas the keyboard is the conventional input device, microcomputers are also capable of accepting inputs from electronic mice, joy sticks, tracker balls, touch screens, bar code readers, and digitizers (each of these devices are defined in Chapter 3). In addition, small computers can receive data from other computer equipment through a communications port (a **port** is an external connection point through which data may be imported or exported). Figure 2–2 depicts the most customary forms of input devices.

Output Devices

The customary output devices are printers and displays. Displayed output is called **soft copy** whereas printed output is called **hard copy.** Printers used with microcomputers typically are capable of printing one character at a time. These are to be distinguished from faster printers, used with minicomputers and mainframes, which are capable of printing a line or even an entire page at one time. An exception is the laser printer, which has become popular in its use with microcomputers. Displays are most frequently **CRTs** (cathode ray tubes), but flat screens are becoming increasingly prevalent in most laptop computers. Cathode ray tubes are used

FIGURE 2–1

Four Basic Components of Computers

INPUT		CENTRAL PROCESSING UNIT		OUTPUT
keyboard bar code reader trackerballs digitizers touch screens mice	→	microprocessor primary storage	→	printers displays plotters

↕

SECONDARY STORAGE

system software
applications software
data files
text files

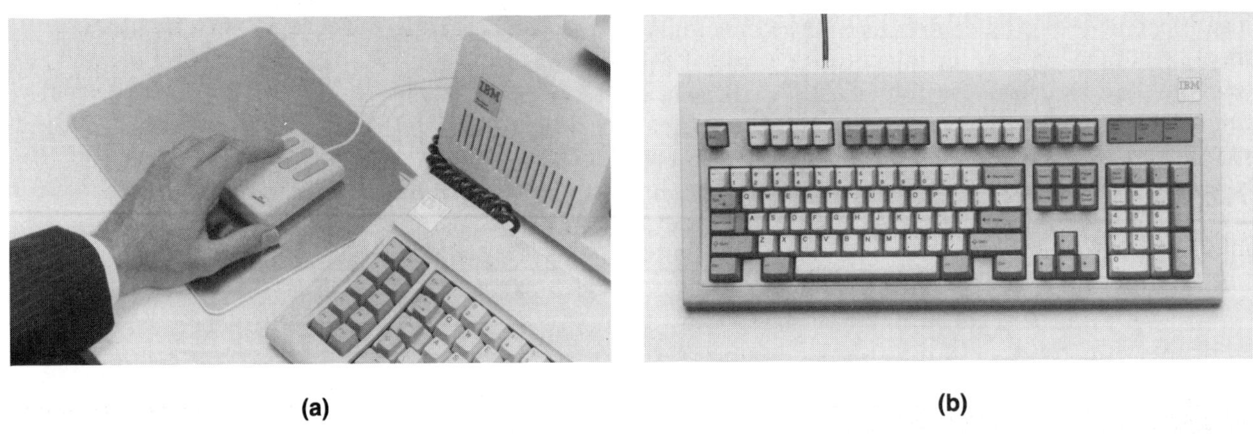

(a) (b)

FIGURE 2–2

Input Devices for Small Computers (a) An Optical Mouse. *(Courtesy of Mouse Systems Corporation.)* (b) An MS-DOS Keyboard. *(Courtesy of International Business Machines Corporation.)*

for the familiar television appliances we have in our homes, but most ordinary television sets are inappropriate for use as displays in business and professional contexts (see Chapter 3 for further details). Figure 2–3 shows the arrangement for a commercial-grade display. Most of the displays associated with microcomputers and terminals alike possess 24 or 25 lines, each consisting of 80 columns of characters.

It is important to characterize the most common input/output device of the 1960s and 1970s, called the **terminal** (see Figure 2–4), in order to distinguish it from the microcomputer. Because terminals look similar to microcomputers, the two appliances are easily confused. The terminal is usually an unintelligent device consisting of keyboard and display or print mechanism. As such it can be used for both inputting data and receiving information from another computer, which could be a microcomputer. Usually, it has little native processing power or memory.

Terminals are a very familiar appliance in our society. Airline reservation clerks use them to communicate with mainframes. With the terminal connected

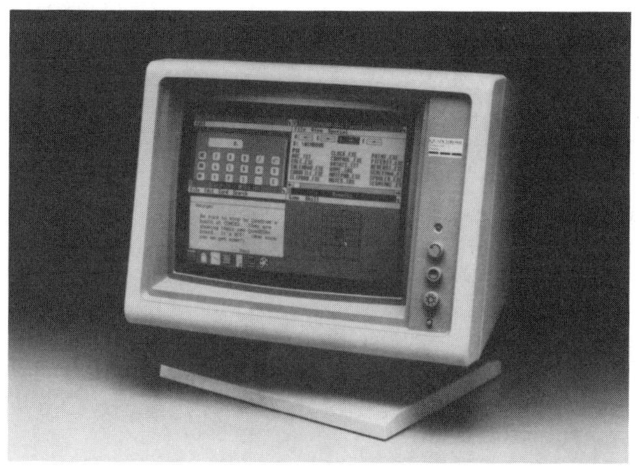

(a)

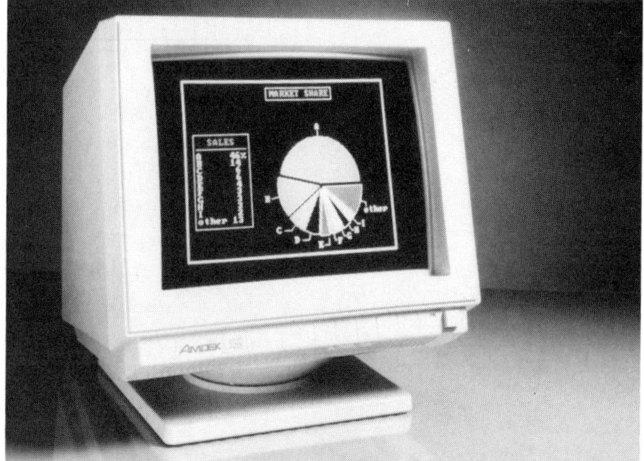

(b)

FIGURE 2–3

Some "Typical" Video Displays (a) Quadram's Quadchrome Enhanced Display. *(Photo courtesy of Quadram.)* (b) Amdek's Color 725 Display. *(Photo courtesy of Amdek.)*

(perhaps over great distances) to a computer, the reservation clerk can determine the flight departure times and fares for a particular city pair, can ascertain whether a particular flight has vacancies, and can confirm a reservation. Terminals are commonplace in grocery stores. Each checkout station is equipped with a point-of-sale terminal that is able to read the bar codes of the products purchased and to calculate the bill. Most of us have used an automated teller machine that tells us the status of our account and furnishes us with cash. This is just another terminal.

Terminals, along with printers, plotters, and storage devices like tape drives and disk drives, are called **peripherals** if they are not part of the system unit. Some microcomputers are capable of supporting several users concurrently. When this

FIGURE 2–4

Some "Typical" Terminals *(Courtesy of West Publishing Company.)*

is the case, each user may interact and communicate with the microcomputer through a terminal.

Central Processing Unit

The **central processing unit** (or CPU) consists of two subcomponents, the microprocessor and primary storage. The **microprocessor** does all arithmetic and logical operations. As the microcomputer's "brain," it is also responsible for overall system control. The microprocessor is usually a single integrated circuit or **chip.** In performing its operations, the microprocessor accepts instructions from **primary storage** only. It is attached or soldered into a **printed circuit board,** which enables it to interact with primary storage by means of etched lines of foil over which data can be transferred between the microprocessor and primary storage.

All programs and data must be placed in primary storage before they can be processed. Unfortunately, primary storage is usually volatile in the sense that when the machine is shut off, the data and programs contained there are lost. Moreover, primary storage is fixed in size and, therefore, unable to simultaneously accommodate all the programs you will want to use. Usually, each program must be loaded and executed separately. Finally, primary storage is expensive when compared with the cost of secondary storage. For all of these reasons, all computers—micros, minis, and mainframes—possess both primary and secondary storage. Primary storage is sometimes referred to as "primary memory" or just "memory."

The reader might wonder why a microprocessor isn't designed to work with secondary storage directly, since secondary storage seems to suffer from none of the shortcomings of primary storage. The reason relates to speed. Secondary storage is slow because it depends on the physical movement of disks and other devices. A processor that performed all of its computations directly with secondary storage would be orders of magnitude slower.

Thus all computers possess both primary and secondary storage. Before any program can be "run," it must first be placed in primary storage. An obvious implication for start-up of a computer follows. When the computer is turned on, the software required to support an application must be loaded from secondary storage into primary storage. The operating system (a part of the system software) is loaded first. This is called **booting.** Then the application software package required to support the specific application desired is loaded. Finally, the user is ready to begin the application.

Primary storage can be thought of as a long array of mail boxes or cells into which information can be stored, as shown in Figure 2–5. Each cell is called a byte. A **byte** is the amount of storage needed to accommodate a single character, such as a letter or number. Like mail boxes, each byte has an address. The microprocessor uses this address when it wants to retrieve data from a specific byte or store data in a byte. For example, if the microprocessor wants to store some data in byte 335542, it first sends the address 335542 to primary storage and informs primary storage to get ready to accept the data. Then it sends the data to primary storage and primary storage places the data in byte 335542.

Shown in Figure 2–5 is a memory map for primary storage. The **memory map** illustrates how programs and data are stored in primary storage. It is worth noting that both programs (software) and data can reside in primary storage at the same time. As we shall discover in Chapter 3, primary storage is also called Random Access Memory (RAM).

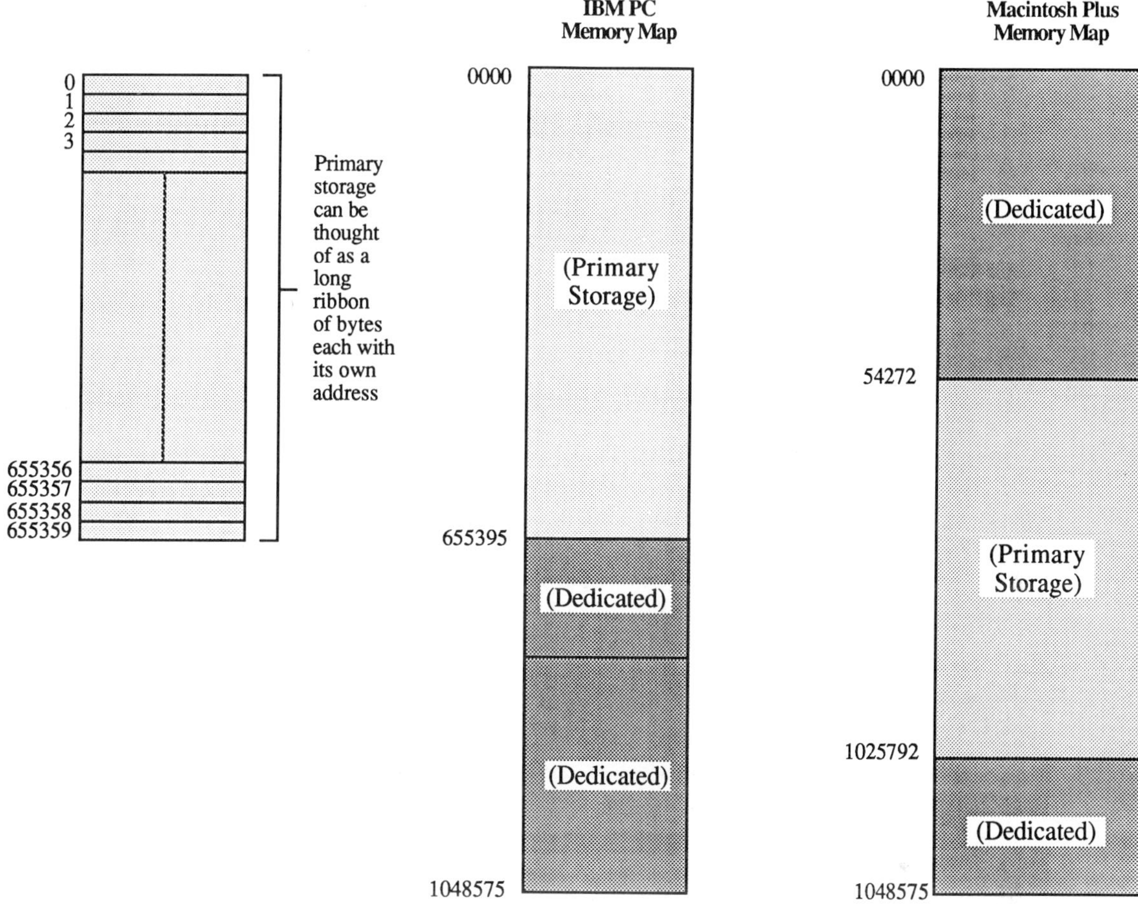

FIGURE 2–5

Organization of Primary Storage

Secondary Storage

Unlike primary storage, secondary storage is permanent (nonvolatile), and inexpensive. Secondary storage is not volatile because it does not depend on electricity to be sustained. The storage medium is usually some magnetizable surface such as magnetic tape or disk. Figure 2–6 depicts some secondary storage devices and media.

At least two basic types of secondary storage are commonly used in small computers: hard disks and floppy disks (also called diskettes). Hard disks generally are nonremovable rigid metallic platters encased in a sealed housing. Hard disks are much faster (by ten times, roughly) than floppies and the density of information storage is much higher than floppies. They are also more expensive than floppy disks. Floppy diskettes are removable media; therefore, an unlimited amount of information may be stored through or retrieved from a single floppy disk drive. Hard, fixed disks are limited to the storage capacity of the single disk itself. The data and software stored on magnetic media are read from and written onto the medium by means of read/write heads that are similar to the read/write heads used in audio and stereo equipment.

Secondary storage, like primary storage, consists of bytes. Moreover, bytes consist of bits. The **bit** is an acronym for binary digit, and is used in both primary

FIGURE 2–6

Some Typical Secondary Storage Devices and Media

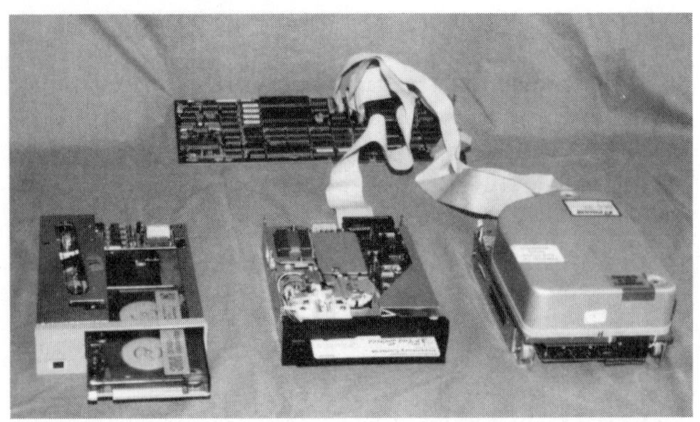

and secondary storage. It is the smallest unit of memory. As the term *binary digit* would suggest, each bit is a zero/one or on/off device. All data and programs are ultimately stored as long strings of zeros and ones called bits, and grouped into bytes. For example, by convention it is agreed that the letter *A* will be represented by the bits 0100 0001. Each byte is comprised of eight bits; clearly, the byte contains exactly the number of bits required to accommodate the letter *A*. Similar conventions apply to all the other letters of the alphabet; each requires eight bits, or exactly one byte. The codes assigned to each letter are called **ASCII codes**. ASCII is an acronym for American Standard Code for Information Interchange.

In addition to bits and bytes, the software, textual material, and data stored on secondary storage devices are grouped into larger entities called files. A **file** is an entire collection of bytes taken together by virtue of their common purpose, function, or identity. As we shall see, all files require a name, called a filename. There are three basic types of files: program files (software), text files, and data files. **Program files** contain either system or applications software. **Text files** contain text that has been entered and saved by means of applications software. In general, text files are files consisting entirely of ASCII codes. Some word processing programs are able to save documents as text files on permanent storage. **Data files** contain data that was entered and saved by means of a spreadsheet, data base management package, or some other applications software package.

System Software

The **system software** is the housekeeping or host software that interfaces directly with the hardware. In fact, the software components interact to support the user in a layered fashion, as shown in Figure 2–7.

The user interacts with the applications software, which in turn interacts with the system software. The system software interacts with the hardware.

Figure 2–8 depicts the major components of system software. The most important part of the system software is the operating system. The **operating system** is a collection of related computer programs used to supervise and direct the tasks and operations engaged in by the hardware. The operating system consists of device drivers (to control communication between the CPU and devices such as printers, keyboards, CRTs, and disk drives), a user interface, and a control program. The operating system is often called the DOS (an acronym for Disk Operating System). **Device drivers** are computer programs (software) which direct the hardware in

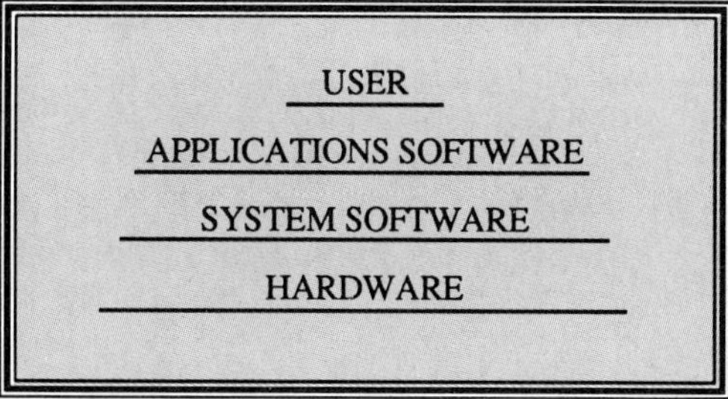

FIGURE 2–7
Layered Support System Used by Computers

specific tasks to be done, such as turning on a floppy disk drive, moving the read/write heads to the appropriate track, and so forth. A printer driver is a program that directs and controls the flow of information to the printer. Printer drivers are hardware-specific. The **user interface** consists of directives that the user enters via the keyboard (or other input device); these directives inform the system software what the user wants done. As will be discussed, a directive might be an item selected from a menu, an icon that has been selected, or a command (memorized by the user) that the user enters. In any case, **directives** are a common set of conventions by which the user communicates with the system software and hence with the computer itself.

In addition to the operating system, the system software may include language translators (BASIC, FORTH, COBOL, C, Pascal, LOGO, etc.), utilities, and communications software. **Utilities** are computer programs that perform housekeeping chores, such as copying a file or computer program from one diskette to another. **Communications software** enables microcomputers to emulate terminals when talking to large computers, and to transmit/receive files to/from other computers. Microcomputers can also communicate with other microcomputers by means of communications software.

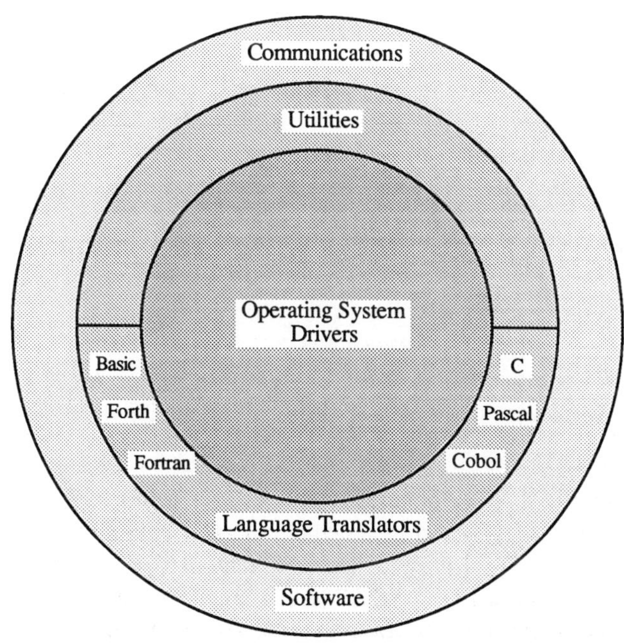

FIGURE 2–8
Major Components of the System Software

Applications Software

Applications software will include all the packages shown in Table 2–1. As its name implies, applications software is computer programs designed to support specific applications. For example, a word processing program is applications software designed to support the entering, editing, formatting, and printing of textual matter. Applications software is usually acquired separately from the purchase of the hardware at additional cost. In addition, users may create (by writing programs) one or more applications software packages of their own.

CLASSIFYING MICROCOMPUTERS ACCORDING TO FORM

Microcomputers are available in a variety of forms to enhance their functionality. Perhaps the most common form is the **desktop computer**. The desktop computer, as shown in Figure 2–9, consists of a keyboard, display, and system unit. The system unit contains the microprocessor, primary storage, and secondary storage, which is usually disk drives of the fixed (hard) or floppy variety. To reduce the space on the desk required by all this equipment, some configurations allow the system unit to stand on its end underneath or beside the desk. In addition, the display can be placed on a movable rack or elevated pedestal that lifts it off of the

TABLE 2–1

Taxonomy of Applications Software

Word Processing Systems

Data Base Management Systems (DBMS)
- File and record management programs
- Relational DBMS

Decision Support Systems
- Electronic spreadsheets
- Financial planning packages
- Simulation languages
- Computer models
- Statistical packages

Managerial Systems
- Electronic calendars/schedulers
- Time management packages
- Personnel management packages
- Project management packages

Accounting and Inventory Systems
- Payroll
- Accounts payable
- Accounts receivable
- Order entry/invoicing
- General ledger
- Sales inventory systems
- Manufacturing inventory systems

(a)

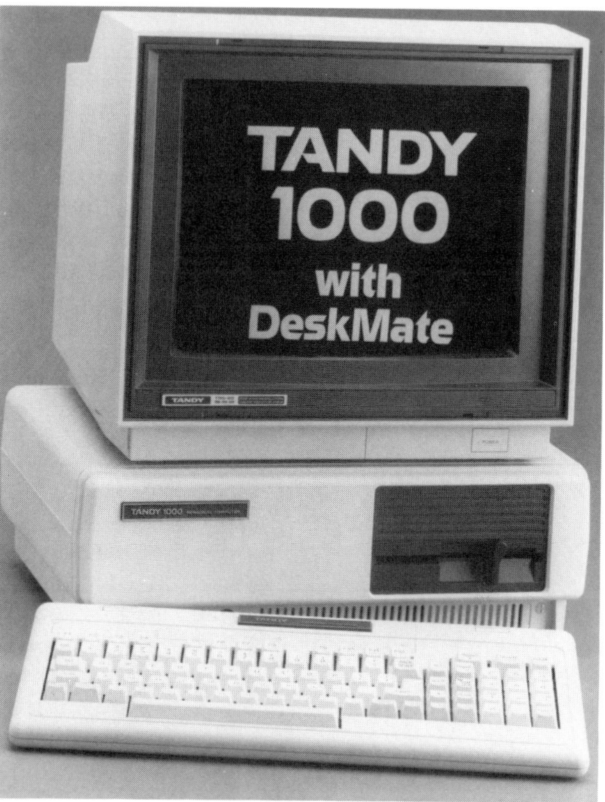

(b)

FIGURE 2–9

Two Popular Desktop Computers The Compaq Deskpro 386.™ *(Courtesy of Compaq Computer Corporation.)* (b) The Tandy 1000 Desktop Computer. *(Courtesy of Radio Shack Advertising.)*

desk top. For our purposes these alternate configurations will also be considered desktop computers.

The desktop computer is the most conventional form of the microcomputer, and the most widely used. It supports all of the applications discussed in Chapter 1. It does have one drawback, however; it is not easily moved or transported.

The Personal System/2 line of personal computers, introduced by IBM in April of 1987, contained several models with system units in vertical cabinets intended to be placed on the floor beside a desk or inside the footwell of a desk. This is true of the Models 60, 70, and 80 of the Personal System/2 line, as depicted in Figure 2–10.

For users who change workplaces occasionally and wish to take their computers with them, the **transportable computer** was developed. The transportable is a microcomputer that can be packaged into a single unit for convenient transport from one work location to another. The display is usually incorporated into the system unit in some way, as shown in Figure 2–11. The detachable keyboard fits into a portion of the unit or attaches to it, permitting all the components to be fitted together into a single unit so they can be transported in one trip, instead of several. Insofar as computing power and capacity are concerned, the transportable is as capable as a desktop.

The transportable might seem to be a more utilitarian form of the microcomputer than the desktop, but it has some drawbacks. First, the display is smaller—usually 7 or 9 in. (measured diagonally) instead of 12 or 15 in., as for desktops.

FIGURE 2–10

The IBM Personal System/2 Model 80. *(Courtesy of International Business Machines Corporation.)*

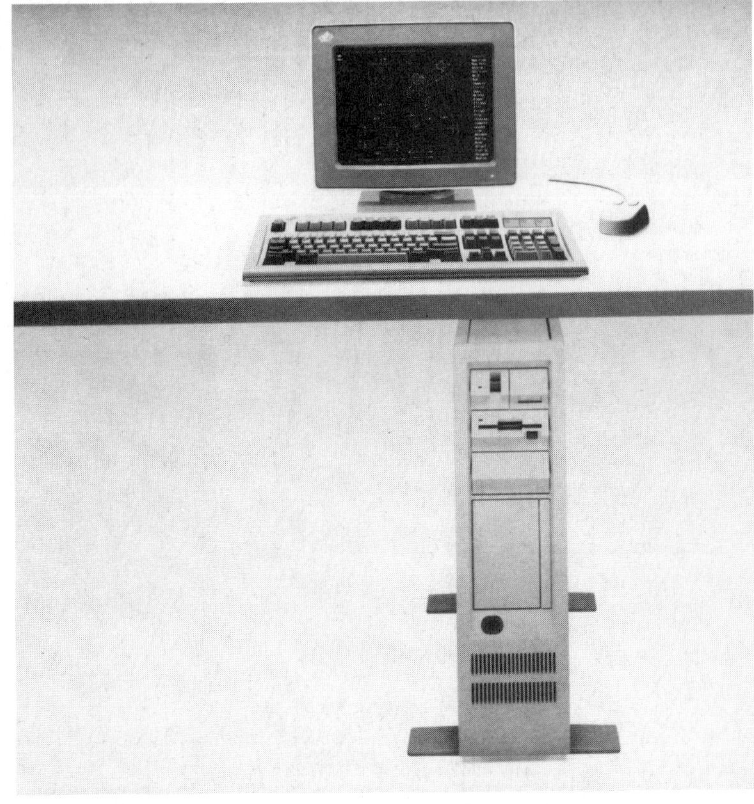

FIGURE 2–11

Two Popular Transportable Computers. (a) The Cordata Transportable AT Computer. *(Photo Courtesy of Cordata.)* (b) The Compaq Portable 286. *(Courtesy of Compaq Computer Corporation.)*

(a)

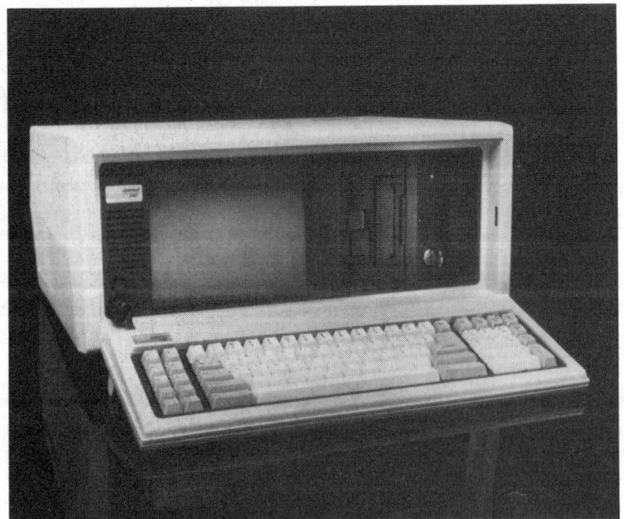

(b)

THE PERVASIVENESS OF THE MICROCOMPUTER

In ten short years, the microcomputer has penetrated our homes, schools, and places of work, like no other technology in the history of mankind. This photo essay graphically portrays the tremendous impact the microcomputer is having in every facet of modern life. In the photos to follow, it will become clear that the microcomputer has permanently changed our ways of working, of communicating, of learning, and of playing.

In what follows we shall consider a variety of contexts in which microcomputers are being used and are having an impact. First, we look at applications of microcomputers in large organizations. Then we shall delineate the use of microcomputers within small business, within the professions (law, medicine, architecture), within schools, and in the home.

Microcomputer Usage in the Professions

In the past half-dozen years, corporate America has spent tens of billions of dollars on microcomputers, but even more has been spent on training corporate professionals in the usage of the machines. As depicted above, microcomputers are used by business professions for such applications as word processing (the preparation of memos, documents, reports, letters), spreadsheets (for cash management, budget control, financial planning), and data base management (for management of information about the companies' labor, material, and capital resources)—topics about which much will be said in Chapters 5 through 10. *(Courtesy of International Business Machines Corporation)*

Above, a computer professional develops a worksheet template (see Chapter 8) for use by others. In recent years the spreadsheet program has given rise to a new kind of "programmer" called a *spreadsheet programmer*. This person is quite skilled in the use of spreadsheets and can develop customized menus, extensive macros, and protected templates within the worksheet so it can be easily used by managers. *(Courtesy of Compaq Computer Corporation)*

The advent of the microcomputer has revolutionized inventory recordkeeping (see Chapter 13) in a warehouse operation. Records on over 100,000 items of inventory are retained on the computer's hard drive. *(Courtesy of International Business Machines Corporation)*

Above, construction workers are logging the data and time of the job they have just completed and of the job they will begin next. The information is used for monitoring and control of the construction project as discussed in Chapter 12. *(Courtesy of International Business Machines Corporation)*

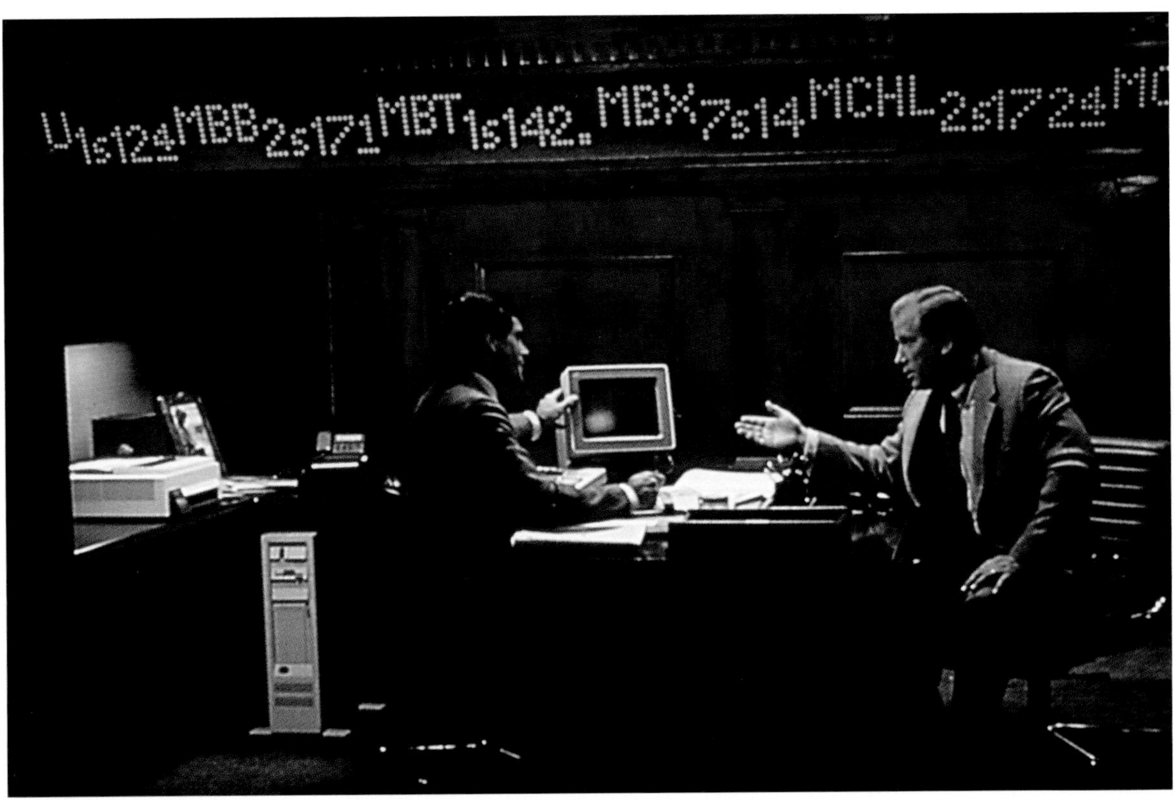

Microcomputers are being used by stock brokers to perform analyses on stocks and bonds, as depicted above. Stock brokers use microcomputers to track stocks, compute moving averages, and issue "buy" and "sell" recommendations. It is possible to have "ticker tape" information communicated directly to the microcomputer via phone lines for up-to-the-minute processing and analysis. *(Courtesy of International Business Machines Corporation)*

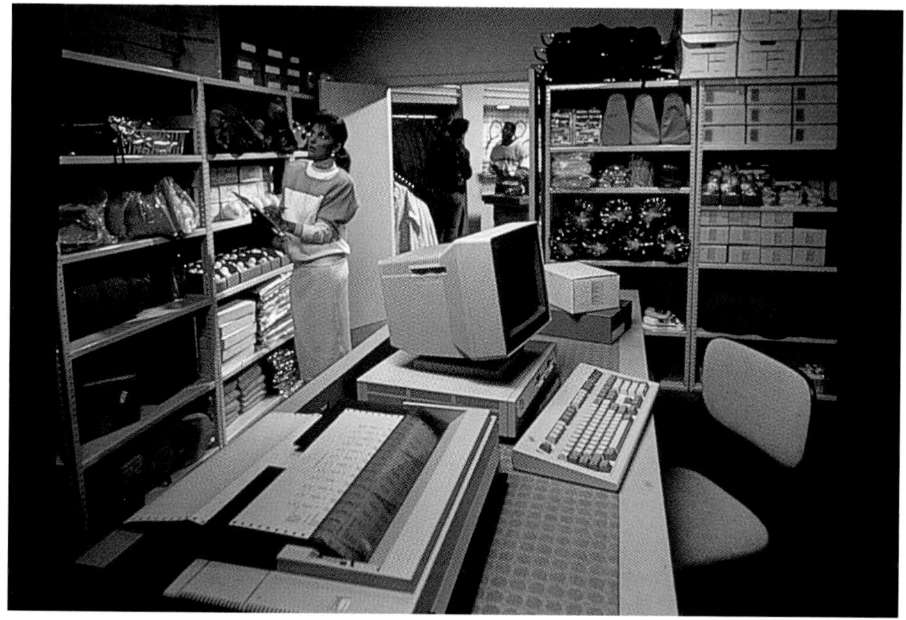

Today, microcomputers are being used in retailing as depicted in the photo to the left to track inventory, bill customers, and even discriminate among vendors when making inventory purchasing decisions. *(Courtesy of International Business Machines Corporation)*

Above, a dispatcher for a small package air carrier is using a portable microcomputer to monitor and control the locations of the delivery and pick-up vans. *(Courtesy of Compaq Computer Corporation)*

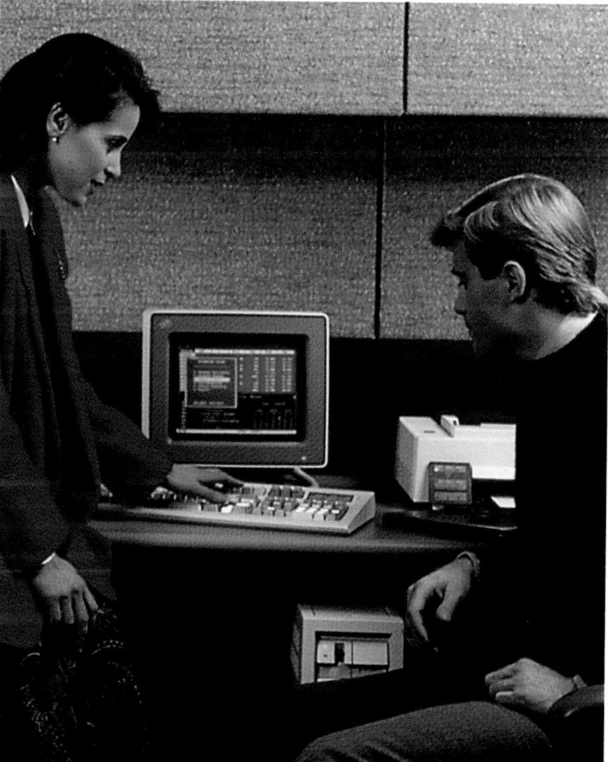

In addition to word processing, spreadsheets, and data base management, microcomputers may be used in small businesses for accounting purposes. Accounting systems enable small businesses to track their receivables (what is owed to them), to control their payables (amounts they owe to others), and to monitor the overall financial condition of the business, as discussed in Chapter 13. *(Courtesy of International Business Machines Corporation)*

Designers and analysts within large organizations make extensive use of microcomputers for the same applications that executives use them. But these professionals also utilize them for computer-aided design, drafting, and drawing. Shown above, a designer is using his microcomputer to develop a pattern for fabric to be used on bed sheets and pillow cases. *(Courtesy of Compaq Computer Corporation)*

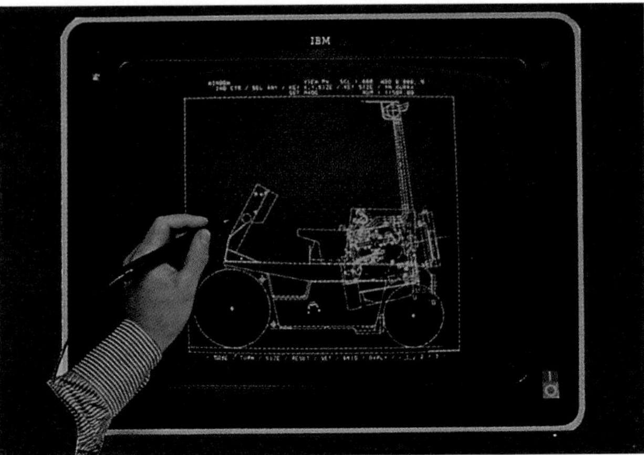

A specialized application for microcomputers is computer-aided design/computer-aided manufacturing. More is said about this application in Chapter 11. *(Courtesy of International Business Machines Corporation)*

An architect is using architectural renduring software to design a tall building in the photo to the right. The software can rotate the image of the building so the architect can view it from an unlimited number of perspectives. Often such software will permit the architect to see the building in the context of its architectural environment. *(Courtesy of Compaq Computer Corporation)*

Shown above, an industrial engineer lays out a manufacturing facility. With the aid of manufacturing layout software, thousands of layout combinations can be tried and tested in minutes, whereas the same process might take days or months by hand. Near optimal layout plans can be obtained. *(Courtesy of International Business Machines Corporation)*

These subdivision planners are using a personal computer to plot a housing addition. Like all computerized applications, this one gives the planners the opportunity to rapidly develop and evaluate a number of alternative housing plans. This can be done with orders-of-magnitude greater speed and efficiency than what was available before computers became pervasive. *(Courtesy of International Business Machines Corporation)*

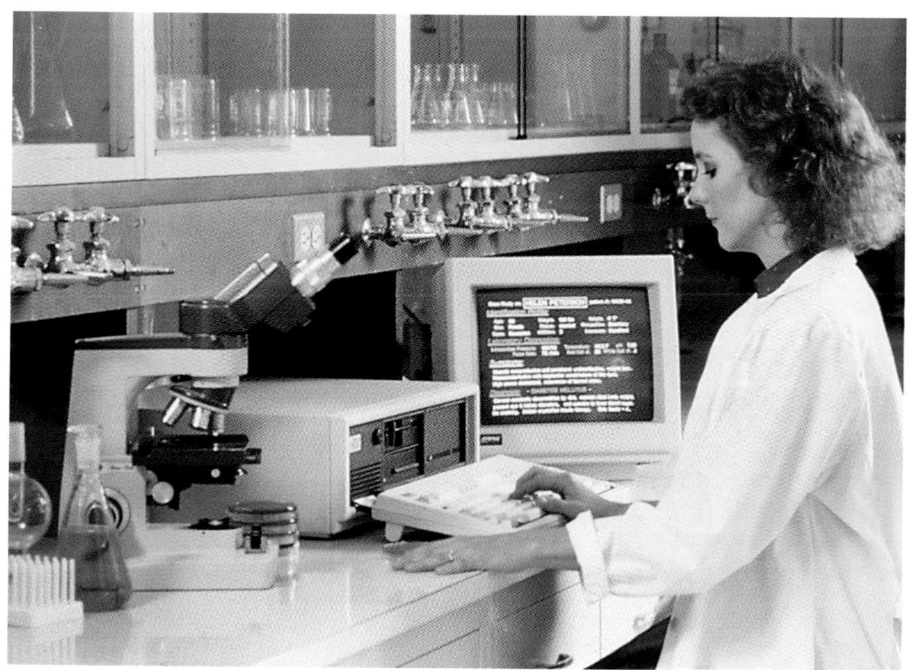

An industrial chemist uses a personal computer for recording the results of an experiment and for calculations in the photo to the left. *(Courtesy of Compaq Computer Corporation)*

Above, a microcomputer is being used to keep medical records in a medical clinic. By networking (Chapter 15) with other microcomputers in the medical office, it is possible to record every service that was performed on a patient, to produce a consolidated invoice or bill showing all services performed, and to present this to the patient prior to the patient's departure. *(Courtesy of Apple Computer, Inc.)*

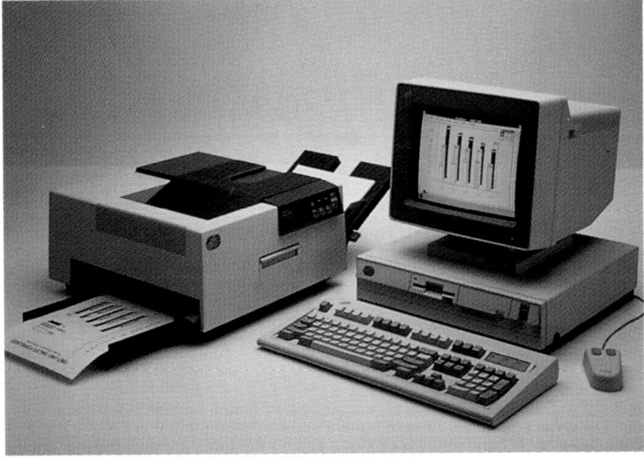

An application which is taking on increasing importance in our information society is that of desktop publishing (discussed in Chapter 6), which has proven so useful to writers, academics, advertising agencies, and print shops, as well as major corporations and governments. *(Courtesy of International Business Machines Corporation)*

Above, an advertising agency president is shown using a personal computer to generate advertising copy. Graphics can be integrated with text to produce camera-ready copy that is ready for publication, as discussed in Chapter 11. All of which happens with far less investment in required hardware and software than what was true just a few years ago. *(Ellis Herwig/Stock, Boston)*

Microcomputer Usage in Education

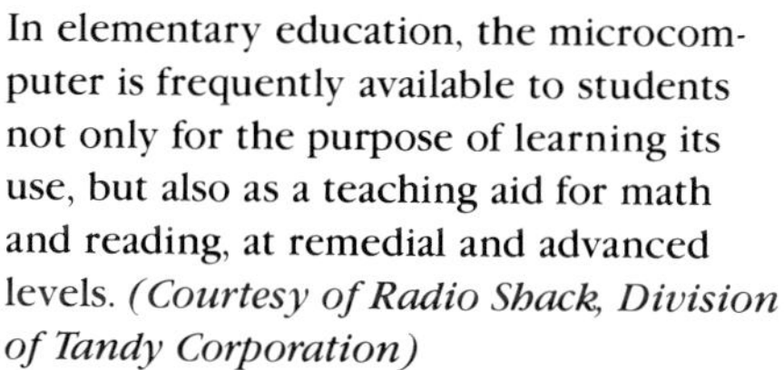

In elementary education, the microcomputer is frequently available to students not only for the purpose of learning its use, but also as a teaching aid for math and reading, at remedial and advanced levels. *(Courtesy of Radio Shack, Division of Tandy Corporation)*

Students are now learning to use microcomputers in their high school classes, not only to study the prevalent computer languages, but also to discover uses such as spreadsheet and other productivity software applications. *(Courtesy of International Business Machines Corporation)*

An instructor, who uses microcomputers in his college classroom, converses with two of his students after class. Projection systems which project the display of the instructor's computer on a large screen for all students to see are now commonplace. *(Courtesy of International Business Machines Corporation)*

Above, a chemistry student is performing molar calculations to determine the precise amounts of ingredients to include in a solution. College students utilize microcomputers in all types of classes. Engineering and chemistry uses as depicted here are just two of the many possible uses to which the microcomputer can be put on college campuses and classrooms. *(Courtesy of Apple Computer, Inc.)*

Microcomputer Usage in the Home

A home owner uses his personal computer to do household budgeting. *(Courtesy of NEC Home Electronics (U.S.A.) Inc., Wood Dale, Ill.)*

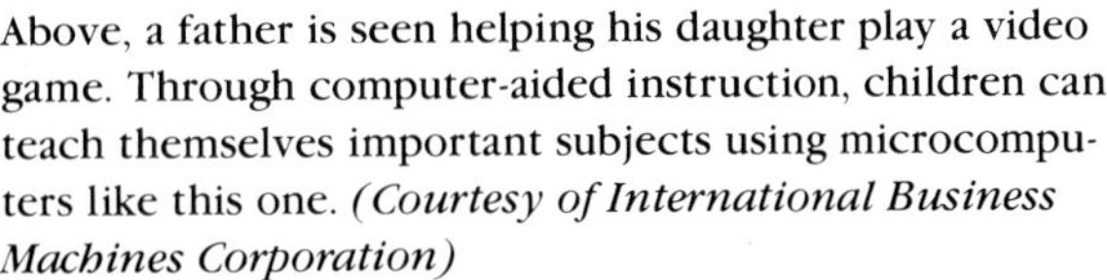

Above, a father is seen helping his daughter play a video game. Through computer-aided instruction, children can teach themselves important subjects using microcomputers like this one. *(Courtesy of International Business Machines Corporation)*

This real estate agent uses a microcomputer for report writing and before coming into the office; she can also take it with her during after-hours property showings for on-the-spot calculations. *(Courtesy of NEC Home Electronics (U.S.A.) Inc., Wood Dale, Ill.)*

From the portrayals above it is apparent that the microcomputer has involved itself with just about every facet of our business and personal lives. Clearly, we must learn well the principles and nuances of using this machine.

(a)

(b)

FIGURE 2–12

Two Popular Laptop Computers. (a) The NEC Multispeed. *(Photo courtesy of NEC Home Electronics (USA) Inc., Wood Dale, IL.)* (b) Zenith Z-181 Laptop Computer. *(Courtesy of Zenith Data Systems, Glenview, IL.)*

Second, transportables are heavy—weighing in at anywhere from 22 to 45 lbs. Third, some transportables are quite bulky. Their weight and size may prevent their being toted between home and work each day. Some transportables are so big they cannot be placed under a standard airline seat, or in the bin above, and you would not want to check them for luggage without placing them in appropriate packaging. Consequently, there is no convenient way to get some of the oversized transportables on board a commercial airline flight.

As a result of the weight and bulkiness of the transportables, the **laptop** or **briefcase computer** has evolved. Weighing in at under 15 lbs. (the average is around 6 or 7 lbs.), these computers have flat displays with attached keyboards. Laptop computers are appropriate for use by traveling professionals such as salespeople. The same set of productivity applications is supported as for transportables and desktops. Expandability is limited as compared with desktop and transportable computers. Due to their smaller size, laptop computers generally do not have expansion slots which permit the user to add additional memory, external ports, hard-disk controllers, and such. Some laptop computers have built-in devices called **modems** that allow text and data to be transmitted to other computers via the phone lines. (More will be said about modems in Chapter 14.) Other laptop computers have built-in hard drives. The use of 3½-inch floppy drives in conjunction with laptop computers is commonplace. As the name suggests, these computers are small enough to fit in a briefcase. Figure 2–12 depicts some laptop computers.

The last classification of microcomputer, and the one we will have the least interest in, is the **hand-held** or **pocket computer**. These computers are used by technicians, businesspeople, and engineers to perform calculations while they are

Focus Feature

A TYPICAL COMPUTER SESSION: HOW IT GOES

This article describes how to bring a microcomputer system up and get it running. It explains how files are created, saved, loaded, edited, and saved again. Finally, this article describes how to terminate a session with the microcomputer.

First, it is important to point out that different computers are turned on and made operational in different ways. We choose to discuss this operation in terms of computer systems classified by the operating systems they use. Two of the more prominent operating systems in use are CP/M and MS-DOS. CP/M is an acronym for Control Program/Microcomputer and DOS is an abbreviation for Disk Operating System. For all intents and purposes, IBM's PC-DOS is a type of MS-DOS in that both were developed by Microsoft, Inc. Minor differences do exist between PC-DOS and MS-DOS, however. There are variations within these two classes, so readers are encouraged to consult their user's manuals if the instructions given here are unsuccessful.

MS-DOS MACHINES

The first thing that must happen in most MS-DOS machines is called booting (loading) the operating system. MS-DOS computers accomplish this in two ways. One way is called a "cold boot" and the other is called a "warm boot." For machines without hard or fixed disks, a cold boot is accomplished as follows. For such machines the system software resides on a single diskette called the *system diskette*. The system diskette is inserted into drive A and the machine is turned on. Drive A is usually the top drive if the disk drive insertion slots are horizontal; otherwise, drive A is the leftmost drive when the diskette drives are vertical. The diskette should be inserted with the label up if the drives are horizontal, and with the label facing left if the drives are vertical. After some testing of its integrated circuits, a *bootstrap program* permanently contained in those same integrated circuits loads the operating system from the secondary-storage diskette into primary storage, where it is activated. At that time, control of the computer is turned over to the operating system. For systems which boot from the hard disk, all that is required is to turn the system on. The bootstrap program will automatically load the operating system from the hard disk.

A warm boot is accomplished after the machine has already been turned on and is useful if a particular software package being used "hangs" the machine, rendering it totally disfunctional. When this happens, the user must reboot the operating system and start over. This is accomplished by *simultaneously* pressing the <Ctrl> key, the <Alt> key, and the <Del> key. (Please note the emphasis on "simultaneously." Pressing these keys in sequence will not work.) The system diskette must reside in drive A for floppy diskette systems. The bootstrap program is reactivated and the operating system is rebooted exactly as in a cold boot.

Figure 2–13 depicts the initial sign-on sequence for an MS-DOS machine. The first four lines are automatic in the sense that all the user has to do is turn the machine on and they will be displayed. They indicate that initial testing was satisfactory, that 384K (approximately 384,000 storage locations) of primary storage are installed and available to DOS. The next line is "Booting . . ." and informs the user that the operating system has been found on the system diskette and is being loaded by the bootstrap program. The next line is "Microsoft MS-DOS version 2.11"; this line indicates that the operating

```
System ROM Version 3.06
Testing Complete
 384K Memory installed
 384K Memory available to DOS
Booting...
Microsoft MS-DOS version 2.11
Copyright 1981,82,83 Microsoft Corp.

Command v. 2.11
Current date is Tue  1-01-1980
Enter new date:  12-19-87
Current time is  0:00:27.36
Enter new time:  15:40

A>_
```

FIGURE 2–13

Typical Sign-on Display for an MS-DOS Machine

system has been successfully loaded and is in control. Before the operating system will accept directives (commands) from the user, it wants to know the date and time. It first informs the user that, according to its records, the "Current date is Tue 1-01-1980," and it then asks, "Enter new date:", to which the user response is **12-19-87** followed by pressing the <**Return**> key. It then displays what it believes to be the current time as "Current time is 0:00:27.36," and asks the user to "Enter new time:", to which the response is **15:40** (40 minutes after 3 P.M.), followed by <**Return**>**.** The operating system uses the values the user provided for date and time to maintain the current time and date within primary storage. The date and time are used to *date stamp* and *time stamp* all files created in a session. Finally, the operating system displays its *prompt* to the user (the A>_), indicating it is ready to accept commands. A partial list of common user commands is shown in Table 2–3. for both MS-DOS and PC-DOS.

The "A" in front of the A>_ prompt tells the user which disk drive is the "default" drive. If no drive is specified in connection with a disk-related command, the operating system assumes the default drive. Most microcomputers have at least two disk drives, designated "A" and "B."

Suppose the user wishes to change the default drive. This could be done by typing **B:** followed by pressing the <**Return**> key. The operating system prompt would now appear as "B>_". The operating system is now ready to accept commands entered by the user at this prompt. If no drive is specified in conjunction with these commands, the operating system will assume the default drive. If the user now typed **DIR** (an acronym for DIRectory) followed by <**Return**> a list of all files on the diskette in drive "B" would be displayed. Of course, the user could have obtained the same list by typing **DIR B:** while still retaining "A" as the default drive. In this latter case a specific drive has been designated—namely drive "B"—and this designation overrides the default specification. Similar statements can be made about all the other commands which relate to a disk drive in some way. In the section on User Interfaces, a thorough discussion of the DIR command is given.

Users learn very quickly that they do not have to enter the date and time to get to the operating system prompt. Simply by pressing <**Return**> twice the user jumps past the "Enter new date:" and the "Enter new time:" prompts and the date and time assume their default values, which for the above-mentioned case are 1-01-1980 and 0:00:27.36. However, it is very important that users develop the habit of actually entering the date and time so newly created and updated files will always exhibit the actual date and time at which they were last updated or created. This is extremely useful in distinguishing the latest file from older files that might have a similar name.

Of importance to first-time users of microcomputers are the conventions regarding naming of files. Fortunately, the rules are essentially the same for both MS-DOS and CP/M. These rules are presented in Table 2–2 and should be studied carefully, because all the applications to be discussed in forthcoming chapters will require use of these same rules. Further discussion concerning use of the MS-DOS, PC-DOS, and other operating systems will be reserved for Chapter 4.

CP/M MACHINES

CP/M (an abbreviation for Control Program/Microcomputer) machines are very similar to MS-DOS in that the operating system must first be booted, the operating system prompt is identical, and the commands are very similar. To boot the operating system, however, the user must place the system diskette in the default drive and turn the machine on just as for an MS-DOS machine. However, unlike MS-DOS, many CP/M machines require that the user must now depress <**Return**> or some other key such as **B** (for "boot"). Upon doing so, the operating system will be booted just as before. All versions of CP/M prior to CP/M 3.0 do not request the current date and time; instead, they display the operating system prompt immediately. When the directory command DIR is issued with these older versions, the user will also discover that the files are not time and date stamped, as in MS-DOS. This makes tracking of files more difficult. Other significant differences exist between the two operating systems, but these are beyond the scope of this article (see Chapter 4).

(*Continued*)

Focus Feature (Continued)

A TYPICAL COMPUTER SESSION: HOW IT GOES

TABLE 2–2

Rules Governing Naming of Files in MS-DOS (PC-DOS) and CP/M

1. Each filename consists of three parts: a drive designation, a primary filename, and a secondary filename or extension. The filename may consist of upper- or lowercase alphabetic characters. Lowercase characters are translated to uppercase automatically.
2. All parts of the filename must be adjacent without interleaving spaces.
3. The first part is a drive letter followed by a ":", such as "A:", "c:", etc. This part may be omitted; in such cases, the system assumes the default (or logged) drive.
4. The primary filename is eight or fewer characters long. All of the characters must be alphanumeric, that is, either alphabetic or numeric.
5. The secondary filename is optional. If used, it is three (or fewer) alphanumeric characters long.
6. A period must appear between the primary and the secondary filename, if the secondary filename is included.
7. The secondary filename is used to designate file type; the user should use the following conventions:
   .DAT—a data file
   .TXT—a text file
   .EXE—a program file
   In some instances, the application program will place its own extension onto the filename, regardless of whether one is specified by the user.
8. The following are legitimate filenames:
   `MYFILE` `a:CHAP1.dat`
   `junkfile.dat` `Chapter5`
   `C:BALANCE.WKS` `EE`
   It should be noted that lowercase letters are usually converted to uppercase and most operating systems do not distinguish between upper- and lowercase.
9. The filename selected for a new file should be unique. A non-unique filename will cause the operating system to overwrite an existing file (with the same filename) on the diskette, destroying the old file.
10. The following are not legitimate filenames:
    1:mydata.dat — drive specification incorrect
    Junk.file —secondary filename too long
    z:DATA —drive specification incorrect
    the.end.fil —only one period
    Mitchells.dat —primary filename too long

LOADING AND EXECUTING PROGRAMS

To execute (or run) an application program in many microcomputer systems, the user merely types the primary name of the program after the operating system (or DOS) prompt followed by the <Return> key. For example, to execute the program file FUNGAME.EXE, the user merely types **"FUNGAME"** and <**Return**> after the A>_. This will cause the program file FUNGAME to be loaded into primary storage and the computer will begin executing the machine instructions in FUNGAME. Suppose FUNGAME is one of six files saved on the diskette in drive A. The other five files can be also executed, if they are program files. Text files and data files cannot be executed because they do not contain machine instructions.

TABLE 2–3

Partial List of Commonly Used Operating System Commands in MS-DOS or PC-DOS

DIR	–Displays a directory listing of the files on a disk, and may give other information such as the size of files, the type of file and its protection level, and the date and time it was created or last updated.
COPY	–Copies a file, usually from one disk to another. In some operating systems this can be used to merge files or to transfer data between machines.
ERASE	–Deletes a file from a disk.
TYPE	–Displays file contents on the screen.
RENAME	–Changes the name of a file on a disk. Abbreviated to REN for some systems.
DATE	–Displays or sets the date for systems that use an internal clock.
TIME	–Displays or sets the time for systems with internal clocks.

Only program files can be executed. Program files generally will end with the extension ".EXE" or ".COM" as part of the filename. Once an application program is executing, the user must follow the instructions provided by the program or by the manual accompanying the program.

SAVING AND RETRIEVING NON-PROGRAM FILES

Most application programs allow the user to save and retrieve work as a file to and from secondary storage. For example, a word processing program allows the user to save the memo, document, or letter that was created as a file (on secondary storage). A spreadsheet program allows the user to save the worksheet that was created, and a data base management program permits the user to save the data as a separate file on secondary storage. These text and data files which the user creates by use of applications software are non-program files in the sense that they cannot be executed and contain no executable machine code. The user can save these files by selecting the **SAVE** directive in the application program being used. The application program will prompt the user for a filename if none is given. The user's response will be consistent with the naming conventions listed in Table 2–2. Invoking the **SAVE** command will cause the file currently being worked on to be copied from primary memory to secondary storage where it is permanently retained.

At some later time, the user may wish to return to work previously saved. This can be done by first loading and executing the application program and then using the application program to retrieve the appropriate non-program file from secondary storage. By issuing a **LOAD** directive, the application program will respond with a prompt for a filename if none was provided at the time the **LOAD** directive was issued. The user then enters the name of the file to be loaded and the application program will open the file and load a portion or all of it into primary storage. The user may now continue with the creation—adding to or enhancing previous creative activities which were saved in the previous session. These concepts are illustrated in Figure 2–14.

Figure 2–15 shows the steps involved in booting up and interacting with the computer when the operating system and the application software reside on the same disk. In the appendix to Chapter 4, a procedure for creating an application disk that contains the operating system as well so both can be loaded from one disk at once is given.

TERMINATING A SESSION WITH A MICROCOMPUTER

The procedure for ending a session with a microcomputer is straightforward and simple. First, the user will want to save whatever work is currently in primary storage so it can be retrieved at a later session. After all work is saved, the user simply removes all floppy diskettes from their drives and turns off the power. There is no need to return to the operating system from the application program. Some machines require that several power switches be shut off: one to the display, another to the system unit, and still another to the printer.

(*Continued*)

Focus Feature (Continued)

A TYPICAL COMPUTER SESSION: HOW IT GOES

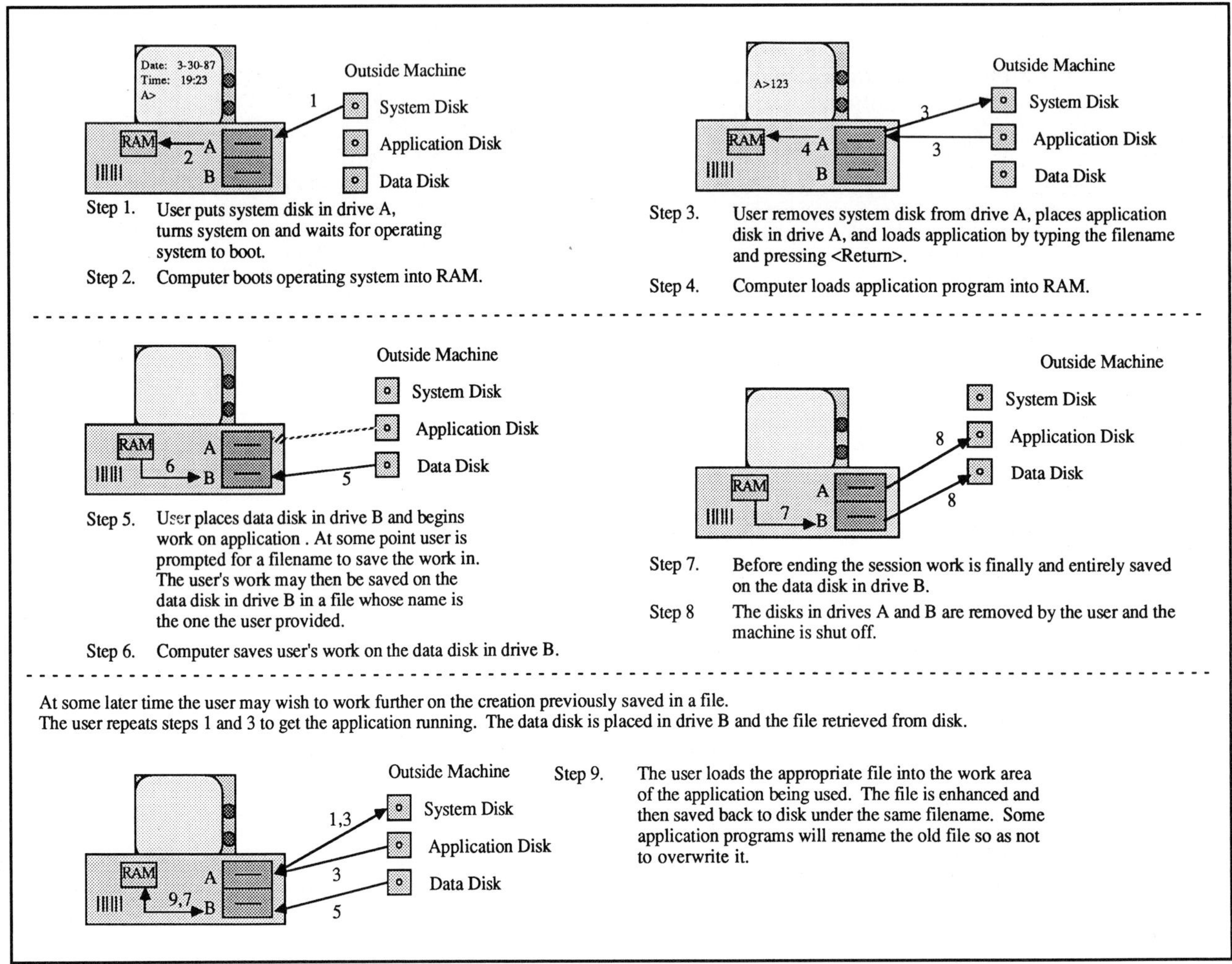

Date: 3-30-87
Time: 19:23
A>
Outside Machine
System Disk
Application Disk
Data Disk
RAM
A
B
Step 1. User puts system disk in drive A, turns system on and waits for operating system to boot.
Step 2. Computer boots operating system into RAM.
A>123
Step 3. User removes system disk from drive A, places application disk in drive A, and loads application by typing the filename and pressing <Return>.
Step 4. Computer loads application program into RAM.
Step 5. User places data disk in drive B and begins work on application . At some point user is prompted for a filename to save the work in. The user's work may then be saved on the data disk in drive B in a file whose name is the one the user provided.
Step 6. Computer saves user's work on the data disk in drive B.
Step 7. Before ending the session work is finally and entirely saved on the data disk in drive B.
Step 8 The disks in drives A and B are removed by the user and the machine is shut off.
At some later time the user may wish to work further on the creation previously saved in a file.
The user repeats steps 1 and 3 to get the application running. The data disk is placed in drive B and the file retrieved from disk.
Step 9. The user loads the appropriate file into the work area of the application being used. The file is enhanced and then saved back to disk under the same filename. Some application programs will rename the old file so as not to overwrite it.

FIGURE 2–14

Steps Involved in Interacting with a Microcomputer Without a Hard Disk

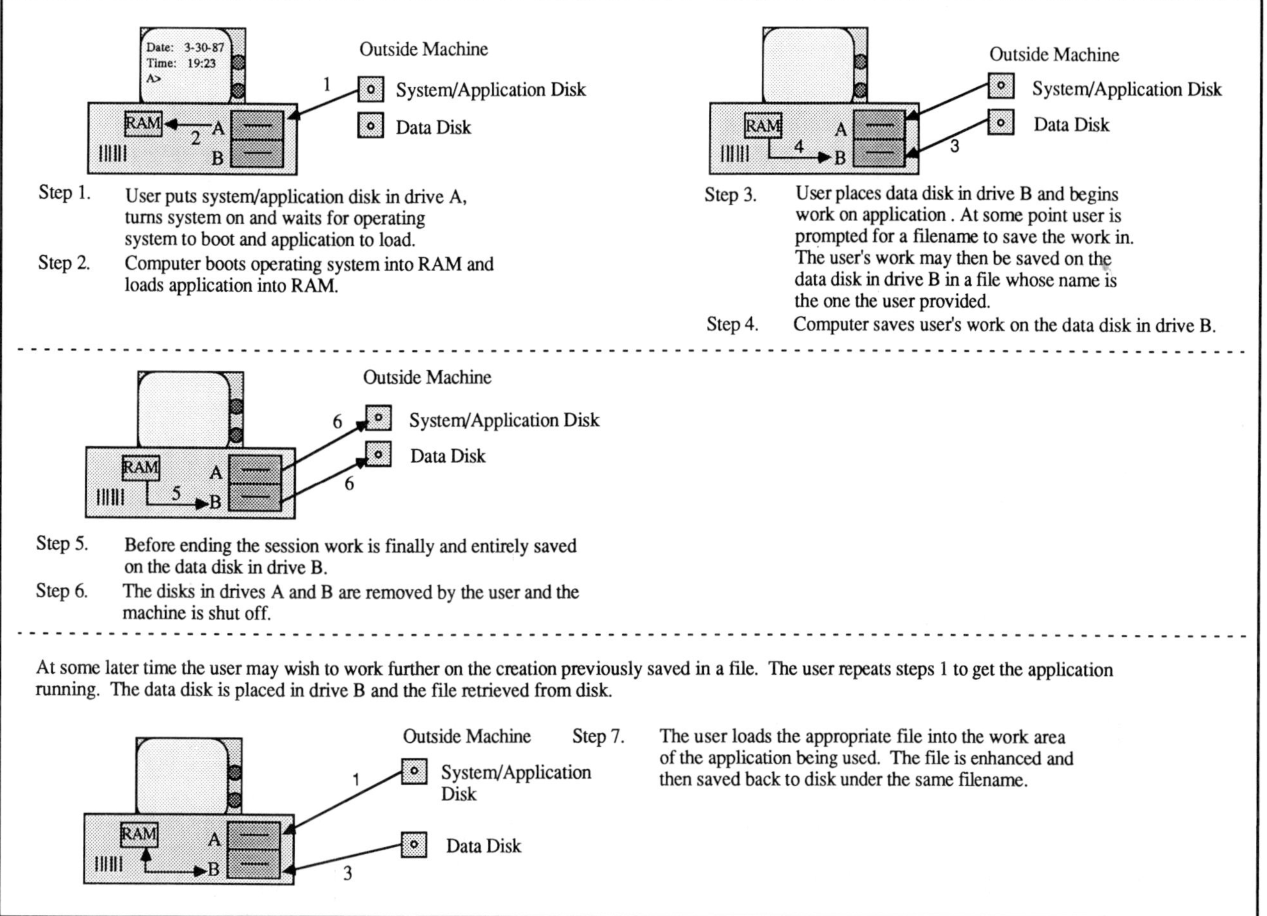

Date: 3-30-87
Time: 19:23
A>
Outside Machine
1
System/Application Disk
Data Disk
RAM
2
A
B
Step 1. User puts system/application disk in drive A, turns system on and waits for operating system to boot and application to load.
Step 2. Computer boots operating system into RAM and loads application into RAM.
Outside Machine
System/Application Disk
Data Disk
RAM
4
A
B
3
Step 3. User places data disk in drive B and begins work on application . At some point user is prompted for a filename to save the work in. The user's work may then be saved on the data disk in drive B in a file whose name is the one the user provided.
Step 4. Computer saves user's work on the data disk in drive B.
Outside Machine
6
System/Application Disk
Data Disk
RAM
A
5
B
6
Step 5. Before ending the session work is finally and entirely saved on the data disk in drive B.
Step 6. The disks in drives A and B are removed by the user and the machine is shut off.
At some later time the user may wish to work further on the creation previously saved in a file. The user repeats steps 1 to get the application running. The data disk is placed in drive B and the file retrieved from disk.
Outside Machine
Step 7. The user loads the appropriate file into the work area of the application being used. The file is enhanced and then saved back to disk under the same filename.
1
System/Application Disk
Data Disk
RAM
A
B
3

FIGURE 2–15

Steps Involved in Interacting with a Microcomputer When the Operating System and Application Software Reside on the Same Disk

away from their desks. In view of their small size, hand-held computers are somewhat limited in what they can do. Generally, these computers have primary and secondary storage limitations, and the display is very much smaller than that of desktop and transportable computers.

USER INTERFACES

Let us digress a moment and discuss the various ways in which system software and applications software may interact with users. We call these interaction schemes **user interfaces**. Interfaces are simply a boundary between two interacting entities: in this case the user and the computer, which is driven by software.

Directives: Commands and Menus and Icons

As previously mentioned, **directives** are the mechanisms by which users issue directions to computers. You discovered that the MS-DOS and PC-DOS operating systems tend to be *command-driven* in the sense that the user is expected to enter commands and the operating system responds. Obviously, such usage requires that the user recall the appropriate command. Less demanding user interfaces are the so-called *menu-driven, screen-driven, query-driven,* and *icon-driven* interfaces. As we shall see, the applications software to be discussed in succeeding chapters may use any one, or combinations, of these four. Some popular word processing programs are command-driven, while others are menu-driven. Most accounting software employs a combination of menus and screens in their user interfaces. A *menu-driven* interface is one in which the user is presented with a list of choices (a menu) and asked to make a selection. *Screen-driven* interfaces are popular in situations where the user is expected to enter a lot of data, and are employed in data base management software and accounting software. Essentially, the user is presented a screen with fields to be filled in. The user merely types the appropriate data into each field. *Query-driven* interfaces simply present to the user a sequence of questions, or queries, to which the user responds. User responses direct the application program to perform the required processing. *Icon-driven* interfaces present the user with small pictures representing the "thing" about which some action is to be taken. This technique is used in the Apple Macintosh's user interface, is very intuitive, and requires very little memory recall on the part of the user. An example of this interface is shown in Figure 2–16.

The Macintosh interface employs what is known as the desktop metaphor, in which the screen is intended to represent a desktop. Executable files may show up as icons on the desktop. By using the cursor to point to these icons, it is possible to load and execute the programs they represent. A sheet of paper will show up as a sheet or "window" on the desktop. The sheets or windows, as they are called, are areas of the screen surrounded by a border and exhibiting the user's creation within their borders. They may be overlapping. Windows are really opened documents that have been loaded from secondary storage into primary storage. By dragging the sheet to the trash-can icon, the sheet (and thus the document it represents) is thrown away. In addition to trash-can icons and windows, there may

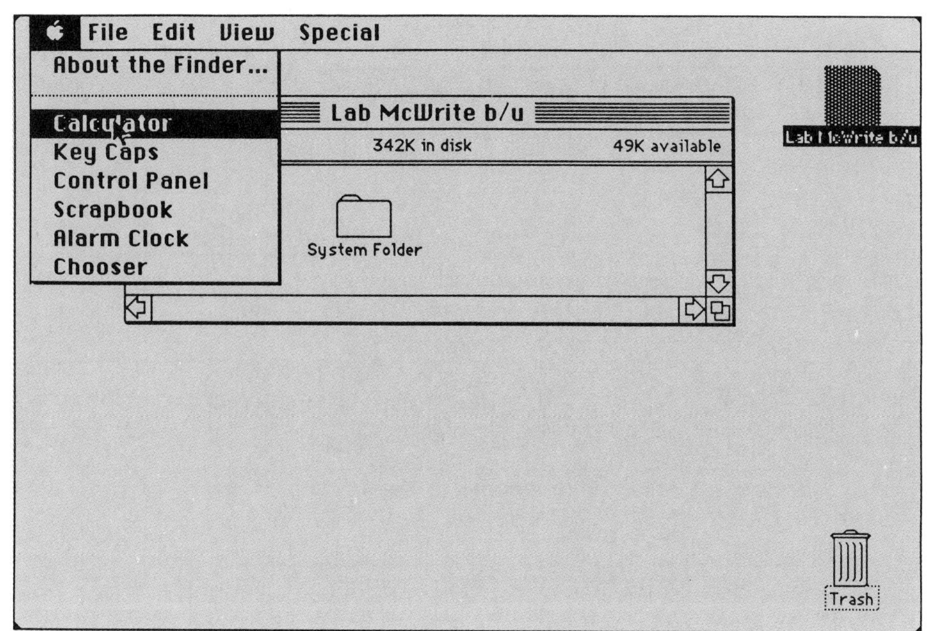

FIGURE 2–16
The Macintosh Interface

be a notepad, a calculator, an alarm clock, a control panel, and other accessories on the Mac desktop as well.

Across the top of the Macintosh screen is a menu bar. By pointing to these with the cursor, the user can "pull down" submenus. Shown in Figure 2–17 is the information that can be stored in conjunction with a file. The following can be recorded in conjunction with each file:

the filename

creation date and time stamp

last-modified date and time stamp

kind of file it is

whether the file is locked (so it can't be thrown away)

which disk and which drive the file is located on

up to three lines of descriptive information about the file

In Figure 2–17 the filename is BurnsFig2.8 (filenames can be more than eight characters long on the Macintosh), the creation date and time stamp is Saturday, February 14, 1987 at 5:48 P.M., and the file is not locked.

As examples of a command-driven interface, we consider MS-DOS and PC-DOS versions 1.00, 1.25, 2.00, 2.11, and 3.00. Provided in Table 2–3 is a partial list of commonly used operating system commands.

Suppose a user wanted a directory list of all files on drive "A." All a user has to do is type the command **DIR** followed by <**Return**> after the A>_ prompt. Displayed on the screen will be the names of the files on the diskette in drive "A" together with their lengths, date stamps, and time stamps, very much like that shown in Figure 2–18. In addition, the number of files (six in this case) and the number of bytes of free space unused on the diskette (222865 in this case) is also displayed.

FIGURE 2–17

Information That Can Be Retained on Any Document Created with the Macintosh

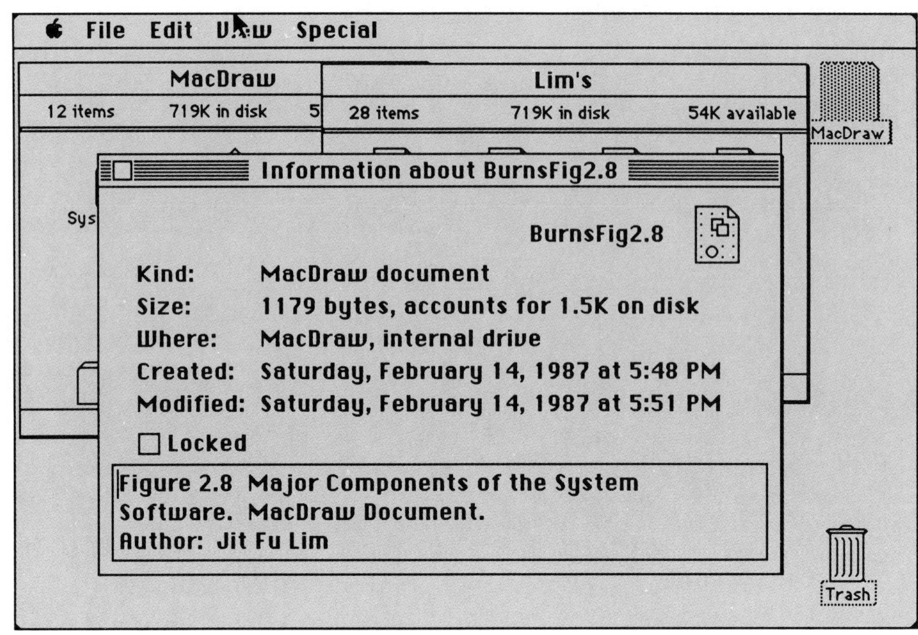

FIGURE 2–18

A Typical MS-DOS Directory Display

```
A>DIR <Return>

 Volume in drive A has no label
Directory of A:\

MEMO                 5888  11-12-87   2:33a
MEMO         .OLD    5765  11-11-87  11:35p
FUNGAME      .EXE   59652  10-25-87  11:37a
JUNK         .TXT   35221   1-10-88   3:52p
MOREJUNK     .TXT   38226   1-10-88   4:23p
STUFF        .DAT    1023   1-05-88   2:35p
        6 File(s)      222865 bytes free
```

Placed on every diskette is a directory containing the information shown in Figure 2–18. When the operating system receives the DIR command, it goes out to the directory on the diskette in the default drive, reads this information, and displays it on the screen.

Let us take a closer look at the files listed in Figure 2–18. In addition to their names, a directory listing will also exhibit their length in characters (column 2), their date stamp (column 3), and their time stamp (column 4). Thus the file MEMO is 5888 characters long and was created on 11-12-87 at 2:33 A.M. If there is ever a need to distinguish that file from another similar file (such as MEMO.OLD) as to which is the most recent, we can do so by means of the date and time stamp. In this case, MEMO is clearly the newer of the two files.

For a complete discussion of the commands listed in Table 2–3, the reader is referred to the MS-DOS TUTORIAL at the end of Chapter 4.

User Prompts, Default Settings, and Such

Occasionally, an application program will use questions (called **user prompts** or queries) to elicit from the user additional details regarding how a requested task is to be conducted or carried out. Prompts expect the user to enter one of several appropriate responses. If the user response is inappropriate, the same prompt will appear again. Some programs will require the user to enter an appropriate response and follow this with a <Return> or <Enter>. A good example of user prompts appears in the word processing program WordStar. When the user directs the program to print a file, the following list of user prompts appears:

```
NAME OF FILE TO PRINT?   letter
For default press RETURN for each question:
     DISK FILE OUTPUT (Y/N):  N
     START AT PAGE NUMBER (RETURN for beginning)?
     STOP AFTER PAGE NUMBER (RETURN for end)?
     USE FORM FEEDS (Y/N): N
     SUPPRESS PAGE FORMATTING (Y/N): N
     PAUSE FOR PAPER CHANGE BETWEEN PAGES (Y/N): N
Ready printer, press RETURN: <Return>
```

With the exception of the first question, each of the prompts has a default value, which is exhibited at the end of the prompt in the list above. The user can select the default value merely by pressing RETURN in response to a particular prompt. For example, the default value for DISK FILE OUTPUT (Y/N): is N, and the default value for START AT PAGE NUMBER (RETURN for beginning) is merely the beginning of the file. If the user is satisfied with the default values at a particular point in the prompt sequence, the user can press the ESC key. WordStar will then use the default values for all the remaining prompts in the sequence and begin printing the file immediately.

All application programs have **default settings** that make assumptions about what the typical user wants. Most word processing programs will assume the user wishes to print on 11-inch paper at 6 lines per inch, for example, and that the width of the paper is 8 1/2 inches with left and right margins of exactly one inch. These default settings can be overridden by the user in various ways, but a deliberate effort on the user's part is required.

CARE OF YOUR COMPUTER

Care of the microcomputer begins with the selection of an appropriate site for the computer, which will be discussed first.

Selecting a Site for the Computer

Several important considerations should be weighed in connection with the choice of a site for the microcomputer. First, the power supplied to the system should be "clean" in the sense that it is relatively free from power surges or sinks. Almost any power line can be affected by these, but this is especially true of ones to which heavy electrical equipment or thermostat-controlled air conditioners have been attached. Sharp power drops can cause the loss of all data currently in memory, whereas strong power surges can destroy microprocessor and RAM chips. The first problem is unfortunate, the second can be devastating. To mitigate this problem an inexpensive surge protection device should be used.

Second, the computer system should be located in a relatively clean, protected environment. A constant temperature is not critical, but it should not be exposed to extremes; exposure to direct sunlight can even cause damage. If there is static in the area an anti-static mat may be useful, or one can spray the rug once a week with laundry fabric softener diluted 10 to 1 with water.

If the printer produces a lot of vibration and shaking, then it is best to place the printer on a table or stand that is separate from the supporting table used for the computer.

The furniture used to support the keyboard and display can be important to the care of yourself and the computer. Displays should be positioned far enough away from the user to avoid unnecessary eyestrain caused by the CRT. Among terminals, there is a trend toward larger displays placed farther away from the user. A detachable keyboard will help accommodate such an arrangement. Similarly, the keyboard should be at a comfortable height for the user. Special computer furniture can allow for adjustment of both the keyboard and display to suit the particular user.

Other Considerations Relating to Care of Your Computer

Frequent power-ons and power-offs are hard on a computer and wear out its integrated circuits faster than if the computer were left on all day and hence turned on and off only once each day. If the computer is not in use for awhile, rather than turning it off, simply turn down the screen intensity (brightness) to prevent the image from being permanently burned into the screen. Do not place liquids close to the computer where they could spill on it; avoid smoking when using the computer. If the computer must be moved, exercise extreme care so as not to drop or otherwise jar it unnecessarily; moreover, the floppy disk drives should have old, unusable diskettes placed in them (with the drive door or latch closed) to protect the heads during the move.

CARE OF FLOPPY DISKS AND THE FILES CONTAINED ON THEM

All floppy diskettes should be treated with care. The purpose of such care is to protect important program and data files stored on the disk from possible erasure or from otherwise being made unreadable. The back of the diskette jacket usually provides brief details regarding the care and handling of diskettes, but a more extensive discussion is provided in this section. It is a good practice to label and date a floppy diskette once files have been saved on it. Obviously, the label ought to reflect the contents of the diskette.

TABLE 2–4

Do's and Don'ts for Handling Diskettes

1. Write on the diskette with felt-tip pen only.
2. Grasp the diskette only by its corner.
3. Always store the diskette in its protective envelope when not in use.
4. Always label your diskettes (once you have placed files on them) with the filename and the date of creation.
5. To protect important files from being overwritten, erased, damaged, or destroyed, cover the write-protect notch.
6. Never use pencils or ball-point pens to write on floppy diskettes.
7. Never touch the exposed area of the diskette (the oval area where the magnetic mylar surface comes in contact with the read/write head.)
8. Never expose the diskette to direct sunlight or high temperatures.
9. Do not bring the diskette into close proximity with machines or devices which produce magnetic fields.
10. Do not attempt to clean the diskette by wiping the mylar surface. There is a self-cleaning feature on the inside of the diskette jacket.

Table 2–4 lists some do's and don'ts to observe in conjunction with handling diskettes.

If copiers, microwave ovens, or other magnetic devices are in the room, be careful to keep floppy diskettes as far away from these machines as possible. Magnetic fields can destroy data on floppy diskettes, and magnets are used in more places than most people would suspect. Most electrical appliances employ magnets, so the list of devices to keep away from diskettes should include printers, tape recorders, video recorders, and even the handset of your telephone.

Protect diskettes from dust and smoke. Smoke and dust permeate the air with small particles which can cause read or write errors during disk operations. If the diskettes are going to be in a smoke-filled room, they require extra care. Keep them in their envelopes, and store them in their boxes or in other storage devices available for floppy diskettes.

Each floppy disk drive on your computer has a small red in-use light which lights up whenever the diskette in the drive is being accessed. Do not attempt to insert the diskette or remove it when the red in-use light is lighted. This can seriously damage the read/write head(s) in the drive and destroy the data on the diskette.

To insert a diskette in a drive, open the drive latch, remove the diskette from its jacket, and insert it gently into the drive until the diskette clicks into place. Close the drive latch. This automatically brings the read/write head into contact with the diskette surface. Do not force a diskette into a drive, and never force-close the latch. Consult your system user's manual to determine if the diskette label should be facing up, down, right, or left when the diskette is inserted.

All diskettes have what is called a *write-protect notch*. Usually, when this is covered, data cannot be written onto the diskette (for protection of the data that is already there). On some 8-inch diskettes, data cannot be written onto the diskette if the write-protect notch is uncovered. In either case, the intent is the same: to protect important data on the diskette from being overwritten or erased.

Before leaving this section on floppy disks, it is worthwhile to note the three sizes of floppy disks currently in use, as shown in Figure 2–20. The 8-inch standard

FIGURE 2–19

A Floppy Disk (3 1/2-inch) with its Protective Cover Opened

FIGURE 2–20

The Three Sizes of Floppies Available for Microcomputers: 8-inch Standard Floppy, 5 1/4-inch Minifloppy, and 3 1/2-inch Microfloppy.

floppy was the original size of floppies when they were first introduced by IBM. The 5 1/4-inch minifloppy got its start in conjunction with the microcomputer and was popular for nearly the first ten years of the microcomputer era. The definite trend is toward the 3 1/2-inch microfloppy. The microfloppy can hold nearly three times as much data as the original standard floppy, yet is so compact that it will fit in a shirt pocket.

Making Backups

You may be asking, "What happens if somehow my important program files are erased or otherwise unreadable? What do I do then?" You contact your dealer to see if you can obtain additional copies from him. If not, you must write or call the vendor and pay their fee for additional copies.

One precaution you can take is to make backups of your program disks. **Backups** are themselves floppy diskettes onto which you have transferred your important files. In the appendix to Chapter 4, we describe several ways to do this. Application software which you have purchased should, as a first step to its use, be backed up before you do anything else. This is possible only when the software is not copy protected. Copy-protected software will generally not permit you to make any backups; if you erase or otherwise damage the program files contained on the disk, you must return the damaged diskette to the vendor (or to your dealer) so the diskette can be rewritten. Some copy-protected application software will permit a maximum of only two backups to be created.

For non-copy-protected application software, you should prepare two mirror-image backup diskettes of each original diskette that came with the software package. Take the original diskettes and one set of backups and lock them up in a safe place. Use the second set of backups for executing the application. If these are damaged in any way, they can be rewritten from the originals or from the first set of backup diskettes.

Summary

In this chapter we have introduced you to the components of microcomputers, that is, computing devices which are able to be used in office environments. We found that the hardware consists basically of four components: input devices, output devices, the central processing unit, and secondary storage. We also learned that there are two software components: system software and application software. Four basic classifications of microcomputers were described: the desktop, the transportable, the laptop, and the hand-held computer. We have also discussed how to log onto (or start up) a microcomputer, and have provided a hands-on guide to what novices need to know for their first computing session. We have presented the basic conventions for filenames. Almost all microcomputer operating systems and applications packages adhere to the filenaming conventions presented in the chapter. We have described how to terminate a session with a microcomputer. Finally, we have provided instructions on how to care for your microcomputer and your floppies.

The next two chapters describe the hardware and system software of microcomputers in much greater detail. For example, Chapter 3 (Hardware for Small Computers) presents, among other topics, five different types of secondary storage in addition to floppies (which were briefly discussed in this chapter). And Chapter 4 describes the basic components that make up any operating system. At the end of Chapter 4 the reader will find a Tutorial on MS-DOS (PC-DOS), the most popular operating system available for the microcomputer today. Readers who require a thorough introduction to the hardware and system software of microcomputers will want to study Chapters 3 and 4 carefully.

Key Terms

ASCII codes
applications software
backup
bit
booting
briefcase computer
byte
central processing unit
chip
communications software
control program
CP/M
CPU
CRT
data communication
data files

default settings
desktop computer
device driver
directive
DOS
file
hand-held computer
hard copy
input devices
interface
laptop computer
memory map
microprocessor
modem
MS-DOS
operating system
output devices
peripheral
port
primary storage
printed circuit board
program files
secondary storage
soft copy
system software
text file
terminal
transportable computer
user interface
user prompts
utilities

Self-Test

1. What are the components of microcomputer systems?
2. What are the forms and sizes that microcomputers take?
3. Describe how to save and retrieve text and data files.
4. Describe how to end a session with a microcomputer.
5. Describe what user interfaces are available.
6. What is meant by user prompts?
7. What are default settings, and how can they be changed?
8. Describe how to use and care for floppy disks.
9. Describe the rules for naming files.
10. Explain the rudiments of MS-DOS and PC-DOS.

Exercises

1. Secondary storage devices may contain four different software or data types. What are they?
2. Discuss why two types of storage are required, and describe how these two types differ.
3. What are the four components that comprise the hardware side of any computer system? List examples of each component.
4. Discuss the process of start-up of a microcomputer that runs MS-DOS or PC-DOS. Why are the operations you described necessary?
5. Discuss the basic structure of data on secondary storage devices.
6. What type of printer is most frequently used with microcomputers? What types of displays are popular with microcomputers?
7. Distinguish between hard copy and soft copy. Do printers produce hard or soft copy?
8. How does the microprocessor interact with primary storage? What gets passed between these two subcomponents? These subcomponents are a part of what larger component?
9. The four basic components of computer systems we described can be quite different from the physical components that make up a microcomputer system. Describe one popular packaging arrangement for microcomputers currently in use. Which of the four components we described are packaged together? Which are packaged separately? What logic would motivate such a packaging arrangement?
10. Classify the following as hardware or software.
    CRT

device drivers
keyboard
language translators
primary storage
utilities

11. Describe the differences between the four basic categories of user interfaces. Which is the most demanding of the user? Which are most popular in accounting applications? Which are most likely to be found in word processing applications?

12. Indicate which of the following filenames are legitimate (acceptable to MS-DOS or CP/M) and which are not.
database.dat
B:document.fil
5:BAL.WRK
me
my.file
stagefive.wks
J.R
Balance.wks

13. Briefly characterize the following user interfaces, especially in view of advantages/disadvantages.
Command-driven interface
Icon-driven interface
Menu-driven interface
Query-driven interface
Screen-driven interface

14. Of the user interfaces listed in Exercise 13 above, which would you feel most comfortable with? Why? Which of the interfaces would frequent, experienced users feel most comfortable with? Which of the interfaces would casual, inexperienced users feel most comfortable with?

15. To which of the four basic computer components does the terminal belong? List three basic uses of terminals in our society. Describe how a terminal differs from a microcomputer.

16. Check the DOS manual of the microcomputer you are using to see if it provides a picture of the machine's memory map. Find the section in the manual that describes the memory map in detail. Describe the memory map of the machine. Illustrate the memory map with a figure like that shown in Figure 2–5.

17. Examine the files listed in Figure 2–18. Some of the file names have extensions. Which ones are they? What is the longest file on the diskette? What is the most recent file on the diskette? If there is a file named MEMO.OLD, what is its length?

18. Which of the following filenames are legitimate in MS-DOS and which are not? (Only one is legitimate.)

BAD:ILLUSTRA.ION
A:CON.BAT
B:HUNT_AND.PEK
C:SLOW.DOWN
B:"HONEY".BEE

Note that A:CON.BAT appears to be a legitimate filename. However, in many versions of MS-DOS it is not because it uses the operating system device name CON (for console). Other device names are PRN, LPT1, A:, B:, C:, AUX, and COM1 and these likewise should not be used as part of the primary portion of the filename. "HONEY" is not legitimate because it uses non-alphanumeric characters.

Additional Reading

Curtin, Dennis P., and Leslie R. Porter. *Microcomputers: Software and Applications.* Englewood Cliffs, N.J.: Prentice-Hall, 1986.

Dologite, D.G. *Using Computers.* Englewood Cliffs, N.J.: Prentice-Hall, 1987.

Dravillas, Paul; Steven Stilwell; and Brian K. Williams. *Power Pack for the IBM PC.* St. Louis: Times Mirror/Mosby College Publishing, 1986.

Fuhrman, Peter H., and Gregory F. Buck. *Microcomputers for Management Decision Making.* Englewood Cliffs, N.J.: Prentice-Hall, 1986.

Gibson, Glen A., and Mary L. Gibson. *Understanding and Selecting Small Business Computers.* Englewood Cliffs, N.J.: Prentice-Hall, 1986.

Goldstein, Larry Joel. *Microcomputer Applications: A Hands-on Approach to Problem Solving.* Reading, Mass.: Addison-Wesley Publishing Company, 1987.

Grauer, Robert T., and Paul K. Sugrue. *Microcomputer Applications.* New York: McGraw-Hill Book Company, 1987.

Johnston, Randolph. *Microcomputers: Concepts and Applications.* Santa Cruz, Calif. Mitchell Publishing Co. (a division of Random House, Inc.), 1987.

Spence, J. Wayne, and John C. Windsor. *Using Microcomputers: Applications for Business.* St. Louis: Times Mirror/Mosby College Publishing, 1987.

Zimmerman, Steven M., and Leo M. Conrad. *Understanding and Using Microcomputers.* St. Paul, Minn.: West Publishing Company, 1986.

CHAPTER

3

Hardware for Microcomputers

CHAPTER OUTLINE

Printed Circuit Board and Printed Circuit Cards 56

Microprocessor 58

Primary Storage 59

Secondary Storage 61

FOCUS FEATURE Factors Affecting Processing Speed of the Microcomputer 68

Displays 71

Keyboards 74

Printers 76

FOCUS FEATURE Printers: Up Close and Personal 78

Other Devices for Input/Output 80

Ports and External Interfaces 82

CHAPTER OBJECTIVES

In this chapter you will learn

1 the important features and concepts of microcomputer components
2 the jargon that purchasers of microcomputers must know
3 what managerial and professional considerations are important in the selection of microcomputer hardware
4 everything you always wanted to know about printers but were afraid to ask
5 how the microcomputer is interfaced with the external world

In Chapter 2, we introduced the basic components that comprise each computer system and provided only brief descriptions of the function of each component. This chapter provides a detailed discussion of the hardware components. The purpose of such information is many-fold. First, this material should make potential purchasers of microcomputers more aware of the features available in the hardware. Second, this material will instruct the reader in the features required to support certain applications. Third, this material should enable microcomputer users to better understand the functions of each hardware component.

As mentioned in Chapter 2, minimal hardware requirements for the microcomputer user include a keyboard, a display, some form of permanent storage for programs and data, a printer, and the computer itself, consisting of microprocessor and primary storage. The microprocessor and primary storage are referred to as the central processing unit, or CPU for short. The manner in which these components are packaged together varies from manufacturer to manufacturer. When separately packaged, each component requires its own switch, plug, and power supply unit, with the possible exception of the keyboard. In integrated form, one switch and power supply provides power to all the required devices, except the printer. The integrated system not only has less equipment to plug in and turn on, it may be less expensive to buy, since fewer power supply units are required. Integrated systems are also easier to move and are less complicated to hook up and install. Typical examples of integrated systems are the so-called "transportables" that contain the CPU, floppy disk drives, display, and detachable keyboard. Just one plug and power switch gets the system up and running. The "system unit" concept popularized by the IBM PC is another example of the integrated system. The **system unit** consists of CPU and secondary storage—of microprocessor, primary storage, and disk drives. Although detachable keyboards are commonplace in the IBM family of personal computers and compatibles, they do not require separate power supplies. The display and printer are purchased separately, enabling owners to select their own output peripherals.

It was also mentioned in Chapter 2 that users are actually going to need two types of storage: (1) internal memory or primary storage, and (2) permanent or secondary storage. In order to be processed, all programs and data must be placed in primary storage, since the microprocessor is designed to accept instructions and data from primary storage only. Hence, the heart of any computer is the central processing unit, consisting of microprocessor and primary storage. Our discussion in this chapter will begin by focusing on the CPU and the printed circuit board on which its components are mounted.

PRINTED CIRCUIT BOARD AND PRINTED CIRCUIT CARDS

All microcomputers have a main printed circuit board to which the integrated circuits (chips) are attached, affectionately called the **motherboard**. The motherboard (also called a *planar board*) has lines of metallic foil on both sides of it. The lines are used to carry small electric signals between the various integrated circuits attached to the board. These lines enable the various integrated circuits to communicate with each other. By means of these lines, the microprocessor can send addresses to primary storage, can send and receive data to and from primary storage, and can receive power from the power supply. This gives rise to four types of lines found on motherboards, called *buses.* There is an address bus, a data bus, a control bus, and a power bus, all of them simply etched lines of foil on the motherboard. The *power bus* is used to provide power to all the integrated circuits. The *data bus* is used for passing data to and from primary storage and the microprocessor. The *control bus* allows the microprocessor to send control signals to the other integrated circuits, and the *address bus* is used to pass addresses (of bytes to be accessed) from the microprocessor to primary storage. The integrated circuits required for primary storage, video interface, processing, keyboard interface, and floppy disk control are either directly soldered into the motherboard or attached by means of sockets. Some motherboards come with sockets for half a megabyte or more of primary storage, with only half or a quarter of these sockets actually filled with memory chips. For a few hundred dollars, the additional memory chips can be purchased and simply pressed into the sockets when the user decides to expand memory at some later time. A typical motherboard is shown in Figure 3–1.

Many microcomputer manufacturers subscribe to the expansion or open architecture concept in that *expansion slots* are provided on the motherboard. The IBM PC and most of its compatibles and clones (machines that are functionally similar to the IBM PC and compatible with its hardware and software) provide expansion slots of the type described here. Optional, add-on printed-circuit cards can be plugged into the expansion slots. These plug-in cards can provide interfaces with external peripherals, such as a color monitor, a hard disk, or a printer. Or, these cards may be multifunctional, in which case they would be able to provide for additional primary storage, for real-time clock/calendars that continuously run whether or not the machine is on, and for other functions that will allow for communication over telephones lines or coaxial cable. At last count, more than fifty different companies manufacture compatible cards that can be inserted into one of the expansion slots. Table 3–1 lists the major categories of printed-circuit cards (and the major manufacturers) that are plug-compatible with the IBM PC and Personal System /2 family of personal computers, and computers that are hardware-

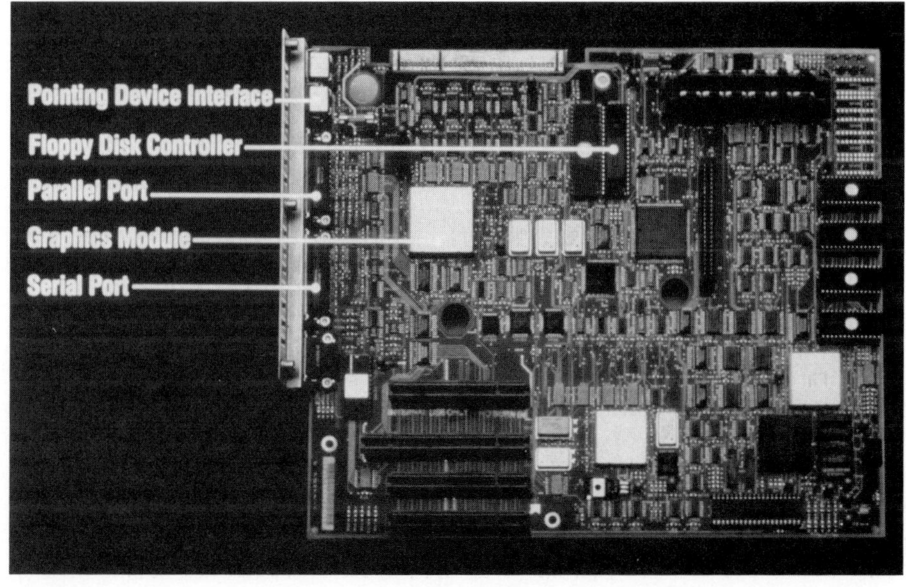

FIGURE 3–1

A Typical Motherboard for a 16-bit Microcomputer.
(Courtesy of International Business Machines Corporation)

TABLE 3–1

List of Plug-in Printed Circuit Cards for the IBM PC and Hardware-Compatible Computers

Accelerator Cards—Cards that are able to increase the processing speed of microcomputers anywhere from two to ten times. Major manufacturers are Orchid Technology Inc., Quadram (Intelligent Systems Corp.), PC Technologies Inc., Fast 86, and Personal Computer Support Group.

Expanded Memory Cards—Cards that increase the available primary storage by as much as 2 million bytes or more. Useful for large spreadsheets. Major manufacturers are Intel Corp. and AST Research Inc.

Hard Disk Controller Cards—Cards used to provide hardware control of hard disks. One major manufacturer is Qubie Distributing.

Input/Output Cards—Cards used to provide external interfaces for peripherals like printers, displays, etc.

Local Area Network Cards—Cards that support data communication between a network of computers. One major manufacturer is Orchid Technology Inc.

Micro-to-Mainframe Link Cards—Cards that enable data communication between a microcomputer and a large mainframe computer. One major manufacturer is Ideassociates, Inc.

Modem Cards—Cards used to enable data communication between computers and among computers and peripherals over phone lines. Major manufacturers are Hayes Microcomputer Products Inc., Promotheus Products Inc., Novation Inc., Quadram (Intelligent Systems Corp.)

Multifunction Cards—Cards used to provide a variety of functions, such as external ports, clock/calendar, additional memory, etc. By including all of these functions on a single card, precious expansion slots are preserved for other purposes. These are the most popular of all the add-on cards. Major manufacturers are AST Research Inc., STB Systems Inc., TECMAR Inc., Qubie Distributing, Orchid Technology Inc., and Quadram (Intelligent Systems Corp.)

Video Cards—Cards that support high-resolution graphics and/or color displays. May include additional memory intended for use by the video. Major manufacturers are IBM, Paradise, and Hercules.

compatible with the IBM PC. Figure 3–2 depicts some typical plug-in printed circuit cards.

Unfortunately, not all manufacturers support the open architecture concept. Machines that do not possess expansion slots are limited in their potential to grow and adapt to the changing needs of the user.

MICROPROCESSOR

Perhaps the most important integrated circuit of the computer system is the microprocessor. The following microprocessors were commonplace among the early single-user computer systems: Zilog Z80A (CP/M machines and Radio Shack TRS-80) and Z80B, MOS Technologies 6502 (Apple and Commodore) and 6510, Intel 8080, Intel 8085, and the Motorola MC6809. These are generally classified as "8-bit" processors, and are able to provide ample throughput to support many single-user applications. These processors gave the microcomputer its start, but are largely being phased out as the newer 16- and 32-bit microprocessors replace them. Most popular among the 16- and 32-bit microprocessors are the following: Intel 8088, Intel 8086, Intel 80186, Intel 80286, or Intel 80386, and the Motorola MC68000 series.

When considering the purchase of a microcomputer, users will probably want to limit their choices to computers using the popular 16-bit processors mentioned

(a)

(b)

FIGURE 3–2

Some Typical Plug-in Printed Circuit Cards for Microcomputers. (a) Intel's 2M byte Above™ Board/AT and Above™ Board/PC. (*Courtesy of Intel® Personal Computer Enhancement Operation*) (b) The Quad 386XT Accelerator Card and Daughter Card by Quadram. (*Courtesy of Quadram Corporation*)

above in order to assure themselves of an adequate software base to choose from. Two of the most popular microprocessors are shown in Figure 3–3.

The 8-bit or 16-bit designation is used in this context to indicate the amount of information that can be internally manipulated by the microprocessor. A 16-bit processor, therefore, should be able to process, in a single operation, the same amount of information that would require two operations from an 8-bit processor. In the past, a 16-bit designation also indicated that the microprocessor loaded its internal components (called *registers*) 16 bits at a time. The emergence of the Intel 8088 confused the issue, however, because it processes 16 bits at a time internally but requires two trips to primary storage to load the registers, retrieving only 8 bits with each trip. This slows the processing speed. More will be said about processing speed in this chapter's article, "Factors Affecting Processing Speed of a Microcomputer."

PRIMARY STORAGE

Primary storage is usually divided into two categories: ROM (read-only memory) and RAM (random-access memory). **ROM** is analogous to a printed page that is read from but not written on. **RAM**, as we have previously defined it, is like a blank page that can be written onto, read from, erased and written onto again, etc. A typical 16-bit processor (such as the Intel 8088 or the Intel 8086) has a memory address space of one megabyte—1,048,576 bytes or storage locations, each with its own address. The **address space** is a hardware limitation on the number of bytes of primary storage that can be accessed directly as a block—usually 64K for 8-bit

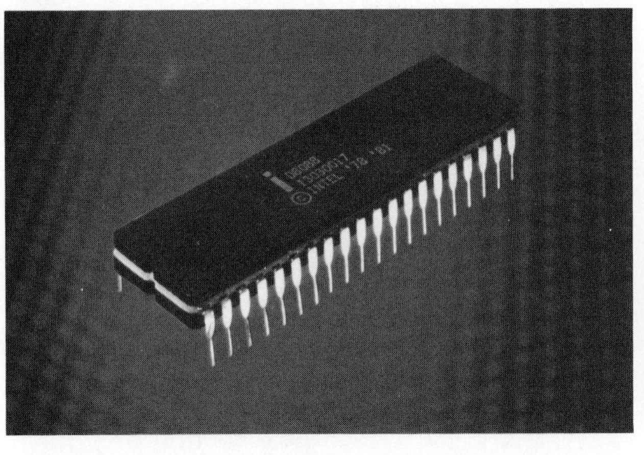

(a)

(b)

FIGURE 3–3

Two Popular Microprocessors.
(a) The Intel 8088 Microprocessor, used in many MS-DOS machines. *(Courtesy of Intel Corporation)* (b) The Motorola MC68000, used in the Apple Macintosh. *(Courtesy of Motorola Corporation)*

micros. (This is 65,536 bytes or characters; 1K equals 1,024 bytes.) The 16-bit microprocessors developed by Intel (the Intel 8088, 8086, and 80186) can address one megabyte of address space. The IBM PC and most of its clones and compatibles use the Intel 8088.

Whereas the hardware permits addressing one megabyte, the system software may limit this area to 640K or 768K bytes of usable address space, with ROM placed above that. Not all of this address space need be filled with ROM and RAM. For example, it is possible to purchase a machine with 20K of ROM and 256K of RAM; this leaves over half of the 1-megabyte address space unused. Such machines are usually expandable to 640K of RAM, filling out the 640K of *usable* address space.

Generally, the software placed in ROM is needed to support some or all of the applications. For example, the bootstrap program required to get the microcomputer running each time it is turned on is always stored in ROM. It loads the system software into primary storage from secondary storage. This activity is called *booting* (defined in Chapter 2), and is one of the first functions the computer performs when switched on.

The address space, it turns out, is solely a function of the number of address lines connecting the microprocessor to primary storage (ROM and RAM). **Address lines** make up the address bus and are used to pass addresses from the microprocessor to primary storage. The older 8-bit micros had only 16 address lines; the 16-bit micros using the Intel 8088, 8086, and 80186 all possess 20 address lines. Each line, like an ordinary bit, can be set either high or low; hence, a line can only be in two states. With 16 address lines, 2^{16} different permutations of addresses can be represented. It turns out that 2^{16} is 64K, or 65,536. On the other hand, 2^{20} is one megabyte, or 1,048,576 different addresses. Since one and only byte is associated with each address, 2^{20} enables exactly 1,048,576 different bytes to be accessed. One of the most significant advantages of the 16-bit micros was the greatly increased address space.

We can expect that increases in the number of address lines will stretch out the address space even further. The Intel 80286 used in the IBM PC AT and AT-compatible computers uses 24 address lines and has a 16-megabyte address space. The Motorola MC68000 used in the Apple Macintosh also has 24 address lines, giving it a 16-megabyte address space.

SECONDARY STORAGE

Secondary storage usually requires the use of a magnetic medium such as tape, flexible diskette, or hard disks of both the fixed and removable variety. Cassette tape drives are suitable mostly for backing up hard disks. In the early days of microcomputing, audio cassette tape recorders were used for secondary storage. They have long since been phased out due to their slowness and unreliability. Consequently, audio tape recorders are judged unsuitable for use in business and professional contexts.

Floppy Disks

As shown in Chapter 2, flexible disk drives come in several sizes: 3 1/2-inch microfloppy, 5 1/4-inch minifloppy, and 8-inch standard floppy. One would be inclined to think that the larger the floppy is, the more data (in numbers of bytes) that can be placed on it. However, density of the information plays an even more important role in determining the storage capacity of the diskette. For example, almost 800K bytes can be stored on the Apple Macintosh microfloppy, while the IBM PC minifloppy diskette may hold as little as 360K bytes of data and programs.

Before a soft-sectored diskette (i.e., a diskette whose sector boundaries are to be established by software) can be used to store data and programs, it must first be formatted. Formatting of the diskette establishes the sector boundaries on the diskette and sets up a directory in which all file names and associated time and date stamps are stored. Once formatted, the diskette will have its storage capacity reduced somewhat (less than 10 percent). After formatting, the diskette is organized into tracks and sectors within tracks, as shown in Figure 3–4.

As an example of the diverse formats and configurations available, consider the 5 1/4-inch minifloppy. You can choose between single-density, double-density, or quad-density formats and between single- and double-sided storage (storage of data on both sides of the diskette). Doubling or quadrupling the density of the data on the diskette is usually accomplished by doubling or quadrupling the number of sectors per track. However, it is also possible to increase the amount of storage on one side of a diskette by increasing the number of tracks on one side. Most 5 1/4-inch diskettes will have either 40 or 80 tracks per side.

The disk drive format is important for more than just capacity considerations, because it also has an impact on the availability and price of software. If a computer has an unusual disk format, its owner may have to wait a long time until popular software packages are available for it. Even then the user may have to pay a premium price for the package, and it will likely be unavailable at the neighborhood software emporium. Theoretically, if a disk is written on two sides with 40 tracks per side (48 tracks per inch), 9 sectors per track, and with 512 bytes per sector (this is the format for the IBM PC with the DOS 2.0 operating system), it can be read from or written to by any other machine with the same disk drive specifications. Numerous machines support this format because of the mature software base that exists for the PC. In practice, however, the potential purchaser is advised to read reviews on prospective machines in one of the publications listed at the end of Chapter 2 to see if disk compatibility may be a problem. The ability to read another computer's diskettes does not ensure that the program will execute on a proposed machine.

FIGURE 3–4

Organization of Data on the Floppy. The diskette shown is formatted with forty tracks and nine sectors.

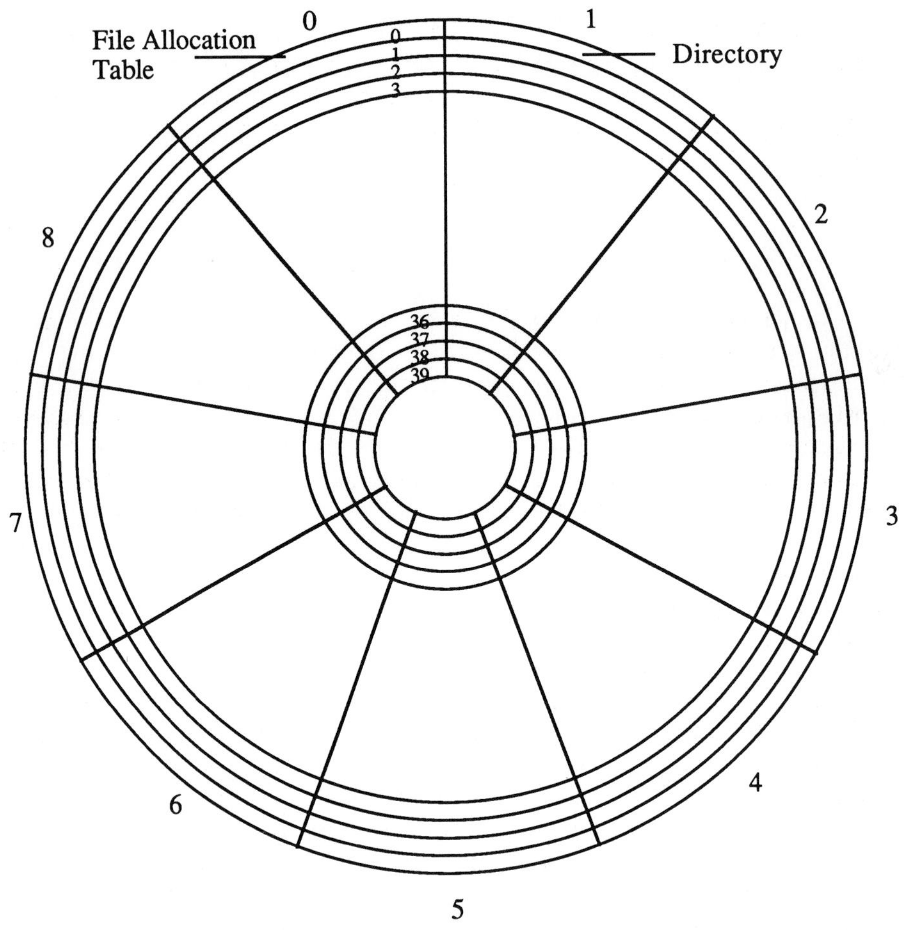

This issue will be explored more fully in the discussion of operating systems (Chapter 4).

Users actually need two disk drives to enable easy backup for their important programs and data. Backing up with a single drive is not impossible, but can be bothersome for most applications. When the Apple Macintosh had only 128K RAM, anywhere from four to ten swaps of source and target diskettes were required to complete a backup with its single 3 1/2-inch microfloppy disk drive. With only one drive, a portion of the data on the source diskette is written to RAM, then the source diskette is removed and the target diskette inserted. The data in RAM is then written to the target diskette, after which the target diskette is removed and the source diskette inserted for transferral of the next segment of data. The entire process is repeated until all the data has been copied. Therefore, most users will want a second disk drive, even though extra cost is involved.

Even though floppy disks are losing some ground to hard disks (see the next section), the floppy disk technology is changing rapidly. The IBM PC standard of 360K bytes of formatted storage capacity on 5 1/4-inch double-sided, double-density diskettes is being challenged by 3 1/2-inch formats and 5 1/4-inch formats with more capacity. IBM adopted a 1.2-megabyte, 5 1/4-inch floppy disk drive for the AT, for example. This drive can read from and write to the older 360K format. Apple offers a double-sided 800K, 3 1/2-inch disk drive for its Macintosh. A similar disk drive is used in IBM's PC Convertible (a small portable computer) and is available as an add-on for the IBM PC, PC XT, and PC AT. Many microcomputer futurists expect the 3 1/2-inch floppy disk drive to play a significantly more important role. Even so, perhaps one day your children may discover a box of dusty floppy diskettes in the attic and ask, "What are these used for?"

Hard Disks

Winchester hard disks (named after the project that originated in the offices of IBM, the developer of the technology) are gaining increasingly widespread use in microcomputers, because they offer considerable advantages over floppies. They provide much more on-line storage and they are much faster. A general ledger application, which takes an hour to complete its operation using floppies, might take only ten minutes to perform the same operation using a hard disk. Hard disks are faster from two standpoints, file access time and data transfer rate. **Access time** is the time required to position the read/write head over the track and sector containing the data and **transfer rate** is the rate at which the data is moved to/from secondary storage and primary storage. A hard metallic platter continuously spins inside a hermetically sealed case at speeds of 3,600 rpm. By contrast, most floppies do not continuously spin and must be started from dead stop to operating speed (300–400 rpm) before they can be accessed. This takes roughly a half second. In both instances, a read/write head must be positioned over the appropriate track for access. The positioning of the read/write head is much faster for hard disks. Then the system must wait for the appropriate sector on the track to rotate under the head. Again, this *rotational delay* (or *latency*) is much shorter for hard disks because of the higher operating rpm. Moreover, the rate at which data is transferred to and from the hard disk is much faster than for floppies (see Table 3–2). Finally, hard disks (see Figure 3–5) support much larger contiguous data files than do floppies. If there is a need for a 1-megabyte data file and the floppies have only a 360K byte capacity, then a hard disk is a requirement.

Although Winchester hard disks are faster than floppies and provide much more on-line storage, they are generally not removable. The removable feature of

TABLE 3–2

Comparison of Secondary Storage Types

NAME	DATA TRANSFER RATE (BITS/SEC)	CAPACITY (KB = 1,024 BYTES) (MB = 1,048,576 BYTES)	ACCESS TIME (SEC)
Floppy Diskette			
5 1/4″ MS-DOS 2.0	250,000	360Kb	0.5
3 1/2″ Macintosh	250,000	400Kb and 800Kb	0.5
3 1/2″ MS-DOS 3.3	500,000	720Kb and 1.44Mb	0.25
Hard Disk	5,000,000	10–100Mb	0.015 to 0.085
Optical Disk	2,500,000	230Mb	0.15 to 0.7
Removable Magnetic Disks	5,000,000	10–20Mb	0.085
CD-ROM	5,000,000	1,000Mb	0.1
RAM Disk	10,000,000	300Kb to 1Mb	Negligible

(a)

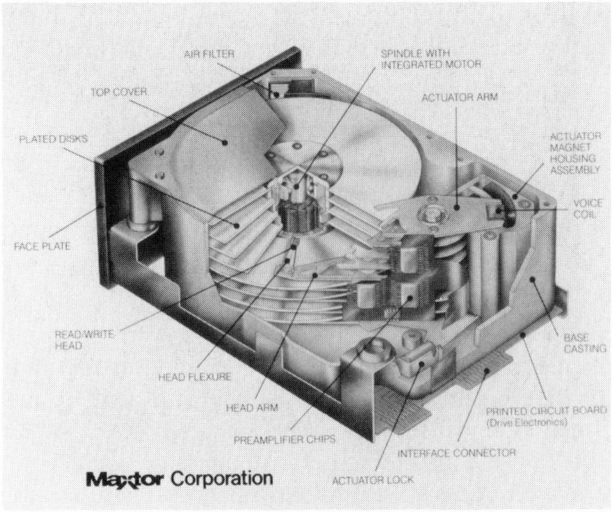

(b)

FIGURE 3–5

Hard Disk Drives. (a) Seagate's ST225 25M byte disk drive. *(Courtesy of Seagate)* (b) A high-capacity hard disk drive. (*Photo courtesy of Maxtor Corporation and* IEEE Spectrum)

floppies enables an unlimited amount of data to be stored through one floppy disk drive, regardless of data density.

Backing up of files on the hard disk is a necessity in any business context where important programs or data could be lost. An infrequent consequence of extensive or abusive hard-disk use is what is known as a "head" crash. A head crash occurs when the read/write head actually comes in contact with the hard-disk surface. This is usually accompanied by a high screeching sound and subsequent destruction of the disk surface (which gets badly scarred and grooved as a result). Of course, the data on the disk is lost as well. Ordinarily, the read/write head floats on a thin film of air just above the hard-disk surface. The distance from the head to the surface is an order of magnitude smaller than a particle of smoke or dust, hence the need for encasing the disk in a sealed enclosure. If disciplined backup procedures are followed, the physical loss of the disk drive itself will seem relatively minor by comparison to the catastrophe that would otherwise have occurred. Backing up is usually accomplished with floppy disks or cartridge tape.

Floppy disk backup can be tedious. Assume double-sided, double-density floppy disks are used, each with 360K bytes storage per diskette. It would take 59 diskettes and several hours of effort to back up one 20-megabyte hard disk. Imagine doing this every night after work. Fortunately, we usually only back up those files that have been changed during the day. But what if the file is 1 megabyte long? Can it be backed up onto three floppies? The answer depends on the system being used. The cartridge tape backup system solves all of these difficulties. In less than ten minutes it is possible to back up the entire 20-megabyte hard disk. Users can then remove the tape cartridge and lock it up in a safe, or place it in some other secure place.

It is noteworthy that head crashes are uncharacteristic of floppy disks. This is because the read/write heads are constantly in physical contact with the disk surface. It is because of this physical contact that the floppy diskette does not continuously spin within the drive. This would cause too much wear on the diskette and the head(s).

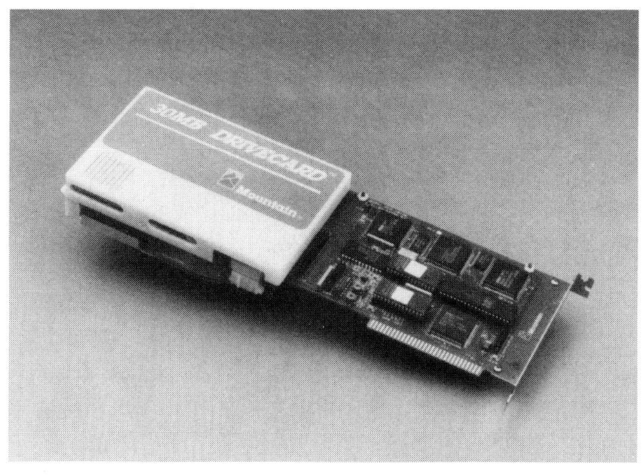

(a)

(b)

FIGURE 3–6

A Hard Disk on a Card.
(a) Mountain Computer's Hard Disk on a Card. This card is the PC industry's first 30 Mb-Winchester hard disk on a card. *(Photo courtesy of Mountain Computer, Inc.)*
(b) Hardcard™ 20, 20 megabyte hard disk drive on a plug-in card. (Shown with exposed head disk assembly.) (© *1986 Plus Development Corporation. All rights reserved.*)

Of increasing popularity is the "hard disk on a card" configuration. This unit simply plugs into any expansion slot of an IBM PC or compatible computer and is ready to run. Currently, 20 megabytes of capacity is common in these units, but 30 and 40 or more megabytes of formatted storage capacity is possible. The hard disk itself is 3 1/2 inches in diameter. Data is stored on both sides of the disk. Access times below 80 msec (milliseconds, or 1×10^{-3} seconds) are currently commonplace. Hard-disk cards are designed to withstand extreme shock and vibration, operate within the power range of the PC power supply, and occupy a single PC slot. These plug-in cards are better suited for use in transportable PCs than conventional hard disks. Figure 3–6 depicts a typical hard disk on a card.

RAM Disks

In addition to the types of secondary storage just mentioned, there is another type of pseudo-secondary storage in common use, called a **RAM** disk. A *RAM disk* is nothing more than a section of RAM that is set aside to act exactly like a disk from the perspective of the operating system. It is set up and controlled by software and can be easily removed when unwanted. It has a directory and a file allocation table. Filenames, date and time stamps, etc. are contained in the directory just like they would be on any other disk. The advantage of a RAM disk is speed; it is much faster than a hard disk, as Table 3–2 would suggest. However, like any RAM, RAM disks are volatile and their contents must be transferred to flexible or hard disks before turning the machine off. They greatly speed up any input/output-intensive processing, such as word processing, DBMS processing when files are stored on disk, and storage/retrieval of files in general.

Removable Magnetic Disk Storage

Removable magnetic disks are desirable when there is a need for lots (many megabytes) of on-line secondary storage and the data stored thereon must be protected from theft or loss from head crashes. The advantages of this type of storage are derived from the removability of the media. This allows an unlimited amount of data to be accessed and stored through a single drive. Removability strongly facilitates backup of important programs and data and greatly enhances security of the data. The removable media can be shipped across the country or walked to the office next door. Moreover, it can be stored in a safe for security purposes.

Among the best-selling disks of this category is the **Bernoulli box**, which was introduced in 1984 by Iomega Corporation. It boasts data access speeds and transfer rates that rival the best hard disks. The on-line storage capacity varies from 10 to 40 megabytes, depending on the configuration purchased. The medium is actually a floppy diskette with a capacity of 10 or 20 megabytes. As the diskette spins, air currents generated by the spinning action cause the diskette to be pushed up near the heads (by virtue of the Bernoulli principle). If any small particle should interrupt the flow of air, the diskette drops back away from the head, preventing damage to the diskette or the head and eliminating the possibility of head crashes. The influx of air that results flushes the particle out of the system and the data is reread or rewritten as necessary. Moreover, the compliant air coupling between the head and the media permits momentary uncoupling in response to vibration or shock, thereby preventing head crashes.

Optical Disk Storage

Two types of optical disk storage devices are available commercially, with more expected soon. **CD-ROM** (Compact Disk–Read-Only Memory) technology is an outgrowth of the compact disk used for audio recording and playback. WORM (Write-Once–Read-Mostly) disks and drives permit data to be recorded only once on a particular location of the disk, but read an infinite number of times.

CD-ROM Disks This revolutionary type of storage allows for data to be read from but not written onto. Its advantage is tremendous storage capacity, which is currently 600 megabytes on a single side, as provided for in a worldwide standard developed by two companies, Philips and Sony. The medium is a compact optical disk (4.72 inches in diameter) similar to the compact disks that are becoming increasingly popular among audio equipment. The disks (see Figure 3–7) are removable. CD-ROM drives come in add-on or add-in versions; the latter install in microcomputers just like minifloppy disk drives.

By 1990 it is expected that CD-ROM disks with a *gigabyte* (1,000 megabytes) of memory will be selling for about $100. An entire encyclopedia along with search and retrieve software could be placed on one of these disks. Dictionaries, telephone directories, reference works, and catalogs are among the applications to which this technology can be put. Recently, a new standard called CD-I allows for storage of more than just data; audio and video information could be stored in digital form as well. This standard could open new markets for compact disk technology not necessarily connected with the microcomputer.

WORMs WORM applications include archival storage and image storage. These applications could replace vast tape libraries currently maintained by large data centers. Public libraries that use microfilm or microfiche for newspaper storage could digitize the pages of newspapers onto WORM disks. The information could

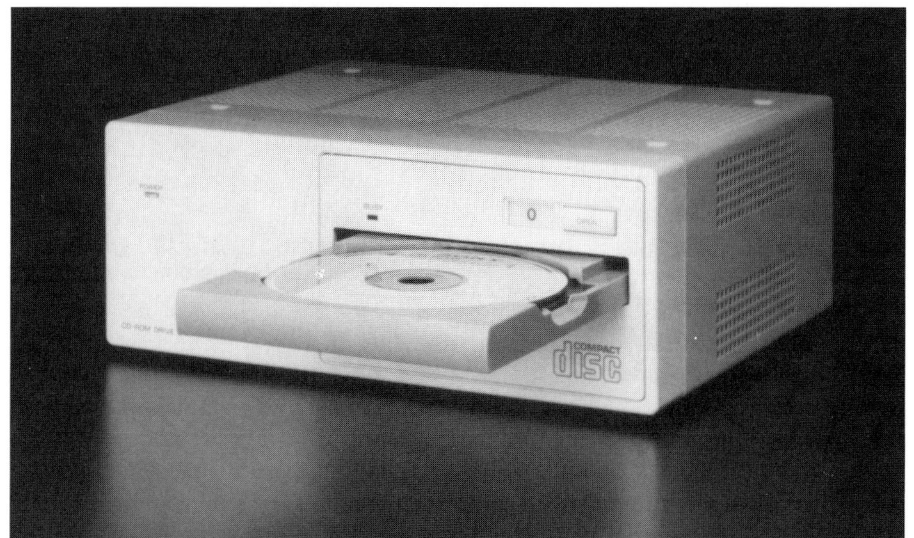

FIGURE 3–7

CD-ROM Disk and Drive. (*Courtesy of Sony Corporation of America*)

FIGURE 3–8

The Information Storage Inc. WORM Optical Disk and Drive. The removable 230 DS cartridge holds 230 Mbytes, has a transfer rate of 2.5 million bits/sec., and an average access time of 150 milliseconds. (*Courtesy of Information Storage, Inc.*)

not be altered after the original writing, but it could be read over and over again. The density of the information would be far greater than what is currently available in microform technology. Shown in Figure 3–8 is a state-of-the-art optical disk drive.

In the future it is expected that devices capable of both reading from and writing to compact disks will be developed. These media may then have most of the assets one could ever expect out of any secondary storage medium: remova-

Focus Feature

FACTORS AFFECTING PROCESSING SPEED OF THE MICROCOMPUTER

The speed with which a microcomputer operates depends on more than the speed of its secondary storage. Microprocessor clock rate, RAM access time, whether the microprocessor processes 8, 16, or 32 bits at a time, whether a floating-point coprocessor is accessible, operating system efficiency, and the efficiency of the application software are also factors.

The *clock rate* of a microprocessor is an indication of the electronic speeds at which the CPU will operate. Measured in megahertz (MHz), it can provide a guide for comparing relative speeds of systems only when all other factors can be assumed to be held constant and are equal across machines. Table 3–3 lists some of the major microprocessors around which most microcomputers are being configured, together with their speed-related characteristics.

RAM access time is the amount of time required for the microprocessor to retrieve data from the RAM chips for processing, and is typically measured in nanoseconds (10^{-9} sec.). Computers with shorter RAM access times can be expected to run faster. The RAM access time must be properly sequenced with the microprocessor to avoid wait states. A **wait state** is a period of time in which the microprocessor waits on primary storage, either to store data or to transmit data to the microprocessor. The effect slows down the processing speed.

The number of bits that can be stored or retrieved in a single operation is a factor affecting the speed of processing. Processors which fetch (store or retrieve) 16 bits at a time will naturally operate faster than processors that fetch only 8 bits at a time, and similarly for 32 bits in relation to 16 or 8 bits. The number of bits that can be fetched is determined by the number of external (data) lines that connect the microprocessor to primary storage. Likewise, processors which are able to (internally) perform arithmetic and logical operations 16 bits at a time will have greater throughput than processors which perform these operations 8 bits at a time, and similarly for 32 bits in relation to 16 or 8 bits.

Another factor strongly affecting processing speed is the number of machine cycles required to execute a single instruction, as suggested in Table 3–4. The time required to execute a single machine cycle is one over the clock rate. For example, if the clock rate is 8 MHz (8 million cycles per second), then the time required to execute a machine cycle is 1/8000000, or 0.000000125 seconds (125 nanoseconds). The time required to execute a machine cycle when the clock rate is 4.77 MHz is

TABLE 3–3
Characteristics of Popular Microprocessors

MICROPROCESSOR	BITS PROCESSED INTERNALLY	BITS PROCESSED EXTERNALLY	CLOCK RATE	ADDRESS LINES
Zilog Z80A	8	8	4 MHz	16
Intel 8088	16	8	4–5 MHz	20
Intel 8088-2	16	8	6–8 MHz	20
Intel 8086	16	16	8 MHz	20
Intel 80186	16	16	8 MHz	20
Intel 80286	16	16	12 MHz	24
Intel 80386	32	32	12–20 MHz	32
Motorola MC68000	32	16	6–12 MHz	24
Motorola MC68020	32	32	12–25 MHz	32

TABLE 3–4

Machine Cycles Required to Execute Several Typical Instructions

INSTRUCTION	IBM PC (8088)	IBM AT (80286)	(80386)
No operation	3	3	3
16-bit integer multiply	128 to 154	21	9 to 22
16-bit integer divide	165 to 184	25	27

1/4770000, or 0.000000210 seconds (210 nanoseconds).

From Table 3–4 it should be evident that the IBM PC requires as a minimum 165*210 = 34,650 nanoseconds to execute an integer divide, whereas the IBM AT operating at 8 MHz requires 25*125 = 3,125 nanoseconds to execute an integer divide—over ten times faster.

The efficiency of an operating system has a marked effect on the speed of certain applications. Whenever information must be retrieved from or written to a disk or displayed to a screen or printer, the applications program will typically call upon the operating system for assistance. An efficient operating system can fill a screen with characters very quickly, whereas a less efficient one can be agonizingly slow. Some operating systems will reserve an area of RAM as a disk buffer. A **disk buffer** is filled with information to be recorded on a disk. Once full, the entire contents of the buffer are written to the disk, thereby lessening the number of disk writes required, since the buffer will hold several "records" of information. Ordinarily, each record would require a separate disk write. The disk buffer operates in the reverse fashion when reading from the disk.

Finally, the efficiency of the code implementing the application being used will greatly affect the processing speed. For example, one of the most time-consuming tasks spreadsheet software has to accomplish is recalculation of the spreadsheet model being exercised. The speed with which this operation is performed varies greatly from one spreadsheet package to the next. The speed of processing is such an important concern that application software reviewers give this attribute an importance ranking among the top five attributes around which the packages are evaluated. The processing speed is generally referred to as the performance, although other factors affect performance as well.

There are several things one can do to speed up an existing PC or compatible. One of those is to add a floating-point coprocessor, such as an Intel 8087, or an Intel 80287. (The 8087 is intended to be used with the 8088, while the 80287 is to be used with the 80286 and 80386.) A **floating-point coprocessor** is a chip designed to do hardware floating-point arithmetic (arithmetic involving fractions and decimal numbers). Without a floating-point coprocessor, all floating-point operations are done on the main microprocessor chip using fixed-point operations and software designed to accomplish floating-point operations with fixed-point operations. This is much slower than hardware floating-point operations. To take advantage of the floating-point coprocessor requires software written specifically for it. The user must also purchase a floating-point coprocessor chip and insert it into the empty socket on the motherboard inlaid especially for it.

Another way to speed up a PC or compatible is to add an accelerator card. As Table 3–1 suggests, some of the major manufacturers are Orchid, Quadram, PC Technologies Inc., and Personal Computer Support Group.

Processing speed relates so strongly to performance that cost of computer hardware increases in rough relationship to processing speed. We can expect to see continuing advances in the processing speed of microcomputers.

bility, reliability, fast transfer rates and moderately fast access times, and a vast storage capacity on a single volume. At that time this technology could challenge all other forms of secondary storage. Current advantages of this type of storage technology include its removability, high reliability, and vast storage capacity.

Cartridge Tape

Cartridge tape drives and media are used to back up hard disks, as previously mentioned. Their usefulness in this regard is substantially better than floppies. The backup process, which could take hours using floppies, takes minutes using cartridge tape and the entire hard disk contents can be transferred to a single tape. The device shown in Figure 3–9 can transfer data from the hard drive to the tape at the rate of 5 megabytes a minute. Likewise, data can be transferred from the tape to the hard disk at the same rate. Moreover, the entire backing up operation can be automated so that at midnight each evening the DOS loads the backup program and executes the backup operation. The next morning the user need only switch tape cartridges.

In addition to hard disk backup, cartridge tape can be used to transfer files easily from a mainframe to a microcomputer, and vice versa. They can also be used to transport large amounts of data from one computer to another of any size. The capability to carry 60 or more hermetically sealed megabytes of precious data around in one's shirt pocket no doubt appeals to some users. Cartridge tape drives will fit in a 5 1/4-inch "half-height" diskette drive position and will require one expansion slot for the printed circuit card on which the controller has been placed. The medium is removable.

The biggest single drawback to the use of cartridge tape as a secondary storage device is the sequential nature of the media. Unlike disks, in which the read/write head can be moved quickly to the track containing the desired data while awaiting

FIGURE 3–9

Mountain Computer's Series 7000 offers tape backup disk storage and disk/tape combo systems with zero footprint for IBM PC/XT/AT, Compaq, AT&T, and compatibles *(Courtesy of Mountian Computer, Inc.)*

the appropriate sector to rotate underneath, tape must be scrolled to the appropriate position where the data is located, making access times unacceptably long. This is the reason cartridge tape is used primarily for hard-disk backup purposes.

DISPLAYS

The display should consist of 80 or more columns and at least 24 lines of characters. A typical single-spaced, typewritten page usually holds up to 55 lines of text, each about 66 columns wide. So an 80-column by 24-line display is sufficient to accommodate a little more than one-third page of text with margins on both sides. Displays with less than 80 columns and 24 lines make word processing and other applications more difficult.

The display should be capable of exhibiting both upper- and lowercase characters. Each character is formed by use of a **dot-matrix character box** consisting typically of nine or more rows and seven or more columns of dots. As mentioned in Chapter 2, the display should be sharp and crisp so that a comma is easily distinguished from a period and a "B" is distinguished from an "8." Green or blue phosphor or amber monochromatic displays are popular. Color displays are also popular.

Also mentioned in Chapter 2 is that ordinary low-resolution television sets are inappropriate for use as displays in a professional or business context because they provide insufficient resolution for 80 columns of characters. A monochromatic display, on the other hand, is a high-resolution, high-persistence monitor that is able to provide excellent character definition and crispness, the best among the displays considered here. Many monochrome displays operate in either a graphics or character (text) mode. In character or text mode, each character is formed from a matrix of dots or *pixels* (picture elements) as shown below in Figure 3–10.

For monochromatic displays, the character box may be anywhere from 7 to 9 pixels wide by 9 to 14 pixels high. The higher the density of the character box in pixels, the better formed the characters are. In graphics mode, the resolution of the display is specified again in pixels. High-resolution displays are generally capable of producing over 700 pixels horizontally, and over 350 pixels vertically.

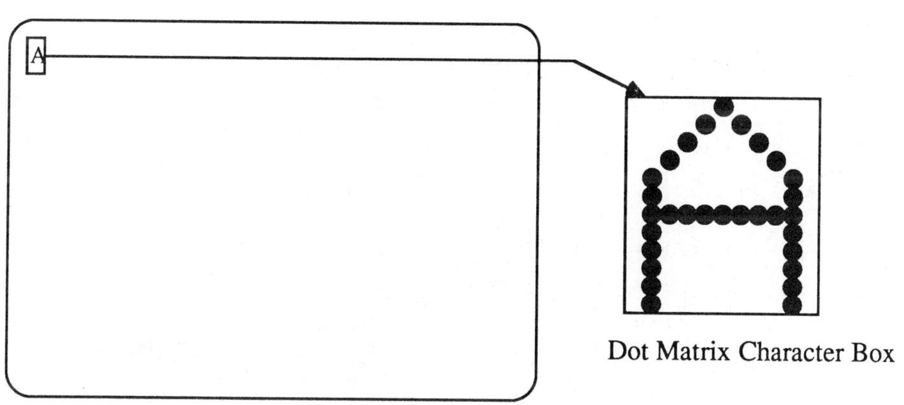

FIGURE 3–10
Typical Dot-Matrix Character Box

There are still other display features of which users should be made aware. Many displays feature reverse video (lighted background with black characters), underlining, and a 256-character character-set consisting of upper- and lowercase letters, numbers, graphics characters, blinking and half-intensity characters. Most monochromatic displays have brightness and contrast controls on the front so users can adjust these to their particular needs. Displays may have an anti-glare surface to prevent glare from overhead fluorescent lights; those that do not can be fitted with a hood or glare filter. Many displays can be tilted and swivelled so the user can adjust the display to a comfortable viewing angle. Displays come in sizes ranging from 5 to 9 inches (diagonal measurement) on some transportables to 11 to 15 inches in most desktop models. Some displays have what is called smooth scrolling while others do not. Scrolling refers to the way a new line of information is exhibited on the bottom of the screen, consequently forcing all other lines to move up, with the top line disappearing from view. Most displays accomplish this in a very "staccato" fashion, making them harder to read when scrolling takes place.

Color displays add a lot of interest and come in two forms, composite color and **RGB** (for Red, Green, and Blue). RGB monitors feature a separate color gun for each of the three primary colors, and are not as likely to produce chromatic fringing as are composite color monitors. "Chromatic fringing" describes the presence of unwanted or muddied colors in the display, usually at the borders of each character. Lengthy sessions spent gazing at displays with perceptible fringing problems can become extremely fatiguing. The price for reduced (but never fully eliminated) fringing afforded by RGB rather than composite color displays is typically $100 to $300 more. Shown in Figure 3–11 is a state-of-the-art color monitor.

Color displays are ordinarily capable of both high-resolution text and graphics. The character box was originally 8 × 8 pixels with descenders; however, the density of the character box is increasing as the newer technology comes on-line. The highest resolution monitors may display as many as 1,024 × 768 pixels or more. The number of available colors in this mode will normally be restricted to 256 or fewer. A medium-resolution display will feature screen resolution of at least

FIGURE 3–11
The NEC MultiSync Color Monitor. *(Courtesy of NEC Home Electronics U.S.A. Inc., Wood Dale, Il.)*

640 × 350 pixels and the ability to display between 4 and 16 colors simultaneously. Sometimes a low-resolution mode is also offered, providing cruder character definition, but a larger number of simultaneously displayable colors. This mode can have a different color for the foreground, background, and border, and may allow the display of between 16 and 64 different colors, selected from a palette of up to 4,096. As with monochrome displays, color displays may have reverse video, upper- and lowercase characters, underlining, and graphics symbols. Brightness and contrast controls are usually included and in some cases the display may be able to tilt and swivel. However, stands on which displays can rest may be purchased for this purpose.

A few flat-screen displays, employing either liquid crystal display (LCD) or plasma technology, are being used with portable microcomputers in order to reduce their size and weight (see Figure 3–12). Recent advances in LCD technology have made it possible to produce flat displays with resolution rivaling or equalling that of the typical monochrome monitor.

Before leaving our discussion of displays, it is necessary to discuss several issues of importance to the equipment buyer. First, a distinction must be made between display characteristics associated with the monitor (the "tube" itself), and those controlled by the video-generating hardware in the system unit of the computer. It is the computer's hardware that will determine the resolution (by the number of vertical and horizontal pixels generated), the design of the dot-matrix character box, the ability to display colors, and special features like inverse video, on-screen underlining, and graphics symbols. A computer that creates characters as an 8 × 8 dot matrix will do so on a 7-inch screen or a 15-inch screen, so that the latter size functions well when the screen needs to be read from great distances but will be perceived as less crisp when viewed up close. Similarly, a color monitor will respond with a less than dazzling display if the computer sends it only monochrome signals. Color graphics capability is often an option on microcomputers, typically costing between $300 and $600. For example, many MS-DOS machines with expansion slots will accommodate color graphics adapter cards to be inserted

FIGURE 3–12

The Compaq Portable III with Flat-screen Display.
(Courtesy of Compaq Computer Corporation)

into one of the slots. These cards will "drive" color displays with varying degrees of quality (in resolution and number of colors displayed). The IBM PC and PC XT require the user to separately purchase a video adapter card. For these machines the purchaser is faced with decisions regarding whether a monochrome or color capability is required, and what quality he or she is willing to pay for. Most IBM-PC-compatible computers will have the equivalent of a monochrome or color video card already built into the motherboard. However, the user can still purchase a separate video card which, when plugged into one of the expansion slots, will provide video capabilities beyond those afforded by the video interface on the motherboard.

Because so many of the characteristics of the display are controlled by computer hardware, selection of a separate display monitor involves relatively few considerations. A monitor should have adjustable brightness and contrast controls, an anti-glare filter, and a crisply displayed dot pattern. On some monitors, the phosphor decay rate is slow enough to make the screen blurry when scrolling or typing very fast, and this can quickly become a nuisance. The choice between monochrome colors (black and white, blue, green, or amber) is largely a matter of personal taste, because the superiority of any of them is far from being established. The decision to purchase a color monitor should probably be contingent upon a clear indication of need, considering their increased costs, the fatigue associated with their extended use, and the availability of software to effectively employ them. Few would argue, however, against the ability of color displays to add a certain "punch" to business graphics, and they are becoming increasingly popular in the development of advertising materials. It should be noted, however, that many commercially available graphics software packages for MS-DOS machines require a color-graphics adapter (video interface) card. Without it, a monochrome display goes blank when graphics software is executed.

Three standards have evolved in conjunction with color video interface cards, referred to as CGA, EGA, and PGC. CGA, an acronym for color graphics adapter, provides the lowest resolution with the least number of colors displayed. EGA, an acronym for enhanced graphics adapter, provides significantly better resolution with more colors displayed than CGA, but at greater cost. The highest levels of resolution and number of colors displayed is offered by PGC (for professional graphics controller), but again at higher expense. These cards may contain additional memory to fill out the address space allocated to video RAM. More will be said about color graphics cards and displays in the graphics chapter, Chapter 11.

KEYBOARDS

For computers that will be heavily used for word processing, the design of the keyboard can make the difference between delight and dismay, which usually translates to increased use (productivity) or disuse (dollars down the drain). Most microcomputer keyboards consist of several groupings of keys: the typewriter layout, a numeric keypad, arrow keys, and in some cases function keys. The keyboard in Figure 3–13 is typical of machines which use the MS-DOS or PC-DOS operating systems.

The keyboard should support **rollover** for fast typists who do not release a key before pressing a second key. To test for this feature, hold one key down and

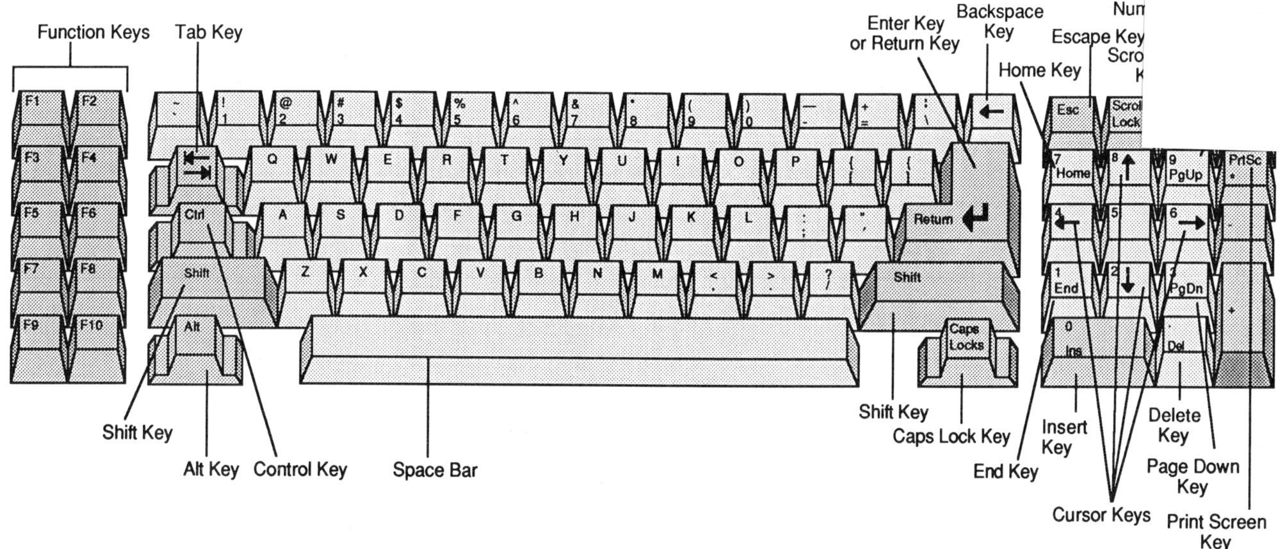

FIGURE 3–13

IBM PC AT and Compatible Keyboard Layout

press a second key. The character corresponding to the second key should appear on the screen. The keyboard should have a "break" key or a "control" key, or both, and should also possess cursor control keys or some other form of cursor control. The **cursor**, as defined in Chapter 2, is a bar, dot, underline, or arrow (usually blinking or in inverse video) that marks the current position on the display. Most keyboards support **auto-repeat**, which causes the character associated with the key to be repeated across the screen when the key is held down for longer than half a second. And most keyboards have a small buffer which will store keystrokes when the processor is busy doing something else. This is called **type-ahead.**

Depicted in Figure 3–13 is a typical MS-DOS keyboard, patterned after the keyboard introduced in October 1984 by IBM in connection with their AT. There are three key groupings and a total of 84 keys on the keyboard. On the left is the function key grouping. Some keyboards place these above the main grouping of keys in the center. These keys are defined to do different functions depending upon the application software in use. The F1 function key is frequently used to provide help to the user when how to proceed becomes unclear. The F7 function key might be used to save the user's work, while the F10 function key could be used to exit the application program.

In the main key grouping is the usual QWERTY keyboard, along with the conventional Tab key and Shift keys. Other conventional keys in this group are the Return key (which also functions as the Enter key), and the Backspace key (which moves the cursor backward one space or character position, usually erasing the character immediately to the left of the cursor). Also included within the main key grouping is the Caps Lock key, which behaves like any caps lock key. Usually this key has a little red light (light-emitting diode) which, when lighted, shows that the caps lock is "on" and all alphabetic entries will be in capitals. The most unconventional keys in the main key group are the Control key and the Alt key. These two keys are used to give all of the other keys alternate definitions. For example, the Control key, when used simultaneously with the Y key in WordStar (a word processing program), causes WordStar to erase an entire line.

On the far right in Figure 3–13 is the third and final key grouping: the cursor-control/numeric-keypad combination. Along the top and second from the rightmost key is the Num Lock key. This key controls which of the two functions this key group will be used for. Ordinarily, this third key group is used for cursor control. However, if the Num Lock key is depressed, this key group will be used as a numeric keypad. Let's consider the cursor-control function first. The Home key moves the cursor to the top-leftmost position on the screen. The cursor arrow keys move the cursor one position in the direction indicated by the arrow. When used with the Control or Alt keys, these keys may be able to move the cursor much farther in the direction indicated. The End key usually moves the cursor to the bottom-leftmost position on the screen, but as with all keys in the cursor control pad, the actual effect may vary depending on the application. The Page Up and Page Down keys usually move the screen up or down one entire screen within the document, worksheet, or file. These keys do not cause any movement on the part of the cursor. The Esc key is used to get out of certain control sequences in many application programs. The Print Screen key does just what its name suggests; it causes the screen to be printed when simultaneously pressed with the Shift key. In effect, the contents of the screen are "dumped" to the printer so that a hard-copy record of the screen can be retained. When used with the Control key, information that gets written to the screen is also sent to the printer at the same time. A second simultaneous depression of the Control key and the Print Screen key is required to shut this off. The effect of the Print Screen key is independent of whether the third key group is in the cursor-control mode or the numeric-keypad mode.

A depression of the Num Lock key puts the third key group in the numeric-keypad mode. Now this key group functions just like any ordinary keypad and is useful for entering numbers rapidly.

Some of the older, outdated technologies involved use of keyboards with chiclet keys. Chiclet (calculator-like) keyboards are unacceptable for all but the simplest of applications involving calculations of a few numbers. Standard typewriter keyboards in the IBM Selectric layout will be the easiest to use by those who have experience with Selectric typewriters. This arrangement of keys is known as the "QWERTY" layout, after the first five characters on the upper left of the board. It was originally designed to reduce the speed of fast touch-typists so that the keys would not jam. An alternative to the QWERTY arrangement is the DVORAK, named after its designer (not the composer). The DVORAK keyboard takes a more logical approach to the arrangement of keys in order to increase speed and reduce fatigue. Although the DVORAK layout has existed for many years, it gained little acceptance until the microcomputer revolution put keyboards in the hands of a whole generation of users without prior experience on QWERTY typewriters. The prospective purchaser is advised to stay with the IBM Selectric (QWERTY) layout, unless he or she is accustomed to the DVORAK keyboard. Noteworthy is the fact that with software it is possible to change the key definitions from QWERTY to DVORAK.

PRINTERS

Machines which translate electronic data and words into hard copy are today a $2.5 billion industry, with sales expected to more than double before the end of the decade. Printers are a "must" for all but the simplest of applications. There are, however, situations in which the result of some scientific or financial calculations is a few numbers which can easily be displayed and written down by hand. Even more than microcomputers, printers come in a diversity of sizes, shapes, types, and price ranges. As explained in Chapter 2, printers designed for use with microcomputers are classified as *character printers,* because they form characters one at a time on the page. Letter-quality (daisy-wheel or thimble) printers and dot-matrix printers, both of which are character printers, are among the most popular printers for microcomputers. An exception is the increasingly popular laser printer, which prints an entire page at one time and is capable of printing six to eight pages per minute.

For word processing, a letter-quality (daisy-wheel) printer has been popular. **Daisy-wheel printers** derive their name from the print element they use, which has the appearance of a daisy with 96 or 100 "petals" on it. Each petal has a character embossed on its tip. The element is rotated until the required petal is in front of a hammer, which is then fired. This brings the character embossed on the tip of the petal in contact with the ribbon, which in turn gets mashed onto the paper. In this way an impression of the character is produced on the paper after the mechanical fashion of a typewriter. The characters produced are fully formed, of typewriter quality. Each character is produced in a single mechanical motion. These printers are often referred to as "full formed" character printers.

Daisy-wheel printers currently sell for $150 to $3,000 and tend to be noisy. Acoustic shields are desirable ancillary devices for trapping the noise they produce in noise-sensitive office environments. Inexpensive daisy-wheel printers are slow, roughly 10 characters a second, and may not support some desirable features like subscripts and superscripts. The more expensive daisy-wheel printers are capable of printing 35 to 65 characters per second.

The other alternative is the less expensive, more reliable dot-matrix printer. The quality of the print is generally not as good, but the dot-matrix printer is much faster—ranging from 30 to 600 characters per second (cps)—and is capable of high-resolution, hard-copy graphics. Some of the newer, more expensive dot-matrix printers can produce a print quality that rivals the daisy-wheel printers, while providing greater speed and reliability. One way this is accomplished is by making multiple passes over each line. Before each pass, the print head is moved slightly so the dots that are added fill in the characters and give them a much more fully formed look. For some dot-matrix printers—costing $800 to $2,500—the print quality is difficult to distinguish from typewritten material.

There are disadvantages associated with the multi-pass dot-matrix printers, however. The additional passes slow them down and wear out ribbons much faster. These difficulties are alleviated by giving the user the option of single-pass printing for draft-quality output, when the print quality is not so important.

Another tradeoff relates to the way that paper is fed through the printer's platen for printing. There are essentially two choices: friction-feed and tractor-feed. Tractor-feed may be an add-on attachment to the friction-feed mechanism already built into the printer. With **friction-feed**, the paper is drawn through by pressing it between rollers and using the friction that exists between the rollers, in much the same way that a typewriter feeds paper through. Friction-feed is satisfactory for low-volume word processing or high-volume word processing when it is used in conjunction with an automatic sheet feeder—a device that automatically feeds sheets between the rollers. An advantage of friction-feed printers is their ability to print on paper that does not have its edges perforated for tractor-feeding (e.g., 3 × 5 cards, envelopes, or narrow slips of paper).

Tractor-feed, on the other hand, is a requirement whenever there is a need to print on forms. Forms printing is common in accounting applications where check-vouchers, invoices, and statements are printed on fan-folded, finished forms.

Focus Feature

PRINTERS: UP CLOSE AND PERSONAL

This article presents a few of the myriad other features of printers that purchaser might wish to acquaint themselves with.

80-COLUMN VS. 132-COLUMN FORMATS

Most printers used in conjunction with the mainframes of the last twenty years printed 132 columns on 15-inch paper. This is a desirable format for heavy data processing output, such as occurs when accounting applications are undertaken by the microcomputer. Another application for which 132 columns are desirable is in the use of spreadsheets (discussed in Chapter 7). For word processing, however, 80 columns is usually quite adequate. Printers that will provide 80 print columns on 8 1/2-inch finished paper are less expensive than printers that will accommodate up to 132 columns on 14- or 15-inch finished forms. Several of the more popular microcomputer printers are available in both widths, with a price difference of $100 to $250. If your printing application requires a lot of columns on a line, you may still be able to use a dot-matrix printer with an 8 1/2-inch platen, since many of these are capable of printing in a compressed mode (15 to 17 characters per inch, or cpi), as well as pica (10 cpi), elite (12 cpi), and perhaps even a wide mode (5 or 6 cpi). In compressed mode you will typically get between 120 and 137 characters on a line, but it may suffer from reduced legibility. Certainly the quality of compressed print is not as good.

DUTY CYCLE AND REPAIR CONSIDERATIONS

Many printers designed for use with microcomputers were never intended for heavy commercial use, and may not hold up well in a large billing office, at an airline ticket center, or in a bank. Commercial-grade printers are often rated in terms of their intended *duty cycle,* which can serve as a rough guide to the type of load that it can reliably withstand. A printer that is advertised as having a 100 percent duty cycle is designed for generating output from morning until night. If it is anticipated that the demands of a microcomputer installation will require the printer to be printing (not merely turned on) more than 20 or 30 percent of the time, the duty cycle of prospective printers must be considered. Since duty cycle ratings are made by the manufacturer (and many fine commercial printers never advertise a duty cycle), the most reliable information is often obtained by examining warranty conditions.

Two other printer specifications that are often found in advertisements are MTBF (Mean Time Between Failures) and MTTR (Mean Time To Repair). These terms may be used when discussing the print head of a dot matrix printer, the part that is most likely to wear out under normal operating circumstances. Ratings of 4,000 hours for MTBF and 15 minutes for MTTR are not uncommon with modern dot-matrix printers. A 15-minute MTTR rating (which considers only the time required to open the printer up, replace the defective part, and close it) will be of little consolation when the nearest repair outlet is in another state. The life of a dot-matrix printer can be prolonged by keeping it away from sources of dust and dirt, using only manufacturer-approved ribbons (they often contain lubricating ink), and installing it in a location where heat from the print head is easily dissipated.

MISCELLANEOUS FEATURES

There are numerous other features of both daisy-wheel and dot-matrix printers that microcomputer users have come to take for granted. For example, most character printers today are bidirectional, logic-seeking, and

Another frequent application of tractor-feed mechanisms is in the use of printing lengthy word processing documents when an automatic sheet feeder is unavailable. Sprockets are used to mesh with the perforations on the edges of the fan-fold paper to pull the paper through the print platen. The sprockets are usually of adjustable width; when they are not, the print-drive mechanism is usually referred to as "pin-

have multiple type fonts to choose from. *Bidirectional* print refers to the capability of printing from both right to left and from left to right. This speeds up the print process because the print carriage does not have to return to the left margin each time it starts a new line.

Logic-seeking refers to the capability of starting a new print line immediately, even when short lines are printed. With logic-seeking, it is no longer necessary for the print head to traverse the full distance of the carriage. The print head is instead sent directly to the location of the nearest printable character, saving considerable time in transit.

Multiple type fonts involve the use of interchangeable print-wheels in the case of daisy-wheel printers. For dot-matrix printers, the various type fonts are burned into ROM. Some dot-matrix printers (notably the Texas Instruments Model 855) have interchangeable ROM cartridges to support multiple fonts. The TI 855 has three slots on the front into which one can load any three typeface ROM cartridges. This allows the user to switch between pica, elite, italic, script, or one of several other available fonts, at the touch of a button.

In addition to these capabilities there are features like reverse line-feed, proportional spacing, and internal RAM buffers. *Reverse line-feed* allows the print mechanism to actually roll the print platen, and hence the paper, back one or more lines. Half-line forward and backward platen control is necessary to print subscripts and superscripts on daisy-wheel printers. The reverse line-feed feature is rarely seen on dot-matrix printers, because they employ a different method of producing subscripts and superscripts.

Proportional spacing is the ability to adjust print spacing to the width of the characters being printed (e.g., an 80-character line with a lot of i's will be shorter than 80-character line with a lot of m's). This should not be confused with either *microjustification,* in which words in a line are spread out by providing even spacing between letters, or normal justification, which alters the spacing between words, usually in character-width increments, such that some words are separated by only one space while others may have several spaces between them. Proportional spacing printers can produce hard copy with between-character spacing that appears to have been professionally typeset.

Internal RAM buffers lessen the number of interrupts required to get the text to the printer and onto the paper, since they allow for much more data to be sent to the printer at one time. This saves precious CPU time and facilitates the execution of other tasks which might be going on concurrently with printing. For printers which do not have an internal buffer, the CPU must send each character separately, wait until it is printed, then send the next character, and so forth. On the other hand, printers with large print buffers will allow the CPU to send an entire text file consisting of thousands of characters and then proceed onto other tasks while the printer takes its own sweet time printing out each character in the buffer. Since the transmission rate is very high—often 9,600 to 19,200 characters/sec.—the interests of CPU utilization are vitally served when larger amounts of data can be sent at one time. For printers with a small buffer that cannot be expanded, or with no buffer at all, several manufacturers supply external devices that will provide this function. A microcomputer with a generous supply of RAM and a print "spooling" software program will also allow this function.

feed." Pin-feed printers have friction-feed drive mechanisms for ordinary paper, with sprockets on the ends of the rubber platen for pulling through 8 1/2-inch forms that have perforated edges. These sprockets, however, cannot be adjusted. High-speed character printers frequently use tractor-feed. Figure 3–14 depicts some popular printers for use with microcomputers.

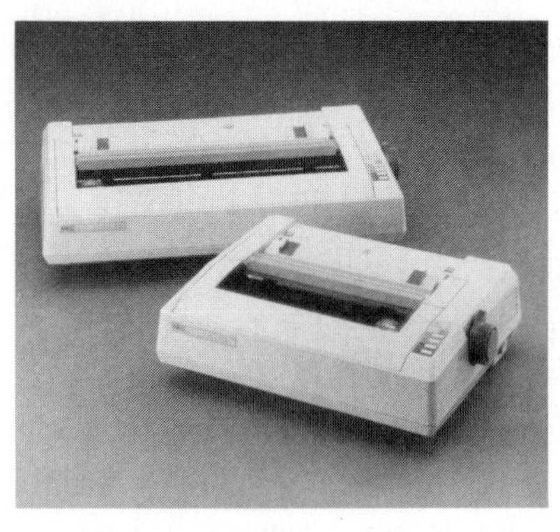

(a)

(b)

(c)

FIGURE 3–14

Some Typical Printers for Microcomputers. (a) Examples of some 24-pin dot-matrix printers. (*Courtesy of NEC Information Systems, Inc.*) (b) An Apple LaserWriter printer. (*Courtesy of Apple Computer, Inc.*) (c) A QMS-PS 800 PostScript-based laser printer. (*QMS PS-800 QMS, Inc. One Magnum Pass, Mobile, Ala. 33618 (205) 633-4300*)

The next generation of printers for microcomputers will most likely use one of the non-impact technologies. (The daisy-wheel and dot-matrix printers available today use impact technologies.) The new non-impact laser printer technology is beginning to appear in the high-price character printer range. Another non-impact technology showing promise is the ink-jet printer. These printers should usher in a new era of print quality, speed, quietness, and reliability. These newer printers can produce near-typeset quality print and will make inexpensive desktop publishing a possibility.

OTHER DEVICES FOR INPUT/OUTPUT

One of the more popular auxiliary forms of input is the mouse. A **mouse** is a small device that the user rolls on a tabletop to control movement of the cursor on the screen. Moving the mouse will cause a corresponding movement of the cursor. One problem with the mouse is that it requires additional desk surface on which to perform.

Mice usually have one, two, or three buttons on them, which can be used to select an item from a menu displayed on the screen. Chapter 2 explained how to discard a document currently being displayed when using the Apple Macintosh. The user moves the cursor (by moving the mouse) to a corner of the page, depresses the single button on the mouse to attach the cursor to the page, then rolls the mouse so that the cursor moves down to the trash-can icon (an image on the screen of a trash can) and depresses the button again. The document is now deleted—literally thrown away. The mouse is an electromechanical device that is intuitive in its use. Novice computer users may find that it makes the machine easier to use, but experienced users or fast touch-typists may be annoyed by having to remove their hands from the keyboard to make a selection.

Similar electromechanical devices for input to the computer are track balls and joysticks. These devices are widely used in computer games to guide the user-controlled images. For **joysticks**, the cursor is controlled by the direction indicated by the movement of the joystick itself (up, down, left, right). A **track ball** is embedded in a panel near the keyboard and the cursor moves in whichever direction the user rolls the ball. Problems can arise in eye-hand coordination and in an interruption of work flow when using a keyboard. Joysticks are used mostly for game playing and graphics input. Track balls have replaced mice as mechanisms for cursor control in some instances.

Touch-sensitive screens have been popularized by the introduction of Hewlett Packard's HP 150 microcomputer. There are four ways that this type of input can be accomplished, which all require use of the finger to point to some object on the screen. The HP 150 method (the only one to be discussed here) is to use an array of infrared light beams in front of the screen. The place where the finger breaks the beam at a certain intersection is the desired input; this is transmitted in code to the computer.

Touch screens make a great deal of sense in certain applications. One advantage they offer is quick interaction between the computer and user. There is no hunting for keys. Touch screens are designed more with managerial and executive needs in mind, where massive data or text entry capability is not important. Another strong use for touch panels is as an information directory.

Scanners (see Figure 3–15) are devices for inputting a paper image into a computer, regardless of whether the image is text, graphics, or some combination. Scanners have dropped in price from over $10,000 to less than $2,000 in recent years and are being increasingly used in desktop publishing applications.

Some of the newer input technologies involve pattern recognition in some way—for example, recognition of a signature or handwritten characters, or voice recognition. This is one area in which humans are better than computers. However, much research is being done in **pattern recognition**; it is only a matter of time before computers will have all the capabilities of humans. Currently, handwriting input is used within special well-defined contexts, and could also be used to send messages from one user to another user without the computer having to understand what the message says.

Speech recognition could be the ultimate method of inputting information into a computer, but is the least well developed. Currently, the recognition devices have small vocabularies, and often they can recognize only one speaker's voice. In view of the low level of development of voice-recognition technology, its applications are limited as well. It has been implemented in inventory position and sales order-entry systems. Despite its limited present use, when the technology is well developed, voice recognition should be the major way of inputting information into computers in the future.

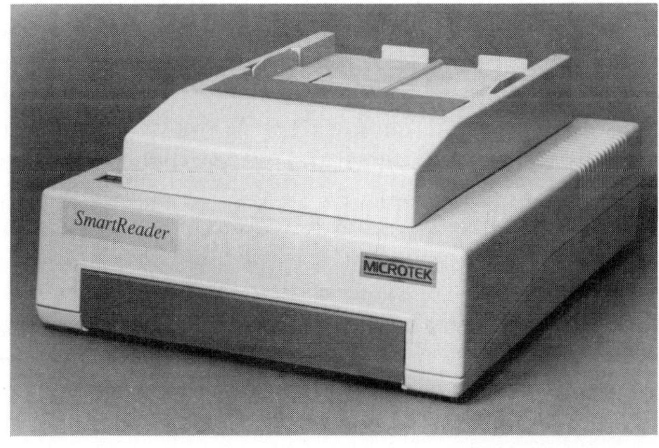

FIGURE 3–15

The Microtek Smart Reader Scanner. *(Courtesy of Microtek Lab, Inc.)*

FIGURE 3–16

External Interfaces on the Back of a Computer

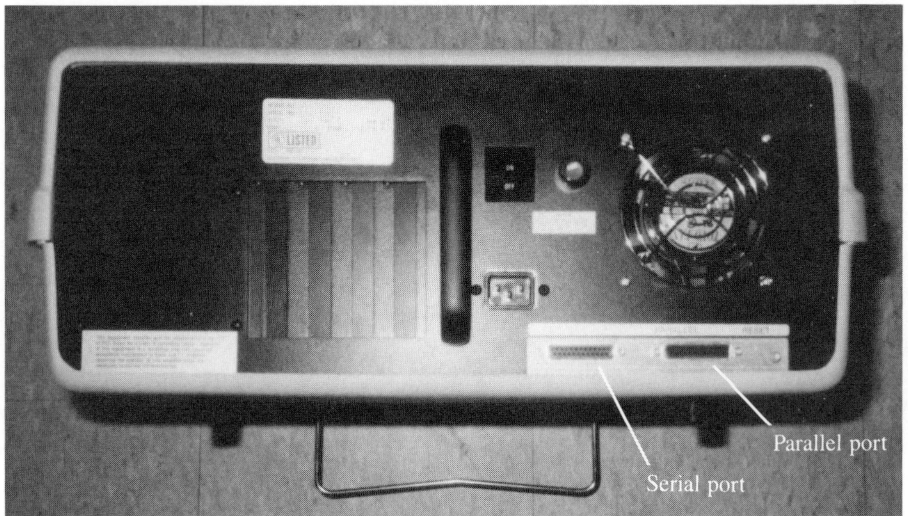

PORTS AND EXTERNAL INTERFACES

Two important external interfaces (also called "ports") are found on the back of many microcomputers. One of these is called a **serial port**; it is used primarily for data communication. The other is called a **parallel port**, it is used primarily as an external interface for the printer. These are depicted in Figure 3–16. Each will be discussed in turn.

The serial interface is technically a RS-232 port. Data transmitted through this port is sent out serially in bits, with one bit following the other sequentially. There are two main wires: a send wire, over which a bit stream is transmitted to the outside world; and a receive wire, over which data is received from the outside world. Additional wires are used for control and handshaking. **Handshaking** is the term used to describe the means by which two data transmission devices get prepared to send and receive data between themselves. More will be said about the serial port in the chapter on data communications (Chapter 14).

The parallel interface is usually an IEEE-488 port, also called a Centronics parallel port (named after the firm that developed the interface). There are eight send wires and additional wires for handshaking and control. The transmission is usually from computer to printer. The eight send wires are each capable of transmitting a single bit at the same instant in time, that is, in parallel. Hence, an entire byte can be transmitted at once. These two ports—the serial port and the parallel port—are the interfaces through which the microcomputer communicates with the external electronic world.

Summary

In this chapter we have described in detail the basic hardware components that make up any microcomputer system. We conclude the chapter by summarizing what we feel are minimal hardware requirements for managerial/professional usage of microcomputers *in the office.* (Field usage of microcomputers would require a different set of specifications.)

The CPU should include a 16-bit (or 32-bit or larger) microprocessor with at least a 1-megabyte address space. Primary storage should include at least 256K of RAM. Expandability to a half-megabyte or more is very desirable.

Insofar as displays are concerned, the standard monochrome green phosphor, blue phosphor, or amber monitor is appropriate where color is not a requirement; otherwise, a color monitor must be selected. In text mode, the monitor must be capable of displaying at least 80 columns with at least 24 lines of text. For color monitors and applications involving color, one should be concerned about (1) the resolution, (2) the number of colors that are simultaneously displayable, and (3) whether graphics can be intermixed with text. Features like smooth scrolling, a glare filter, and brightness and contrast controls should be given careful consideration.

Secondary storage, including floppies, hard disks, Bernoulli boxes, and CD-ROMs, was discussed at length. Larger capacity floppy disk drives can contribute in important ways to the productivity of a managerial work station. A hard disk can further improve productivity by greatly speeding up the reading and writing of data to and from the disk. Capacity planning for both primary storage and secondary storage will be taken up in Chapter 16. As a minimum, one would want double-density, double-sided drives in the IBM PC format (360 Kbytes per drive) if using the 5 1/4-inch minidiskettes. Two drives will facilitate the backup of important files and enable programs and data to be segregated. A second drive will also put more data within easy reach of the microprocessor.

The keyboard should have the familiar typewriter layout (the so-called QWERTY keyboard), with standard typewriter keys. Features like rollover, auto-repeat, type-ahead (the ability to enter a limited number of keystrokes while the processor is still performing a previous request), function keys, and numeric keypad are mandatory for managerial or professional use. Some keyboards are difficult to get used to; the user may want to test the "feel" of the keyboard for "mushiness," placement of keys, and accuracy of typing before considering the purchase of a new system. If the computer is being purchased as a word processor for someone else in the office (e.g., a secretary or typist), it is probably wise to have them test the keyboard and participate in the purchase decision.

The printer, like the other hardware components we have discussed, should be selected on the basis of the applications it must support. The volume of printed output should be the determinant of such considerations as print speed, paper width, and duty cycle. If word processing is a primary intended use, the quality of print must be an important consideration. The new low-cost laser printers have ushered in a new era of print speed and quality.

These are the main components that have been discussed in this chapter. When considering the purchase of a new hardware system, be certain to use the checklist at the end of the book to compare each hardware alternative. In Chapter 16 we present a methodology for grading each hardware alternative and for considering that alternative in relation to its price. In addition, we will describe how to get the vendors to design the system for prospective purchasers at no cost (usually).

Key Terms

access time
address lines
address space
auto-repeat
Bernoulli box
CD-ROM
cursor
daisy-wheel printer

- disk buffer
- dot matrix
- dot-matrix character box
- floating-point coprocessor
- friction-feed
- handshaking
- icon
- joysticks
- mouse
- parallel port
- pattern recognition
- RAM
- RGB
- rollover
- ROM
- scanner
- serial port
- system unit
- touch screens
- track balls
- tractor-feed
- type-ahead
- wait state

Self-Test

1. What are the important features of
   (a) primary storage?
   (b) floppy disks?
   (c) microprocessors?
   (d) displays?
   (e) keyboards?
   (f) printers?
   (g) hard disks?
   (h) CD-ROMs?
   (i) WORMs?
2. Discuss the operation of floppy disk drives.
3. Discuss the operation of hard (Winchester) disk drives.

Exercises

1. Contrast integrated systems with component systems. Find examples of each in the literature.
2. What managerial and professional considerations are important in the selection of microcomputer hardware?
3. How is the microcomputer interfaced with the external world?
4. Contrast floppy diskettes with hard disks in terms of
   (a) access time
   (b) transfer rate
   (c) rotation speed
   (d) susceptibility to head crash
5. Describe what is meant by "backing up" important programs and data. Why is this necessary?
6. Characterize the following microprocessors with respect to
   (a) clock rate
   (b) number of data lines
   (c) number of address lines
   (d) address space
   (e) word length (number of bits it processes at one time internally)

Not all of this information is available in Chapter 3, so you will have to do some research. Refer to the list of periodicals at the end of Chapter 2.

Intel 8080
Intel 8085
Intel 8086
Intel 8088
Intel 80186
Intel 80286
Intel 80386
MOS 6502
MOS 6510
Motorola 6809
Motorola 68000
Motorola 68010
Zilog Z80A
Zilog Z80B
Zilog Z8000

7. RAM chips come in the following sizes: 16K bits, 64K bits, 256K bits, and 1M bits. How many of each size are required to supply 256K bytes of primary storage (excluding the 1M bit chip)? How many of each size are required to supply 1M byte of primary storage?
8. Distinguish between RAM and ROM. Would you say that ROM is RAM?
9. List as many media as you can that could be used for secondary storage.
10. Arrange the list of microprocessor chips from Exercise 7 in descending order of speed. Which of these chips is likely to support multiuser operation?
11. Describe the function and operation of the following devices.

touch screen	joystick
mouse	track ball

12. List the important buying considerations relative to printers.
13. List the important buying considerations relative to displays.
14. Choose a hardware system of interest to you. Collect as much information as you can about it. Write a report on it in which you describe the system using the checklist contained in the appendix that follows Chapter 16 at the end of this book.
15. Use the "Printers: Up Close and Personal" article to define the following terms.
    bidirectional printing
    duty cycle (of printers)
    internal RAM buffers (as applied to printers)
    logic-seeking
    microjustification
    proportional spacing
    reverse line-feed
16. The Intel 80386 is expected to be the microprocessor of the future. Why do you think this is likely? Table 3–3 suggests that the 80386 has 32 address lines. How large is its address space? Why is the Intel 80386 faster than the Intel 80286?
17. It has been suggested that the Intel 80386 microprocessor is a true mainframe processor on a chip. Compare the chip with the Intel 8088, assuming the 8088 runs at 5 MHz and the 80386 at 20 MHz. Software written for the 8088 will run on the 80386. How much faster is this software likely to run?
18. Some experts have suggested that CD-ROMs have a fundamental shortcoming and should not be marketed. What do you think that shortcoming is?
19. Describe the operation of Bernoulli boxes. What are the advantages of Bernoulli boxes? The disadvantages?

20. What advantage would a floating-point coprocessor provide for a word processing application? A spreadsheet application?
21. List the peripherals you believe would be important in any desktop publishing application.

Cases

1. A real estate company decided to purchase a personal computer for word processing and other applications. The company already owned an expensive typewriter/printer with a serial port, which it wanted to interface with the new computer. After due consideration of several machines, the company decided on an expensive microcomputer for which very little software was available. When the computer finally arrived and was installed, it was discovered that the word processing software was designed to work only with printers made by the computer manufacturer, and there were no provisions for installation of other printers. Furthermore, all printing was directed to the parallel port (apparently the serial port was designed primarily for attaching a modem). What preventive measures should have been taken to avoid this dilemma? What solutions would you recommend to ameliorate this problem?
2. A small tavern decided to purchase a microcomputer to automate its nightly close-out, a simple inventory and cash drawer reconciliation. In order to save money, the tavern owner purchased the minimum configuration of a popular computer, a 256K byte, one-disk drive machine with no software. After discovering that none of the available accounting packages would run on a one-drive machine, and that even if they did they would still only be minimally acceptable, the tavern owner hired a local consultant to design a custom program. The consultant spent several hours studying the close-out procedure, after which he described a marvelous-sounding system to the tavern owner. He also delivered an estimate of $600 for the completed program and a bill for $100 for the study (included in the $600 if the tavern owner gave the go-ahead). The tavern owner was very upset, because he thought the entire program could be done for $50 or $60. He is aware that for $400 (plus the $100 to the consultant) he can buy a second disk drive ($100) and an accounting package ($300). What are the arguments in favor of having the consultant prepare the custom program? What arguments favor the purchase of the disk drive and accounting package? Can you think of any other alternatives?

Additional Reading

Books

Canning, Richard G., ed. *So You Are Thinking About a Small Business Computer.* Vista, Calif.: Canning Publications, Inc., 1980, 1983.

Connolly, Edward S., and Philip Lieberman. *Introducing the Apple Macintosh.* Indianapolis: Howard W. Sams & Co., Inc., 1984.

Cortesi, David E. *Your IBM Personal Computer: Use, Applications and Basic.* New York: Holt, Rinehart, & Winston, 1982.

Osborne, Adam, and David Bunnell. *An Introduction to Microcomputers, Vol. 0: The Beginner's Book.* 3d ed., Berkeley, Calif.: Osborne/McGraw-Hill, 1982.

Peltu, Malcolm. *Introducing Computers.* New York: NCC Publications, 1983.

Silver, Gerald A. *Small Computer Systems for Business.* New York: McGraw-Hill Book Company, 1978.

Traister, Robert J. *The IBM Personal Computer.* Blue Ridge Summit, Pa.: Tab Books, Inc., 1983.

Veit, Stanley S. *Using Microcomputers in Business: A Guide for the Perplexed.* Rochelle Park, N.J.: Hayden Book Company, Inc., 1981.

Wilkenson, Barry, and David Horrock. *Computer Peripherals.* Toronto, Canada: Hodder and Stoughton, 1980.

CHAPTER

4

System Software and Operating Systems

CHAPTER OUTLINE

A Few Definitions 88

Operating Systems 89

FOCUS FEATURE Humble Beginnings . . . 91

FOCUS FEATURE Operating System Compatibility Issues 92

FOCUS FEATURE The Evolution of DOS 96

Applications Environments 101

Language Translators 102

FOCUS FEATURE What Is Structured Programming, and Why Is It Preferred? 105

Utility Programs 110

FOCUS FEATURE Description of Utility Programs Available 110

Advanced Features of Operating Systems 111

MS-DOS TUTORIAL 116

CHAPTER OBJECTIVES

In this chapter you will learn

1 the components of system software
2 the components of operating systems
3 compatibility issues relating to software
4 what application environments are and how they are used
5 what language translators are and how they are used
6 what utilities are and how they are used

Recent advances in computer hardware have produced systems that can be marvelous productivity tools for an individual or a small business. But they are little more than expensive paperweights without software packages to run on them. The most fundamental, and in some ways the most important, of these packages is the system software. It is the system software that greets you when the machine is first turned on, and the system software that controls virtually all of the computer's activities until the time it is turned off. Small computer installations may vary in the amount and type of both hardware and software components, but all of them will have system software.

System software will affect the types of programs you can run. It may determine the number of activities and users that the system can simultaneously accommodate. It is likely to affect the speed and flexibility of the hardware and software, and it provides so much of the character and personality of the computer that it may make the difference between an enjoyable session at the computer or a frustrating one. Since system software affects so many aspects of a computer system, it is an important consideration in the acquisition of a small business computer, and in certain circumstances should be selected before applications software.

A FEW DEFINITIONS

System software is a term applied to a broad spectrum of programs that perform functions not normally found outside a computerized environment. It would be easy for a business manager who is completely unfamiliar with computers to identify the business functions that are performed by a payroll program, a word processing package, or an inventory program. It might be considerably more difficult for her to imagine the usefulness of a print queue manager or a hard-disk backup program. System software programs, then, are principally concerned with controlling and enhancing the computer system's hardware and software components, rather than performing a specific business function.

There is little agreement as to what types of programs should be included in this category. Many microcomputer users consider system software to be the operating system and associated utilities that were provided with their machines when they purchased them. Even with this simple definition there will be some confusion when different operating systems are examined. The UNIX and the UCSD p-system, for example, have language translators; the PICK system has a fully operational data base system; and some implementations of MS-DOS have sorting programs. In this chapter we will consider as system software the following categories of programs:

operating systems
applications environment programs
language translators
system utility programs

An **operating system** is a program that controls the interactions between the hardware and software components of a computer system. Whenever a computer is turned on, it is unable to process any programs or instructions until the operating system is loaded into primary storage, usually from a disk. Once in primary storage it will remain there until the machine is turned off, which is why the operating system is sometimes known as the "resident" portion of system software. Most computer manufacturers package an operating system with their hardware, but the user can usually purchase other operating systems that will work on the same hardware.

Applications environment programs are a relatively new category of software; the first commercially available package (DESQVIEW by Quartermaster) was introduced in 1983. Application environment programs resemble operating systems in that they reside in primary storage while application programs are running, yet they may still require an operating system to interface with the hardware components. These programs typically provide an easy-to-learn (or menu-driven) set of commands to perform operating system functions, and may include windowing or data transfer capabilities (more on this later).

Language translators allow a programmer to develop custom applications programs to run on a microcomputer. The costs associated with the development of a large-scale applications program are usually not justified when suitable packaged software is available. Low-cost commercial packages, however, are designed to reach the widest possible market, so a business with unusual software requirements may find the need to develop their own programs or hire someone to produce them. The availability of fast, flexible, and easy-to-use languages can be an important consideration when purchasing a computer system.

Utility programs are programs designed to extend the flexibility and ease of use of an operating system. Operating systems, by virtue of the size limitations imposed by their primary storage resident nature, provide only a few essential functions (called "commands" in Chapter 2). Other nice, but nonessential, functions have been relegated to separate programs to be called from the disk when needed. A wide assortment of utility programs is typically bundled with the operating system, yet some are written by independent software houses, hardware manufacturers, or other users. These programs may perform functions as diverse as recovering files from a damaged disk, altering the shape of the characters displayed on the CRT, or reserving a portion of primary storage to emulate a floppy disk. We will discuss the major types of utility programs later in this chapter.

OPERATING SYSTEMS

Operating systems are typically supplied with the purchase of a computer system. Most microcomputers, however, will run more than one operating system, so the user is not restricted to the one supplied with his or her equipment. This section will explore some of the differences between operating systems by looking at operating system components, factors that affect software compatibility, and single versus multiuser systems. Four of the more popular operating systems—CP/M, MS–DOS, operating systems for the Apple Lisa and Macintosh, and UNIX—will then be looked at in more detail. To give the reader a clearer idea of operating system functions, the following article provides a brief historical perspective.

Modern operating systems for microcomputers perform the same services as the efforts of early programmers described above. They control the activities of the hardware components by providing the link between the microprocessor and the user or programs as depicted in Figure 4–1.

FIGURE 4–1
The Role of Operating Systems

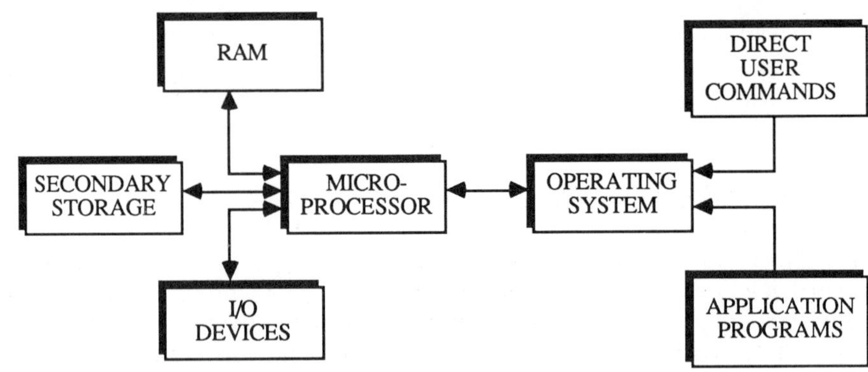

Every operating system has three main segments: the Console Command Processor (CCP), the Basic Input/Output System (BIOS), and the Basic Disk Operating System (BDOS). The BDOS contains a number of routines that are used by the CCP or are called directly from applications programs. These routines handle everything from getting information to and from disks to displaying output on a CRT or printer. The BDOS routines call upon the BIOS to interact directly with the hardware. Since only the BIOS needs to be rewritten for different machine implementations, and since applications programs make calls only to the BDOS (which is essentially the same from machine to machine), programmers can develop applications without concern for the hardware environment. This is the essence of program transportability. Unfortunately, many programs have been written which make calls directly to the BIOS, making them unusable for all but a single machine. It should be noted, moreover, that in some operating systems, there is no distinction between the BDOS and the BIOS, and both components are included under the term BIOS. Figure 4–2 depicts the relationship between the user, the application program, and the components that make up the operating system.

The Console Command Processor

The **Console Command Processor (CCP)** interprets the user's commands and directs processing to the appropriate routines within the input/output program in order to accomplish the user's directive. CCP is resident in primary storage, since it is loaded when the operating system is loaded. For MS-DOS and PC-DOS, the CCP is the COMMAND.COM file resident on the system disk, which gets loaded during booting. Console commands that are available in the MS-DOS and PC-DOS operating systems were partially listed in Table 2–3. A more complete list is found in Table 4–4 in the MS-DOS TUTORIAL at the end of this chapter. These commands are to be entered after the operating system prompt (i.e., not during the execution of an application program).

The Input/Output System

A command to produce a directory listing like the one in Figure 2–18 probably doesn't appear too remarkable to most people, because we have come to take a facility like this for granted. In truth, a fairly complicated program segment is

Focus Feature

HUMBLE BEGINNINGS . . .

In the mid-1970s, when microcomputers first began to be produced commercially, programming a microcomputer was not an easy task. If you were not fortunate enough to have an input keyboard and a display device, you had to load your program into primary storage by positioning a row of toggle switches on the front of your computer. Up meant on. Down was off. When you had eight of them positioned in the manner you wanted, you had a byte ready to load—as soon as you entered the primary storage location through another set of switches. When the program ran, you could get your results by reading the values contained in the memory locations where the results were to have been stored. You merely set the switches to the appropriate memory addresses and read the values from a bank of light-emitting diodes (LEDs), with each diode showing the value of a single bit.

Those who could afford terminals (and many of the early hobbyists could not) found that they still had a formidable task ahead of them before their terminal was usable. When the computer was first turned on, they had to use the toggle switches to enter a program that would cause the computer to recognize the existence of the terminal. This program informed the computer that all subsequent input would come from the terminal's keyboard and that all output would be directed to the terminal's display. This was not an insignificant programming job, either, because it had to contain instructions to tell the computer to periodically scan the keyboard to see if a key was pressed, and directions concerning what to do if the user pressed a key.

It did not take long before the early programmers began storing their terminal driver programs on ROM chips so that they did not have to be entered upon every power-up. With the passage of time came an increase in the sophistication of these start-up programs. They were expanded to include routines which would read and write programs and data on secondary storage devices—cassettes in the early days and later floppy disks. Soon the programs became too large to be economically stored on ROM chips, so the majority of the routines were put on a floppy disk with only enough in ROM to load the remainder into primary storage from the disk.

called upon to perform this simple function, and it requires many steps. Each step in turn involves dozens of instructions to complete, all of them transparent to the user. The major procedure that would be followed by many operating systems is listed in Table 4–1.

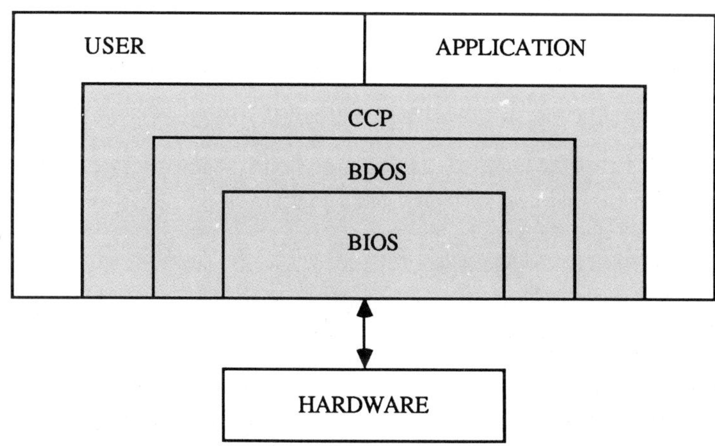

FIGURE 4–2
The Operating System Components

Focus Feature

OPERATING SYSTEM COMPATIBILITY ISSUES

One principal consideration in the selection of a small computer system is its software compatibility. The degree of a hardware-software combination's *compatibility* (the ability of a given computer to properly run a particular software package) is often difficult to discern. Generally speaking, if two computers run *exactly* the same operating system, and an application program is designed to run with that operating system, then the program should perform properly on either machine. Problems arise, however, when software publishers develop multiple versions of the same operating system for different computers. Applications programmers, having no desire to develop their own operating systems, rely heavily upon operating systems to perform hardware controlling functions. This means that the operating system routines called by the applications program must always be in the same location and handle the requested function in the same manner from machine to machine. When a hardware manufacturer develops a computer with distinctive features, an existing operating system for similar machines is usually modified slightly to work on the new computer. Such minor differences in operating systems can arise from virtually any hardware configuration differences, but they are usually attributable to the choice of hardware/software characteristics in one or more of the following areas: (1) operating system version number; (2) the type of microprocessor; (3) the disk format; (4) the video attributes, and (5) the operating speed, or clock rate, of the microprocessor.

OPERATING SYSTEM VERSION NUMBER DIFFERENCES

An applications program that is advertised as running under "MS-DOS" may in fact be designed for versions 2.0, 2.1, 2.05, or 2.11 only. It may not run at all under versions 3.0 and higher. Users may not be aware that their operating system is different. Even the version number is not always a sufficient clue to the degree of program compatibility. CP/M-80 version 2.2 is available for a wide assortment of computers with markedly differing disk formats, speeds, and video attributes, preventing programs from being readily transported from computer to computer.

MICROPROCESSOR DIFFERENCES

An operating system is written to use the instruction set of a particular microprocessor. The *instruction set* is the language of the microprocessor, the collection of singleton operations that the microprocessor can perform. It is easy to see why a new microprocessor, with a different set of control instructions, would require a different operating system. Thus, an operating system that works with a Zilog Z8000 would not be usable on a computer with a Mostek 6502. Occasionally a new chip will appear with an instruction set which includes that of an earlier chip, but perhaps offers greater performance or flexibility. Chips that share a common core of instructions are said to be in the same microprocessor family. Different computers

TABLE 4–1

Principal Processing Steps for a DIRectory Command

1. Reserve an area of primary storage (memory) to store the disk information.
2. Store the name of the file to be searched for in a particular area of primary storage so that it can be compared for a match with each filename read from the disk. If no filename has been specified, the area is filled with wild-card characters, thereby allowing anything to match.
3. Send the control signals to start up the drive and position the read/write head at the starting address for the directory information.
4. Read a portion of the directory tracks into the reserved area of primary storage.
5. Process the information in primary storage into a readable form and display it on the CRT.
6. Repeat steps 4 through 5 until no more filename matches are found.
7. Return control of the computer to the user.

based upon chips within the same family can frequently use the same operating system, and hence run the same applications programs.

DISK FORMAT DIFFERENCES

When a computer manufacturer wishes to offer a higher disk capacity than is available on other machines employing the same microprocessor chip, the operating system for the earlier machines may have to be altered before it can run on the new computer. Usually, the later version of the operating system can read and write in the format of the earlier version. If this is the case, and no other system features have been altered, there is a high probability that programs written for the earlier machine will run the same on the newer one (but not vice versa). When a disk format deviates radically from earlier ones, or when the operating system has been altered to change the number or type of drives that may be used, the computers may be software incompatible.

It was pointed out in Chapter 3 that the disk format of a Macintosh is totally incompatible with that of the PC and its compatibles. To further ensure their incompatibility, the disks are different sizes to begin with.

VIDEO ATTRIBUTE DIFFERENCES

Some MS-DOS-compatible software is designed to run only with the IBM color graphics adapter card or its equivalent. When used with machines having only the IBM monochrome card or its equivalent, the screen goes blank. To overcome this problem, many application software packages provide several screen drivers and let the user pick the one that is appropriate for his or her machine. This is usually done when the package is installed. Most application software packages come with an install program that lets the user pick screen, printer, and keyboard drivers that are appropriate for the hardware configuration on which the software is to be used.

OPERATING SPEED DIFFERENCES

Many microprocessors are operated at well below their maximum theoretical speed, usually so that slower (and less expensive) RAM chips and coprocessors can be used. An applications package designed to run on an Intel 8088 at 4.77 MHz may not work at all on the same chip running at 8 MHz, for a variety of complex technical reasons. Minor speed variance (no more than 10 or 15 percent) usually poses no difficulty, but applications programs must occasionally have new versions developed for faster computers.

The lesson to be learned from this brief introduction to software compatibility factors is that the buyer of hardware and software must be especially cautious when selecting either. The ultimate test of compatibility is to have the desired applications program *demonstrated* on the user's computer.

Steps 1 through 5 as listed in Table 4–1 are each performed by a different routine. These routines are but a small portion of the many functions that make up the *input/output program* of an operating system. Each routine controls the hardware to perform a specific function. When used in combination they can accomplish virtually every task that is within the capability of the hardware, generally with great efficiency and speed.

The input/output system (also called the BIOS, for Basic Input Output System) contains all of the necessary functions to control the activities of the microprocessor, and all of the other hardware, even if it is peripheral. Since BIOS is always resident in primary storage, application programs usually rely upon the routines in the BIOS rather than develop routines of their own. Because a given operating system will always be loaded into the same primary storage locations, the task of an applications program developer is greatly simplified. Some word processing programs, for example, save text to a disk in the following manner:

1. The starting address in RAM of the text to be saved is sent to a predetermined primary storage (memory) location or register.
2. The stopping address in RAM of the text to be saved is placed in another predetermined storage location.
3. The code(s) for a disk-write operation are sent to another memory location or register.
4. Processing is turned over to the BIOS until the operation is completed.

If the operating system was not available, the applications programmer would have to develop routines for

determining which areas of the disk were not being used

grouping the text into blocks that fit the disk format

directly controlling a number of hardware activities, such as spinning the disk, moving the read/write head, and so forth.

Directly controlling the hardware of a microcomputer system is often extremely complicated, even for simple tasks. A programmer who decides to develop a versatile applications package, such as a word processor, without using the operating system will face a monumental task. Since the input would most likely come from a keyboard and the output would be directed to a CRT, he or she would have to write keyboard input routines and video driver routines. In order to save text on a disk, there would have to be a number of routines for reading and writing to disks. Since text produced by the word processor would ultimately be printed, the programmer must develop routines that direct the microprocessor to interface with the printer. At an even more basic level, routines must be written to tell the microprocessor where in RAM to store each character as it is entered. In short, by the time the program was developed, the programmer would have replicated most of the functions of the typical operating system, and at a very high developmental cost. It is easy to see, then, why virtually all applications packages rely upon operating systems to control the system's hardware, and why operating systems remain in a designated portion of memory while other programs are run.

Single-user, Multiuser, and Multitasking Operating Systems

Operating systems for microcomputers may be classified as either single-user, multiuser, or multitasking systems. An understanding of the differences and limitations of these systems is important in planning for small-computer acquisitions.

Single-user Systems Most operating systems for small computers are designed for a single user running a single application at a time. In many situations they afford all the performance and flexibility that the user will ever need. A small retail establishment, medical office, or manufacturing facility might have only one individual who directly interacts with the computer system. In a larger organization, a single-user system can serve as an excellent executive workstation, used as a terminal to the corporate mainframe for large jobs and as a local processor for quick analysis of data transported from the mainframe. Single-user systems, then, impose no obvious restrictions on a large segment of small-computer users, and can be run on some quite powerful machines. CP/M-80, CP/M +, CP/M-86, MS-DOS, PC-DOS, AppleDOS, ProDOS, TRSDOS, TurboDOS, ProDOS, and the Apple Macintosh operating system are all examples of single-user operating systems.

Multiuser Systems When it is anticipated that several users will require simultaneous access to the computer or to the same data, a choice must be made between networked single-user systems, file-server systems, multiprocessor systems, or time-sharing systems. Each type of multiuser system is discussed in Chapter 15. It is sufficient to remark here that specialized system software is required for each category (and manufacturer) of a multiuser system.

Multitasking Operating Systems A **multitasking** operating system is designed to allow a single user to run more than one job at a time. Many multiuser operating systems are also multitasking, and multitasking systems such as Concurrent CP/M-86 are available for the single user environment. In a multitasking system the computer will alternate between jobs in the same manner that the time-sharing system alternates between users. Different programs, or program segments, will reside in different areas of memory. The operating system will control swapping activities and display the output for each program in different areas of the display (each area is called a *window*). Imagine being able to analyze corporate financial data on a spreadsheet while a word processor prints the minutes from the last board meeting and the computer is communicating with a remote device, such as another computer.

CP/M, MS-DOS, UNIX and UNIX Work-alikes, and Macintosh and Lisa Operating Systems

Many operating systems have been developed to work on small computers. In this section we will take a brief look at four operating systems that have played a significant role in the history of microcomputers. Each one has spawned imitators and prompted the development of thousands of programs.

CP/M *CP/M* (for Control Program/Microcomputer) was developed in 1973 by Gary Kildall, a consultant to Intel Corporation, as a by-product of the development of a language (called PL/M) for Intel's 8080 microprocessor. When Intel showed no interest in Kildall's program, he left the company and formed his own, Digital Research Corporation. It was not long before many companies discovered that they could license CP/M from Digital Research at a much smaller cost than developing their own operating system. Since those early days, CP/M has been either a primary or an optional operating system on hundreds of different computers.

Versions of CP/M exist for several microprocessors. For computers using the Intel 8080 or Zilog Z80 (8-bit processors) families with 64K bytes or less of RAM, there is CP/M-80. For computers with more memory there is a version called CP/M +. For the Intel 8086 and 8088 microprocessors, there are two CP/Ms: a single-tasking version called CP/M-86 and the multitasking Concurrent CP/M. There is also a multiuser version for 8-bit computers called MP/M. All of these versions are structured in the same manner and have similar commands.

Because of its small size (the first version took less than 4K) CP/M's Console Command Processor has only a few built-in commands. **DIR** provides a directory listing. **TYPE** followed by a file name will list the file's contents to the CRT. **ERA** will erase the files listed after it. **REN** will rename a file. **USER** changes directories from the current one to another in the range of zero to nine (storing similar files in different user numbers helps keep track of them if a great number of files are on a disk). To handle more complex matters, like copying files, a utility must be called from a disk.

Focus Feature

THE EVOLUTION OF DOS

DOS got its start in connection with an agreement worked out between IBM and Microsoft in 1980. In its original form, DOS 1.xx strongly resembled CP/M. Microsoft acquired rights from Seattle Computer Products to market the CP/M-like operating system they had developed. It did not support hard disks and it was strictly a single-user, single-tasking operating system. The IBM version was referred to as PC-DOS and versions for all other machines were marketed and produced under the name MS-DOS. There were minor technical differences between these DOSs. Later versions of DOS 1.xx added support for hard disks.

MS-DOS/PC-DOS 2.0

MS/PC-DOS 2.xx offered the following significant advantages over the previous versions of DOS.

Installable Device Drivers. This feature permits the user to install device drivers appropriate for such hardware as the keyboard and monitor. The user, at installation time, could load any device driver into memory that was appropriate for the particular system. This capability greatly facilitated the use of PCs in foreign countries with non-English language displays and non-American keyboards. The installable device driver provides the gateway to sophisticated networking systems.

Xenix Compatibility. The second most important feature of DOS 2.0 is its Xenix compatibility, which is divided into several areas. First are the file primitives, which provide a very efficient way of invoking the operating system to perform a file management function. The parsing of filenames, for instance, is handled in a more sophisticated way. DOS 2.0 also makes it possible to create programs that can run in either a Xenix or an MS-DOS environment.

An Improved File Directory. Another example of MS-DOS 2.0's compatibility with Xenix is its enhanced directory system. Logically consistent with the Xenix file structure and physically consistent with the existing MS-DOS file structure, the directory is a hierarchical system that permits the logical organization of user files. It allows users, for example, to partition a hard disk shared by several office workers into several areas. The hierarchical structure eases storage and retrieval of files to and from the hard disk. Subdirectories can be defined to permit the user to organize his or her files into logical subdirectories.

Input/Output Enhancements. In addition to modifying the file structure of DOS 1.xx, Microsoft added the capability to redirect the input and output in DOS 2.0. Output from standard devices, such as a keyboard, display, and communications port, can be redirected either to files or other devices. The redirection can be either a dynamic one (performed on the command line) or one that invokes a utility to redirect the output permanently. One type of redirection, for example, would be to send output intended for the screen to the printer. The capability of redirecting the input and output is closely coupled to the concept of installable device drivers.

DOS 2.0 also provides a limited form of piping, a means of interprocess communication available in Xenix. This type of piping permits the user to take the output of one process and have the operating system automatically feed it to another process as input. The SORT utility, a type of filter, is a standard utility that is very helpful for this kind of piping. Other utilities include a simple one called MORE, which suspends output on the screen every 24 or 25 lines so that the user doesn't see all his

MS-DOS/PC-DOS When IBM introduced its Personal Computer (PC) in 1981, many industry people felt that it would have little impact upon the market. IBM, after all, was a manufacturer of large computers, and was making its small computer debut with what some felt was an overpriced product based on a mediocre microprocessor (the Intel 8088 was far from the state of the art in speed and memory capacity). The IBM name, however, was enough to overcome most objections, as

output go by without being able to read it. Still another utility, called FIND, helps locate a given string of characters within a file.

Background Tasking. DOS 2.0 makes it possible to support a limited background/foreground multitasking environment. The actual capability is called background tasking. A print spooler provided as part of DOS 2.0 makes extensive use of this capability.

MS-DOS/PC-DOS 3.0

IBM introduced DOS 2.0 when it announced its PC-XT, because earlier versions would not support the XT's fixed disk and many changes to DOS 1.xx were required to operate the new hardware. Similarly, the primary function of DOS 3.0 was to provide the necessary hardware support for the PC AT's new disks—the 1.2-megabyte floppy and the optional pair of 20-megabyte hard disks—and the Intel 80286 processor chip.

Thus DOS 3.0 was introduced in September 1984, along with the PC AT. Its biggest advantage was the special support required by the dual-mode, high-capacity hard-disk drive which makes DOS 3.0 essential to AT users. Other major changes include the introduction of internal networking features like file sharing and data locking (a technique that prevents the data from being shared by one program while it's being changed by another). Significant changes were made to certain utilities, and a few utilities were added. For example, the new DOS 3.0 FORMAT utility is capable of formatting the 1.2-megabyte floppies in addition to the older 360-kilobyte floppy format. However, to actually format a floppy with 1.2 megabytes of storage requires the special AT floppy drive. Some of the additional utilities include

ATTRIB—lets the user control the read-only attribute of each file. The read-only attribute protects files against being changed or deleted. However, ATTRIB won't let the user change each file's archive attribute, which informs the BACKUP program of the files that have been changed since the last backup copy. When backing up the hard disk, for example, it is necessary only to back up files that have changed since the last backup.
LABEL—lets users add or change the volume label on the hard disk and floppies.
SELECT—gives users in foreign countries the ability to customize their IBM keyboards for their particular key layouts.

MS-DOS/PC-DOS 3.2. This DOS is designed to support IBM and compatible products that use the 3- and -1/2-inch floppy-disk drives. In addition, four more utility files were added to the 37 files already a part of MS-DOS/PC-DOS 3.1.

MS-DOS/PC-DOS 4.0

Microsoft's DOS 4.0 allows PC users to run several tasks at once. Under DOS 4.0, for example, users can simultaneously print a file, sort through a data base, compile a program, and write a letter. In addition, programs written to run under DOS 4.0 can make use of "virtual" memory space in excess of 640K bytes. This means that DOS 4.0 applications could consist of many megabytes of code, but would execute like any PC-DOS/MS-DOS 2.0 application program. Currently, users can implement multitasking under DOS 2.0 with windowing products such as Microsoft's Windows. These products have been criticized for their heavy memory requirements and burden on system performance. The advantage of DOS 4.0 is that multitasking can now be done inside the operating system,

(*Continued*)

THE EVOLUTION OF DOS (Continued)

which is a much more efficient way than to overlay a windowing environment onto a single-tasking DOS.

Unlike a windowing environment, which typically creates multiple windows within one screen, DOS 4.0 has six so-called virtual screens. Each virtual screen occupies the entire monitor, and can display one application as it executes. Other tasks can continue to execute in the background, but they may not be displayed on the screen.

MS-DOS/PC-DOS 5.0

DOS 5.0 runs on 80286-based PCs equipped with 1M byte of memory and a hard disk, and will support up to 16M bytes of memory. Its internal processes resemble those in Microsoft Windows. With this DOS, the 16M-byte address space of the 80286 is divided into two main regions, the lower 1M-byte region and the upper 15M-byte region. The lower 1M-byte region is able to accommodate conventional MS-DOS application programs, while the upper 15M-byte region will accommodate newer applications. These applications will be able to run concurrently with the application running in the lower 1M-byte region. Software that runs in the upper 15M-byte region is said to run in the "protected mode."

To speed processing of multiple applications, and to conserve system memory, DOS 5.0 will be able to allocate and deallocate regions of memory based on a least-recently-used algorithm. For example, should memory be needed by an application, DOS 5.0 could send a rarely used program segment to disk, subsequently reloading it to memory when again needed.

DOS 5.0 also has an asynchronous task scheduler that will allow multiple applications to run concurrently in the 1M to 16M region. The mechanism will allow applications to gain the attention of the 80286 microprocessor according to three different criteria: the priority level of the application, preemption of other tasks according to the need of the application, or processor time-slicing.

DOS 5.0 was introduced by IBM on 2 April 1987 under the name OS/2. A joint development of IBM and Microsoft, the Microsoft version is called MS-OS/2. Before its introduction, the operating system was also referred to as protected mode DOS, DOS 286, ADOS, CP-DOS, and new DOS. The new operating system incorporates much of the current functionality in Microsoft's Windows and has a graphical user interface. The operating system was released late in 1987. It has broken the 640K-byte memory barrier that applications software was previously limited to and created a new generation of application software.

MS-DOS/PC-DOS 6.0

DOS 6.0 is being created to run on 80386-based machines. This product is said to create "virtual machines" under the 80386, meaning that the user can run several programs in any of several concurrent PC/MS-DOS sessions. The programs need not load entirely into primary storage because of the virtual capabilities of the hardware and software. Each DOS session behaves as if it has complete control over the 80386. DOS 6.0 is being designed so that it can run applications written for the original 8088 chip, as well as for protected mode capabilities of the 80286 and 80386.

the PC rose to top position in dollar sales volume in less than a year. By 1984, dozens of other companies had developed computers that promised to run the same software as the PC, and the PC-compatible applications programs numbered in excess of ten thousand.

IBM chose Microsoft Corporation to provide an operating system for their new machine. As previously mentioned, Microsoft, principally a developer of language translators (the BASIC language of most microcomputers was written by Microsoft), developed an operating system called PC-DOS (or simply DOS) for the PC, and a very similar one called MS-DOS to run on the PC-compatible computers of other companies.

MS-DOS (and hence PC-DOS) is very similar to CP/M in its command structure and features, but is a much larger program. It contains friendlier error handling features (MS-DOS allows the user to recover all or most of his data when disk errors occur, while CP/M disk errors can have disastrous consequences) and provides internal (CCP) commands for activities that require utility programs in CP/M (such as file transfers). MS-DOS also changed certain command structures, so that CP/M's awkward "REN B:TWO.COM = ONE.COM" has become a more intuitive "RENAME B:ONE.COM TWO.COM."

UNIX and UNIX Work-Alikes UNIX was developed by Brian Kernighan and Dennis Ritchie of Bell Laboratories (the research and development subsidiary of AT&T) in the late 1960s. A major design goal was to provide a computing environment that was not tied to a particular brand and model of machine, so that programs written on one computer could be used on another. Originally designed for DEC minicomputers and later expanded to other brands, UNIX became commercially available in 1973. The popularity of UNIX on minicomputers has increased steadily over the years as more and more programmers are exposed to its flexibility through universities (Bell Labs will license UNIX free to universities). In the early 1980s UNIX was licensed to some companies for use on microcomputers, and is available in several versions. UNOS (Charles River Data Systems), XENIX (Microsoft Corp.), VENIX (VenturCom), and U-II (Unidos Systems) are licensed versions of UNIX for small computers. UNIX work-alikes (UNIX-compatible operating systems not licensed from Bell Labs) also abound. QNX (Quantum Software Systems), uNETix (Lantech Systems), IDRIS (Whitesmiths, Ltd.), and Coherent (Mark Williams Co.) are all UNIX work-alikes.

Unix is a very large system, and is generally appropriate only for computers with a fast processor, a hard disk, and a large main memory (UNIX System V requires nearly two megabytes to fully implement on the AT&T 3B2/300 computer). Smaller versions of UNIX will not provide all of UNIX's features, but the user may find it very easy to write utility programs that will work with UNIX.

UNIX is a multiuser, multitasking operating system with numerous mainframe operating system features. UNIX provides system accounting functions (it keeps track of the time and resources used by jobs) and extensive communications features (like electronic mail, file transfer programs, and mainframe dial-up facilities).

For many users, the two most important features of UNIX are its enhanced user interface and its data interchange features. The user interface is known as the **shell**, a small collection of commands and functions at the user's disposal. In the UNIX system, the shell can be easily modified by the user. Commands can be changed to suit the user, and new commands are easily added. Data interchange between programs is accomplished through pipes and filters. A **pipe** is the UNIX name for a channel through which data flows. **Filters** are program modules that transform the data in the pipe. Filters are designed to receive data in a standard input form, operate on the data, then output it to the next filter in a standard output form. UNIX systems generally come with a wide assortment of modules that can be used as filters, and with facilities for easy development of other modules. By combining several modules, the user can perform highly complex data processing jobs, with data passing from one program to the next. When the same process is to be used repeatedly, you can give it a name and add it to the shell so that it may be invoked by a single word.

Macintosh and Lisa Operating Systems In early 1983, Apple Corporation startled the microcomputer world with the introduction of the Lisa (for Large Integrated System Architecture) computer. Lisa's operating system or user interface was such a radical departure from systems available on other microcomputers that it was the topic of numerous articles, even in non-computer publications. It was not such a hit at the box office, however; Lisa's price put it out of reach for most small-computer users. A year later, a lower-priced computer, Macintosh, was introduced. It incorporated most of the design objectives and user interface features of Lisa at a $2,595 base system price.

The basic concepts for the Lisa and Macintosh operating system were not new. Most of the ideas emanated from research by Xerox Corporation's Palo Alto Research Center (PARC) in the mid-1970s, and were used on Xerox's Star series of computers. The Star systems, like the early Lisa, were expensive office tools that found little acceptance in the marketplace. With Macintosh, Apple produced "the computer for the rest of us."

Lisa and Macintosh use graphic symbols (called *icons*) to turn the computer into an electronic metaphor for a desktop (see Figure 4–3). Do you want to save a document? In an office, this is normally accomplished by placing it in a file folder and storing it away. On the Macintosh, the cursor (a small arrow) is moved to the "paper" by moving a mouse. The button on the mouse is pushed to pick up the paper, and by moving the mouse, the paper is moved over to the icon of the folder. A second push on the mouse's button will store the document in the folder.

Apple prides themselves on the ease with which the Macintosh and Lisa systems can be learned. Commands do not have to be remembered, because they are available in "pull-down" menus.

The Macintosh system comes with features and development tools not found in most other systems. Most of these reside in 64K bytes of ROM and are always available to the user. A program called Quickdraw maintains the high-resolution graphics display on both Macintosh and Lisa. It is used by other system modules to draw letters and shapes on the screen, and can fill closed shapes with any of a wide selection of patterns. A font manager lets the user choose how characters will be displayed. Anything from very small italics to very large Old English text can be selected. A desk manager controls the activities represented by the icons, and a

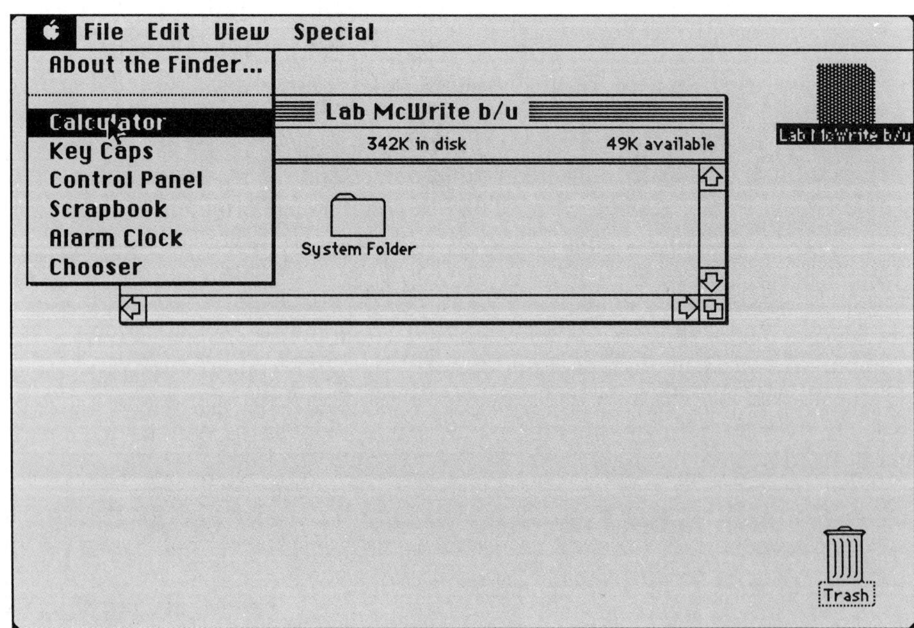

FIGURE 4–3
The Macintosh Desktop with Desk Accessories Menu Shown

menu manager directs the display and processing of commands from the pull-down menus. The Macintosh system also allows data transfer capabilities similar to those available from applications environment programs. To move data from a spreadsheet to a word processor, the Macintosh user first attaches the data to a piece of electronic scratch paper, then uses the mouse to drag the paper to the word processor, where it is released.

Various desk accessories are built into the system software of the Mac, including a scrapbook, an alarm clock, a notepad, a calculator, key caps, a control panel, and a puzzle. The pull-down menu associated with the apple on the menu bar at the top of the Mac screen reveals these accessories, as shown in Figure 4–3. To pull this or any menu down from the items on the menu bar, first place the cursor by use of the mouse on the item—in this case, the Apple logo. Then press the button on the mouse while dragging the cursor down through the list in the pull-down menu. By moving the cursor down through this list, you highlight each item as the cursor moves through it. By releasing the button on the mouse, you cause the highlighted menu item to be selected and displayed.

The size and complexity of the Lisa and Macintosh operating systems can adversely affect the speed of operations. The first Macintosh systems sold well but were widely criticized for their limited 128K-byte memory size and the single 400K-byte disk drive. Disk drives soon became available from Apple and independent manufacturers, and in October 1984, Apple announced an upgrade of primary memory to 512K bytes (nicknamed the "fat Mac"). The very popular Mac Plus was introduced in 1985 and sports a half-megabyte of primary storage and one 800K double-sided disk drive.

APPLICATIONS ENVIRONMENTS

In 1983, computer users saw the emergence of a new category of software for microcomputers, the applications environment. Sometimes called shell programs, these programs bear a resemblance to both multitasking operating systems and integrated software packages (see Chapter 11). From the user's viewpoint, an applications environment will function very much like an operating system. Most of the operating system's CCP commands will be handled through the shell, and programs will be run inside it. Shells are not operating systems, however, because they must rely upon an operating system to perform most of the hardware controlling tasks.

Applications environments offer some interesting capabilities. DESQVIEW and Microsoft's Windows can simulate a multitasking environment. The user can divide the CRT's display into several different areas, called "windows," and run separate programs in each. The user can move freely from window to window, moving data around or starting new operations. Some applications environments are designed to work only with a select group of software. VisiCorp's VisiOn system was designed to provide a unified command structure and a data transfer capability for other programs within the same product lines. It has been discontinued. IBM's Topview worked with a wide variety of programs, but offered enhanced features when the software producer had adapted a program specifically for the Topview environment. It, too, has been discontinued.

One important consideration of all the applications environment programs is their resource utilization. They all require a large amount of primary memory (usually more than 256K), and work best when all the applications programs are on the same disk. This will generally mean that the user must have a hard-disk drive for easy access to the programs that will run in the shell. Some operating environments appear to sacrifice speed for ease of operation and data transfer capability. Users should also be careful when making data transfers between different programs. If a great deal of time was spent generating spreadsheet data, it is a good idea to save it to a second disk file before transferring it to the word processor through the shell.

LANGUAGE TRANSLATORS

Programmers working on small computers will find an astonishing number of languages at their disposal. Most major mainframe languages like ADA, APL, COBOL, FORTRAN, LISP, and PL/1 are available for computers as small as a 64K-byte, 8-bit machine, although they have not met with overwhelming acceptance. In this section, we will briefly survey several languages that have achieved widespread use on small computers, either because of their power and flexibility or their ease of use.

All computers have a set of machine instructions that their associated processors are able to execute and perform. This instruction set differs from one microprocessor type to another. The instruction set for an Intel 80386 is very different from the instruction set for the Motorola 68020, for example. Before the processor can act on any set of directives, the directives must be reduced to machine instructions. The high-level languages used by most programmers must therefore be translated to machine instructions that the microprocessor can understand. This is the purpose of **language translators.** One high-level language statement could translate into up to 20 machine instructions. From a programmer productivity point of view, the benefits of writing code in a high-level language are obvious—one line of code might do what would have required 20 lines of code at the machine instruction level. An exception is assembly language.

Assembly Language

Assembly languages are languages having a **mnemonic** equivalent for each instruction in a microprocessor's instruction set. A mnemonic is a memory aid, and in an assembly language the term refers to the use of from one to four letter commands to replace binary strings. For example, the assembly language for the Intel 8080 replaces "00101010" with the easier to remember "ADD." Since each microprocessor has its own instruction set, each one must have its own assembly language.

All programming languages require a language translator to convert the high-level language statements that the programmer has written, known as **source code**, into machine instructions consisting of zeros and ones, called **object code**, that the microprocessor can understand. The translator for assembly languages is called an **assembler**, and many operating systems come equipped with one.

```
TITLE   ROUTINE TO CLEAR THE SCREEN AND HOME THE CURSOR
PAGE 60,132
CODE    SEGMENT BYTE PUBLIC "CODE"
ASSUME  CS:CODEX
PUBLIC  CLS
CLS     PROC    FAR
        MOV     CX,0
        MOV     DX,2479H
        MOV     BH,7
        MOV     AX,600H
        INT     10H
        RET
CLS     ENDP
CODE    ENDS
        END
```

FIGURE 4–4

An Assembly Language Program to Clear the Screen for the Intel 8088, 8086, 80186, and 80286

Assembly language programming can be extremely difficult. It requires intimate knowledge of how the microprocessor works, and because it operates in extremely small steps, the sheer number of statements required to perform even simple operations will cause it to be loved by very few programmers. Assembly language does have its virtues, however. It generates, by a considerable margin, the fastest-running programs available. It also produces object code that is much smaller than even the most efficient higher-level language translators. Assembly language also makes it possible to control any activity in the microprocessor's repertoire, a feat most higher-level languages cannot accomplish. Assembly language was used in developing many of the most popular operating systems and applications programs for these reasons. An example of a simple program in 8088 assembly language for use with MS-DOS is shown in Figure 4–4.

BASIC

BASIC (For Beginner's All-purpose Symbolic Instruction Code) was developed by John Kemeny and Thomas Kurtz at Dartmouth College in the early 1960s in an effort to find an easy language for student programmers. Because BASIC can be used in computers with very small amounts of RAM, it quickly became the predominant language on microcomputers.

BASIC is available in two forms: interpreted and compiled. In an **interpreted** language, the computer will convert a line of source code into object code, run the object code, then begin work on the next line of source code. A **compiler** will convert the entire source code program to object code before any of it is run. In fact, the object code is saved to an object program file that is executable. Interpreters, on the other hand, are not capable of producing an object program file. Compiled languages can run several times faster than interpreted ones, yet they require time to translate a large source code program into object code. Imagine waiting five minutes for a program to compile, only to be rewarded with a notice that a syntax error was found in line 15240. An interpreter would process the same program, displaying any resulting output as it went, up to the point of error. It might even have allowed the programmer to make a quick correction of the error, and would proceed with the processing from that point.

Interpreted languages, then, are excellent for use during the development of programs. Compilers offer speed advantages once the program has reached its final form. BASIC is one of the few languages for small computers that can offer the advantages of both, because compilers are available that can convert code originally developed with an interpreter.

On the negative side, BASIC is often criticized on several counts. It is said to lack speed, standards, control, and structure. Interpreted BASIC is indeed slow when compared to compiled languages, and a compiled BASIC program will often run slower than C, Forth, Pascal, FORTRAN, and, most certainly, assembly language. BASIC suffers most in applications requiring a great deal of reading and writing on a disk. BASIC, unlike mainframe COBOL or FORTRAN, does not have a standardized convention for commands and syntax. However, (with the notable exception of Applesoft BASIC) most BASIC interpreters were developed by the same company (Microsoft Corporation, Redmond, Washington); and the different versions are remarkably similar. A program written in BASIC-80 on a KAYPRO computer will usually run without alteration on a Compaq using BASICA. The same cannot be said for most languages on microcomputers, because the same standards established for a mainframe C or Pascal compiler are often ignored in their microcomputer implementations. It is difficult to argue with the last two criticisms, however. BASIC does not offer the degree of control over hardware operations that can be found in assembly language or C. Nor does it have the modularity that a structured language (see Pascal) should have. (Microsoft's Quick BASIC compiler does support structured programming.) These are major factors in the consideration of a language for serious application development. What BASIC does best is offer an easy-to-learn environment for the rapid development of easy-to-read code. Figure 4–5 shows a simple BASIC program to compute prime numbers.

FIGURE 4–5

A Sample BASIC Program to Compute Prime Numbers

```
10 ' PROGRAM TO COMPUTE PRIME NUMBERS
20 TRUE = 1
30 FALSE = 0
40 SIZE = 8191
50 DIM FLAGS(SIZE +1)
60 ' PROCESSING BEGINS HERE
100 FOR ITER = 1 TO 10
110    COUNT=0
120    FOR  I = 1 TO  SIZE
130        FLAGS(I) = TRUE
140        NEXT I
150    FOR I = 1 TO SIZE
160        IF FLAGS(I) <> TRUE THEN  230
170            PRIME = I + I + 1
180            FOR K=I+PRIME TO SIZE STEP PRIME
190                 FLAGS(K) = FALSE
200                 NEXT K
210       COUNT=COUNT+1
220       ' ENDIF
230       NEXT I
240     PRINT ITER,  COUNT,   "PRIMES"
250     NEXT ITER
260 END
```

Focus Feature

WHAT IS STRUCTURED PROGRAMMING, AND WHY IS IT PREFERRED?

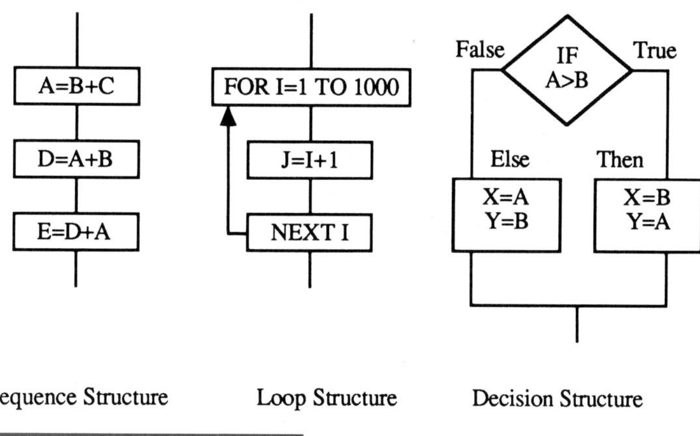

FIGURE 4–6

Control Structures Used in Structured Programming

Over twenty years ago computer linguists like Niklaus Wirth examined conventional program code in high-level languages like BASIC and FORTRAN, and decided that the unreadability of the code was due in large part to the unstructured way in which it was written. Studies showed that any program segment could be implemented with just three fundamental control structures: the sequence structure, the decision structure, and the loop structure, as shown in Figure 4–6.

In the sequence structure, statements are executed in sequence—in the order of their appearance, or one after the other. The loop structure executes the statements within the loop over and over until some condition is satisfied. The decision structure tests a condition using an IF statement and then executes the block of statements following THEN if the condition is true, or executes the block of statements following ELSE if the condition is false. If no ELSE is provided, control proceeds to the next statement following the IF when the condition is false.

Pascal and Modula-2

Pascal (named after French mathematician Blaise Pascal) was developed by Swiss computer scientist Niklaus Wirth in the late 1960s. In recent years it has become extremely popular, replacing BASIC as the instructional language in many colleges. Sophisticated applications packages and even operating systems have been written in Pascal.

Pascal was the first major language to be developed incorporating certain "structured" programming principles that were the topic of much discussion and controversy in the 1960s and early 1970s. **Structured programming** is a process in which a complicated procedure is broken down into successively smaller portions until each portion takes the form of one of several recognized control structures, such as the loop structure, the decision structure, or the sequence structure (see article on structured programming). This top-down approach results in code that is easy for programmers to read and debug, and can be a great asset in the development of programming logic for large, complex tasks. BASIC programs, on the other hand, tend to become progressively unreadable and difficult to debug with increases in size.

A Pascal program has three main segments: a program header, which provides a title for the program; a declaration section, which lists the variables that will be used, along with the variable type (real, integer, etc.); and the program body, made up of modules (called **procedures**) that perform the actual processing. Figure 4–7 shows a Pascal program that calculates prime numbers.

Pascal has always been a compiled language, unlike BASIC and C, which are both compiled and interpreted languages. This may seem to be an impediment to the use of Pascal for those who are just learning programming, or for program development. Recently, the appearance of editors able to interact with very fast compilers that do all compiling exclusively in primary memory has alleviated such concerns. A 100-line program compiles in just seconds; if there are any compilation errors, the development system returns to the editor at the point in the source code where the error occurred, telling the user what went wrong. If there are no errors, the compiled program runs.

Pascal can help promote good programming habits and is relatively easy to learn; it therefore makes an excellent language for learning programming principles. It does have a few drawbacks as a language for business application development, however. Its disk I/O handling is only moderately satisfactory, although better than BASIC. Also, relatively few standards are available for microcomputer-based Pascal compilers. In an effort to correct some of Pascal's shortcomings, Wirth introduced a new language in the early 1980s, called **Modula-2**. A Modula-2 program looks very much like one written in Pascal, but the new language offers better input/output capability, more functions, and an extension of Pascal's modularity. With Pascal, a program might be highly modular (broken into discrete program segments, called modules), and these modules could be called from various points in the program. With Modula-2, useful modules can be saved in external module libraries so that they can be called from many programs. This feature, similar to external subroutines in mainframe FORTRAN, can save considerable effort in program development since each successive application might have fewer modules to encode.

C

Around 1970 or 1971, Bell Laboratories wanted to move its recently developed UNIX operating system from the little used Digital Equipment Corporation PDP-7 computer to the more popular PDP-11 model. To accomplish the transformation in a reasonably short period of time, Dennis Ritchie, one of the UNIX designers (with Brian Kernighan), needed to develop a new language. The outcome of his efforts was a language called "C" (its PDP-7 predecessor was called "B"). As UNIX became popular as a minicomputer operating system, there developed a great deal of interest in C, the language in which UNIX was written. Nearly 10 years later, C was made available on microcomputers, and it quickly gained wide acceptance among system developers and applications programmers.

```
PROGRAM primes;
{ This program calculates the number of prime numbers between 1 and 8191 10 times.}
CONST
  true: INTEGER = 1;
  false: INTEGER = 0;
  size: INTEGER = 8191;
VAR
  flags : array[1..8192] OF REAL;
  count, i, iter, k : INTEGER;
(* The program begins below.*)
BEGIN
FOR iter := 1 TO 10 DO
  BEGIN
    count:=0;
    FOR i := 1 TO size DO
      BEGIN
        flags[i] := true;
        END;
    FOR i := 1 TO size DO
      BEGIN
        IF flags[i] = true THEN
          BEGIN
            prime := i+i+1;
            k = i+prime;
            WHILE k <= size DO
              BEGIN
                flags[k] := false;
                k := k + prime;
                END;
              count := count + 1;
              END;
            END;
          WRITELN('Iteration =',iter,count,' primes');
        END;
      END. (* OF PROGRAM primes *)
```

FIGURE 4–7

Primes in Pascal

There are many reasons for C's success. Like Modula-2, it is highly modular. Functions and utilities can be stored in libraries, to be called by any program, or even from the operating system level (when working in UNIX). C has a very small compiler, which means that it can be run easily on most 8-bit computers. It also allows a very high degree of control over the activities of the microprocessor. This last feature, along with the large assortment of data and character types available in C, has made it a very good choice for complex applications programs or operating system development. Many C compilers generate quite fast running code.

With all of its charms, C is probably not the ideal language for everyone. It is not the easiest language to learn, and many preprogrammed facilities that the programmer will have become accustomed to in other languages may be missing from C. For example, there may be no direct way of comparing two strings or of manipulating an array in C. Functions or modules may have to be written to accomplish this.

There appear to be many differences in the commercially available C compilers. Most C versions are a subset of the commands and data types available in minicomputer C compilers, which means that a C program written on a microcomputer stands a good chance of running on a larger computer. There are some major differences in the number of minicomputer C features that have been implemented among the microcomputer versions. Since C is a small language that is meant to make heavy use of a function library, most C compilers come with a number of useful functions included. Some compilers come with libraries containing hundreds of modules, while others have only a few. An example of a C program that finds prime numbers is shown in Figure 4–8.

FORTH

FORTH is the principal language in a category known as **Threaded Interpreted Languages**. A threaded language uses a powerful sequence of user-defined functions to do virtually all of the processing in a program. The user begins a program by defining small functions. As the program proceeds, these small functions are used to define larger and larger functions. Finally, after all the functions have been defined, the main program is written. Due to the manner in which the functions have been created, the main portion of the program is often astonishingly short.

FORTH was developed in 1970 by Charles Moore for controlling radio telescopes. It was not until the early 1980s that it became popular as a language for applications programming. As an applications development language, FORTH has several desirable features. It is a very compact language. An entire FORTH development system, including an editor, can be contained in 10K or less. Programs written in FORTH are usually small, as well. The development of programs is aided because FORTH is an interpreted language, yet it too can be compiled. In fact, unlike most languages, FORTH programs can be compiled in parts, without the

FIGURE 4–8

A C Program that Finds Prime Numbers

```
#define true 1
#define false 0
#define size 8191
    char flags[size+1];
main() {
for(iter = 1; iter <=10; iter++) {
    count=0;
    for(i = 1; i <= size; i++)
        flags[i] = true;
    for(i = 1; i <= size; i++) {
        if(flags[i]) {
           prime = i + i + 1;
/*         printf("\n%d",prime);*/
           for(k=i+prime; k<=size; k+=prime)
               flags[k] = false;
           count++;
        }
     }
     printf("\n%d primes.",count);
}
}
```

```
8190 CONSTANT SIZE
0 VARIABLE FLAGS  SIZE ALLOT
:DO-PRIME
     FLAGS SIZE 1 FILL   (SET ARRAY)
     0 SIZE 0   (0 COUNT)
     DO FLAGS I + C@
        IF  I DUP + 3 + DUP I +
        BEGIN     DUP SIZE<
        WHILE     0 OVER FLAGS + C! OVER +
        REPEAT    DROP DROP 1+
        THEN
     LOOP
     .  ."PRIMES";
```

FIGURE 4–9

A FORTH Program to Calculate Prime Numbers

complicated linking procedures required by more modular languages. FORTH programs can also be very fast, depending upon the methods used to build functions.

For every programmer who loves FORTH (it has been called a "cult" and an "addiction"), there are just as many who hate it. A FORTH program is virtually unreadable to anyone but the individual who wrote it. FORTH uses a curious way of arranging values and the variables to which they are assigned, an arrangement known as "reverse Polish notation." Writing a FORTH program requires a fairly intimate knowledge of the inner workings of the computer since FORTH directly manipulates the "stack" (an area of memory for temporary storage of values). Most programming languages handle these low-level operations for the user in a transparent manner. FORTH is also a nonstandardized language, and different versions will offer a very different set of initial functions (called "words" in FORTH). Most versions of FORTH are incapable of generating native code, that is, machine language code that is "native" to the machine, and cannot be run in the absence of the interpreter or compiler.

In short, FORTH is an interesting language that offers a great deal of power and speed to the programmer. Its drawbacks include the nonstandardization of the language and the unreadability of the code, making programs difficult to debug. For most users these difficulties will make it an unsuitable choice for software development. An example of a FORTH program is provided in Figure 4–9.

As a summary to this section, Table 4–2 exhibits side-by-side comparisons of syntax for five statement types in BASIC, Pascal, and C.

TABLE 4–2

Comparison of Statement Types in BASIC, Pascal, and C

STATEMENT	BASIC	PASCAL	C
assignment	A=B+C	a:=b+c;	a=b+c;
IF	IF A<B THEN	IF a<b THEN	if(a<b){
DO group	all statements on same line	BEGIN...END	{ }
FOR statement	FOR I=1 TO SIZE	FOR i:=1 TO size DO	for(i=1;i <=size; i++)
PRINT statement	PRINT A,B,C	WRITELN(a,b,c);	printf(a,b,c);

Focus Feature

DESCRIPTION OF UTILITY PROGRAMS AVAILABLE

DISK AND FILE UTILITIES

A **disk formatter** will magnetically arrange a new disk into a track and sector layout arrangement that the operating system can read. **Disk recovery programs** take two forms. Some will mark bad sections of a disk so that no attempt is made to write on them, while others can restore files that had been erased. **System tracks generators** will save the operating system at a special location on the disk. **File transfer programs** make copies of files from one disk to another (or on the same disk). **File comparison programs** will evaluate, byte by byte, two disk files, and note the differences between them. This is useful for programmers who need to examine changes between program versions, or for writers trying to remember which file contained the latest version of a manuscript.

Sort programs are available to arrange data (or text) in virtually any conceivable manner. **Search programs** can scan through one or more files for key words supplied by the user, then display or print any records in which the key words are present. **Hard-disk backup programs** allow the user to attend to other matters while the hard disk contents are being backed up on another storage device. **Disk format designators** can control a disk drive to read and write disks in the format of another computer. These are extremely useful for sharing text and data with another computer owner whose disk format is different.

CONFIGURATION PROGRAMS

Device allocation programs are used to control the input and output channels on a computer. Using these programs, it is possible to instruct the computer to receive all input from a serial port (to which a terminal is attached) rather than from the keyboard, direct output simultaneously to the CRT and a printer, adjust the transmission rate of a modem port, or make any of dozens of other possible device assignments. **Device status programs** usually display the current device assignments. **Key definition programs** allow the user to write command sequences, long strings, or even entire paragraphs; and store them in memory to be called up with only one or two keystrokes. With some key definition programs, the commands of an operating system or word processor can be changed to something the user is more likely to remember, and can make even the most difficult-to-learn program a great deal easier. With these programs a user can change the conventional QWERTY keyboard definitions to those of DVORAK.

Character generators allow the user to alter the design of the characters displayed on the CRT or printer by altering the character matrix. Thus, it is possible to have scientific symbols or foreign language characters in a text file. **RAM disk emulators** set aside a portion of the user's available RAM to be used as if it were another disk drive. The purpose of this is to obtain speed. A word processor that requires 20 seconds to search for a particular

UTILITY PROGRAMS

A wide variety of utility programs are available for the small-computer user. Many of them are supplied with the purchase of an operating system. Others have been developed by hardware manufacturers because of special characteristics of the computers. Computer users groups have developed some of the most widely used utility programs. Still others are written by independent software producers. If there is any non-application task you ever wanted your computer to do (within the bounds of reason and the computer's capabilities), someone has written a utility to do it. The variety of programs makes them difficult to categorize, so we suggest the arrangement listed in Table 4–3.

word on a disk file might take only a second to perform the same operation in RAM. Since RAM is volatile, it is important for the user to save a RAM disk file (using a file copy command) onto a floppy or hard disk before turning the computer off.

MISCELLANEOUS UTILITIES

Batch processors can process a sequence of operating system or applications program command statements stored in a file (called a "batch" file). A batch processor can be a major time-saver for frequently used sequences of activities. A single command can trigger an entire chain of events, such as (1) set the date and time for stamping files; (2) set function key definitions for a word processor; (3) run a utility to send output to the printer on the parallel port; (4) run a spelling checker on the filename you input on the command line, and tell it to mark misspelled words and print a list of them; (5) redirect output back to the CRT; and (6) enter the word processor, call up the file you are working on, and find the first marked word.

Print queue managers (also called print spoolers) can send files to the printer while the computer is being used for other jobs. Some print queue managers print files stored in RAM (this is fast, but requires large memory and is often restricted to printing only one file) while others print from files on a disk (slow, but the user can give a list of files to be printed). **Disk access method controllers** determine where files are found or stored. If a program is called for by the user, these programs can search on different disks until the file is found. Some also control such activities as storing or retrieving files in libraries or subdirectories (groupings of related files). Many operating systems have a **help facility,** a program that accesses a text file for information on the computer's features or commands. **Date and time utilities** work with a computer's internal clock circuit to record information about when a file was created or modified. This is almost a necessity for keeping track of files that undergo multiple revisions.

When disk space is limited, a **data compression program** can be used to store a file in a more compact form. This is useful only for little-used files, since a file must be restored to its expanded form before it can be run or edited. **Data protection programs** can encode or otherwise protect a file so that persons without the proper password may not access it. **Program debuggers** are used to display and alter the contents of a disk program file. Most of these are complicated for inexperienced users, since they might require some assembly language knowledge.

ADVANCED FEATURES OF OPERATING SYSTEMS

Some of the newer, more advanced operating systems can support features previously found only on mainframes and minicomputers. Included in these features are virtual memory, program overlays, program segmentation, swapping, and security. With the exception of security, all of these features have the capability to make secondary storage appear to be primary storage from the perspective of the microprocessor. This enables programs that are larger than the actual primary storage available to be executed without difficulty.

Virtual memory is a technique for extending primary memory by employing secondary storage devices to store program pages that are not being executed at

TABLE 4–3
Types of Utility Programs

DISK AND FILE UTILITIES	CONFIGURATION PROGRAMS	MISCELLANEOUS UTILITIES
Disk formatters	Device allocation programs	Batch processors
Disk recovery programs	Key definition programs	Print queue managers
System tracks generators	Character generators	Disk access method controllers
File transfer programs	RAM disk emulators	Help facilities
File comparison programs	Device status programs	Data compression programs
Disk format designators		Data protection programs
Sort programs		Program debuggers
Search utilities		Date and time utilities
Hard-disk backup programs		Line editor
		Linker

any instant in time, and then alternating these pages in and out of memory as they are needed. The facilities required to do this involve a microprocessor specially designed for this purpose, such as the Intel 80286 and 80386, and software. Figure 4–10 illustrates how this works. Virtual memory will allow very large programs to be executed on a small computer.

Overlays is a computer processing technique in which programs not actively being processed are held on secondary storage devices and alternated in and out of memory with other programs as they are required. Overlays are employed by some word processing packages and some integrated software packages. A print program would not necessarily reside in primary storage until it was invoked, at which time it would be loaded into primary memory, thereby overwriting (overlaying) the program that was previously loaded there. *Swapping* is nearly identical to overlays, except that portions (pages) of programs can be overlayed.

FIGURE 4–10
An Illustration of Virtual Memory

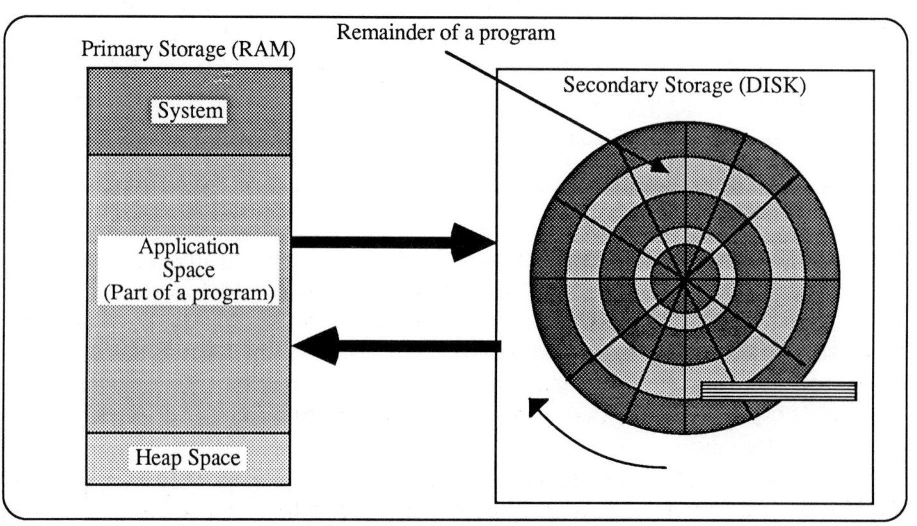

Most single-user operating systems provide only very limited security. **Security** relates to maintaining the integrity and accuracy of files stored on disks, either floppy or hard. This is accomplished by limiting access to the records within a file. Access control is usually accomplished by the use of passwords. MS-DOS versions 2.11 and lower do not provide any form of password protection. For this reason some spreadsheet and data base management programs provide their own forms of password security. More sophisticated multiuser operating systems provide quite extensive forms of password security. Access to the computer itself is usually password-controlled, as it is on mainframes and minicomputers.

Summary

This chapter presents an overview of system software and of its nucleus, the operating system. Operating systems were described as consisting of a command console processor and an input/output program. Some operating systems also have a component called the basic disk operating system. In general, however, this component is submerged within the input/output program. Operating systems may be classified as single-user, multiuser, and multitasking. An article describing operating system (and related) compatibility issues was presented. The more popular operating systems were discussed, including CP/M, MS-DOS, PC-DOS, Apple DOS, and UNIX, as well as the Macintosh and Lisa operating systems.

Application environments were described briefly as regards capabilities. Four commercial application environments were presented as having multitasking capabilities, and a windowing capability.

Language translators were discussed in some detail. Interpreters are distinguished from compilers in that interpreters run 5 to 20 times slower, but are much easier to work with when a program is being developed. BASIC, the most popular language for microcomputers, has both advantages and disadvantages. Some of its advantages are that it is both an interpreted and a compiled language, it is easily learned, and source codes in BASIC are fairly easy to read. Its disadvantages include its slow running time and its limited ability to write and read massive amounts of data to and from a disk.

Pascal and Modula-2 are languages designed to enforce certain rules for structured programming. The purpose of structured programming is to make the source code more readable. Pascal is an excellent language for learning programming principles, but is no better than BASIC at handling disk input/output. Modula-2 looks very much like Pascal, but offers better disk input/output capability, more functions, and an extension of Pascal's modularity. C and FORTRAN may be the best choices for scientific computing on a microcomputer. Depending on the specific compiler chosen, both can generate the fastest-running compiled codes available today. FORTH and assembly language have a reputation for generating very fast code, but both are difficult language environments in which to develop programs; as a result, development times will be longer.

Utility programs were categorized and described in some detail. There are three categories of utility programs: disk and file utilities, configuration programs, and miscellaneous utilities. Individual utility programs within each of these major categories were briefly discussed.

The chapter ends with a discussion of advanced features of operating systems and system software.

At the end of this chapter, you will find a tutorial on learning to use the MS-DOS operating system. This tutorial describes how to format, back up, and copy diskettes. It also describes how to copy, erase, rename, and display files. This material should be sufficient preparation for the most important section of this book—the managerial productivity tools, Chapters 5 through 11.

Key Terms

applications environment
assembler
assembly language
BASIC
batch processing
BDOS
BIOS
character generators
compiler
Console Command Processor (CCP)
data compression program
data protection programs
date and time utilities
decision structure
device allocation programs
device status programs
disk access method controllers
disk format designators
disk formatter
disk recovery program
file comparison programs
file server
file transfer programs
filter
hard-disk backup program
help facility
icon
instruction set
interpreter
key definition programs
language translator
loop structure
microprocessor family
mnemonic
Modula-2
multiprocessor
multitasking
multiuser
object code
operating system
pipe
print queue managers
procedure
program debuggers
RAM disk emulators
search programs
security
sequence structure
shell
sort programs
source code
structured programming
system software
system tracks generator
threaded interpretive language
time sharing
utility program
virtual memory

Self-Test

1. What are the major components of system software?
2. What are the subcomponents of operating systems?
3. List the compatibility issues relating to software.
4. Describe what application environments are, and how they are used.
5. Describe what language translators are, and how they are used.
6. Describe what utilities are, and how they are used.

Exercises

1. What are the possible advantages of having operating systems contained in ROM chips? What are the disadvantages?
2. What are the differences between the functions of a basic input/output system (BIOS) and the basic disk operating system (BDOS)?
3. Discuss the basic purpose of the operating system components CCP and BIOS.
4. Discuss the important issues with respect to operating system compatibility.
5. List and briefly describe four different application environment packages.
6. Programs such as Lotus 1-2-3™ and Microsoft Flight Simulator are often used as a test of compatibility between two computers. Why? (Lotus 1-2-3 is discussed in Chapter 8).
7. Occasionally a computer can pass the Lotus and Flight Simulator tests (indicating IBM PC compatibility) and still can't run certain programs designed for the IBM PC. What other factors might be involved?
8. UNIX is considered too large and complex for most small businesses and users to handle (most UNIX implementations require a system operator). Yet many magazines are predicting that UNIX will sweep the microcomputer world. At the opposite end of the spectrum are operating systems like the Macintosh system and Digital Research's Graphics Environment Manager (GEM). In the power versus ease-of-use race, which is likely to attain the largest sales?
9. Describe the capabilities afforded by application environments.
10. List some of the reasons why a programmer might want to code an application in assembly language. Why might he not want to?
11. Some programmers have been known to comment that assembly language is the easiest programming language to learn *if you learn it before exposure to other languages.* Is there any reason to believe this could be true? What reasons can you think of that would not support such a claim? What advantages do high-level languages have over assembly language in general?
12. List the advantages and disadvantages of compiled languages and interpreted languages.
13. Compare the various language translators available for microcomputers with regard to speed, ease of use, modularity, and ability to write/read to/from a disk.
14. Most serious program development being done today on microcomputers is written in Pascal or C. Why do you think this is true?
15. Suppose that running (execution) speed was the most important criterion for selection of a language translator. What language would be your choice?
16. What are the potential uses for some of the capabilities provided by applications environment programs (windowing, interfile data transfers, etc.)? Do most people need these capabilities?

Additional Reading

Banahan, Mike, and Andy Rutter. *The UNIX Book.* New York: Wiley Press, 1983.

Dahmke, Mark. *Microcomputer Operating Systems.* Berkeley: Osborne/McGraw-Hill, 1981.

Ettlin, Walter A., and Gregory Solgerg. *The MBASIC Handbook.* Berkeley: Osborne/McGraw-Hill, 1983.

Grogono, Peter. *Programming in Pascal.* Reading, Ma.: Addison-Wesley, 1980.

Hogan, Thom. *Osborne CP/M User Guide.* 3d ed. Berkeley, Calif.: Osborne/McGraw-Hill, 1984.

Kernighan, Brian W., and Dennis M. Ritchie. *The C Programming Language.* Englewood Cliffs, N.J.: Prentice-Hall, 1978.

Waite, Mitchell, and Robert LaFore. *Soul of CP/M.* Indianapolis: Howard W. Sams & Co., 1983.

TUTORIAL

MS-DOS

We present, in this tutorial, a description of some of the more commonly used MS-DOS commands that were not discussed in the main body of this chapter. In view of the strong similarities between MS-DOS and PC-DOS, what will be described herein applies equally well to PC-DOS. The objectives of this tutorial include, but are not limited to, the following:

to become acquainted with MS-DOS

to be able to FORMAT diskettes

to be able to back up application diskette originals

to be able to create bootable application diskettes

Table 4–4 lists the more common MS-DOS (PC-DOS) commands. These commands are generally classified as either "external" or "internal." Internal commands are contained in the file COMMAND.COM, which is loaded during booting. After booting these commands reside in primary storage and are immediately available without requiring a disk access. The external commands are really references to utilities in the sense that an external program on the system disk is invoked and loaded into primary memory. Hence, to invoke an external command the system diskette must reside in the default drive, unless some other drive is specifically designated as the source drive for the external command. The external commands will show up as .EXE or .COM files when the directory of the system diskette is displayed; such is not the case for internal commands.

In what follows, we will describe how to format a diskette, how to back up your application diskettes, and how to transfer your important files from one diskette to another. In addition we will show you how to make the backup copies of your application diskettes bootable. Finally, we will present some odds and ends like how to display or print text files, how to rename files, how to erase files, and so forth. If you have difficulty in getting the commands we suggest to work, consult your computer system's user manual.

Formatting a Diskette Before you can actually use a diskette as a secondary storage medium, you must first format (or initialize) the diskette. This involves use of an MS-DOS utility called **FORMAT.** By typing **FORMAT** <**Return**> after the DOS prompt, you can invoke this utility. It will tell you to insert the diskette in the default disk drive and press any key when ready. Having done so, it will then proceed to format the diskette. Formatting involves checking each storage location on the diskette to make certain it is working, establishing sector boundaries on the diskette, and placing a directory on the diskette. All flexible diskettes consist of tracks (concentric circles,

TABLE 4–4

List of Major MS-DOS Commands

NAME	TYPE	PURPOSE
ARCHIVE	external*	Copies hard-disk files onto floppies
CHKDSK	external	Scans the directory and checks for consistency
COMMAND	external	Loads COMMAND.COM into primary storage
CONFIG	external	Sets the hardware options
COPY	internal	Copies file(s) specified from one disk to another
DATE	internal	Displays and sets date
DEBUG	external	Makes alterations to a machine language program
DIR	internal	Lists requested directory entries
DISKCOMP	external	Compares two floppy diskettes
DISKCOPY	external	Copies one entire diskette onto another
DISKTEST	external*	Tests the accuracy of the hard-disk read/write heads
EDLIN	external	Creates and edits small files one line at a time
EQUIP	external	Lists hardware/memory installed in the system
ERASE	internal	Deletes files designated
EXE2BIN	external	Converts an .EXE file to a .COM file
FORMAT	external	Formats (initializes) a diskette
LINK	external	Links object modules into an executable module
MEMTEST	external	Tests RAM and indicates location of bad chip
MODE	external	Specifies certain system options
PAUSE	internal	Pauses for input in a batch file
PREPARE	external*	Erases and formats (initializes) the hard disk
REM	internal	Provides a comment within a batch file
REN	internal	Renames a file
RESTORE	external*	Copies archived floppies onto the hard disk
SIZE	external*	Allocates space for four partitions on the hard disk
SYS	external	Transfers DOS system files from system disk to another
TIME	internal	Displays and sets time
TYPE	internal	Displays the contents of a designated file

*Designates commands applicable to a hard disk.

usually 40 or more) and sectors (pie-shaped wedges) as shown in Figure 3.4. Locations of files stored on the diskette are retained in the file allocation table by track number and sector number.

If your system has two floppy disk drives and you wish to format a double-sided diskette, then place the system disk in drive A and type

(*Continued*)

MS-DOS (Continued)

FORMAT B:

and press <**Return**> following the DOS prompt A>_.
Your screen will display a prompt to insert the new diskette in the B drive and strike <**Return**> when ready. When formatting is complete, you will see the prompt

```
Format another (Y/N)?
```

This option permits you to format multiple diskettes by repeating the response <**Y**>**;** otherwise, type <**N**> and you will again see the DOS prompt

```
A>_.
```

If you wish to have system tracks placed on the diskette along with the file COMMAND.COM, then type

FORMAT B:/S

and press <**Return**>**.** This will inform the FORMAT utility to transfer onto the newly formatted diskette the minimal requirements for the MS-DOS operating system. Doing so will enable the diskette to be a "bootable" diskette—one that can be used to start up the computer system as described in the main body of this chapter.

Since the operating system files take up space on a diskette and are not needed on a data diskette that would normally reside in drive B, omitting the /S parameter when formatting will omit the operating system files and produce a "data" diskette.

Backing Up Your Important Diskettes Many vendor-original diskettes furnished to you (for such applications as word processing, spreadsheets, and data base management systems) are not copy-protected. This makes it easy for the user to make backup copies. You are well advised to make two backup copies of any original application diskettes and put the master and one copy in a safe place. Use the other backup as your working copy. It is also good advice to back up important data diskettes; in fact, a good practice to get into is to back up all data files that have been created or modified during the business day *at the end of the business day.*

To make an image backup (a track-for-track, sector-for-sector duplicate) of a diskette, you should first have your computer at the operating system level with the DOS prompt displayed and a disk containing the utility DISKCOPY.COM in the A drive. Before proceeding, place a *write-protect tab* over the *write-protect notch* on the diskette that you want to back up. This will prevent your overwriting the source disk you wish to make a backup of. It is easy to get the source and destination diskettes confused and thereby copy in the wrong direction. Covering the write-protect notch makes sure that it is the source diskette that gets backed up onto the destination diskette. Now type

DISKCOPY A: B: <Return>

Wait for the DISKCOPY utility prompt to be displayed on the screen. Then remove the system diskette from drive A and place your write-protected "source" diskette in the A drive and your formatted "target" diskette in the B drive and press **<Return>.** It is not necessary to format the target diskette in drive B, because the DISKCOPY utility will do this for you automatically if it discovers that the diskette is not formatted. The DISKCOPY utility will make an image backup of the disk in drive A; that is, the disk in drive B will be identical to the disk in drive A when finished. Obviously, any files previously on B are going to be lost unless they also reside on A.

When DISKCOPY is finished, it will tell you so, and ask if you want to copy another. However, the DISKCOPY may not have been successful, and if there are errors, DISKCOPY will inform you of these and tell you that the target diskette may not be usable. DISKCOPY tells you when it has difficulty reading a source diskette or writing to a destination diskette. Nevertheless, DISKCOPY doesn't check the destination diskette to see if it matches the source diskette. Another utility, the DISKCOMP utility, will do this, however. DISKCOMP is designed to verify the results of DISKCOPY by performing a byte-for-byte comparison. If any byte pairs do not match, DISKCOMP complains by informing the user of the disk sector in which the match does not occur.

Making Application Diskettes Bootable To use an application diskette efficiently, you will need to prepare a *bootable application diskette.* Be sure that your computer is at the system level (i.e., in DOS), with the DOS prompt showing, and that you have a system disk with system utilities in the left or A disk drive. If you do not have the DOS prompt on the screen, then insert a DOS diskette in the (A) drive and close the drive door. If your computer is already on, you can do a "warm boot." On many MS-DOS machines, this is done by pressing the <Del> key while simultaneously holding down the <Ctrl> and the <Alt> keys.

We recommend preparing one bootable diskette for each application diskette (that is not copy-protected). To copy the application program(s) onto

(Continued)

the formatted bootable diskette, place your working backup of the application diskette in the A drive, place your destination bootable diskette in the B drive, and type

COPY *.* B: <**Return**> or **COPY A:*.* B:** <**Return**>

This will transfer the files to your bootable diskette in drive B. The use of the * here is called a *wild card.* The use of *.* within the COPY command causes DOS to transfer all of the files from the default drive to drive B. The application now resides on a bootable diskette which can be used to start up your computer system. Now it is not necessary for you to swap diskettes (removing the system diskette and replacing it with a nonbootable application diskette) after start-up to load the application of interest, as was shown in Figure 2.14.

You may be wondering why we used the internal command, COPY, rather than the external utility, DISKCOPY, as we did for making backups of the original (master) application diskette. The DISKCOPY utility creates a track-for-track, sector-for-sector mirror image of the original diskette on the destination diskette. Since the destination diskette already contains system tracks and the COMMAND.COM file, we do not wish to disturb these. The DISKCOPY would copy over any files already on the destination diskette. The COPY *.* B: command, however, transfers one file at a time from the original diskette to the destination diskette. The files will not necessarily be copied into the same locations (tracks and sectors) as they were in on the original diskette. Whenever possible, it is usually advantageous to use COPY *.* B: as opposed to DISKCOPY. The reason for this is that whatever form the file was in on the original diskette, it is always written onto the destination diskette as a contiguous file; that is, all sectors containing data belonging to the file are together in adjacent sectors. Such may not have been the case on the original. When a file is noncontiguous and therefore saved in nonadjacent sectors all over the diskette, the read/write heads have to be positioned all over the diskette to access the file, thereby slowing the access time.

You may also wish to transfer some of the utilities from your operating system diskette to this diskette. To do so, remove the working backup of the application diskette and place your system diskette in the A drive. Now transfer the following utilities to the bootable application diskette as follows:

COPY FORMAT.COM B:

COPY CHKDSK.COM B:

COPY DISKCOPY.COM B:

This will copy the FORMAT, DISKCOPY, and CHKDSK utilities to your bootable application diskette so that these can be used without swapping (without removing the bootable application diskette and inserting the system diskette). It should be recognized that each of these utilities exists as a separate file on the system diskette and, if you performed the transfers using the COPY utility just mentioned, would now reside on your bootable application diskette as well.

Next, the user should create an AUTOEXEC.BAT file and save it on the bootable application diskette. Suppose the application to be booted has the name SW.COM. The following AUTOEXEC.BAT file will request the date and time from the user, and then will load the operating system and the application whose name is SW automatically, anytime the small computer system is booted with this disk in the A drive.

```
DATE
TIME
SW
```

An AUTOEXEC.BAT file is a file of operating system commands batched together so they can be executed as a group. It is a very special type of batch file that is executed by the operating system just after bootup, when it is present. Regardless of type, batch files must be created by the user. With the exception of the AUTOEXEC.BAT file, batch files are also executed by the user like ordinary commands from the operating system prompt. Batch files always end with the extension .BAT.

The procedure for start-up of any application can now be merely to place your bootable application diskette in the A drive, a data diskette in the B drive, and boot up the system by turning on the power or by simultaneously pressing <**Ctrl**>-<**Alt**>-<**Del**> for a warm boot. Both DOS and the application software will be loaded into primary storage and executed.

Erasing, Renaming, Displaying, and Printing Files In this section we will show you how to manage your files in other ways besides making copies. There are occasions when you may wish to delete a file, when you will want to rename a file, and when you will want to display a file's contents.

To erase a file you use the command ERASE followed by the file specification and a <**Return**>**.** For example, to erase the file MYJUNK.DAT on drive B, all you need do is enter

(Continued)

MS-DOS (Continued)

ERASE B:MYJUNK.DAT <**Return**>

after the DOS prompt, and it will be done. As in all previous commands, if the file is on the default drive it is not necessary to mention the drive letter in the file specification. Hence, the following commands will have the same effect (assuming that drive A is the default drive), namely, to erase the file CHAPTER1.TXT on drive A.

ERASE CHAPTER 1.TXT <**Return**>
ERASE A:CHAPTER1.TXT <**Return**>

To rename a file, you use the command RENAME as follows:

RENAME B:OLDJUNK.DAT B:MYJUNK.DAT <**Return**>

This will cause the file OLDJUNK.DAT on the diskette in drive B to be renamed MYJUNK.DAT. Nothing else is changed.

To display the contents of a file on the screen, you use the command TYPE, as follows:

TYPE BALSHEET.DAT <**Return**>

This will cause the file BALSHEET.DAT on the default drive to be displayed on the screen so you can ascertain its contents. The entire file contents will be displayed, and this will most likely cause the screen to scroll. It should be noted that although all files can be TYPEd, only some files will cause decipherable characters to appear on the screen. Only text files—files consisting exclusively of alphabetic, numeric, and other discernible characters—produce decipherable displays when TYPEd. Text files are also called ASCII files, since ASCII is an acronym for the codes of displayable characters—American Standard Code for Information Interchange—about which much will be said later. Binary files, executable program files, even some word processing data files cannot be deciphered when TYPEd.

To transfer the contents of a file to the printer for printing, most versions of MS-DOS support the following:

COPY {file specification} PRN: <**Return**>

Here PRN is the device name for the printer. Some versions of PC-DOS allow you to use a simpler directive:

PRINT {file specification}. <**Return**>

CREATING, CHANGING, AND DELETING SUBDIRECTORIES

Because there is so much space on a hard disk, it is useful to partition this space into subregions by subject area. The same is true of the newer high-capacity floppy disks. Each subregion is of arbitrary length and is not user-specified. Without such a capability, a directory command might produce a list of several hundred files. MS-DOS versions 2 and higher utilize a hierarchical directory structure that permits users to define subdirectories, even subdirectories within subdirectories. This turns out to be a very useful way to organize and manage the hundreds of files that eventually accumulate.

When a hard disk or floppy disk is formatted, a single directory is created. This is called the *root directory*. Each subdirectory is like a disk unto itself. In order to access files within a particular subdirectory, you must either make the subdirectory the working directory (analogous to a logged disk drive) or specify the path to the subdirectory.

To create and use subdirectories, you need only be familiar with the following commands:

Name	**In-Brief**	**Description**
CHDIR	CD	used to change to a different working directory
MKDIR	MD	used to make (create) a subdirectory
PATH		used to specify an additional directory in which to search for files
RMDIR	RD	used to remove a directory

In what follows you are going to create a directory tree. You don't need a hard disk to do this. MS-DOS or PC-DOS versions 2.0 and higher will support what you are about to do.

1. Turn on your PC or compatible computer and boot the operating system. Make "A" the logged drive.
2. Remove the system disk, if you used one, from drive A and replace it with a formatted data disk.
3. Create six subdirectories as follows. Each command is issued after the DOS prompt.

(*Continued*)

MS-DOS (Continued)

md	\WORD-PRO	<Return>	md	\WORD-PRO\WORDPERF
md	\SPRDSHET	<Return>	md	\WORD-PRO\WORDSTAR
md	\DBASEIII	<Return>	md	\SPRDSHET\LOTUS123

4. Now do a **DIR**. Each subdirectory requires 1K or 1024 bytes of space.

Use the command **PROMPT PG <Return>** to change the DOS prompt to reflect the subdirectory you are in and use the command **cd \word-pro** to enter the subdirectory WORD-PRO that you just created.

EXERCISES

1. Find an MS-DOS or PC-DOS manual, look up, and describe 10 MS-DOS (PC-DOS) commands not described here.
2. Describe how to change the logged disk drive.
3. Which of the following is a reference to all files on the A drive?
   (a) A:?.?
   (b) A:*.*
   (c) A:?.*
   (d) A:????????.???
4. The following commands are called internal MS-DOS (PC-DOS) commands and are contained in a file called COMMAND.COM. Use an MS-DOS (PC-DOS) manual to determine the effect or purpose of these commands.
   COPY REM
   DATE REN
   DIR TIME
   ERASE TYPE
   PAUSE
5. The following MS-DOS (PC-DOS) commands are external commands, since each consists of a program module on the system diskette. Use an MS-DOS (PC-DOS) manual to determine the purpose of each command.
   CHKDSK EDLIN
   DISKCOPY DISKCOMP
   FORMAT SYS
6. Explain why a bootable version of an application diskette cannot be obtained by invoking DISKCOPY A: B: from your system diskette in drive A, removing the

system diskette, replacing it with a (nonbootable) copy of the application diskette in drive A, placing a bootable formatted diskette in drive B, and pressing <**Return**>.

7. Consider the following list of tasks:
   (a) copying files onto a target diskette without erasing files already resident on the target diskette
   (b) displaying the contents of a file
   (c) printing a file
   (d) making an exact mirror-image of an entire diskette
   (e) checking the integrity of a target diskette in relation to a source diskette
   For which of the above tasks would you use DISKCOPY? For which of the above tasks would you use COPY? ERASE? DISKCOMP? TYPE?
8. Which of the following commands will create a mirror image of the source diskette in drive A on the target diskette in drive B, and why?
   (a) A>DISKCOPY A: B:
   (b) A>DISKCOPY B: A:
   (c) A>DISKCOPY B:
   (d) A>DISKCOPY
   Must the target diskette first be formatted?

DISK EXERCISES

1. Using the diskette that came with this book, obtain a hard copy of the directory of the disk by use of **DIR>PRN.**
2. Obtain a hard-copy listing of the file COMMANDS.BAT. Explain what the file is, and what each line in the listing of the file does.
3. Using a blank disk of your own provision, FORMAT that disk. (Do not format the diskette that came with this text.)
4. Using the formatted disk you created in disk exercise 3 above, use the COPY command to copy all files from the diskette that came with this book onto your formatted diskette. What do we call the disk you just created?
5. Using your formatted disk, which now contains a copy of the contents of the diskette that came with this book, erase all files on your formatted disk except COMMANDS.BAT. Turn in this disk as a part of your homework assignment.

PART II

PRODUCTIVITY TOOLS

Consisting of Chapters 5 through 11, Part II introduces the applications software that has come to be known as the productivity tools—word processing, spreadsheets, file and data base management systems, graphics packages, and packages which integrate these applications into a single program.

The section is broken down as follows. Chapters 5 and 6 present the rudiments of word processing. *Word processing* applications support the organization, entering, editing, formatting, and printing of textual material (memos, letters, papers, documents, and books). Chapter 6 is followed by tutorials on WordStar and WordPerfect, two of the leading commercial packages available.

In the next chapters, 7 and 8, spreadsheets are described in detail. While word processing programs facilitate working with words, *spreadsheet* programs facilitate working with numbers. Following Chapter 8 is an extensive tutorial on Lotus 1-2-3—for two years running, the best selling software package in the industry. A tutorial on Microsoft Excel™ is also included. Excel™ is available for MS-DOS machines as well as for the Apple Macintosh.

Programs which facilitate the storage, retrieval, and manipulation of data are called *file management systems* or *data base management systems*. File management systems are discussed in Chapter 9. Following Chapter 9 is a tutorial which describes how Lotus 1-2-3 can be used as a file management program. Data base management systems are described in Chapter 10. Chapter 10 is followed by a tutorial on dBASE III and dBASE II Plus.

Chapter 11 discusses graphics and the importance it plays in business and the professions. Included in Chapter 11 as well is a discussion of software packages which integrate all of the above applications into a single program. At the end of Chapter 11 is a tutorial that illustrates and describes how to use Lotus 1-2-3's graphics capability.

These are the chapters and tutorials which comprise Part II. For many readers, Part II will be the most important section of the book.

CHAPTER

5

Word Processing Concepts

CHAPTER OUTLINE

A Bit of History 129

Business and Personal Uses for Word Processors 131

FOCUS FEATURE The Processed Word 133

Software Concepts and Design Philosophies 134

FOCUS FEATURE Customizing a Word Processor 140

FOCUS FEATURE About Spelling, Grammar, and Style Checkers 144

Using a Word Processor: An Overview 146

FOCUS FEATURE Toward Better Writing and Composition 148

Hardware and Software Requirements for Word Processing 150

FOCUS FEATURE The Future of Word Processing? 151

CHAPTER OBJECTIVES

In this chapter you will learn

1 how word processing was done in the past
2 basic word processing features
3 word processing design considerations
4 how word processing is used by students, businesspersons, and professionals

Even a cursory examination of a typical office will provide ample evidence of the importance of the written word in transacting business. Trays are filled with letters to be typed and correspondence to be answered. File cabinets overflow with legal documents and employee records. Forms exist for recording virtually any type of business occurrence. Memos abound. Well before the first business computer, the UNIVAC-1, was installed at General Electric in 1954, the typewriter had become a central fixture in every office. It remains less so today. In the same way that hand-crank adding machines have been made obsolete by the advent of electronic data processing, there is reason to believe that the days of the conventional typewriter are numbered.

Computers were originally designed to deal with numerical data. Their remarkable ability to rapidly and accurately manipulate numbers has been the most important source of change in the manner of conducting business for more than thirty years, and affects each of us daily. But computers are not merely number-crunchers. In recent years, more attention has been given to their ability to handle textual information, or words. **Word processing** is the entry, manipulation, storage, and retrieval of written communication, and it can enable businesses, as well as individuals, to handle textual information with a speed and accuracy not available in ordinary typewriters. With a word processing system, a document can be entered, checked for spelling, and printed several times (with individual addresses and greetings to several different people), all in the time it would take for a single document to be produced on a typewriter. And the output from the word processor will be free from erasure marks and typewriter correction fluid, and is more apt to be free from other errors, as well. Are the margins a bit too small? No problem. Changing margins will not require retyping with a word processor. Did you forget to leave enough space at the bottom of the page for your footnotes? A word processor will allow you to mark your footnote as a block and move it until it fits properly on the page. Some word processing programs will automatically leave enough space on the page to fit the note. Do you need to center a heading? It usually takes only one or two keystrokes to accomplish this with a word processor.

A BIT OF HISTORY

Word processing is a term coined by International Business Machines in 1964. IBM developed the phrase to describe their latest product, the Magnetic Tape/Selectric Typewriter, or MT/ST. The MT/ST, as its name implies, was a Selectric typewriter that used magnetic tape (similar to a cassette tape) for storage and retrieval of documents. This device allowed the user to type a letter or other document, make corrections until it was error-free, then print multiple copies through the same typewriter. MT/ST was responsible for some major office productivity improvements: frequently used documents and correspondence could be printed as often as necessary, requiring only the entry of a new name as addressee. A few years later IBM introduced the Magnetic Card (see Figure 5–1), a small storage medium that held a single page of text, making document storage and alteration a bit easier.

In the 1970s, microprocessor technology and reduced computer storage costs prompted several companies to enter the market with word processing equipment that used computer terminals, rather than typewriters, to enter textual information. Instead of using costly (and often inconveniently located) company mainframe

FIGURE 5–1

An IBM Magnetic Card/ Selectric Typewriter. *(Courtesy of International Business Machines Corporation)*

computers, these were often **dedicated word processors**, computers that were designed solely for textual processing (see Figure 5–2). Companies like Wang, Lanier, CPT, Xerox, Exxon, and even IBM introduced lines of dedicated word processors, costing between $6,000 and $25,000. These systems generally consisted of a video terminal with keyboard, a letter-quality printer, and a central processor unit with floppy-disk storage capable of holding anywhere from sixty to several hundred pages per disk.

The advent of the microcomputer in the mid-1970s has had a profound effect on word processing, and for good reason. The typical microcomputer has all the basic components of the dedicated word processor (video screen, keyboard, floppy disks, and a microprocessor CPU), and is not restricted to a single word processing program.

In the late 1970s, the word processing software has blossomed from the Electric Pencil (Mark Shrayer Software—generally considered the first true word processor for microcomputers) to over two hundred different programs currently on the market. Many of the most recent word processing programs rival dedicated word processors in the number of features they offer, and can even offer a few that the expensive systems do not have. Using the bit-mapped graphics capability of the typical microcomputer, some word processing programs can display text that is raised or lowered for super- and subscripts, brighter than normal for bold print, or even displayed in italics.

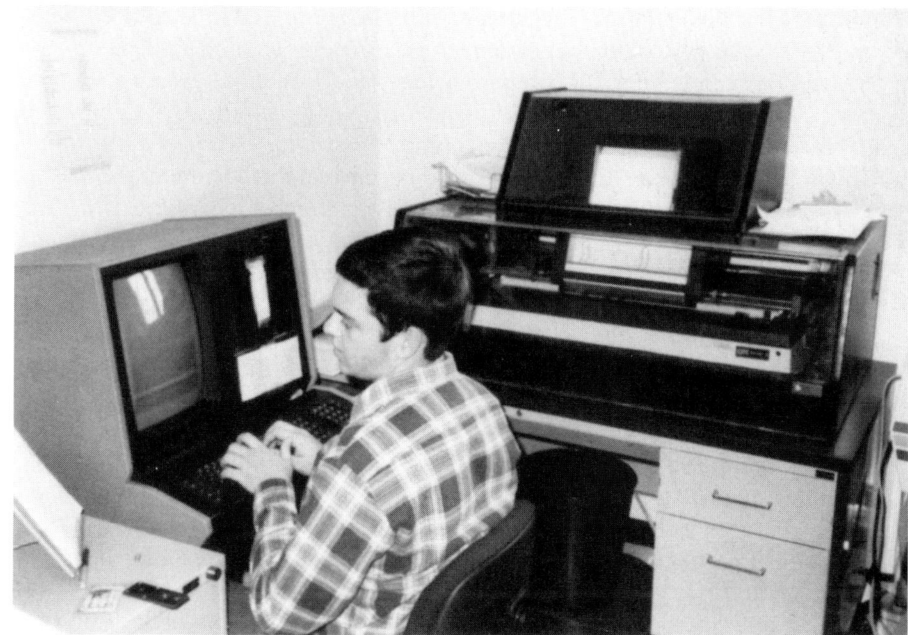

FIGURE 5–2
A Dedicated Word Processing System

The most important aspect of word processing on a microcomputer, of course, is its low cost. Many businesses can find adequate equipment for their word processing needs for less than $3,500, and an individual with less demanding requirements can find a wealth of hardware and software combinations for well under $2,000. As microcomputer prices come within the reach of more and more people, many individuals who would never have believed they would own a computer have purchased microcomputers for the power and flexibility of the word processing programs they can use. Not all of us center our lives on ensuring that Accounts Receivable come in before Accounts Payable are due, but everyone from the family doctor to the parish priest must deal with the written word.

BUSINESS AND PERSONAL USES FOR WORD PROCESSORS

Word processing programs excel in the creation of documents: documents for business, documents for publication, even documents for personal correspondence. The speed with which an experienced word processing user can transform thoughts into written communication has made word processing programs extremely popular with professional writers, academics, students, and businessmen of all varieties. Some programmers even use them to enter high-level language programs.

Word Processing for Business

Not too many years ago, proportional spacing typewriters were a standard tool in the legal profession. These typewriters used different spacing for each alphabetic character, so that the word *ill* was considerably shorter than *wow,* even though each has three letters. This feature was often required in legal documents to ensure that changes could not be made to crucial contracts and agreements. But it was a tedious undertaking to prepare a lengthy document, because the typist would have to start a page again if a single incorrect key was struck. Adding words to an already full page was almost catastrophic.

Word processors can make a dramatic difference in the document processing of most businesses. For the legal secretary, changing a word or inserting a paragraph can all be done before the document is printed. If errors are noted later, the document can be recalled from the disk, corrected, and another copy printed in very rapid form. If a copy of the contract is required by the New York office before 5:00 P.M., it can be transmitted via phone lines and stored in yet another computer. If a similar agreement occurs in the future, the old document can be recalled, and with the insertion of a few new names, amounts, and items, a new contract has been created.

If the document is produced routinely, it can be modified so that variable names such as FIRSTNAME, LASTNAME, ADDRESS, CITY, STATE, and ZIPCODE are placed in the text, rather than the actual client information. As new clients are obtained, they can be added to a list and periodically a **list processor** (also known as a print merge program) can combine the form letter and the mailing list to produce an unlimited number of "personalized" documents. List processing programs make it possible for a single person to duplicate the output of dozens, and are largely responsible for the dramatic increases in "junk" mail over the past decade. (The reader might find some consolation in knowing that while the U.S. Postal Service gives a moderate discount for presorting and bundling large mailings, personalized letters do not qualify for the lowest-cost bulk rates.)

Productivity gains from the use of word processing equipment or programs are often in the range of 100 to 400 percent. These gains derive from several sources. The most obvious gains occur when frequently used documents are processed as forms by a list processing program. With new documents, the ease of making corrections and restructuring paragraphs or margins can typically be accomplished in minutes, rather than the hours it might take to retype. Other productivity gains develop in more subtle ways. As word processing users become more comfortable with the editing commands at their disposal, typing speed often increases. For most typists, the anxiety caused by the errors they know are waiting to pounce onto their page can slow them down considerably and is often, itself, a source of errors. A word processor, with its ease of correcting errors, will relieve the anxiety and allow the fingers to follow the thoughts more closely.

Word Processing for Writers and Academics

In recent years, professional writers have discovered that although a word processor will not help them generate new ideas, it can help them organize their thoughts and record them while they are still fresh in the mind. Writers who compose their material while entering it at a keyboard sometimes find that the word processor's ability to mark a portion of text as a block and move it elsewhere in the work allows them to experiment with the arrangement of ideas and the flow of arguments. With some authors, this experimentation can stimulate stagnant creative processes. Others find that with a word processor they are compulsively editing and re-editing text as they write it, making progress difficult. Writing out material before entering it at the keyboard, or composing at the keyboard with the

Focus Feature

THE PROCESSED WORD

Most individuals who have ever subscribed to a magazine, owned a credit card, or belonged to a record or book club have probably seen a personalized form letter like the one shown on the left. The form used to generate the letter (created with WordStar and Mailmerge) is shown on the right.

Acme Insurance Company
1 Acme Circle
Ajax, Iowa 70707

Ed Wilson
123 Main Street
Chicago, Ill 60609

Dear Ed,

Happy 25th Birthday!! You've reached another milestone in your life, and perhaps it's time to reflect. Are you, Ed Wilson, reaching your personal financial objectives? Do you sleep at night secure in the knowledge that your family will be provided for financially should tragedy befall you? Call Dave Pinkham or Bob Thomas and let them explain to you how Acme's **Preferred Whole Life Term Policy** can give you security now and *cash payments to you* upon retirement. You see, Ed, we at Acme Insurance **really care about *you*.** Call us today at (319) 412-5161.

Bob Reynolds
General Sales Manager

Acme Insurance Company
1 Acme Circle
Ajax, Iowa 70707

&FNAME& &LNAME&
&STREETADDRESS&
&CITY&, &STATE& &ZIP&

Dear **&FNAME&,**

Happy **&BDAY&**th Birthday!! You've reached another milestone in your life, and perhaps it's time to reflect. Are you, **&FNAME& &LNAME&,** reaching your personal financial objectives? Do you sleep at night secure in the knowledge that your family will be provided for financially should tragedy befall you? Call Dave Pinkham or Bob Thomas and let them explain to you how Acme's **Preferred Whole Life Term Policy** can give you security now and *cash payments to you* upon retirement. You see, **&FNAME&,** we at Acme Insurance **really care about *you*.** Call us today at (319) 412-5161.

Bob Reynolds
General Sales Manager

screen display turned off can help overcome this writing block. When the manuscript is completed, having it on disk can help with revisions and may allow the book or article to be published in less time.

Academics enjoy the same benefits of word processing as other writers. In some disciplines, word processing has become essential; several journals are beginning to require accepted articles to be delivered on diskettes. These journals can save time and clerical expense by not having to reenter the text from written copies of the articles. This method also eliminates the possibility of errors created during the reentry process.

Word Processing for Students

It's late at night, the evening before the 15-page research paper is due. The library is closed. All the thoughts and quotations have been collected and were periodically entered into small files on the computer over the previous three weeks.

Now it's time to assemble the paper and print it out. Using a program with outline processing capability, such as Thinktank (Living Videotext, Inc.) or Framework (Ashton-Tate), you quickly arrange and rearrange the order of material until you are satisfied with the flow of arguments. After adding a few print formatting controls to the text, you print it out.

Much to your dismay, you find that you had not checked the length of your research paper before printing, and it falls nearly two pages short of the requirement. You also have forgotten to center headings and underline book titles and names of publications in your bibliography. After some quick calculations, you find that by altering your left and right margins by a single character apiece, adding one line to both top and bottom margins, and switching your line height from 16/48ths of an inch (3 lines per inch, or standard double-spaced) to 18/48ths (2 2/3 lines per inch), you can reach the 15-page minimum with a bit to spare. After approximately 5 minutes of entering your corrections, you again print the paper. Whew, it looks as if you made it home free. The finished product is well organized, free of errors (you ran the text through a spelling checker and grammar checker), is beautifully printed, and meets the length requirements while remaining virtually indistinguishable from a properly spaced paper.

In a more serious vein, many students are finding that a word processor can free them from a great deal of the drudgery associated with preparing a class paper. Data base systems and outline processors simplify the collection, review, searching, and organizing of information, serving as the electronic counterpart of the 3 × 5 card of the past. When combined with easy editing and foolproof printing, a word processing system allows the student to concentrate more on content and less on form. Many students find that during the course of a four-year college career, a word processor can more than pay for itself in better grades, more free time (available for other studying, of course), and less money spent for typing services.

Text Processing for Programmers

Word processing software is frequently used by programmers to write program code. The code is then saved onto disk in a text file with no extraneous, non-ASCII characters so it can later be compiled. Some word processing programs have certain capabilities that make them particularly suitable for this purpose; the most notable is being able to save the file as a pure ASCII file on disk. Beyond this, the capability to move and copy blocks of text is highly desirable. Global-search-and-replace is another extremely useful feature.

Some compilers have their own built-in text editors to assist in writing program code. The advantage of using a built-in text editor is its interactive operation with the compiler, all of which is contained in one program. If an error is detected during compilation or execution, control returns to the text editor at the point where the error occurred.

SOFTWARE CONCEPTS AND DESIGN PHILOSOPHIES

Word processing programs differ considerably in the features they offer, as well as in the philosophy of their design. The "perfect" word processor is not difficult to describe. It contains all of the features described in Table 5–1. Of course,

TABLE 5–1
The Perfect Word Processor

Ease of learning	All commands can be mastered and retained in five minutes or less.
Speed	Is blindingly fast at entering, editing, saving, retrieving, and searching through text.
Mistake-proof	Never allows even a single keystroke to be lost through error.
Compatible	Can export and import text to and from other programs, and interfaces well with writing aids like spelling and grammar checkers. It also runs on any computer and works with any printer.
Powerful	Has every conceivable editing and formatting capability.
Great display	Shows, at minimum, a full page of text exactly as it would appear in print, complete with italics, underlines, and raised superscripts.
Inexpensive	Preferably free.
Voice-driven	No keyboard required.
Intelligent	Understands what you meant to say, rather than what you said, and makes suggestions when you are at a loss for words.

such a program has not yet arrived on the market, and buyers are advised not to hold their breath until it does. Most of the currently available products can offer only a few of the first seven features; which features are offered will depend on the program creator's design philosophy and the word processing needs of the intended consumer (some of the features, such as ease of learning and power, presently appear to preclude other features).

This section examines the major tradeoffs that must be made in designing a word processing program (or, indeed, any application program), and surveys some of the features that are currently available in better word processing programs.

Ease of Learning vs. Power

With the current offering of word processing programs (over two hundred products are being marketed), most can be classified as either robust in features or easy to learn and use. Rarely does a product achieve both of these design objectives.

Easy-to-learn word processors are typified by a command structure that does not require extensive memorization or a reference volume within arm's reach in order to use them. Several methods can be employed to make a word processor easier to use. **Menus**, or on-screen listings of available commands, are the approach used by most word processing programs. Many programs use menus merely as a reminder of the keys that access the various commands, and some packages allow more experienced users to increase the amount of text displayed by reducing or eliminating the number of commands that are displayed (see Figure 5–3). A program is termed "menu-driven" if the user accesses editing and formatting features by leaving the text entry mode and moving the cursor to the desired selection. Pull-down menus and bottom-of-screen menus (Figure 5–4) are often employed so the user can keep the text in view while making changes.

The difficulty with menu-driven word processing programs is that as the number of functions increases, users may have to search several levels of menus

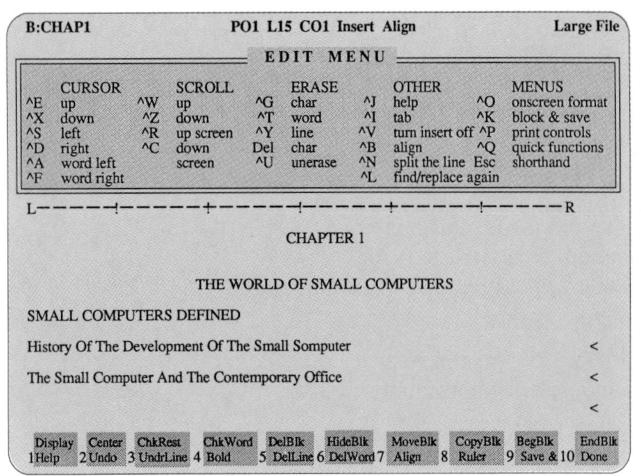

B:CHAP1 PO1 L15 CO1 Insert Align Large File
.he CHAPTER 1--The World of Microcomputers
.mt 6
.mb 5
.po 9
.mh 3
.pn 1
CHAPTER 1
THE WORLD OF SMALL COMPUTERS
SMALL COMPUTERS DEFINED
History Of The Development Of The Small Somputer
The Small Computer And The Contemporary Office
Display Center ChkRest ChkWord DelBlk HideBlk MoveBlk CopyBlk BegBlk EndBlk
1Help 2Undo 3UndrLine 4Bold 5DelLine 6DelWord 7Align 8Ruler 9Save & 10Done

(a) (b)

FIGURE 5–3

Variable Help Menus.
(a) Wordstar at Help Level 3.
(b) Wordstar at Help Level 2.

to accomplish simple editing tasks (e.g., to mark the beginning of a block of text so that it can be moved, you may have to select EDIT from the main menu, BLOCK from the edit menu, then MARK BEGINNING from yet a third menu). These systems may be ideal for the beginner and infrequent user, but they can become a nuisance to the experienced writer. On some systems, the word processing program must read each menu from overlay files on a disk before they can be displayed, greatly affecting editing speed.

Careful design of a word processing program yields a reasonable compromise between power, speed, and ease of use. Some menu-driven systems allow the user to enter the first letter of commands without actually moving the cursor through the menu. A built-in delay period before the computer retrieves a menu can allow experienced users to enter the commands entirely by letters, or to wait, if they are uncertain about which command is appropriate. The use of **mnemonics**, or memory aids, will make a program more "user-friendly." In a mnemonic system, func-

FIGURE 5–4

Different Menu Types. (a) Pull-down menu (Macwrite). (b) Bottom-of-screen menu (Microsoft Word, MS-DOS Version).

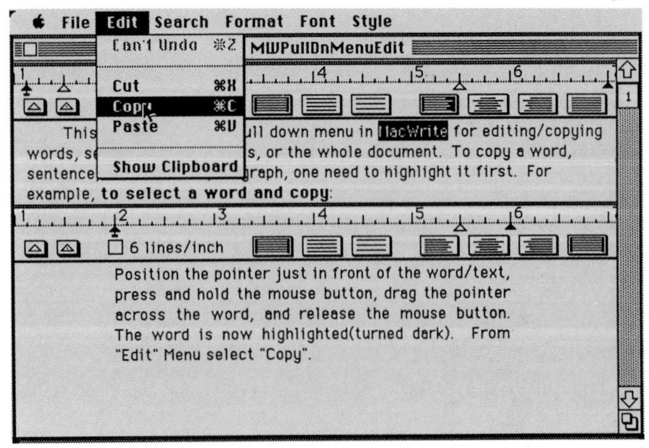

(a)

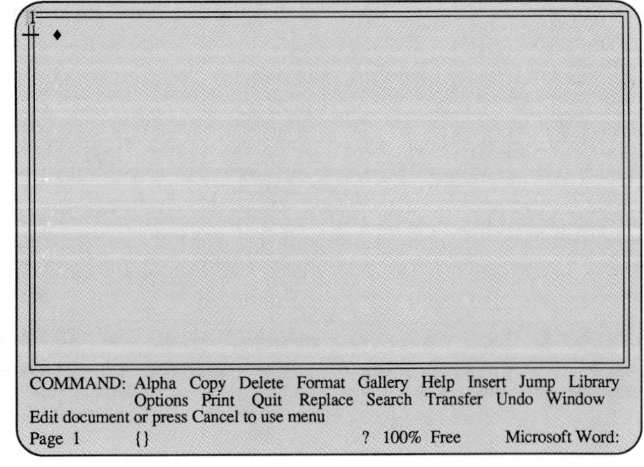

(b)

tions are assigned to keys in a logical, easy-to-remember manner, such as "Alt-T" to jump to the top of the text, or "ctrl-P" to force a page break. Keyboard overlays, stick-on key labels, and reference charts (Figure 5–5) can help complex word processors become more manageable. A HELP key that describes options available at a given point can make life easier, as can placing frequently used commands on special function keys. Hands-on computerized tutorials and well-written manuals with indexes are becoming the rule in today's offerings, and are essential until the user becomes familiar with the system.

Other Word Processing Considerations

One way that word processors are classified is according to display characteristics. One group of word processing programs is generally referred to as "what-you-see-is-what-you-get," or **screen-formatted.** With this type of program, text that is **justified** (spread so that both left and right margins are straight) or double-spaced appears on the screen just as it would on the printed page. Newer word processors in this category display text in graphics mode and can show raised superscripts, underlining, and even italics on the screen. Proponents of screen-formatted word processors have very little tolerance for the other type, the **embedded-command** word processor (see Figure 5–6).

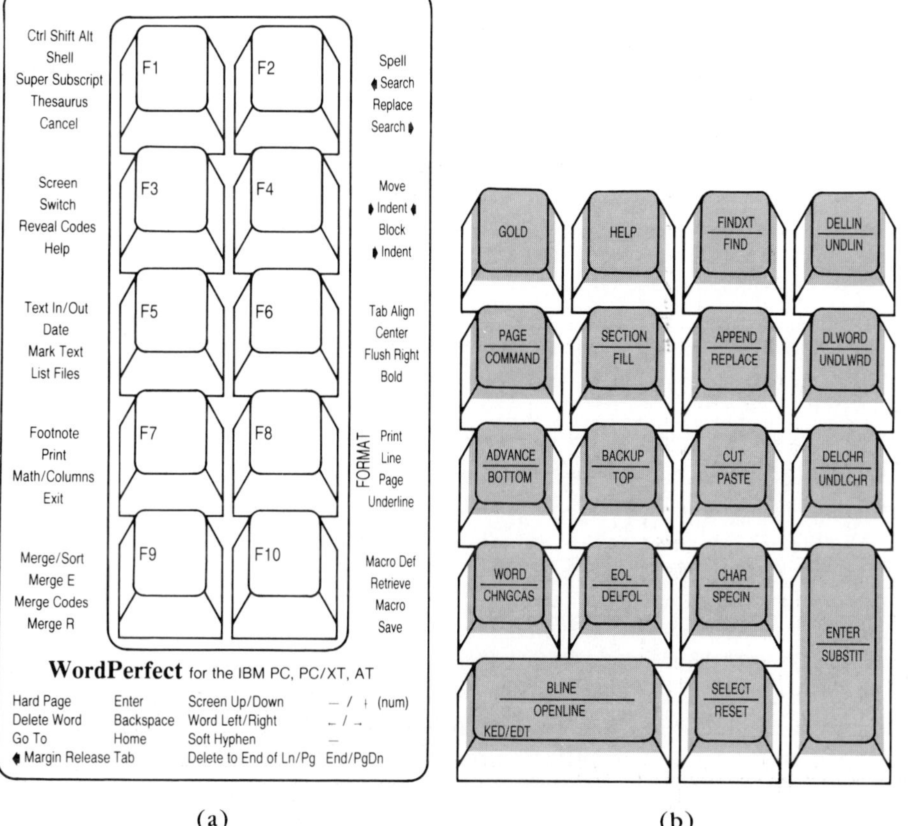

FIGURE 5–5

Word Processing Aids.
(a) Keyboard overlay for WordPerfect 4.2. *(Reproduction of the template courtesy of WordPerfect Corporation)* (b) Stick-on labels for DEC (Digital Equipment Corporation) VT-220 Keyboard.

FIGURE 5–6

Embedded-Command vs. Screen-Formatted Display.
(a) Microsoft Word (Macintosh) Screen-formatted display.
(b) WordStar embedded commands.

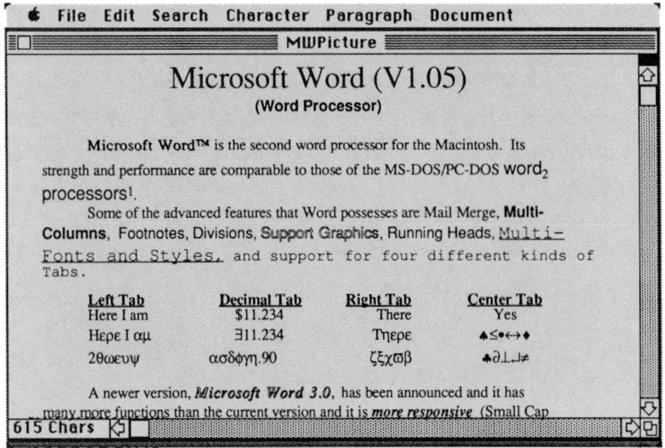

(a)

.heWORDSTAR DOT COMMANDS
.po 9—a page offset of 9
.mt 7—a top margin of 7
.mb 6—a bottom margin of 6
.hm 4—header starts in line 4
.fm 2—footer starts two lines up from bottom
.fo PAGE #

WordStar dot commands always begin in column 1 and are never printed. They are embedded commands to the print routine which inform it how to format a particular document. The above commands specify a top margin of 7 lines with the header WORDSTAR DOT COMMANDS to appear on line 4 left justified. The bottom margin is to consist of 6 lines. By implication there are 66-7-6 = 53 printed lines between the top and bottom margin. A footer will print PAGE followed by the page number in line 64.

(b)

Embedded-command programs use special symbols to direct the format during printing. A typical embedded command might be @DS, to double-space text, until another embedded command alters the line spacing. Embedded-command word processors are typically quite fast and very powerful in their editing and formatting capabilities. They are also relatively difficult to master. Writers who compose at the keyboard will find that this type of word processor reduces the urge to compulsively edit text and allows them to concentrate more on content. Most programs in this category have a "print to screen" function that allows them to view a document as it might appear when printed.

Another way in which word processing programs can be distinguished is whether they are memory-based or disk-based. Memory-based word processors are the fastest because they eliminate the need for frequent disk accesses. Disk-based word processors are, however, the most powerful and work best with a hard disk.

In **memory-based** word processors, all the required software is loaded into memory at start-up. Then the document to be worked on is read entirely into whatever available RAM is left. Once all the available primary storage is used, the document must be saved to disk and a new document is started. Obviously, however, this imposes a limitation on the document's length. Since the document is entirely contained within memory, it is possible for the word processor to perform searches and transitions from one end of the document to the other very rapidly. Also, no disk accesses are required to retrieve print utilities, search functions, specialized menus, or whatever, because these are all read into primary storage at start-up.

Disk-based word processors are just the opposite and work reasonably well even when there is limited primary storage. Unlike memory-based word processors, only a portion of the required software may reside in primary storage with the remainder available on disk. Print modules, global search-and-replace modules, and block operation modules may first have to be read in from disk before they can be executed. Similarly, submenus may reside on disk to be invoked upon demand. There is an apparent saving of primary storage, but the disk accesses slow the operations down. As primary storage becomes larger and less expensive to enlarge, the trend has been to place more and more of the operating word processor software directly in primary storage.

The most important aspect of disk-based word processor software is that it does not have to load the entire document into primary storage. Instead, the document is opened and just the first few pages are read in. When it becomes necessary for the user to proceed beyond these pages in memory, the word processor writes the current pages to a new temporary disk file and reads in the next few pages. This paging capability supports the creation of much larger documents than memory-based word processors are capable of. Moreover, the paging of text in and out of primary memory does slow things down. As primary memory increases, the trend will be toward greater use of memory-based word processing because it is faster.

Word Processing Features

Modern word processing programs have myriad features. This section looks at the features that might be found in a very powerful word processor. Most of these features fall in one of five categories: display features, formatting and printing features, editing features, file handling features, and utilities and external interfaces. Because everyone's needs are different, some of the features listed below remain unknown to even experienced users. Certain capabilities, however, can be agreed upon as essential to all types of users. The program must be able to control any of the special print features (change the character width, change to italics, etc.) that are available on a printer and may be needed in a document. It should allow recovery of a user's text if a disk is too full to contain the document. And, it should allow default settings (line spacing, margins, etc.) to be changed by the user so that a tedious setup procedure is not required with each editing session.

Display features affect how the text appears on the screen. In addition to the screen formatting found in many word processors, some have **graphics capability**, and can display foreign characters or scientific symbols (it should be noted, how-

Focus Feature

CUSTOMIZING A WORD PROCESSOR

(a)

(b)

FIGURE 5–7

Alternative Input Devices. (a) Word processing with a mouse. *(Courtesy of Mouse Systems Corporation)* (b) Microtek MS-300A intelligent image and text scanner. (c) Koala Technologies 6- by 8-inch Koala Pad + TouchTablet. *(Courtesy of Koala Technologies Corporation)*

Even a powerful, complex word processor can be made friendlier and much faster with some of the aids currently on the market.

In a system with lots of primary memory (preferably 256K bytes or more), using a portion of RAM to emulate a disk drive can provide tremendous speed advantages. Some word processors have too many features to reside entirely in memory, and must store some in overlay files on the disk. This results in frequent delays as these functions are accessed during editing. Other delays result from the interaction between buffers and scratch files. Some word processors keep only a small portion of a

ever, that this is of little value if the printer cannot print them). **Color**, although usually not well suited to word processing because of its low resolution, can be used effectively to highlight words that are to be underlined or superscripted. **Page break** marks (typically a horizontal line across the screen) eliminate guesswork about where pages will end. **Status lines** are used to show which page, line number, and column number is being worked on. Status lines usually appear at the top or bottom of the display.

Formatting and printing features are important in determining how the printed page will appear. Word processors allow the user to control top, bottom, left and

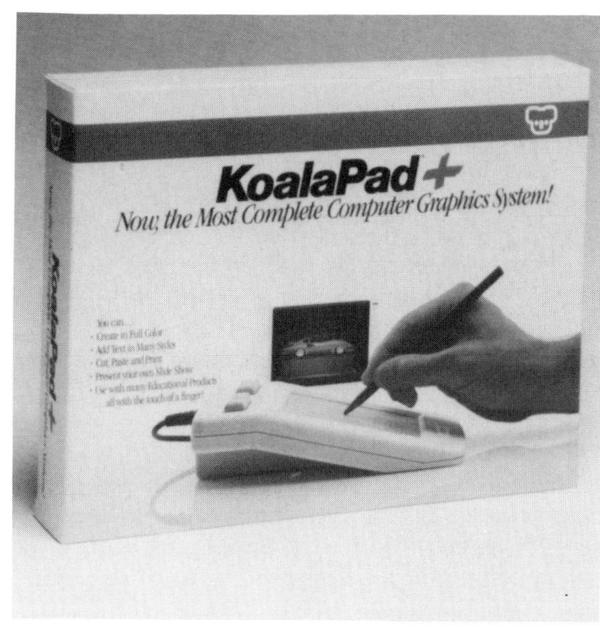

(c)

large text file in memory, in a special work area of RAM called a buffer. Whenever the buffer area is full (from entering new text), its contents are written to a temporary scratch file on the disk (at the end of the editing session, the scratch file is used for saving the text). When the word processor is scanning from the top to bottom of a long document, the buffer contents are frequently emptied to the scratch file and refreshed with new material from the disk. With a RAM disk emulator, both the word processing program (and its associated overlay files) and the text to be processed can be placed in memory. All of the disk accesses will now occur dozens or even hundreds of times faster.

A key definition utility such as Prokey or MagicKeys can allow a user to program his or her own mnemonics, permitting any key to contain a word processing function. Having trouble remembering the WordStar command to search for text (ctrl-QF, usually written as ^QF)? Key definition programs will let you store the WordStar definition into a shorter and easier-to-remember key combination, such as "Alt-F" (for Find) or "Ctrl-S" (for Search). Key definitions can be complex combinations of commands (for example, the combination ^K1^QC^KV^Q1^K1 will make a copy of a marked section of text to the end of the file and return you to your current position in WordStar). They can even contain entire phrases or paragraphs (The party of the first part . . .).

Special input devices, such as a light pen or a mouse (see Figure 5–7), can make movement of the cursor through text or menus considerably easier. Koala Technologies manufactures a touchpad with overlays for principal commands of several word processors (or users can create their own overlays), allowing commands to be issued by merely touching a large, clearly marked square.

With RAM disk emulators, key definition programs, and special input devices, any word processor can be fast and easy to use.

right **margins**, and to alter them within the text. Most word processors have automatic centering for titles and have methods for **indenting** without physically spacing to the right. A word processor may allow considerable flexibility in the placement and content of **page numbers** and **headings** (titles that are automatically printed on each page). The **linespacing** (number of lines printed per inch) and **character width** (number of characters in an inch) is often adjustable in very small increments for dot-matrix printers that offer these features. The word processor should be able to control all of these features on a large number of printers. Other formatting and printing features are shown in Table 5–2.

TABLE 5–2

Other Formatting and Printing Features

Headers and footers	These elements can occupy multiple lines on more powerful word processors and can even alternate between the right and left side for documents printed on both sides of the page.
Superscripts and subscripts	Text can have multiple levels, if the printer will scroll in both directions. This is necessary for scientific and mathematical text, such as $Z_{X_{ij}}$.
Page breaks	Page breaks can be inserted at any point. Conditional page breaks tell the printer to go to a new page if the specified number of lines will not fit on the current one. This prevents pictures and tables from being broken up.
Editing during print	This allows the computer to be used during long printing periods for editing other documents.
Multiple-file printing	This feature will let the user print several documents without constant attention to the computer.
Multiple-copy printing	With this feature, the user can print as many copies as desired of a single document.

Editing features make a word processor powerful, flexible, and easy to use. Most word processors allow the typist to select either **insert** or **overwrite** modes for text entry. In insert mode, new text is entered at the location of the cursor, and any previously entered material is shoved to the right. The overwrite mode replaces text at the cursor with the new entries. All word processors employ **word wrap** and can **justify** text. With word wrap, the user enters text without concern for where a line will end. As the right margin is reached, the cursor and any word that will not fit automatically go to the next line. If justification is turned on, the word processor will adjust the spacing so that both left and right margins are straight. Some word processors allow flush right columns for tables.

Search and replace features (see Table 5–3) will find words in a text, allowing them to be corrected or replaced. **Text movement** is important for changing the order of events in a document, because it allows entire paragraphs or pages to be relocated. This is usually accomplished by marking the beginning and end of the block of text to be moved, placing the cursor at the new location (where the text will be moved to), and issuing the move command.

Cursor movement is accomplished by using the arrow keys. Some word processors, however, allow the user to move the cursor in any direction a word, line, sentence, paragraph, or page at a time. Other commonly found editing features are listed in Table 5–3.

File handling features control the activities occurring on the disk during editing. Some word processors impose a limit upon the **size** of the file that can be created, because the text file resides entirely in memory. Others are limited only by the capacity of the disk but might make automatic **backup** copies, effectively reducing the maximum file size to one-half the disk size. Some word processors are **page-oriented**; that is, they store documents in a separate file for each page, reducing the risk of losing an entire document if a disk error occurs (page orientation can become cumbersome if text is to be moved between pages). These

TABLE 5–3
Other Editing Features

Search and Replace Options	These options can be extensive on some word processors, allowing backward searches, searches over a selected range of text, search for whole word occurrences only, and search without regard to upper- and lowercase.
Reformatting	Reformatting is the adjustment of text to fill the area between margins. If several words are deleted in the middle of a paragraph, the text will be pulled up from subsequent lines to fill the gap created. This is done automatically on some word processors, manually on others.
Case change	This feature allows text to be converted from lower- to uppercase (or vice versa) without having to reenter it.
Hyphenation help	This feature will break a long word at the end of a line into two parts by inserting a hyphen. This can be overridden by the user.
Block write	Block write allows a portion of text marked, as a block, to be written into a newly created disk file.
File insertion	File insertion pulls other disk files into the current text.
Windows	Windows will let the user view several portions of the text simultaneously.
Undo command	This command retracts the last command issued. This can be a lifesaver if you have just deleted an important section.
Programmability	This feature allows the user to define special function keys or special printer controls as he or she desires.
Column blocks	Column blocks allow any regular-shaped portion of text (say, from column 6 through 20 and lines 10 through 20) to be moved, copied, deleted, or saved, in the same manner as other block functions.
Block move	Block move allows a block of text to be moved elsewhere within the document.
Block copy	Block copy allows a block of text to be copied elsewhere within the document.
Block delete	Block delete allows a block of text to be deleted.

programs often have an **automatic save** feature at page intervals. **Multiple files** can be edited in some systems, allowing transfer of information from one document to another.

Various **utilities** are available to make the job of writing and proofreading easier. List processors are discussed above under "Word Processing for Business." Many word processors have built-in **spelling checkers**, and independently produced spelling checkers are available for those that don't. Spelling checkers may be used after the text has been entered and saved. Each word in a document is checked against a dictionary file containing from 10,000 to 100,000 words. As errors are found, the word (and usually surrounding text) is displayed. Better spelling

Focus Feature

ABOUT SPELLING, GRAMMAR, AND STYLE CHECKERS

For almost as long as there have been word processors, there have been tools to help you overcome spelling and grammar difficulties. Most writers who have used these aids learn to depend upon them. No matter how good a speller you are, you will probably benefit from a spelling checker. Most word processing users will find that no matter how careful they are, any document over a few pages is bound to contain errors, if only from missed keystrokes.

SPELLING CHECKERS

Spelling checkers come in two varieties: those that are used while in the edit mode of your word processing program (often called "in-context" spelling checkers, and those that are run outside the editing process (external spelling checkers), whether accessed from the main menu of the word processing program or run from the operating system level. Each type has its adherents, and each type has its strong and weak points.

External spelling checkers can often correct a document in less time than an in-context checker. The Word Plus, a popular spelling checker for CP/M-based computers (it is also the spelling checker for Microsoft Word) will compile a list of all unique words in a document (each word is listed only once). The list is then sorted and checked against a dictionary containing approximately 45,000 words and errors are noted along the way. When the checking process is completed the user reviews the words, marking or correcting them in a brief time.

Contrast that mode of operation with the in-context spelling checker. When the checker is invoked, it begins at the top of the document and checks each word in order until the first error is found. At this point the program will stop to allow you to correct the error or continue if the word is spelled as you intended. The program will then continue until another misspelled word is found or the end of the text is reached. Because the list of words is not sorted, and because of the frequent starts and stops, the in-context checker usually takes longer to use than the external spelling checker. The principal advantages of this type of processor are that you can see the surrounding context.

The principal features to look for in a spelling checker are

Speed. The speed of a spelling checker is dependent upon the size of its dictionary, the mode of operation (in-context or external), the efficiency of the program coding, and the type of data compression used to store the dictionary.

Dictionary size. Spelling checkers come with dictionaries ranging from 10,000 to 150,000 words in size. Virtually all spelling dictionaries use some type of compression scheme to fit more words in a file and to make the program run faster. A dictionary that is too small or does not include the plurals of words or commonly prefixed words will fail to recognize many correct words and will mark them as incorrect. This will slow down the proofing process and can becoming annoying.

Auto correction. After entering corrections, most of the better spelling checkers will correct misspelled words within the text file, even checkers that are run externally. An external checker usually will not be able to reformat paragraphs when a word changes length, however, but will mark the word so that you may re-edit the document.

View in context. In-context checkers, of course, show you the surrounding text so that you may judge what the correct word should be. Some external checkers can do this also, usually by saving a line or two of surrounding text into a special file used when reviewing the misspellings.

Suggestions. Many spelling checkers will make suggestions as to what word you intended to enter. Using a few simple algorithms (humans have a tendency to misspell in a consistent fashion), the dictionary is searched for words that are close to the misspelled word. With some spelling

checkers allow the user to enter the correct word (and may provide suggested spellings) and will automatically change the document wherever the misspelled word occurs.

Grammar checkers can locate a number of simple grammatical mistakes and will catch errors that a spelling checker can't, such as the same word entered twice

checkers you may correct a word by selecting one of the suggestions that have been made.

User dictionaries and dictionary updates. Most spelling checkers will allow the dictionary to be expanded by the user. If you are writing technical works or frequently use certain names or foreign terms, you may want to add them to the dictionary so you will not constantly be stopped when these words are encountered during checking. A few spelling checkers allow multiple special dictionaries for different uses (e.g., one for statistical papers, one with computer terms, etc.). During proofing these are checked after the main dictionary because including the terms in the large dictionary might hamper speed.

Spelling dictionaries can be a great aid to word processing users, but they are not perfect. They will not know if you meant "hill" when you typed "gill," since both are acceptable words. Because of limitations on dictionary size and performance, they also do not distinguish between upper- and lowercase words, so they will not be able to inform you that the first word in your sentence should be capitalized.

Early proofreading products even contained a few misspellings themselves (what typist would you trust to enter 100,000 words flawlessly?). Nowadays, a new spelling dictionary is likely to have been checked against an existing (and known to be reliable) dictionary before it is compressed into its final form. On the other hand, how many of us can really be certain that our spelling dictionary knows how to spell "etiquette" (ettiquette?)?

GRAMMAR AND STYLE CHECKERS

Grammar checkers have never received the kind of praise that is heaped upon spelling checkers, and with good reason. Most of the current offerings can be of diminishing value with extended use. A grammar checker can be a great asset to turn to periodically, but is unlikely to be used on every document you produce. It's just too much trouble.

What a grammar checker does is check for certain common types of grammatical errors, including:

Forgetting to close quotation marks and parentheses.

Putting less than two spaces after a period or colon, or less than one after a comma or semicolon.

Beginning a sentence without capitalization.

Placing the period or comma outside the quotation marks.

Repeating the same word twice.

In addition to these common errors, grammar checkers can check a file (similar to a spelling checker's dictionary) for commonly misused words or phrases. The dictionary can contain problematic phrases of all types, pointing out redundancy ("collaborate together"), awkwardness ("as per"), or wordiness ("equally as good as"). With most grammar checkers, the user can add to the list of phrases to flag.

Using a grammar checker can be a revealing process. Most users find that the first time they use one, it will flag phrases throughout the text. It can be genuinely rewarding, causing you to think about the way you phrase sentences. Helpful suggestions will allow you to make a readable document out of academic or bureaucratic gibberish. Most writers also find that with repeated use, they are conscious of the kinds of errors the grammar checker will find, and do not use them in their documents.

The education provided by a grammar checker can easily be worth its purchase price to a professional writer. However, individuals who write only occasionally are advised that grammar checkers often are not used after the first few times.

in a row. **Footnote programs** can control page spacing so that sufficient room is left at the bottom of a page for the corresponding footnotes. They can also collect them to be placed at the end of a document in bibliographical form. **Index generators** are useful to anyone preparing a large document. They will find all occurrences of specified key words and phrases and create an index or table of contents with the correct page numbers. The computerized **thesaurus** has become increasingly popular, because it is usually on-line and can be used to immediately look up synonyms of an overused or trite word.

The **external interface** of a word processing program allows interaction and information transfer with programs outside the word processing program. Some word processors place special characters in the text that prevent material from being used by other word processors, utility programs, or data base and spreadsheet programs. Most programs allow access to operating system commands in order to delete, copy, and rename files.

The Bottom Line

Since word processors run the gamut from simple and inflexible to powerful and complex, the selection of a word processor can be difficult. Not everyone needs the array of editing and formatting features offered by some of the more powerful entries in the market, and might find them so complex that the program receives little use. The choice of word processors should be made based on the frequency of intended use and the degree of formatting capability desired. For example, playwrights and screen writers have complex indentation rules to follow, and must find a word processor that can handle multiple indentation easily. College professors preparing articles for journal submission are likely to require a powerful word processor with many formatting features. Table 5–4 can serve as a rough guide in determining which word processors might be best suited to an individual's need.

USING A WORD PROCESSOR: AN OVERVIEW

Document generation with a word processing program consists of the following steps:

1. Creating the document
2. Entering the text
3. Editing, or making any necessary corrections
4. Saving the document
5. Getting it printed out

Creating a document occurs at the opening menu on a word processor and is usually done by selecting the "create a file" or "open a file" option and specifying a filename. Since most word processing programs need to stay in the "A" disk drive during use, the user must be careful to identify the file as being on drive "B." The user should also ensure that the disk in drive B has adequate space left to hold the document to be created. Approximately 2K bytes of disk space should be allowed for each double-spaced page, with one-inch margins on all sides. In MS-DOS, the disk space can be checked with either the DIR B: or CHKDSK B: command (CHKDSK B: requires the program CHKDSK.COM to be on the disk in drive A). If the user wants to work on an existing document, the word processor will display the beginning portions on-screen and place the cursor in the upper left corner. To append

TABLE 5–4

Selecting a Word Processor

In this table, a user is classified as "infrequent" if periods of two or more weeks are likely to occur between use of the word processor (just enough time to forget most of the commands). His or her formatting needs are termed "complex" if the documents to be produced require special indentation, include mathematical formulas or illustrations, or might contain a variety of line spacing and character widths in the same document.

		FORMATTING NEEDS	
		SIMPLE	**COMPLEX**
Frequency of use	**Infrequent**	Choose simplest menu-driven program available.	Choose fast word processor, possibly with a menu bar and pull-down menus.
	Frequent	Choose powerhouse that uses menus and mnemonics. Screen formatting important.	Choose powerful word processor that doesn't interrupt work to cycle through menu layers.

new material, the END OF FILE (or similar) command causes the cursor to go to the bottom of the text. Shown in Figure 5–8 are the opening menus of several popular word processing packages.

Entering the text is done in the same manner as with a typewriter. The principal difference between the use of a typewriter and a word processor is in the use of the <Return> key. With a word processor, words will wrap when the right margin is reached. The only time the <Return> key is pressed is when the end of a paragraph is reached. If margins need to be adjusted, this can be done either at the beginning, or after the material is entered (the text may have to be reformatted to the new margins). It is not necessary to insert spaces manually to set the left

CORONA PC
Exclusive version of MULTIMATE Rel 3.12C

1) Edit Old Document
2) Create New Document

3) Print Document Utility
4) Printer Control Utilities
5) Merge Print Utility

6) Document Handling Utilities
7) Other Utilities

9) Return to DOS

DESIRED FUNCTION:
Enter the number of the function, press RETURN

(C) Copyright 1982
Software Systems, Inc.

(a)

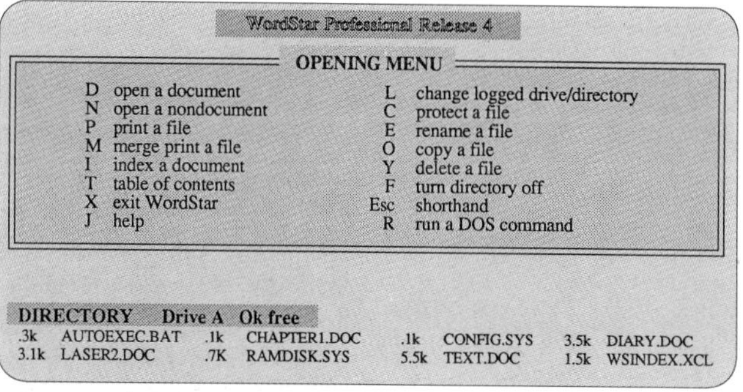

(b)

FIGURE 5–8

Opening Menus. (a) Multimate. (b) WordStar.

Focus Feature

TOWARD BETTER WRITING AND COMPOSITION

All too frequently we as educators hear employers complaining about the writing skills of their new hires who, only months before, were our students. This article presents a procedure for improving your writing skills. This procedure is not concerned with the steps required to operate a word processor that were presented in the main body of this chapter. If you can stomach a bit of alliteration, several issues bear consideration in writing compositions: creativity, content, consistency, completeness, and clarity. Beginning with creativity, the procedure consists of the following steps.

Step 1: Create an Outline. How many times have we been told this before? It works, and there is no substitute for it. If you can't outline the document you're going to write, then you are unprepared to write it. Creation of any written manuscript must be directed by a well-defined mission or purpose. The purpose of the paper or publication will largely determine content, coverage, and style. Write out the major section headings of the document first and then add subsection headings to the major section headings based upon a careful consideration of content and coverage as they relate to the purpose. Relevance is the main issue here. Then decide what will be the basis for sequencing the sections and subsections. It could be chronological order, methodological order, deductive order, inductive order, or some other order. As a general rule, any formal document will consist of an abstract, or executive summary in which the author tells the readers what they will read, an introduction, a main body in which the major content of the document is unraveled, and a summary or conclusion in which the readers are reminded of what they have read.

The good news is that there is software to help with this step. Called an *Outline Processor* or *Idea Processor,* this software also facilitates the development of content, the reorganization for clarity, and the addition of content for completeness.

Step 2: Concentrate on Content by Filling in the Outline. You may enter ideas and thoughts anywhere in the outline as these thoughts come to mind. At this point

margin, because a word processor will allow the user to shift all the text to the right when ready to print.

As errors occur, the document will need to be **edited**. This involves moving the cursor to the location of the error and overwriting it with corrected text (or deleting the incorrect and inserting correct text). The ability to scroll through a large document a screen or page at a time can be helpful. If the user finds that a word used throughout a large document has been consistently misspelled, the search and replace function will allow corrections to be made rapidly. Shown in Figure 5–9 are the editing displays (screens) of several popular word processing packages.

When the text is completed, it must be **saved.** Some word processors allow the user to quit without saving anything from the current editing session. This is convenient if a user changes his mind about the revisions just made to a previously saved work, because it does not destroy the prior version. In systems that do not make backup copies of work, users should create duplicate copies of important documents before altering them, unless they are certain that they will never need the old version. In a system that backs up files, an old version of a file called BIOPAPER would automatically be renamed something like BIOPAPER.BAK when the new version is saved. Thus, the user can always go back to the earlier version if not satisfied with the changes just made.

Printing a document is relatively simple if the word processor has been installed for a particular printer. Since each printer uses different commands to signify such things as "begin superscript" or "print boldface," word processors come with con-it isn't necessary to be concerned with spelling, grammar, or style. With the word processor writers can focus exclusively on content and concern themselves with spelling and grammar later.

Step 3: Concentrating on Consistency, Revise the Outline as Necessary. Reconsider the sequencing of the material. Is it consistent with the sequencing criterion you decided upon in Step 1? Combine content areas that develop the same idea in different places. Develop transitional material that bridges the movement from one major content area or section to another.

Step 4: Add Content as Necessary for Completeness. Try to convey to the reader all that is necessary to fully develop and present your ideas. This may require some research on your part to sufficiently develop the content areas of your manuscript. Thus some prior analysis and investigation may be necessary to support the synthesis of appropriate content.

Step 5: Proof the Manuscript for Correctness and Clarity. Proofing always involves printing a rough draft of the manuscript so it can be read and marked on. It's easier to proof hard copy than soft copy because you have it all in front of you. Proofing may involve further reorganization of the material; this is easier when it's all there in front of you—not just 24 or 25 lines at a time.

Run your manuscript through spelling and grammar checkers to help locate spelling errors and style problems.

Step 6: Make Corrections. With the marked hard-copy draft in front of you, edit the manuscript using the word processor. Repeat steps 2 through 6 until you are satisfied with the final product.

A primary advantage of word processors is that they facilitate the revision and editing of the document. This makes it possible for the writer to concentrate on just one dimension of the writing, such as content, rather than all of them simultaneously, as used to be the case before word processors.

figuration programs that should be run before the word processor is used for the first time. An **installation program** will have a menu of printers for which it already knows the codes, and will allow the user to enter printer codes if his printer is not represented in the list. The installation program need only be run once, because it permanently (or until the configuration program is run again) alters the word processing program to send the correct codes to the printer. Installation of a printer

FIGURE 5–9

Editing Displays. (a) Wordstar. (b) Word-Perfect.

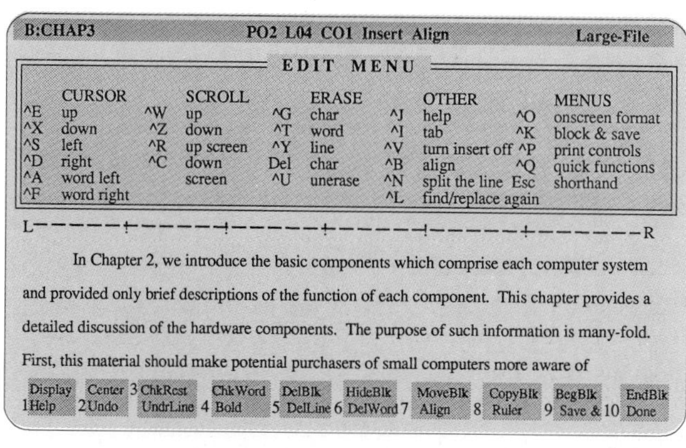

(a)

Ms. Katherine R. Haley
Executive Vice President
Corporate Relocation Division
Merrill Lynch Realty
94 Wall Street
New York, NY 10022

Dear Ms. Haley:

As you may have read in the January issue of Corporate World, Corporate Communication Associates is planning to transfer twenty-four of our executive families from New Orleans to Atlanta in May. We believe we can facilitate their moves by contracting with a real estate firm such as Merrill Lynch Realty to set up appointments for our executives and their spouses to see houses that are tailored to their specific family needs. Because of the large number of homes involved (which CCA will help finance) and because of the substantial settlement fees and real estate commissions resulting from the sale of such a block of property, we are planning to invite four national real estate companies to submit their proposals for relocating our families.

Doc 1 Pg 1 Ln 1 Pos 10

(b)

that cannot be selected from the menu is quite complex, and advice should be sought from experienced users of the word processor/printer combination.

Once the printer is installed, saved documents can be printed by specifying PRINT at the main menu. The program will then present a list of options, such as printing to a disk file instead of using the printer, making multiple copies, setting the left-hand margin, or starting and stopping the printing at certain page numbers. Shown in Figure 5–10 are the print options of several popular word processing packages.

HARDWARE AND SOFTWARE REQUIREMENTS FOR WORD PROCESSING

To get maximum benefit from a word processing system, the user should have the following hardware:

A screen that displays 80 columns.

A full-travel keyboard.

Two disk drives.

A printer capable of producing the print quality required: often, but not always, a laser printer.

Although word processing can be done on a 40- or 64-column screen, it will become very difficult to visualize how the text will appear in print if the screen width is less than the line length (text will either disappear off the right side of the screen, or wrap onto the next line). We have become accustomed to an 8 1/2-inch page width with 1- to 1 1/2-inch margins on each side, allowing 62 to 72 characters per line. Hence, 80-column screens are sufficient. Fortunately, few computers are offered today with less than 80-column video output. Several screen characteristics strongly affect a user's ability to work on a word processor during extended periods without fatigue. Crisp, clear characters that appear to be filled in, rather than a collection of dots, are easier on the eyes. Video output that does not flicker when

FIGURE 5–10

Print Options. (a) Multimate. (b) Wordstar.

```
                    Submit a Document for Printing

                  Drive: B        Document:  Lim

Current Time is:   13:35:54                Delay Print Until Time is: 13:35:54
Current Date is:   02/27/1987              Delay Print Until Date is: 02/27/1987

              Print Document Summary Screen?               N
              Print Queue Statistics?                      N
              Delete Queue Entry when done?                Y
              Print in Background or Foreground (B or F)?  B

Left Margin                        000   Pause between Pages?        N
Start Print at Page Number         001   Right Justification?        N
Stop Print at Page Number          999   Draft Print                 N
Header/Footer First Page Number    001   Default Print               4
Printer Number                     001   Printer Type            EPSON
Number of Original Copies          001
Document Page Length               066

Printer types available:
EPSON  TTYCRLF  PRISM    BROTHR1  CITHOHF10  DIABL620  DIABL630
IBM    NEC3550  NEC7730  NEC5510  NEC3515    SMITHCOR  OKDATA82
```

(a)

```
P                       WordStar Professional Release 4

To skip further questions, press the Esc key at any point.  Press ↲ at any question to use the default
answer.

Document to print? Chap1
↲  done ^U  cancel  ^R  repeat  | ^S  Left  ^D  right  | Del  char  ^G  Char  ^Y  all
^X directory  ^P  literal       | ^A  wd lf ^F  wd rt  | ^H  left  ^T  word

                 Number of copies?  1
       Pause between pages (Y/N)?  N
            Use form feeds (Y/N)?  N
                   Starting page?  1
                     Ending page?  50
              Nondocument (Y/N)?  N
                Name of printer?  IBMPRO

Directory (DRAFT)  Printers  ^W  scroll up  ^Z  scroll down

630ECS  630WP   ASCII  AUTOLF  C1550   CITMSP  CUSTOM  D2100P  DIABLO
DRAFT   FX80    FX85   GEM10X  HPL:AD  HPLJ:B  HPLJ:U  HPLJ:Y  HPLJET
HPTJI   IBMCLR  IBMGR  EBMPRO  IBMQUI  IBMWP   IBMWPE  LBP8    LP300
LP4080  LQ1500  LQ800  LX80    ML182   ML182I  ML192   ML192I  ML292
```

(b)

Focus Feature

THE FUTURE OF WORD PROCESSING?

Word processing, particularly on microcomputers, has swept a sizable portion of our population and will continue to grow in popularity over the next several years. Yet many people with both a demonstrated need and available funds will not join this trend until the technology has changed sufficiently to overcome a major problem. The problem? Getting pages full of words into the computer in under an hour when your typing is of the hunt-and-peck variety. Several approaches exist that go a long way toward alleviating this problem, and one of them might provide a permanent solution.

One answer is to rearrange the keyboard. The standard typewriter key layout (called "QWERTY" for the first five letters of the top alphabetic row) is difficult for most people to learn. At least one alternative exists, called "DVORAK" for its inventor, August Dvorak. The DVORAK keyboard is arranged so that cumbersome reaches are all but eliminated, the typing load is more evenly distributed between the hands, and moving a finger from the first to third rows for consecutive letters occurs infrequently (try typing "Greece" a few times on a QWERTY keyboard). DVORAK proponents claim that the new system can be learned in a fraction of the time taken to learn QWERTY, that it greatly reduces typing fatigue, and that it can provide considerable gains in typing speed. DVORAK may not be the answer to everyone's typing problem. It has been around for over 50 years and hasn't yet supplanted the QWERTY keyboard, mostly because of the time and money already invested in acquiring and learning QWERTY typing. But in an age when people who have never used a typewriter are turning to micros, the DVORAK keyboard has suddenly begun to receive serious attention.

Wouldn't it be nice to be able to take that long passage from the book and put it directly into the computer, where you can modify it? It is possible with **Optical Character Recognition** (OCR). Several manufacturers market OCR devices that can read a variety of typestyles and feed the information directly to a disk in your computer. The best-known of these is the DEST PC Scan Plus (see Figure 5–11), an under-$10,000 device. As the technology improves, OCR will allow handwritten input with virtually flawless recognition.

FIGURE 5–11
The DEST PC Scan Plus.
(Courtesy of DEST Corporation)

(*Continued*)

THE FUTURE OF WORD PROCESSING? (Continued)

The obvious shortcoming of both methods described above is that they still require the operator to write out the text, either upon or before entry. The solution? **Voice recognition.** In a voice recognition system, the computer takes in each word separately, extracts a small set of distinguishing characteristics (e.g., the frequency at each minute time slice), and compares it against a data base of words until it finds a match. Since each of us pronounces words differently, supplying unique combinations of pitch, timing, and inflection to all of the words in our vocabulary, voice recognition devices must be "trained" to individual voices. Voice recognition is one of the few areas of computer technology that has lagged behind predictions of progress, due to the massive storage requirements and high-speed processors that it requires. Progress is being made, however, and several companies, most notably Texas Instruments and IBM, have already begun to market voice recognition devices. These early devices will recognize only a limited number of words; the Texas Instruments device is perhaps best used to store computer commands rather than a written vocabulary (e.g., you can program it to insert left and right margins by five spaces whenever you say "indent"). As search and pattern recognition algorithms improve, and with the advent of high-speed parallel processors, voice recognition may become a usable alternative to keyboard input by the early 1990s.

scrolling and that has pleasantly rounded characters will also allow users to stay at the computer longer.

The keyboard should have full-travel keys, with a pleasant feel. A **palm rest**, a large surface where hands can relax, will also help reduce fatigue. If no palm rest is available, a very thin keyboard sometimes allows the hands to be placed on the table. **Detached keyboards** are the standard for microcomputers. Their greatest benefit is the viewing angle and distance to the screen can be adjusted. If a user has a large screen and short arms, a fixed keyboard will become annoying in a very short time. Key placement is also important. Some word processors make heavy use of the <Control> key, and there are keyboards that place it out of reach without moving the left hand. Most important, however, is the "feel" of the keys. Try it out. Type as fast as you can. Do you notice an increase or decrease in typing speed while you test it? Do your wrists become sore from awkward key placement or a poor angle? Do your fingers fall naturally on the "home" row (left and right index fingers on F and J, respectively)? Can you consistently hit the <Shift>, <Control>, and <Return> keys without looking? If you anticipate doing a great deal of word processing, the feel of the keyboard may make the difference between a pleasant experience and a painful one.

Two disk drives are necessary for virtually all modern word processors. Unlike many applications packages, the program disk must reside in drive A (or a hard disk) during the entire editing process, because frequent calls are made to overlay files and utility files. Since these files are typically quite large (especially with a spelling checker), little room remains for text files.

If speed is important (remember, most of the time the program is idly waiting for the next keystroke), try moving the cursor left and right, jumping from the top to bottom in a large file, and deleting a full line of text from right to left. A word processor that cannot scroll or delete quickly (and several are lacking in these areas) may not be suitable.

Word processing has become the domain of laser printers. In recent years, however, advances in dot-matrix technology have produced faster and less expensive printers with high-quality output. The choice of printers must be governed by the answer to two questions: (1) what print quality is demanded by the intended audience, and (2) what printers can be used by the existing word processors? Most businesses will use laser printers to give a "typed," professional appearance to correspondence going outside the firm. On the other hand, high-quality dot-matrix output, especially when photocopied, is impossible to tell from a typed letter. Unless the user is a good programmer, it is advisable to ensure that any printers under consideration are listed in the menu of the word processor's installation program.

Summary

Word processing—the entry, manipulation, storage, and retrieval of written communication—is a mainstay of most businesses. Since their introduction in the mid-1960s, word processors have advanced from typewriters that stored text to highly sophisticated microcomputer-based systems that will probably use voice input in the next decade.

Productivity gains from the use of word processors (versus typewriters) often range from 100 to 400 percent. The largest gain comes from not having to reenter text when changes are made. Other major gains come from the use of list processing features, and from the reduction in errors that often accompanies their use.

Programs that are easy to use are excellent for the infrequent user, but may not have sufficient editing or formatting power for complex texts. With the use of key definition programs and other word processing aids, even a complex program may be made more "user friendly." Word processors can also be classified as using either screen formatting or embedded commands, and each type has a strong following.

A wealth of features are offered on most word processors. Display features such as on-screen boldface, underlining, and superscripting help the user more clearly visualize the printed outcome. Formatting and printing features allow flexibility in the appearance of printed output, and automate such tasks as centering headings, numbering pages, and spacing margins. Editing features can be the most important aspect of a word processor, because they dictate the speed and ease with which a document can be generated. Block moves, search and replace functions, and cursor movement commands allow changes to be made very quickly, even in large files. Spelling and grammar checkers will aid the proofreading of a document, and most word processors can execute a limited number of operating system commands without leaving the program.

Using a word processor involves five stages: creating, entering, editing, saving, and printing. If further changes must be made, only the last three steps are needed. Good writing quality has five considerations: creativity, content, consistency, completeness, and clarity.

Word processing programs can work as well on 16-bit computers as on their larger 32-bit counterparts. An 80-column video output, a good keyboard, and two disk drives are, however, necessary. The selection of a printer is becoming more difficult with better dot-matrix models entering the market. Most businesses, however, will continue to use laser printers because of the professional appearance of their output.

Key Terms

automatic save
backup
block move
character width
color
cursor movement

dedicated word processor
detached keyboard
disk-based word processor
display features
editing
embedded-command word processor
external interface
file handling
footnote programs
grammar checkers
graphics capability
indenting
index generators
insert mode
installation program
justified
linespacing
list processor
margins
memory-based word processor
menu
mnemonic
multiple files
optical character recognition
overwrite mode
page break
page headings
page orientation
palm rest
screen-formatted word processor
search and replace
size
spelling checkers
status line
text movement
thesaurus
utilities
voice recognition
word processing
word wrap

Self-Test

1. Describe how word processing software and applications got their start.
2. Describe the uses to which word processing software is generally put.
3. Describe what features one can generally expect in word processing software.
4. Describe what steps are generally involved in using a word processor.
5. Describe what hardware and software are required for word processing.

Exercises

1. Discuss the differences between word processing programs that use screen formatting and those that use embedded commands. Under what circumstances would an embedded-command word processor be preferable?
2. Compare WordStar (based on the information here and in the tutorial at the end of Chapter 6) with the "perfect" word processor in Table 3–1 (ignore the last three). How many of the perfect features does WordStar have? Concerning which items does WordStar show the greatest shortcoming? Analyze another word processing package, such as Microsoft Word. Does it come any closer?
3. An insurance agency is considering purchasing a word processing program. It will be used constantly by highly skilled typists who have never used a word processor. Documents to be prepared are from one to five pages long. Which of the following products would you recommend to them, and why? (1) A very fast word processor that is difficult to learn but has powerful formatting capability, (2) a fast word processor that is made friendly by the lack of commands (features) that must be learned, or (3) a menu-driven program that offers a large number of features and is simple to learn, but is very slow in editing.

4. Using the same three choices as in exercise 3, select a word processing program for a college professor, a law office, and yourself. Explain your answers.
5. Under what circumstances would typewriters be more appropriate than a word processing program?
6. Does the DVORAK keyboard stand a chance of catching on? Why or why not?
7. Why would WordStar (and several other word processors) still offer ^E, ^X, ^S, and ^D as alternatives to the up, down, left, and right arrow keys, when virtually all computers are equipped with arrows? (Hint: The answer is *not* that some computers do not have arrows.)
8. Do you agree with the statement that the typewriter may become as much a relic as the hand-crank adding machine? Discuss why or why not.
9. How important is the ability to have the screen reflect exactly how the printed page will look?
10. Why do word processors offer justification? Is this style of print acceptable in business correspondence? On school projects?
11. Some word processors offer a multiple-column mode, in which the text in each column can be either left- or right-justified. When might each of these be used?
12. Two basic categories of word-processing design philosophies were discussed. What are they? How do they differ?
13. List and describe the five categories of features associated with any word processing program.
14. Describe your own method for writing and composition. Compare your method with that described in the article, "Toward Better Writing and Composition." What can you do to improve your writing skills? How has the technology of word processing made good writing easier to achieve?
15. What advantages can be had from customizing a word processor?
16. Assuming you are already familiar with a word processing package, describe the word processing package you use in light of the material presented in this chapter. Is the word processor disk-based or memory-based? Is the word processor screen-formatted or does it use embedded commands? Describe some of the features of your word processor that are especially important to you.
17. Discuss how you can improve your word processing skills and thereby become more efficient and effective at processing words (creating and editing text). Considering the following list, what specific skills would you consider especially useful beyond mere entering and editing of text, and why?

    (a) how to use a spelling checker
    (b) how to use macros
    (c) how to use list processing
    (d) how to use an on-line thesaurus
    (e) how to use an outline processor

    Many of these skills are covered in the next chapter.

Additional Reading

McWilliams, Peter A. *The Word Processing Book.* Los Angeles: Prelude Press, 1982.

Waite, Mitchell, and Julie Arca. *Word Processing Primer.* New York: Byte Books/McGraw-Hill, 1983.

Webster, Tony. *Office Automation & Word Processing Buyer's Guide.* New York: Byte Books/McGraw-Hill, 1984.

Periodicals

The following publications frequently carry articles on the use of word processing software, as well as reviews of recent product offerings.

BYTE
INFOWORLD
PC
PC WORLD

CHAPTER

6

Word Processing Mechanics

CHAPTER OUTLINE

The Screen Display 158
The Printed Page 159
Typing, Editing, and Revising Text 161
Formatting and Printing Text 168
FOCUS FEATURE Mechanics of Enhancers 171
FOCUS FEATURE Desktop Publishing 180
Classifying and Characterizing Existing Word Processing Programs 182
WORDSTAR TUTORIAL 191
WORDPERFECT TUTORIAL 202

CHAPTER OBJECTIVES

In this chapter you will learn

1 how word processing packages present textual material on the screen, and how this might differ from the printed version of the document
2 the rudiments of entering, editing, and revising the manuscript
3 how word processors differ with respect to saving the document and creating old backup versions of the document
4 how to format and print documents
5 the major product offerings and how they compare

The previous chapter introduced the usage, functions, and features of word processing. This chapter introduces the mechanics of word processing. The features which were only briefly presented in the previous chapter will be described in considerable detail in this chapter.

The chapter begins with back-to-back discussions of soft and hard copy—the screen display and the printed page. This will lay the groundwork for many of the explanations to follow. Then the process of typing, changing, and revising text is described. This is followed by the steps of formatting and printing the text. The chapter concludes with tutorials on WordStar and WordPerfect.

THE SCREEN DISPLAY

As we observed in Chapter 5, most word processing programs are capable of displaying a variety of screens to the user. Shown in Figure 6–1 is a typical entry/edit screen—perhaps the most important of the screens exhibited by the word processor. Like an empty page, most of the screen consists of the text area, which awaits the keyboarding of text by the user.

In addition to the entry/edit area, most word processors exhibit a **status line**, which shows (1) the name of the document being worked on; and (2) the location

FIGURE 6–1
Screen Display in Detail

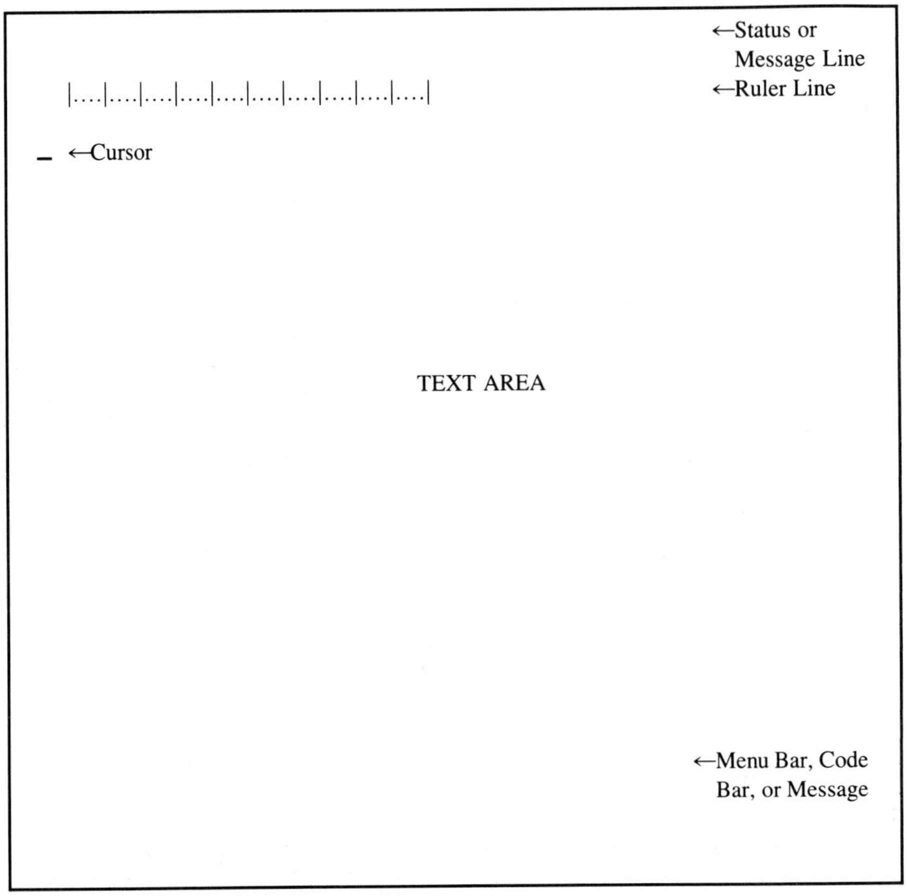

of the cursor within the document, by page number, column number, and line number. As shown in Figure 5–4b and Figure 5–9, status lines usually appear at either the bottom or the top of the screen. The status line will also show what commands are currently being executed and will provide brief messages to the user, such as whether the word processor is in insert mode or typeover mode.

Below the status line is the **ruler line**. The tab stops are shown on the ruler line as vertical bars or other symbols on the line. Depression of the <Tab> key will cause the cursor to jump to the next tab stop. Tab stops can be used to indent paragraphs and to create tables and lists with aligned columns. Like typewriters, word processor tab stops are adjustable. If changed, the tab stops may get saved with that portion of the document to which they apply. Starting a new document may reset the tab stops back to their default positions.

Along the bottom of the display, function key definitions may be exhibited as a reminder to the user.

As the screen display fills up with text, each beginning of a new line at the bottom of the page will cause all lines of text to move up one line on the screen. The top line at the top of the screen moves off the screen to make room for the new line being entered at the bottom of the screen. This is called **scrolling**. The screen can be scrolled up, down, left, or right. Scrolling occurs in word processing programs whenever there is an attempt to move the cursor beyond the boundaries established by the screen. For example, if the user tries to move the cursor above the top line of the screen, the screen will scroll down. Similarly, if the user attempts to move the cursor beyond the rightmost displayed column, the screen will scroll left, once the cursor reaches the rightmost displayed column of the screen. Scrolling occurs only if text extends beyond the boundaries established by the screen display.

Split Screens and Windows

Some word processing programs do not let the user look at text on two different pages at the same time. After viewing one page, the user must enter a command or sequence of commands to see the other page. Word processing programs that do display the two pages together do so by means of a split screen or by use of windows. Some word processing programs allow the user to view different parts of the same document by splitting the screen. Screens may be split either horizontally or vertically. The result is two viewing areas in which two different portions of the document may be viewed at the same time. This may be useful when transferring a block of text from one place to another, for example.

Other word processing programs allow users to work on two or more different documents at the same time by viewing portions of those documents through windows, which may be overlapping. Microsoft Word and WordPerfect both support this capability. Windows differ from split screens in that more than two may be open and viewed at the same time. Moreover, windows generally are overlapping, whereas split screens are never overlapping.

THE PRINTED PAGE

When in edit mode, word processing programs do not show on-screen *exactly* what a document will look like when printed. Part of the reason for this is the limited size of the hardware displays, especially when driven in text mode. On screen, the user will most likely see everything but the headers and footers, the pitch, type size, subscripts, and superscripts. All of these will be seen on the printed output, however. What is displayed versus what is printed is covered in detail in this chapter's section entitled "Formatting and Printing Text." Figure 6–2 depicts the typical printed page.

Several terms depicted in Figure 6–2 are commonly used in the manuals that describe how to use the word processing software, and therefore require definition. First and foremost is the distinction between "space" and "line." A **line**, as shown in Figure 6–2, is an entire row of text and/or blank space on the sheet. A **space** is simply a character position, within a line, filled with nothing. The **top margin** refers to the top of the page before text begins. Headers (defined in Table 5–2 of Chapter

FIGURE 6–2
The Printed Page

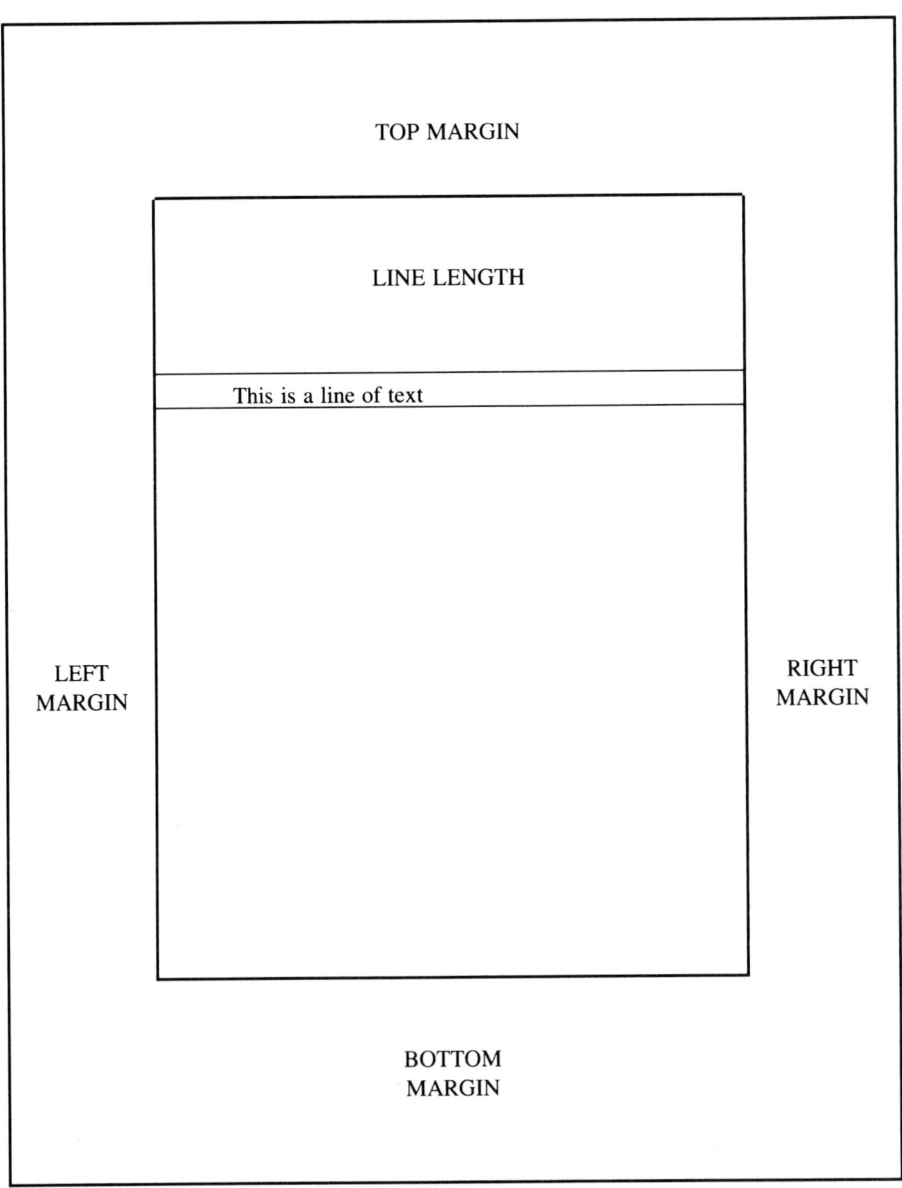

TABLE 6–1

Definition of Terms Used in Conjunction with the Printed Page

TERM	DEFINITION
Bottom margin	The blank lines that appear at the bottom of the page, sometimes containing a footer.
Left margin	The blank space along the left edge of the paper.
Line length	The number of spaces of text from the left margin to the right margin. If the left margin is set at 9 and the right margin is set at 74, the line length is 65.
Page length	The length of the page in lines of print.
Right margin	The blank space along the right edge of the paper.
Top margin	The blank lines that appear at the top of the page, sometimes containing a header.

5) may appear in this area, which may be left-justified, right-justified, or centered, and may consist of several lines. The user is able also to control the actual line number(s) on which the header appears. The blank area at the bottom of the page is referred to as the **bottom margin.** Footers (also defined in Table 5–2 of Chapter 5) may appear in the bottom margin. Like headers, these may consist of one or several lines and be left-justified, right-justified, or centered. And the user has control over the actual lines they appear on. One use to which footers may be put is to print the date at the bottom of each page. The top margin, number of lines of print, and bottom margin must total to the page length. The **page length** is the total number of lines on the page; for 11-inch paper at 6 lines per inch, there are 66 lines.

In addition to top and bottom margins, there are left and right margins. The blank column(s) on the far left side of the page is referred to as the **left margin.** The blank column(s) on the far right side of the page is the **right margin.** Table 6–1 lists these and other terms and definitions associated with a printed page.

TYPING, EDITING, AND REVISING TEXT

Typing text on a microcomputer is similar to typing on a typewriter, except when the text approaches the right margin. When using an electric typewriter, a typist must press the carriage return key to return the carriage back to the left margin. With a word processor, the cursor is automatically returned to the left margin and any words extending beyond the right margin are automatically "wrapped" back to the left margin on the line below. This is called a **word wrap**; it will insert a soft carriage return at the end of the line, whereas actual depression of the <Return> key on the keyboard inserts a hard carriage return. Hard carriage returns are used between paragraphs. They are one means the word processing package has to detect the end of a paragraph. In fact, a paragraph can be broken up into two paragraphs simply by pressing the <Return> key at the point where the break is to occur.

As the user types in text, characters appear on the screen at the position the cursor was in when typing began. Eventually, the screen fills up with characters. Once this happens, the cursor is on the bottom line of the screen and each word wrap causes the screen to scroll up one or more lines.

Document Navigation

Document navigation refers to movement of the cursor within the document itself to positions where revisions and corrections to the document are required. Such movement is accomplished by use of the cursor arrow keys, by use of the <Home>, <End>, <PageUp>, and <PageDown> keys, or by the use of commands, which may involve the <Ctrl> and <Alt> keys. It may be possible, for example, to move both forward and backward a character, word, sentence, paragraph, screen, or page at a time. By themselves, the left and right cursor arrow keys will generally move the cursor one character at a time. The up and down cursor arrow keys will move the cursor up or down one line at a time. When used with the <Ctrl> or <Alt> key, these same keys may be able to move the cursor much farther. For example, when the <Ctrl> and right arrow keys are pressed simultaneously, most word processors will move the cursor right one word.

Some word processing packages must be used with a mouse. Movement of the mouse directs movement of the cursor to the desired position. Cursor behavior is similar to its behavior when controlled by cursor arrow keys, as described above. Each character is highlighted as the mouse-controlled cursor is dragged over it, so the user can detect immediately which character the cursor is currently pointing at.

Correcting Typos: Insertion vs. Type-over

Almost all MS-DOS and PC-DOS machines have an <Ins> key directly below and to the left of the numeric keypad. This key controls the insert/type-over mode of operation when working with a word processor. The appropriate mode becomes very important when editing a manuscript. When correcting typos, the appropriate mode is "type-over" when a wrong character has been typed, and "insert" when characters have been left out. The current mode is usually displayed on the screen. The <Ins> key is actually an insert/type-over toggle. (A **toggle** is any key that acts as a two-state—on/off—switch. Many such keys are defined this way in word processing and other applications.)

To delete or remove characters, the <Del> key or the <BackSpace> key is used. Generally, the <BackSpace> key deletes characters immediately to the left of the cursor while the <Del> key erases characters highlighted by the cursor. But there are important exceptions. In WordStar 3.3, for example, the nondestructive <BackSpace> key does nothing but move the cursor backwards without deleting anything, while the <Del> key deletes the character immediately to the left of the cursor. Release 4 of WordStar works in the usual way, however. In addition, some programs allow the user to delete a character, sentence, line, lines, or paragraph at a time without marking these larger text strings as blocks. Any time a deletion is requested, any text below or to the right of the deleted text is moved up or to the left, over the deleted portion.

Reforming Paragraphs

Paragraph reforming is necessary whenever insertions or deletions have taken place while editing the paragraph. As a consequence, lines may extend beyond their right margins or may not reach their right margins. Most programs have a

This text is unreformed. The right side is very jagged and the boundary set by the margin is exceeded as a result of much editing.	This text is reformed. The right side is very even and runs out to the margin exactly.
Unreformed ↑ {right margin}	**Reformed**

FIGURE 6–3

Unreformed vs. Reformed Paragraphs

command that reforms the paragraph when the user is through editing it. Some programs do it automatically. Automatic or dynamic paragraph reforming can be distracting if the program does not wait until the user has finished editing the paragraph before reforming it. The completion of editing of a paragraph could be detected by the movement of the cursor above or below the paragraph. (Otherwise, the program reforms the entire paragraph for each change that is made.) The purpose of paragraph reforming is to bring lines back within their right margins, regardless of whether the right margin is justified or not. Figure 6–3 illustrates the difference between unreformed, edited paragraphs and reformed, edited paragraphs for right-justified text.

Block Manipulation

Sometimes called "cut and paste," **block manipulation** refers to marking a block of text and then moving, copying, or deleting the block of text. These functions are very important when doing major revision and reorganization of a document.

The first step in any block maneuver is to mark the text so it can be treated as a block. This is done by positioning the cursor at the start of the block and placing a beginning-of-block mark and then moving the cursor to the end of the block and placing there an end-of-block mark. This will cause the block to be highlighted or half-shaded, so it will stand out as a block from the rest of the text. Having done this, it is possible to delete the block or to copy or move the block within a document file, or between two documents. We reserve discussion about how to transfer a block from one document file to another for the next section, on "Writing and Reading Files."

When moving or copying text within a file, place the cursor at the position where the marked block is to be copied or moved to, and then issue the appropriate command to copy or move the block. The marked block will appear, beginning at the position designated. Text below the point at which the marked block is to be moved or copied is moved down to make room for the newly inserted block of text. If the block is moved, the "hole" created by vacating the former position of the moved block is filled with text from below. This is illustrated in Figure 6–4 below.

It is generally not possible to copy or move a block of text to a position within the block itself. It is, however, possible to move or copy a block of text adjacent to another column of text so as to create two side-by-side columns of text. To do this, however, the word processor must be informed that column block operations are to follow. This procedure is described in detail in a forthcoming section.

Before	After
Meal preparation involves the following steps: 2. cook meal 1. shop for food 3. set table 4. serve	Meal preparation involves the following steps: 1. shop for food 2. cook meal 3. set table 4. serve

FIGURE 6–4

Moving a Block of Text within a Document

Writing and Reading Files

Two approaches are taken to the task of copying or moving a block of text in one document into another existing document, depending upon whether the word processor can have more than one file open or not. For word processors that can have more than one file open, the procedure is to open the origination document, mark the block to be copied or moved, open the destination document, move the cursor to the position where the block is to be moved or copied, and issue the command to move or copy the block, as shown in Figure 6–5. The effect is evident in the windows opened for the two documents.

For word processing programs that can only open one document at a time, the procedure is quite different and varies from package to package. One approach is first to open the origination document, mark the block of text, and write it to disk as a separate and distinct disk file. The word processor will ask for a filename into which the marked block of text is to be written. The word processor will then create the file and write the block to the file.

In order to insert the block of text into another document file, it is necessary to close the first open document file. Then the second document file must be opened, just as would ordinarily be done to edit and add to the file. Then the cursor must be moved to the place within the document where the block of text, which was previously saved to a disk file, is to be entered. Next, the command must be issued to the word processor to read a document file. The word processor will then ask for a filename. The proper response will be the filename of the file containing the marked block of text. The word processor will then read this file in; the file will be inserted, beginning at the point where the cursor was placed. This second file must then be closed by saving it back to a disk file. This procedure is illustrated in Figure 6–6.

Block Column Move Operations

Another set of block operations widely supported by the word processing software includes the block column operations: move, copy, and delete. It is possible to mark a block as a collection of character-position columns and to remove, copy, or move it. The beginning marker marks the starting column and row of the block, just as it does for ordinary operations. The ending marker marks the ending

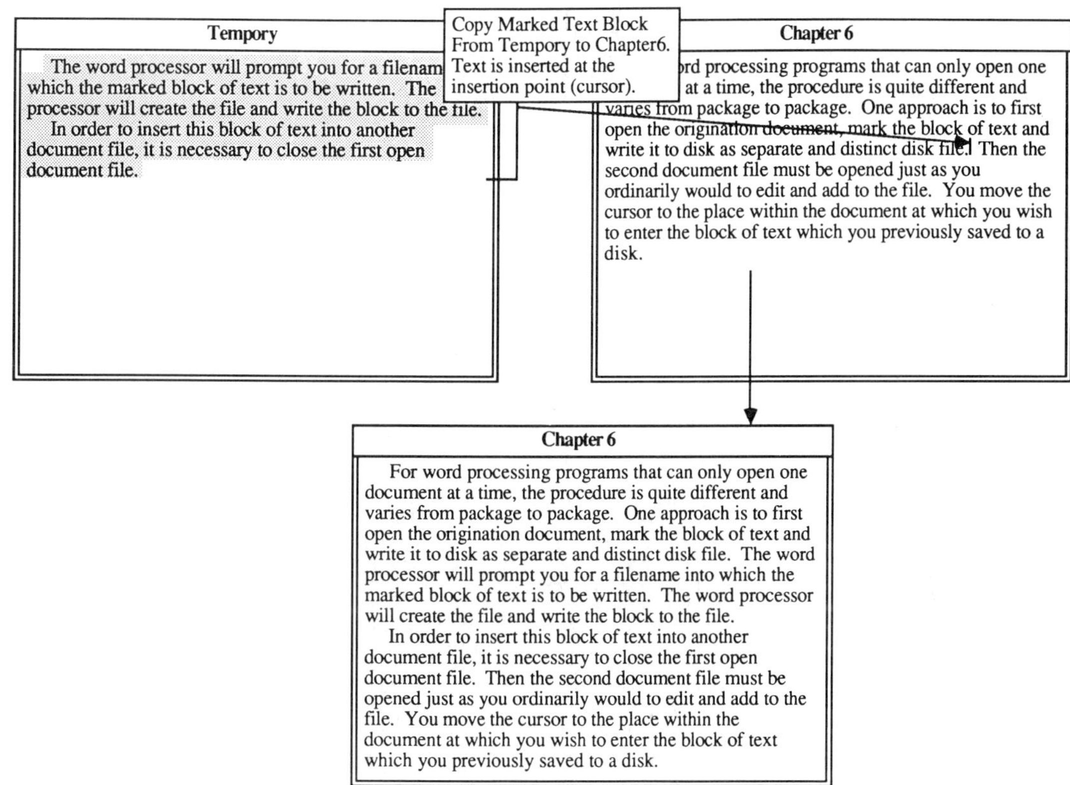
Tempory
The word processor will prompt you for a filenam
which the marked block of text is to be written. The
processor will create the file and write the block to the file.
In order to insert this block of text into another
document file, it is necessary to close the first open
document file.
Copy Marked Text Block
From Tempory to Chapter6.
Text is inserted at the
insertion point (cursor).
Chapter 6
rd processing programs that can only open one
at a time, the procedure is quite different and
varies from package to package. One approach is to first
open the origination document, mark the block of text and
write it to disk as separate and distinct disk file. Then the
second document file must be opened just as you
ordinarily would to edit and add to the file. You move the
cursor to the place within the document at which you wish
to enter the block of text which you previously saved to a
disk.
Chapter 6
For word processing programs that can only open one
document at a time, the procedure is quite different and
varies from package to package. One approach is to first
open the origination document, mark the block of text and
write it to disk as separate and distinct disk file. The word
processor will prompt you for a filename into which the
marked block of text is to be written. The word processor
will create the file and write the block to the file.
In order to insert this block of text into another
document file, it is necessary to close the first open
document file. Then the second document file must be
opened just as you ordinarily would to edit and add to the
file. You move the cursor to the place within the
document at which you wish to enter the block of text
which you previously saved to a disk.

FIGURE 6–5

Moving a Block of Text from One Document to Another When Both Documents Can Be Open at the Same Time

column and row of the block, but blocks are not assumed to proceed to the rightmost margin as they are for ordinary operations. The ending marker must always be at least one column to the right of the beginning marker. Figures 6–7 and 6–8 illustrate column block move operations. In Figure 6–7 a long list is halved and the second half is moved up parallel with the first half, thereby saving half the lines required to exhibit the long list.

In Figure 6–8 there are six columns; it is desired to move column "aaaa" over to the far right, where it would become the rightmost column. Column "aaaa" is marked as a column and the cursor is moved to the position where column "aaaa" is to be moved. The COLUMN MOVE command is issued to the program, the column is moved to the cursor position, and all the other columns are moved left to fill in the vacated position left by the moved column.

Using Find and Replace

The FIND command lets the user search for a particular string of characters. The command will prompt the user for the particular character string to be found. After specifying the string, the command may then prompt the user for specific options, like finding all occurrences of the character string that was entered, or searching backward from the present cursor position, etc. Table 6–2 lists some of the various options found in the FIND or FIND AND REPLACE commands of most word processors. the "Find" functions of some word processing packages allow the use of wild cards like "*" and "?". And the user can always enter spaces as part

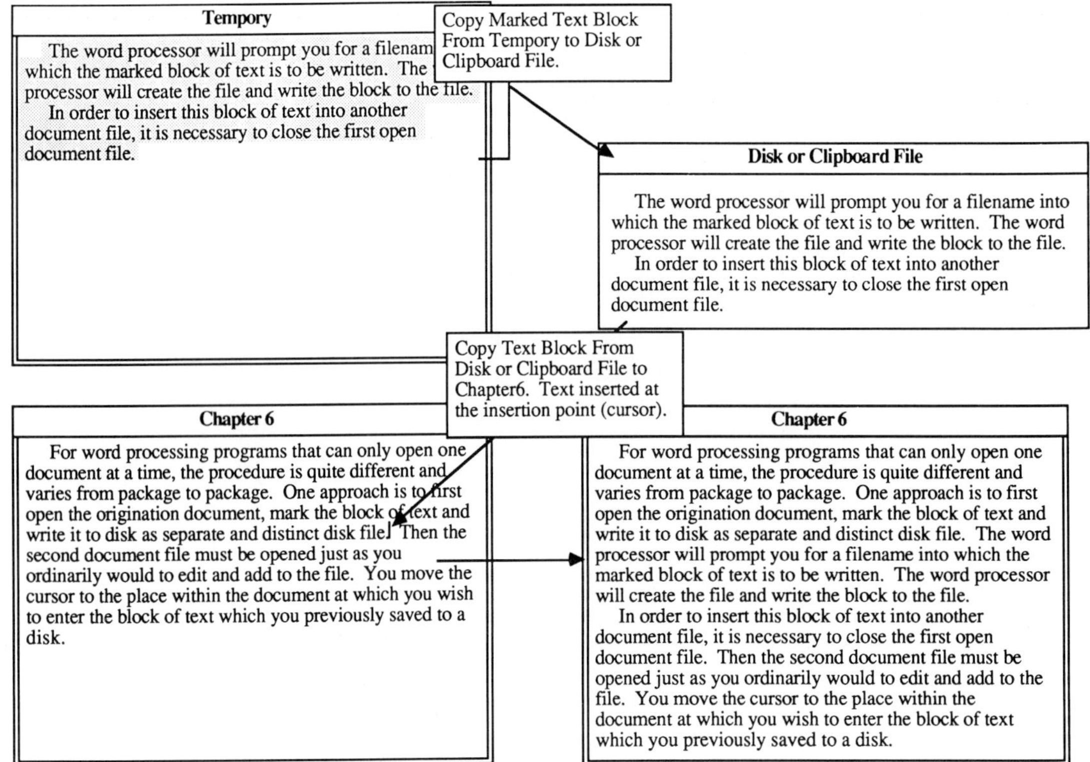
Tempory
The word processor will prompt you for a filenam
which the marked block of text is to be written. The
processor will create the file and write the block to the file.
In order to insert this block of text into another
document file, it is necessary to close the first open
document file.
Copy Marked Text Block
From Tempory to Disk or
Clipboard File.
Disk or Clipboard File
The word processor will prompt you for a filename into
which the marked block of text is to be written. The word
processor will create the file and write the block to the file.
In order to insert this block of text into another
document file, it is necessary to close the first open
document file.
Copy Text Block From
Disk or Clipboard File to
Chapter6. Text inserted at
the insertion point (cursor).
Chapter 6
For word processing programs that can only open one
document at a time, the procedure is quite different and
varies from package to package. One approach is to first
open the origination document, mark the block of text and
write it to disk as separate and distinct disk file. Then the
second document file must be opened just as you
ordinarily would to edit and add to the file. You move the
cursor to the place within the document at which you wish
to enter the block of text which you previously saved to a
disk.
Chapter 6
For word processing programs that can only open one
document at a time, the procedure is quite different and
varies from package to package. One approach is to first
open the origination document, mark the block of text and
write it to disk as separate and distinct disk file. The word
processor will prompt you for a filename into which the
marked block of text is to be written. The word processor
will create the file and write the block to the file.
In order to insert this block of text into another
document file, it is necessary to close the first open
document file. Then the second document file must be
opened just as you ordinarily would to edit and add to the
file. You move the cursor to the place within the
document at which you wish to enter the block of text
which you previously saved to a disk.

FIGURE 6–6

Moving a Block of Text from One Document to Another When Only One Document Can Be Open at a Time

of the string to be searched for. Most Find functions are case-sensitive. Hence, if the user enters the string "The," she may be surprised to discover that none of the strings "the" will be found. Most word processors will let users specify as an option whether they want all occurrences of the string "the" to be found, regardless of case. Another approach is to leave off the first letter of the word being searched for if the word could be placed at the beginning of a sentence. For example, if the misspelled word "becuase" was to be found and replaced with "because," then searching for "ecuase" and replacing that with "ecause" everywhere would do the job.

As the example above suggests, the Find-and-Replace option lets the user search for a particular character string and replace it with another. This can be a time-saving feature when extensive document revision is required. A proper name, for example, could be searched for and replaced with another proper name.

TABLE 6–2

Options Typically Found in the Find-and-Replace Command of Most Word Processors

1. Search backward from cursor position; default is forward from the cursor position.
2. Perform global search—find all occurrences of a string.
3. Pause for replacement approval.
4. Ignore case.
5. Find whole words only.
6. Perform multifile search—mostly in-memory word processors.

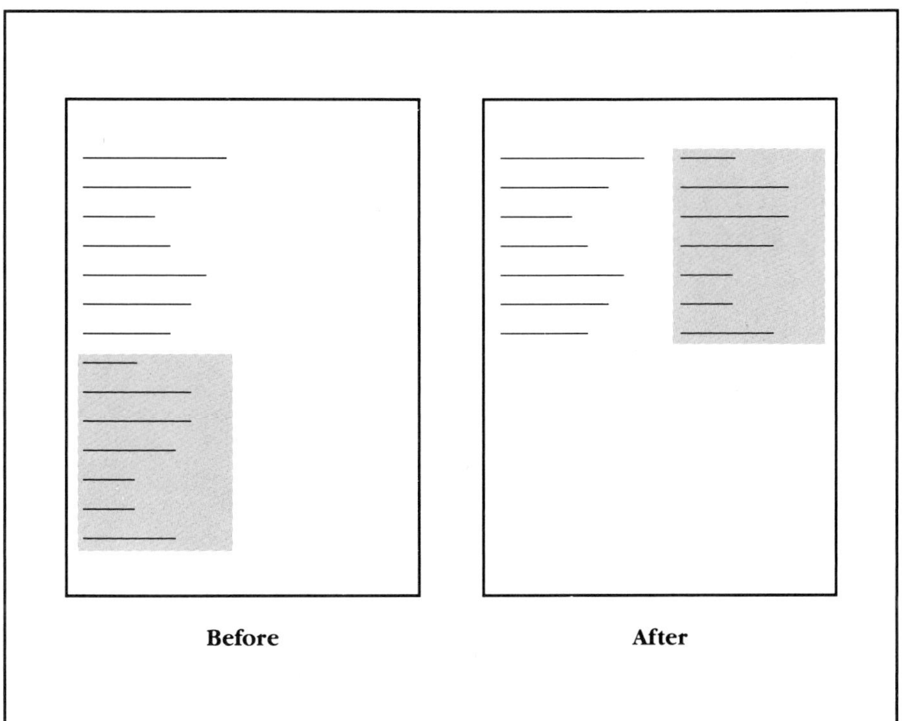

FIGURE 6–7
A Column Move Operation

Saving the Document

Disk-based programs will generally require that the document be saved on disk before it can be printed. Some in-memory programs permit the user to print the document while it remains in memory. Nevertheless, it is good practice to save the document onto secondary storage before printing it. Some programs maintain a backup file on the disk. When the file is saved, the most recently edited version of the file is written to disk and saved under the filename. The backup of the file contains the version of the file before the editing accomplished in the current session was performed. The previous backup may be retained or erased. If it is not erased by the word processor program, the disk will quickly fill up with old backup versions of the file; it becomes the user's responsibility to manage and remove unwanted old backups from the disk. Other word processing programs do not automatically maintain backups, but permit the user to change the filename before saving the file so that old versions of the file can be retained if wanted.

Of Libraries and Macros

Libraries are indexed collections of text files saved on a floppy or hard disk. These can be easily retrieved when required. Law offices can make expeditious use of this capability. When preparing a will, affidavit, suit, or other legal instrument, carefully prepared paragraphs containing the precise legal language needed can be pulled into the document from the library. These paragraphs are called **boilerplate.**

Macros are a sequence of keystrokes or commands that are saved so they can be played back when needed. A command is used to inform the program to begin

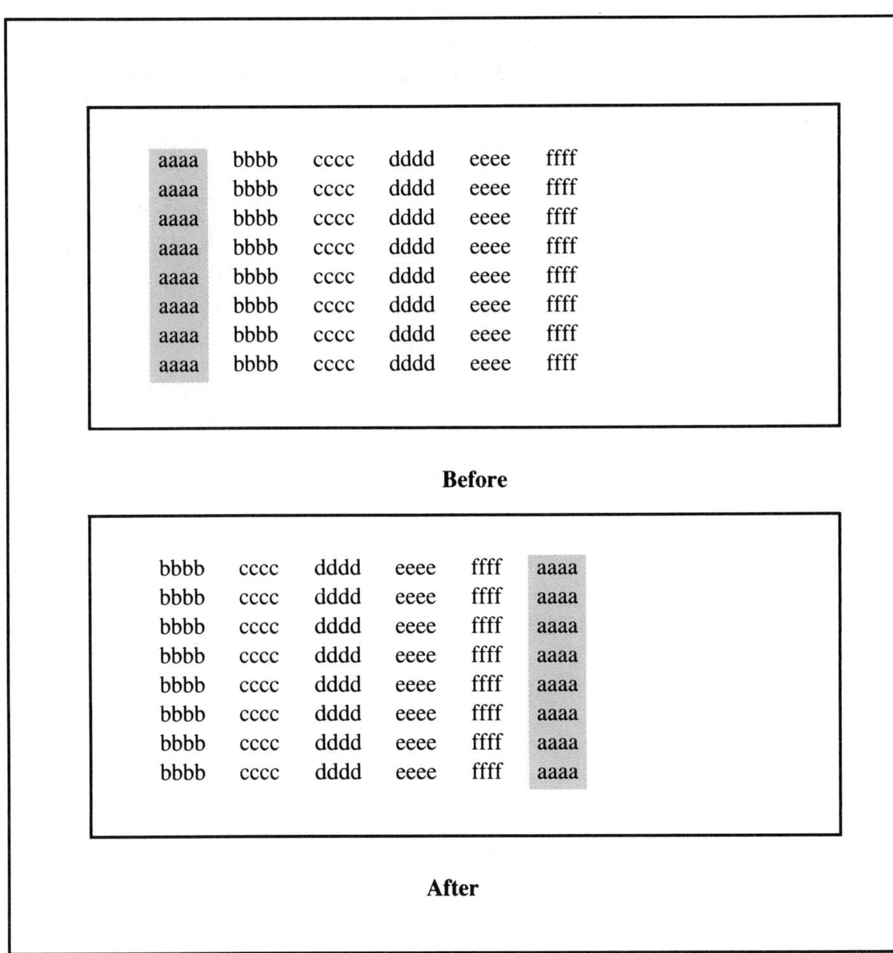

FIGURE 6–8
Another Column Move Operation

recording keystrokes. Then the keystrokes are assigned a name, which is usually one or two characters. Next, the keystrokes to be saved are entered. Finally, a command is issued to terminate the recording of keystrokes. The program will then save the recorded keystrokes under the assigned name. There is a limit to the number of keystrokes (for some programs, 128 keystrokes) that can be assigned to a key. Whenever that sequence of keystrokes is needed, they can be invoked simply by pressing <Alt> or <Ctrl> in conjunction with the assigned name. The stored sequence of keystrokes will then appear on the screen and in the text at the cursor position, if they are not commands. If the stored sequence consists of commands, they will be executed.

FORMATTING AND PRINTING TEXT

Once you're satisfied with the content of your document, it's time to print the document so you can proofread it, add content as necessary, and allow others to study it. However, before you can print the document, you must first check the print format on screen to make sure you have specified appropriate print directives.

TABLE 6–3

The Levels of Print Format Control and What They Affect

PRINT FORMAT CONTROL LEVEL	SETTING AFFECTED
Character and Word	□ typeface □ boldface □ underlining □ subscripts and superscripts □ italics
Line and Paragraph	□ paragraph indents and outdents □ spacing between lines □ spacing between paragraphs
Page	□ top and bottom margins □ left and right margins □ headers and footers □ page offsets □ page breaks

As we shall see, there are basically three levels of print format control. These are listed in Table 6–3.

Since these format controls are concerned with printing the document files, it may not be possible to actually see the effect of these controls on the screen. Word processing programs that control the screen in text mode are usually incapable of exhibiting the chosen typeface (font) and pitch (pica at 10 characters per inch or elite at 12 characters per inch, for example). The same is true of type size and italics. Only the control characters used to produce these effects can be seen. However, word processing programs which drive the display in bit-mapped mode can do all of these. Other word processing programs may not display the page offset on the left side of the page, especially when the page offset is not the same as the left margin. Headers and footers are usually not displayed on the screen, nor are the top and bottom margins, because of the traditionally small screen size (24 or 25 lines of text).

Default Format Settings

Most word processing programs are set by default to print text single-spaced with 65 columns, right-justified. As it turns out, there are default settings for all margins, for page length, for the number of lines of text on a page, for right justification, for line length, and for page numbers, all of which can be changed by the user. The advantage of the default settings is simply that the user does not have to set any of these to start producing documents right away. MacWrite's (Figure 6–9) default settings are unusual—justification is off, for example.

Focus Feature

MECHANICS OF ENHANCERS

Features that enhance the power of word processors are appearing more and more often in the highly competitive marketplace of word processing software. Conceptual discussions of spelling and style checkers, idea (outline) processors, and electronic thesauruses appeared in Chapter 5. This article discusses the mechanics of these increasingly commonplace features.

OF MACROS AND SHORTHAND

Release 4 of MicroPro's WordStar refers to macros as "shorthand," and indeed they are. Suppose you are using the word *philanthropic* in more than a dozen places throughout a paper you are preparing. Each macro's name consists of a single character, and up to 80 keystrokes can be stored in a single macro. To define a macro, you press **Esc** and then **?.** WordStar will list all of the macro names currently in use. At the prompt `Character to be defined?`, type **H.** (Our choice of *H* here rather than *P* is because we would like to use *P* to name a print macro.) Next, you are prompted for a longer descriptive name that WordStar can use to remind you what this macro does: `Description for ESC menu?`. The response is **philanth** followed by <**Return**>**.** Next, WordStar Release 4 prompts you for the definition of the macro itself: `Definition?`. Your response is **philanthropic** followed by <**Return**>**.** You will notice that the shorthand character and definition are now listed with the other shorthand characters in alphabetical order in the ESC menu. To stop the creation of macros simply press **ˆU,** (we have used the ˆ to represent the <Ctrl> key). At the prompt `Store changes onto disk?`, your response is **Y;** these changes are stored in a file on the program disk, after which the screen is rewritten to look like it did before you started the definition of the macro.

Now, when you need the difficult-to-type-word *philanthropic,* you simply hit the Esc button and then type H and the word magically appears.

For word processing programs that do not have a built-in macro capability, you can purchase keyboard enhancers like Prokey and Magickeys. Prokey and Magickeys belong to a collection of software called "memory-resident utilities," which are discussed further in Chapter 12. They were also discussed in the article "Customizing a Word Processor."

SPELLING CHECKERS: SPEEDY AND SUPPORTIVE

We begin by invoking the spelling checker (**ˆF2** in WordPerfect). At this point you must know how you want to use the spelling checker. For example, you may be able to check spelling of a word before you enter into a document, to check spelling of a specific word in the document being edited, to check spelling of all words on the current page being worked on, or to check spelling of the entire document. Our choice is to check spelling of the entire document before printing it. In WordStar Release 4, we would depress **ˆQL** to select the spelling checker and to inform it to check the entire document. The following discussion is procedurally similar to WordPerfect.

The speller begins. After a brief wait, suppose it stops at the word *ferward* in the text. The speller suggests `A. forward` and `B. foreword`. You choose *forward* by pressing the A key and *ferward* is automatically replaced with *forward.* Alternatively, you could have chosen

1. to accept none of the suggested spellings and to go on;
2. to add the word to the dictionary;
3. to edit the word;
4. to continue looking up other possible spellings, possibly using phonetics.

Item 1 above would give you the option of skipping this word or all appearances of this same word in this document.

Next, suppose the speller detects the double word *the the.* You are given a choice of

1. skipping the detection;

2. deleting the second appearance of the word simply by selecting option 2;
3. editing the document; or
4. disabling double-word checking altogether.

Some word processing packages (notably WordPerfect) provide a speller utility to create dictionaries, add or delete words, display the common word list, or check the location of a word. In WordPerfect, you invoke this module by typing **SPELL** followed by <**Return**>**.** The main dictionary is broken up into two components, the common word list and the main word list. By careful selection of the words within these two dictionaries, you can optimize the speed with which searches are conducted, given your vocabulary and frequency of word usages.

ON-LINE THESAURUSES: TERRIFIC

Suppose you reach a point in a document where you wish to avoid overworking a particular word that you may have used several times already. To avoid triteness, you begin by centering the cursor on the word you wish synonyms of. Then you invoke the on-line thesaurus by issuing the appropriate command, and the synonyms are displayed before you on the screen. You select an appropriate alternate word. It replaces the word you requested synonyms of, and you continue with entering or editing the text.

If you are not satisfied with the list of synonyms presented, you can still select the synonym that works best and then request a new search on the newly selected word. This brings up still another list of synonyms, from which an even better word can be selected.

The usefulness of on-line thesauruses derives from the immediacy with which searches are performed. When the command is issued, the list of synonyms is displayed in a window or other portion of the screen. The search requires a fraction of the time and effort that pulling a thesaurus off the shelf and looking up one or more words would require. Moreover, the larger the thesaurus, the richer and more helpful its suggestions will be.

IDEA (OUTLINING) PROCESSORS

In Chapter 5 (the article on "Toward Better Writing and Composition"), we suggested that any extensive writing project should begin with an outline. You may wonder if there is any software to assist in developing an outline. The answer is yes, and the software is called **idea processors,** or **outline processors.**

Idea processors do several things for you. First, they are designed to give you an overview of your proposed writing within the boundaries of a single screen. This is accomplished by exhibiting only major headings and submerging subheadings as necessary to get the entire outline to fit on one screen. Second, they facilitate the fleshing out of each heading and subheading in your outline. The actual paragraphs that make up the content under any heading or subheading can be worked on at random. If, at a later time, you decide to rearrange certain headings or subheadings, the paragraphs and content under that heading or subheading will go wherever you take the heading or subheading. For example, if you are working with the outline displayed on the screen and you move a heading from the beginning to near the end, then the heading and all the textual content you had entered under that heading would also be automatically moved from the beginning to near the end within the document itself. On the other hand, if you were working through the actual text of the document and you used a block move operation to move a subheading and all material under it, then the outline would also be revised automatically for you to reflect the move.

FIGURE 6–9

A Partial Page of Output Using Default Page Settings (MacWrite)

The formula in cell G4 needs clarification. The logical function AND(D4="",E4="") within the IF function tests to see whether both the contents in cells E4 and E5 are null strings — nothing in them (blank spaces are considered zero in Excel and thus are different from null strings). If both cells have nothing in them, then the AND() function returns a logical value "True", and the content right after the first comma, "," will be placed in cell G4 in this case a null string,"", which is exactly what you wanted since you did not make an entry. If either D4 or E4 contain a number or text, then the AND() function returns a logical value "False" and the content or reference right after the second comma will be placed in cell G4, in this case, the formula G3-D4+E4. G3 is the previous balance, D4 the current check amount, and E4 the current deposit amount. Thus,

Current Balance = Previous Balance - Current Check Amount + Current Deposit.

Since each row beyond row 4 signifies a cash outlay — a check or a deposit, the formulas in column G cells should be very similar to each other. Essentially, only the row number changes and the column identifier in the formula remains the same. Instead of reentering each and every formula in G5 through G50 (assuming you don't write more than 47 checks as in this example) you can use a "Fill Down" command in Excel to fill in the formulas.

Saving Formats

Some word processing programs permit the user to define and save frequently used formats independently of the documents themselves. Other word processing programs save the formats with the documents only. Still other programs have no provision for saving user-specified formats, but will retain any document in the format set up at the time the document was created or last updated. The problem with this last approach is this: if the writer changes the format, the entire document must be reformatted. Such is not the case for the first two methods of saving formats. The possibility of *permanently* changing the default settings is provided for in some programs by use of install or setup utilities.

Page Formats

As Table 6–3 suggests, page formats are concerned with margins, page offset, headers and footers, and page length. In many word processing programs, the number of character columns to the right of the left edge of the paper in which the text begins is the page offset plus the left margin. If the **page offset** is 10 (which is the default setting in some word processing programs) and the left margin is set at 10, then text will begin printing 20 columns to the right of the left edge of the paper. However, this is not true of all word processing programs, because some assume only a left margin without a page offset, as was suggested in Figure 6–2.

Different word processors take different approaches to user control of the margins, page, and line length. Some word processors allow the user to control these settings by embedded commands. Embedded commands which control page formatting may be commands starting in the leftmost column with a dot (.); an example appears in Figure 6–10. Other word processors let the user specify these settings by use of a separate screen containing fields for each setting. Just a keystroke or two is all that is necessary to bring up the format control screen, on which the user may make changes to any of the settings shown. Figure 6–11 shows the format control screen used by Microsoft Word. Format control screens may get saved as **style sheets**. Depressing the <Esc> key gets the user out of this mode, and the original text display returns with the cursor in exactly the same position.

```
.he WORDSTAR DOT COMMANDS
.po 9 — a page offset of 9
.mt 7 — a top margin of 7
.mb 6 — a bottom margin of 6 (there are 66 – 7 – 6 = 53 printed lines)
.ps — turns proportional spacing on
.hm 4 — header starts in line 4
.fm 2 — footer starts two lines up from bottom
.fo                              PAGE #
.lh6 — sets line height at 8 lines per inch
```

FIGURE 6–10

Dot Commands Used to Control Page Format (WordStar)

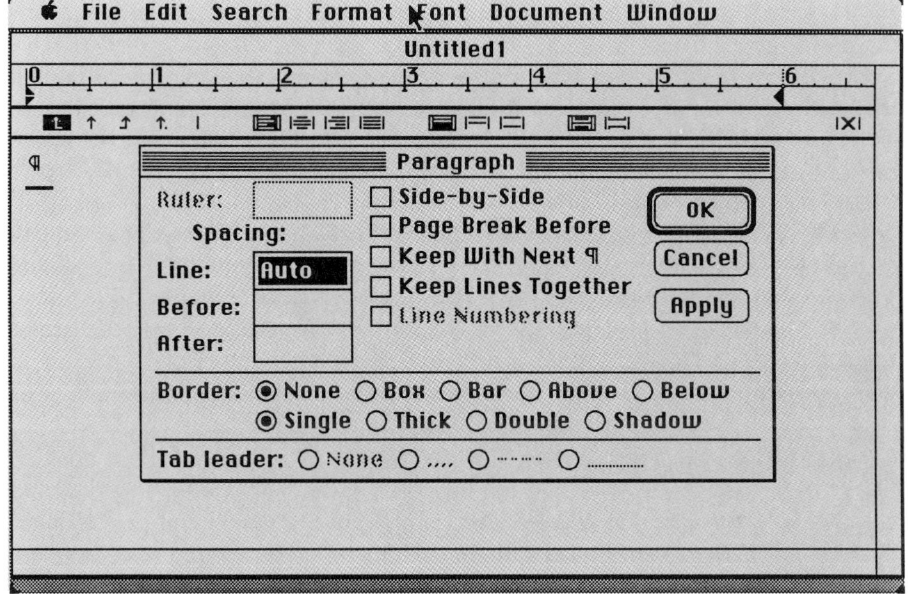

FIGURE 6–11

Microsoft Word's Format Control Screen for the LaserWriter (Macintosh Version)

One great advantage of style sheets as implemented in Microsoft Word is the ability to make changes to the format of a document simply by changing the style sheet. The document, or portion thereof to which the style sheet applies, will be automatically reformatted.

For 8½-inch-wide paper, there are 85 print columns when printing 10 characters per inch. Thus if 10 columns are set aside for both left and right margins, 65 columns are left for printing. This is typical of the default margin and line-length settings of word processors. Again, these are adjustable by the user.

Word processing programs may use a ruler line to specify the left margin, line length, and right margin. The user may adjust the ruler directly or, in the case of programs that provide a format control screen, the ruler may be determined from the user-alterable settings on the format control screen. The ruler line marks the line length, position of the line, and tab settings. The position and length of the ruler line determine the left and right margins. Word processing programs may allow the right margin on the printed page to be determined by the sum of the page offset, left margin, and line length settings. Assume 10 columns per inch and an 8½-inch page. If the page offset is 10, the left margin is 0, and the line length is 65 columns, then the right margin will be 10. Once the user has specified the page offset, left margin, and line length, the right margin is automatically determined as it gets whatever columns remain after the other settings are made.

The same holds true for the top and bottom margins. Once the top margin, the number of lines per page, and the bottom margin are specified, the number of lines in the main body of the printed text have also been determined automatically. At 6 lines per inch, there are 66 lines on any 11-inch piece of paper. Many word processing programs assume 55 lines of text with 6 lines for the top margin and 5 lines for the bottom margin by default. Of course, it is possible to change these, to use different lengths of paper, or to specify eight lines per inch instead of six.

Changing the settings of headers and footers can also be accomplished with special control characters embedded in the text. Other word processing programs use the format control screen to specify margins, page offset, and format controls for headers and footers. Headers print in line 3 or line 4; footers print in line 64 or 65. However, the user can generally control the position and alignment of headers and footers. Some word processing programs offer the option of printing different headers (and footers) on odd- and even-numbered pages. And, multiple-line headers and footers are also offered with some programs.

With many word processing programs it is possible to print page numbers, as well as the date and time of printing, on each page. Many word processing programs will number, date, and time-stamp pages of a document as it is printed, perhaps in a footer. By printing the date and time of printing in a footer at the bottom of a document, it is possible to control the version number of the document better. Page numbers can generally be set to begin with any number; the user generally controls where the page number is printed on the page.

Pagination, the determination of where page breaks occur, can be controlled by the user. However, if not instructed by the user, the word processing program will use its own pagination routine. For example, if the number of printed lines per page is 55, then every 55 lines the program will insert a page break. Unfortunately, this may result in widows and orphans. **Widows** occur when the last line of a paragraph prints at the top of a page. **Orphans** occur when the first line of a paragraph prints at the bottom of a page. Other concerns are a heading that appears at the bottom of a page with no text below it, or a business letter that ends with the closing on a page by itself. This is why the user should do an on-screen check of the page breaks of a document, adjusting them as necessary, before it is printed. Adjustments can be performed by adding/deleting lines between paragraphs, and by inserting page-break control characters. To overcome the problems of widows and orphans, some word processing programs support conditional page breaks. If the remaining section will not fit into the remaining space of a page, the word processing program is told to advance to the next page.

Line and Paragraph Formats

As Table 6–3 suggests, line and paragraph formats are concerned with paragraph indents and outdents, spacing between lines, and spacing between para-

This is single spacing. It is the default setting for most word processing programs. Up to 540 words can appear on an 8 1/2 by 11 inch piece of paper when the line length is 65 and there are 54 lines.

This is double spacing. It is the spacing most frequently used for proposals and manuscripts. It permits up to 270 words per letter-sized 8 1/2 by 11 page.

This is triple spacing. It is used to permit lots of writing between the lines--hence for rough manuscript development. Up to 180 words can appear on a triple-spaced page, roughly.

FIGURE 6–12
Single, Double, and Triple Line Spacing

graphs. Not all word processing programs display the spacing between lines, but all word processing programs support single, double, and triple line spacing when the document is printed, as shown in Figure 6–12.

Character Formats

Character formats are concerned with font, pitch, boldface, underlining, italics, and subscripts-superscripts. Figure 6–13 illustrates typical fonts, and other character formats that are selectable on a word processor which drive the display in bit-mapped mode.

Print Options

Print options include proportional spacing, number of copies of the same document to be printed, which printer to print the document on, starting page number for headers and footers, whether printing is to occur in the foreground or background, and whether or not to print to a disk file. In addition, some word processing programs will query the user for starting page number and stopping page number, or will expect the user to provide these in a special print-document screen.

FIGURE 6–13

Typical Fonts, Pitch, Boldface, etc.

Plain Text Size 12	**Bold Size 12**	*Italic Size 12*	Shadow Size 12	Outline Size 12
Times Roman	**Times Roman**	*Times Roman*	Times Roman	Times Roman
Helvetica	**Helvetica**	*Helvetica*	Helvetica	Helvetica
Courier	**Courier**	*Courier*	Courier	Courier
Σψμβολ	**Σψμβολ**	*Σψμβολ*	Σψμβολ	Σψμβολ
Geneva	**Geneva**	*Geneva*	Geneva	Geneva
New York	**New York**	*New York*	New York	New York

Size 14	**Size 14**	*Size 14*	Size 14	Size 14
Times Roman	**Times Roman**	*Times Roman*	Times Roman	Times Roman
Helvetica	**Helvetica**	*Helvetica*	Helvetica	Helvetica
Courier	**Courier**	*Courier*	Courier	Courier
Σψμβολ	**Σψμβολ**	*Σψμβολ*	Σψμβολ	Σψμβολ

Size 18	**Size 18**	*Size 18*	Size 18	Size 18

Bold & Italic Size 12 ***Bold, Italic, & Shadow Size 12***

Bold, Italic, Shadow, & Outline Size 12

Times Roman Underline, ~~Strikethru,~~ Dotted Underline, Word Underline, SMALL CAP
Double Underline

Background Printing

Background printing refers to the capability of the word processing program to send text to the printer for printing while the user edits, revises, or otherwise enhances the text files with the word processor in the foreground. Without this capability, the printing task will tie up the system, and the user has neither access to nor use of the computer until printing is essentially over. Another way to overcome the problem of having the printing task tie up the system is to use a printer buffer, which can accept a large amount of text at one time so the CPU does not have to continually feed small blocks of text to the printer.

Print Queues

Print queues allow the queueing or chaining of a number of document files that are to be printed in a specific order. Print queues are supported by several word processing programs. The program may sequentially number each page, so that if the last page of the fourth file ends with page 100, the first page of the fifth file in the print queue starts with page 101.

Printing to a Disk File

Some word processing programs permit the user to print a document to a disk file. Print commands are usually interpreted so that if the TYPE command from the operating system prompt is used, the document will appear on-screen pretty much as it would look if printed. The file may then be printed using the DOS directive COPY {filename} PRN.

Printing in Columns

Some programs allow the user to specify that the text be printed in two or more columns, even though the text is ordinarily printed in a single column. Other programs (notably, WordStar) require that text be formatted on-screen into two or more columns if the user wants it printed out that way. To do this in WordStar, the COLUMN MOVE command must be used to move text from the original single-column arrangement into a multiple-column arrangement.

Merge Printing

Merge printing (also called list processing) is used, as suggested in Chapter 5, mostly to create personalized form letters as part of a promotion or solicitation. (Recall the article in Chapter 5, entitled "The Processed Word.")

Two files are required for merge printing: a primary file and a secondary file. The primary file contains the form letter while the secondary file contains the mailing list. Inserted within the form letter are references to specific fields that are included as part of the information associated with each addressee on the mailing list. During printing, these references are used to merge information contained in the mailing list into the form letter. This will cause the line lengths to vary. The word processing software, may, however, reformat the text during printing so that all lines are within their margins.

We return to the Acme Insurance Agency, described in the article on "The Processed Word" in Chapter 5. Figure 6–14 shows an example of a primary file for a letter from Acme Insurance to an addressee on their mailing list.

Next, the user prepares a secondary file (Figure 6–15) containing the list of names and addresses. Using the word processing editor, this file can be prepared in the usual way and in this case is saved under the name list.dat. Each line of the secondary file is a record for an addressee. Each line consists of fields separated by commas; in fact, each field is delimited by a comma that marks the endpoints of the field.

Of importance are the two dot commands .df and .rv that appear at the beginning of the file in Figure 6–14. The .df command defines the secondary file to be used when merging data into the primary file for printing, and is used by the merge print utility. In this case, the file is list.dat. The .rv command defines the names of the fields in the order they will appear in each addressee record within the secondary file. For example, the second field is named LNAME, which is a reference to "Wilson" in the first record, to "Lockman" in the second record, and so forth. Anywhere that the reference &LNAME& is found in the primary file will cause "Wilson" to be substituted when the first personalized form letter is printed, "Lockman" to be substituted when the second form letter is printed, and so forth.

FIGURE 6–14

An Example of a Primary File

```
.op
.df list.dat
.rv FNAME,LNAME,STREETADDRESS,CITY,STATE,ZIP,BDAY

                                   Acme Insurance Company
                                   1 Acme Circle
                                   Ajax, Iowa 70707

          &FNAME& &LNAME&
          &STREETADDRESS&
          &CITY&, &STATE& &ZIP&

          Dear &FNAME&,

               Happy &BDAY&th Birthday!!  You've reached another
          milestone in your life, and perhaps it's time to reflect.
          Are you, &FNAME& &LNAME&, reaching your personal
          financial objectives? Do you sleep at night secure in
          the knowledge that your family will be provided for
          financially should tragedy befall you? Call Dave
          Pinkham or Bob Thomas and let them explain to you how
          Acme's Preferred Whole Life Term Policy can give you
          security now and cash payments to you upon retirement.
          You see, &FNAME&, we at Acme Insurance really care about
          you. Call us today at (319) 412-5161.


                                Bob Reynolds
                                General Sales Manager
.pa
```

FIGURE 6–15

Secondary File Consisting of Addressees' First Name, Last Name, Street Address, City, State, Zip Code, and Age at Next Birthday

```
Ed,Wilson,123 Main Street,Chicago,Ill,60609,25
Jay,Lockman,33568 Gunbarrel Road,Boulder,CO,81125,45
Joe,Martinez,4496 Rural Drive,Logan,UT,87719,33
Bill,Smith,5678 Canyon Road,St. Louis,MO,35547,51
```

Shown in Figures 6–16 and 6–17 are examples of printed form letters for the first two addressee records in the secondary file.

Of Footnotes, Indexes, and Tables of Contents

Some word processing programs support automatic footnoting of documents. The user types the footnotes into the document and places a code in the main text of the document where the footnote is to be referenced. Upon printing of the document, the codes entered into the document are converted to a series of sequential numbers, and the footnotes they refer to are printed on the bottom of the appropriate page. If the document is revised and new footnotes are inserted or old ones deleted, all renumbering and positioning is done automatically.

Acme Insurance Company
1 Acme Circle
Ajax, Iowa 70707

Ed Wilson
123 Main Street
Chicago, Ill 60609

Dear Ed,

Happy 25th Birthday!! You've reached another milestone in your life, and perhaps it's time to reflect. Are you, Ed Wilson, reaching your personal financial objectives? Do you sleep at night secure in the knowledge that your family will be provided for financially should tragedy befall you? Call Dave Pinkham or Bob Thomas and let them explain to you how Acme's **Preferred Whole Life Term Policy** can give you security now and *cash payments to you* upon retirement. You see, Ed, we at Acme Insurance **really care about** *you*. Call us today at (319) 412-5161.

Bob Reynolds
General Sales Manager

FIGURE 6–16

Printed Letter for the First Record in the Secondary File

Acme Insurance Company
1 Acme Circle
Ajax, Iowa 70707

Jay Lockman
33568 Gunbarrel Road
Boulder, CO 81125

Dear Jay,

Happy 45th Birthday!! You've reached another milestone in your life, and perhaps it's time to reflect. Are you, Jay Lockman, reaching your personal financial objectives? Do you sleep at night secure in the knowledge that your family will be provided for financially should tragedy befall you? Call Dave Pinkham or Bob Thomas and let them explain to you how Acme's **Preferred Whole Life Term Policy** can give you security now and *cash payments to you* upon retirement. You see, Jay, we at Acme Insurance **really care about** *you*. Call us today at (319) 412-5161.

Bob Reynolds
General Sales Manager

FIGURE 6–17

Printed Letter for the Second Record in the Secondary File

Focus Feature

DESKTOP PUBLISHING

Call it desktop publishing, personal typography, personal publishing, desktop typography, typesetting with a micro-computer, or whatever, advances in the printer and page composition/typesetting software technologies have brought this capability to the personal computer user. As mentioned in Chapter 3, laser printers are capable of producing near-typeset-quality output, whereas the daisy-wheel and dot-matrix printers are capable of only letter-quality or near-letter-quality output. Today, laser printers costing less than $1,800 make the technology affordable. Still it must be admitted that laser printers with 300-dot-per-inch resolution cannot match the sharp 1,000 or greater dot-per-inch images of high-quality phototypesetters, printing on photographic paper.

Exactly what does it take to get into the personal publishing act, anyway? For starters, you need a laser printer, word processing software specially geared for desktop publishing, a certain amount of patience, and knowledge of the jargon and nature of typesetting and publishing. This last requirement is the theme of this article.

The desktop typesetting software commercially available varies from slightly modified word processors to professional-quality commercial typesetting programs. If your purpose is merely to intelligently operate a laser printer, and that is your sole source of output, then your typesetting software requirements will be minimal. On the other hand, if you intend to send your unprinted, typeset manuscript on a disk to a commercial typesetter in a form that is immediately ready for output, then your software should possess sophisticated typesetting capabilities that are compatible with commercial typesetter's hardware.

Desktop publishing involves more than just turning your text into typeset print, as Figure 6–18 would suggest. It involves the ability to produce high-quality graphics (discussed in Chapter 11), and to lay out each page consisting of graphics integrated with text, a process called **page composition.** To be good at it, you may have to become familiar with graphics, page composition, and typesetting programs, in addition to mastering the centuries-old art of typesetting. Typographic terms like *kerning, tracking, point-size, justification, hyphenation, leading,*

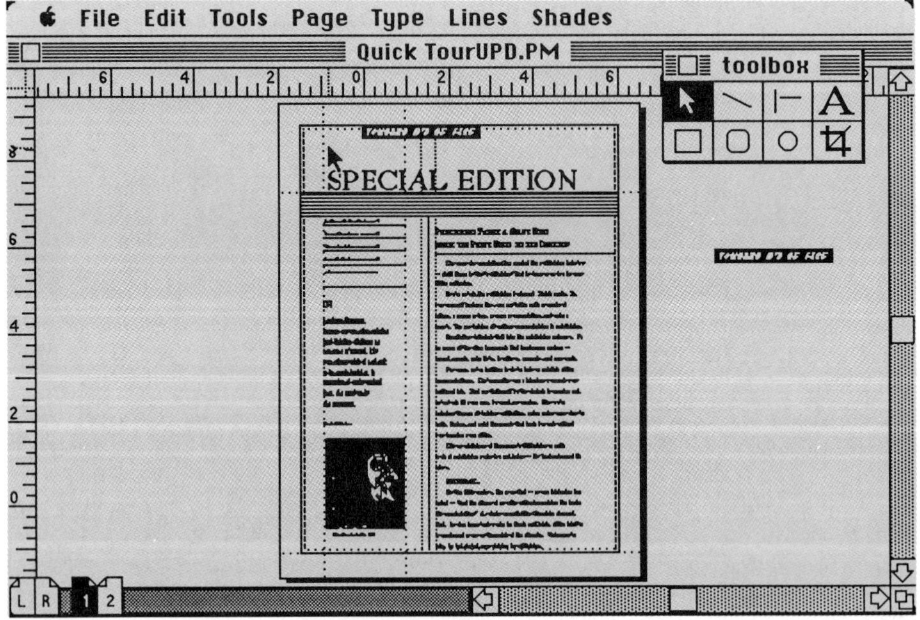

(a)

FIGURE 6–18

Examples of Pages Produced by two State-of-the-Art Desktop Publishing Systems. (a) A Macintosh screen showing a full-page view using Aldus' PageMaker page layout software. (b) The same page printed on a laser printer. (c) A page prepared with Macintosh® Word Version 3.01 for Apple® Macintosh™ systems and printed with an Apple Laser + Writer™.

Chapter 1

The World of Small Computers

Everywhere we turn these days computers can be seen. The checkout person at the cash register runs a bar code across a scanner and a digitized voice tells us we've just spent $1.33 for a loaf of bread. The register then tabulates the total and the same digitized voice comes back to tell us how much we owe.

Elsewhere in the store a cautious shopper zips out a hand held calculator and quickly figures he can save 3 percent by buying coffee at Jiffy-Quick. The calculator probably contains more memory and programmability than the first huge mainframe computers.

Small computers. The concept of microcomputes was born out a need to give people access to the power of a cc nputer in their homes. Texas Instruments' discovery of the silicon based microchip revolutionized the industry. Now components that a few years earlier were measured in feet were now being measured in inches. Now storage components that used to take up a large room were placed on disks that could be easily carried in a jacket pocket. Now computing power that used to require enormous buildings with equally enormous air conditioning units, were placed on people's desks at work or at home. The future had dawned; the future was microcomputing.

IBM, previously the only name in the computer company game in the industry, was threatened by companies with names like Osborne, Tandy, and the Mac. MS-DOS, user friendliness, floppies, icons, and the like added a new dimension to the already dynamic English language.

More and more computer users were not satisfied with what at one time had been the industry standard, the cutting edge of high technology. Now they demanded more. And much to the credit of the industry, it responded. Users were able to access the super powerful mainframes from the comfort of their homes and the comfort of their friendly micros. Poor quality dot-matrix

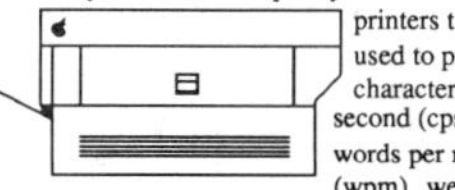

printers that used to print in characters per second (cps) or words per minute (wpm) were replaced by near-typeset-quality laser printers. Those

(b)

Chapter 2

STELLAR OPACITY

Four components make up the opacity, or lack of opaqueness within stars: electron scattering, free-free transitions, free-bound transitions, and bound-bound transitions. This section will demonstrate how to calcuate the mean opacity that these components contribute to.

We must consider two areas in our calculations: (1) the average over all of the radiation frequencies, giving greater weight to those frequencies which have the greatest radiation density gradient. and, (2) the frequency ranges where the opacity is the smallest can sometimes make the greatest contribution to the energy transport, so we would rather average over $1/\kappa(\nu)$ than $\kappa(\nu)$.

Luminosity within the star, $L(r)$, depends on the energy density of radiation $\rho(\nu)$ at frequency ν and temperature T. The complete formulae appear below:

$$U = \int_0^\infty \rho(\nu)\, d\nu = aT^4 \quad \text{and} \quad L(r) = \int_0^\infty L(r,\nu)\, d\nu \qquad [2.1]$$

U, the total energy density, is set equal to the black body energy density. Using $\kappa^*(\nu)$ as the opacity and ν as the frequency, and taking account of stimulated emission, the following formula is possible:

$$\kappa^*(\nu) = [\kappa_{bf}(\nu) + \kappa_{ff}(\nu)]\,(1 - e^{-h\nu/k}) + \kappa_e \qquad [2.2]$$

The *Rosseland mean opacity* can be defined in the following as long the previous relation for κ^* (2.41), and substituting it for $d\rho(\nu)/dT$ is recalled:

$$\frac{1}{\kappa} = \frac{\int_0^\infty \frac{1}{\kappa^*(\nu)} \frac{d\rho(\nu)}{dT} \frac{dT}{dr} d\nu}{\int_0^\infty \frac{d\rho(\nu)}{dT} \frac{dT}{dr} d\nu} \qquad [2.3]$$

The mean opacity favors the frequencies important to the transfer process, by using the energy density gradient $d\rho(\nu)/dr$ as a weighting function for $1/\kappa^*(\nu)$ (which is a measure of the mean free path at frequency ν). The sum of contributions from both bound-free and free-free transitions, and from electron scattering (e) is the opacity at any frequence.

Figure 6-18c. This document was prepared with Macintosh® Word Version 3.01 for Apple® Macintosh™ systems, and printed with an Apple LaserWriter™.

(c)

and *letterspacing* must become well understood. You must learn to wear the hats of the typesetter, designer, and draftsman combined if you are to efficiently carry out this activity within the confines of your computerized electronic drafting, page-makeup, and typesetting table. Clearly, desktop publishing is no casual affair, but the benefits may far outweigh the drawbacks.

Most measurements in typesetting are done in picas and points. A **pica** is 0.166040 inch (about 1/6 of an inch). A pica is in turn divided into 12 points. Thus a **point** is 0.0138366667 inch. Even so, much of the typesetting software lets you work in inches or centimeters if you choose to do so.

One of the first decisions a typesetter must make is choosing the typesize and font of the type. For example, Times Roman is a popular typeface, and 12-point type might be selected. Then the leading must be specified. If 12-point type is set with no leading, then the lines of type are said to be set *solid*. The designation 12/12 is used to

(Continued)

DESKTOP PUBLISHING (Continued)

TABLE 6–4

Definitions of Typography Terms

TERM	DEFINITION
Hyphenation	As in word processing, refers to where words should be broken when the word will not entirely fit on a line. Can be done by use of rules or by use of a dictionary; should be automatic.
Justification	As in word processing, refers to both left and right margin alignment. Left justification usually carries with it the presumption that the right margin is jagged.
Kerning	Software that adjusts the spacing and tightness of letterspacing by giving consideration to the specific letter pairs involved.
Leading	The number of vertical points (of lead in the old typesetting machines) separating lines of type, hence the vertical spacing between lines of type. This is also called linespacing.
Letterspacing	Adjusting spacing between letters and words to justify a line to its margins.
Point size	The selected height of the type from the bottom of the lowest extending character (descender) to the top of the tallest character (ascender).
Tracking	Software that controls the spacing and tightness of letterspacing, regardless of the letter pairs involved.

denote a solid spacing between lines of type. In the early days of typesetting, if more space between lines was desired, the typesetter added thin lines of lead, each a point in thickness. This was (and is) called **leading,** as defined in Table 6–4. Leading increments offered by the typesetting software vary in thickness from a half-point to a tenth-point.

Some word processing programs offer a limited typesetting capability as well as printer drivers for various laser printers. Among them are Microsoft Word and XyWrite III. Other programs, notably PageMaker from Aldus Corp., facilitate page composition. Code-oriented publishing programs may be more powerful than screen-oriented, although screen-oriented typesetting and page-makeup programs let the user visualize what the output will look like and make adjustments to it before it is printed. An inexpensive desktop publishing system might consist of an inexpensive laser printer and one of the word processing programs with typesetting capabilities and laser-printer drivers, and a microcomputer.

CLASSIFYING AND CHARACTERIZING EXISTING WORD PROCESSING PROGRAMS

As mentioned in Chapter 5, word processing programs may be classified as disk-based and memory-based. Disk-based programs may be further classified depending upon whether the word processing software is entirely loaded in memory or whether certain functions and utilities have to be read in to an overlay area from disk before processing of that function can begin. The trend has been toward loading all the necessary software at the time the program is booted, because the

PROGRAM	VENDOR, ADDRESS
DisplayWrite 3	IBM Corporation, Boca Raton, FL 33432
Word	Microsoft Corp., 16011 N.E. 36th Way, Box 97017, Redmond, WA 98073
WordPerfect	WordPerfect Corporation, 288 West Center Street, Orem, UT 84057
WordStar	MicroPro International Corporation, 33 San Pablo Avenue, San Rafael, CA 94903
XyWrite III	XyQuest, Inc., 3 Loomis Street, Bedford, MA 01730
PC Write	Quicksoft, 219 First N. #224r, Seattle, WA 98109
Multimate and Multimate Advantage	Multimate International Corporation, 52 Oakland Avenue, East Hartford, CT 06108-9911

TABLE 6–5

Major Disk-Based Word Processing Programs

PROGRAM	VENDOR, ADDRESS
MacWrite	Apple Computer Corporation (for the Macintosh), Cupertino, CA
PFS:Write and PFS:Professional Write	Software Publishing Company, Mountainview, CA
IBM Writing Assistant	IBM Corporation, Boca Raton, FL 33432

TABLE 6–6

Major Memory-Based Word Processing Programs

greatly expanded memory sizes of the 16-bit processors could easily accommodate the entire program. Doing so made the program faster because the function to be executed did not have to first be loaded into memory. Examples of the former type of operation are the older versions of WordStar. If the user wanted to perform a search and replace, the old versions of WordStar had to first load this function into memory before the actual search operation could begin. The major disk-based word processing programs are listed in Table 6–5.

The other major category of word processing programs is the memory-resident programs. These programs are capable of producing text files whose length is limited by the amount of primary memory available. Once all available memory is used up, the text must be saved to disk and a new in-memory file started. If the user is writing a document whose length must necessarily be longer than the memory available, the document must be spread over several files.

Increasing competition among vendors of word processing programs has created a major features war. Standard word processing features have been augmented by inclusion of built-in spelling checkers, thesauruses, keyboard macros, and outline processors, as well as built-in math functions, tutorials, extensive on-line help facilities, and text sorting (of a bibliography, say).

Descriptions of a few major product offerings among word processing packages are provided below. We reserve discussion of WordStar for the tutorial at the end of this chapter. All the offerings mentioned below support various printers and displays. An **install program**, with which the user selects the appropriate printer driver and screen driver for his or her system, must be executed before using these programs. Install programs come with the various packages and usually allow the program to be customized to the user's needs, including specifying to the word processing system the characteristics of a printer for which no explicit printer driver is included.

Microsoft Word

Microsoft Word is certainly a full-featured word processor, with more features than most of the offerings. It supports a wide variety of printers; newer versions provide typesetting capability and support for laser printers. It can be used in a menu-driven mode or in a command-driven mode, and it can be used with a mouse. Versions exist for both MS-DOS (PC-DOS) and the Macintosh. The Macintosh version is considered among the most powerful and versatile for that machine.

Microsoft Word has an extensive windowing capability, which allows the user to simultaneously display different pages of the same or different documents. In this way, text from two different locations can be easily compared, or text can be moved from one location to another. Version 3.0 allows up to eight different windows to be open at one time.

Microsoft Word's real power is in its ease of formatting and its devotion to almost perfect precision in the printed document. Formatting is almost automatic: it formats the entire document file at once, simply by attaching a format file (or style sheet) to the document file. It provides several preset format files and also permits users to completely design their own. Since it is less expensive than most of the other offerings and is available to the student at a substantial discount, it appears to be an excellent choice for students. The Microsoft Word enter/editing display is shown in Figure 6–19 below.

WordPerfect

WordPerfect versions 4.1 and following have received rave reviews in the literature. It is very fast, full-featured, and requires fewer keystrokes to accomplish each task than most other word processing programs. It is entirely menu-driven,

FIGURE 6–19

(a) The Enter/Edit display of Microsoft Word for the Macintosh. (b) The Page Setup display of Microsoft Word for the Macintosh.

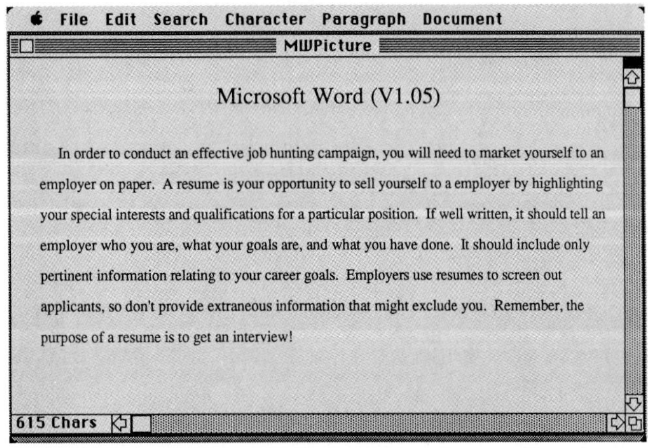

(a)

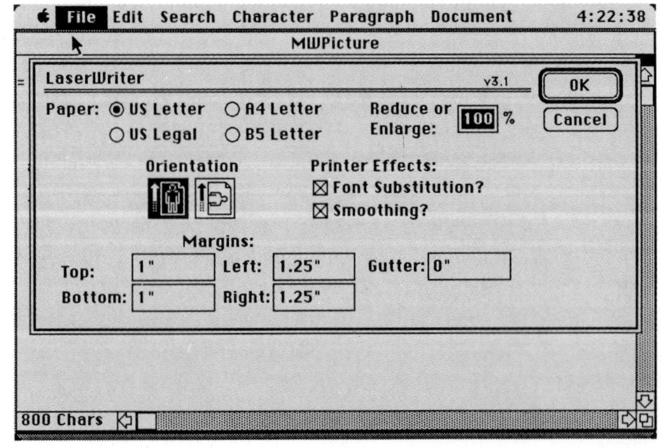

(b)

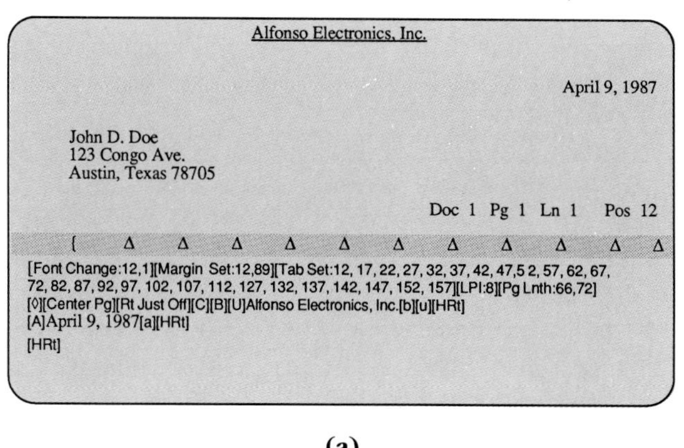

(a)

Printer Control

1 - Select Print Options
2 - Display Printers and Fonts
3 - Select Printers

C - Cancel Print Job(s)
D - Display All Print Jobs
G - "Go" (Resume Printing)
P - Rush Print Job
S - Stop Printing

Selection: 0

Current Job

Job Number: n/a
Job Status: n/a
Message: The print queue is empty

Page Number: n/a
Current Copy: n/a

Job List

Job Document Destination Forms and Print Options

Additional jobs not shown: 0

(b)

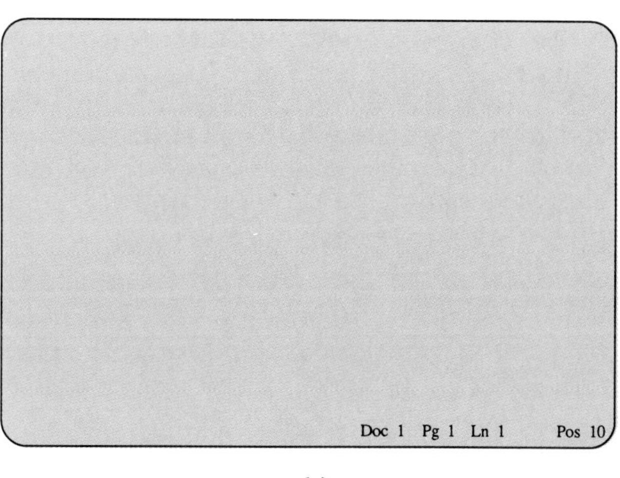

(c)

FIGURE 6–20

(a) The reveal codes display of WordPerfect. (b) The printer control screen of WordPerfect. (c) The entry/edit screen of WordPerfect.

with 40 function keys (F1–F10 combined with the Alt, Shift, and Ctrl keys) and their submenus. And it has one of the largest dictionaries, with over 100,000 words, which can be added to by the user. It has an extensive keyboard macro capability, with which macros can invoke still other macros. Like Microsoft Word, it supports footnotes, multi-window displays, and automatic reformatting of edited paragraphs.

WordPerfect has several interesting displays, including its reveal codes display, its page format menu, and its entry/edit screen (shown in Figure 6–20). Its uncluttered entry/edit screen is considered a plus. No menus are displayed, because these are included on the function key template.

Multimate Advantage

Multimate was first developed to mimic the Wang dedicated word processor, which had a rather large user base. As a result, Multimate caught on rapidly. Mul-

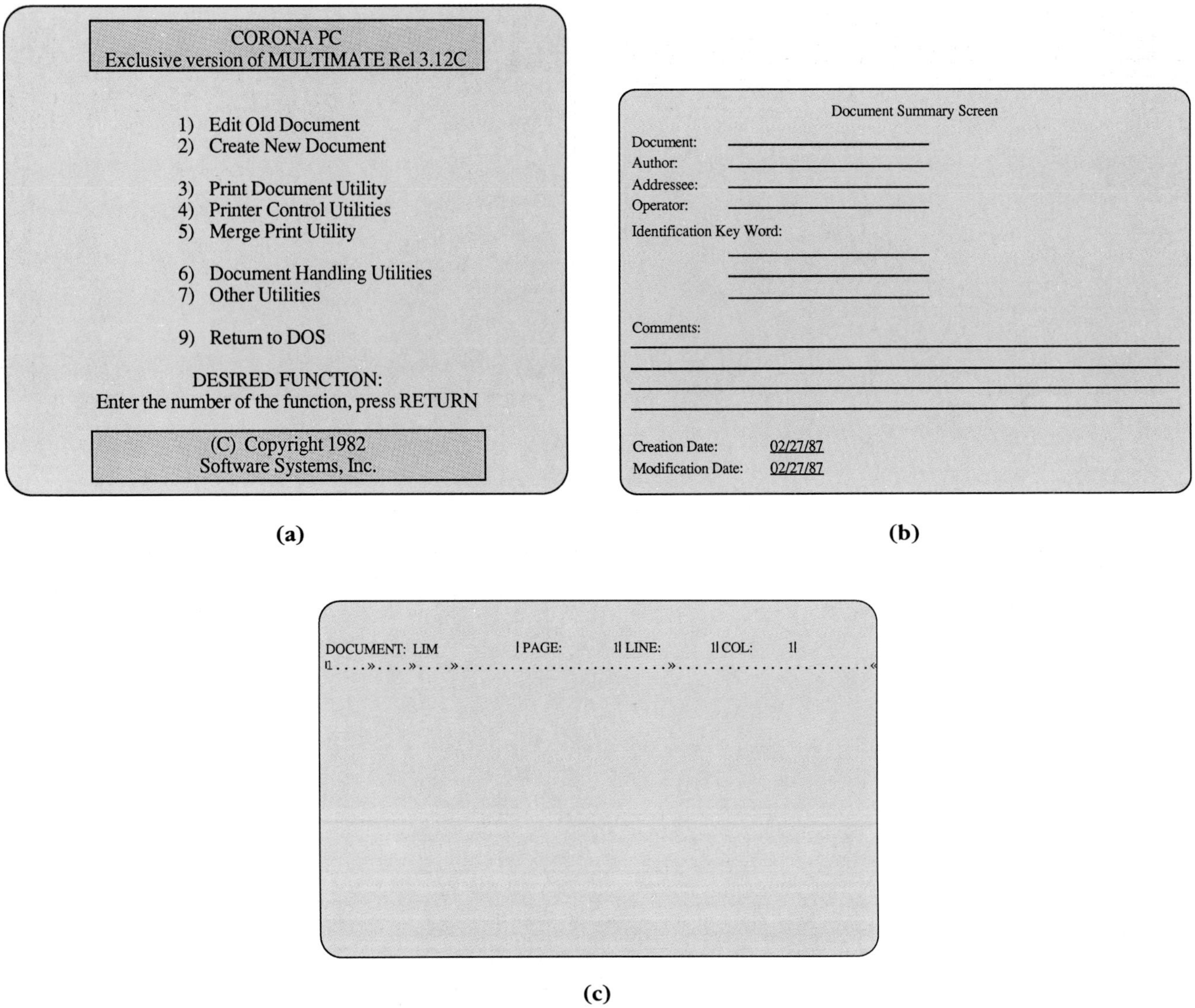

CORONA PC
Exclusive version of MULTIMATE Rel 3.12C

1) Edit Old Document
2) Create New Document

3) Print Document Utility
4) Printer Control Utilities
5) Merge Print Utility

6) Document Handling Utilities
7) Other Utilities

9) Return to DOS

DESIRED FUNCTION:
Enter the number of the function, press RETURN

(C) Copyright 1982
Software Systems, Inc.

(a)

Document Summary Screen

Document: ____________
Author: ____________
Addressee: ____________
Operator: ____________
Identification Key Word:
____
____
____

Comments:
____
____
____
____

Creation Date: 02/27/87
Modification Date: 02/27/87

(b)

DOCUMENT: LIM | PAGE: 1| LINE: 1| COL: 1|

(c)

FIGURE 6–21

(a) The Multimate main menu. (b) The Multimate document summary sheet. (c) The Multimate entry/edit screen.

timate has since been upgraded to Multimate Advantage, which overcomes most of the shortcomings of the earlier offering.

Multimate Advantage is driven by the main menu, shown in Figure 6–21. Like WordStar, Multimate uses a status line and a rule line at the top of the document edit screen. Associated with each document is a document summary screen, containing the name of the document, the name of the author, and comments about the document's content, as shown in Figure 6–21. The document summary also contains the creation date and the date of the last update, which are both automatically entered by Multimate.

PC Write

PC Write is a disk-based, command-driven program that is quite fast and has an abundance of features. Its most remarkable attribute is its marketing strategy.

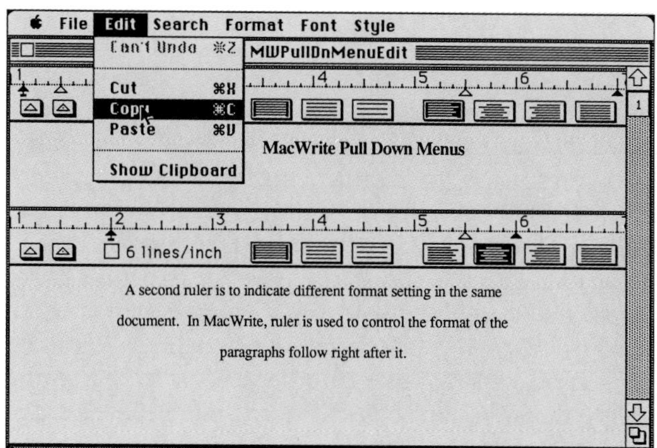

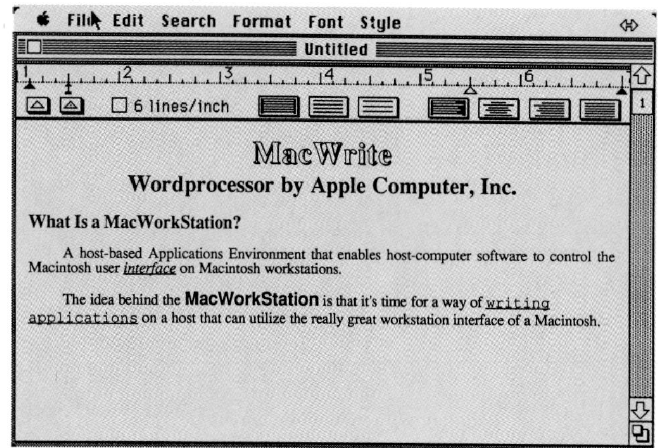

FIGURE 6–22

(a) The MacWrite pull-down menus. (b) The MacWrite entry/edit screen.

PC Write is **shareware**, which means it can be freely distributed. Avid users of PC Write can become registered users for a nominal fee that entitles them to support, a manual, and upgrades. The program makes extensive use of the function keys for its commands, and is comparatively easy to use; for example, the <F1> key brings up the Help screen. In view of its low cost and ease of use, PC Write is an excellent product for students.

MacWrite

MacWrite is a memory based, menu-driven program for the Apple Macintosh. It is designed to be used with a mouse and makes extensive use of pull-down menus. The mouse is used to select (or invoke) commands from the menus, and to mark the cursor position on the display. Menus are "pulled down" from the top line of the display by pressing and holding the mouse button down when the cursor is on the desired item on the menu bar. The associated menu is then pulled down by MacWrite. Still holding the mouse button down, the user drags the cursor (via the mouse) over the desired submenu item and selects the item by releasing the mouse button. Each menu item or subitem is highlighted as the cursor is dragged over it. This is shown in Figure 6–22.

Summary

This chapter has described in detail the myriad mechanical details of word processing programs. Beginning with the screen display, its function and form, the chapter explained how to use the screen display to maximum advantage. The usage and purposes of split screens and windows were discussed. The chapter also described how the appearance of a document on-screen was likely to differ from the printed version.

Next, the printed page was considered. The differences between the printed page and on-screen displays were described. The general terminology of the printed page was defined. Regardless of the hype about the "paperless" office, printed matter has become more important and more profuse with the advent of the microcomputer. The quality of printed matter has improved drastically as a direct consequence of the move toward desktop publishing.

The chapter then turned to the mechanics of typing, editing, and revising text. Procedures for navigation within a document were discussed at length. Cut-and-paste capabilities were considered in the subsection, "Block Manipulation." Most block operations require the user to mark the beginning of the block, mark the ending of the block, move the cursor to the desired position, and insert the desired operation. The insertion versus typeover modes of operation were explained. The ability to reform a paragraph after it has been edited was described in detail.

Still other topics concerned with entering and editing text were covered, such as the "Find and Replace" capability, which allows the user to search for every occurrence of a word or phrase and to replace that word or phrase with another. Also described were keyboard macros, which allow the user to define a key to be a long phrase that is likely to appear many times in a document. By use of the <Alt> key and some other key, the long phrase is called up and displayed at the cursor position on the screen, and is thereby entered into the document. Possible uses for libraries of paragraphs were also considered.

Next, the chapter discussed at some length the mechanics of formatting and printing text. All word processing programs have default format settings that specify page length, margins, line length, and so forth. Two methods customarily used by word processors for altering these settings were described: embedded commands and format control screens. Some programs save the format control settings in a separate file, while others may save the settings along with the document itself. Still others do not save the settings at all; instead, they save the document itself in the format specified by the settings. It was discovered that while some of the settings were concerned with page format, others were concerned with line and paragraph formats, and still others were concerned with character formats.

The chapter went on to describe print routines and the various options they offer. Most word processing programs support background printing, enabling the user to continue editing in the foreground. Some programs support print queues, in which a sequence of files is to be printed off with pages numbered sequentially. Some programs allow the user to print to a disk file so the file can be printed later without using the special print utility. Printing in columns is supported either by formatting the document in columns or by directing the print routine to print the file in columns.

Automatic footnoting, indexing, and generation of tables of contents supported by some programs were then described. Special utilities are included for each of these purposes. For example, the WordStar indexing program is able to create an index file consisting of all underlined words and phrases and their associated page numbers. Desktop publishing was then discussed at length in an article by the same name.

The chapter ended with a section that characterized and classified existing word processing software.

Key Terms

background printing
block manipulation
boilerplate
bottom margin
font
idea processors
indents
install program
leading
left margin
library
line
line length
macro

merge printing
number of lines to print
orphans
outdents
outline processors
page composition
page length
page offset
pagination
pica
point
print queue
right margin
ruler line
scrolling
shareware
space
spacing
status line
style sheets
toggle
top margin
typeface
widows
word wrap

Self-Test

1. Describe what is meant by document navigation. Describe two ways in which document navigation may be accomplished.
2. Of the insertion/typeover modes, which is used for editing text? Which is used for entering text?
3. Describe what is meant by block manipulation.
4. Describe how paragraph reforming may be accomplished.
5. List the ancillary functions of word processors (we have called these functions enhancers.) Briefly describe the utility of each.
6. Describe what hardware and software is needed to support desktop publishing.

Exercises

1. Of the terms listed above, which are concerned with line and paragraph format control?
2. Of the key terms listed previously, which are concerned with page format control?
3. Explain what actions taken by the user will cause the screen to scroll. Describe the scrolling action in detail.
4. Describe what windows and split screens are used for. How are they different?
5. Explain how a block move or copy is accomplished when the maneuver is to be accomplished within a single document.
6. Explain how a block move or copy is accomplished when the maneuver is from one document to another, and the word processor program can open several documents at one time.
7. Explain how a block move or copy is accomplished when the maneuver is from one document to another, and the word processor program can open only one document at a time.
8. Describe two ways in which page format control can be accomplished.
9. List all of the print format attributes, and indicate which of these are likely to be displayed on-screen.
10. For each of the print format attributes you listed in the exercise above, indicate, as best you can, what the default format settings are likely to be.
11. Describe what a ruler line is used for.
12. What is the relationship between line length, left margin, right margin, and number of columns in the page?

13. What is the relationship between page length, top margin, bottom margin, and lines of print?
14. Explain why personal desktop publishing involves a substantial time commitment if it is to be fully used.
15. Define the following terms used in desktop publishing.

    hyphenation
    justification
    kerning
    leading (linespacing)
    letterspacing
    pica
    point
    point size
    tracking
16. Compare, feature by feature, three disk-based word processing programs.
17. Compare, feature by feature, three memory-based word processing programs.
18. Reread the article on "Of Macros and Shorthand" and describe another way in which the same sort of efficiency can be accomplished without the use of macros.

Additional Reading

Ditlea, Steve. "Word Processing." *Personal Computing* 10, no. 10 (October 1986): 73–77.

Felici, James, and Ted Nace. "Typesetting Point by Point." *PC Magazine* 4, no. 6 (July 1986): 170–81.

Knorr, Eric, and Robert Luhn. "Personal Publishing in Black and White." *PC World* 4, no. 6 (July 1986): 182–88.

Winkler, Connie. "Desktop Publishing." *Datamation* 32, no. 23 (December 1986): 92–96.

Wiswell, Phil. "Word Processing: The Latest Word." *PC Magazine* 4, no. 17 (August 20, 1985): 110–35.

WordPerfect 4.2 User Manual. Orem, Ut.: WordPerfect Corporation (288 West Center, Orem, Ut. 84057), 1986.

WordStar Professional Release 4. San Rafael, Calif.: MicroPro International Corporation (33 San Pablo Avenue, San Rafael, Calif. 94903), 1979 and 1987.

TUTORIAL

WordStar

PRELIMINARIES

For this tutorial, we will assume that WordStar has already been correctly installed. In order to run WordStar, you need a computer with two disk drives, a formatted diskette for data, and a WordStar program diskette.

The WordStar program disk must be placed in disk drive A (this is the drive on the left in side-by-side configurations, or on top if the disk drives are stacked). The data diskette should be placed in drive B. Once the computer has been turned on, you should have an operating system command prompt, either A> or C>. At this point you should assure yourself that the WordStar files are indeed present in drive A. This is done by entering **DIR**. While you are at it, make certain that the disk in drive B is formatted and has enough unallocated space to contain your files. In MS-DOS or PC-DOS, this is accomplished by typing **DIR B:**. You will need less than 4,000 bytes free to complete this tutorial.

In this tutorial, we will follow the outline established earlier in Chapter 5.

1. Create the document.
2. Enter the text.
3. Edit the text.
4. Save the document.
5. Print it out.

A few conventions will be followed in this tutorial. The <Control> key (to the left of the letter *A*) will be indicated by the "^" symbol. For example, if the tutorial asks you to enter **^PS**, this means, "hold the <Control> key down with one finger and simultaneously enter a 'P', and an 'S'." Also, the <Return> (or <Enter>) key will be indicated by <**CR**>. In this tutorial, the response that you enter will be in boldface. Messages generated by WordStar are not boldfaced. WordStar Professional Release 4 differs from version 3.3 in some respects (different function key definitions, for example). We will point these out.

CREATING A DOCUMENT

The first step you must take is to load WordStar into primary storage as follows.

A> **WS<CR>**

(Continued)

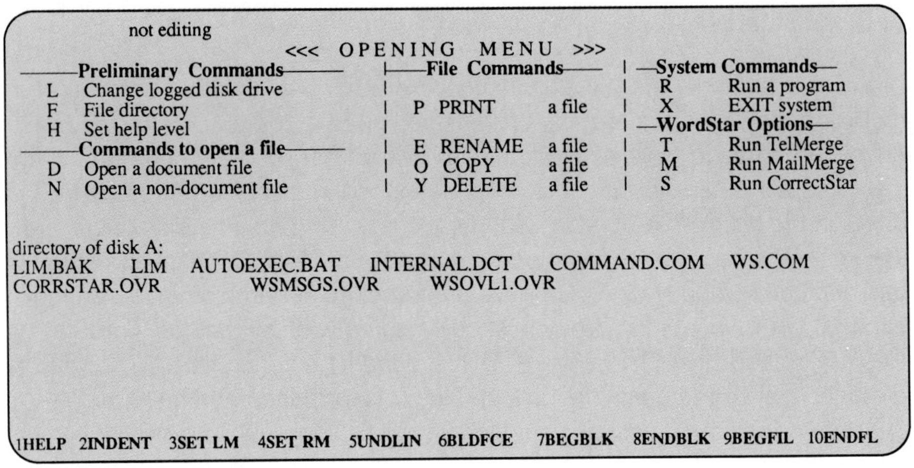

WordStar (Continued)

FIGURE 6–23
WordStar 3.3 Opening Menu

```
              not editing
                          <<<  O P E N I N G   M E N U  >>>
 ----Preliminary Commands----      |----File Commands----   | --System Commands--
   L   Change logged disk drive    |                        |   R      Run a program
   F   File directory              |  P  PRINT     a file   |   X      EXIT system
   H   Set help level              |                        | --WordStar Options--
 ----Commands to open a file----   |  E  RENAME    a file   |   T      Run TelMerge
   D   Open a document file        |  O  COPY      a file   |   M      Run MailMerge
   N   Open a non-document file    |  Y  DELETE    a file   |   S      Run CorrectStar

directory of disk A:
LIM.BAK     LIM    AUTOEXEC.BAT    INTERNAL.DCT     COMMAND.COM    WS.COM
CORRSTAR.OVR             WSMSGS.OVR         WSOVL1.OVR

1HELP  2INDENT  3SET LM  4SET RM  5UNDLIN  6BLDFCE  7BEGBLK  8ENDBLK  9BEGFIL  10ENDFL
```

After a brief delay, the opening menu will appear on your screen, looking like that shown in Figure 6–23. Take a moment to look at the options available to you. (If you are not working on an IBM or IBM-compatible computer, the bottom row of function key definitions will not appear.)

At this point, we want to change our logged disk to drive B. Type **L**, followed by **B**<**CR**>. This means that all "text" files will be found or stored on drive B. A listing of the files on the disk in B should appear immediately below the menu.

WordStar has two types of files you can create, listed in the lower left of the menu. The non-document mode (N) does not wrap words, and is useful for writing computer programs. All characters are standard ASCII characters so they can be recognized by a compiler. Select **D** to open a document file. When asked for the name, enter **MUSIC342**<**CR**>. Release 4 of WordStar will respond with

```
"Can't find that file. Create a new one (Y/N)?"
```

Your response should be **Y**.

ENTERING A DOCUMENT

You have a new menu, shown in Figure 6–24, and the cursor is on the first line of your text area, awaiting input. On the left side of the menu are

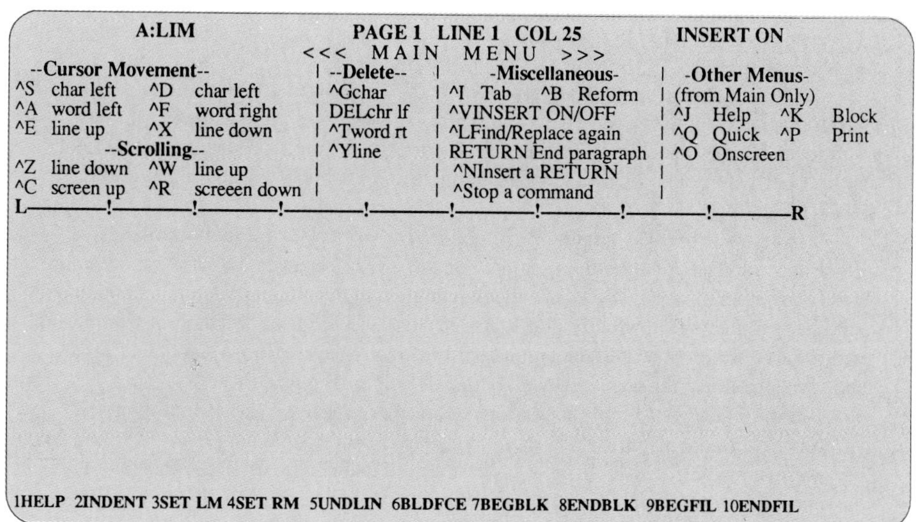

FIGURE 6–24
WordStar 3.3 Main Editing Menu

several commands that can be used to move the cursor around in the text. For simple left, right, up, and down movement, the arrow keys will accomplish the same thing as ^S, ^D, ^E, and ^X. Note that you may also move a word or screen at a time. ^G will delete the character at the cursor and shift the remainder of the line to the left. ^- deletes characters to the left of the cursor; this function can also be accomplished by using the ^ and <BackSpace> keys. Release 4, like most word processors, uses <BackSpace> to delete characters to the left of the cursor, and <Del> to delete the character at the cursor.

A few cursor movements and deletion options are not shown on this menu. ^QR and ^QC move you to the top or bottom of a file, respectively. ^Q- deletes to the beginning of a line, while ^QY deletes to the end of the line.

On the right is a listing of other menus available. You might want to browse through them before entering your document. Of particular interest will be the ^J menu, which accesses a fairly extensive help file. To view a menu without using any of its commands, enter ^ plus the letter of interest. When done, press the space bar or <**ESC**> key.

Now we begin to type. Enter the text listed in Figure 6–25. *Do not press* <**Return**> at the end of each line, only between paragraphs. Do not worry about errors, since we will correct mistakes in the next section.

While you enter text, look at the status line at the top of the screen. It will tell you the current line and column of the cursor. At the upper right, you are

(Continued)

WordStar (Continued)

FIGURE 6–25

Sample Text Arnold Schoenberg (1874–1951)

Arnold Schoenberg (1874–1951)

Arnold Schoenberg, "the twelve-tone man," has played a major role in the development of contemporary musical thought. Although his compositions were not well received in his lifetime, Schoenberg's theories, teaching, and the attention gained by his pupils Berg and Webern have made him the most important musician of the modern era.

His early work was largely romantic, but by World War I it had become dark, mysterious, and decidedly unharmonious. As his music began to depart more and more from conventional works, Schoenberg found a need to develop a structure and theory to serve as a framework for future development. His 1921 lecture, "Method of Composing with Twelve Tones," became the springboard for many later writings (including Style and Idea) that form the basis for twelve-tone or polytonal music theory.

Born into a poor family in Vienna, Schoenberg received early training on the violin but could not afford formal musical training. By the time he was in his teens, he was performing with small chamber orchestras and had composed entire symphonic movements for orchestra.

Schoenberg's best known work, Transfigured Night, is a remnant of his earlier romantic period. As if sensing that his novel ideas would gain more prominence from teaching than from his composition, his later years were devoted to instructing young musicians and writing essays on music. After leaving Nazi Germany in 1933 (although converted to Catholicism, he was Jewish-born), he held teaching posts at the University of Southern California and UCLA. In his lifetime, he profoundly influenced the music of Alban Berg, Anton von Webern, Gustav Mahler, and Igor Stravinsky.

informed that you are operating in the insert mode. To change to overwrite mode, enter **^V** or press the <**Ins**> key. The <Ins> key and ^V are toggles.

If your copy of WordStar has not been modified, your text will be *justified,* spread out between columns 1 and 65, and will not appear on-screen exactly as it does on this page. We can always correct this later, so do not erase any of the spaces created in the justification process.

EDITING THE TEXT

Let's have some fun with our text. To begin with, *unharmonious* (second line, second paragraph) is, perhaps, not the best word we could have selected. Let's replace it with *dissonant.* Now, there are several approaches to making this change, and for the sake of becoming familiar with WordStar, you are encouraged to try all of them.

METHOD 1: Move to *unharmonious,* erase, insert *dissonant.*

Step 1. Use the <**up arrow**> key to scroll upward to the line.

Step 2. Use the <**right arrow**> key to move just past *unharmonious*.

Step 3. Press the **^-** key until the word has been deleted (Release 4 requires that you use the <BackSpace> key).

Step 4. Type **dissonant**.

That was easy enough, wasn't it? Now let's try a few other methods. Leave *dissonant* in place and we'll change it back to *unharmonious* (it will eventually wind up as *dissonant*). Move the cursor to the end of the file (with arrow keys) before you begin.

METHOD 2: Same approach, using different functions.

Step 1. Enter **^R** twice to move up two screensful. You can also do this by pressing the <**PgUp**> key on the keypad twice. If you are at the highest help level and did not press <**CR**> at the end of the text, the cursor should be on the same line as the target word. If you aren't, use the arrow keys to get there.

Step 2. Press **^F** until the cursor arrives at the beginning of our target word. The cursor will be over the letter *d*.

Step 3. Enter **^T** to delete the word.

Step 4. Type **unharmonious.**

Our second method is clearly faster, but more difficult to remember. This is generally true of WordStar. With extended use comes the knowledge of faster ways to edit your text. Try experimenting with the cursor movement commands below. When you are done, move the cursor to the end of the file to start method 3.

Up one screen	→ ^R or <PgUp>
One word right	→ ^F
To beginning of line	→ ^QS
To beginning of file	→ ^QR
Down one screen	→ ^C or <PgDn>
One word left	→ ^A
To end of line	→ ^QD
To end of file	→ ^QC
Move cursor to top of display	→ <Home>
Move cursor to bottom of display	→ <End>

(Continued)

METHOD 3: Find the target word and change it.

Step 1. Type ^**QR** to go to the beginning of the file.

Step 2. Enter ^**QF** to access the Find function.

Step 3. Type **unharmonious**<**CR**> in response to WordStar's prompt, `Find?`. Press <**CR**> for `Options?`.

Step 4. We should now be at the beginning of our word. Press ^**G** until the word has been erased.

Step 5. Type **dissonant.**

Text Movement From looking at the text in Figure 6–25, it is apparent that some rearranging is in order. The second paragraph should probably be the third, and vice versa. To correct this problem, we will do the following:

Step 1. Move the cursor to the beginning of the second paragraph (at the left margin, not the first word). Select any method you want to get there.

Step 2. Type ^**KB** to mark the beginning of a block of text.

Step 3. Move the cursor to the beginning of the next paragraph, or one space past the end of the text to be moved.

Step 4. Type ^**KK** to end the block. The <B> at the beginning of the paragraph should disappear and the entire block will either turn dim, appear in inverse video, or change color, depending upon your monitor.

Step 5. Move the cursor to the left margin at the start of the last paragraph. This is where our second paragraph will go.

Step 6. Enter ^**KV.** Voila! Our text is now in proper order, and we can get it ready to do some formatting. If you want, you can "unmark" the block with ^**KH,** but it will not affect anything if the block remains marked. Since WordStar does not save the block markers in a file, they cannot print out.

Centering, Underlining, and Bold Print Before we print our text, we should do a few things to help its appearance. Specifically, we will center the essay title, underline the book title *Style and Idea,* and put Schoenberg's major work, *Transfigured Night,* in boldface print.

Step 1. ^**QR** to move to the top of the text.

Step 2. ^**OC** will center the text.

Step 3. Move the cursor to *Style and Idea,* near the end of the third paragraph.

Step 4. ^**PS** to begin underlining. Your screen should show ^S before *Style.*

Step 5. Move to the end of *Idea.* Your cursor will be on the right parenthesis.

Step 6. ^**PS** to tell the printer to stop underlining.

Step 7. Move the cursor to *Transfigured Night* in the first line of the last paragraph.

Step 8. ^**PB** to start boldface print. You will see ^B.

Step 9. Move to the end of *Night,* over the comma.

Step 10. ^**PB** to end boldface print.

Margins, Double Spacing, and Reformatting The paper is starting to look a bit better, but it is too wide and should be double-spaced. In order to have a 1½-inch margin on the left and 1 inch on the right, we should only print a 6-inch line of text. At 10 characters per inch, our right margin should be 60. We could adjust our left margin to 15 (1½ inches) and our right to 75, but there is an easier method. With a *dot command* (an embedded command that begins with a period in the first column), we can control the printer to offset (indent) the page by 15 characters. However, we must still adjust the right margin to shorten our lines. Dot commands will also be used to set the top and bottom margins. Once margins are fixed, we will set the line spacing to 2 and change the entire document to fit our new format. This last step, called *reformatting,* is important whenever changes are made that alter the length of a line. Inserting or deleting words will create a line of text that is either too long or too short for our margins. Reformatting will adjust our text from the cursor location to the end of the paragraph.

Step 1. ^**QR** to get back to the beginning of our paper.

Step 2. **.MT9<CR>** This stands for Margin, Top, 9. At 6 lines per inch (normal spacing), this is 1½ inches.

Step 3. **.MB6<CR>** Six lines, or one inch at the bottom.

Step 4. ^**OR60** sets the right margin at 60.

Step 5. ^**OS2** sets it to double spacing.

Step 6. Move to the beginning of the first paragraph.

Step 7. ^**OJ** turns justification off to obtain a ragged right margin. Many people prefer this format.

(Continued)

Step 8. **^B** will reformat the paragraph to our new margin and linespacing settings. Repeat this for each paragraph. In the third paragraph, reformatting will be stopped by the hyphen help. The word *including* will not fit easily on the line, and might leave too much space if wrapped onto the next line. The hyphen help asks us if we want to hyphenate the word at the cursor location. The choice is yours. To break the word, enter – (dash or minus). To send it to the next line, enter **^B.** Hyphen help can be turned off completely by entering **^OH.**

SAVING YOUR WORK

If you are satisfied that your work is in the form you want it, we can now save it. In WordStar, you save a document by entering

^KD

At some later time, you may wish to make further changes to this document. To do this, merely enter your old filename (**MUSIC342** <**CR**>) when you select **D** (open a document file) from WordStar's first menu. If you then make changes and save the file with ^KD, WordStar will rename your original document as MUSIC342.BAK, and save the new one to MUSIC342. This backup system serves as protection against editing errors and disk problems. If you inadvertently delete a large portion of text, you will still have your most recently saved version of the document in a backup file.

Periodically saving the work as you enter it is a good habit to develop on any word processing system. WordStar allows you to save the document without exiting, by entering ^KS. After saving, you can return to your place in the text by typing ^QP (required in versions 3.3 and earlier only).

If for some reason you do not wish to save your file, you can quit with ^KQ. Any previously saved versions of the text will remain intact on the disk.

WordStar always saves a file under the name you used to open it. Occasionally, this is not appropriate. For example, you may be editing a previously saved file and make a great number of changes. You like the current version, but you also want to keep the old one around without having to deal with backup files (they must be renamed before they can be edited in version 3.3). The best alternative would be to save the current text under a different name, but WordStar does not allow this. Using a simple trick, it can be accomplished.

Simply mark the entire file as a block (place **^KB** at the beginning and **^KK** at the end). Then enter **^KW** to write the block out to a file. When asked for a file name, enter the name for your newly created second version. Then quit (**^KQ**) the current session. No backup version will be made, so the original version will not be disturbed. The opposite of ^KW is ^KR, the FILE READ command. With this command you can pull other files into the file currently being edited, which allows you to work with small portions of a document in separate files and later to combine them into a single file.

PRINTING YOUR FILE

When the document has been saved, you are returned to the main menu. Pressing **P** will begin the printing process. WordStar will ask for the name of the file to be printed. Enter **MUSIC342**. You can go immediately to printing by pressing <**ESC**>, or you may wish to look at some print options by pressing <**CR**>.

WordStar 3.3 print options allow you to (1) print your file to a disk, rather than the printer; (2) print only a portion of your file by specifying the beginning and ending pages; (3) have your printer control formfeeds, or page ejects (WordStar normally controls these); (4) print out your dot commands with the text, rather than act upon them; and (5) have the printer pause between pages for use with single-feed sheets rather than fanfold paper. These options may be useful at some time, but for the present, press <**CR**> in response to each one.

Congratulations. You have just created a document with a word processor. WordStar, as you can see, is relatively easy to learn for creating, entering, saving, and printing a simple document. It is the editing and formatting features of WordStar that may be difficult to master. They also give WordStar the power and flexibility required by professional writers, academics, and word processing professionals. We have only touched the surface of commands available to the WordStar user. To learn about more commands, go through the help menu (available only from the editing menu inside a document in version 3.3), or consult either MicroPro's WordStar manuals or one of the many books written on using WordStar.

EXERCISES

1. WordStar develops a "scratch" file as you enter text. What implications does this have on required disk capacity when working with large files? Does this qualify WordStar as a program that automatically saves?

(Continued)

2. Develop a mnemonic system for WordStar functions and commands, as if you had a key definition program. How would you handle assignment of such items as superscript and subscript commands that might contend for the same key?
3. WordStar allows you to set up to ten place markers in your text by entering **^K0** through **^K9**. Once they are set, you can move automatically to the correct marker by typing **^Q1**, **^Q2**, etc. How could you use the combination of place markers and block moves to rearrange an outline? What other uses can you think of for place markers?
4. Under what circumstances would you use the "disk file output" option on WordStar's print menu?
5. As is apparent from the tutorial, WordStar allows a great deal of latitude in the methods used for correcting text. Considering the difficulty of learning some of these methods, is this wise? Would a simpler system be better? Why or why not?
6. Experiment with the formatting commands on the sample text from our tutorial. Adjust the margins and reformat the document, both with and without the hyphen help feature.
7. Try using the column block move in WordStar. You switch the block commands to column mode with **^KN**. Next, reformat our sample text (beginning with the first paragraph) with a right margin of 35, then set the right margin to 80. Mark a block beginning at the start of the first line on the second page (you must find the page-break marker). Move to the last line on the second page, place the cursor in column 36, and enter your end-of-block marker. Now move to column 40 of the first line of text (not the title) on the first page, and issue the block move command. What type of documents might require this function?
8. Just for fun, reformat the first page of the document after completing exercise 7. What happened? Why did this occur?
9. Enter the form letter shown on the left side of the first article in Chapter 5 (entitled "The Processed Word"). Change the names and addresses in the text several times. Practice this in both the insert mode and the overwrite mode. Which do you prefer? Now try using Find and Replace. Is it easier? Turn in all of your work.
10. Use a version of WordStar containing merge-printing (list processing) capabilities to actually implement the merge print example described in the main body of this chapter.
11. Write a tutorial for using the on-line thesaurus of WordStar Release 4.0.

DISK EXERCISES

1. Use the file REFORM.DOC on your exercise disk to reform the document contained in the file REFORM.DOC with a left margin at 8, a right margin at 72, and double spacing. The first line should begin in column 6 and the last line should end on or before line 60. The right margin should also be ragged (^OJ). Save the result on your own diskette and then print the file. (Recall that margin settings consist of a page offset specified by the dot command .PO N, where N is the columns to the right of the left edge plus the on-screen left-margin setting.)

2. Use the file MISSPELL.DOC to search for and replace all of the misspelled words in the document. You may do this with or without the use of a spelling checker. If you choose not to use a spelling checker, you must manually look up all words that are suspect, check their spelling, and then use global search and replace to correct all misspelled words of that type. Save the result on your own diskette and then print the file.
3. Use the file ENTER.DOC to enter the following text at the end of the document.

    Word processing programs are one of the great time-savers and money-savers for students going through college today. With word processing programs, students can prepare papers more rapidly and at less expense than previously. Prior to low-cost word processing, students had to carefully write each paper and then either type it themselves or hire a typist to type it at some expense to them. Today students can prepare their papers as they research the content that goes into them, save their work, and return to it later for further refinement and polishing. Misspellings and typographic errors are less likely because of the ease with which these can be detected and corrected.

    Now reform the entire document to fit within left and right margins of 15 and 70. Double-space the document with justified left and right margins. Save the document on your own diskette and print the document.

TUTORIAL

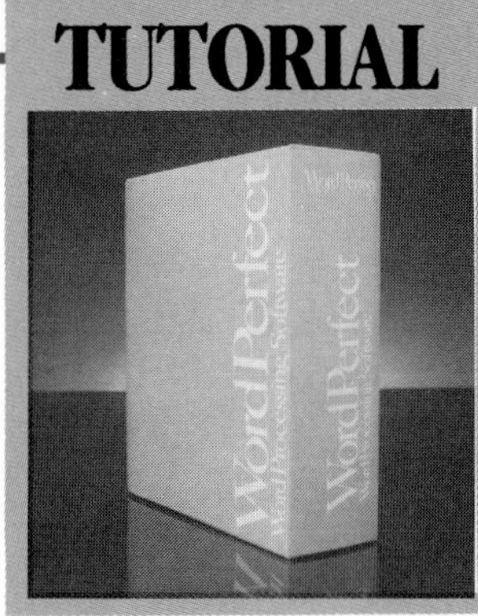

WordPerfect*

GENERAL INFORMATION

WordPerfect is generally considered to be among the front-runners in new-generation word processing software. Version 4.2 of WordPerfect to be described here leaves little to be desired in a complete word processing program. It is a powerful and relatively easy to use screen-oriented word processing system.

Although WordPerfect software is available for many popular computers and operating systems, this tutorial is specifically concerned with the MS/DOS version, which operates on the IBM PC and compatibles. Minimum system requirements are 256 Kbytes of memory, two disk drives, and DOS version 2.0 or later. WordPerfect 4.2 comes on a formidable six diskettes (5¼″ double-sided, double-density or equivalent higher-density media), of which two are dedicated to the support of some 270 different printers. After the initial setup of printers, the working system will require four diskettes in order to access all available features of the software, including an extensive help facility. At least one additional data diskette is necessary for saving documents separate from the program files.

Many other files may be on each diskette. These are usually related to specific printer setups, the on-line tutorial, or other files created by the WordPerfect system for housekeeping.

The instructions in this tutorial will assume that you will be using WordPerfect on a dual floppy system. If you have installed WordPerfect on a hard-disk system, the program will operate the same except that you will not be required to switch diskettes.

To start WordPerfect, place the WordPerfect diskette in drive A (the left or upper disk drive) and enter **A:WP** at the operating system prompt (usually an `A>`). After a brief period, you should see the WordPerfect copyright notice and after a few more moments, a blank screen with the message `Doc 1 Pg 1 Ln 1 Pos 10` in the lower right corner (if your copy of WordPerfect has been modified, the `Position` indicator may be a value other than ten). This message indicates that the cursor is now in document number one, on page one, line one of the typing area, ten spaces from the left edge of the printed page. This blank screen can be thought of as a clean sheet of paper, just

*Anderson, Mickey R. "WordPerfect Tutorial," Term Project. Lubbock, Texas: Texas Tech University, 1987.

rolled into a typewriter. WordPerfect is now ready for you to type a new document or retrieve and edit a previously saved document.

The syntax conventions that will be followed in this tutorial are as follows:

Named keys on the keyboard will be shown inside angle brackets. Examples: <Ctrl>, <Shift>, <Alt>, <Home>, etc. Function keys will be shown as <f1>, <f2>, etc. You may need to refer to your system manual to determine the location of some named keys, such as <Tab>, <Backspace>, and the arrow keys <Left>, <Right>, <Up>, <Down>.

A hyphen will be placed between any two keys that must be pressed simultaneously. Example: <Ctrl>-<Rtrn> indicates that the Control key should be pressed and held while the return (or enter) key is pressed.

A comma will be placed between named keys that must be pressed in sequence (one after the other). Examples: <Home>,<End> indicates that the Home key should be pressed once and released, then the End key. <Ctrl>-<Home>4<Rtrn> indicates that the Control and Home keys should be pressed simultaneously, then the four key, then the return key.

If a key is available in two places on the keyboard, and their functions are differentiated by WordPerfect, then a comment such as (numeric) will indicate which is to be used. Be sure to use only the top row of keys for entry of numbers, and press the <NumLock> key once if the Pos indicator in the lower right corner of the WordPerfect screen is flashing. Other special cases will be explained in the tutorial as necessary.

Before you begin using WordPerfect you should commit at least one command to memory. This is the CANCEL command. It is involved with the <f1> function key on all versions of WordPerfect from 4.0 on. Earlier versions used the <Alt>1 key sequence, and later versions also honor this entry. CANCEL can be used to interrupt most commands before serious damage results from an unintentional keystroke. You may also exit from menus and prompts without making a selection. The latest versions of WordPerfect also use the <cancel> key to UN-DELETE the most recent two deletions made in the document.

CREATING A DOCUMENT

If you have not already done so, start WordPerfect as described above. At the blank screen, WordPerfect has already created an empty document for

(Continued)

you. The document is unnamed until you save the document to disk or attempt to exit WordPerfect.

ENTERING A DOCUMENT

Text is entered at the current cursor position. The arrow keys are generally used to move the cursor to the position on the screen where text is to be entered; however, the cursor cannot be moved past the end of the document. The space bar, <Return> key, or any other character key will cause the cursor to move within, or expand the boundaries of, the document. After text is entered, the arrow keys will move the cursor anywhere within the text area of the document.

Enter the text in Figure 6–26 exactly as shown. Use the <Return> key only at the end of each paragraph. Don't worry about any typing errors you make, because you will see how to correct these in the next section.

FIGURE 6–26

Sample Text The Old English Sheepdog

The Old English Sheepdog

The Old English Sheepdog, or Bobtail, is well suited as a family pet, with the breed's only disadvantages being a profuse coat to maintain and an insatiable desire to keep the family "herded up" with occasional nips at the heel.

The exact origins of the Old English Sheepdog are something of a mystery, with similar breeds developing in countries as far away as Russia and Ireland. It is generally believed, however, that the modern breed came from Sussex, England about 200 years ago.

As wild wolf packs and other roaming predators became less numerous, smaller, more agile and intelligent sheepdogs were adopted to help with rounding up and moving the sheep herds. The Old English Sheepdog soon became a popular herding breed. The Old English Sheepdog's physical resemblance to the sheep is sometimes credited with making the herds less nervous. And certainly, the Old English Sheepdog's somewhat casual disposition helps in keeping the herd calm. Although considered a reasonably large dog by today's standards, the Old English Sheepdog completely retains its gentleness, intelligence and instinctive herding ability.

As you enter the text, notice the status indicators in the lower right of the screen. The line number and position of the cursor are given as you type. When the cursor passes position 75, the current word is automatically wrapped to position 10 on the next line down. This is because the unmodified WordPerfect program defaults to a left margin of 10 with a 65-character print line. Do not be concerned if your text does not wrap at the same position as that in the sample document, since we will adjust the margins in the next section.

EDITING THE TEXT

Use the arrow keys to move the cursor back to any typing errors. Use the delete key <**Del**> to erase each incorrect character, then retype the corrections. Notice as you press <Del> that the text moves in to fill the empty space and the correction spreads the surrounding text. Even if you made no typing errors, try deleting and replacing a few letters anyway.

If you are using a version of WordPerfect less than 4.1, you may need to rewrite (reformat) the text on your screen after any significant changes. Check in your user's manual for the location of the <Rewrite> key. Later versions of WordPerfect automatically rewrite the screen text as the cursor moves through it, however you may use the SCREEN command, <Ctrl>-<f3>,<Rtrn>, to rewrite the whole screen without moving the cursor.

If your copy of WordPerfect has been modified to use margins other than 10 left and 74 right, your text may not have wrapped in the same places as that in the sample text. Move to the top of the document with <**Home**>,<**Home**>,<**Up**>. Use the LINE FORMAT command, <**Shift**>**-**<**f8**>, to view the menu. Select item 3, Margins. You should be prompted `[Margin Set] xx yy to Left =,` where xx and yy are the current left and right margins. Enter **10**<**Rtrn**>**74**<**Rtrn**>**.** This should set the margins to 10 and 74 until they are changed again within the document. Use the <Rewrite> key to adjust the margins on the screen, if necessary.

Press the insert key <**Ins**>. Notice the message in the lower left of the screen: `Typeover.` This indicates that new text will type over, rather than squeeze into, existing text in the document.

Move the cursor to the beginning of the word *generally* in the seventh line of the text (ninth line of the document). With typeover turned on, type in **commonly** and press <**Del**> once. Now let's put *generally* back with

(Continued)

another method. Turn typeover off by pressing the <**Ins**> key a second time. Be sure the cursor is somewhere in the word *commonly.* Press <**Ctrl**>-<**Backspace**>, then type **generally** . Be sure to include the space at the end.

WordPerfect provides many methods of moving the cursor other than with the arrow keys. Some of the most common are listed in Table 6–6. Experiment with some of the cursor movement commands. The commands involving page moves will function correctly only if multiple pages exist in the document, so the cursor will remain on the single page of our sample text.

Another means to move the cursor is with the use of WordPerfect's <Repeat> key. First move to the end of the sample document by using <**Home**>,<**Home**>,<**Down**>. If you did not press <Rtrn> at the end of the text (if your cursor is immediately to the right of the last period), then press <**Rtrn**> now. Press the <**Esc**> key. You should see the n = 8 indicator in the lower left corner of the screen. Press the **4** key, then the <**Up**> key. The n = 8 should have changed to n = 4, then disappeared from the screen. This should have positioned the cursor exactly four lines up from the end of the text. The <Esc> key will repeat almost any movement command (and many other commands) the specified number of times. The default of eight may be changed by using <Esc>*n*<Rtrn> where n is the number you wish to

TABLE 6–6
Cursor Movement Commands

MOVEMENT	KEY SEQUENCE
Character/Line	<One of four Arrow Keys>
Word Left/Right	<Ctrl>-<One of left or right Arrow Keys>
Edge of Typed Area on Current Screen	<Home>-<One of four Arrow Keys> (May be repeated to go to next screen)
Top/Bottom of Current Screen	– or + (numeric keypad only)
End of Current Line	<End>
Top of any Page #	<Ctrl>-<Home>,page number,<Rtrn>
Top of Current Page	<Ctrl>-<Home>,<Up>
End of Current Page	<Ctrl>-<Home>,<Down>
Top of Previous Page	<PgUp>
Top of Next Page	<PgDn>
Top of Document	<Home>,<Home>,<Up>
End of Document	<Home>,<Home>,<Down>

Note: <Up> and <Down> are references to the up and down arrow keys.

change the default to. The repeat key can then be used by pressing <Esc>, then issuing any cursor movement command.

By using the SEARCH commands, WordPerfect will move the cursor to any position where a specified text string is found. WordPerfect allows forward or backward searches using <f2> or <Shift>-<f2>, respectively. To demonstrate, move the cursor to the beginning of the sample text with <**Home**>,<**Home**>,<**Up**>. From this position we will locate all the occurrences of *Old English Sheepdog* in the sample text. Begin by pressing <**f2**> to bring up the prompt `-> Srch:` . The right-pointing arrow indicates that this will be a forward search. Enter the text string **old eng**, then press <**f2**> again to begin the search. WordPerfect will always match lowercase letters to lower- or uppercase, but uppercase are matched only with uppercase. To repeat the search, press <**f2**> and WordPerfect will display the search prompt and the default search string. Press <**f2**> again to repeat the same search. To edit the default search string, press one of the arrow keys before any other key. The `^X` wild-card character (analogous to the Dos ? character in file names) is also available. To enter `^X` into the search string, you must use <Ctrl>V<Ctrl>X. The `^X` wild card will appear in the search string in bold print in order to distinguish it from the "^X" string.

A REPLACE command (<Alt>-<f2>) is available, but should be used with some care. The prompt `w/confirm? (Y/N) N` is provided to prevent unwanted replacement throughout the remainder of the document. REPLACE can be used in a forward direction from the current cursor position only. For example, our sample text contains redundant use of the term *Old English Sheepdog.* Changing every occurrence of *Old English Sheepdog* to the term *Bobtail,* after its definition in the first line, could be accomplished by the following:

<Home><Home><Up>	Move to the beginning of the document.
<f2>bobtail<f2>	Move to the text "Bobtail".
<Alt>-<f2><Rtrn>old english sheepdog<f2>	Invoke replace command, accept default of replace without confirm, and enter the search string.
Bobtail<f2>	Enter replacement string and begin replacement throughout remainder of document.

Text Movement We will use the MOVE command to move the first paragraph to the last paragraph position. First, position the cursor anywhere within the first paragraph. Press <**Ctrl**>**-**<**f4**> to see the menu at the bottom

(Continued)

of the screen. Choose option 2, `paragraph`. The first paragraph should be "highlighted" as the current paragraph, and a second menu should be available. Option 1, `cut,` means that WordPerfect will remove the selected text (a paragraph in this case) and hold it in a buffer so you can retrieve it at a later time. Press **1** now. To retrieve the paragraph, place the cursor at the location where the text is to be inserted, the end of the document in our case. Now use the MOVE command <**Ctrl**>**-**<**f4**> again and select option 5, `retrieve text`, by pressing **5**. The restored paragraph should now be after the others.

Only one cut is available at a time, so don't try to make several and paste them all back at once. The other two move options, `sentence and page`, operate identically to the paragraph move.

Another move procedure involves the use of the BLOCK command. This allows movement of any block of text which may not be adequately described as a sentence, a paragraph, or a page. The block move procedure is similar to the regular move except block mode must be toggled on and the desired segment of text identified to WordPerfect before issuing the MOVE command.

To demonstrate the block move, we will put the document back in original order by moving the first two paragraphs as a block. First, move the cursor to the beginning of the first paragraph. Be sure to move to position 10, since we want the paragraph indentation moved also. Toggle block mode on with <**Alt**>**-**<**f4**>. You should see the message `Block on` flashing in the lower left of the screen. Notice the block highlighting as you begin moving the cursor to the end of the second paragraph. To ensure that the carriage return character (probably not visible on your screen) is moved with the block, position the cursor over the first character in the line *after* the second paragraph. The block will include everything up to, but not including, the current cursor position.

If your block does not appear to be highlighted correctly, you must toggle block mode off (<**Alt**>**-**<**f4**> again) before correcting the original cursor location. As a convenience, the block may also be marked by starting at the end of the desired text and moving the cursor toward the beginning.

When you are satisfied with the highlighted block, and before toggling block mode off, invoke the MOVE command (<**Ctrl**>**-**<**f4**>). The move menu is changed slightly for block mode, but option 1, `Cut Block`, will accomplish the task at hand, so press **1**.

To retrieve the cut text, the procedure is identical to the paragraph retrieve performed previously. After setting the cursor at the desired location (at the end of all the text), use the following key sequence: <**Ctrl**>**-**<**f4**>**5**. The document is now back in original order.

Text Appearance Centering titles, underlining, and boldfacing the print can be used to improve the appearance and readability of the printed text. First we will see how WordPerfect accomplishes these functions during text entry, then we will learn how to apply them to previously typed material.

WordPerfect provides toggle keys which are turned on to begin the function(s), and then turned off to resume normal text. To illustrate their use, move the cursor to the end of the sample text with <**Home**><**Home**> <**Down**>. Press <**Rtrn**> once to separate the previous text, then enter the line below. As you press each of the named keys, notice the cursor location and the `Pos` numerals in the extreme lower right of the screen. In some manner, depending on the type of monitor you are using, the numerals change to indicate when underline and bold are toggled on.

> <**Shift**>**-**<**f6**><**f8**><**f6**>**This line is centered, underlined, and boldfaced.**<**f6**><**f8**><**Rtrn**>

Even though several functions were used on the line, you may have been able to tell which key(s) invoked each function. The CENTER command, <Shift>-<f6>, began centering the text, and continued until the <Rtrn> key was pressed. Next, the UNDERLINE command, <f8>, was toggled on and continued until the next <f8> was entered. Finally, BOLD was started with <f6>, and continued until <f6> was pressed again. Of course, each of these functions may be used independently or in any other combination.

WordPerfect also has available the FLUSH RIGHT command, which is invoked with <Alt>-<f6>, and terminated with a <Rtrn>. It would make little sense to mix this with the CENTER command, so WordPerfect honors whichever is turned on first. You may, as with CENTER, mix FLUSH RIGHT with UNDERLINE and/or BOLD.

The example just given describes methods of changing text appearance *only* during text entry. In order to apply the Underline and Bold functions to existing text, we must define the text to be modified as a Block, just as we did in the "Text Movement" section above. When you have highlighted the appropriate section of text using the BLOCK command, and while the `Block on` message is flashing in the lower left of the screen, simply press the appropriate key to perform the desired modification. If the operation automatically cancels block mode, the <Go To> key, <Ctrl>-<Home>, can be used to re-highlight the block for multiple operations.

(Continued)

WordPerfect (Continued)

To try out the process, we can underline and boldface the title of the sample text. First move to the beginning of the document, then turn block mode on with <Alt>-<f4>. Pressing the <End> key should move the cursor to the end of the line and highlight the title. While the block-on indicator is flashing, UNDERLINE <**f8**>, will underline the highlighted block and turn block mode off automatically. To boldface the same block, simply turn block mode back on, press the <Go To> key twice (<**Ctrl**>**-**<**Home**>,<**Ctrl**>**-**<**Home**>), then press BOLD, <**f6**>.

The CENTER and FLUSH RIGHT commands applied to existing text do not require the block function, unless you wish to center or flush right a group of lines. To center the title of our sample text, move the cursor to the first letter of the title. It will be necessary to move the cursor to the extreme left until the Pos marker is neither bold nor underlined. This extra movement is required because of the hidden control codes in the document, which are discussed in the next section. With the cursor positioned under the *T,* press CENTER, <**Shift**>**-**<**f6**>. The cursor should move to the center of the screen, and push the title too far to the right. The title will center itself as soon as you move the cursor away from the current line. Flush right positioning works in exactly the same manner, except the CENTER command is replaced with FLUSH RIGHT, <**Alt**>**-**<**f6**>.

Text Formats WordPerfect inserts control codes in the document to indicate when a certain change should be made in the document as it prints or in the way it is displayed on the screen. With the exception of setting the margins of the sample text, our document has used WordPerfect's default settings of line spacing, tab settings, and many others too numerous to cover in this tutorial. Before discussing the methods of setting document formats, we will look at the manner in which WordPerfect changes these formats, and how to change or correct an incorrect format setting.

The control codes are not displayed on the normal screen so our text can be viewed in a format as close to the final printed text as possible. WordPerfect has supplied the REVEAL CODES command, <Alt>-<f3>, which allows us to see and manipulate these codes.

To see some of the codes, move the cursor to the top of the sample text and press <**Alt**>**-**<**f3**>. You should see a normal section of text in the top half of the screen, and the text with control codes displayed in the bottom half. The control codes appear in bold text and are surrounded by square brackets. If you reset the margins of your document earlier in the tutorial, you should see the `[Margin Set ...]` code. You should also see the codes used for centering, underlining, boldfacing, and the `[HRt]` and `[SRt]` codes. Notice the `[C]` code. This causes the title to be centered. In the previous section, it was necessary to move the center code beyond the margin set. If REVEAL CODES had been used, it would have been easy to tell how to position the cursor at the beginning of the text line. The `[HRt]` code indicates a Hard Return, and appears everywhere the <Rtrn> key was pressed. The `[SRt]` is the code used by WordPerfect to wrap each line as it reaches the right margin. You will be unable to delete Soft Returns and some other codes inserted by WordPerfect.

The cursor can be moved in the reveal codes screen as usual; however, you will not be able to position the cursor directly under any character or code. You may delete the character or code to the immediate right of the cursor with the <Del> key or to the left with the <Backspace> key. When *any* printing key is pressed while you are at the REVEAL CODES screen, you are returned to the normal text screen.

Viewing the codes on the screen is usually helpful when you wish to delete a setting. For example, to change an underline to normal text, move the cursor next to either the [U] or [u] code and use <Del> or <Backspace>. To change the margins back to the default (or those set by an earlier margin adjustment), locate the code and delete it.

The block mode may be used while in the REVEAL CODES screen to mark an exact block of text and codes. This enables you to copy some, but not all, of the codes, such as margin and tab sets (described below), to another part of the document. Without this capability, you would have to manually enter these functions each time a change was desired.

The search capability may be used to find the codes contained in your document, and the replace facility can change many of these codes. The codes are entered into the search or replace strings by pressing the keys that activate a particular code.

You may display a tab ruler at the bottom of the screen by using the SCREEN command, <Ctrl>-<f3>, and selecting option 2, `Window`, from the menu. Set the window to 23 lines to display the ruler.

Setting a window from 2 to 20 lines results in a second document, `Doc 2`, being partially displayed in the lower portion of the screen. The <Switch> key, <Shift>-<f3>, moves the cursor between the two documents. You may also use the <Switch> key to change to the second document before splitting your screen. Doc 2 is always available in addition to (or instead of) Doc 1. The MOVE command is used to easily copy text between the two documents.

(Continued)

WordPerfect (Continued)

The <Block> and <Switch> keys may also be used together to convert a block to all upper- or all lowercase letters. To capitalize the title of the sample text, first move to the beginning of the title. Turn BLOCK on (<**Alt**>-<**f4**>) and mark the title as the desired block. Press the <Switch> key and select option 1 to convert the block to uppercase, then turn Block off (<Alt>-<f4>).

Option 4, `Spacing`, on the LINE FORMAT menu is used to select the spacing set to be used in a document. The value (1 for single, 2 for double, etc.) sets the spacing on screen as well as at the printer. The line spacing may be changed as often as desired within the document.

The PRINT FORMAT command, <Ctrl>-<f8>, is used to select the various fonts and pitches available with your printer. Underline styles and right margin justification can also be selected. WordPerfect always displays text on-screen with an unjustified (ragged) right margin, regardless of the settings. A Preview option is available to view justified text on-screen from the Print menu; <Shift>-<f7>, option 6. Printing the document will be discussed in a later section.

One other formatting command is available, the PAGE FORMAT command, <Alt>-<f8>. Like the PRINT FORMAT commands, these options affect only the printed document. These optional features include headers, footers, page numbers, and page break controls.

SAVING THE DOCUMENT

For this section, you must place a data disk in a drive other than the one containing the WordPerfect disk. The instructions will assume this drive is B:.

WordPerfect provides an easy method to save the work periodically. The <Save> key, <f10>, prompts for a file name or presents a default of the last name used to save the document. Press the <**Save**> key and respond to the prompt with **B:SHEEPDOG.WP**. Your document will be saved on drive B: and the cursor returned to its previous position in the document. If you have previously saved a document in the current WordPerfect session and wish to overwrite the prior copy, you may press <Rtrn> at the `Document to be Saved:` prompt, and respond with a `Y` to the `Replace ...? (Y/N)` prompt.

The EXIT command, <f7>, is used to exit a document (and WordPerfect). WordPerfect always asks if you would like to save the current document and issues a message if the text has not been modified since the last

SAVE. If another document is in use, the cursor is placed in that document; otherwise you are given the opportunity to exit WordPerfect, continue editing the current document, or begin a new document.

WordPerfect's RETRIEVE command is <Shift>-<f10>. This is used when a new document is brought in from disk, or when a document file is to be included in the current document. The command is the same in either case, depending on whether the current document is clear.

An alternative to the RETRIEVE command is the LIST FILES command, <f5>. LIST FILES will retrieve a disk file in addition to providing much information about the file and the disk it resides on. You must indicate which drive (and path) WordPerfect is to use after issuing the command, and then a directory of all files in the directory is displayed. At the top of the screen, along with information about the current document and the selected disk, a highlighted bar will indicate "current" directory. This bar may be moved among the listed files, like a cursor, and any of the menu options at the bottom of the screen will apply to the highlighted file.

PRINTING THE DOCUMENT

WordPerfect provides two general methods of printing a document. One is printing from the screen, the other is printing a disk file. The screen print is somewhat wasteful in disk space and time required, because WordPerfect must create a temporary file in order to print. The disk file print method avoids creation of the temporary file, but does not reflect changes made to the document since the last save. Both options can be selected from the PRINT command, <Shift>-<f7>. Options 1 and 2 will print the document on screen, either the full text or the current page. Option 4, `Printer Control`, allows printing of the most recent save of the current document, or any other file. Both print methods allow editing during printing, with WordPerfect giving the keyboard operator precedence over the printer during conflicting computer tasks.

OTHER WORDPERFECT FEATURES

Additions to many of the more powerful word processors are the spelling checker and thesaurus. WordPerfect 4.2 includes both of these capabili-

(Continued)

ties plus an extensive on-line help facility. All are relatively easy to use, and are started by temporarily replacing the *data* disk with the Speller, Thesaurus, or Learn disk. The command keys required to access each of the functions are <Ctrl>-<f2>, <Alt>-<f1>, and <f3>, respectively.

The spelling checker provides options for checking words, pages, or the document. When the speller locates an unknown word, the word in context is highlighted and a list of possible replacements is offered. A menu at the bottom of the screen also allows a word to be skipped once, skipped for the rest of the document, added to a supplemental dictionary, edited, or allows you to "look up" another possible spelling.

To look up words in the thesaurus, position the cursor in the word before starting the search. Alternatively, you may type in a word at the `Word:` prompt while the thesaurus is running. After an initial word is supplied, certain suggested synonyms may be selected for further searching. Columns of words are built on the screen for each successive look-up. The cursor movement keys are used to switch between columns and scroll the columns. Words may be automatically replaced by available synonyms contained in the columns.

The help facility is used by typing either a letter corresponding to the first letter of a topic or command, or by pressing the WordPerfect command key associated with starting a command. Pressing the <Help> key again from within the help facility displays the function key layout and names of each command associated with the 40 <Ctrl>, <Shift>, <Alt>, and <fn> key combinations.

Many of the most powerful features of WordPerfect 4.2 have not been mentioned in this brief tutorial. Included in this category are the merge and math/column functions, which provide the software package with fairly extensive file management and math capabilities. The package also supports footnote and endnote editing and positioning as well as automatic generation of tables of contents, lists, and indexes. A macro generation facility can be used to permanently or temporarily store complex or frequently used commands and keystrokes. Macros may be chained, allowing the software to be programmed to automate many routine functions or to be used effectively by inexperienced users.

WordPerfect is an extremely flexible word processor that is readily learned with the aid of the keyboard template. Its power grows as the experience of the user grows. When you become comfortable with the basic commands and procedures covered in this tutorial, experiment with the vast array of editing enhancements, and with the data base and spreadsheet capabilities covered in the WordPerfect manuals.

EXERCISES

1. List several ways multiple document editing might be advantageous in producing a single final document.
2. Type a hyphenated word in a WordPerfect document. Use the REVEAL CODES command to see the results. Why does WordPerfect treat hyphens differently than ordinary characters? What is meant by the term *hard hyphen*?
3. Describe the method of re-highlighting the same block after a function is performed on it. What do you think the GO TO command entered twice does? How might this be used after a SEARCH command is issued?
4. When moving the cursor with the left and right arrow keys, why does it occasionally remain at the same position?
5. What advantages do you see in having the on-screen text unjustified even when justification is turned on for the printout? Do you think viewing justification is the only reason WordPerfect provided the PREVIEW option on the PRINT command? Why or why not?
6. After naming your document on the first save, why does WordPerfect prompt you for a file name on subsequent saves?
7. If your computer had exactly 384 Kbytes of RAM, WordPerfect could be started with the /R option, which loads all of the program into memory. If /R is combined with the /D option, which directs work and overflow files to another disk drive, the WordPerfect disk could be removed. How would this increase maximum document size on the floppy drive system? Could you create a document too big to save on one diskette? How might this make the system easier to operate with smaller documents? Hint: WordPerfect will ask where certain files are located if they can't be found.
8. If you used the start-up options described in exercise 7, how would you save a document larger than one diskette? Are there any applications which would require a document larger than 360 Kbytes?

DISK EXERCISES

1. Retrieve the file **SHEEPDOG.WP** that you created during the tutorial. Place the cursor in line 3, at the far left position of the first line of text, and double-space the document. Use <**Alt**>**-**<**f7**>**4**, **Y** to define two evenly spaced columns of newspaper style, with two spaces between columns. Accept WordPerfect's suggested column positions by pressing the Exit key. Press **5,** `Column Display`, and press **"Y"** to set display columns side by side. Use <**Alt**>**-**<**f7**> again and press **3**, `Column On/Off`, to display the columns. You will need to move the cursor down or use the REWRITE command to see the changes. Use REVEAL CODES to explain what has happened to the text. Save the document as **DOGNEWS.WP**.
2. Use the file **MISSPELL.WP** to search for and replace all of the misspelled words in the document. You may do this with or without the use of a spelling checker. If you choose not to use a spelling checker, you must manually look up all words that are suspect, check their spelling, and then use global search and replace to correct all misspelled words of that type. Save the result on your own diskette and then print the file.

CHAPTER

7

Spreadsheet Concepts

CHAPTER OUTLINE

Some Definitions 218

A Brief History of Spreadsheet Programs 219

Business and Personal Uses for Spreadsheet Programs 221

Software Concepts and Design Philosophies 224

FOCUS FEATURE Spreadsheet Size and Memory Management 228

Using a Spreadsheet Program: An Overview 229

FOCUS FEATURE Financial Modeling Programs 230

FOCUS FEATURE A Few Spreadsheet Caveats 234

Hardware and Software Requirements for Spreadsheet Programs 236

CHAPTER OBJECTIVES

In this chapter you will learn

1 what spreadsheets are
2 how spreadsheets are used
3 how spreadsheets work
4 how to use spreadsheets
5 hardware and software requirements for spreadsheets

In recent years, the electronic spreadsheet has become nearly indispensable to a large number of business and professional users. Loan officers, financial analysts, and investment brokers use spreadsheets for cash management or portfolio analysis. Engineers and building contractors use spreadsheets to determine cooling capacities or to trace circuit current loads. Inventory managers and marketers use spreadsheets for tracking stock levels and forecasting product demands. Although the spreadsheet is largely viewed as a financial planning tool, there are surprisingly few nonfinancial business applications in which spreadsheets have not already been successfully employed.

The success of spreadsheet programs is not difficult to understand. Essentially the electronic counterpart of a pad and pencil, spreadsheet programs offer speed, ease of learning and use, permanent storage of worksheets, and rapid recalculation when parameters are changed. A less tangible, but perhaps more important, benefit of spreadsheet programs is the increased confidence in decisions that comes from being able to evaluate a larger number of decision strategies and from reducing the possibility of computational error.

The spreadsheet's speed can be attributed, in part, to the ordinary gains that might be expected from performing calculations with modern microcomputer technology rather than a calculator or pad and pencil. For the most part, however, a spreadsheet's time savings are made possible by its automatic recalculation feature. In virtually all business calculations, certain numbers are derived from the value of other numbers. With automatic recalculation, whenever a number in a worksheet is changed, all the corresponding dependent values are also adjusted and displayed. (In this chapter and in Chapter 8, we will use *spreadsheet* in referring to the program and *worksheet* in referring to the model entered by the user.) In a loan amortization schedule, for example (see Figure 7–1), all of the figures are derived from three primary values: the loan amount, the Annual Percentage Rate (APR), and the number of compounding and payment periods (the term of the loan). To change the interest

	A	B	C	D	E
1	Loan Amount?		$1,500		
2	Ann. Int. Rate?		16.50%		
3	# Of Months?		12		
4	Payment Amount		$136.45		
5					
6	Month	Payment	Interest	Principal	Balance
7	-----------------	-----------------	-----------------	-----------------	-----------------
8	0				1500
9	1	136.45	20.63	115.83	1384.17
10	2	136.45	19.03	117.42	1266.75
11	3	136.45	17.42	119.03	1147.72
12	4	136.45	15.78	120.67	1027.05
13	5	136.45	14.12	122.33	904.72
14	6	136.45	12.44	124.01	780.71
15	7	136.45	10.73	125.72	654.99
16	8	136.45	9.01	127.45	527.55
17	9	136.45	7.25	129.20	398.35
18	10	136.45	5.48	130.97	267.38
19	11	136.45	3.68	132.78	134.60
20	12	136.45	1.85	134.60	0.00

FIGURE 7–1
Loan Amortization Schedule (Monthly Payments and Compounding)

rate to 17%, simply enter 17 in place of 16.5 and the table will be automatically recalculated. Changing the loan amount from $1,500 to $2,000 is just as simple, with the same rapid results.

SOME DEFINITIONS

An **electronic spreadsheet** is a computerized calculator designed to solve almost any type of mathematical problem for which the data can be arranged into rows and columns. At the intersection of a row and a column is a **cell.** In a spreadsheet that uses letters for designating columns and numbers for rows, the first column in the first row will be called A1, the fourth column of the seventh row is D7, etc. (Figure 7–2). The letter and number corresponding to the column and row of a particular cell are referred to as the *coordinates* or *address* of the cell.

An individual cell in a worksheet may house values, formulas, or labels. A **value** can be a simple number, such as 50,000 or 0.0675, or it may be character data. Character data can be comments, titles, or even necessary data elements, as in a list of clients. Spreadsheet programs allow users to enter text to identify a column (e.g., January) or row (Units-sold). These descriptors are called **labels,** and can be used in place of the ordinary cell designations in some spreadsheet programs. Most users find that worksheets are easier to read and less prone to errors if they can refer to a cell as "1995 taxes" instead of as D27 or R6C14. With some spreadsheets, labels are placed in the top row or the left-hand column and stay on the screen at all times, making it easy to ensure that data is being entered in the correct location.

The highlighted horizontal and vertical bars along the top and left-hand sides of the display are the top and leftmost **borders** of the spreadsheet. Any attempt to

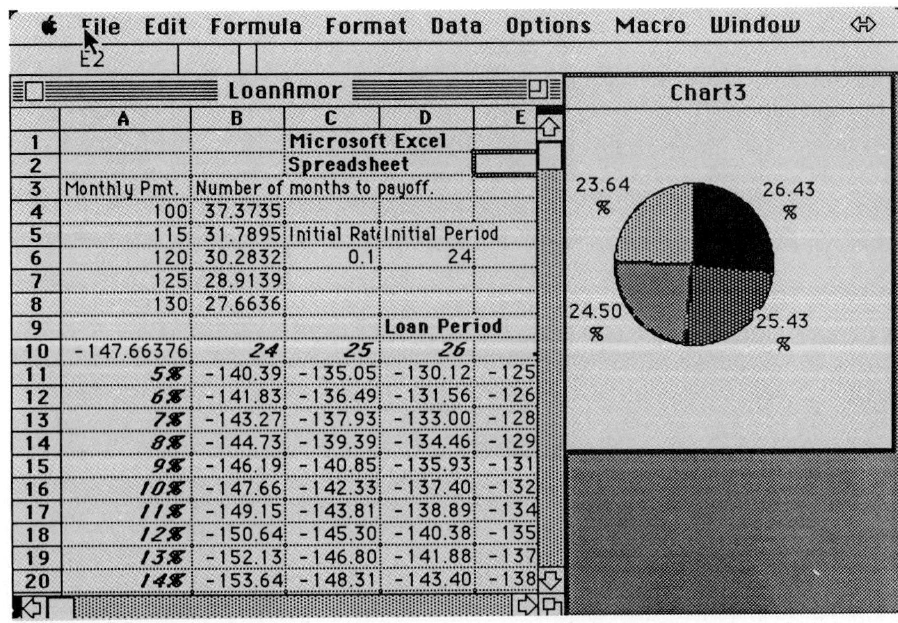

FIGURE 7–2

Loan Amortization Schedule in Microsoft Excel (Macintosh) Showing Rows, Columns, and Cells along with Chart

	A	B	C	D
1	***Objective is to maintain a minimum of $50,000 n***			
2				
3			**1/1/1987**	**2/1/1987**
4	Income		20000	20000
5	Previous Balance		=B10	=C10
6	Expenses		30000	30000
7				
8	Amount To Borrow		=IF(C4+C5-C6<50000,50000-(C4+C5-C6),0)	=IF(D4+D5-D6<50000,50000-(D4+D5-D6),0)
9				
10	Balance	100000	=C4+C5+C8-C6	=D4+D5+D8-D6

FIGURE 7–3

Some Formulas Used in a Cash Management Worksheet

move the cursor above or to the left of these borders will initiate a "beep" response from the spreadsheet program. The same goes for attempts to go beyond the bottom and rightmost borders of the spreadsheet. The cell on which the cursor resides is highlighted, and is always referred to as the **active cell.**

A spreadsheet **formula** uses a cell name or coordinates in the same way an algebraic formula uses a variable name. Formulas may be very simple, as in `1.15*C4` (literally, take the contents of cell C4, multiply by 1.15, and display the result in the current cell). Whenever the value in C4 changes, the amount displayed in the current cell also changes. A formula may also contain a **function**, a predefined process or calculation. The financial, logical, mathematical, and statistical functions of a spreadsheet give it considerable power. Finding the average of a column of twenty numbers is far easier with `@AVG(A1..A20)` (Lotus 1-2-3) than with `(A1+A2+ ,..., +A20)/20`. Functions and formulas can usually be combined, as in `.0675*@SUM(INCOME)`. Shown in Figure 7–3 are some formulas used in a cash management worksheet.

A BRIEF HISTORY OF SPREADSHEET PROGRAMS

Spreadsheet programs have a unique history among microcomputer software products. It is likely that the spreadsheet, more than any other application tool, is responsible for the major inroads made by microcomputers into the business world. Also, whereas most other applications categories existed for mainframe computers well before the introduction of microcomputers, spreadsheet programs were first developed on the smaller machines, then later adapted for mainframes.

In 1978, Harvard Business School student Dan Bricklin, in search of a better way to deal with the financial analysis required by Harvard's case study approach, teamed up with programmer Robert Frankston. Forming a company called Software Arts, they developed a "visible calculator" program that would run on the early 16K byte Apple and Radio Shack microcomputers. Dan Fylstra, also a student, acquired the marketing rights to the program for his company, Personal Software. By the time the program was released, the product was known as VisiCalc (see Figure 7–4) and Fylstra's company had changed its name to VisiCorp Personal Software (later simply VisiCorp).

VisiCalc dramatically altered the attitude of business toward microcomputers. In these early days, before the advent of the 80-column screen, and before sophisticated data base management tools were introduced, the microcomputer was largely thought of as an expensive toy for the electronics hobbyist. Soon after VisiCalc was

FIGURE 7–4
VisiCalc

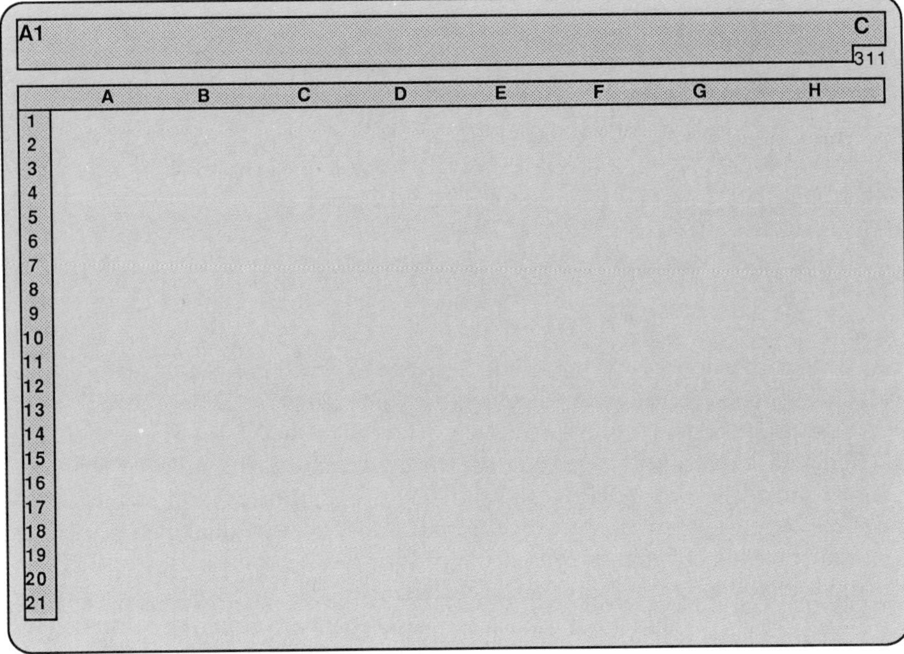

introduced, microcomputer sales boomed. Some industry analysts credit VisiCalc with having strongly influenced the purchase of as many as 250,000 Apple II computers.

If VisiCalc can be credited with sparking Apple sales, the same credit must be accorded to Lotus 1-2-3 (Lotus Development Corporation) for its impact upon the sales of IBM PCs and PC-compatible computers. IBM's original PC, an anemic 16K byte machine with a single 160K byte disk drive and built-in cassette interface, suffered from sluggish sales between the time of its introduction in 1981 and late 1982. Virtually all industry watchers surmised that IBM had entered the micro market too late, and with too little. But in late 1982, IBM microcomputer sales began to skyrocket, giving them a dominant market share within a year and a half. Meanwhile, software sales surveys, such as those conducted by Infocorp and the Softsel Hot List, show that Lotus 1-2-3 (which runs only on IBM and compatible computers) was the highest-selling software product for over two years (early 1983 to early 1985). Figure 7–5 depicts the Lotus 1-2-3 spreadsheet display.

The success of VisiCalc and Lotus 1-2-3 caused a succession of spreadsheet products to enter the market, but none has come close to the phenomenal sales of either of these programs. The two closest competitors have been SuperCalc from Sorcim (now Computer Associates) and Multiplan from Microsoft Corp. The original SuperCalc program (a close replica of VisiCalc in both form and function) sold very well to users of CP/M-based machines, a market ignored by VisiCalc's creators. Multiplan's formula for success appears to have been a combination of relatively early entry into the spreadsheet arena, the large number of computers that can run the program, powerful features (advanced financial functions and sorting capability), and the financial and advertising resources of a very large software development firm.

Early spreadsheet programs like VisiCalc were quickly surpassed in speed, power, and capacity by the next wave of spreadsheet programs. This second generation of spreadsheet products offered many more built-in functions; the ability

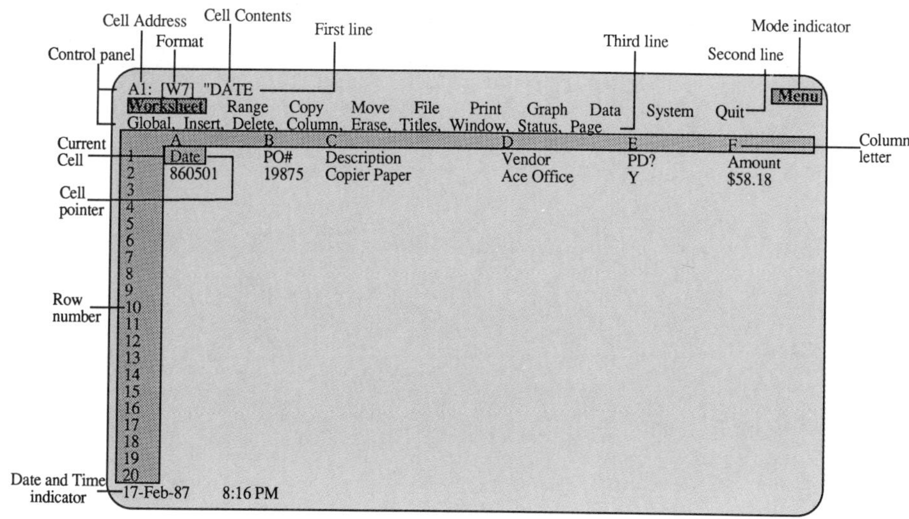

FIGURE 7–5

Lotus Development Corporation's 1-2-3

to refer to cells by labels instead of row numbers and column letters; and, by taking advantage of a 16-bit processor's larger address space, the ability to create very large spreadsheet applications. Some, like Lotus 1-2-3, SuperCalc[3], and Context's MBA program can create graphics or perform record management functions with the worksheet's numbers.

BUSINESS AND PERSONAL USES FOR SPREADSHEET PROGRAMS

With its familiar ledger sheet format of columns and rows, a spreadsheet program conforms naturally to the computational processes employed in most decision-making situations. This has made the spreadsheet an easy tool to use for virtually all types of calculations, whether for business, scientific, or personal use.

Spreadsheet programs have found the most use in financial and accounting applications. These applications include cash flow management, portfolio management, financial statement or ratio analysis, forecasting, and budgeting.

As a cash flow management tool, the spreadsheet is unrivaled (see Figure 7–6). By entering projected income and expense figures on a period-by-period

FIGURE 7–6

A Cash Management Worksheet

	A	B	C	D	E	F	G	H	I	J	K	L	M	N
1	*Objective is to maintain a minimum of $50,000 monthly balance, borrow if necessary.*													
2														
3			**Jan**	**Feb**	**Mar**	**Apr**	**May**	**Jun**	**Jul**	**Aug**	**Sep**	**Oct**	**Nov**	**Dec**
4	**Income**		$20,000	$20,000	$15,000	$15,000	$20,000	$60,000	$40,000	$45,000	$30,000	$60,000	$120,000	$180,000
5	**Previous Balance**		$100,000	$90,000	$80,000	$55,000	$50,000	$50,000	$80,000	$90,000	$80,000	$60,000	$65,000	$109,000
6	**Expenses**		$30,000	$30,000	$40,000	$40,000	$45,000	$30,000	$30,000	$55,000	$50,000	$55,000	$76,000	$85,000
7														
8	**Amount To Borrow**		$0	$0	$0	$20,000	$25,000	$0	$0	$0	$0	$0	$0	$0
9														
10	**Balance**	$100,000	$90,000	$80,000	$55,000	$50,000	$50,000	$80,000	$90,000	$80,000	$60,000	$65,000	$109,000	$204,000

FIGURE 7–7

A Portfolio Management Worksheet

	A	B	C	D	E	F	G	H	I
1	Company	# of Share	Curr. Price	Purchased Price	Est. Divdend	Curr. Yield	$ Amount	Gain (Loss)	% of Portfolio
2									
3	Apple Computer	5000	55.250	20.500	0.15	0.27%	276250.00	173750.00	19.79%
4	Acme	500	13.000	11.250	0.40	3.08%	6500.00	875.00	0.47%
5	Adobe	500	10.000	8.500		0.00%	5000.00	750.00	0.36%
6	Alcan	1000	45.250	47.500	0.80	1.77%	45250.00	-2250.00	3.24%
7	Bank of Boston	300	32.750	35.240	1.00	3.05%	9825.00	-747.00	0.70%
8	Boeing	2000	45.125	44.750	1.40	3.10%	90250.00	750.00	6.47%
9	Bristol Meyer	1500	96.750	95.750	2.80	2.89%	145125.00	1500.00	10.40%
10	Colgate Pal	400	43.125	43.000	1.36	3.15%	17250.00	50.00	1.24%
11	Coca Cola	3000	41.125	40.500	1.12	2.72%	123375.00	1875.00	8.84%
12	Data General	500	31.250	30.250		0.00%	15625.00	500.00	1.12%
13	Digital Equp.	1000	165.500	150.750		0.00%	165500.00	14750.00	11.86%
14	IBM	3000	165.250	155.750	4.40	2.66%	495750.00	28500.00	35.52%
15									
16	**Total $ Amount**	$1,395,700					**Total Gain**	$220,303	
17									
18									
19									
20									
21									
22									
23									
24									
25									
26									
27									
28									
29									
30									
31									
32									
33									
34									
35									

basis, it is possible to tell at a glance whether the cash reserves in any period will be sufficient to meet operating expenses. By careful manipulation of the numbers, managers can determine the optimum time to borrow funds, decide how to dispose of excess monies, or develop strategies to smooth out cash flows over upcoming periods.

Spreadsheets are used both by individuals and investment professionals as a tool for managing investment portfolios. The typical portfolio management worksheet for tracking stocks might use columns to record the stock's name, the number of shares held, the purchase price per share, the book value of shares, the current price per share, estimated (or most recent) dividend, current yield, percentage of the portfolio invested in the stock or category of stocks, and capital gain or loss, as shown in Figure 7–7. Once the worksheet has been set up, entry of new data is very easy, and the template can be used to evaluate other investments being considered.

Students of corporate finance are aware that ratio analysis can be a powerful tool for analyzing the financial statements of corporations. Figures such as the average collection period (accounts receivable × 360 ÷ annual credit sales), the quick ratio ([current assets − inventories] ÷ current liabilities) and the debt-to-equity ratio (total debt ÷ total equity) can provide considerable information about a firm's short- and long-term solvency or profitability, as shown in Figure 7–8. Most financial analysts have developed spreadsheet templates that contain formulas to calculate many such ratios. Using annual reports, 10K reports, or interim financial statements, the analyst merely enters a few selected figures into the model; the program generates the desired ratios almost instantly, making it possible to analyze dozens of companies in the time it formerly took to analyze one.

The tedious number crunching required by most of the commonly used forecasting methods can be greatly reduced with a spreadsheet program. In only a few minutes, sales figures from a previous period can be transformed into pro-

LIM Manufacturing Company Balance Sheet(In Thousands of Dollars)

	December 31, 1986		December 31, 1985	
Assets:				
Current Assets:				
Cash		$2,540		$2,750
Marketable Securities		$1,800		$1,625
Accounts Receivable, net		$18,320		$16,850
Inventories		$27,530		$26,470
Total Current Assets		$50,190		$47,695
Fixed Assets:				
Plant and Equipment	$43,100		$39,500	
Less: Accumulated depreciation	$11,400		$9,500	
Net Plant and Equipment		$31,700		$30,000
Total Assets		$81,890		$77,695
Liabilities & Owners' Equity				
Current Liabilities:				
Accounts Payable		$9,721		$8,340
Notes Payable—Bank(10%)		$8,500		$5,635
Accrued Taxes Payable		$3,200		$3,150
Other Current Liabilities		$2,102		$1,750
Curr. Portion of Long-Term Debt		$2,000		$2,000
Total Current Liabilities		$25,523		$20,875
Long-Term Debt(9%)*		$22,000		$24,000
Total Liabilities		$47,523		$44,875
Owners' Equity				
Common Stocks($10 par)	$13,000		$13,000	
Contributed Capital Excess of Par	$10,000		$10,000	
Retained Earnings	$11,367		$9,820	
Total Owners' Equity		$34,367		$32,820
Total Liabilities & Owners' Equity		$81,890		$77,695

*Mortgage Bonds require a $2000 annual payment to sinking fund

Ratio Analysis

Quick Ratio	0.888
Current Ratio	1.966
Average Collection Period	87.893 days
Inventory Turnover	3.159
Fixed Assets Turnover	3.557
Total Assets Turnover	1.377
Debt Ratio	0.580
Debt To Equity	1.383
Times Interest Earned	3.646
Fixed Charge Coverage	1.631
Gross Profit Margin	24.35%
Net Profit Margin	3.86%
Return On Investment	5.31%
Return On Equity	12.65%

(a)

LIM Manufacturing Company Balance Sheet(In Thousands of Dollars)

For Year Ending December 31, 1986		
Net Sales		$112,760
Cost of Goods Sold		$85,300
Gross Margin		$27,460
Operating Expenses:		
Selling	$6,540	
General & Administrative*	$9,400	
Total Operating Expenses		$15,940
Earnings before Interest & Taxes		$11,520
Interest Charges:		
Interest on Bank Notes	$850	
Interest on Mortgage Bonds	$2,310	
Total Interest Charges		$3,160
Earnings Before Taxes		$8,360
Federal & State Income Taxes(@48%)		$4,013
Net Income		$4,347
Dividends Paid on Common Stock		$2,800
Earnings Retained		$1,547

*Includes $150 in annual lease payments.

(b)

FIGURE 7–8

Financial Statement Analysis. (a) An illustration of the use of a spreadsheet for financial statement analysis. (b) An income statement for LIM Manufacturing Company computed using a spreadsheet (Microsoft Excel).

jected sales by either adding (or subtracting) a fixed percentage amount or calculating the average of several periods and using that for the projections. More involved methods, such as exponential smoothing or even linear regression, are so easy to set up in a spreadsheet that users frequently find no need to purchase special programs for these methods. A typical sales forecasting worksheet is shown in Figure 7–9.

Applications for spreadsheet programs are by no means limited to business finance or accounting. Many people use a simple spreadsheet model to balance their checkbook or budget their home expenses. Instructors have found that spreadsheet programs make a fine tool for recording class grades. Farmers use spreadsheets to calculate fertilizing and irrigation schedules. In fact, almost any type of calculation can be performed more rapidly with a spreadsheet program. Table 7–1 lists some of the more interesting spreadsheet uses found in recent popular computer magazines.

Although spreadsheet programs have many applications in the business world, they do have limitations. Before a worksheet model can be developed for analyzing some financial aspect of a firm, the user must first be aware of the underlying relationships of the data at his or her disposal. Even then, making any type of

FIGURE 7–9

A Sales Forecasting Worksheet

Sales and Profit Forecast

	1985	1986	1987	1988	1989	1990
Sales (in Million $)	35.31	38.30	41.61	45.28	49.36	53.90
Cost Of Sales (in Million $):						
Normal	23.45	23.12	20.81	18.73	16.85	15.17
ExtraOrdi. Start-Up	0.00					
Total Cost Of Sales	23.45	23.12	20.81	18.73	16.85	15.17
Depreciation	1.60	1.60	1.60	1.60	1.60	1.60
Gross Income	11.86	15.18	20.80	26.55	32.50	38.73
Nonmanufacturing Expense	3.09	3.59	3.19	3.24	3.25	3.25
EBIT	8.77	11.59	17.61	23.31	29.25	35.48
Interest	0.00	0.00	0.00	0.74	0.54	0.54
Income Before Taxes	8.77	11.59	17.61	22.57	28.71	34.94
Taxes @approx. 45%:						
Current	3.94	5.22	7.93	10.16	12.92	15.72
Deferred	0.00					
Total	3.94	5.22	7.93	10.16	12.92	15.72
Less Invest. Credit						
Net Provision	3.94	5.22	7.93	10.16	12.92	15.72
Net Income (Million $)	**$4.82**	**$6.38**	**$9.69**	**$12.42**	**$15.79**	**$19.22**
Forecasted Sales:	Fiber Volume Growing at 20% and Price drop 1% per Year.					
Polyester Fiber (Millions !bs)	16.00	19.20	23.04	27.65	33.18	39.81
Price Per LB	0.31	0.31	0.30	0.30	0.30	0.29
Sub-Total	4.96	5.89	7.00	8.32	9.88	11.74
	Tire Cord Volume Grow 20% and Price Drop 11% per year.					
Polyester Tire Cord (Millions lbs)	52.50	63.00	75.60	90.72	108.86	130.64
Price Per LB	0.58	0.51	0.46	0.41	0.36	0.32
Sub-Total	30.35	32.41	34.61	36.97	39.48	42.16
Total Forecasted Sales (Million $	**35.31**	**38.30**	**41.61**	**45.28**	**49.36**	**53.90**

projection is risky at best. Analysis using worksheet models should be considered an aid to, not a replacement for, sound financial judgment. Later in the chapter, the article "A Few Spreadsheet Caveats" discusses cautions that should be observed when using spreadsheet programs.

SOFTWARE CONCEPTS AND DESIGN PHILOSOPHIES

Spreadsheet programs are relatively simple in both concept and design. But to become truly useful beyond their basic function of storing (in primary storage) and calculating *worksheet* information, spreadsheet programs should also provide a convenient method of performing the following basic operations:

Worksheet navigation and entry

Copying, moving, inserting, and deleting material in the worksheet

Formatting and editing the worksheet appearance

Inputting and outputting worksheet information to and from disk (secondary storage)

With so few primary operations, and an intuitively appealing model (the manual ledger method) to follow, it is no wonder that so much similarity exists in the look, feel, and operating principles of different commercial spreadsheet programs.

TABLE 7–1

Some Nonfinancial Uses for Spreadsheets

- The Fire Research Lab in Richmond, California (affiliated with the University of California at Berkeley) uses a spreadsheet to determine sprinkler system requirements by calculating hydraulics and friction loss. Spreadsheets are also used to simulate heat transfer during critical fire stages.
- A physician uses spreadsheets to determine drug dosages, track disease stage progress, and calculate intraocular lens specifications for cataract surgery patients.
- A cattle feedlot manager uses his spreadsheet to monitor feeding schedules and calculate weight gain ratios, as well as to determine feedlot costs and develop invoices for customers.
- A lawyer has developed a spreadsheet program for analyzing blood alcohol levels in drunk driving cases.
- A homeowner's association uses spreadsheet templates to monitor swimming pool usage among its members.
- In a project during the 1984 Olympics, Levi Strauss used a spreadsheet to count over 70,000 pieces of art contributed by 300,000 school children and to calculate the percentage of involvement for each Los Angeles area school (to award prizes).

Spreadsheets are so similar, in fact, that it is usually possible to switch from program to program with minimal retraining.

The commands and common features used to implement basic spreadsheet operations will be covered in the next section on spreadsheet use. But first, a brief look at how a spreadsheet operates, and at some approaches used in solving the size and speed problems plaguing frequent spreadsheet users.

A Spreadsheet's Internal Operations

Spreadsheets operate by using clever schemes for manipulating primary memory (RAM). One area of RAM is reserved to store values and formulas in much the same form that they were entered. Also stored in this area is information about how the contents of a particular cell will be displayed; for example, whether it will be right- or left-justified, in inverse or normal video, how many digits will be displayed, etc. In most spreadsheets, another (smaller) area of RAM is used to store the worksheet's evaluated cell contents as they will be displayed on the screen. This second area of memory is then used for the screen display, and will be updated with each change or new entry in the worksheet. For example, if `5` were placed in cell A1, and `3*A1` were put in A2, the second area of memory would have a `15` in A2 while the first would house the underlying formula.

It is easy to see why a spreadsheet would maintain both areas of memory. Storing the underlying formulas in memory, rather than merely the results of the formulas, makes it possible to change previously entered values. If cell A1 in Figure 7–10 were changed to `7`, a spreadsheet that did not store the underlying formula for A2 would still show `15` in that location, rather than the correct `21`.

The display memory, on the other hand, speeds things up whenever the user scrolls horizontally or vertically in a large worksheet. When the cursor reaches the edge of the screen and a new row or column appears on-screen, programs that do not use display memory must calculate what the new area should look like. The screen displays only a small window on what may be a very large worksheet. Consequently, some programs will, upon recalculation, calculate only those cells

FIGURE 7–10
Two Spreadsheet Memory Areas

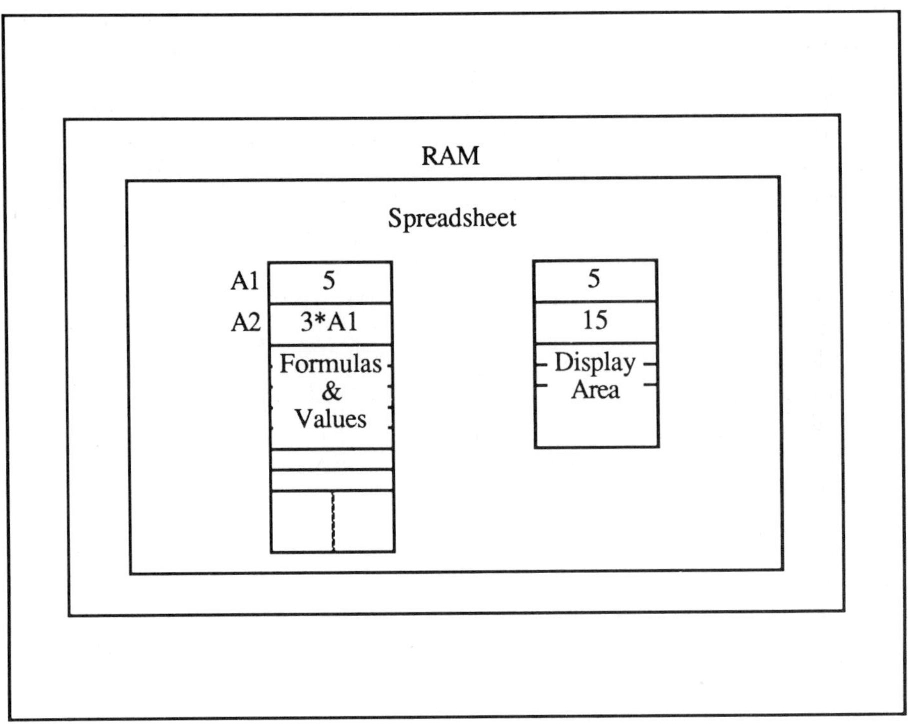

currently being displayed. And scrolling will cause the program to recalculate any newly revealed cells.

Using a separate area of RAM to hold values for display will speed up the process of scrolling through a large worksheet, but it costs extra time whenever the worksheet must be recalculated (with each new entry), and it takes up valuable internal memory. Lotus 1-2-3 uses a hybrid approach to this problem. In 1-2-3, a separate display area of memory is maintained, but it is only large enough for a single screenful, not the entire worksheet. When recalculation takes place, only a small portion of that time is required to update the display memory, thus speeding up recalculation. When the user is scrolling beyond the screen's boundaries, a delay occurs as each new column or row is calculated, but the delay is not nearly as long as on systems that update the entire worksheet display memory at one time.

Spreadsheet Speed

Spreadsheet programs can be blindingly fast with small worksheets. As the worksheet grows, however, recalculation takes longer and longer. Since (for most spreadsheets) recalculation of the entire worksheet is performed between each cell entry, adding new information or making changes to a large model can become an exercise in frustration. The time required to perform recalculation will vary with the number and complexity of the formulas and functions used in the worksheet, but it is not uncommon for a large corporate financial model to take 15 or more seconds to recalculate, even with the fastest programs.

Spreadsheet designers use several methods to enhance their programs' operating speeds. First, the programs are almost always written in assembly language.

Newer spreadsheet programs are designed to take advantage of a high-speed math co-processor (the 8087 or 80287 chip in IBM PC and PC AT computers and compatibles) if one is present in the system.

The spreadsheet user can also take measures to reduce delays. Spreadsheets allow the user to switch from automatic to **manual recalculation.** Manual recalculation allows the user to decide when to recalculate, usually by pressing a specially designated function key. It is wise to switch to this mode for long data entry sessions, recalculating the worksheet only after all entries are made.

Sparse memory management methods (in which empty cells need not be calculated) and recalculation schemes can also significantly improve a spreadsheet's performance. Most spreadsheets recalculate by beginning at the upper left (A1) and calculating all cells across the first row; they then move on to recalculate all cells across the second row, the third row, and so forth. This method is satisfactory when all formulas refer to cells that are above them. Suppose, however, that cells derive part of their values from areas that follow them in the calculation order, as in Figure 7–11.

This situation is called a **forward reference**, and some first-generation spreadsheets did not respond well at all to them. In the row-wise recalculation method described above, the spreadsheet program cannot look forward to the last referenced cell, so it will place a 0 in cell C2 and continue calculating. When it reaches the last cell, it can begin calculating the worksheet again from the top left. With this method, a recalculation is required for each forward reference, until, finally, all cells have the correct values. Some of the early spreadsheets refused to handle forward references at all, or required the user to repeatedly press the manual recalculation key until all values had stabilized.

Several of the newer spreadsheets use **natural recalculation order** to speed things up. With this method, a record is kept of how many times a cell is referenced by other cells. When recalculation time comes, the cells with the most references are calculated first, then the cells with the next most references, and so on. For example, in the loan amortization table (Figure 7–1), the underlying formulas for each of the cells in the INTEREST column references the annual interest rate at the top. With natural recalculation order, this cell would be calculated first, no matter where it was placed in the worksheet.

Another problem is presented when a worksheet contains **circular references.** A circular reference occurs when two or more cells depend upon each other to compute their value. Figure 7–13 shows a simple circular reference. The value of cell C1 depends upon the value in A3. A3, in turn, depends partly upon C1 for its value. Lotus 1-2-3 will continue to calculate these cells until their values stabilize, and will display an error message (such as CIRC, for circular reference) if the values cannot be resolved. Multiplan requires the user to specify the number of times the worksheet will be recalculated.

	A	B	C	D
1	Quarter	Actual Values	Estimated Values	
2	1	100	@A2*$C$9	
3	2	250	@A3*$C$9	
4	3	320	@A4*$C$9	
5	4	490	@A5*$C$9	
6				
7				
8				
9			@(B2+B3+B4+B5)/4	

FIGURE 7–11

A Forward Reference

Focus Feature

SPREADSHEET SIZE AND MEMORY MANAGEMENT

Because most spreadsheet programs store the entire worksheet in the computer system's main memory, large models can present problems, and many business applications for spreadsheets are very large, indeed. A corporate income statement may have dozens of columns and hundreds of rows. Tracking daily prices for a large number of stocks can require even more space. In their advertisements, most spreadsheet programs cite an impressive figure for the number of rows and columns available to the user. These range from a modest 254 rows by 65 columns (VisiCalc and SuperCalc^2) to a staggering 32,000 by 32,000 (Framework). These figures are of little value, however, in determining how large a useful spreadsheet may be entered.

The number of cells that can be filled with values is a function of both the cells' contents and the efficiency of the storage method employed by the program. In Lotus 1-2-3, for example, storing a small integer value (e.g., 123) in a cell uses about four bytes of storage. A real number (1.234) occupies eight bytes. Storing the letter *A* takes approximately 10 bytes. Thus, in an MS-DOS computer that is loaded with the full complement of 640K bytes (only about 512K will be available for a worksheet after the operating system and Lotus 1-2-3 are loaded into memory), you can fill a worksheet with roughly 50,000 cells containing *A,* or 100 columns with 500 rows each. Or you may fill the same area with 130,000 cells containing 123. At best, you can use less than 10% of Lotus 1-2-3's 2,097,152 available cells (8,192 rows by 256 columns). If a worksheet contained the names and addresses of clients, that percentage would be dramatically reduced.

A worksheet can even run out of operating room when there are very few occupied cells. Some spreadsheet programs allocate a fixed amount of internal storage to all cells in the **active area,** defined as the rectangle beginning with row 1, column 1 and extending as far down and to the right as the last cell with an entry. Thus, if you place *A* in row 400, column Z and leave all other cells blank, the spreadsheet would define the active area as a rectangle of 400 rows and 26 columns, an area of 10,400 cells, These blank cells would cut deeply into the amount of memory available for calculations. Most spreadsheet users learn to leave very little blank space, and begin their worksheets in the upper left-hand corner. Depicted in Figure 7–12 is an example of wasteful spreadsheet usage.

In recent years, several approaches have been taken to defeat size limitation problems. Some programs do not allocate space to empty cells. Other programs use highly efficient storage methods for recording information internally, so that textual contents require only as many bytes as the number of characters they contain, and a small number may be stored in two bytes instead of four. With some systems, it is even possible to have a worksheet that is larger than the computer's available memory.

FIGURE 7–13
A Resolvable Circular Reference

	A	B	C
1	500		=A3
2	=C1-A1		
3	=A2-C1		
4			

FIGURE 7–14
An Unresolvable Circular Reference

	A	B	C
1			
2			
3			
4	=10+C4		=3*A4

	A	B	C	D	E	F	G
1			December 31, 1986			December 31, 1985	
2							
3	**Assets:**						
4	Current Assets:						
5	Cash			$2,540			$2,750
6	Marketable Securities			$1,800			$1,625
7	Accounts Receivable, net			$18,320			$16,850
8	Inventories			$27,530			$26,470
9	**Total Current Assets**			$50,190			$47,695
10							
11	**Fixed Assets:**						
12	Plant and Equipment		$43,100			$39,500	
13	Less: Accumulated depreciation		$11,400			$9,500	
14	Net Plant and Equipment			$31,700			$30,000
15	**Total Assets**			**$81,890**			**$77,695**
16							
	Break point						
400	**Liabilities & Owners' Equity**						
401	**Current Liabilities:**						$5,635
402	Accounts Payable			$9,721			$8,340
403	Notes Payable—Bank(10%)			$8,500			
404	Accrued Taxes Payable			$3,200			$3,150
405	Other Current Liabilities			$2,102			$1,750

FIGURE 7–12

Wasteful Spreadsheet Usage

Release 2.01 of Lotus 1-2-3 uses such a swapping method, with worksheet overflow stored entirely on RAM disks.

An earlier approach to solving this problem was introduced by Microsoft in their Multiplan spreadsheet. Instead of expanding the computer's memory to fit the worksheet, the Multiplan solution is to break the worksheet into smaller sections that fit the computer. These smaller sections can be linked together so that changes in a cell in one worksheet affect the values of dependent formulas in other worksheets. In Multiplan, up to eight worksheets can be linked in this way, making the effective worksheet area up to eight times the size of the memory available.

It should be noted that some circular references cannot be resolved, as in Figure 7–14. With proper planning, unresolvable circular references should not occur; they are usually the result of an omission or entry error. In most cases, users should avoid circular references altogether.

USING A SPREADSHEET PROGRAM: AN OVERVIEW

Shown in Table 7–2 are the steps required to formally construct a worksheet model. It is assumed that the user will save the worksheet, both from time to time and from session to session, so this is not listed as a step. The steps from Table 7–2 are described and illustrated in what follows.

Focus Feature

FINANCIAL MODELING PROGRAMS

Spreadsheets are not the only packages available for solving financial calculations, nor were they the first. Long before the spreadsheet made its debut on microcomputers, **financial modeling programs** were running strong on minicomputers and mainframes.

A financial modeling program generates the same type of worksheet output as a spreadsheet program. Creating the worksheet, however, is quite different. Instead of directly entering data and formulas into appropriate cells, a financial modeling program allows you to define the worksheet's contents and relationships (formulas) in a simple method that uses truly descriptive variable names.

Financial (or business) modeling programs come in two types. One type has a number of predefined standard financial forms. To use this program, you merely select the type of worksheet you want to generate, enter the variables you are interested in, and input the appropriate data values. Venture, from Weiss Associates, uses this method. The more common type of financial modeling program is really a programming language. The user defines rows and columns in a data definition section then lists the relationships between the variables. Microcomputer-based modeling languages are patterned after their large computer counterparts, and offer a wide assortment of formatting features and built-in financial functions.

There are several reasons why a company might choose to use a financial modeling program instead of a spreadsheet:

1. Financial modeling programs, unlike spreadsheets, are not limited by the internal memory of the computer. The models used to create a worksheet are typically quite small, even though the worksheets they generate can be any size.
2. With certain types of analysis, a modeling program can be much simpler to set up. This is usually the case when only a few formulas are replicated in a large number of columns or rows (a cash-flow worksheet, for example, might have only ten or twelve formulas repeated for each month being analyzed).
3. The modeling language programs keep data values in a separate file from the model formulas, allowing the user to easily change the data or model as the need arises.
4. Modeling programs often have advanced financial functions and other features that are not generally available in spreadsheets. Their most notable feature is **goal seeking,** or iterative recalculation to reach a specified objective. With a spreadsheet, finding the amount of sales necessary to generate $5 million net profit usually involves repeatedly plugging different amounts into the cell for sales until the bottom line equals $5 million. With goal seeking, $5 million is specified for net profit, and a program statement instructs the modeling package to adjust the sales figure accordingly.
5. The model programs are easier to check for validity than the worksheets of a spreadsheet program. There are too many ways to introduce errors into a large worksheet of a spreadsheet program. Values can be pulled from the wrong column, a formula multiplier can be off slightly, etc. Large worksheets can be difficult to debug because of their cryptic row and column references, and no convenient method exists

Determine the Purpose

A well-understood and clearly defined purpose is essential to the successful formulation of any worksheet. The purpose will determine what is included and what is left out of the worksheet. If the purpose is to study strategies for reducing production costs, there is no point in including a forecast of the gross revenues, for example.

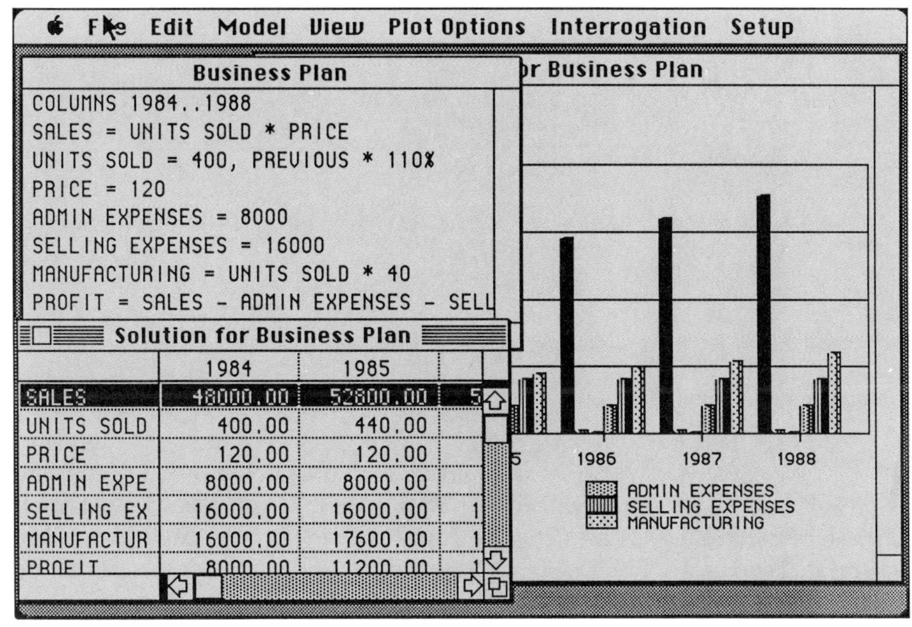

FIGURE 7–15

The Business Model Program MindSight (Macintosh). *(Courtesy of Execucom Systems Corporation.)*

for printing out their formulas. The model listing from a modeling package, on the other hand, is usually brief, easy to read, and uses descriptive variable names that simplify checking formulas.

For all their advantages, modeling programs do have limitations. They are not as versatile as spreadsheet programs for nonfinancial uses. They are often expensive (some of the better ones cost upwards of $1,000). Most important, however, they are not as easy to use as the simple spreadsheet method, although they are becoming increasingly user friendly (see Figure 7–15 above). Modeling programs can be valuable assets for corporate financial officers, but it is unlikely that other busy executives will spend the time required to learn how to use them. We will discuss financial modeling programs again in Chapter 12, under the heading "Decision Support Systems."

Synthesize a Well-conceived Title

The title should reflect the focus, subject matter, and content of the worksheet. Along with the title, or perhaps as part of the documentation (step 11), it is helpful to describe the problem being addressed, why there is an interest in the problem, and who is interested.

TABLE 7–2

Steps for Constructing a Worksheet

1. Determine the purpose
2. Synthesize a well-conceived title
3. Specify date and authorship
4. Determine independent and dependent variables
5. Lay out the worksheet on scratch paper
6. Enter labels, independent variables, and values
7. Enter base formulas
8. Copy base formulas
9. Adjust format (global and local) and column width
10. Verify and validate the worksheet
11. Document the worksheet
12. Develop the necessary graphics
13. Perform "what-if" analyses
14. Print the required outputs

Specify Date and Authorship

This can be very important when the worksheet is to be used by individuals other than the original author. Other users will want to know when the worksheet was created and by whom, should they encounter any difficulties or have questions about the worksheet model.

Determine Independent and Dependent Variables

The variables chosen for inclusion in the worksheet will depend directly on the purpose set forth for the worksheet. These can be categorized into two classes: independent and dependent. **Independent variables** do not depend on any other values contained in the worksheet, and usually represent parameters (or constants) around which the user performs "what-if" analyses. Generally, independent variables are mere values as far as the worksheet is concerned. **Dependent variables,** on the other hand, have their values determined from formulas involving cell references that can ultimately be traced back to the independent variables.

Lay Out the Worksheet on Scratch Paper

A little planning can go a long way in making the worksheet model easier to enter and maintain. A good practice is to sketch the displayed appearance of a worksheet on scratch paper first. Shown in Figure 7–16 is a general format (or template) for layout of a worksheet.

To avoid forward references, it is best to place independent variables ahead of dependent variables: in the upper left-hand corner of the worksheet, as suggested in Figure 7–16. As far as possible, dependent variables should be laid out so that all base formulas appear in the same column or row. This allows them to be copied into the rest of the worksheet by means of a single copy command.

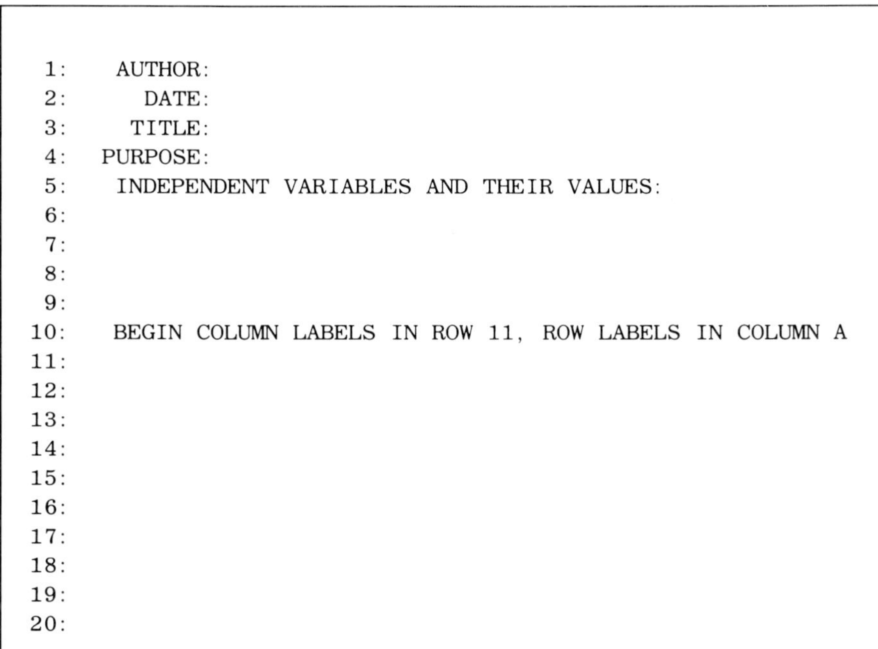

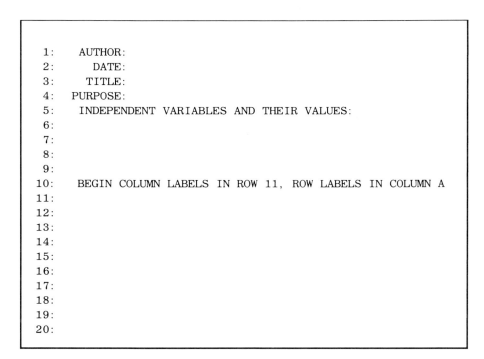

```
 1:   AUTHOR:
 2:     DATE:
 3:    TITLE:
 4:  PURPOSE:
 5:   INDEPENDENT VARIABLES AND THEIR VALUES:
 6:
 7:
 8:
 9:
10:   BEGIN COLUMN LABELS IN ROW 11, ROW LABELS IN COLUMN A
11:
12:
13:
14:
15:
16:
17:
18:
19:
20:
```

FIGURE 7–16
General Format for a Worksheet

Enter Labels, Independent Variables, and Values

Row and column labels, as well as labels for the independent variables, should be entered first. The user should be careful to follow the format laid out on scratch paper. When "What If" analyses are conducted, the user will be changing *only* independent variables which are well identified and labeled in this format. Changing a dependent variable is likely to replace a formula with a value and thereby introduce a multitude of errors. This could happen in worksheets where there is no careful distinction between independent and dependent values, since all values appear as numbers in cells on the display.

Enter Base Formulas

Next the base formulas should be entered. The user must exercise utmost care to mark references to independent variables as absolute. **References** are cell coordinates or cell names that appear as part of a formula in other cells. References may be either relative or absolute. Generally, references to cells containing independent variables are absolute. Forgetting to denote absolute cell references as absolute will most certainly result in "garbaged" output, and is an error that is hard to detect. Relative cell references get adjusted when the formula is copied.

Copy Base Formulas

Next the base formulas are copied. Usually, a single column of base formulas can be copied across successive columns by a single copy command (replicate command in some spreadsheet programs). Likewise, base formulas can be copied from a single row down into successive rows by use of a single copy command.

Focus Feature

A FEW SPREADSHEET CAVEATS

Recently, financial newspapers and business magazines have been reporting horror stores resulting from the use of spreadsheet programs. A firm nearly suffers bankruptcy because of a spreadsheet budget calculation that was $6 million in error. Another firm, using a simple formula for sales projections, narrowly escapes disastrous consequences when another manager, doubting the overly optimistic report, decides to check the calculations by hand. The list goes on.

Analysis of financial data can be so seductively easy with a spreadsheet program that many users are not nearly as cautious as they should be. Because spreadsheets perform calculations with such speed and precision, they are being used for more and more kinds of calculations, and with larger and larger models. Whenever spreadsheets become very large, it becomes more difficult to ensure their accuracy. In both of the situations described above, the program users had entered seemingly correct formulas, but inadvertently were rounding numbers by not specifying enough precision in some major variables. Listed below are some suggestions for spreadsheet use that can help you avoid unpleasant financial consequences.

1. *If you don't understand the worksheet, don't use it.* Because of the popularity of spreadsheet programs, and the complexity of certain kinds of financial calculations, a booming market has developed for spreadsheet applications books, spreadsheet seminars, and packaged spreadsheet templates. When using anybody else's worksheets, extreme caution must be employed. If a worksheet contains a formula such as F9*C5/1200, there should be no mystery as to what the numbers in F9 and C5 represent and why their total is being divided by 1200. If the reasons are not apparent, either revise the template or find out from the author (if you did not write it) what the formula does.
2. *Always document your worksheet, even if you will be the only user.* As spreadsheets become larger and

Adjust Format (Global and Local) and Column Width

Once the entire worksheet is up and running, the user can begin to concentrate on improving the appearance of the displayed worksheet by adjusting formats. The numeric format of some numbers may be inappropriate, for example. Formats representing dollars should have two digits to the right of the decimal point and commas after every third digit to the left of the decimal point, for example.

After the format has been adjusted, column widths should be adjusted as appropriate so that the displayed values will fit easily in the column width specified. If the spreadsheet program is unable to get the displayed value to fit within a prescribed width, it will display asterisks (or other unexpected characters) in that cell.

Verify and Validate the Worksheet

Next comes verification and validation. Verification will usually involve a manual calculation for comparison with the computerized calculations. A manual calculation for all dependent numeric values in the worksheet is required for at least one set of independent variable values. **Verification** ensures that the worksheet model operates as intended—that it does what it is supposed to do.

more complex, it becomes difficult to remember all the relationships between the values they contain. Even though it is always possible to display the formula for a cell rather than the result of that formula, most spreadsheet users will only look at this when first developing the template. It is a good idea to reserve an area on your worksheet for comments that explain (in English, rather than cell designations) any formulas you are using.

Most spreadsheet programs have a way of printing out the contents of all cells (with the underlying formulas) in addition to printing out what is displayed (the results of the formula calculations). For small spreadsheets, this will allow you to look at your formulas and verify their correctness. With larger spreadsheets this is not nearly as useful, because the printout is likely to be listed vertically down the page, with the contents of A1 on the first line, A2 on the second, etc. A large worksheet model will span many pages and require hours of page-flipping to confirm relationships that go across rows rather than down columns. For these programs, the serious spreadsheet user should consider purchasing one of the inexpensive *spreadsheet documentation programs,* such as Docucalc, from Micro Decision Systems, or Spreadsheet Auditor, by Columbia Software. These programs enable you to print out your worksheet model with formulas listed in the same relative position as their display on the screen.

3. *Always test your worksheet by hand.* Before inserting critical data into your worksheet model, try it out with some known values. Use past data or easy-to-calculate figures, such as tens or hundreds. When the model is very large, try breaking it up into smaller portions and checking the output of each portion before integrating it into a large model. Then check the large worksheet to ensure that your integration was successful.

In addition, the worksheet model should be submitted for scrutiny by others closely associated with the project so that they can exercise judgment regarding the appropriateness of the worksheet parameters, formulas, calculated results, and format. This is called **validation.**

Document the Worksheet

Documenting the worksheet involves inserting textual material. What each formula does, for example, should be documented. Some spreadsheet programs permit the user to insert comments into cells containing formulas that describe what the formula does. The comment is placed after the formula and the program recognizes the comment by a special character that precedes it.

Develop the Necessary Graphics

At this point the user can begin to concentrate on developing graphics to help interpret and understand the data better. Although this is a necessary step in the formal evolution of any worksheet model, a discussion of graphics is reserved for Chapter 11.

Perform "What-if" Analyses

Guided by rationale and with a set of goals in mind, the user now systematically changes the independent variable values to observe their effects on the final outcomes. These effects might be graphed in some way to lend better comprehension.

Print the Required Outputs

The required outputs are printed or outputted so they can be presented to others. Almost all spreadsheets support printing of the worksheet to a disk file so the worksheet can be merged into a word processing document. More will be said about this in Chapter 8.

HARDWARE AND SOFTWARE REQUIREMENTS FOR SPREADSHEET PROGRAMS

Spreadsheet programs are available to run on both large and small microcomputers, and for most of the common operating systems. When the computer's memory is small, however, the spreadsheet will compromise either features or performance to fit the machine. One compromise is to severely limit the number of features offered. Spreadsheet programs that run on a 32K byte laptop portable are useful for quick calculations and personal use, but would be unable to handle the demands of a corporate financial officer or an investment analyst.

Another compromise often made is to place most of the spreadsheet's functions in an overlay file, and to call them in only as they are needed. This approach is taken by many programs designed for the 64K byte CP/M-based computers. These programs may offer most of the features of a second-generation spreadsheet, but perform slowly because of frequent disk accesses.

The point of the preceding paragraph should be evident: memory size is the principal requirement for heavy spreadsheet users. Release 2 of Lotus 1-2-3 will not operate with less than a 256K byte computer, and really needs at least 512K to create a decent-sized worksheet.

Two other hardware features that can be classified as helpful, but not absolutely necessary, are a wide-carriage printer and a terminal or video screen with a 132-column mode (the normal display shows 80). A wide-carriage (15 or more inches) dot-matrix printer can normally print at least 120 characters across a line in normal print mode, and may print 230 or more in a condensed mode. When a spreadsheet cannot print all of its columns within the boundaries of a page, it will print a vertical portion of the worksheet from top to bottom. When that is finished, it will print the next vertical section to the right, and continue this process until the full width of the worksheet is on paper. Thus, the first 50 or 60 rows of columns A through G may appear on the first page of the printout, while column H does not show up until the next page. Funk Software has created an innovative program called Sideways that, as its name implies, prints a wide spreadsheet lengthwise on continuous-form paper, allowing for a virtually unlimited width, as shown in Figure 7–17. It works on Epson and IBM Graphics printers, and with several spreadsheet programs.

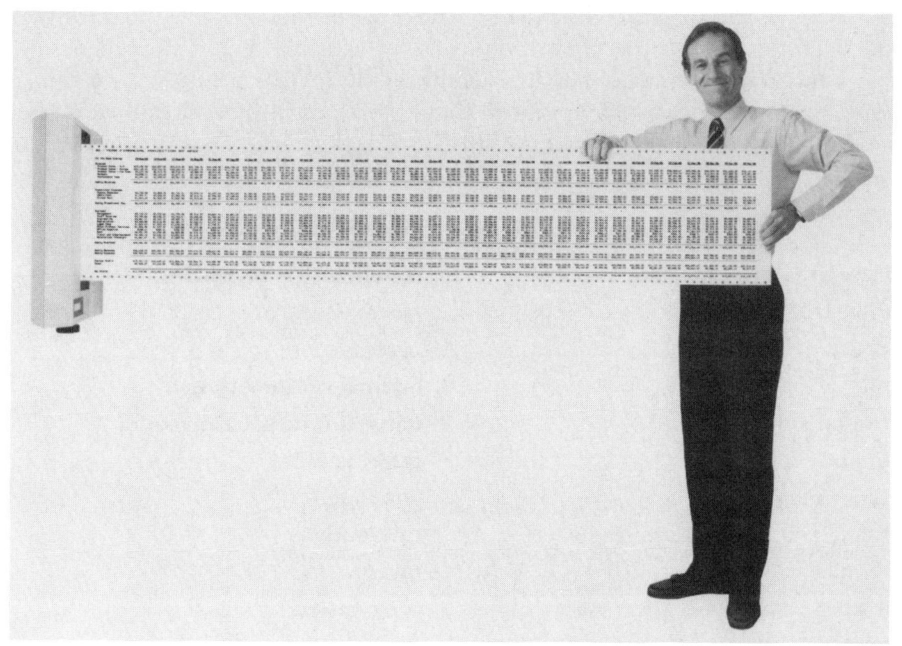

FIGURE 7–17
A Sideways Spreadsheet.
(Courtesy of Funk Software)

To facilitate the development of extremely large worksheet models, Lotus, Intel and Microsoft developed a standard whereby hardware manufacturers could build a card that would plug into an expansion slot of the PC or compatible and be able to provide up to 2 additional megabytes of user-accessible RAM. Various products were developed to do exactly this, and are commercially available in the marketplace.

Summary

Electronic spreadsheet programs are row-column (matrix) calculators designed to ease the burden of repetitive calculations that would otherwise have to be performed manually. In addition, these programs have the capability to store, retrieve, and print the worksheet. The row-column format of the spreadsheet conforms to the computational requirements of thousands of business, scientific, and professional applications.

A second generation of spreadsheets began with the introduction of Lotus 1-2-3 in January of 1983. In addition to a much larger worksheet capacity, the second generation of worksheets provided some graphics and data base capabilities that enhanced the usefulness of these programs. During that time spreadsheet programs became faster when asked to recalculate the worksheet, and enhanced the user interface by providing both command and menu-driven facilities.

At the intersection of each row and column of a spreadsheet is a cell into which three basic types of information can be stored: numbers, labels, and formulas. In addition, it is possible to store formatting information, titles, comments, even commands in the cells. Formulas are arithmetic expressions that include numeric constants, cell references, and built-in functions. Cell referencing may be relative or absolute. Absolute cell references do not change when a copy or replicate command is used to copy the formula into other cells, whereas relative references will.

Spreadsheet displays will consist of one or more windows in to the worksheet and a control panel at the top or bottom of the screen. When a menu bar is not always displayed, commands are invoked by typing "/". Doing so will bring up the main menu bar, from which a command can be selected. Most spreadsheets offer the flexibility to be used in a menu-driven mode or in a command-driven mode.

Key Terms

active area
active cell
border
cell
circular reference
dependent variable
electronic spreadsheet
financial modeling programs
formula
forward reference
function
goal seeking
independent variable
label
macros
manual recalculation
natural recalculation order
references
template
validation
value
verification
worksheet

Self-Test

1. Describe how spreadsheet software and applications got their start.
2. Describe to what uses spreadsheet software is generally put.
3. Describe what features one can generally expect in spreadsheet software.
4. Describe the steps that are generally involved in using a spreadsheet program.
5. Describe the hardware and software required for spreadsheet applications.

Exercises

1. Which of the following situations could be analyzed by use of a spreadsheet program? Why? Why not?
   (a) portfolio management
   (b) management of a list of clients
   (c) management of personnel data
   (d) production cost management
   (e) management information system for inventory
   (f) management of the accounting records (including their storage) for a large corporation
   (g) management of a story for a major newspaper
2. Describe some not-so-common usages of spreadsheet programs.
3. List some applications of spreadsheet programs that were not described in the chapter.
4. Why do you believe the spreadsheet program has been so successful? What features have contributed to the success of the spreadsheet program?
5. Two distinct areas of memory are used for storing the user's worksheet model. Describe why two areas are used, and what is contained within them.
6. Describe the method Lotus 1-2-3 uses for management of the display area RAM.

7. How many bytes are required to store a three-digit integer number in a cell in Lotus 1-2-3? How many bytes are required to store the real number 5.678 in a cell in 1-2-3? How many bytes are required to store a letter?
8. Explain why it is a good idea not to leave a lot of blank space in the middle of your worksheet.
9. What techniques are employed in some newer spreadsheets to overcome worksheet size limitation problems?
10. What advantages result from Multiplan's approach to management of worksheet size? What is unique to this approach?
11. What techniques are employed to speed up the process of recalculating a worksheet? What is meant by *manual recalculation*?
12. It is a good idea to avoid forward and circular references. Why? What is meant by *natural recalculation order*? Why are some circular references unresolvable? How might a spreadsheet program detect this?
13. Explain why a well-defined purpose is essential to the successful formulation of any worksheet model.
14. In Figure 7–16, a general format for a spreadsheet was presented. What benefits might result if the format is rigorously adhered to?
15. Explain what independent and dependent variables are.
16. Explain why it is important to verify and validate the worksheet model. Describe several ways of doing this.
17. Discuss various ways in which a worksheet model could be documented.
18. What is meant by *what-if analyses*?
19. The section titled "Software Concepts" lists only four basic functions of a spreadsheet program. What are they?
20. The section titled "Using a Spreadsheet Program" suggests fourteen steps in building a worksheet model. What are they?
21. Why do you think there are so many more steps to building a worksheet model than there are spreadsheet functions?
22. What are the hardware and software requirements of spreadsheet programs?
23. Describe how circular references are handled in Lotus 1-2-3. Distinguish between resolvable and irresolvable circular references and give examples of each.
24. Lay out a worksheet for keeping the hole-by-hole score for a foursome in the game of golf. You will want to make provisions for displaying the par of each hole. For each hole you would want to show a hole tally and a cumulative score for each player. Show the labels you would use for each row and column.
25. Lay out a worksheet for keeping track of your favorite football teams on a week-by-week basis. For each football game, show the opponent's name, the opponent's score, the score of one of your favorite teams, and whatever other statistics you would like to retain, such as passing yardage, field goal percentage, etc. How might this information be used?
26. Lay out a worksheet for keeping track of your grades in each of the courses you are taking. Have the worksheet compute a running current course grade for each course.
27. Lay out a worksheet for tracking the stocks you are invested in on a daily basis. If you aren't invested in any stocks, pick a half-dozen stocks at random from the listing for the New York Stock Exchange. For each stock-day pair, enter the high, the low, and the close. Do this for a half-dozen stocks and include a week's worth of data. For each stock include a column showing its annual high and low. How might this information be used?

Additional Reading

Douglas Ford, Cobb, and Geoffrey T. LeBlond. *Using 1-2-3.* Indianapolis: Que Corporation, 1983.

The Power of Multiplan. Management Information Source, 1983.

The Power of SuperCalc. Management Information Source, 1983.

The Power of VisiCalc. Management Information Source, 1983.

The Power of VisiCalc Volume II. Management Information Source, 1983.

CHAPTER

8

Spreadsheet Mechanics

CHAPTER OUTLINE

Typing, Editing, and Revising the Worksheet 242
Formatting and Printing Worksheets 255
Operators and Functions 259
Building Worksheets for Use by Others 265
File Management and Operations 267
Classifying and Characterizing Existing Spreadsheet Programs 270
LOTUS 1-2-3 TUTORIAL 278
MICROSOFT EXCEL™ TUTORIAL 312

CHAPTER OBJECTIVES

In this chapter you will learn

1 how to create worksheets, including (a) how to enter labels, constants, and titles; (b) how to enter formulas
2 how to edit worksheets
3 how to reorganize/revise worksheets
4 how to format worksheets
5 how to save and print worksheets
6 how to build worksheets for use by others
7 how to manage worksheet files

The previous chapter introduced the usage, functions, and features of spreadsheets. This chapter introduces the mechanics of spreadsheets. Features that were only briefly presented in the previous chapter will be described in considerable detail in this chapter.

A study of the working habits of spreadsheet users is likely to reveal a wide diversity in operational styles and organization of tasks. Not only do different users perform spreadsheet operations in different order, but individual users will vary their style according to the complexity and length of the problem! In light of this, the arrangement of spreadsheet operations presented in the previous chapter is probably as good an order as any, and will be particularly useful for handling large worksheet problems. For small models, the order is simply this: after defining the model (determining which values will be used and the relationships between values), arrange the information on paper into rows and columns in a way that places formulas below or to the right of the values that are needed for their calculation. Then start the spreadsheet program, *load* the general template suggested in Chapter 7, *change* the title, date, and other preliminaries, *enter* the independent variable values, *enter* the base formulas, *copy* or replicate the base formulas and values, *format* the worksheet into the required (or pleasing) form, *save* the worksheet, *validate* the model, *print* the worksheet, and *document* it.

This chapter looks at the principal commands used to support these basic spreadsheet operations, and explores some special features that lend versatility or power to a spreadsheet. Most of the discussion centers on major spreadsheet programs like Lotus 1-2-3 (or simply 1-2-3), Multiplan, and SuperCalc^3, because they embody most of the commonly used spreadsheet presentation and command formats. A figure illustrating a screen from SuperCalc^3, for example, will come very close to what would be seen in SuperCalc4, SuperCalc^2, VisiCalc, and dozens of other spreadsheet programs. Likewise, anything written about 1-2-3 or Multiplan will hold true for a number of similar products.

TYPING, EDITING, AND REVISING THE WORKSHEET

Loading the Spreadsheet Program

The first step to using a spreadsheet is, of course, loading the program from the disk into memory. Many spreadsheet programs require the use of two disk drives. The program disk is kept in the A: drive, while a disk to store data files is placed in B:. Second-generation spreadsheets ordinarily load the entire program into memory; nevertheless, these programs may still require the program disk to reside in drive A:. The use of a separate data disk (in drive B:) is strongly advised even if ample space remains on the program disk. Lotus's 1-2-3 assumes a separate data disk by default. To load 1-2-3, simply type **123** followed by **<Return>**; to load SuperCalc^3, type **SC3** and **<Return>**, and to load VisiCalc, merely type **VC** and **<Return>**.

The Worksheet Display

Once loaded, the user is presented with a blank worksheet, such as the one in Figures 8–1 and 8–2. There are several noteworthy features in this initial display.

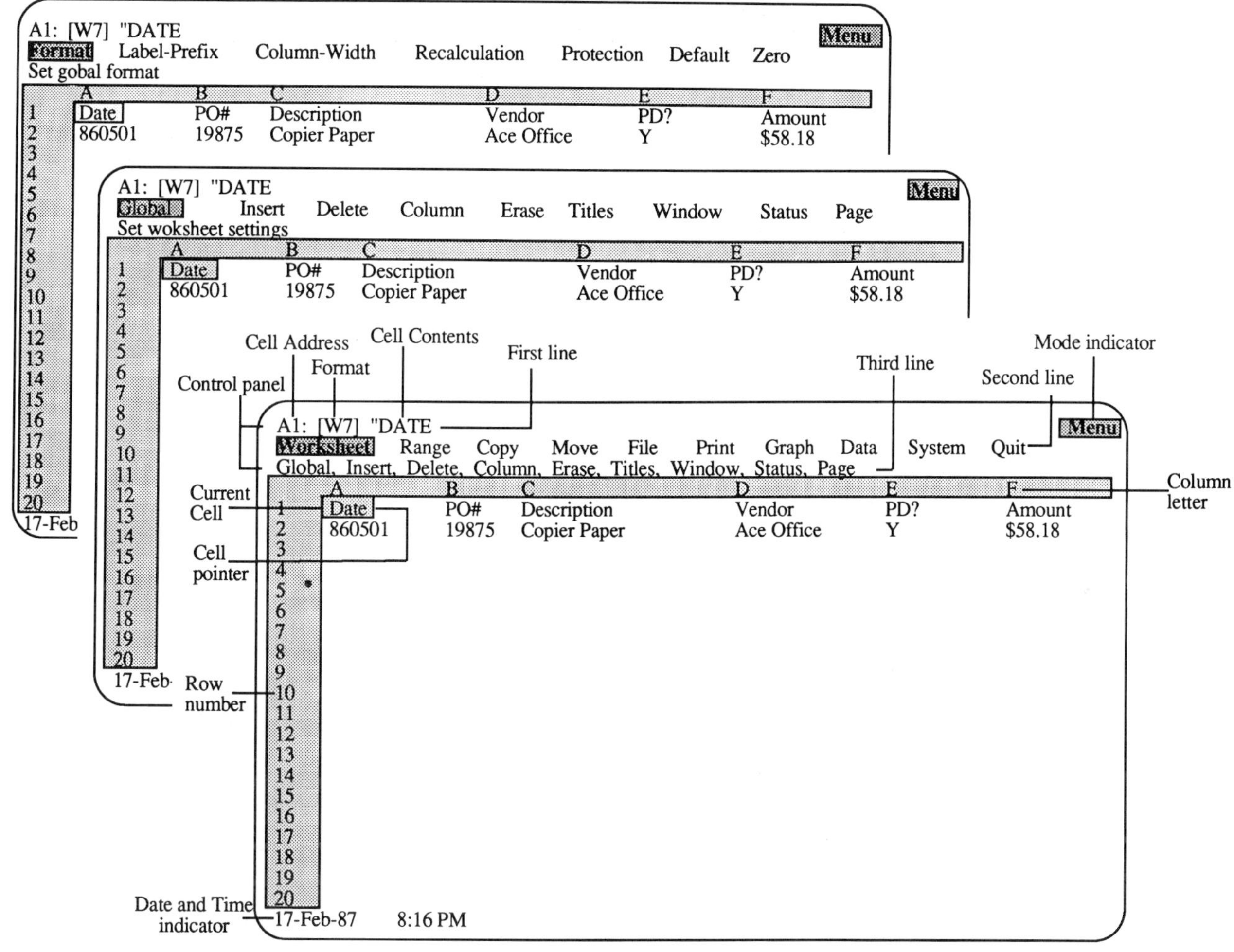

FIGURE 8–1

Worksheet Window with Control Panel at Top (Lotus 1-2-3)

The largest area of the screen is blank. This is the **worksheet window**, where the results of all entries will be displayed. Since no data has yet been entered, the cursor will be at the beginning point of the worksheet, the upper left-hand corner. The location of the cursor identifies the **active cell**, the one that is currently being entered or viewed.

Surrounding the worksheet window is the **border**. The border displays the row numbers and column designations, and provides a reference point for locating cells within the grid. The border in Figure 8–1 shows that the worksheet window has six columns (labeled A through F) and twenty rows. This is only a small portion of the work area available. If the user scrolled to the right, past the edge of the screen, the border will move also, revealing new column or row designations. In most spreadsheets, once the user goes past column Z she encounters column AA, then AB, etc.

Outside (above or below) the worksheet window are several special lines which make up the **control panel**, as shown in Figure 8–3. A **status line** displays the current location of the cursor, and gives the user a view of the active cell's current contents. Since the worksheet window only displays a cell's calculated value, the status line is the only way of viewing the underlying formulas in some spreadsheets.

FIGURE 8–2

Worksheet Window with control panel at Bottom (MS-DOS Version of Microsoft Multiplan)

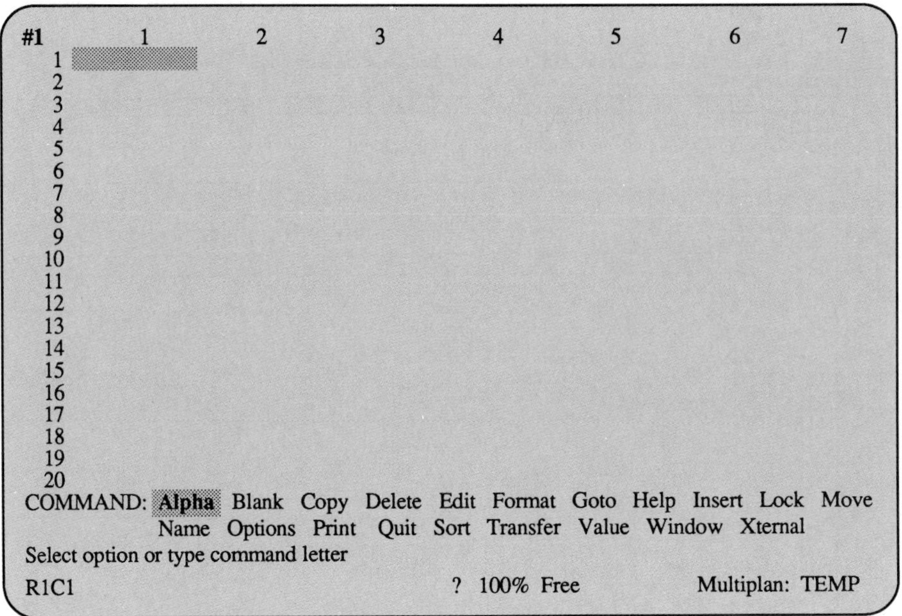

A **menu line** (or lines) is used to display the major options available to the user. If there are more choices within one of these options, a new menu will be displayed in the same area after the option is selected.

A **prompt area** is for displaying messages while the user is making menu selections or entering commands. Menu prompts help clarify the choices available, or the kind of input expected of the user. They are responsible for a large portion of the spreadsheet's ease of use, because even novices need rarely consult a manual if they pay close attention to these prompts.

The **entry area** is where all data, formulas, and commands are entered. In 1-2-3, this occupies the same line as the menu. If the user begins by entering a "/," the menu line will appear; otherwise, the area is used for cell entries. Once a cell entry is completed (by pressing <Return> or <Enter>), the spreadsheet is recalculated with the new value, and the outcome of the user's new entry will appear in the cell highlighted by the bar cursor in the worksheet window.

Cell and Range Specification

In 1-2-3 and SuperCalc^3, a cell is identified by its row number and column letter(s). Cell AA34, for example, uniquely identifies the cell at the intersection of the 34th row and the 27th column. In Multiplan, however, columns also have

FIGURE 8–3

A Closer Look at the Control Panel of Lotus 1-2-3

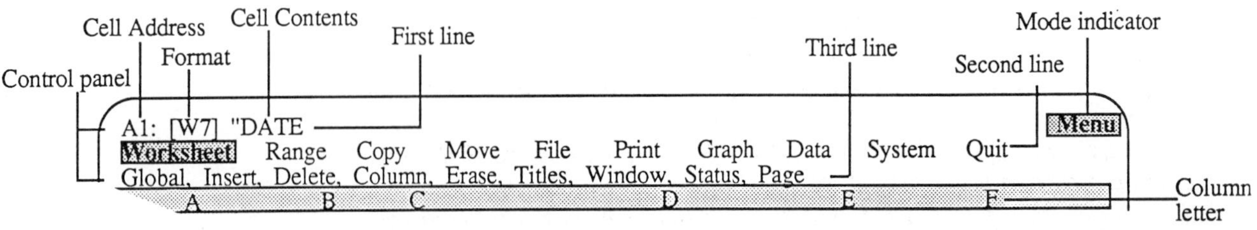

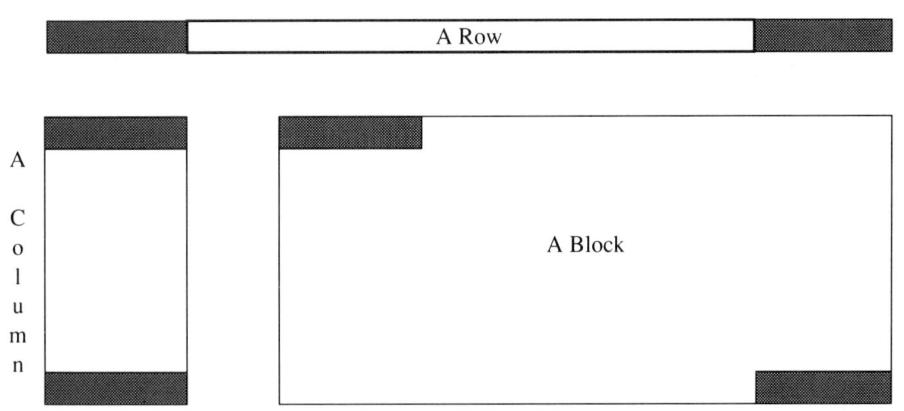

FIGURE 8–4

Worksheet Ranges (Beginning and Ending Cells are Shaded)

numeric designations, so that the same location would be identified as R34C27. A **range** is any rectangular area of the worksheet. Spreadsheets can perform many operations on a rectangular area, and might be able to do the same with an irregular shaped area of cells if it weren't for the fact that there is no convenient way of identifying a diagonal or circular grouping of cells. Any rectangular area, however, is neatly defined by specifying the beginning (upper left) and ending (lower right) cells, as shown in Figure 8–4 where beginning and ending cells are shaded. The ten vertical cells that begin at the top of column C, for example, can be specified as C1:C10 in SuperCalc^{3} or C1..C10 in 1-2-3. The block beginning with D4 and ending at F9 is simply D4:F9 or D4..F9.

Some users may find Multiplan's cell identification method (RmCn for the cell in row m and column n) inconvenient, but other ways of identifying cells are available. Most of the need for cell identification comes when the user is building a formula, moving worksheet information, or altering (formatting) the display. In all three of the programs under discussion, a cell can be specified by moving the cursor to that location and pressing a special key or key sequence. To sum a column of ten numbers in 1-2-3, for example, the user can begin writing the formula in the normal fashion. At the point where the range of values (to sum) is required, the user can move the cursor to the beginning of the column and press <.> (period). This specifies the beginning of the range and *anchors* the cursor. Moving the cursor down to the last value desired and pressing <Return> completes the range. This is called *cursor pointing,* and is an alternate way of referencing cells without having to type in cell ranges. Almost all spreadsheets support it.

Worksheet Navigation and Entry

In all spreadsheets, entering a simple value into the worksheet is just a matter of moving the cursor to the cell desired and making an entry. The end of the entry is signaled by pressing <Return>. In SuperCalc^{3}, if values are being entered in an orderly fashion (across a row or down a column), pressing <Return> will move the cursor to the next cell in the same direction. In 1-2-3, the arrow keys can be used instead of <Return> to end an entry, and the cursor will be moved in the direction of the arrow.

The arrow keys are used to move around the worksheet a column or row at a time. For more rapid movement around a large worksheet, some programs have special keys defined for scrolling in all directions a screenful at a time. In 1-2-3,

FIGURE 8–5

Lotus 1-2-3 Commands Showing All Menu Bars, and How They are Linked

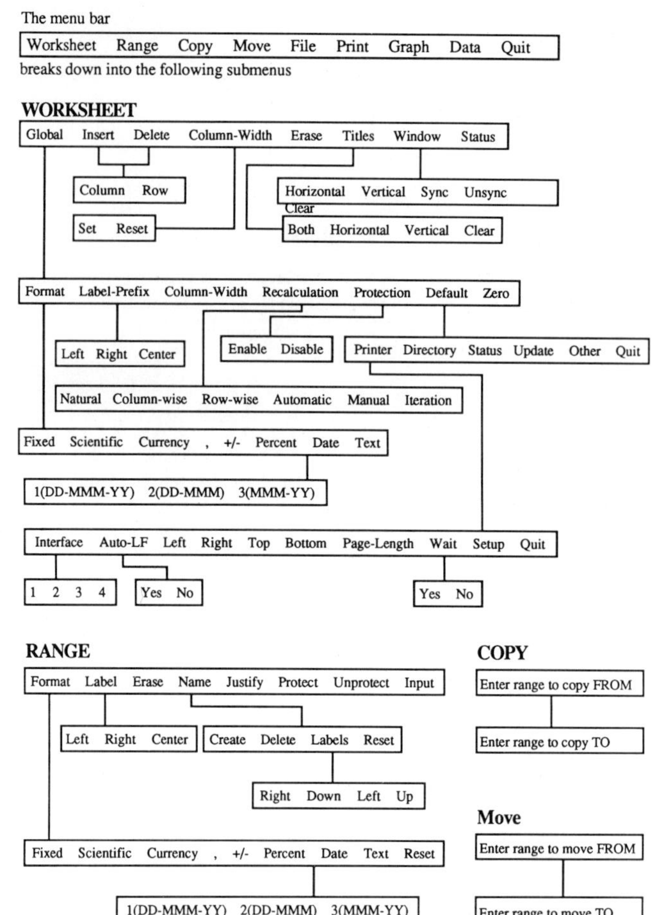

the <Pg Up> key (on the numeric keypad) will move the cursor up a screenful at a time, and the <Home> key will place the cursor in the first cell (A1) of the worksheet. The <Pg Dn> key moves the cursor down a screenful each time. <Tab> is used for rapid scrolling to the right, and by pressing <End> followed by an arrow key, the user can jump quickly to the edges of a worksheet (in any direction). To use these special keys (or the arrow keys), however, the <Num Loc> key must be off, which is inconvenient for most spreadsheet users. SuperCalc and VisiCalc programs offer a GOTO command (summoned by pressing =). To move directly to cell D48, the user would enter =D48. In 1-2-3, depressing the function key <F5> invokes the GOTO command, which prompts for the cell the user wishes to jump to.

Command Entry

The method of entering commands will differ from program to program. In 1-2-3, SuperCalc, VisiCalc, and many other spreadsheets, a command is issued by first pressing /. This causes the menu options to appear on one or more menu bars. (With Multiplan, the command mode is entered by pressing <Return> before other

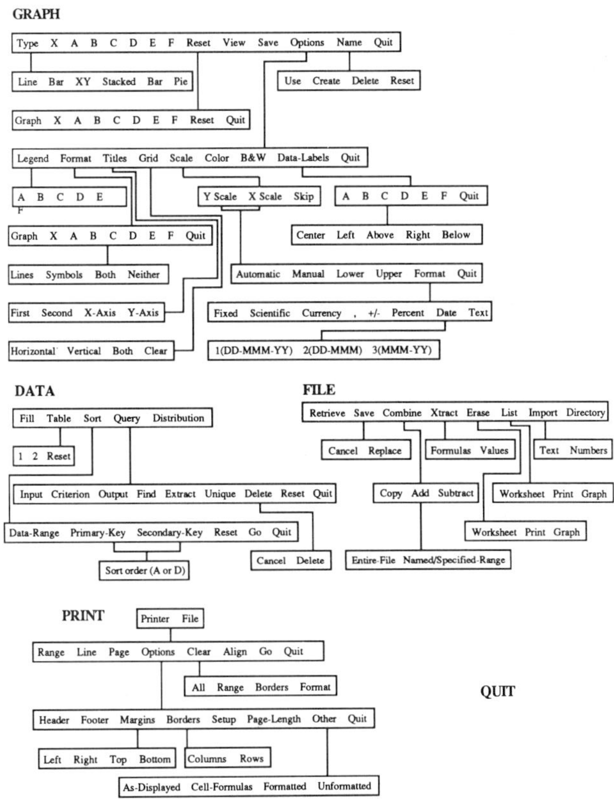

entries are made.) The command on the menu bar that the cursor currently resides on—the first command, usually—is highlighted. The user moves the cursor to the desired selection and presses <Return> (or releases the mouse button in the case of the Macintosh). Doing so may bring up a submenu from which a selection must be made. In some instances the user must work through as many as four menus and submenus. In Figure 8–1, the item WORKSHEET was selected from the first menu bar, the item GLOBAL was selected from the submenu bar associated with the menu item WORKSHEET, and the menu item FORMAT was selected from the sub-submenu bar associated with the submenu item GLOBAL. Note that the third line of the control panel lists the submenu associated with the currently highlighted item on the second line of the control panel *for the worksheet menu bar only,* which is the opening menu bar that appears once the / key is depressed.

Spreadsheet designers have enabled the programs to be both menu- and command-driven. This permits novice users to use the menus and experienced users to use the commands. Rather than working through long lists of menus and submenus, it is much easier for an experienced user to invoke specific tasks by command. The designers have carefully named their commands so that no two (major) commands begin with the same letter. This allows the user to select a command merely by entering its first letter, following the /. It also creates problems when there are a great number of commands and only 26 letters available. To overcome this obstacle, 1-2-3 commands are grouped into a limited number of major categories (no more than will fit across one row of the screen at one time). The Lotus 1-2-3 menu "tree" is shown in Figure 8–5.

One problem with clustering commands into groups is that either the name given to a command or the group it is placed in may seem highly contrived or arbitrary. It also requires the user to cycle through multiple levels of menus and commands to accomplish a single task. For example, deleting column F of a 1-2-3 worksheet is accomplished by entering /WDCF1..F1, for "put me in command mode, please" (/), "let me adjust the WORKSHEET" (the DELETE command has been put in this group), "by allowing me to DELETE a COLUMN—specifically allow me to delete from F1 to F1" (more on 1-2-3 range specifications later).

In SuperCalc^3, the same deletion can be made with /DCF. The price paid for saving the extra step is menu options that will not all fit on-screen if they are completely written out. Instead, only the first letter of each command is shown. If the user presses /P in hopes of *P*rinting his worksheet, he will have just entered the PROTECT command (printing is found under /O for OUTPUT). As soon as the first letter of a command has been entered, the rest of the command will be written in the entry area. This is called **interpretive prompting.** SuperCalc^3 begins commands with every letter in the alphabet except J, K, N, and, curiously, H (the HELP command is obtained with the <?> key). Part of the SuperCalc^3 menu tree is shown in Figure 8–6, along with some SuperCalc^3 commands.

Occasionally, the user may find that he has inadvertently entered the wrong command. The command may be abandoned by pressing the <Backspace> key in SuperCalc^3, or <Esc> in 1-2-3. The multiple questions and menu levels can be useful in this case, because they provide plenty of room to back out before the user does something he might regret, such as erase the entire worksheet.

Entering Formulas and Functions

In 1-2-3, a value or formula must begin with one of the following characters:

0 1 2 3 4 5 6 7 8 9 0 . + – (@ # $

Thus, a simple formula to multiply A1 by 3 will be written as 3*A1 or +A1*3. Entering it as A1*3 will cause it to be interpreted as a label, and A1*3 will appear in the cell, rather than a formula that is evaluated to a number. SuperCalc^3 assumes that any entry is a candidate for calculation unless it is prefaced with a single quotation mark (which identifies it as a label). Shown in Figure 8–7 are valid formulas for Lotus 1-2-3 and SuperCalc^3. SuperCalc4 has a way of determining whether a cell entry is a formula or text (a label or title).

Copying and Moving Worksheet Information

Imagine a worksheet that contains payroll information (Figure 8–8). Column C contains the wage rate for each job category. To give the president a 5% raise, the user could move the cursor to an unoccupied cell (E3 might be a good choice) and enter 1.05*C3. This would yield the correct figure (36750) for the president's new salary. Upon moving back to C3, the user would enter the new value.

This method would certainly give the correct result, but it would become extremely tedious to perform if the 5% raise went to all job titles, and there were 200 of them instead of only 5. Fortunately, spreadsheet programs provide several commands for manipulating blocks of cells.

/Arrange
/Blank
/Copy
/Delete
/Edit
/Format
/Global
/Insert
/Load
/Move
/Output
/Protect
/Quit
/Replicate
/Save
/Title
/Unprotect
/View
/Window
/X (execute)
/Zap
//Data mgt

Each command is the beginning of a command tree as shown below for /Move and /Output:

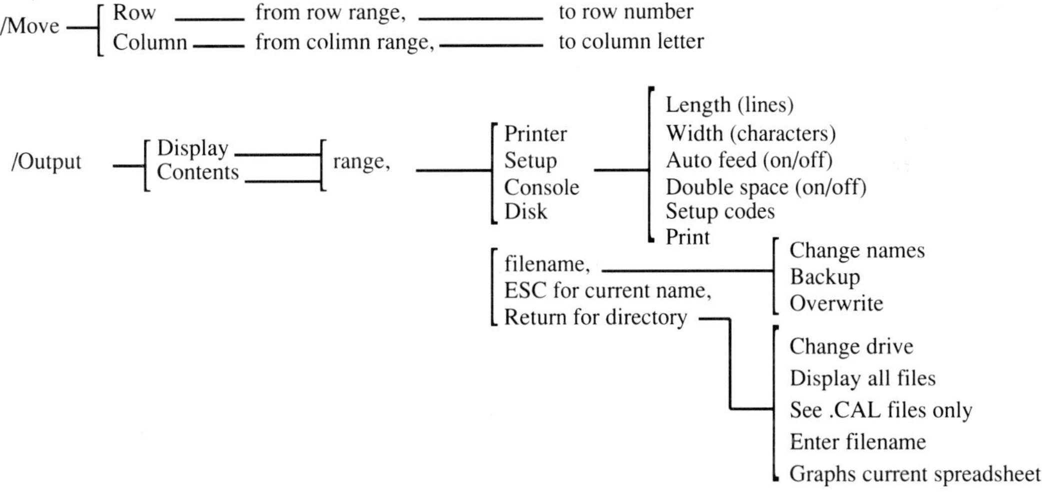

FIGURE 8–6
SuperCalc^3 Commands

A COPY command can be used to make a duplicate of a cell or group of cells at a different location in the spreadsheet. SuperCalc^3 actually has two commands, REPLICATE and COPY, to duplicate worksheet entries. The REPLICATE command is used to copy a single cell into a range of cells. COPY does the opposite, duplicating a range of cells to another location (addressed by its starting, or upper left-hand cell). 1-2-3 and Multiplan both use the command COPY to perform these functions.

A MOVE command will take a column, row, or rectangular block of cells and place them elsewhere in a worksheet, as shown in Figure 8–9. Unlike the COPY command, moving data does not create duplicate information. The purpose of the MOVE command is to improve the appearance and organization of the worksheet. In SuperCalc^3, moving a column out from between two columns will collapse the surrounding columns to fill in the gap, as shown in Figure 8–10. Moving a column into a position between two columns will, accordingly, cause the column to the right of the new location to move farther right to accommodate the new column. 1-2-3 handles the MOVE command quite differently. When moving a column or row, 1-2-3 will leave a gap (an empty column or row) in the old location. The destination column or row will be overwritten as 1-2-3 doesn't bother to bump them over. Therefore, it may be necessary to first use the INSERT command to clear the destination area.

FIGURE 8–7
Some Valid Formulas

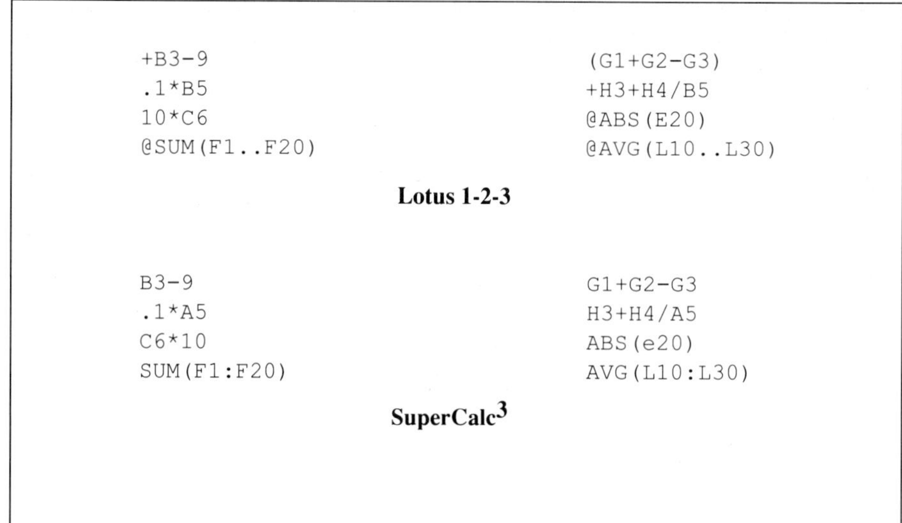

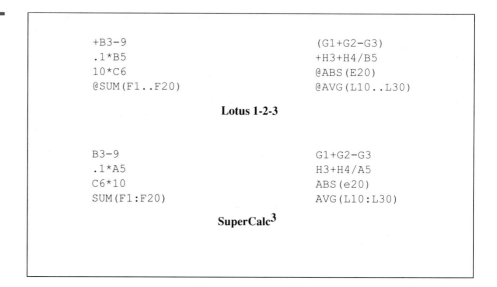

```
+B3-9               (G1+G2-G3)
.1*B5               +H3+H4/B5
10*C6               @ABS(E20)
@SUM(F1..F20)       @AVG(L10..L30)
```

Lotus 1-2-3

```
B3-9                G1+G2-G3
.1*A5               H3+H4/A5
C6*10               ABS(e20)
SUM(F1:F20)         AVG(L10:L30)
```

SuperCalc^3

FIGURE 8–8
A Payroll Worksheet

	A	B	C	D
1	**Title**	**# Workers**	**Rate**	**Total $**
2	-----------	-----------	-----------	-----------
3	Pres.	1	35000	35000
4	Sr. V.P.	2	30000	60000
5	Jr. V.P.	6	26000	156000
6	Secty.	1	12000	12000
7	Janitor	1	31000	31000
8	-----------	-----------	-----------	-----------
9	Total	11		294000

Each method has its advantages and disadvantages. The 1-2-3 approach requires the user to clear the area (by using the INSERT command) before moving material in a crowded worksheet, and may leave unsightly gaps (that can be deleted). SuperCalc^3, on the other hand, is limited to moving columns and rows, and is unable to move a rectangular block of cells (it cannot handle pushing surrounding cells both down and to the right even though SuperCalc4 can do this). It is noteworthy that rows can be moved into other rows only, columns can be moved into other columns only, and, in 1-2-3, rectangular blocks can be moved into other blocks. Thus it is not possible to move rows into columns or blocks, columns into rows or blocks, and blocks into rows or columns.

The DELETE command (found beneath the WORKSHEET heading in 1-2-3) will eliminate an entire column or row, and can be used to close up any gaps in a worksheet. The INSERT command will create a new, empty column or row for new material.

Returning to the initial problem of the 5% across-the-board raise, the block manipulation commands could make short work of the task. The procedure might go like this:

1. Move to E3 and enter the formula, 1.05*C3 (entering this formula directly over the old value in C3 will create an unresolvable circular reference).

	A	B	C	D	E
1	**Title**		**Rate**	**Total $**	**# Workers**
2	----------	----------	----------	----------	----------
3	Pres.		35000	35000	1
4	Sr. V.P.		30000	60000	2
5	Jr. V.P.		26000	156000	6
6	Secty.		12000	12000	1
7	Janitor		31000	31000	1
8	----------	----------	----------	----------	----------
9	Total		134000	294000	11

The result of moving Column B to Column E. Column B is left blank and Column E is overwritten. Note that references in Column D now refer to Column E instead of B.

	A	B	C	D
1	**Title**	**# Workers**	**Rate**	**Total $**
2	----------	----------	----------	----------
3	Pres.	1	35000	35000
4	Sr. V.P.	2	30000	60000
5	Total	16	242000	432000
6	Secty.	1	12000	12000
7	Janitor	1	31000	31000
8	----------	----------	----------	----------
9				

The result of moving Row 9 to Row 5. Row 9 is left blank and Row 5 is overwritten. The numbers in cells C5 and D5 are incorrect and 1-2-3 advises that there are circular references.

	A	B	C	D	E	F
1	**Title**	**# Workers**	**Rate**	**Total $**		
2	----------	----------	----------	----------	----------	----------
3	Pres.	1	35000	35000		
4	Sr. V.P.	2	30000	60000		
5	Jr. V.P.			156000	6	26000
6	Secty.			12000	1	12000
7	Janitor	1	31000	31000		
8	----------	----------	----------	----------	----------	----------
9	Total	11	96000	294000		

The result of moving Block B5..C6 to E5..F6. Block B5..C6 is left blank and Block E5..F6 is overwritten. Formulas in D5 and D6 now refer to cells E5 to F6.

FIGURE 8–9

Some MOVE Operations in 1-2-3 as Applied to the Payroll Worksheet in Figure 8–8

2. Use the COPY command to duplicate this formula in the cells below it.
3. Change the formulas for column D so that they are calculated from the new column E times column B (cell D3 would read +E3*B3 in 1-2-3).

The new spreadsheet would appear as shown in Figure 8–11 on page 253.

Figure 8–11 is useful for illustrating several points about spreadsheet operations. First, note that the revised worksheet does not look quite like the original (there are now five columns instead of four). To remedy this, the user might at first think that column E should be moved between columns B and D, and that the old column C should be deleted. Unfortunately, the result of such an attempt is shown

FIGURE 8–10

Some MOVE Operations in SuperCalc³ as Applied to the Payroll Worksheet in Figure 8–8

	A	B	C	D	E
1	**Title**		**Rate**	**Total $**	**# Workers**
2	------------	------------	------------	------------	------------
3	Pres.	35000	35000		1
4	Sr. V.P.	30000	60000		2
5	Jr. V.P.	26000	156000		6
6	Secty.	12000	12000		1
7	Janitor	31000	31000		1
8	------------	------------	------------	------------	------------
9	Total	134000	294000		11

The result of moving Column B to Column E. Columns C and D are automatically moved left by SuperCalc³ to fill the vacated Column B. Cell references in the new column C are appropriately adjusted. Column D is now vacant.

	A	B	C	D
1	**Title**	**# Workers**	**Rate**	**Total $**
2	------------	------------	------------	------------
3	Pres.	1	35000	35000
4	Sr. V.P.	2	30000	60000
5	Total	22	268000	588000
6	Jr. V.P.	6	26000	156000
7	Secty.	1	12000	12000
8	Janitor	1	31000	31000
9	------------	------------	------------	------------

The result of moving Row 9 to Row 5. Rows 5 through 8 are automatically moved down to Rows 6 through 9. The numbers in Cells C5 and D5 are incorrect. There are circular references.

	A	B	C	D
1	**Total $**	**Title**	**# Workers**	**Rate**
2	------------	------------	------------	------------
3	35000	Pres.	1	35000
4	60000	Sr. V.P.	2	30000
5	156000	Jr. V.P.	6	26000
6	12000	Secty.	1	12000
7	31000	Janitor	1	31000
8	------------	------------	------------	------------
9	294000	Total	11	96000

The result of moving Column D to Column A. Columns A through C are automatically moved right by SuperCalc³ to Columns B through D. Formulas in the new Column A have been appropriately adjusted and the numbers are correct.

in Figure 8–12 ("ERR" indicates that an error has occurred in calculating the cells). The formulas in the new column E depend upon column C for their values, so column C may not be eliminated.

Another spreadsheet feature should be apparent from the creation of the revised payroll worksheet (Figure 8–11). When the formula was copied from E3 to the cells below it, all of the cells in column E were calculated from column C values within the same row! It was not necessary to adjust each cell's formula to

	A	B	C	D	E
1	**Title**	**# Workers**	**PR Rate**	**Total $**	**New Rate**
2	----------	----------	----------	----------	----------
3	Pres.	1	35000	36750	36750
4	Sr. V.P.	2	30000	63000	31500
5	Jr. V.P.	6	26000	163800	27300
6	Secty.	1	12000	12600	12600
7	Janitor	1	31000	32550	32550
8	----------	----------	----------	----------	----------
9	Total	11		308700	

FIGURE 8–11

Revised Payroll Worksheet

	A	B	C	D
1	**Title**	**# Workers**	**Rate**	**Total $**
2	----------	----------	----------	----------
3	Pres.	1	ERR	ERR
4	Sr. V.P.	2	ERR	ERR
5	Jr. V.P.	6	ERR	ERR
6	Secty.	1	ERR	ERR
7	Janitor	1	ERR	ERR
8	----------	----------	----------	----------
9	Total	11		ERR

FIGURE 8–12

The Result of Inadequate Information

calculate from within its own row, the spreadsheet did this on its own. By looking at the status line while scrolling down column E it is obvious that, indeed, all the formulas are different. This is known as **relative cell referencing**, and it is the default mode for the spreadsheet copy command.

There are times when relative cell referencing is not appropriate, as when copying cells that should refer to the same location for a critical value. For example, in a sales forecasting worksheet, a single cell can be used to enter a number for expected sales percentage growth. This cell can then be used by an entire column of formulas, each one multiplying the sales amount in the adjacent column by the single growth factor. For these situations, spreadsheets use **absolute cell referencing** (sometimes called fixed referencing). In 1-2-3, the user designates a fixed reference by placing a dollar sign before the cell coordinates when entering the formula in the first cell (before copying it throughout the column). In SuperCalc^3, the formula is written without regard to absolute or relative references. When the user copies the formula to the cells below, however, she will be asked to specify which formula references are absolute and which are relative (i.e., should be adjusted by the program). Figure 8–13 shows what would have resulted if the formula in E3 had been entered as 1.05*$C$3.

Editing the Worksheet

Before a worksheet is printed or saved, the user will want to take some time to correct any errors that may have been made, and to design the final appearance

FIGURE 8–13

Absolute Cell Referencing

(a) Personnel file. (b) Forecast formulas. Note $ signs. The forward references are satisfactorily handled by Microsoft Excel.

	A	B	C	D	E
1	**Title**	**# Workers**	**PR Rate**	**Total $**	**New Rate**
2	-------	-------	-------	-------	-------
3	Pres.	1	35000	36750	36750
4	Sr. V.P.	2	30000	63000	36750
5	Jr. V.P.	6	26000	163800	36750
6	Secty.	1	12000	12600	36750
7	Janitor	1	31000	32550	36750
8	-------	-------	-------	-------	-------
9	Total	11		308700	

(a)

of the work. Several editing and formatting features exist to help accomplish these objectives.

The DELETE command can be used to remove a gap that extends across an entire row or column. Occasionally, relative referencing can leave zeros in cells after copying a formula. The zeros may be necessary in the final display, but if they are not, they can be erased. The ERASE command (called BLANK in SuperCalc^3, and CLEAR in other programs) will produce empty cells in any specified range, without causing movement of the surrounding cells. It can also be used to clear the entire worksheet and start over (SuperCalc^3 uses ZAP for this).

The user will probably also want to add some information to the worksheet, such as comments, or column and row headings. The INSERT command can create an area for entering these items. Text that is too large to fit the column width (columns are usually between eight and eleven characters wide) will be displayed in (spilled over into) the cell to the right if it is not occupied. If the adjacent cell is filled, however, the user may want to adjust the **column width** because no spillover is allowed in this case. A column may be made up to 240 characters wide, and some programs allow unlimited width. The column may also be made smaller, down to zero characters in width. A column that is zero characters wide is said to be "hidden." There are security-related uses for such a feature.

Creating Windows

Some manipulation of the worksheet is done to aid in using the spreadsheet, rather than for appearance. Creating windows allows the user to view two or more widely separated areas of the worksheet simultaneously. A window splits the screen into multiple worksheet areas and has some important uses. Important data may be kept in a central location at the top of a worksheet. A **horizontal window** can keep this area in view at all times as entries are made into other worksheet areas. For an instructor's grade roster (Figure 8–14), a **vertical window** can keep the students' names visible as she enters grades several columns to the right. Both windows can also be **synchronized**, so that both scroll vertically as the user moves down the column making entries.

With 1-2-3 and SuperCalc^3, a special command allows the user to display the underlying formula in a cell instead of its calculated value. In SuperCalc^3, the user may go one step beyond this and have one window display values while another

	A	B	C	D
1	Quarter	Actual Values	Predicted Values	
2	1	100	=A2*$C$9+$D$9	
3	2	250	=A3*$C$9+$D$9	
4	3	320	=A4*$C$9+$D$9	
5	4	490	=A5*$C$9+$D$9	
6				
7				
8			**Trend: y = mx + b**	
9			**=LINEST(B2:B5)**	**=LINEST(B2:B5)**

(b)

shows the formulas used for calculation. This can be a tremendous aid in tracking down spreadsheet errors.

FORMATTING AND PRINTING WORKSHEETS

Once the worksheet model has been created and validated, the next major task is to format it neatly and then to print it. Formatting involves specifying exactly

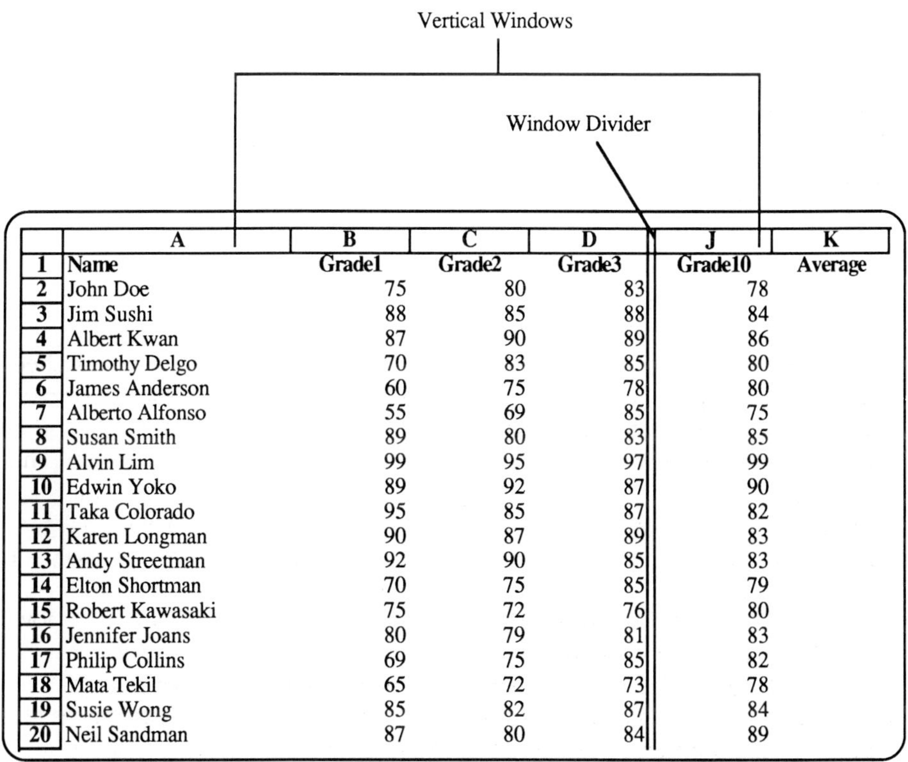

	A	B	C	D	J	K
1	Name	Grade1	Grade2	Grade3	Grade10	Average
2	John Doe	75	80	83	78	
3	Jim Sushi	88	85	88	84	
4	Albert Kwan	87	90	89	86	
5	Timothy Delgo	70	83	85	80	
6	James Anderson	60	75	78	80	
7	Alberto Alfonso	55	69	85	75	
8	Susan Smith	89	80	83	85	
9	Alvin Lim	99	95	97	99	
10	Edwin Yoko	89	92	87	90	
11	Taka Colorado	95	85	87	82	
12	Karen Longman	90	87	89	83	
13	Andy Streetman	92	90	85	83	
14	Elton Shortman	70	75	85	79	
15	Robert Kawasaki	75	72	76	80	
16	Jennifer Joans	80	79	81	83	
17	Philip Collins	69	75	85	82	
18	Mata Tekil	65	72	73	78	
19	Susie Wong	85	82	87	84	
20	Neil Sandman	87	80	84	89	

FIGURE 8–14

A Synchronized Vertical Window

TABLE 8–1
Format Settings Likely to Be Available

SuperCalc³	
Integer	123
General	123.45678
Exponential	1.2345e3
Money	$123.46
Right-justified values	
Left-justified values	
Right-justified text entries	
Left-justified text entries	
Linear display (the use of *'s to display a simple graph)	
User-defined format	
Hide a cell	

Lotus 1-2-3	
General	123.45678
Fixed	123.46
Scientific	1.23E+02
Currency	$123.46
Percent	12345.68%
Date-1	28-May-91
Date-2	28-May
Text	123.45678

how the numbers and labels are to be displayed. This may be followed by adjusting the column widths of certain columns. Ultimately, the worksheet developer will want to print the worksheet model so it can be presented to others.

Format Settings

Initially, all cells have a predefined **general format** by default. Once the model has been created, it is possible to change the formats to improve readability. Value cells, or cells defined by formulas, employ a different collection of format settings than those used by label cells. The entire collection of format settings that are likely to be available is shown in Table 8–1. Format settings can be global or local. In the latter case, the user is expected to specify a range, which can be as small as a single cell.

The user can specify that all text or numbers will be right-justified (aligned on the right) or left-justified. By default, a spreadsheet will left-justify text and right-justify numbers, but either or both of these can be reversed. 1-2-3 also allows text to be centered.

Formatting a worksheet is not done merely to please the eye. The nature of the report might require numbers to be displayed in scientific notation (e.g., 4.231E5) or as a dollars-and-cents amount, with two digits to the right of the decimal, a dollar sign, and commas after every third digit to the left of the decimal. Spreadsheet programs offer several formatting styles, as indicated in Table 8–1.

Adjusting Column Widths

The adjustment of column widths should take place after the cells have been formatted. Generally, the cell widths should be adjusted so that the displayed values and labels of all cells are clearly readable. Values that are too large to fit in certain cells might be displayed in scientific notation, or the cell may simply be filled with ********, >>>>>>>>, ########, or !!!!!!!. The goal of column width adjustments is to remove all appearances of "fill" characters within cells by enlarging their widths as necessary. (At least one commercial spreadsheet program adjusts column widths automatically so the numbers or labels are clearly visible.)

Users can adjust column widths globally or locally. If the request is for local adjustment, the user must specify a range (of one or several columns) over which the adjustment is to be applied. Necessarily, however, the adjustment must be applied down the entire column. It is not possible for cells within the same column to have different cell widths. Global column width adjustments apply to all columns in the worksheet.

Several considerations affect the number of characters required to display the value of a cell: the cell's magnitude (numeric size), the format selected, and the number of decimal places required by the selected format.

Saving Formats

Once the user is satisfied with the format settings, it is a good idea to (again) save the worksheet model. Doing so will preserve the effort that went into specifying the format settings. Generally, saving the worksheet model causes the format settings to get saved right along with the worksheet model itself in the same file. However, some spreadsheet programs will save the format settings independently of the file containing the model.

Print Options

To print the worksheet model it must be active (loaded and in memory) for most spreadsheet programs. The PRINT command is invoked, and the program then prompts the user for a range. If the user's response is not **All**, then he must specify the range to be printed—usually, the upper-left cell and the lower-right cell of the range. The user can do this by typing in the cell coordinates of the upper-left cell and lower-right cell, or by cursor pointing.

Some options offered by most spreadsheet programs include headers and footers that can be added, showing page numbers, date, and time. Borders showing the row numbers and column letters can be toggled on or off for the hard-copy output only. While debugging the program, the user can refer to these borders to trace cells and cell references within formulas by using the border's number and letter coordinates. But, when the final product is to be printed, it is convenient to turn the borders off for readability and polish in appearance.

Unlike word processing packages, most spreadsheet programs do not support background printing. Consequently, the system is unavailable for use when printing of the worksheet is in progress.

Printing reports is one of the weakest areas of a spreadsheet, in part because no printer-specific drivers are usually included with the program, even though

FIGURE 8–15

Display and Contents Outputs of a Sales Forecasting Worksheet. (a) Display output. (b) Contents output (Microsoft Excel).

Sales Forecast

Quarter (Base Year 1985)	Actual Sales	Trend Estimates	Seasonal Factor	Average Seasonal Factor
1	$300.00	$228.33	1.31	1.25
2	$200.00	$280.60	0.71	0.79
3	$220.00	$332.86	0.66	0.70
4	$530.00	$385.12	1.38	1.28
5	$520.00	$437.38	1.19	
6	$420.00	$489.64	0.86	
7	$400.00	$541.90	0.74	
8	$700.00	$594.17	1.18	

Trend Equation (y = mx + b)
52.26 176.071

Sales Forecast For 1987 Quarter	
9 I	$808.93
10 II	$548.66
11 III	$525.32
12 IV	$1,025.83

(a)

Sales Forecast

	A	B	C	D	E	F	G	H
1		Actual Sales		Trend Estimates		Seasonal Factor		Average Seasonal
2	Quarter (Base Year 1985)							Factor
3								
4	1	300		=A4*$A$15+$B$15		=Actual_Sales/Trend_Es		=(FirstYrFactor+SecondYrFactor)/2
5	2	200		=A5*$A$15+$B$15		=Actual_Sales/Trend_Es		=(FirstYrFactor+SecondYrFactor)/2
6	3	220		=A6*$A$15+$B$15		=Actual_Sales/Trend_Es		=(FirstYrFactor+SecondYrFactor)/2
7	4	530		=A7*$A$15+$B$15		=Actual_Sales/Trend_Es		=(FirstYrFactor+SecondYrFactor)/2
8	5	520		=A8*$A$15+$B$15		=Actual_Sales/Trend_Es		
9	6	420		=A9*$A$15+$B$15		=Actual_Sales/Trend_Es		
10	7	400		=A10*$A$15+$B$15		=Actual_Sales/Trend_Es		
11	8	700		=A11*$A$15+$B$15		=Actual_Sales/Trend_Es		
12								
13								
14	**Trend Equation (y = mx + b)**							
15	=LINEST(B4:B11)	=LINEST(B4:B11)						
16								
17								
18		**Sales Forecast For 1987**						
19		**Quarter**						
20	9	I		=(A20*$A$15+$B$15)*H4				
21	=A20+1	II		=(A21*$A$15+$B$15)*H5				
22	=A21+1	III		=(A22*$A$15+$B$15)*H6				
23	=A22+1	IV		=(A23*$A$15+$B$15)*H7				

(b)

quite a few print options may be supported. A word processing program can usually be installed for a specific printer by selecting the printer model from a menu. From that point on, the program merely looks at a printer driver file or table to select the correct code to switch into letter-quality or expanded print modes. Since most older spreadsheets do not have printer installation programs and printer drivers, the user must consult the printer manual to find the correct codes. The reason this is important is that worksheets can be very wide, and users often want to print them in a compressed print mode.

Most spreadsheet programs allow the user to control the left and top margins, as well as to designate the number of lines to print per page. They also have a special mode that can be used to send printer control codes directly to the printer. It is this mode that is used to switch print styles or character widths. Novice users are apt to find that this can be difficult, depending upon the clarity of their printer's manual.

A worksheet may be printed in two formats, as shown in Figure 8–15. The **display format** creates an image on paper that duplicates the screen display. This is the normal manner of printing work. The **contents format** will print the formulas (and some screen formatting information) of each cell. This is used for documentation and debugging purposes, although it has limited value when a worksheet model is large. Special spreadsheet documentation programs exist, however, to facilitate documentation and debugging needs.

Most spreadsheet programs offer the user the option of printing to a disk file instead of directly to the printer. A filename must be provided for the output to be stored under. As shall be seen in the 1-2-3 tutorial at the end of this chapter, 1-2-3 has the capability to print (in this case send) several ranges to the same file. Each successive printing will append the new range of information to the existing data in the file when the same filename is used, rather than overwriting the existing information in that file. This feature allows printing of several sections of the worksheet without having to print the entire worksheet, as shown in Figure 8–16.

OPERATORS AND FUNCTIONS

The essential fabric of formulas are cell coordinate addresses (or references by the use of cell names), which are operated upon by operators and functions. This section deals with operators and functions.

Precedence Order of Operators

As discussed earlier, formulas consist of cell references separated by operators, but formulas may also contain functions. Strict rules exist for evaluating formulas. First, a precedence order of operators, as indicated in Table 8–2, is used to determine in what order the operators should be evaluated. When ties occur, the evaluation order proceeds left to right.

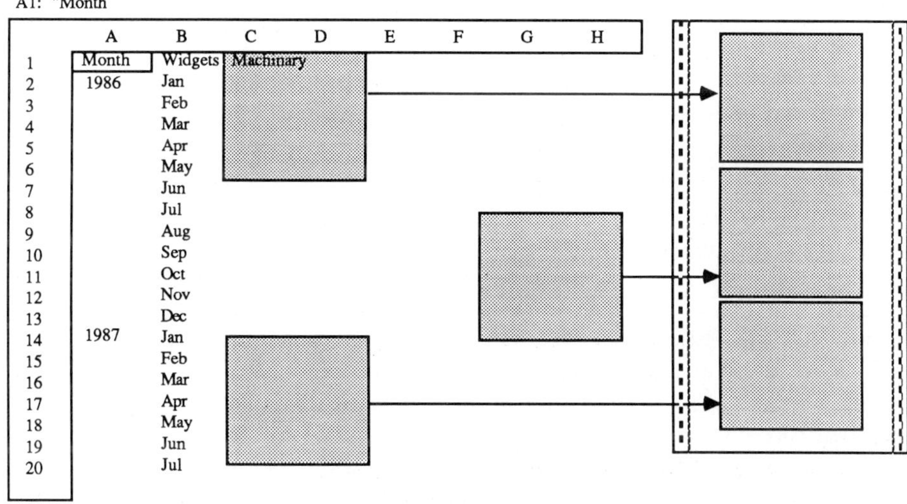

FIGURE 8–16

A Print Job with Several Parts

TABLE 8–2
Precedence Order of Operators

	DESCRIPTION	OPERATOR	ORDER
Algebraic Operators	Parentheses	()	1
	Exponentiation	^	2
	Multiplication	*	3
	Division	/	3
	Addition	+	4
	Subtraction	−	4
Relational Operators	Less-than-or-equal-to	<=	5
	Less-than	<	5
	Greater-than-or-equal-to	>=	5
	Greater-than	>	5
	Equal-to	=	5
	Not-equal	<>	6
Logical Operators	Logical AND	AND	7
	Logical OR	OR	7
	Logical NOT	NOT	7

For example, consider the formula +C10+D5^2/D2*E8. (Note that the first operator—the "+" sign—serves only to inform the spreadsheet program that what follows is a formula.) According to Table 8–2, this formula would be evaluated as follows:

1. Evaluate D5^2.
2. Take the result of step 1 and divide by D2.
3. Take the result of step 2 and multiply by E8.
4. Take the result of step 3 and add C10.

Suppose that, in algebraic notation, the expression to be evaluated was

$$\frac{C10+D5^2}{D2*E8}$$

Would the spreadsheet formula have performed the job correctly? To properly evaluate this expression, the following steps must be taken:

1. Evaluate D5^2.
2. Take the result of step 1 and add C10.
3. Find the product of D2 and E8.
4. Take the result of step 2 and divide it by the result of step 3.

Clearly, the spreadsheet formula does not get the job done. To get the spreadsheet to properly evaluate the expression above, parentheses must be used. The formula should be written as (C10+D5^2)/(D2*D8). Because the formula now begins with an open parenthesis, the spreadsheet will recognize it as a formula and no initial "+" is necessary. The use of parentheses causes the expressions they contain to be evaluated first, before operations outside the parentheses are performed. Of course, the precedence rules apply within parentheses as well, so the exponentiation operation is performed first and then the addition operation.

The second set of parentheses causes the multiplication operation between D2 and D8 to be performed before the division operation involving the two parenthesized expressions is performed. Again this is because the precedence order of operations (Table 8–2) requires that the spreadsheet do operations inside parentheses before doing any operations outside of parentheses. As shown, the evaluation process *proceeds left to right* whenever the precedence rules permit. Such is the case when a sequence of operations of the same order is to be performed, such as +A1/B2*C3. First, A1 would be divided by B2 and the result of that would be multiplied by C3. It is worth noting that the precedence order of operators is used in nearly every high-level computer language.

Functions

Spreadsheet functions are used by entering the name of the function and enclosing its **arguments** (all the values necessary for calculation) in parentheses, as shown in Figure 8–17. In 1-2-3, the user must precede the function name with @ (the "at" symbol). @AVG(C1..C40) will find the average of the range extending from C1 to C40. AVG is the function name, and the average requires only one parameter, a range of values. Functions may be combined or used in formulas just like any other value, with extremely powerful results. For example, a statistician (or an instructor calculating grades) can use (A4 – @AVG(A1.. A100))/@STD(A1.. A100) to find the difference between cell A4 and the average of cells A1 through A100 divided by the standard deviation. This calculates a useful statistic known as the Z-score for the student whose individual test score had been placed in cell A4.

Generally, arguments may be either single-valued or ranges. Single-valued arguments can be any of the following: number, cell address, function, range name that names a single cell, or a formula. Range arguments may be ranges of the form C4..E50 (or C4:E50 for SuperCalc^3) or a range name when the spreadsheet program permits the user to name a range of cells. Cell ranges may be specified by pointing to the range or typing the range in.

Second-generation spreadsheets have a large number of mathematical, statistical, financial, logical, date, and special functions. Table 8–3 shows a small sampling of SuperCalc^3's functions (SuperCalc^3 has 42 functions altogether), along with their required arguments. Tables 8–4 and 8–5 list similar functions for Lotus 1-2-3. The functions provided by the Lotus programs Symphony and Jazz would be very similar.

Financial Functions Among the most important of the functions provided by a spreadsheet program are its financial functions. These will include functions to compute the internal rate of return, the net present value, the future value of an annuity, the present value of a loan, and the payment of a loan. These functions effectively determine the effect of interest rates upon sums of money over time.

```
@FUNCTION-NAME (ARG1, ARG2, . . . , ARGN)
                \________Arguments________/
```

FIGURE 8–17

The General Form of a Function

TABLE 8–3

Some SuperCalc^3 Functions

Mathematical

SQRT(number or cell)
Calculates the square root of the argument.

LOG(number or cell)
Determines the logarithm (base 10). Natural logs are found with LN(number or cell).

PI
No argument required. PI is accurate to 15 decimal places.

SIN(number or cell)
Gives the sine in radians, not degrees. Also available are functions for cosine, arc sine, arc tangent, and both two- and four-quadrant arc tangents.

Financial

PMT(principal,interest,term)
Determines the payment per period for a loan with the given parameters.

FV(payment,rate,term)
The future value of an annuity. If you deposit $1,000 per year (payment) for 5 years (term) at 10% interest (rate), how much will that be worth?

PV(payment,rate,term)
The present value of an annuity. How much should it cost to purchase a plan that will pay you $1,000 per year for 5 years if current interest rates are 10%?

NPV(discount rate,range)
The net present value. Similar to present value, it determines the current value of a series of evenly spaced cash flows of differing amounts. It has many financial uses, including calculating how much the balloon payment on a mortgage is really going to cost you. The discount rate is usually the current cost of capital, or the rate of return you would expect if your money were invested elsewhere (often called opportunity cost).

Statistical

SUM(range)
Finds the total for the range.

MIN(range)
Finds the minimum value in the specified range. Also available: MAX.

Logical

IF(condition,value 1,value 2)
If the condition is true, put value 1 in the cell, otherwise use value 2. 'IF(GRADE>69,"pass","fail")' might simplify an instructor's end-of-semester work.

TABLE 8–4

Lotus 1-2-3 Financial Functions

@PMT(principal,interest,term)
Determines the payment per period for a loan with the given parameters.

@FV(payment,rate,term)
The future value of an annuity. If you deposit $1,000 per year (payment) for 5 years (term), at 10% interest (rate), how much will that be worth?

@PV(payment,rate,term)
The present value of an annuity. How much should it cost to purchase a plan that will pay you $1,000 per year for 5 years if current interest rates are 10%?

@NPV(discount rate,range)
The net present value. Similar to present value, it determines the current value of a series of evenly spaced cash flows of differing amounts.

@IRR(guess,range)
Calculates the internal rate of return.

TABLE 8–5

Statistical Functions in 1-2-3

	@AVG(range) Finds the average of all items in the range.
	@COUNT(range) Finds number of items in the range.
	@MAX(range) Finds the maximum value in the specified range.
	@MIN(range) Finds the minimum value in the specified range.
	@STD(range) Finds the standard deviation of all items in the range.
	@SUM(range) Finds the total for the range.
Statistical Functions for File Management	@DCOUNT(input,offset,criterion) Finds the number of items in the field. @DSUM(input,offset,criterion) Finds the sum of items in a field. @DAVG(input,offset,criterion) Finds the average of items in a field.

Statistical Functions Statistical functions are used to compute descriptive statistics on a collection of data. Statistics are used in virtually every area of business: from marketing to management, from accounting to finance.

Logical Operators and Functions Logical functions are used to set conditional values in cells. For example, if an instructor is keeping a gradebook and wishes to assign a grade of A, B, C, D, or F depending upon the averaged numeric grade, this could be accomplished by use of the following logical functions and operators in 1-2-3: @IF(D9>89,"A",@IF(D9>79,"B",@IF(D9>69,"C",@IF(D9>59, "D","F")))).This formula assumes the numeric grade was placed in cell D9. The formula will display the letter grade into whichever cell the formula is placed in. Like any other function, the @IF function can be embedded in itself or any other function, as the formula above suggests.

The algebraic and relational operators shown in Table 8–2 are binary since they relate a constant, variable, or expression on their left to a constant, variable, or expression on their right.

Relational operators like ">", "> = ", " = ", "< = ", and "<" (see Table 8–2) are used within the logical function @IF (see Table 8–6) as the operator that goes within the first argument of the @IF logical function. In fact, the first argument of every @IF function must have at least one relational operator. The relational operator is preceded and followed by expressions that could be simple constants or complicated algebraic expressions. *Algebraic expressions* are expressions contain-

TABLE 8–6

Lotus 1-2-3 Logical Function

@IF(condition,value 1,value 2)
If the condition is true, put value 1 in the cell, otherwise use value 2.

ing **algebraic** ("^", "*", "/", "+", "−") **operators** only. The **logical operators** AND, OR, must be preceded and followed by logical expressions only. *Logical expressions* are simply algebraic expressions with one or more relational and/or logical operators in them.

Date and Time Functions Date and time functions (see Table 8–7) enable the user to calculate dates and times. For example, to find the number of days from September 2, 1990 to December 18, 1990, simply use @DATE(1990,12,18) − @DATE(1990,9,2).

Lookup Functions With most spreadsheet programs, lookup functions come in two varieties: vertical lookup functions and horizontal lookup functions, as shown in Table 8–8.

A lookup function will look for a specified value on a row or column of the table and return a corresponding value in an adjoining row or column that is offset from the row or column specified in the *range* argument by the number specified in the *offset* argument. If the value specified in the lookup function does not exactly match one of those listed in the table, the function will match on the value that is equal to or just less than the value specified in the lookup function. For example, suppose the following tax rate table had been placed in columns F and G (rows 3 through 6) of a worksheet:

	F	G
1	SALARY	TAX RATE
2		
3	0	0
4	10000	0.1
5	25000	0.27
6	50000	0.33
7		

Then if a vertical table lookup function @VLOOKUP(33000,F3..F6,1) were placed in cell C10, that cell would contain the value .27. The vertical lookup function @VLOOKUP looks through the range F3..F6 for the largest value that is less than or equal to 33000. It comes up with 25000. It returns the value in the adjoining

TABLE 8–7

Lotus 1-2-3 Date and Time Functions

@DATE(year,month,day)
Calculates number of days since 31-Dec-1899.

@TODAY
Provides today's date.

@DAY(date)
Returns the day number of the year from the date.

@MONTH(date)
Returns the month number.

@YEAR(date)
Returns the year number.

TABLE 8–8
Lotus 1-2-3 Table Lookup Functions

@CHOOSE(x,v0,v1,...,vN)
Select argument value.

@HLOOKUP(value,range,offset)
Horizontal table lookup.

@VLOOKUP(value,range,offset)
Vertical table lookup.

TABLE 8–9
Lotus 1-2-3 Mathematical Functions

	@SQRT(number or cell) Calculates the square root of the argument.
	@LOG(number or cell) Determines the logarithm (base 10). Natural logs are found with @LN(number or cell).
Mathematical	@PI No argument required. PI is accurate to 15 decimal places.
	@SIN(number or cell) Gives the sine in radians, not degrees. Also available are functions for cosine, arc sine, arc tangent, and both two- and four-quadrant arc tangents.
	AND A DOZEN OTHERS

column that is offset one column to the right: namely, .27. Horizontal lookup functions expect a range argument that is a row, while vertical lookup functions expect a range argument that is a column. Horizontal table lookup functions return the value in the matching column that is offset by the number specified in the offset argument *below* the range specified.

Algebraic and Trigonometric Functions Algebraic and trigonometric functions are used greatly by engineers and scientists, and less significantly by business. They include SIN( ), COS( ), TAN( ), LOG( ), and SQRT( ) among others, as listed in Table 8–9.

BUILDING WORKSHEETS FOR USE BY OTHERS

Particularized needs must be met when a model builder designs a worksheet model for use by others. If the generalized model contains all labels and formulas necessary for calculations but does not contain any problem-specific data, it is referred to as a *template.* Some portions of the worksheet should never require updating or access by users. These cells can be protected from erasure and from being changed in some way. Other portions of the worksheet may contain sensitive data that is not intended for general consumption. Cells containing this data can be hidden from view and protected. In addition, specialized commands may be created and named so the worksheet model is made easier to use. Entirely new menu bars can be created. Finally, the entering of data into the worksheet can be greatly facilitated by the use of forms. All of these capabilities can make worksheet models intended for use by others much easier to use.

Templates

As previously defined, templates are simply worksheet models devoid of problem-specific data. A retailer with fifty retail outlets might develop a single standardized template for use by each outlet in performing end-of-period profit analyses. Each outlet would enter their revenue and cost data into the template and return a copy of the parameterized template with live data in it back to the head office for analysis each month. Each retailer would also use the parameterized template to analyze its own operations.

Hiding and Protecting Cells

The easiest way to hide cells is to set their column width to zero. Doing so will prevent the cell from being printed or displayed. However, it would be a trivial task for a seasoned spreadsheet user to reset the column width to something other than zero. SuperCalc^3 uses the format designation "H" to designate a cell as "hidden."

To prevent the contents or format of cells from being changed in any way, the cells must be protected. Most spreadsheets start with all cells unprotected so the user can enter data into them. Once a model has been entered and validated, its developer can protect all or part of the cells that make up the model. For example, the developer may decide to hide and protect only those cells containing formulas and sensitive data, and to leave the cells defining independent variable values unprotected so that other users can change them to perform what-if analyses.

Many spreadsheet programs offer two levels of protection, with the second level of protection requiring a password to be penetrated. These programs will prompt the developer for the password at the time the protection is set or applied.

Macros and Macro Languages

Like any other application containing macros, spreadsheets use macros to permit a sequence of commands to be stored so they can later be invoked by a single keystroke or combination of keystrokes. For example, to update the disk file for an updated worksheet, the command sequence in 1-2-3 is, FILE, SAVE, YES, where the last item in the sequence is a response to whether the user wants to replace the old disk file with the new one. Under such circumstances the spreadsheet program is usually smart enough to remember the filename of the file retrieved from disk. It will then save the updated worksheet under this filename, thereby overwriting the old file. With the terse command entry mode of 1-2-3, the command is /FSY. It would be possible to save this sequence and attach to it the letter *S*. The command could then be invoked at any later time simply by typing <ALT> S, and saving two keystrokes in the process.

```
SAVE GET PRINT GRAPH QUIT
```

FIGURE 8–18
User-Defined Menu Bar

Creating Menus

Spreadsheet programs with a macro language capability will permit the user to assign a name to the stored sequence of commands. Such programs also allow users to create their own menu bars. The name will then appear on a menu bar of the user's own creation, where it can be invoked as another command. Figure 8–18 illustrates a user-defined menu bar.

Creating Forms

Some spreadsheets specifically accommodate the creation of forms for the purpose of entering or outputting data. An example appears in Figure 8–19.

FILE MANAGEMENT AND OPERATIONS

Spreadsheet programs require a filename whenever they are called upon to perform a file-related operation. And they will prompt the user for the same when the user is loading in a file from disk, or whenever it is not obvious what the filename should be. This is because file operations involve a disk file in some way. Most spreadsheet programs expect the user to specify only the primary filename; the program will supply the extension or secondary filename. Lotus 1-2-3 uses WKS (.WK1 for Release 2) for worksheet files, .PRN for disk files containing the

	A	B	C	D	E	F
1		**Lim Manufacturing**				
2		**123 Tango Street**				
3		**Austin, Texas 78705 Tel: (512) 764-7677**				
4						
5	**Name**	John Jones	**Date:**	7/5/87	**No:**	3271
6	**Address**	2207 10th Street, Apt. #856				
7	**City**	Debuque	**State**	Iowa	**Zip**	51137
8	**Tel.:**	(405) 127-3741				
9						
10	**Product #**	**Description**	**Unit Cost**	**Unit**	**Subtotal**	
11	125456	Transmission	346.23	1	$346.23	
12	580977	Spark Plugs (8)	11.92	1	$11.92	
13	769113	Carburetor	159.77	2	$319.54	
14						
15						
16						
17				**Taxes**	$40.66	
18					-------------	
19				**Total**	**$718.35**	
20					-------------	

FIGURE 8–19
A Form Created by Use of a Spreadsheet. Field names are in bold print. User-specified entries are in ordinary print. This is an invoice.

output of a print-to-file operation, and .PIC for files that contain data for printing of graphs.

In addition to the usual saving and retrieving of files, it is possible to merge files, combine (add or subtract) files, and extract files. The user also can save files so they can be read by other programs: word processing programs, other spreadsheet programs, and file management programs (next chapter).

Saving and Retrieving Files

Saving a worksheet can be accomplished through two methods: A SAVE command (found under the FILE heading in 1-2-3) will retain all cell entries including labels, values, formulas, and formatting information so that the worksheet may be loaded and worked on in the future. The RETRIEVE command (also under the FILE heading in 1-2-3) will do just the opposite: retrieve the file the user designates from disk and load it into primary memory. The short form of these commands is /FS for saving files and /FR for retrieving files. Both will prompt the user for a filename.

ASCII and Print Files

The PRINT command has an option that lets the user print a worksheet to a disk file instead of a printer. This is extremely useful for creating an image of a worksheet as ASCII characters that can be incorporated into a word processing file and edited with the user's word processing program. These are the .PRN files briefly discussed earlier. Such files do not contain formulas, nor do they contain formatting information. Any special format codes for headers, footers, margins, or page numbers are interpreted when the file is written to the disk.

It is generally possible to save a worksheet to disk as an ASCII file. Doing so will cause the spreadsheet program to append the extension .TXT to the user's primary filename. Like .PRN files, these files do not contain formulas and may be read into any other program capable of reading an ASCII file.

The user may save all of a worksheet or only a portion, as suggested by Figure 8–20. Saving portions (defined as a range or rectangular block) is one way of

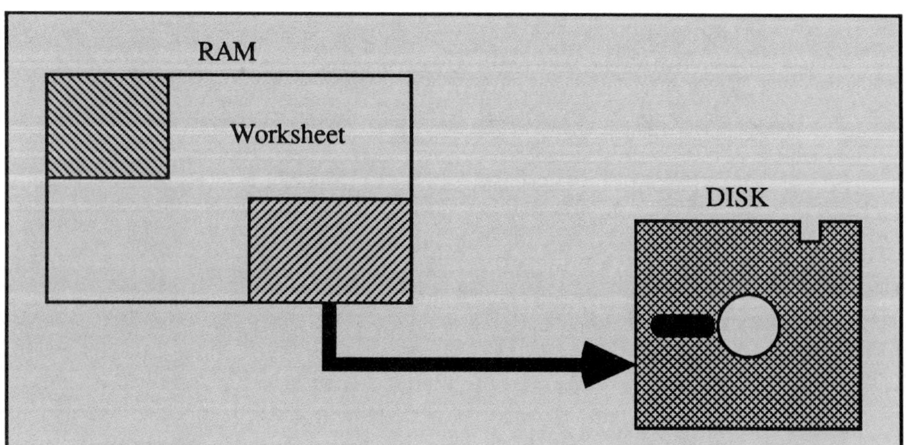

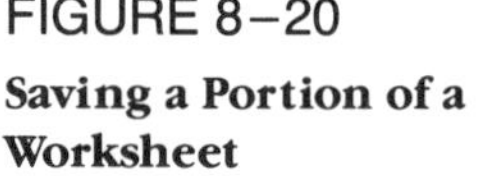
FIGURE 8–20
Saving a Portion of a Worksheet

breaking up a large worksheet into smaller modules: simply save different areas into different files. This is called **extracting**, and the user may be given the option of extracting the displayed contents of cells or the cell formulas. When extracting formulas the user must exercise care with regard to cell references to cells that were not extracted. When reloading an extracted file, cell references to cells that were not extracted will be assumed to have zero values.

When loading worksheets, the user can employ the exact reverse of the extraction concept. Pull in one file (or portion of one), move to a clear area of the worksheet, then load another file. This process, which can be repeated until internal memory runs out, is called worksheet **merging**.

Merging (Importing) Files

When merging worksheet files, the user must have one worksheet file in memory while the other resides on disk. The worksheet file residing on disk is copied (literally imported) into the one in memory. The location of the in-memory worksheet where merging is to begin is specified by the user, and copying begins from that point. If there are contents in cells into which merging is to take place, these contents will be destroyed by the merging process. The purpose of merging is to allow two worksheets to interact so that a model reflecting the effects of both submodels in the two merged worksheets can be created. It is possible to merge several worksheets into the in-memory worksheet. This allows a large problem to be broken up into several smaller problems, so each can be separately developed by an analyst. The resulting submodels can then be merged (as shown in Figure 8–21) and made interactive so the overall problem can be analyzed.

Combining Files

In addition to merging, which copies a file resident on disk to a worksheet in memory as just explained, it is possible to *add or subtract* a disk file from an in-memory file. In the latter case the calculated values of the file on disk are added to or subtracted from the values they are copied into within the in-memory worksheet. Labels are generally not copied from the disk file when doing an add or subtract operation—just the values.

File Interchanges with Other Programs

Most spreadsheet programs have the capability of *interchanging* data with other programs. VisiCalc established a popular spreadsheet storage method called DIF (Data Interchange Format), and most spreadsheets can translate a worksheet into this form or convert a DIF file to their own format. This makes it possible for users of different spreadsheet programs to share the worksheets they have developed. It also makes possible the importing of spreadsheet data saved as a DIF file into a data base management system file such as dBASE III, and vice versa.

Another common input and output format is the Comma-Separated Values file (CSV). This format separates the values (display, not contents) of a worksheet row with commas, and places quotation marks around all non-numeric values. This format is used by MicroPro's MailMerge (and other mailing list programs), and is

FIGURE 8–21
Merging Files

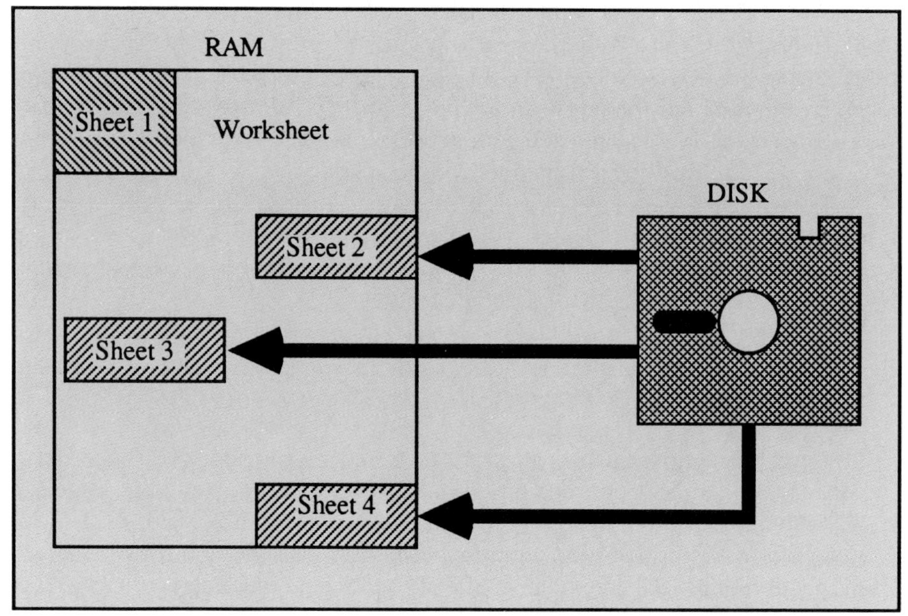

equivalent to a sequential file in BASIC programming. SuperCalc³ also allows the user to save a spreadsheet in a format that retains only the values for cells, not the underlying formulas. This differs from the screen image file described above, since the information is kept in SuperCalc³'s own format and requires no translation. Although 1-2-3 does not allow this, the same effect is accomplished by *loading* into memory only the values from a worksheet file, and not the formulas.

CLASSIFYING AND CHARACTERIZING EXISTING SPREADSHEET PROGRAMS

Microsoft Multiplan

Available for both MS-DOS machines and the Macintosh, Multiplan was one of the earliest spreadsheet programs widely available. It supported most of the same features available in VisiCalc, but differed from it in some rather interesting ways. First, unlike VisiCalc and Lotus 1-2-3, rows were labeled R1,R2,R3,.....,Rn and columns were labeled C1,C2,C3,....,Cn. To reference the cell in the second row and third column, the designation R2C3 was used. Thus to enter cell coordinates required a bit more keystrokes than in most of the other spreadsheets.

Although the Multiplan worksheet was small (256 rows by 64 columns), the worksheets could be linked by use of standardized naming conventions. Hence, a formula within a cell in one worksheet could reference cells within other worksheets. This feature added significantly to the power of Multiplan. Shown in Figure 8–22 is a Multiplan spreadsheet implemented on a Macintosh. Multiplan's biggest shortcomings are the absence of graphics and record management capabilities.

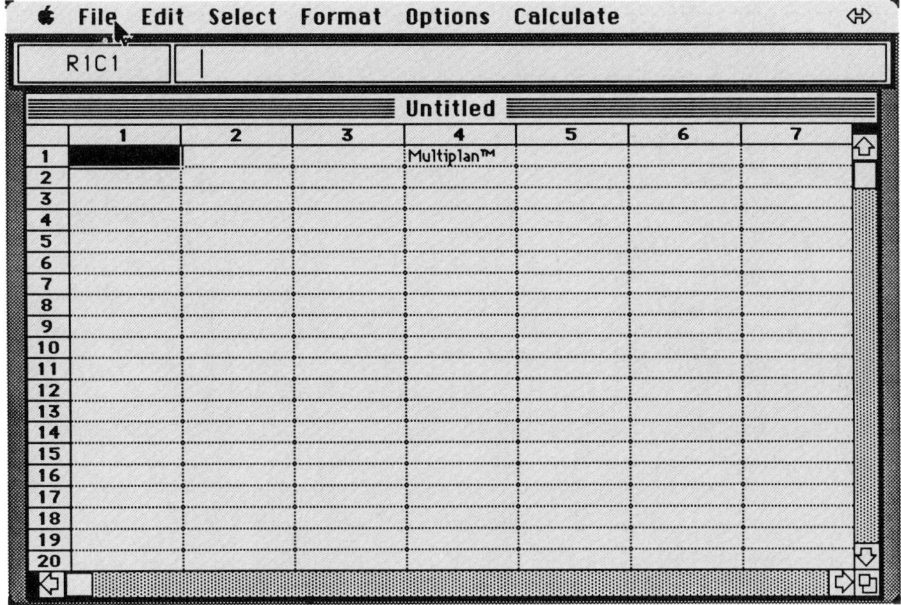

FIGURE 8–22

Microsoft Multiplan on the Macintosh

Microsoft Excel

Multiplan was Microsoft's first spreadsheet for the Macintosh; it was no match for Lotus 1-2-3 running on MS-DOS, even though it was easier. Consequently, power spreadsheet users looked upon the Macintosh as something of a toy when heavy number-crunching was the order of the day. Microsoft Excel put this case to rest, however. Developed especially and exclusively for the Macintosh, Excel may just be the most powerful spreadsheet program ever produced for any computer. Excel comes complete with business graphics and data base capabilities. The graphics module in Excel rivals many stand-alone charting programs in the MS-DOS world.

Spreadsheet Module Excel's size measures 256 columns by 16,384 rows. This works out to over four million cells—double that of Lotus 1-2-3, Release 2. What really matters is not the number of cells available but the amount of worksheet space that is actually for use, and the amount of data that can fit into it. A test performed by The Seybold Group, Inc. shows that around 57,088 cells are available on a Mac Plus.

All the options and functions on the Excel menu are accessible via macros. Each macro in Excel is stored in a separate file and can be easily shared among many different worksheets. Excel offers a macro recording feature, which learns and records all the mouse clicks and cursor movements. For simple macros, all the user has to do is turn on the macro record feature and point and click on the functions to be included in the macro. Macros in Excel can also be treated as functions. If a desired function is not built into Excel, the user can construct a macro function and use it in a formula as if it were built-in.

Unlike any other spreadsheet, Excel supports arrays—ranges of values. Arrays are useful when the user wants to create functions that use multiple values and produce multiple values as results. Excel offers three regression functions to support forecasting—something almost no other spreadsheet has.

Excel offers great flexibility in formatting the worksheet. There is great breadth of choice in fonts, style (italic or bold on a cell-by-cell basis), and border, along with very flexible numeric and text formatting.

In addition, Excel supports selective recalculation, in which only those cells directly or indirectly affected by a change are recalculated. The selection of formulas from a menu is also supported, which allows the user to avoid directly typing in a long function name. Cells can be given descriptive names instead of the conventional cell coordinates. And worksheets can be linked, as in Multiplan; in effect, data from another worksheet is imported into the cell whose formula references the external data. The Excel spreadsheet also supports multiple worksheets opened at one time and accessible through windows. Cell contents can be copied from one worksheet into another.

Charting Module More than 40 predefined types of charts are available. Excel supports all the usual chart types (see Chapter 11), each with several options to choose from. Axes can be easily scaled to the user's liking. Text can be added anywhere on the graph. Arrows and legends can be added to the graph, to indicate a specific location or to clarify a point or two. Many symbols, as well as a variety of patterns and different line widths, are available to further enhance the output.

Data Base Module The data base capabilities of Excel are similar to those of Lotus 1-2-3. The usual capabilities of "find" and "extract" are available. The built-in functions for file manipulation are similar if not superior to those of Lotus 1-2-3.

There is no question that Excel has made the Macintosh a serious business machine and has helped increase its sales, just as VisiCalc has helped sales of the Apple II and Lotus 1-2-3 has helped sales of the IBM PC. Excel is now available for MS-DOS and OS/2. Both Multiplan and Excel are vended by Microsoft, Inc., 16011 N.E. 36th Way, Box 97017, Redmond, WA 98073–9717.

Javelin

A new program called Javelin, intended specifically to support calculations, received the *InfoWorld* Product of the Year Award in 1985. Javelin gives the user over ten different views of the data. For example, Javelin will display the formulas, the calculated worksheet, a diagram of the relationships between the variables, a variety of tables representing calculated values, a graphic representation of the values, and several other views including a macros view, an errors view, and a notes view of the model. Some of these views are shown in Figure 8–23. Moreover, Javelin makes it possible to enter data and formulas from a variety of views. For example, if the user is viewing a graph of the values which does not appear to be quite right, the graph can be adjusted and the numbers are automatically changed by Javelin so every view shows the same information. Each view gives the user a different way to look at and manipulate the same underlying information.

In Javelin, the user can assign descriptive variable names like *Gross Revenues* or *Net-After-Tax Profits* instead of *G33* or *H44*. If the user's variables vary over time, Javelin is especially well suited for accommodating such a problem, because Javelin understands how days, weeks, months, quarters, and years are related. Javelin supports all the built-in functions users have come to expect within a spreadsheet. When the user is writing formulas, Javelin helps by letting her point to variable

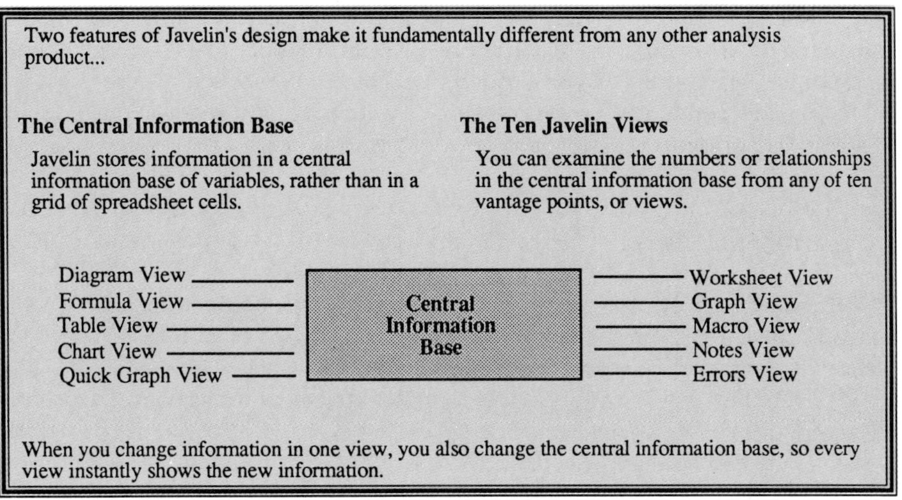

(a)

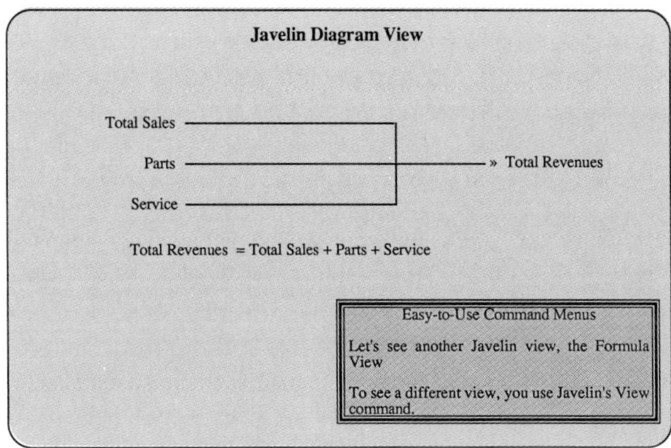

(b)

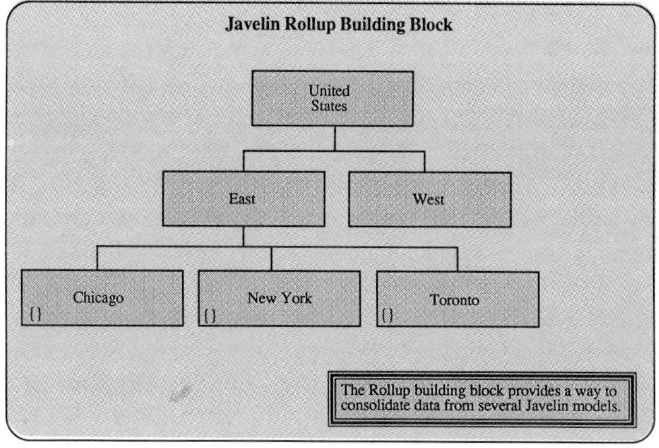

(c)

FIGURE 8–23

(a) Some of the views of a model provided by Javelin. (b) The Javelin diagram view. (c) The Javelin rollup building block.

names that have already been entered; thus a long variable name need not be reentered in formula after formula. Because it offers so much that is unconventional and unique, yet useful, Javelin is bound to become a best-seller.

Javelin is vended by Javelin Software Corporation, One Kendall Square, Building 200, Cambridge, MA 02139.

SuperCalc4

SuperCalc4 is a very fast, powerful spreadsheet that in many respects is superior to Lotus 1-2-3, even though it has never sold as well. For example, SuperCalc4 offers a larger spreadsheet that uses sparse memory management techniques (255 columns by 9999 rows). In SuperCalc4, only cells containing data consume primary storage (regardless of where they are located); in Lotus 1-2-3, even the blank cells located between non-empty cells use memory. SuperCalc4 offers a broad range of formatting options and supports convenient movement, insertion, or deletion of blocks of cells. Because of the conventions used by SuperCalc4, the "@" symbol in front of functions is not required, nor is it necessary to begin a formula with a "+" sign or other arithmetic symbol. SuperCalc4's broad menu structure allows access to menu items with fewer keystrokes. SuperCalc4 has a learn mode that makes it easy for the casual user to create macros, since SuperCalc4 captures the keystrokes. Unlike SuperCalc^3, SuperCalc4 allows for rectangular ranges to be moved and copied. SuperCalc, which has been around since 1980, has always had a reputation for being fast; SuperCalc4 is no exception. Its graphics are brilliant, it supports the 8087/80287 numeric coprocessor and the Lotus/Intel/Microsoft expanded memory specification. In short, SuperCalc4 is a beautifully executed and articulated spreadsheet. The product is vended by Computer Associates, 2195 Fortune Drive, San Jose, CA 95131.

As a summary to this section, Multiplan, Excel, and SuperCalc4 all belong to the same genre of spreadsheet as Lotus 1-2-3. Although the differences between Excel, SuperCalc4, and 1-2-3 are more than subtle, these spreadsheet programs are certainly not clones of each other. Several software vendors have produced 1-2-3 clones; most notable are Paperback Software's VP Planner, and another product called The Twin Classic from Mosaic Software. Javelin, however, is a spreadsheet and business planning system of a totally different kind. Its perspective is much more general and its philosophy more analytical.

Summary

This chapter has endeavored to impart a flavor for the mechanics of spreadsheet usage. The chapter opened with a description of the general layout of a spreadsheet and continued with a discussion of the control panel as well as navigation within the worksheet. How to enter, edit, and revise the worksheet was discussed. Concepts like anchoring the cursor, cursor pointing, interpretive prompting, relative references, and absolute references were discussed in detail. Lengthy discussions of COPY, MOVE, DELETE, and INSERT commands were provided.

How to format and print the worksheet were next described, as was how to build formulas using operators and functions. Printing of the worksheet is perhaps the weakest aspect of many spreadsheets and for this reason spreadsheet users will print their worksheets to a disk file where they can be read, edited, and printed by a word processor program. This capability also enables the spreadsheet user to embed the worksheet in text which describes the worksheet and possibly its spreadsheet-generated graphs, thereby creating a single integrated hard-copy report and associated report file. Such a file could then be electronically mailed anywhere.

The chapter described at some length the operators and functions that make up formulas. The precedence order of operators shown in Table 8–2 was described together with its implications for writing correct formulas. One of the biggest shortcomings of spreadsheets is the fact that the formulas are usually hidden from view on the display, the active cell excepted. Hidden formulas discourage the proofing that is necessary to eradicate the errors that might exist within them. Although these erroneous formulas generate innocuous-looking numbers, they are wrong.

In addition, discussions of how to build worksheets for use by others were provided. In this context, templates, cell protection, macros, menus, and forms were discussed. Also described were the types of files spreadsheets could be saved in.

Finally, the chapter described some of the major product offerings, such as Microsoft Multiplan and Excel, Javelin, and SuperCalc4. It is expected that in the future spreadsheet programs will continue to add features, flexibility, power and convenience in order to maintain competitiveness. The Javelin capability to observe one's model from a variety of different viewpoints, coupled with the ability to enhance and edit the model in many of those views, is an idea that is certain to obtain an enthusiastic following.

A recent innovation in spreadsheet technology is the three-dimensional spreadsheet program that supports layers of ordinary spreadsheets linked together. These are vaguely similar to Microsoft's Multiplan and Excel in this respect. In the discussion of templates, the chapter described how a retailer with fifty retail outlets might use a template that is identical for each outlet. The retailer would require each outlet to return a copy of the template with live data in it to the head office at the end of each accounting period. Each parameterized template would comprise a "layer" of the ultimate three-dimensional corporate worksheet and would be linked into the master worksheet so that a corporate-wide aggregate analysis could be performed.

Immediately following this chapter, the reader will find tutorials on Lotus 1-2-3 and Microsoft Excel.

Key Terms

absolute cell referencing
active cell
algebraic operator
arguments
arrays
border
column width
contents format
control panel
display format
entry area
extracting from a worksheet
horizontal window
interpretive prompting
logical operator
menu line
merging
prompt area
range
relational operator
relative cell referencing
status line
synchronized windows
vertical window
worksheet window

Self-Test

1. Describe how the worksheet display is organized.
2. What three types of entries can be made within a spreadsheet?
3. Describe how to copy and move worksheet information.
4. Indicate what the major concerns are when formatting a worksheet.
5. Explain how and when the precedence order is used.
6. What functions are generally available within spreadsheets?
7. What are the major considerations in building worksheets for use by others?
8. What are the major product offerings among spreadsheets, and how do they differ?

Exercises

1. Briefly describe the function of the following 1-2-3 commands. Illustrate how to use each.

   COPY
   DELETE
   INSERT
   MOVE
2. Contrast 1-2-3 with SuperCalc^3 relative to copying a cell or range of cells.
3. Describe generally the method for cell addressing and range specification used in programs like 1-2-3 and VisiCalc.
4. Describe the methods used for worksheet navigation and data entry.
5. Describe the methods for command entry used in 1-2-3, VisiCalc, and SuperCalc^3. Do this again for Multiplan. Contrast the command-driven user interface with the menu-driven one as regards efficiency and convenience. Why do most spreadsheet programs offer both interfaces?
6. Describe the method Lotus 1-2-3 uses for distinguishing a cell formula from a number or label. What method does SuperCalc^3 use? How are functions identified in 1-2-3?
7. Discuss the commands used for copying and moving the contents of cells within a worksheet. How does REPLICATE differ from COPY in SuperCalc? Does 1-2-3 have a REPLICATE command?
8. Contrast 1-2-3's cell movement facilities with those of SuperCalc^3. Discuss what is meant by relative cell referencing, and how it differs from absolute cell referencing. When would relative cell referencing be required? When would absolute cell referencing be essential?
9. Describe generally the features for editing and formatting the worksheet found in most spreadsheets.
10. How are windows used within spreadsheets? What types of windows do most spreadsheets offer?
11. What facilities are generally available for saving and retrieving worksheets? For printing worksheets? How does a saved worksheet differ from a saved worksheet print file? What advantage does saving the worksheet as a .DIF file have? What is a comma-separated value file, and when would such files be useful?
12. Describe what is meant by the options *display* versus *contents* when printing a spreadsheet. Do spreadsheet programs generally have their own printer-specific print-driver programs that the user can select from when installing the program? What advantage is there to writing a print file to a disk?
13. Find a reference manual or pocket guide of a spreadsheet that interests you. Describe the features offered by the spreadsheet for

    (a) worksheet navigation
    (b) formatting

(c) editing
(d) printing
(e) graphics

14. Find reference manuals (or pocket guides) for two or more spreadsheets. Compare their capabilities with regard to worksheet size and features.
15. Construct a worksheet model of a new-product break-even situation in which production costs are initially running $100 per unit but are declining at the rate of 1% a month. The selling price of the unit is constant at $150 per month. The development costs were $3,000,000 and the overhead runs $15,000 a month. Sales are expected to be strong at 3,000 units a month, and will grow at the rate of 2% a month. The marketing costs are running $17,000 a month, but are expected to decrease by 5% a month during the next 12 months and then remain constant. Run this model for 36 months. Determine when the break-even point will be reached. How much profit, if any, will be generated?
16. Construct a worksheet model of a new-product break-even situation in which production costs are initially running $500 per unit but are declining at the rate of 1% a month. The selling price of the unit is constant at $950 per month. The development costs were $5,000,000 and the overhead runs $15,000 a month. Sales are expected to be strong at 1,000 units a month, and will grow at the rate of 1% a month. The marketing costs are running $23,000 a month, but are expected to decrease by 1% a month during the next 12 months and then remain constant. Run this model for 48 months. Determine when the break-even point will be reached. Perform appropriate what-if analyses and graph the important concepts and results. How much profit, if any, will be generated?
17. Giving consideration to such issues as compatibility with existing worksheets, ability to provide significant financial analyses, ability to support forecasting, hardware available, and size of worksheets anticipated, describe which of the major spreadsheet product offerings are most appropriate for which situation. Characterize several situations and describe what the clear product choice would be for each.

Additional Reading

Close, Kenneth S. *Integrated Software: Principles and Applications Using Lotus 1-2-3.* Cincinnati: South-Western, 1986.

Ewing, David Paul. *The Using 1-2-3 Workbook and Disk.* Indianapolis: Que Corporation, 1984.

Holt, Jack A. *Cases and Applications in Lotus 1-2-3.* Homewood, Ill.: Irwin, 1986.

LeBlond, Geoffrey, et al., *Using 1-2-3.* Indianapolis: Que Corporation, 1984.

Lotus 1-2-3: User's Manual. Cambridge, Mass.: Lotus Development Corporation, 1983.

Ross, Steven C. *Understanding and Using Lotus 1-2-3.* St. Paul, Minn.: West Publishing Company, 1986.

SuperCalc^3: User's Guide & Reference Manual. Documentation 1.0, January 1984, Fifth Ed., San Jose, Calif.: Sorcim, 1983.

TUTORIAL

Lotus 1-2-3

Lotus 1-2-3 has set a standard that other spreadsheet programs have tried to emulate (imitation is the sincerest form of flattery). As a spreadsheet, it is fast, versatile, and relatively easy to use. But 1-2-3 is more than just a spreadsheet; it is an integrated program that has a graphics capability, as well as an assortment of disk and file management facilities. The program is available from Lotus Development Corp., 55 Cambridge Way, Cambridge, MA 02142.

ABOUT THIS TUTORIAL

Because Lotus 1-2-3 has so many functions and features to offer, this tutorial is rather large. In order to allow you to select only the sections that interest you, this tutorial is divided into three modules, covering the three principal components of 1-2-3: the spreadsheet, the file management system, and graphics. The file management module follows Chapter 9 (File Management Systems) and the graphics module follows Chapter 11 (Graphics and Integrated Software Packages). Certain material in the file and graphics modules will be more understandable if the corresponding chapters are read beforehand.

This tutorial is concerned only with the Lotus spreadsheet; it is divided into an introduction and six segments, each building upon the previous segment. The introduction describes the task and shows the spreadsheet that will be our ultimate objective. The six segments are brief. The longest should take no more than 30 minutes for the novice, and an experienced user might be able to complete all six segments in less than an hour at the computer. Even if you choose to go through all the segments in a single session, we advise that you save your worksheet at the end of each segment.

THE LOTUS SYSTEM AND HARDWARE REQUIREMENTS

The Lotus 1-2-3 comes on four disks: a System Disk, a Utilities Disk, a Print Graph Disk, and a Tutorial Disk. The System Disk contains the principal Lotus program, called 123.EXE. 123.EXE performs all of the spreadsheet, graphics, and data base functions of the Lotus 1-2-3 system, but can generate 1-2-3 graphs only to the monitor. To print graphs on paper requires the Print Graph Disk. Also included on the System Disk is a large Help file that can be accessed while running 1-2-3, several small files used for configuring the system to your specific hardware setup, and LOTUS.COM, a menu program that provides access to all of Lotus 1-2-3's capabilities.

The Tutorial Disk has one of the better interactive tutorial programs found in commercial software. You do not need the System Disk to run the tutorial, because it has its own modified 1-2-3 program. To enter the tutorial, place the Tutorial Disk in drive A and enter **TUTOR<CR>.** Since most of the lessons contained on the disk will be covered in this tutorial, you will not need the Tutorial Disk. However, you may wish to browse through the disk-based lessons for reinforcement of the learning you will gain through our tutorial, or merely to see how an interactive tutorial works.

Lotus 1-2-3 requires an IBM PC or IBM-PC-compatible computer, either PC-DOS or MS-DOS for an operating system, and two disk drives (double-sided). The minimum amount of internal memory is 192K bytes, but at least 256K bytes is recommended in order to develop reasonably sized worksheets. If 1-2-3 is to be used in conjunction with other memory-resident programs (operating environments, desktop organizers, keyboard enhancement programs, etc.), even 256K bytes may not be enough. For example, loading the Lotus 1-2-3 system after MS-DOS, Sidekick (a desktop organizer), and Prokey (a keyboard enhancer) were in memory took over 200K bytes of memory, before any worksheets had been created. Releases 2 and following of 1-2-3 use the 8087/80287 coprocessor when it is available and support the Lotus/Intel/Microsoft expanded memory specification.

In order to display graphics on-screen, you must have a graphics adapter (1-2-3 will work with either the IBM or Hercules graphics adapter, and other compatible boards). If you do not have a graphics adapter, you can still print the graphs, but will not be able to view them before printing.

SPECIAL KEYS AND CONVENTIONS

1-2-3 has special uses for many of the keys on an IBM-compatible keyboard. Their placement is shown in Figure 8–24, and a brief description of their functions follows in Table 8–10. You will become more familiar with their use during the tutorial lessons.

(Continued)

Lotus 1-2-3 (Continued)

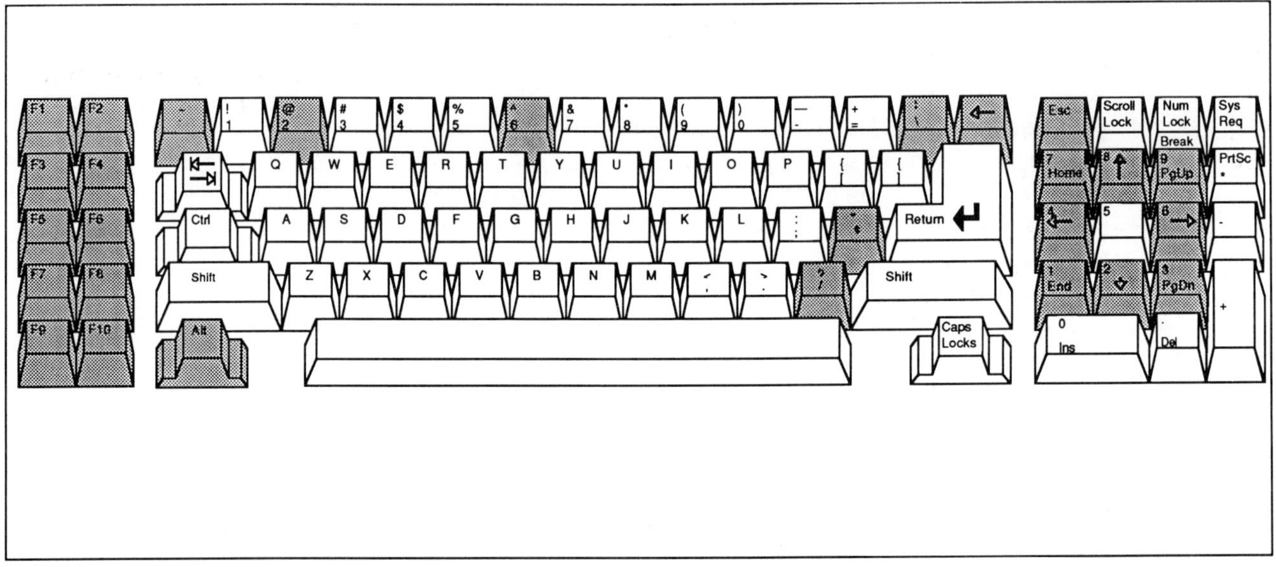

FIGURE 8–24

Special Keys Used By 1-2-3 (represented by shading)

GETTING STARTED

After you have placed the System Disk in drive A and a formatted work disk (for storing worksheet files) in drive B, there are two methods of entering Lotus 1-2-3. Using the first method, you would enter **LOTUS**<**CR**> at the command prompt (A> or C>). This brings up the screen shown in Figure 8–25.

The options available from the 1-2-3 main menu are the following:

1-2-3. The main spreadsheet/graphics/data base program.

PrintGraph. Requires the Print Graph Disk.

Translate. Performs file conversion between the 1-2-3 format and other popular formats, including those used by VisiCalc, dBASE II, and the DIF format. Also requires the Utilities Disk.

Install. Used to install the Lotus system: specify hard disk or floppy system, designate device drivers and so forth.

View. Provides explanations and views of 1-2-3.

Exit. Leaves 1-2-3 and returns to the operating system.

TABLE 8–10

Special Keys Used in This Tutorial

KEY	DESCRIPTION
<U>	The up arrow key, for cursor movement.
<D>	The down arrow key.
<L>	The left arrow key. This causes a nondestructive backspace when editing cell contents.
<R>	The right arrow key.
<BS>	The backspace key. Erases as it moves left.
<CR>	The carriage return key, used to terminate all entries. Its function is duplicated by <Enter> on the numeric keypad.
<F1>	This accesses the help facility, with information about the use of any 1-2-3 command or function.
<F2>	Enters the edit mode. This is used by moving the cursor to the cell you wish to edit, then pressing <F2>.
<F4>	This makes a cell reference absolute when in the POINT mode.
<F5>	The goto key. This allows you to jump directly to any cell in the worksheet.
<F6>	Moves the cursor between windows on-screen.
<Esc>	Retract last entry. If you enter a command or menu that you change your mind about, this allows you to back out. When entering cell contents, <Esc> will clear your entry.
<Home>	During worksheet navigation, this sends the cursor to cell A1. While editing a cell, it sends the cursor to the beginning of the edit string.
<End>	During worksheet navigation, this sends the cursor in the direction of the arrow key that follows it, moving it to the end of the worksheet. <End><D>, for example, sends the cursor down to the last entry in that column (more on this later). In the edit mode, it sends the cursor to the end of the edit string.
<Del>	Deletes the character under the cursor in edit mode.

Note: In this tutorial, keys enclosed by < and > (as with those above) provide functions accessed with a single keystroke.

Most of the facilities in the Lotus main menu are used only occasionally, if at all. The vast majority of work is done with the 1-2-3 program, which can be selected from the main menu by moving the cursor to 1-2-3 (it is already there unless you have moved it) and pressing <**CR**> or <**Enter**>. This will bring up the Lotus copyright notice, and pressing any key places you into the 1-2-3 program.

If you wish to use only the 1-2-3 program, and do not need the special utility programs, there is a more direct method of entering Lotus. Simply type

(Continued)

FIGURE 8–25
Lotus 1-2-3's Main Menu

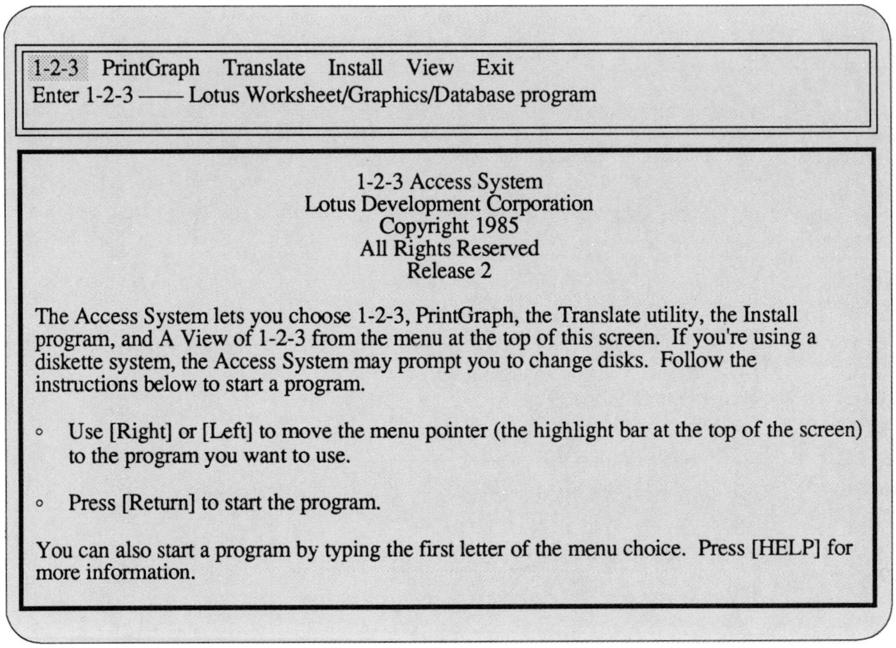

1-2-3 PrintGraph Translate Install View Exit
Enter 1-2-3 —— Lotus Worksheet/Graphics/Database program

1-2-3 Access System
Lotus Development Corporation
Copyright 1985
All Rights Reserved
Release 2

The Access System lets you choose 1-2-3, PrintGraph, the Translate utility, the Install program, and A View of 1-2-3 from the menu at the top of this screen. If you're using a diskette system, the Access System may prompt you to change disks. Follow the instructions below to start a program.

- Use [Right] or [Left] to move the menu pointer (the highlight bar at the top of the screen) to the program you want to use.
- Press [Return] to start the program.

You can also start a program by typing the first letter of the menu choice. Press [HELP] for more information.

123<CR> and you will be shuttled into the spreadsheet/graphics/data base program, without using the preliminary menu. Since this is simpler and saves some time, this is the method we will use throughout this tutorial.

AN OVERVIEW

In the segments that follow, we will create and explore the spreadsheet's capabilities by constructing a worksheet that can forecast sales demand. Each segment will add new features to our worksheet. This introduction will explain some of the theory behind the model we build so that you will understand the formulas used in the lesson. If you are already familiar with forecasting models (or don't care), this section may be safely skipped. After completing all the segments, you will have a worksheet that looks like the one in Figure 8–26.

Exponential Smoothing In the segments, we will create a small worksheet that can be used for forecasting sales demand, since it provides ample

	A	B	C	D	E	F	G
1			Exponential Smoothing Model				
2							
3	Product:	XL Tire			Alpha:	0.3	
4	Price:	$50.00					
5							
6		1st Q	2nd Q	3rd Q	4th Q	1st Q	2nd Q
7		LAST YR	LAST YR	LAST YR	LAST YR	THIS YR	THIS YR
8	**Sales**						
	Actual	950	1350	1160	1160	990	1015
10	Forecast	950	950	1070	1097	1116	1078
11	**Inventory**						
12	Begin	100	0	0	0	0	126
13	Produce	850	950	1070	1097	1116	952
14	End	0	0	0	0	126	63
15	**Costs**						
16	Holding	$125.00	$0.00	$0.00	$0.00	$157.38	$236.29
17	Stockout	$0.00	$2,000.00	$450.00	$315.00	$0.00	$0.00
18							
19	Total	$125.00	$2,000.00	$450.00	$315.00	$157.38	$236.29

FIGURE 8–26

Our Final Objective

opportunity for performing "what-if" analysis and will illustrate the use of a wide variety of 1-2-3 features. Dozens of methods are in common use for forecasting sales demand. No method achieves high success in all markets; most experienced sales forecasters will use several methods, depending upon the type of product, seasonality (lawn furniture sells better in the summer months), growth of sales, and many other factors.

The method we will be using is called *exponential smoothing* (or, more correctly, single exponential smoothing). The basic idea is to calculate how far off from actual demand the last period's forecast was. You then take a certain percentage of the amount missed and add it to last month's forecast, and you have your forecast for the next period. For example, if last month's forecast was 100 units too low (we sold 100 more than expected), this month's forecast will be last month's plus a percentage of the 100 units missed. The percentage used to correct forecasts is normally called alpha, and the formula is

$F_t = F_{t-1} + \text{alpha} * (A_{t-1} - F_{t-1})$, where

F = the forecast

t = the period being forecast

A = the actual demand for the period

(Continued)

Why not use the amount of your miss and add it directly to the last period's forecast, or in even more straightforward fashion, simply use last period's actual demand? Other forecasting methods do precisely that, but they will not perform well under certain situations. If demand is erratic (displays no particular pattern or trend), taking a percentage of the amount missed will tend to "smooth" our forecasts, ensuring that our forecasting errors will not become excessively large.

As we can see, a new forecast depends upon the previous forecast, which in turn depends upon the forecast before it, etc. The most recent forecast will play the largest role in the new forecast, with each preceding forecast being of "exponentially" diminishing importance. How rapidly this importance diminishes is determined by the alpha level (for those fascinated by mathematics, see the note below). With a high alpha value (say, 0.8) almost all (96%) of the information for the current forecast comes from the last two periods. With a low value (0.2), the forecast from three periods ago is only marginally less important than the most recent one. The alpha value, then, determines how rapidly our forecast reacts to fluctuating demand.

Deciding upon what alpha value to use for a given product is difficult, usually a mixture of design and guesswork. A low alpha provides very smooth (small fluctuations) forecasts, and keeps you from producing a product heavily one period and lightly in another (this may entail heavy hiring or layoff costs), while a large alpha will allow forecasts to more easily track a rapidly changing demand. Some companies, therefore, select an alpha value without regard to how well it fits the data.

Guesswork enters the picture when a company decides to try different alpha values on past data to select the one that would have provided the most accurate forecasts. Because of the large number of computations involved in producing a single forecast, trying a number of different alpha values can take several days of tedious calculation. The "ideal" alpha that results is then only applicable to a single product.

The real value of a spreadsheet program should become apparent from the exercises that follow. In a very short period of time, we will construct a model that allows us to try out new alpha values. When completed, we can try as many values as we like, at the rate of 10 or 20 per minute (1–2 seconds to recalculate each, the remaining time to type in the number). Furthermore, the same worksheet can be used for all products in the company's

Note: The "weight" of a previous forecast is calculated as alpha$(1 - \text{alpha})^{x-1}$, where x is the number of periods prior to the current forecast. Thus with alpha = 0.6, the forecast of three periods ago accounts for $0.6(1 - 0.6)^{3-1}$, or 0.064 (6.4%) of the present forecast.

offerings, with each new product taking only a minute or two before a forecast is produced.

Our Task Our mythical firm is finally going to automate its sales forecasting. We have the records for sales for all of its products over the past six periods. We will begin by evaluating our major product, the XL tire. Our objective is to try different values for alpha to see how they would have performed if we had been using this method throughout the six periods. The best value will then be used for forecasting future periods.

One way to determine which alpha is best is to see which produces smaller errors over the long run. This would work except that some errors are more costly than others. The cost of storing or holding products (when our forecast is overly optimistic and we produce too many) averages 5% of the item's cost per quarter for each item stored (20% per year is typical for many industries). The cost of running out (*stockout*), however, will be much more, due to ill will, effect upon future sales, and the costs of back-ordering goods. Our best guess places this figure at 10% of the cost of the product per quarter in our firm.

Our final alpha, therefore, will be the one that yields the lowest total costs (for holding and stockout) over the six-period test span.

All businesses involved in selling products (or services) need to make forecasts in order to plan for production and staffing. For a small business with highly stable demand, a simple average of several prior periods, or even an eyeball estimate, might work well. The larger the firm and the more complex the factors that create demand, the greater the need for a sophisticated model to aid decision making. Mathematical models, such as the very simple exponential smoothing method described herein, can save a large firm thousands or even millions of dollars, and are very common in the business world. They are only models, however. In the real world, forecasts are acted upon after being "adjusted" with common sense, experience, and hunches. Let's begin.

ENTERING THE TITLE AND HEADINGS

Topics covered:

Worksheet navigation	Editing cells
Range specifications	Copying cells
Label entry and formats	Saving the worksheet
Setting column-widths	

(Continued)

Lotus 1-2-3 (Continued)

The first step in building our worksheet is to enter the Lotus spreadsheet. At the A> prompt, enter **123**<**CR**>. Press any key to move past the copyright display, and you're in. The status line in the upper left corner indicates that the current active cell is A1. Directly beneath this line is the entry area, currently occupied by a blinking cursor (on most IBM-compatible computers) because no entry has yet been made. The active cell location is verified by the bar cursor, which is currently highlighting cell A1 in the worksheet area (the area below and to the right of the borders). Note the [READY] indicator in the upper right-hand corner. This area will indicate our current mode.

Indicator Lights Before we make any entries, let's become more familiar with our indicators. Try entering a word, such as **HELLO**, without pressing <**CR**>. Note that the mode indicator changes to [LABEL]. Try erasing a letter or two by pressing the <**BS**> (backspace) key. Now enter <**Esc**>. This removes our last entry and returns us to the [READY] mode. There are three indicators along the bottom of the screen to show the status of the <Caps Lock>, <Num Lock>, and <Scroll Lock> keys. Press each of these keys to see this display. The <Num Lock> key should be off for most of our tutorial, because it prohibits the use of the arrow keys and special cursor positioning keys located on the keypad (if you have a keyboard that uses separate keys for these functions, you will probably prefer to have the <Num Lock> on).

The <Scroll Lock> key is used to shift the worksheet around while keeping the cursor in the same cell. <Caps Lock> can be pressed to make all entries in uppercase letters. Pressing <Shift> produces lowercase letters when <Caps Lock> is on.

Worksheet Navigation Let's move around the worksheet a bit. Try the arrow keys to move the bar cursor up, down, and to the right and left. Note how the status line always reflects the active cell location. To get back to A1 in a hurry, press <**Home**>. To move to the last row, press <**End**><**D**>. Try <**End**> followed by each of the arrow keys. Table 8–11 lists the cursor movement commands used in 1-2-3.

Moving around one screen at a time is accomplished with the <PgUp>, <PgDn>, and <Tab> keys. <PgDn> jumps one screen down (20 lines), and <PgUp> sends the cursor up the same amount. Jumping a screen to the right is done by pressing <Tab>, while <Shift><Tab> sends you one screen left. Try each of these.

Entering the Heading Our first entry will be the worksheet's title, which we will place in cell C1. Use the arrow keys to move there, then enter **Expo-**

KEY	ACTION
<U>	Up one cell.
<D>	Down one cell.
<L>	Left one cell.
<R>	Right one cell.
<PgUp>	Up one screen.
<PgDn>	Down one screen.
<Tab>	Right one screen.
<End><U>	To top of column.
<End><D>	To column bottom.
<End><L>	Left edge of row.
<End><R>	Right edge of row.
<Home>	To A1.
<Shift><Tab>	Left one screen.

TABLE 8–11

1-2-3 Cursor Movement Commands

nential Smoothing Model <**CR**>. When you have finished your entry, note the status line at the top. It contains a single quotation mark at the beginning of the string. 1-2-3 placed this here to indicate that the value is a left-justified (or aligned) label. Unless you are entering numbers or special symbols for formulas and functions, 1-2-3 assumes that the entry is a label. You should also observe that our entry extends well beyond the width of column C, yet is still displayed in full. Placing an entry in cell D1 will write over a portion of our title.

Correcting Mistakes If you make any errors while entering, remember that <BS> (backspace) will erase backward and <Esc> will clear your entry to begin again. If an entry has already been completed, correct it by moving to the cell and pressing <**F2**>. This places you in the edit mode (watch the mode indicator in the upper right corner). Several special key functions are available in edit mode. The right and left arrow keys, for example, now allow you to move back and forth within the entry area. The <Home> key will send you to the beginning of your line, while the <End> key sends you just past the last character entered in the cell. <BS> is still used to delete backwards, and the <Del> key will erase the character directly above the cursor. The <Insert> key has no effect, because 1-2-3 always operates in the insert mode. Experiment for awhile with the editing features by altering our title, then move to A3 (try <**Home**><**D**><**D**>) for our next entry.

(Continued)

Lotus 1-2-3 (Continued)

Column-Width You may have noticed from Figure 8–24 that our first column is wider than the rest, so that we have ample room to enter row labels. This is done with the following command: **/WCS15<CR>**, which stands for / (brings up our first menu), Worksheet, Column-Width, Set, 15 (our desired width).

Label Formats Our next step is to enter the values "Product:", "Price:", and "Alpha:" in cells A3, A4, and E3, respectively. We will later make our entries for these parameters in adjacent cells to the right of each. For appearance's sake, we want these labels to line up with the right-hand sides of their cells. 1-2-3 allows labels, or text values, to be left-aligned, right-aligned, or centered by prefacing them with either a single quote mark, a double quote, or a caret (^), as shown in Table 8–12.

As you enter each label, try moving directly to the next cell by pressing the appropriate arrow key rather than <CR>. When you are done with the "Product," "Price," and "Alpha" labels, move to cell B6 to begin entering column headings. Your worksheet should appear as shown in the lower part of Figure 8–27.

Copying Enter the first column heading **(^1st Q<R>)** along with corresponding entries for the second, third, and fourth quarters in cells B6 through E6 (the caret [^] is entered as <Shift><6>, rather than <Ctrl>). When F6 is reached, we will use the COPY command to make duplicates of our first three headings. The values we need for cells F6 through H6 are the same as those in B6 through D6, so why bother retyping them?

There are several ways to copy cells, but each of them involves invoking the COPY command (/C) and specifying first the range of cells to copy, then the location for making the copy. For our first use of COPY, enter **/CB6..E6<CR><CR>**, for /Copy, from B6 to E6, to the current cell (F6). The worksheet should now appear as shown in the lower part of Figure 8–28.

TABLE 8–12
Label Entry Formats

Entering		Produces (left)	(center)	(right)
entering → ^hi	produces →		hi	
entering → "hi	produces →			hi
entering → 'hi	produces →	hi		
entering → hi	produces →	hi		

Note: Entering *hi* directly produces left alignment, the default mode for Lotus 1-2-3.

Recap

Keystrokes	Action
<R><R>Exponential Smoothing Model<CR>	Title
<Home><D><D>	Move to A3
/WCS15<CR><U><R><R><R>	Col-wid to 15
"Product:<D>"Price:<R>"Alpha:	Enter labels
<D><D><D><L><L><L>	Move to B6

The screen should now show

	A	B	C	D	E	F
1			Exponential Smoothing Model			
2						
3	Product:				Alpha:	
4	Price:					
5						
6		<cursor>				
7						
8						
9						
10						

FIGURE 8–27

Worksheet After Entering Title and Labels

Using the <End> Key to Move Quickly Notice that column H is not visible on the screen. To ensure that it says "3rd Q," use the arrow keys to scroll to the right. To move quickly back to B6, try entering <**End**><**L**>. The <End> key, when used in combination with an arrow key, will move to the directional extreme of a group of entries. Notice that you are not sent all the way back to A6. The <End><L> sequence will send you left only until a blank column is encountered. This is useful if you are accustomed to dividing your worksheet into blocks separated by blank rows or columns.

Now, move down to B7 and enter **^LAST YR**. We will copy this to C7..E7, using a slightly different approach from our first COPY. Enter **/C**<**CR**>**C7..E7**<**CR**>. Try <**End**><**R**><**R**> to move to F7. At F7, enter **^THIS YR** and copy it to G7..I7. The worksheet appears as shown in the lower part of Figure 8–29.

Saving the Worksheet Before concluding this segment, we will save our worksheet (it will be used in the upcoming segments). When working long sessions, a worksheet should be saved at frequent intervals, because disruptions might cause the loss of data. To save a worksheet, make certain

(Continued)

Lotus 1-2-3 (Continued)

FIGURE 8–28
Worksheet After Entering More Labels

Recap

Keystrokes	**Action**
^1st Q<R>^2nd Q<R>^3rd Q<R>^4th Q<R>	Enter headings for quarters
/CB6..D6<CR><CR>	Copy B6..D6 to F6

The screen should now show

	A	B	C	D	E	F	G
1			Exponential Smoothing Model				
2							
3	Product:				Alpha:		
4	Price:						
5							
6		1st Q	2nd Q	3rd Q	4th Q	<1st Q>	2nd Q
7							
8							
9							
10							

Note: the brackets <> show the location of the cursor

that a formatted disk is in B drive, and that it has at least 20K bytes available on it. Then enter /**F**ile **S**ave **EXPSMO<CR>** to save our file under the name EXPSMO. Once your work is saved, exit 1-2-3 with /**Q**uit **Y**es.

ENTERING THE ROW LABELS

Topics covered:

Retrieving worksheets	Inserting	Using Point
Numeric formats	GOTO	

In this session, we will enter the row labels and a few of the numbers that will appear in our final worksheet. Before we begin, let's retrieve our worksheet from the disk. Enter /**FR** and wait a moment. You should see the file you saved highlighted on the menu line. Press <**CR**> to retrieve the worksheet.

Move to cell A8 and enter *row labels* as shown in Figure 8–31.

Inserting Rows and Columns Our worksheet would look a bit better if we had a summation line between "Stockout" and "Total." To create this line, we must first clear some space for it. Move to B18 and enter **/WIR<CR>**

Recap

Keystrokes	Action
<End><L><D>	Move to B7
^LAST YR<CR>	Enter heading
/C<CR>C7..E7<CR>	Copy "LAST YR" to C7..E7
<End><R><R>^THIS YR<CR>	Enter "THIS YR" in F7
/C<CR>G7..H7<CR>	Copy it to G7..H7

The screen should now show

	A	B	C	D	E	F	G
1				Exponential Smoothing Model			
2							
3	Product:			Alpha:			
4	Price:						
5							
6		1st Q	2nd Q	3rd Q	4th Q	1st Q	2nd Q
7		LAST YR	LAST YR	LAST YR	LAST YR	THIS YR	THIS YR

FIGURE 8–29

Worksheet After Entering Still More Labels

(/Worksheet Insert Row<CR>). Deleting a row or column will work in the same manner. To create a row of dashes, enter \-<**CR**>. The backslash key indicates that characters that follow are to be repeated across the entire cell width.

Using POINT to Copy To copy this cell across the row, let's use a powerful feature of 1-2-3, the POINT mode. Enter /**C** to invoke the COPY command, then press <**CR**> to indicate the range for copying from. Notice that the mode indicator in the upper right corner shows "POINT," allowing us to point to the range we will copy *to.* To use this feature, move the cursor to C18 and enter **.** (period). The period "anchors" the cursor for expansion. Watch what happens as you use the arrow keys to make the cursor area grow larger. Try expanding and contracting the cursor in all directions to get the feel of this process, then return to C18 and expand it across the row to H18. When done, press <**CR**> to set our range and have the copy operation proceed.

The GOTO Key To move around rapidly in a large spreadsheet, the <F5> key acts as a direct cursor location key, called the GOTO key. To use it, simply press <**F5**> followed by the address of the cell to jump to and a <**CR**>. Use <**F5**>**B3**<**CR**> to jump to the entry area for our product name, and type **XL Tire**<**D**>.

(Continued)

Lotus 1-2-3 (Continued)

FIGURE 8–30

Keystrokes Required to Save the Worksheet and Exit 1-2-3

Keystrokes	Action
/FSEXPSMO<CR>	Save the worksheet
/QY	Quit 1-2-3

Numeric Formats In B4 we will enter the price of our product, *50*. To give this value the appearance of a dollar amount, we will use one of the many formatting options provided by 1-2-3. Enter /**RFC**<**CR**><**CR**> (/Range Format Currency). Use <**F5**>**F3**<**CR**>**.3**<**CR**> to enter 0.3 as our initial guess at an alpha level. Your worksheet should now appear as shown in Figure 8–32.

To finish the session, save the worksheet (use the same name) and exit 1-2-3. Select **R** for the Cancel/Replace option. This will erase our previous worksheet (1-2-3 does not keep backup copies).

ENTERING THE DATA

Topics covered:

Formulas

Functions

In this session we will enter the initial data for our forecasting model, and some of the initial formulas. We begin by moving to B9 and entering our demand figures for the past six quarters across the ninth row (from B9 to G9). The figures are

First quarter last year	950
Second quarter last year	1350
Third quarter last year	1160
Fourth quarter last year	1160
First quarter this year	990
Second quarter this year	1015

After these entries have been made, move to B10 to begin entering the values in column B. For the first-quarter forecast amount, we will use the same value as our first-quarter demand figure, because our model cannot produce a forecast based upon only a single-period demand figure. Once

Keystrokes	Action
/FR<CR> or /FREXPSMO	Retrieve worksheet
<Home><D><D><D><D><D><D><D>	Move to A8
SALES<D>"Actual<D>"Forecast<D>	Enter first 3 labels
INVENTORY<D>"Begin<D>"Produce<D>"End	Next 4
COSTS<D>"Holding<D>"Stockout<D>"Total<CR>	Last 4

FIGURE 8–31

Worksheet After Entering Row Labels

The screen should now show

	A	B	C	D	E	F	G
1			Exponential Smoothing Forecasting Model				
2							
3	Product:	XL Tire		Alpha:	0.3		
4	Price:	$50.00					
5							
6		1st Q	2nd Q	3rd Q	4th Q	1st Q	2nd Q
7		LAST YR	LAST YR	LAST YR	LAST YR	THIS YR	THIS YR
8	SALES						
9	Actual						
10	Forecast						
11	INVENTORY						
12	Begin						
13	Produce						
14	End						
15	COSTS						
16	Holding						
17	Stockout						
18	<Total>						
19							

this starting forecast has been entered, all future forecasts will have a previous one to be based upon.

Rather than simply entering 950 in B10, we would like the worksheet to use whatever the initial value is in B9. We tell 1-2-3 to take the value from B9 by entering **+B9**. The plus symbol identifies this entry as a formula rather than a label. Try entering this value with and without the plus symbol to see the difference.

Once the initial forecast has been entered, move down to B12 and enter 100 for the beginning inventory of this first period. The amount to produce (B13) should be the forecasted demand (B10) less the amount on hand at the beginning of the period (B12). Enter this as **+B10−B12** to distinguish it from a text or label entry. Notice that the result of our formula (B10−B12) appears in B13, rather than the formula itself. Your worksheet should now appear as shown in Figure 8–33.

(Continued)

Lotus 1-2-3 (Continued)

FIGURE 8–32
Worksheet After Entering Product, Price, and Alpha

Recap

Keystrokes	**Action**
<U><R>/WIR<CR>	Insert row 18
\-<CR>	Dashes in B18
/C<CR><R>.<R><R><R><R><R><CR>	Copy to C18..H18
<F5>B3<CR>XL Tire<D>50<CR>	Enter product and price
/RFC<CR><CR>	Format to currency
<F5>F3<CR>.3<CR>	Enter alpha

The screen should now show

	A	B	C	D	E	F	G
1			Exponential Smoothing Model				
2							
3	Product:	XL Tire			Alpha:	0.3	
4	Price:	$50.00					
5							
6		1st Q	2nd Q	3rd Q	4th Q	1st Q	2nd Q
7		LAST YR	LAST YR	LAST YR	LAST YR	THIS YR	THIS YR
8	SALES						
9	Actual						
10	Forecast						
11	INVENTORY						
12	Begin						
13	Product						
14	End						
15	COSTS						
16	Holding						
17	Stockout						
18		----------	----------	----------	----------	----------	----------
19	Total						

1-2-3 @ Functions The amount of inventory on hand at the end of the period should be our beginning amount (B12), plus the amount we produced (B13), minus the demand for the period (B9). However, if we did not produce enough to meet the demand, the simple formula +B12+B13−B9 would result in a negative ending inventory. To prevent this occurrence, we can use a special 1-2-3 function.

Most Lotus functions have three parts: the "@" symbol (which identifies the entry as a function), the function name, and the values (called *arguments*) that will be used in computing the function. Arguments are placed in parentheses and are separated by commas if more than one is required. For situations such as ours, 1-2-3 has a special decision function, @IF. The @IF

Recap

Keystrokes	**Action**
<F5>B9<CR>950<R>	Enter first quarter
1350<R>1160<R>1160<R>990<R>1015<CR>	Rest of row 9
<F5>B10<CR> +B9<D><D>	Enter first forecast
+B10-B12<D>	Enter production amount

The screen should now show

FIGURE 8–33

Worksheet After Entering the Data

	A	B	C	D	E	F	G
1			Exponential Smoothing Model				
2							
3	Product:	XL Tire			Alpha:	0.3	
4	Price:	$50.00					
5							
6		1st Q	2nd Q	3rd Q	4th Q	1st Q	2nd Q
7		LAST YR	LAST YR	LAST YR	LAST YR	THIS YR	THIS YR
8	SALES						
9	Actual	950	1350	1160	1160	990	1015
10	Forecast	950					
11	INVENTORY						
12	Begin	100					
13	Produce	850					
14	End						
15	COSTS						
16	Holding						
17	Stockout						
18							
19	Total						

function takes three arguments. The first argument is the condition that will be checked, the second is the value that the cell will have if the condition is true, and the third is the value of the cell if the condition is false.

In our case, if the beginning inventory plus the production amount is less than the demand (the condition to be evaluated), then we want a zero for ending inventory (all stock was sold); otherwise, we want the amount by which production and beginning inventory exceeded demand. This would be entered in B14 as **@IF(B12+B13<B9,0,B12+B13−B9)**. In other words, if B12 plus B13 is less than B9, then enter zero; otherwise enter the value of B12 plus B13 minus B9. After entering this formula, move to B16 to compute holding costs.

Holding costs are 5% of the average inventory value. Average inventory value for the period is usually computed by adding the beginning and ending

(Continued)

inventory counts and dividing by two, then multiplying by the value of each product in inventory. Even though 850 tires were produced during this first period, an assumption of steady demand allows us to assume that these tires were shipped fairly quickly after production, so that inventory levels declined throughout the period. To find 5% of the average inventory value for the period, enter **.05*B4*(B12+B14)/2** in cell B16. Note that parentheses must be used around B12+B14 to ensure that we don't simply divide B14 by 2, and that we used the cell reference (B4) to find our price (this might be subject to change).

For our stockout cost (B17), we have another complex decision function. If we did not produce enough tires (in which case B14 would be zero), the stockout cost should be 10% of the value of the number we were short. If we were not short, this cell should be zero. For B17 enter **@IF(B14=0,(B12+B13−B9)*.1*B4,0)**.

Cell B19 will display the costs incurred by errors in our forecasting model during the first period. This is simply the sum of cells B16 and B17. Move to B19 and enter **@SUM(B16..B17)**. Since we have our initial row and column of data and formulas, this would be an appropriate place to save the worksheet, which should appear as shown in the lower part of Figure 8–34.

ENTERING THE FORECASTING MODEL

Topics covered:

- Building formulas with POINT
- Copying formulas
- Relative and absolute cell referencing

Begin this section by moving to C10 to enter our exponential smoothing formula. Recall that we will take the previous period's forecast (B10) and add to it the product of our alpha value (F3) and our forecasting error. Since we have no error in our first forecast, our second period's forecast should remain at 950. We will use 1-2-3's POINT feature to build our formula. First, type **+** to indicate that we are entering a formula. Then move the cursor left to cell B10. Notice that the mode indicator shows POINT and the entry line displays +B10. Press **+** again to continue the formula. The cursor will jump back to our starting place at C10.

The next part of our formula is the alpha value in F3. Move the cursor to F3 and press <**F4**>. The <F4> key designates that this is an *absolute,*

Recap

Keystrokes	Action
@IF(B12 + B13<B9,0,B12 + B13 − B9<D><D>	Ending inventory formula
.05*B4*(B12 + B14)/2<D>	Holding cost formula
@IF(B14 = 0,(B12 + B13 − B9)*.1*B4,0) <D><D>	Stockout cost formula
@SUM(<U><U><U>.<D><CR>)<CR>	Total costs formula

The screen should now show

	A	B	C	D	E	F	G
1			Exponential Smoothing Model				
2							
3	Product:	XL Tire			Alpha:	0.3	
4	Price:	$50.00					
5							
6		1st Q	2nd Q	3rd Q	4th Q	1st Q	2nd Q
7		LAST YR	LAST YR	LAST YR	LAST YR	THIS YR	THIS YR
8	SALES						
9	Actual	950	1350	1160	1160	990	1015
10	Forecast	950					
11	INVENTORY						
12	Begin	100					
13	Produce	850					
14	End						
15	COSTS						
16	Holding	125					
17	Stockout	0					
18							
19	Total	125					

FIGURE 8–34

Worksheet After Entering Formulas

rather than a relative cell address. If we create a formula totaling a column and then copy that formula across several columns, 1-2-3 will adjust the copied formulas so that each one totals its own column rather than the initial column. This is relative cell referencing. This is not appropriate for our current formula because when we copy it across row 10, F3 would become G3, H3, etc., cells that do not have values. By pressing F4, we are telling 1-2-3 to leave this cell reference unchanged no matter where the formula appears.

To complete our formula, we will multiply F3 by the forecasting error. Enter ***(**, move to B9, enter **−**, go to B10, and close the formula with **)**. When we press <**CR**>, the result of our formula will be displayed. If all went well, the status line should show our formula as B10 + $F$3*(B9 − B10), and cell C10 should be 950.

(Continued)

Use the pointing method to get the entry for C12. Our beginning inventory for the second quarter will be the ending amount of the first quarter. Enter **+**<**D**><**D**><**L**><**CR**> to get this value.

Copying Formulas We should now have all the necessary formulas to fill in the remainder of the worksheet. Enter /**C**<**U**><**U**><**CR**>. This defines the area to be copied. Now move one cell to the right (D12), anchor the cursor (**.**), expand the cursor upward and to the right to cover the area from D12 to G10, and press <**CR**>. Do not worry if some of the values do not make sense at the moment. We will correct them later. Now use the same method to copy all the cells from B13 through B19 into columns C through G. The resultant worksheet should look like the one in Figure 8–35. After the worksheet has been filled in, save it before beginning the next section.

CLEANING UP THE WORKSHEET

Topics covered:

Formatting worksheets	More on functions
Correcting errors	Recalculation

Several things are wrong with our current worksheet. To begin with, the zeros in cells C17 through G17 are troublesome. By moving the cursor across row 17, we can examine each formula as it is displayed on the status line. We can also see that when we copied B17 across the row, our formula (originally @IF(B14=0,(B12+B13−B9)*0.1*B4,0) was adjusted for each column. This is appropriate for all but one value. The price of the tire is only in B4, not across the entire fourth row. Apparently, we should have made this an absolute cell reference. To change our formula, return to B17, press <**F2**> to edit, and place a "**$**" before both the B and the 4 in B4. Now copy the corrected formula across the screen on row 17.

Our worksheet now shows the correct stockout costs, but those costs should be positive values, rather than negative. We might alter the middle argument to read (B9−(B12+B13))*0.1*$B$4 or we can leave the expression as it is and retain its absolute value. Let's try the last method to see if 1-2-3 will allow functions within functions. Press <**F2**> again and enclose the entire area between the commas within the parentheses in **@ABS()**. Copy this latest version across the same row to see if it has the desired effect.

Recap

Keystrokes	**Action**
<F5>C10	Go to L10 to enter model
+<L>+<U><U><U><U><U><U><U><R><R><R><F4>	First part of formula
*(<L><U> − <L>)<CR><D><D>	Remander of formula
+<D><D><L><CR>	Beginning inventory
/C<U><U><CR><R>.<U><U><R><R><R><CR><D><L>	Fill rows 10–12
/C<D><D><D><D><D><D><CR>	Copy from B13..B19
<R>.<D><D><D><D><D><D><R><R><R><R><CR>	To C13..G19

The screen should now show

	A	B	C	D	E	F	G
1			Exponential Smoothing Model				
2							
3	Product:	XL Tire			Alpha:	0.3	
4	Price:	$50.00					
5							
6		1st Q	2nd Q	3rd Q	4th Q	1st Q	2nd Q
7		LAST YR	LAST YR	LAST YR	LAST YR	THIS YR	THIS YR
8	SALES						
9	Actual	950	1350	1160	1160	990	1015
10	Forecast	950	950	1070	1097	1115.9	1078.13
11	INVENTORY						
12	Begin	100	0	0	0	0	125.9
13	Produce	850	950	1070	1097	1115.9	952.23
14	End	0	0	0	0	125.9	63.13
15	COSTS						
16	Holding	125	0	0	0	0	0
17	Stockout	0	0	0	0	0	
18							
19	Total	125	0	0	0	0	0

FIGURE 8–35

Worksheet After Copying Formulas

We have another difficulty that does not materialize with the current data, but may present a problem later. Our formula for the amount to produce in a quarter takes the forecast for the period and subtracts the beginning inventory. However, if demand dropped off sharply from one quarter to the next, we might wind up with a starting inventory that is more than we need to produce to meet demand. Our production for the quarter should be zero in this case, but the current formula would yield a negative number. To correct this, go to B13 and enter a better formula, **@IF(B12>B10,0,B10 − B12)** (if starting inventory is more than forecasted demand, produce nothing, otherwise produce the amount of the difference). Copy this formula across row 13. This will not change any of

(Continued)

the current values, but will eliminate problems that might occur with different input data.

Before moving on, note that the holding costs are now incorrect. Can you determine why? Look at B4 in the formula in B16 and compare with C16. Correct cell B16, copy across the row, then save the worksheet. After fixing B16, try entering /WGRM <CR> to see its effect. Most spreadsheet users will enter their data and formulas from left to right or from top to bottom. If a cell in the interior of the worksheet is changed, it most often affects only those cells below or to the right of the current one. By not having to recalculate the entire worksheet with each entry, 1-2-3 can keep its operating speed at an acceptable level. When you want the spreadsheet recalculated, you can press <**F9**>. Explore the other recalculation methods available when you enter **/WGR** (Worksheet, Global, Recalculation). Your worksheet should now appear as shown in the lower part of Figure 8–36.

1-2-3 Formats Although our worksheet is mostly correct, the values in the last two columns can present problems. The production personnel may not be able to produce 0.9 or 0.23 tires, and the warehouse personnel would probably throw these portions away if they did. These numbers should be integer values only. We could use the @INT or @ROUNT functions to force integer values in our formulas, but 1-2-3 provides a simpler method. Move to B9 and enter /**RFF0**<**CR**> (/Range Format Fixed decimal places). When asked for the range, expand the cursor bar to cover the area from B9 to G14 and press <**CR**>.

The RANGE command is selected because we want 1-2-3 to change the display appearance of a portion of the worksheet. If an entire worksheet required the same format, we could use a similar format command found under /WG (/Worksheet Global).

Just as fractional parts of tires make little sense, rows 16 and 19 display too many decimals for dollars and cents. To correct this, move to B16 and enter /**RFC**<**CR**> (/Range Format Currency 2 decimal places) and select B16 through G19 for the range. Notice that our formatting command only changes numeric entries, and does not alter row 18.

Our final change is made necessary by the appearance of a line of asterisks in C17. When we changed to currency format, with its dollar sign and commas, C17 changed from 2000 to $2,000.00 and is now too large to fit in the cell. The solution is to widen column C from 9 to 10 or 11 places. To do this, move the cursor to column C and enter **/WCS10**<**CR**> (/Worksheet Column-width Set 10). When done, your worksheet should look like the one in Figure 8–37. Save it.

Recap

Keystrokes	Action
<F5>B17<CR><F2><L><L><L><L><L>$<R>$<CR>	Move to and edit B17
/C<CR><R>.<R><R><R><R><CR>	Copy across the row
<F2><R> (24 times) <R> (21 times, to comma))<CR>	Insert absolute value function
/C<CR><R>.<R><R><R><R><CR>	Copy across the row
<F5>B12<CR>@IF(B12>B10,0,B10 – B12)<CR>	Correct production formula
/C<CR><R>.<R><R><R><R><CR>	Copy it across the row
<F9>	Recalculate

The screen should now show

	A	B	C	D	E	F	G
1			Exponential Smoothing Model				
2							
3	Product:	XL Tire			Alpha:	0.3	
4	Price:	$50.00					
5							
6		1st Q	2nd Q	3rd Q	4th Q	1st Q	2nd Q
7		LAST YR	LAST YR	LAST YR	LAST YR	THIS YR	THIS YR
8	SALES						
9	Actual	950	1350	1160	1160	990	1015
10	Forecast	950	950	1070	1097	1115.9	1078.13
11	INVENTORY						
12	Begin	100	0	0	0	0	125.9
13	Produce	850	950	1070	1097	1115.9	952.23
14	End	0	0	0	0	125.9	63.13
15	COSTS						
16	Holding	125	0	0	0	157.375	236.2875
17	Stockout	0	2000	450	315	0	0
18							
19	Total	125	2000	450	315	157.375	236.2875

FIGURE 8–36

Worksheet After Some Cleaning Up

FINDING THE BEST ALPHA

Topics covered:

Windows*   Macros   Printing the worksheet

The real advantages of spreadsheets are seen when changing a single number alters all other values in the worksheet. In our forecasting model, we are

*Note: Inoperative on the student version.

(Continued)

Lotus 1-2-3 (Continued)

Recap

Keystrokes	**Action**
<F5>B9<CR>/RFFO<CR>	Select integer format
<D><D><D><D><D><R><R><R><R><R><CR>	Select the range
<F5>B16<CR>/RFC<CR>	Select currency format
<D><D><D><R><R><R><R><R><CR>	Select the range
<R>/WC10<CR>	Widen column C

The screen should now show

	A	B	C	D	E	F	G
1			Exponential Smoothing Model				
2							
3	Product:	XL Tire			Alpha:	0.3	
4	Price:	$50.00					
5							
6		1st Q	2nd Q	3rd Q	4th Q	1st Q	2nd Q
7		LAST YR	LAST YR	LAST YR	LAST YR	THIS YR	THIS YR
8	SALES						
9	Actual	950	1350	1160	1160	990	1015
10	Forecast	950	950	1070	1097	116	1078
11	INVENTORY						
12	Begin	100	0	0	0	0	126
13	Produce	850	950	1070	1097	1116	952
14	End	0	0	0	0	126	63
15	COSTS						
16	Holding	$125.00	$0.00	$0.00	$0.00	$157.38	$236.29
17	Stockout	$0.00	$2,000.00	$450.00	$315.00	$0.00	$0.00
18							
19	Total	$125.00	$2,000.00	$450.00	$315.00	$157.38	$236.29

FIGURE 8–37

Worksheet After Adjusting Formats and Column Width

interested in finding the value of alpha that yields the lowest total inventory costs over the previous six quarters, and using it to forecast the next period. Before we do this, we should make a few minor changes to our worksheet.

Move the cursor to any cell on the sixth row and enter **/WIR<CR>** three times. This will insert three new rows at the cursor location, giving us more room to work at the top of the screen. Next, move the cursor to the ninth row and divide the worksheet into two separate areas by entering **/WWH** (/Worksheet Window Horizontal). The WINDOW command is useful for viewing information from one area of the worksheet that is too far away from the current working area to remain on the screen. It does not create a separate worksheet, but allows the user to view two different areas simultaneously. You can move back and forth between the two windows by pressing the <**F6**> key.

Try jumping to the lower window and moving the cursor down until the bottom row appears on-screen, then return to the top.

We created a window in order to have a straightforward method of entering the essential data for any new products we want to evaluate with our model. We will now line up our entries with the MOVE command. Go to A3 and move the range of cells from A3..B4 to C3. To do this, enter **/M<D><R><CR><U><R><CR>.** Using the same MOVE command, place E3 and F3 (Alpha: .3) immediately beneath the product price. Below this (C6), enter **"Costs: <D>"Frcast:<U><R>**.

The formula for our cost total in D6 is the sum of B22 through G22. **@SUM(B22..G22)** should do nicely, but it is more fun to build the formula using the POINT method. It will not matter if you move to row 22 in the top or bottom window. Try it each way. After creating the formula, you should format the result in either the currency or fixed formats. The fixed format will not require altering the column width in order to fit.

Obtaining a value for cell D7 is a bit more difficult. This cell will be used to hold a projection for the current quarter based upon our model, and we would like to be able to copy the formula from another cell instead of having to reenter it. Unfortunately, the COPY command will not work properly because it will adjust all of our cell references (try it!). The move command is also insufficient, since it will remove vital information from the lower work area. 1-2-3 lacks any single command that will accomplish our purpose.

One solution (there are several) to the problem would be to copy cell G13 to H13. This will correctly adjust our formula to refer to the most recent quarter, yielding a forecast for the current quarter. Once this has been done, we can move the formula from H13 to D7.

Our model is complete. After saving it to disk, we can return to our original objective of refining the forecasting process. We need to find the best alpha value for our XL tire—the one that would have yielded the least costly total of holding and stockout costs. Move the cursor to D5 and try entering several different alpha values. You should see the resultant total costs and current-quarter forecast appear in the cells below almost instantaneously. Keep adjusting your entry up to two decimal places, until you have found the lowest possible inventory cost. The top portion of your final worksheet will look like the one in Figure 8–38.

Printing the Worksheet A good worksheet model can be useful to the person who created it, but usually the information it contains will be more valuable if it can be shown to someone else. Because not everyone who needs the information will be able to visit your computer to view the work,

(Continued)

Recap

Keystrokes	**Action**
<F5>A6<CR>/WIR<CR>/WIR<CR>/WIR<CR>	Insert three rows
<D><D><D>/WWH<F6>	Create window
<D> (13 times) <F6>	Position lower window
<F5>A3<CR>/M<D><R><CR><U><R><CR>	Move A3..B4 to C3
<R><R><R><R>/M<R><CR><D><D><L><L><CR>	Move "Alpha: 0.3"
<D><D><D><L><L>"Costs:<D>"Frcast:<U><R>	Enter next two labels
@SUM((F6<L><L>.<R><R><R><R><R><CR>	Total cost formula
<F5>G13<CR>/C<CR><R><CR>	Get new forecast at H13
<R>/M<CR><F5>D7<CR>	Move it to D7

The top portion of your screen should now show

	A	B	C	D	E	F	G
1			Exponential Smoothing Forecasting Model				
2							
3			Product:	XL Tire			
4			Price:	$50.00			
5			Alpha:	0.3			
6			Costs:	3283.66			
7			Frcast:	1059			
8							

FIGURE 8–38

Top Portion of Worksheet After Inserting Rows

there must be a way to get the information on paper. Lotus 1-2-3 allows two basic methods of accomplishing this: you may send the worksheet directly to the printer, or you may store it on disk in a form that can be edited by a word processor.

To use either of these methods, select the Print option from the primary menu (/**P**). You are then presented with a choice of output to either a printer or a file. For now, select the printer. The next menu, designed to help you control the printed appearance, has the following options:

```
Range   Line   Page   Options   Clear   Align   Go   Quit
```

The Line, Page, and Align selections mimic the actions of three buttons found on most printers. Line sends a line-feed signal (an ASCII control character) to the printer and the paper advances one line. Page sends the printer a page feed (again, an ASCII control character) so that the paper will scroll to the top of the next page. Align will tell the printer that the current location should be treated as the top of the page (most printers have a top-of-form button). Choosing Clear will allow you to cancel any or all of the current printer settings. Quit will return you from the print menu to the previous main menu.

For our report, we will use Range to select the areas we wish to be printed, Options for setting margins and other print characteristics, and Go to begin the actual printing.

Range must be selected before Go in order to indicate the area of the worksheet we want printed. You can enter the cell range by typing the first and last cells in 1-2-3's normal range format—A1..G22 in our case. Remembering the cell addresses is difficult, however, especially if the end of the worksheet is not on-screen. You may find that selecting a range with the point method is easier. With a large spreadsheet even this can become tedious, and 1-2-3 does not offer a choice of selecting an entire worksheet. This is accomplished fairly easily, though, by entering <Home>. <End><Home> <CR> when asked for the range. This will send the cursor to the last occupied cell in the active worksheet, and all of the information will have been selected.

Selecting Options will present you with yet another menu:

```
Header  Footer  Margins  Borders  Setup  Page-length  Other
```

The Header and Footer selections will allow you to print titles or messages that appear at either the top or bottom of each page of a multi-page report. They also allow you to place page numbers and the date on the header or footer lines, and will center or left- or right-justify specific portions of your title or message. The Border option is a toggle, which when turned on will print the row and column coordinates of the cells along the top and left of the page, just as it appears on-screen.

The Margins command will allow you to set top, bottom, left, and right margins on the printed output. On multiple-page printouts, top and bottom margin settings allow you to control how many lines get printed on each page. The Page-length will let you work with forms of varying length, and works with the margin setting to determine how many lines are printed before it will skip to the top of the next page.

Choosing Setup allows you to define a string of characters that are sent to the printer before printing begins, usually to select a print mode offered by the printer. If you have a worksheet that is too wide to be printed in normal typesize on your 8½-inch paper, your printer may have a compressed print mode available, and the code to activate this mode should be sent to the printer before actual printing begins. On an Epson, or Epson-compatible printer, for example, you would enter **\018** to switch to compressed print. The slash (\) is required by 1-2-3, and the numbers that follow are the ASCII code

(Continued)

required by the printer in a three-digit format. Printer control codes can be found in the printer's operating manual.

The last selection, Other, contains a very useful feature—printing the formulas contained in a cell rather than their displayed results. With this listing one line is devoted to each occupied cell in the worksheet, which makes it somewhat difficult to read. It is, nevertheless, very useful for tracking down spreadsheet errors, and can be used to document the worksheet so that others may understand how it operates. It also provides a paper record that can be used to rebuild the entire worksheet if anything should happen to your disk, or if you need to send it to someone.

After exploring the print features for awhile, we should be able to obtain a printout with minimal difficulty. For Range, select all of the worksheet by entering <**Home**>. <**End**><**Home**><**CR**>. Make sure the margin settings are appropriate for your paper size. We do not need a header because our worksheet has its own title line. Now select Go by pressing **G**.

Printing to a file presents you with the same options. In addition, you must provide a filename for it to be stored under. Filenames follow normal DOS conventions, and if you omit a file extension, 1-2-3 will provide one (.PRN). This means that you may use the same name as your worksheet, which will have a .WK1 extension. The file that is created will look just like the worksheet on your monitor. It uses no embedded codes, so most word processing programs will have little difficulty working with it. A nice aspect of 1-2-3's print-to-file feature is that it appends the currently selected range to the end of a file, rather than overwriting the file upon using the print-to-file facility on the second and succeeding times. This means that you can print several noncontiguous segments of a worksheet while skipping over areas you wish to omit.

Automating the Worksheet with Macros Experienced users find that 1-2-3's *macro* capability is one of its most powerful features. A macro is a series of commands that is stored in the worksheet in such a way that it can be called up at any time with a simple two-key combination. Macros can hold difficult-to-remember sequences of keystrokes, or can be used to ensure that the necessary input values are obtained from the user. 1-2-3's macro feature even contains a number of special commands that can only be used in macros, giving the user the power to create fully automated, menu-driven programs.

A 1-2-3 macro contains two parts, a macro name and the macro contents. The macro name consists of a backward slash (\) and a single letter or number between 0 and 255. Macro names are entered with a special command, /Range Name Create. The macro contents are placed in a nearby cell (usually the adjacent cell to the right of the name), and are entered as text (just like any label), prefaced with a single quotation mark. You may create either the macro contents or the macro name first. Once a macro has been created, it is invoked or executed by holding down the <Alt> key and pressing the letter (or number on the numeric keypad) that was selected for its name.

An example might help. When we printed our worksheet, we entered a lengthy string of commands (see Figure 8–39, below). To simplify this operation, we could place the entire sequence in a macro (this would be particularly useful if there was a special printer setup string required). To do this, move to an unused area of the worksheet, such as B30, and type in the following sequence: **'/PPRA1..G22~OMT5~QGQ<CR>** (/ Print Printer Range A1..G22 <CR> Other Margin Top 5 <CR> Quit Go Quit). The single quotation mark is required so that this sequence gets entered into a cell, rather than acted upon as you type it. Note that we explicitly specified the range as A1..G22, rather than typing <End><Home>, because we have just expanded our worksheet area with our macro and do not wish the macro to be printed. The squiggly line, called a *tilde,* represents a carriage return, and is found next to the carriage return key on most keyboards (if your keyboard does not have one, hold down the <Alt> key and enter 126 on the numeric keypad).

Once the macro has been created, it must be named. Move to A30 and enter /**RNC** (/ Range Name Create). When asked for a name, enter **P** (for Print, so we can remember it). You will then be asked for the range that contains the macro. Enter **B30.** Once this has been done, your macro is ready for use. To try it out, enter <Alt>P (press <Alt> and <P> simultaneously). We have just reduced the job of printing our worksheet to a single, two-finger keystroke.

FIGURE 8–39
Keystrokes Required to Print Worksheet

Recap

Keystrokes	**Action**
/PP	Print to the printer
R<Home><End><Home><CR>	Select all for range
OMT5<CR>Q	Set a top margin of 5
GQ	Print it.
/PFEXPSMO<CR>	Print to a file
GQ	Range is already set

(Continued)

Lotus 1-2-3 (Continued)

1-2-3's macro capability has several special features. A special key, such as <Esc> or <PgUp>, can be included in a macro by enclosing the key name in brackets (either [] or {}). For function keys, use the name of the function (e.g., {GOTO} rather than {F5}). Arrow keys are {UP}, {DOWN}, {LEFT}, and {RIGHT}. A question mark enclosed in brackets will accept user input until <CR> is pressed. Thus {GOTO}B13~{?}~{GOTO}C5~ will jump to cell B13, wait for the user to input a value, and then jump to cell C5. Another special macro feature is the ability to enter a macro with multiple lines. Successive lines should be placed beneath one another, and can be invoked with a single macro name. A special macro name, \0 (use *zero,* not the letter O), is automatically invoked any time the worksheet is loaded, effectively automating any process you desire.

To automate our worksheet so it will prompt the user for the necessary demand figures and prices, try entering the sequence listed below as a macro with the name \0. Then save the worksheet and reload it. The first line of the macro clears the window, repositions the screen, then gets input for the product name and price. The second line gets an initial alpha value and the first two demand figures. The third line gets the remaining demand figures and reestablishes the window. The fourth line positions the lower window so that the Totals line is in the display. The fifth line relocates the cursor at D6 for experimentation with the alpha value. The last line names the macro as \0 so that it will be automatically invoked when the worksheet is loaded in the future.

Cell	**Entry**
B31	'/WWC{HOME}{GOTO}D3~{?}~{GOTO}D4~{?}~
B32	'{GOTO}D5~{?}~{GOTO}B12~{?}~{RIGHT}{?}~{RIGHT}{?}~
B33	'{RIGHT}{?}~{RIGHT}{?}~{RIGHT}{?}~{GOTO}D9~/WWH
B34	'{WINDOW}{PGDN}{UP}{UP}{UP}{UP}{UP}{UP}{UP}{UP}
B35	'{WINDOW}{UP}{UP}{UP}
A31	/RNC\0<CR><R>.<D><D><D><D><CR>

EXERCISES

1. Name the disks that Lotus 1-2-3 comes on. Which disk contains the 123.EXE program file? What is the Print Graph Disk needed for? Which program provides access to all of the Lotus 1-2-3 facilities?
2. Describe the hardware required to fully support Lotus 1-2-3.
3. Function keys have special meanings in Lotus 1-2-3. What are they?
4. In addition to the function keys, Lotus 1-2-3 makes judicious use, for control

purposes, of other non-alphabetic and non-numeric keys. Which ones are they? What are their defined uses within Lotus 1-2-3?

5. What five options are available from the Lotus access system, and which one is used most often? What is each used for?

DISK EXERCISES

1. Load the worksheet CASH.WK1 into Lotus 1-2-3. Add a row NON-TAX INCOME between rows 6 and 7 with the amounts shown below for each column.

Jan	0
Feb	2000
Mar	4000
Apr	3000
May	1000
Jun	1000
Jul	0
Aug	0
Sep	1000
Oct	1000
Nov	0
Dec	0

   The contents of this row are to be added to the Balance row in the same way that Income is added. Adjust the Balance row formulas appropriately.

   Add column O (letter O) after column N, which is the column for December. Label it TOTALS in row 3. Total the Income and Expenses rows into this column. In cell O10, subtract the total income from the total expenses. Label this cell NET INCOME in cell O9. Print the modified workseet.

2. Load the worksheet BALANCE.WK1 into Lotus 1-2-3 and do the following. Move all rows down one row by simply inserting a row before row 1. Use the INSERT command to do this, with the cursor in cell A1. Specify the INSERT directive under the WORKSHEET menu item. Then specify ROW, and finally specify the range as A1.. A1. Now add, in Row 1, the following title: BALANCE SHEET FOR GENERAL MANUFACTURING COMPANY. To do this, move to A2, request the TITLES directive under the WORKSHEET command. Specify a HORIZONTAL title and then try to move to A1. Print the modified worksheet and save the modified worksheet under the same filename on your data disk.
3. Do exactly the same work as requested in Disk Exercise 2 above, only use the MOVE directive rather than the INSERT directive to create a row of empty cells in Row 1 for the title.
4. Use the INSERT directive to produce 10 empty rows at the beginning of the BALANCE.WK1 worksheet. Using the general format for a worksheet suggested in Figure 7–16, specify an AUTHOR, a DATE, a TITLE, and a PURPOSE. Use your

(Continued)

name for the AUTHOR; use the current DATE; use BALANCE SHEET FOR GENERAL MANUFACTURING COMPANY as the TITLE; and use TO SPECIFY CORPORATE NET WORTH, ASSETS AND LIABILITIES as the PURPOSE. Print the modified worksheet and save the worksheet on your data disk under the filename BALANCE1.WK1.

5. Load the worksheet MINI.WK1. (The extension .WK1 is the one Lotus 1-2-3 Release 2 uses to distinguish worksheets created using Release 2 from those created using Release 1A, which have the .WKS extension.) Print the entire unmodified worksheet. Add a column in column J, starting in Row 51, which calculates for each row the "PV Cash Flows." Use the formula PV Cash Flows = PVIF*(Aftertax Cash Flows) as shown in the worksheet. Label this column appropriately in cells J47 and J48. Print the worksheet again.
6. Load the worksheet MINI.WK1. Delete rows 1 through 3. Do this by invoking the WORKSHEET, DELETE, ROW directives. In response to the RANGE request, type A1.. A3 or use the cursor to point to these. Change the TITLE to read "Cash Flows Adjusted for Inflation." Print the worksheet.
7. Do both Disk Exercises 5 and 6 above and then print the modified worksheet.
8. As best you can, modify the worksheet OIL.WK1 so that it fits the general format suggested in Figure 7–16. Save the worksheet on your own data disk. Print the modified worksheet. You are free to use your own discretion in this exercise; you should not feel that there is only one exactly right answer.
9. Use the worksheet OIL.WK1 by loading it from the work disk. Print the entire unmodified worksheet. Add in row 18 the TOTALS of columns C through M. Label this row in cell A18 'TOTALS. Print the modified worksheet. Note: To do this effectively, you must first create an appropriate formula in cell C18 and then COPY the contents of this cell into cells D18 through M18. Save the modified worksheet on your data disk under the filename OIL1.WK1 and print it.
10. Use the worksheet OIL.WK1 by loading it from the work disk. Move row 20 between rows 6 and 7. Change or modify column H cells H12 through H18 so that these cells get their value from the cell in column A containing the ".875." For example, if cell A7 contains .875, then cell H12 should be modified to read +$A$7. What kind of cell reference is this? Copy the contents of cell H12 into cells H13 through H18. Print the modified worksheet.
11. Use the worksheet OIL1.WK1 by loading it from your data disk. (See Disk Exercise 9 above.) Now, in row 19 compute averages for each total you found in row 18 by dividing the contents of each cell in row 18 by 7. Label this row, in cell A19, 'AVERAGES.
12. As best you can, modify the worksheet MINI.WK1 so that it fits the general format suggested in Figure 7–16. Save the worksheet on your own data disk. Print the modified worksheet. To do this you will want to move rows 21 through 24 so they appear before (or above) the table. You are free to use your own discretion in this exercise; do not feel that there is only one exactly right answer.
13. Use the worksheet LEVERAGE.WK1 by loading it from the work disk. Enter your name and the current date in cells A5 and A6. Save the worksheet under the

same name on your data disk. Print the worksheet. Print the cell contents as well. You do this by specifying the Print, Printer, Options, Other, and Cell-Formulas directives. Now use the Escape key to get back to the Range Line Page Options Clear Align Go Quit menu bar. Select Go from this list. Examine the contents of cells in Column B. Note that these cells have a [W24] prefix before anything else (text, formula, value, or whatever in the cell). What does this mean? Now examine the contents of cells D11 through D16. These have a (C2) [W20] prefix specification. What does this mean? Note that the brackets [ ] are used to specify column width and the parentheses ( ) are used to specify format. Consult your Lotus 1-2-3 manual. Examine the contents of cells B11 through B20 again. What does the ′ mean? What is the width of column C? Is it possible to specify different cell widths within a column, or must all cells in a column retain the same width?

14. Examine the contents of cells B21 through D28 of the LEVERAGE. WK1 worksheet on your work disk. What do these cells have in common? What does the U specification mean? Hint: Examine this part of the worksheet on a color monitor. Now change the total sales figure to $9,000,000.00 How does this change the rest of the worksheet? Print the worksheet again and compare with the former printed version.
15. Load the worksheet MACRO.WK1. Describe what this worksheet does. Print the worksheet contents. Analyze how this worksheet works and explain how it works.

TUTORIAL

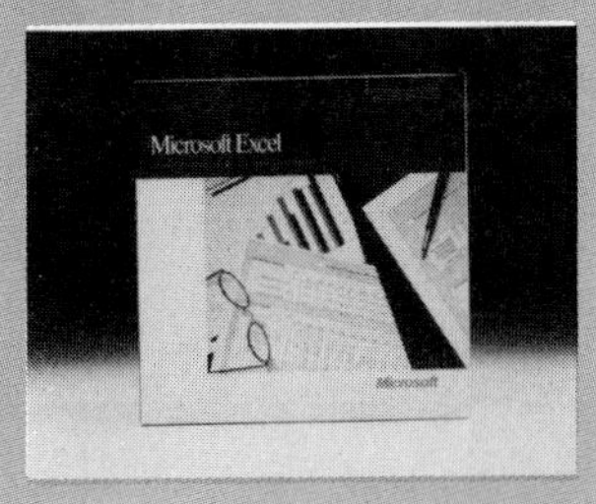

Microsoft Excel™

In this tutorial, you will learn to set up a worksheet for maintaining a simple checkbook register. This tutorial will guide you through some basic concepts of Excel, such as entering information and formulas in cells, and saving and printing a worksheet. You will use the fill function and paste formulas, and you will modify the appearance of the worksheet by changing the column width, font typeface, and styles. We will use the term *click* to refer to a depression and release of the mouse button in what follows. **Minimum Hardware Requirement:** Macintosh 512K, two 400K drives. **Recommended System:** Macintosh 512K, Mac Plus, or Mac SE with an 800K external drive.

STARTING EXCEL AND CURSOR MOVEMENT

Starting Excel

1. Turn on your Macintosh.
2. Insert Excel Program Disk (with a System file) into the internal disk drive. In about 45 seconds you should see the disk icon on the display.
3. Insert your Data disk into the external drive.
4. Double-click the Excel Program Disk icon to open the disk. Double-click the Excel icon to start Excel and create a new worksheet. Excel will name the new worksheet "Worksheet1."

Cursor Movements You can use the <Tab> key to move the cell pointer one cell to the right, use <Shift Tab> to move one cell to the left, or use the cursor to point at the cell you wish to select. Click once. The reference to the active cell will be indicated at the top left corner of the screen. The <Return> key will enter your data/information into the active cell and move the pointer one cell down. <Shift Return> will move the cell pointer one cell up. Clicking at the gray part of the vertical scroll bar will move one screen up or down, depending on whether you click above or below the square box. Clicking at the gray part of the horizontal scroll bar will move one screen to the right or left, depending on whether the mouse is to the left or right of the square box. To select/highlight a range of cells, click and drag the mouse left or down. If you need to go to a specific cell that is not currently shown on the screen, the GO TO command from the formula menu quickly scrolls the worksheet and selects the reference/cell you specify.

CREATING A SIMPLE CHECKBOOK REGISTER

If you haven't started Excel, start Excel by following the instructions just given. You should see a blank worksheet, titled Worksheet1. The current active cell, A1, has a heavy black border (highlighted). Excel's worksheet has 16,384 rows by 256 columns. Rows are numbered 1 to 16,384; columns are labeled A to Z and continued with AA through AZ, BA through BZ, and so on through IV.

You create a worksheet by entering text, numbers, and formulas in the cells. Before entering information into the cells, you need to select or specify the cells you want to work with.

1. Move the cursor to cell A1 and click the mouse to select the cell. In what follows the word *select* will always have this meaning.
2. Type **Trans.** and then press the <**Tab**> key to enter the text and move on to select the next cell, B1. If the content of the cell begins with an alphabetic character, it is assumed to be text or a label. If you make any mistakes before pressing the <Tab>, <Enter>, or <Return> key, you can use the <Backspace> key in combination with the cursor to correct your mistakes. If you pressed any of the <Tab>, <Enter>, or <Return> keys, reselect the cell that contains mistakes and position the cursor in the "Formula Bar" (Figure 8–40) and backspace to correct the mistakes.
3. In cell B1, type **Check** and press <**Tab**> key to enter the text and move on to select the next cell, C1.
4. In cell C1, type **Description** and press <**Tab**> key. Repeat the same process again to enter **Amount** in cell D1, **Amount** in cell E1, **Clear** in cell F1, and **Balance** in cell G1.
5. Position the cursor to cell A2 and click the mouse button to select the cell. Type **Date** and then press the <**Tab**> key to enter the text and move on to select the next cell, B2. Proceed, entering **Number** in cell B2, **Check** in cell D2, and **Deposit** in cell E2.
6. Position the cursor to cell A3 and click the mouse button. Proceed to enter the text, dates, and numbers in cells A3 through F9 as shown in Figure 8–41. Notice you have yet to enter formulas.

Formulas begin with an equal sign: =. As mentioned earlier, cells are referenced by columns and rows, A1, B1, etc. In this tutorial you will be dealing

(*Continued*)

Microsoft Excel™ (Continued)

FIGURE 8–40
The Excel Worksheet

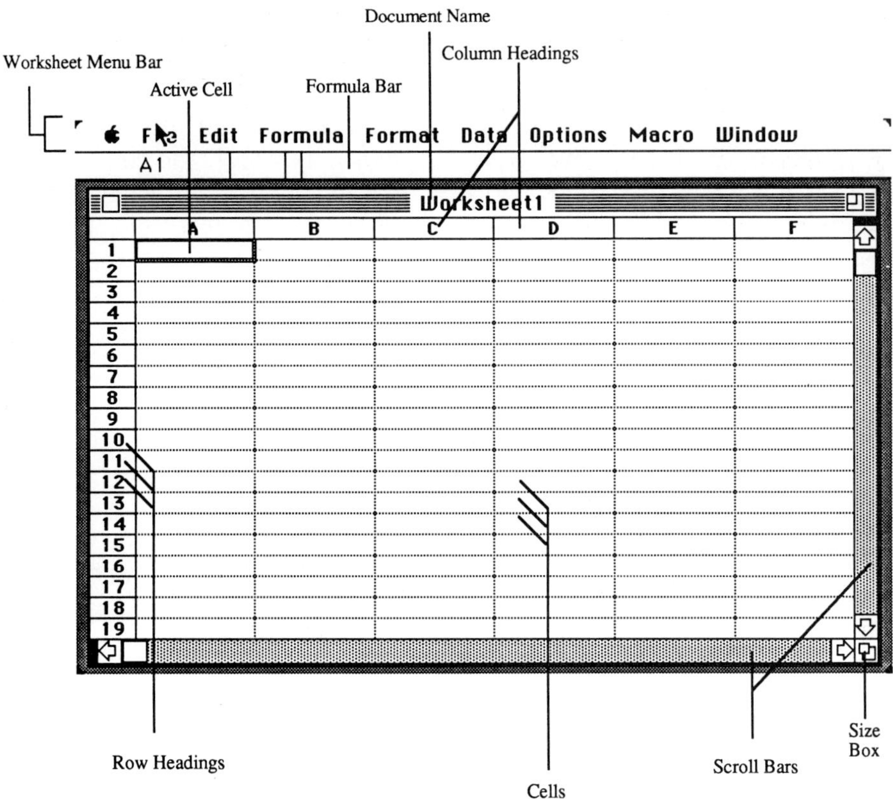

with some simple formulas that involve addition and subtraction, and some more complex formulas such as logical IF and AND functions to make the worksheet look better. A function begins with an equal sign followed by the name of the function, which in turn is followed by an expression that is enclosed in parentheses.

7. Select cell G3, and type **=E3,** then press the <**Return**> key. Because we start an account by first depositing some cash into the account, the balance will be the same as the first deposit, that is, the contents of cell E3. Notice that the cell G4 is currently selected after you press the <Return> key.
8. Type **=IF(AND(D4="",E4=""),"",G3−D4+E4)** and press the <**Enter**> key—the key just right of the spacebar. Notice that the cell G4 is still the active cell. If you press the <**Return**> key instead, the current active cell will be cell G5.

	A	B	C	D	E	F	G
1	**Trans.**	**Check**	**Description**	**Amount**	**Amount**	**Clear**	**Balance**
2	**Date**	**Number**		**Check**	**Deposit**		
3	7/5/1987		Cash to Open new account		1000	Y	=E3
4	7/10/1987	100	Furrs - Groceries	25.88		N	=IF(AND(D4="",E4=""),"",G3-D4+E4)
5	7/10/1987	101	Hair Design - Perm	40		N	=IF(AND(D5="",E5=""),"",G4-D5+E5)
6	7/10/1987	102	Dillards - Blouse	43.99		N	=IF(AND(D6="",E6=""),"",G5-D6+E6)
7	7/13/1987	103	Western, Inc.	200.5		N	=IF(AND(D7="",E7=""),"",G6-D7+E7)
8	7/15/1987		Paycheck		1050.6	N	=IF(AND(D8="",E8=""),"",G7-D8+E8)
9	7/16/1987	104	Food Emporium - Groceries	29.76		N	=IF(AND(D9="",E9=""),"",G8-D9+E9)
10							=IF(AND(D10="",E10=""),"",G9-D10+E10)
11							=IF(AND(D11="",E11=""),"",G10-D11+E11)
12							=IF(AND(D12="",E12=""),"",G11-D12+E12)
13							=IF(AND(D13="",E13=""),"",G12-D13+E13)
14							=IF(AND(D14="",E14=""),"",G13-D14+E14)
15							=IF(AND(D15="",E15=""),"",G14-D15+E15)

FIGURE 8–41

The Excel Worksheet After Step K

The formula in cell G4 needs clarification. The logical function AND(D4 = "",E4 = "") within the IF function tests to see whether both the contents in cells D4 and E4 are null strings—that is, have nothing in them (blank spaces are considered zero in Excel and thus are different from null strings). If both cells have nothing in them, then the AND( ) function returns a logical value "True," and the content right after the first comma (,) will be placed in cell G4, in this case a null string, "", which is exactly what you wanted because you did not make an entry. If either D4 or E4 contain a number or text, then the AND( ) function returns a logical value "False" and the content or reference right after the second comma will be placed in cell G4, in this case the formula G3 − D4 + E4. G3 is the previous balance, D4 the current check amount, and E4 the current deposit amount. Thus,

Current Balance = Previous Balance − Current Check Amount + Current Deposit

Because each row beyond row 4 signifies a cash outlay—a check or a deposit—the formulas in column G cells should be very similar to each other. Essentially, only the row number changes and the column identifier in the formula remains the same. Instead of reentering every formula in G5 through G50 (assuming you don't write more than forty-seven checks, as in this example) you can use a FILL DOWN command in Excel to fill in the formulas.

9. Position the cursor in cell D4. Click and hold down the mouse button and drag the mouse down until all the cells from G4 through G50 are selected. Release the mouse button. You have just selected a range of cells, G4:G50. Excel uses the colon to indicate a range of cells.

(Continued)

Microsoft Excel™ (Continued)

10. Select **FILL DOWN** from the Edit menu. To do this you have to position the cursor on Edit and hold the mouse button in as you drag the cursor down to the FILL DOWN option. Release the mouse button. In a moment the correct formulas will be entered into these cells. Cells G5 through G9 will have the correct balance. Cells G10 through G50 will contain null strings (nothing), since no data entries were entered in cells D10 through D50 and E10 through E50. If you use a simple formula like G3 – D4 + E4 in cell G4 instead of = IF(AND(D4 = "",E4 = ""),"",G3 – D4 + E4) the content in cells G10 through G50 will indicate the same amount as in cell G9.

MODIFYING THE APPEARANCE OF THE WORKSHEET

When you create a new worksheet in Excel, the column width defaults to a ten-character width in the Geneva font (typeface). There are two methods of widening or narrowing the column width in Excel. One is by positioning the cursor to the border of the column headings and dragging to widen or narrow the column. The cursor changes from a "Cross Bar" to a "Straight Line With Two Arrows." The second method is to use the COLUMN WIDTH command.

Changing Column Width

1. Select column A by clicking at the column A heading. The whole column will be highlighted.
2. Select COLUMN WIDTH from the Format menu. Type **8** upon seeing the dialog and then click OK.
3. Select column B. Select COLUMN WIDTH from the Format menu. Type **6** upon seeing the dialog and then click **OK.** Repeat the same process for columns C and F—Column C equals **25** characters wide and Column F equals **5** characters wide.

Changing Text and Number Formatting

1. Position the cursor to cell A1. Click and drag the mouse down and to the left to select cells A1 through G2.
2. Select **STYLE**... from Format menu.

3. Select **BOLD** by clicking at the appropriate check-box and click **OK** or press the <**Return**> key. All the cell contents in cells A1 through G2 will be displayed in bold characters.
4. Select **ALIGNMENT**... from the Format menu. Select **CENTER** by clicking the appropriate check-box and click **OK** or press the <**Return**> key. The contents in cells A1 through G2 will now be displayed in bold characters and centered in the column.
5. Select the range of cells A3 through A50. Select **NUMBER**... from the Format menu and then select the option **m/d/yy.** The contents in cells A3 through A50 will be displayed in the "Date Format": month/day/year.
6. Select the range of cells D3 through E50. Select **NUMBER**... from the Format menu and then select the option **$#,##0.00;($#,##0.00).** The contents in these cells will be formatted in "Currency" format with negative numbers in parenthesis.
7. Format the range of cells G3 through G50 in "Currency" format as you did in step 6.

SAVING AND PRINTING THE WORKSHEET

1. Select **SAVE** from the File menu. Type **CheckBook Register** upon seeing the dialog for the SAVE command. Make sure the disk you're saving to is the data disk instead of the program disk. The name of the disk is indicated at the top of the "Save" dialog. Click **SAVE** when ready. This command will save the worksheet to the disk with a file name "CheckBook Register."
2. Select **PRINT**... from the File menu. Upon seeing the Print dialog, click at the **Preview** check-box at the lower left corner and then select **OK.** This command will give you a preview on the screen of how your worksheet will actually look if printed.
3. Select **PRINT**... again, but this time unselect the Preview check-box by clicking at it again. Position the cursor to the rectangular box next to From, click once, and type **1.** Press the <**Tab**> key once and type **1.** This command will inform Excel to print only page one of your worksheet. If you wish to print the entire worksheet, leave these two boxes blank, or select **All** by clicking at the appropriate "Radio" button.

(*Continued*)

Microsoft Excel™ (Continued)

FIGURE 8–42
The Excel Completed Worksheet

	A	B	C	D	E	F	G
1	**Trans.**	**Check**	**Description**	**Amount**	**Amount**	**Clear**	**Balance**
2	**Date**	**Number**		**Check**	**Deposit**		
3	7/5/87		Cash to Open new account		$1,000.00	Y	$1,000.00
4	7/10/87	100	Furrs - Groceries	$25.88		N	$974.12
5	7/10/87	101	Hair Design - Perm	$40.00		N	$934.12
6	7/10/87	102	Dillards - Blouse	$43.99		N	$890.13
7	7/13/87	103	Western, Inc.	$200.50		N	$689.63
8	7/15/87		Paycheck		$1,050.60	N	$1,740.23
9	7/16/87	104	Food Emporium - Groceries	$29.76		N	$1,710.47

Once you have completed the last step, your worksheet should look like the one shown in Figure 8–42. This concludes the tutorial for setting up a simple checkbook register in Microsoft Excel.

CHAPTER

9

Record and File Management Systems

CHAPTER OUTLINE

Record and File Management Systems Defined 320

The History of Record and File Management Systems 321

FOCUS FEATURE Manual versus Computerized File Operations 323

Business and Personal Uses for Record and File Management Systems 326

Software Concepts and Design Philosophies 329

FOCUS FEATURE Methods of Searching for Records Within Files 332

Using a File Management System 333

FOCUS FEATURE Using a Spreadsheet like Lotus 1-2-3 as a Flatfile Manager 340

Hardware and Software Requirements for File Management Systems 340

LOTUS 1-2-3 FILE MANAGEMENT TUTORIAL 343

CHAPTER OBJECTIVES

In this chapter you will learn

1 what a flatfile manager is

2 why file and record management systems are important

3 what features to expect in file management systems

4 how file management systems differ from other kinds of data base software

5 how file management systems came about

6 what file management systems can be used for

7 how to use a file management system

8 how to select an appropriate file management system for you

With the ever-increasing use of microcomputers, software packages and systems that support the storage, manipulation, and retrieval of information and data take on ever-increasing importance. In the 1950s, information was generally perceived as bits and pieces of knowledge trivia, such as "Who won the World Series in 1955?" or "How many home runs did Babe Ruth hit?" Today, we have a very different perception of information; we recognize it as the essential fabric of all rational behavior and decision making. We have entered the Information Age.

This chapter and Chapter 10 are concerned with software packages that improve our information-handling ability. These packages enhance our organizational skills by never forgetting where a particular record or item of information has been stored. Before computers, business and professional people stored important items of information in file cabinets. If that particular item wasn't carefully and systematically placed in its proper position within the drawers of the file cabinets, one could literally spend hours looking for a particular file folder. With microcomputers and software for data management, this is no longer a problem. The computer never "forgets" where a particular file is stored.

Quick and efficient retrieval of information is only a small part of the many advantages business and professional people are discovering as inherent within file and data base management systems. Ease of data entry, editing, reporting, searching, and sorting are just a few of the capabilities and advantages that such systems are presenting to potential users over and above manual methods of data handling.

RECORD AND FILE MANAGEMENT SYSTEMS DEFINED

There are two basic categories of software for data management. Record and file management software is the simpler of the two, and the subject of this chapter. With this type of software, only one file may be "open" (and hence, accessible to the user) at a time. The second category of software—**data base management systems**, or DBMS—permits several files to be open at the same time, and is the subject of Chapter 10. Having several files open at the same time can be advantageous in certain situations. For example, if the user wishes to prepare a report using data contained in several files, a DBMS can do that.

Thus, a **file management system** is distinguished by its ability to manipulate only one file at a time. Most file management systems store, organize, and output data sequentially. Although this is the most basic type of data organization, its simplicity does not mean this category can't be useful.

File management systems are usually considerably less expensive than full-blown DBMSs and are quite sufficient for many applications. Why use an eighteen-wheel diesel truck when moving a few pounds of dirt to the dumpster? In such instances, a small wheelbarrow works wonders.

Organization of Data Files

All of us have used files before. A phone book is a file, as is a book of recipes organized into alphabetized categories. A dictionary is a type of file, as is an encyclopedia. An ordinary novel or book would not be considered a file because these have no logical, consistent structure or organization.

Files can be decomposed into smaller data groupings called records. A **record** is all the information associated with a given entity in a file. For example, a parts file would consist of a record for each part, a personnel file would consist of a record for each employee, each listing in a phone book is a record, and an invoice file would contain a record for each invoice. A record is usually all the information contained in a single row of a file. When the record structure is the same for each record, file management systems are called **flatfile managers.**

Essentially, a hierarchy of data components, beginning with files and ending with bits, is found in most data files, as shown in Figure 9–1. Records can be decomposed into a smaller data component called a **field.** The fields of a phone book listing are the name, the address, and the phone number. Shown in Figure 9–1 are the fields that might make up a record for a simple personnel file. Finally and ultimately, fields can be broken down into bytes, which we know are composed of bits.

For example, suppose a manager has a simple personnel file containing the names of the individuals shown in Figure 9–1. For each individual, the manager has a record consisting of a name field, an address field, and a department field. Record number three, for example, contains pertinent information on Hugh Hill. Hugh's address is 80 Pass Street, and his department is ACCT, according to the information contained in the file. Thus there is an address field, a department field, and other fields which make up the record for Hugh Hill.

It must be pointed out, however, that not all secondary storage files are organized this way. Word processing files and machine language program files will consist of bytes, but the bytes may not be grouped into fields or records. As such, the file is just a very long string of bytes. Source program files, when saved as ASCII files, consist of a byte for each character; whereas a line of source code is the basic record, with the entire file consisting of records (lines of source code).

THE HISTORY OF RECORD AND FILE MANAGEMENT SYSTEMS

Record and file management programs first got their start in conjunction with the microcomputers of the late seventies—the Apple II and Radio Shack TRS80. Application software developed back then created and maintained its own file(s). A different program had to be learned and used to access and maintain each file. Finally, somebody suggested, "Why don't we develop a single program that can be used to access, update, and search all files?" Out of that thought arose the concept of a file management program. Today, such programs are prolific in the microcomputer marketplace.

Before microcomputers, most records and files were maintained manually. Consider the file management needs of an insurance salesperson, for example. Certainly, this individual would want to maintain a file of clients, containing their names and addresses, city and state, zipcode, telephone numbers, and their birth dates. (Knowing the client's birth date enables the insurance salesperson to send them birthday cards, and to determine premiums for various life insurance products.) Such a file is shown in Figure 9–2 on page 322. Each line of the file is called a *record,* and contains the essential information associated with a particular client. In a manual system each record would be placed on a 3 × 5 card and kept in a

File (a collection of records)

Record #	Name	Address	Department
1	Johnson, Judy	2000 Yards Place	ACCT
2	Brown, Ben	218 Touchdown Lane	MKT
3	Hill, Hugh	80 Pass Street	FIN
4	White, Wendy	11 Overda Hill	MGMT
5	Smith, Susan	44 New Home Avenue	ACCT
6	Pearson, Paul	88 Old Lane	MKT
7	McDaniel, Mary	86 Quake Street	ACCT

Record (a collection of fields)

field 1	field 2	field 3	field 4
1	Johnson, Judy	2000 Yards Place	ACCT

Field (a collection of bytes--characters)

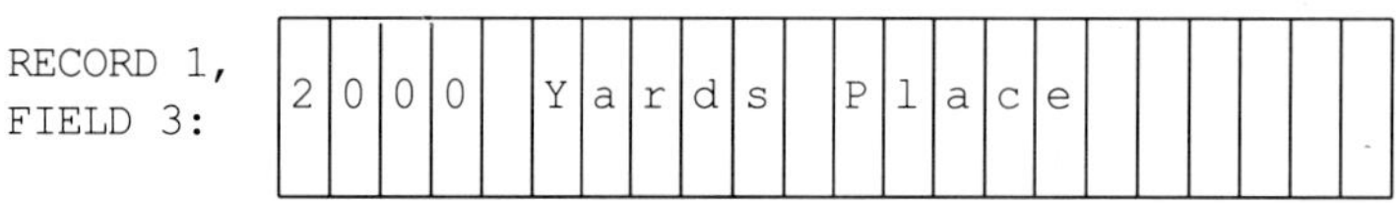
RECORD 1, FIELD 3: | 2 | 0 | 0 | 0 | | Y | a | r | d | s | | P | l | a | c | e | | | | | | |

Byte (a collection of bits)

RECORD 1, FIELD 3, BYTE 1: | 0 | 0 | 1 | 1 | 0 | 0 | 1 | 0 | (the code for "2")

FIGURE 9–1

Hierarchy of Information Groupings

NAME	ADDRESS	CITY, STATE	ZIP	PHONE	BIRTH DATE DA	MO	YR
Kennedy, Kirk	122 Knobby Lane	Willoby, TX	76301	806-731-9888	23	07	44
Norris, Norbert	3004 15th St.	Texline, TX	79999	806-112-1134	04	04	65
Neuman, Nancy	8605 Ave. Q	Ultra, TX	43321	817-692-5390	01	12	50
Ford, Floyd	85 Willow Lane	Happy, TX	77345	806-775-3421	01	01	38
Fisher, Freda	4th & Quinton	Sundown, TX	79123	806-665-0000	31	10	65

FIGURE 9–2

A Typical "Client" File

Focus Feature

MANUAL VERSUS COMPUTERIZED FILE OPERATIONS

The following manual file operations would be possible. A client could be added to the file shown in Figure 9–2. Since the file is in no particular order, the associated 3 × 5 card for the new client would be placed at the end of the stack. For example, suppose we wanted to add the following record to the file:

NAME:Redmond, Rob

ADDRESS:484 Canyon Lane

CITY, STATE:Logan, Utah

ZIP:90113

PHONE:707-866-4321

BIRTH DATE: DAY:07 MONTH:09 YEAR:38

Then the file would appear as shown in Figure 9–3 below.

The list could be sorted or ordered in any one of several ways. For example, the list could be sorted in alphabetical order on the client's last name. Doing so would cause the list of records to appear in the order shown in Figure 9–4 on page 324. Now it becomes clearer why we organized the names with the last name first. What would we do with a list alphabetized on the client's first name? Actually what we have done here is to sort the list of records in ascending order on the NAME field. Thus ascending order is alphabetic order, whereas descending order would be reverse alphabetic order. If two of our clients had the same last name, the first name would automatically be used to determine the appropriate alphabetic order.

Maintaining the file in alphabetic order helps us find the client we are looking for. We don't have to search through the entire file. Imagine what a nightmare searching for a phone number in a phone book with the names listed in completely random order would be. For a large metropolitan area this could take days if done manually. If, on the other hand, we were planning a mass mailing of promotional materials, we would want the file ordered by ZIP code to save money on postage. (The Postal Service actually offers a discount on presorted mail when it is sorted in ascending order by ZIP code.) Clearly, several different sorting orders could be useful to us, including a sorting in ascending order on birth MONTH. This would allow us to determine who is having a particular birthday in a certain month without having to search through the entire file.

We could maintain three different files for this purpose: one sorted in alphabetical order on NAME, one sorted in ascending order on ZIP, and one sorted in alphabetical order on BIRTH DATE. Doing so would take a lot of 3 × 5 cards, a lot of space for the cards, and a lot of time to maintain three different files. Any changes required to a phone number or to an address would have to be performed consistently to all three. Rather than doing this, we might choose to maintain just one sorted file, called the master file, and to maintain two index files.

FIGURE 9–3

A Typical "Client" File with One Record Added

NAME	ADDRESS	CITY, STATE	ZIP	PHONE	BIRTH DATE		
					DA	MO	YR
Kennedy, Kirk	122 Knobby Lane	Willoby, TX	76301	806-731-9888	23	07	44
Norris, Norbert	3004 15th St.	Texline, TX	79999	806-112-1134	04	04	65
Neuman, Nancy	8605 Ave. Q	Ultra, TX	43321	817-692-5390	01	12	50
Ford, Floyd	85 Willow Lane	Happy, TX	77345	806-775-3421	01	01	38
Fisher, Freda	4th & Quinton	Sundown, TX	79123	806-665-0000	31	10	65
Redmond, Rob	484 Canyon Lane	Logan, UT	90113	707-866-4321	07	09	38

(Continued)

NAME	ADDRESS	CITY, STATE	ZIP	PHONE	BIRTH DATE		
					DA	MO	YR
Fisher, Freda	4th & Quinton	Sundown, TX	79123	806-665-0000	31	10	65
Ford, Floyd	85 Willow Lane	Happy, TX	77345	806-775-3421	01	01	38
Kennedy, Kirk	122 Knobby Lane	Willoby, TX	76301	806-731-9888	23	07	44
Neuman, Nancy	8605 Ave. Q	Ultra, TX	43321	817-692-5390	01	12	50
Norris, Norbert	3004 15th St.	Texline, TX	79999	806-112-1134	04	04	65
Redmond, Rob	484 Canyon Lane	Logan, UT	90113	707-866-4321	07	09	38

FIGURE 9–4
"Client" File Sorted in Alphabetical Order on NAME

FIGURE 9–5
Two Index Files

NUM	NAME
1	Neuman, Nancy
2	Kennedy, Kirk
3	Ford, Floyd
4	Fisher, Freda
5	Norris, Norbert
6	Redmond, Rob

A ZIP Code Index File

NUM	NAME
1	Ford, Floyd
2	Norris, Norbert
3	Kennedy, Kirk
4	Redmond, Rob
5	Fisher, Freda
6	Newman, Nancy

A BIRTH DATE Index File

For example, we might choose to maintain the file in alphabetical order on NAME, and to maintain two index files as shown in Figure 9–5 below. Clearly, the order of the records is indicated by using the NAME as an index.

There are other more efficient ways in which the index could be done. For example, a record number could be attached to each record in the original master client file, as shown in Figure 9–6. What we have done is to add another field to each record. Now we can reference each record by means of its record number in the NUM field, as shown in Figure 9–7. Such a field is referred to as a **key field.** Each number under the RECORD__NUM field in the index files in Figure 9–7 is, in fact, a *pointer* to the appropriate record (3 × 5 card) in the original file. Thus, in ZIP code order the first record should be record number 4 in the client file, whereas in birth MONTH order record number 2 should be the first record.

Of course, when computerized, these index files pose a problem in that only one file can be open at once

NUM	NAME	ADDRESS	CITY, STATE	ZIP	PHONE	BIRTH DATE DA	MO	YR
1	Fisher, Freda	4th & Quinton	Sundown, TX	79123	806-665-0000	31	10	65
2	Ford, Floyd	85 Willow Lane	Happy, TX	77345	806-775-3421	01	01	38
3	Kennedy, Kirk	122 Knobby Lane	Willoby, TX	76301	806-731-9888	23	07	44
4	Neuman, Nancy	8605 Ave. Q	Ultra, TX	43321	817-692-5390	01	12	50
5	Norris, Norbert	3004 15th St.	Texline, TX	79999	806-112-1134	04	04	65
6	Redmond, Rob	484 Canyon Lane	Logan, UT	90113	707-866-4321	07	09	38

FIGURE 9–6

Sorted "Client" File with Record Number Included

NUM	RECORD_NUM
1	4
2	3
3	2
4	1
5	5
6	6

A ZIP Index File

NUM	RECORD_NUM
1	2
2	5
3	3
4	6
5	1
6	4

A BIRTH DATE Index File

FIGURE 9–7

Two Index Files Indexed by Record Number

in file management systems. It would seem that to retrieve the client records in ZIP code order, both the ZIP index file and the client file would have to be open at the same time. Since index files are very small by comparison to ordinary files, it is possible to open them, read them entirely into primary storage, and then close them. Then the client file can be opened, and the indexes which are now in memory used to access the master file.

Now suppose that we wish to add another record to the client file, yet maintain the sorted alphabetical order of the file. The record must be inserted into its appropriate position within the file. This requires that a search be performed to find the appropriate position of the new record. Then all records which logically come after the record to be inserted must be moved back to make room for the additional record. For example, suppose that the following record is to be inserted in the master file.

(Continued)

MANUAL VERSUS COMPUTERIZED FILE OPERATIONS (Continued)

NUM	NAME	ADDRESS	CITY, STATE	ZIP	PHONE	BIRTH DATE		
						DA	MO	YR
1	Carter, Cari	9000 Mountain Rd	Salida, CO	88200	303-987-6789	10	08	40
2	Fisher, Freda	4th & Quinton	Sundown, TX	79123	806-665-0000	31	10	65
3	Ford, Floyd	85 Willow Lane	Happy, TX	77345	806-775-3421	01	01	38
4	Kennedy, Kirk	122 Knobby Lane	Willoby, TX	76301	806-731-9888	23	07	44
5	Neuman, Nancy	8605 Ave. Q	Ultra, TX	43321	817-692-5390	01	12	50
6	Norris, Norbert	3004 15th St.	Texline, TX	79999	806-112-1134	04	04	65
7	Redmond, Rob	484 Canyon Lane	Logan, UT	90113	707-866-4321	07	09	38

FIGURE 9–8
Sorted "Client" File with Carter Record Added

NAME:Carter, Cari

ADDRESS:9000 Mountain Rd.

CITY, STATE:Salida, Colorado

ZIP:88200

PHONE:303-987-6789

BIRTH DATE: DAY:10 MONTH:08 YEAR:40

A search reveals that this record must go at the beginning of the file and all of the other records must be moved down. Then the file would appear as shown in Figure 9–8. It would then be necessary to adjust the index files to reflect the newly included record.

Including a record in a sorted file is more difficult and time-consuming than including it within a file whose records are random. In a random file the record could simply be appended to the end of the file. No search for the appropriate position is required.

Another operation frequently applied to files is that of file maintenance. Suppose that Norbert Norris has changed addresses and is now living at 1003 Overton Lane, Aurora, CO 88651, phone number 303-754-3345. It would be necessary to find (search for) and retrieve the

little metal 3 × 5 card file. Taken together, the collection or list of records comprises the client file. Each component of each record—for example, the NAME, is called a *field*. There are eight fields associated with each record in Figure 9–2.

BUSINESS AND PERSONAL USES FOR RECORD AND FILE MANAGEMENT SYSTEMS

File management systems are useful in many applications. They are typically quite easy to learn and use, offer flexibility in the types of information requests

NUM	NAME	ADDRESS	CITY, STATE	ZIP	PHONE	BIRTH DATE		
						DA	MO	YR
1	Carter, Cari	9000 Mountain Rd	Salida, CO	88200	303-987-6789	10	08	40
2	Fisher, Freda	4th & Quinton	Sundown, TX	79123	806-665-0000	31	10	65
3	Ford, Floyd	85 Willow Lane	Happy, TX	77345	806-775-3421	01	01	38
4	Neuman, Nancy	8605 Ave. Q	Ultra, TX	43321	817-692-5390	01	12	50
5	Norris, Norbert	1003 Overton Lane	Aurora, CO	88651	303-754-3345	04	04	65
6	Redmond, Rob	484 Canyon Lane	Logan, UT	90113	707-866-4321	07	09	38

FIGURE 9–9

Sorted "Client" File with Kennedy Record Deleted

record so it could be updated. With a manual 3 × 5 card system, the appropriate 3 × 5 card must be found, the address fields updated, and the 3 × 5 card placed back into its appropriate position within the list. Computerized file maintenance involves a file search, a record retrieval, record updating or editing, and finally storage of the record back onto secondary storage into its appropriate location.

The last file operation to be considered is that of record deletion. For one reason or another, Kirk Kennedy has decided that he doesn't want to be a client any more, and wishes to have his name removed from the file. A search takes place to find the appropriate record. Once Kirk Kennedy's card is located, it is removed from the file and discarded. The file now appears as shown in Figure 9–9.

Computerized file management systems are very similar to manual ones in that records may be added, edited and altered, deleted, searched, sorted, and so forth. It is even possible to add a field to every record, as we did above.

that can be made, and can find information quickly. Even though only one file can be open at a time, the user may create as many different files as desired.

Examples of applications for which a file management system might be suitable include: a catalogue of a stamp collection; a list of addresses, phone numbers, and personal information about clients like the one in the previous section; a list of recipes; a homeowner's inventory of all appliances, furniture, and other perishables, together with an approximate value of each; an instructor's records of students and their grades; or a student's list of friends together with phone numbers and addresses. Each of these can be handled with a single file system, so an inexpensive file manager might be appropriate. A file manager may also provide extensive search capabilities. A recipe file, for example, could be used to store ingredient lists and instructions; it might also be used to compile a shopping list for a dinner menu. It might just as easily handle a request such as, "Find a recipe that uses chicken and oregano, but does not require tomatoes."

An easy way to determine if a file management system can handle particular data requirements is to visualize the process of finding the required information with a manual office system. Do some information requests require cross-referencing of two or more files, as shown in Figure 9–10? For example, a customer calls a hardware store to find out about a replacement wheel for his lawn mower. With a manual file system, the clerk might first consult a parts list for the particular model of lawn mower to find the wheel's part number. With the wheel's part number, the clerk could then consult a second list to find out if it is currently in stock. If it is not in stock, the clerk might then consult a third file of vendors who could supply the item.

Or, suppose that a firm ships its products to Salt Lake City, Utah, via Acme Freight Lines. Acme has just gone out of business and all customers serviced by Acme must be informed that there will be a three-week delay in upcoming shipments. The shipping department will have the information on regions that were serviced by Acme, but it is unlikely that they would know which customers live in those regions. A tedious process of matching the list of regions serviced by Acme with the customer list lies ahead. Computerized, this process would require that two files be open at the same time.

A file management system could only handle these situations if all of the information were kept in one file. A file of shipping carriers could, conceivably, contain information about all of the firm's customers, but this is not a logical way to run a business. Furthermore, the file required to contain all the information would be excessively large and access times would be very poor. For multiple file

FIGURE 9–10
Cross-referencing Files

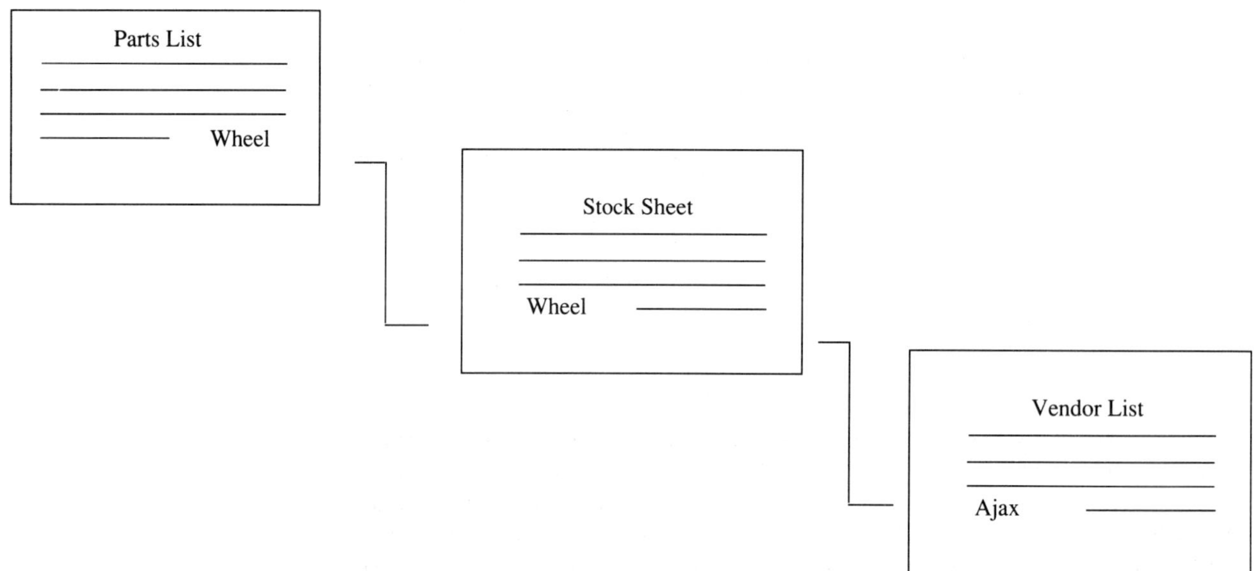

situations, a relational data base management system (the subject of Chapter 10) is needed.

The use of a DBMS eliminates redundancy in the data, thereby increasing the accuracy of the data and lessening the amount of secondary storage required. **Data redundancy** is simply having the same data appear in more than one file or place. For example, suppose that in one file is maintained a list of customer names, addresses, their credit limits when making purchases, and the amount of credit they have used up. In another file is maintained the customer names and addresses for mailing lists. There would be a need for both files, to support the two different applications, in a file management system. If the address of one of the customers changes, both files must be updated. In a DBMS, there is only one file of customer names and addresses. Customer credit data would be contained in a separate file because both files would be open when customer billing and credit-check applications were deployed.

Evidently, having two (or more) files with the same data in them is undesirable because this increases the redundancy of the data. Data redundancy requires more secondary storage; it also increases the likelihood of introducing errors, because the data has to be entered accurately in more than one place. Furthermore, changes might be made in some redundant files but not in others, and some data might be entered correctly in one file and incorrectly in the others. Consequently, operations which require multiple files to be open at once are better off using a DBMS.

SOFTWARE CONCEPTS AND DESIGN PHILOSOPHIES

File Management System Categories

File management systems may be distinguished on the basis of their inclination to "look" like relational data base management systems, their ability to manipulate text files as well as data files, and their ability to be integrated with graphics, statistics, or spreadsheet components. A few file management systems are able to open more than one file at a time, but they cannot relate these files to each other by means of the usual relational operators, so they are not relational data base management systems. Some file management programs are especially well suited to manipulation of text files. This can be useful if the user is searching for notes on a client stored in a file whose "key" is the last name of the client. It can also be useful if the user is trying to pull together a document consisting of twenty or so paragraphs, each of them contained in a separate file. By and large, however, file management systems are a fairly homogeneous class of software.

The User Interface

Many file management systems have a combined menu- and command-driven interface, after the fashion of Lotus 1-2-3 and Microsoft Multiplan. Menu bars, pull-down menus, or pop-up menus are displayed. In some file management programs the menu selection is made by function key. For example, if you want menu item five, you press function key five. In others, either the mouse or one of the cursor arrow keys is used to point to (or highlight) the appropriate item on the menu list, and the <Return> key or mouse button is used to select the marked menu item.

In addition to menus, many file management systems will use queries (questions) to request specific information from the user about a report that is to be displayed or about a file that is to be created.

Many file management systems will provide an on-line help facility, which can enable a confused user to determine what to do next. If at any time during the session the user is uncertain about what to do, the help function key can be depressed; the screen will then display suggestions and advice about how to accomplish the particular task at hand. The <Escape> key is commonly used to return to the original place in the session, and the user, now knowing exactly what to do, can continue working.

Some file management systems provide on-line tutorials that teach a user how to use the software. In general though, the goal of this category of software is to provide a tool that is absolutely straightforward and simple to use. Unlike the more sophisticated data base management software to be discussed in the next chapter, this category of software is aimed at unsophisticated users whose file management needs are simple, and who do not wish to embroil themselves in a lot of complicated commands and capabilities. Thus a software tutorial is usually unnecessary for file management systems. Moreover, unlike the data base management systems to be discussed in the next chapter, file management programs never include a procedural or command language as part of the package, so a user interface that is programmable is not possible in any robust sense.

File Management System Features

Flatfile management system features can be classified according to the functions they are associated with: data input, searching and sorting, reports, data import/export capability, and file restructure capability.

Data Input Early file management systems insisted that users design their own data input "screens" by entering row and column coordinates of every field to appear on the screen. Many newer file management systems allow users to "paint" their own screens by placing the cursor at the point where the field should begin, while others supply a preprogrammed format. Still other packages are capable of both preprogrammed screens and user-designed input screens.

Once the input screen is specified or designed, it will be used for data entry in all subsequent sessions involving data entry into the file. Some lengthy records may require several input screens to be designed to facilitate data entry of the record. Figure 9–11 illustrates a typical data-entry screen. All file management systems come with a full-screen data editor that allows the user to move the cursor anywhere on the screen and make changes, as with a text editor in a word processing application.

Updating/Deleting Records File management systems allow the user to respecify a record when an address, a name, or a phone number changes. The user must inform the system what record is to be updated. It will then search for, retrieve, and display the record. Each field value will be displayed beside its name. The user may then move the cursor to those fields to be changed, make the changes in those

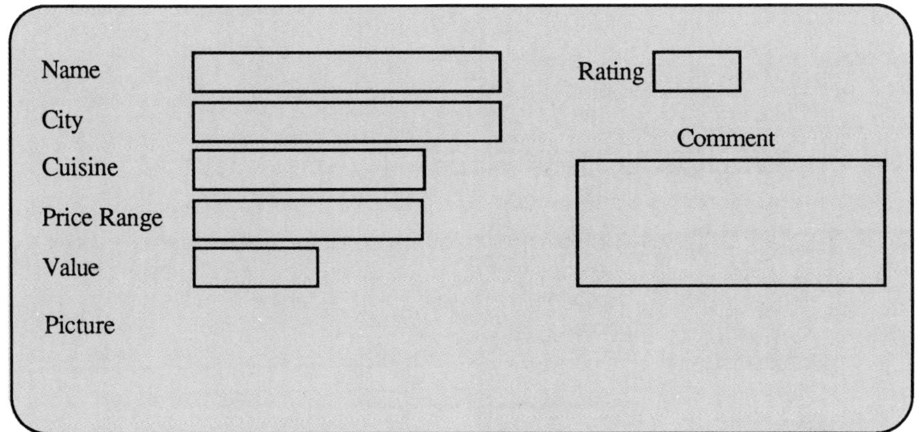

FIGURE 9–11
A Data Entry Screen

fields, and then press <Return> twice to inform the system he is finished. The file management system will then rewrite the record on the secondary storage device in the same location over the old record, destroying its contents.

Deletion of records is also a feature that file management systems are expected to do. Again, the user must be able to specify to the system what record is to be deleted.

Searching and Sorting Records Finding the appropriate record is a process that may be sequential, direct, or indexed-sequential. See the focus feature "Methods of Searching for Records Within Files" for descriptions of these processes. It is sufficient to remark here that **sequential search** is the simplest and takes the most time (because it involves a search), **direct search** is the fastest (because it doesn't involve a search), and **indexed-sequential search** is the most sophisticated (because it involves the use of pointers and index files) but takes a little more time than direct.

All file management systems require keys for searching and sorting. **Search keys** are one or more fields, each with a specified value or range. Search keys are said to be simple if only one field and its associated value or range are required, and compound if more than one field (and associated values, ranges) is involved.

Sort keys involve one or more fields as well. Usually, there are no values or ranges to be concerned with. In sort keys there is usually a primary key (or field); if a "tie" occurs, a secondary key (or field) is used to break the tie. Tertiary keys may even be used to break ties in both the primary and secondary keys. Of concern to the user of these systems would be the speed with which searches and sorts can be carried out, and the flexibility in defining searching and sorting keys.

Reports Some flatfile managers provide automatic reports, but do not allow users flexibility in defining their own report formats. Others will provide both automatic reports, or will allow users to define their own report formats should they wish to do so. Still others require users to define their own report forms, and provide no preprogrammed forms. Each report presents selected fields taken from selected records within the file. Figure 9–12 depicts a typical report for the insured/client file discussed in the opening pages of this chapter. This report shows only customer names in ascending order of ZIP code. Reports like that in Figure 9–12 are usually in table format so numbers across rows can be compared. Generally,

Focus Feature

METHODS OF SEARCHING FOR RECORDS WITHIN FILES

SEQUENTIAL

The sequential search is the simplest. It allows for a record-by-record check on any field. It is slow because the record-by-record check takes time.

DIRECT

The direct method of finding records is fastest. The user must specify a computer-assigned record number. This number is "hashed" or translated to a physical address on the disk where the record is stored. The system goes to that address "directly" and copies the record into primary storage, where it can be displayed or printed.

INDEXED

One or more index files are maintained in addition to the original file. The index files are files of pointers that enable the records to be retrieved in a different order than the order of the original master file itself. Still, individual record retrievals are only slightly slower than direct.

reports consist of headings, subheadings, and the columns (fields) that were selected, together with totals and subtotals.

Most file management systems provide report generators, which might merely consist of providing preprogrammed forms, or of providing flexible menu-driven and query-driven report form specification modules.

Some flatfile management systems provide a graphics capability that enables charts and graphs of various and sundry kinds (see Chapter 11) to be generated. Certainly this is true of Lotus 1-2-3, which provides a flatfile capability within the larger context of a spreadsheet. It is also true of integrated programs in general, such as Framework, Symphony, Enable, and many others, because integrated programs always have a graphics component. However, a few programs that are exclusively flatfile managers also have incorporated a graphics component. Most notable in this category is Borland's Reflex.

Data Import/Export Capability If data are to be imported from a spreadsheet or other application, or if reports are to be exported to a word processing application, then the data import/export capability of the file management system can be important. An **import capability** entails reading into primary memory a file created by another application. The file manager must have the capability of reading the file in its original format and of creating another file, in a format specified by the user, into which the imported data will be read. Usually, import capabilities are limited to the formats of a few very popular spreadsheet programs and data base management programs.

On the other hand, files created by the file manager may not be readable by any application program other than the file manager itself. An **export capability** involves being able to create a file that can be read by another application program.

NAME	ZIP CODE
Neuman, Nancy	43321
Kennedy, Kirk	76301
Ford, Floyd	77345
Fisher, Freda	79123
Norris, Norbert	79999
Carter, Cari	88200
Redmond, Rob	90113

FIGURE 9–12
A Typical Report Form

File Restructure Capability Suppose you have created a file with several hundred records in it, only to discover that you need some additional fields in the file. For example, suppose you wished to add the field AMT OWED (amount owed) to the client file we have been discussing. You might want to do this so you could track the amount each of your clients owe you. At this point you would not want to reenter from the keyboard the entire file of clients, consisting of several hundred records. Rather, you would like to create a new file similar to the old client file depicted in Figure 9–2, but with the additional field added. Then you would want to "import" each record from the old client file, thereafter adding the appropriate information regarding AMT OWED and then saving the new record in the new file. One way of restructuring a file is to read in all records from the old file and write them into the new one, thereby avoiding having to reenter all of the records from the keyboard by hand. If the original file is so large that not all of the records can be read in at once, the file is read up to the maximum capacity of primary storage, and closed. The new file is then opened and the records in memory are written into the new file. This process is continued until all records in the old file are written into the new file with the new format involving additional fields.

Miscellaneous Features Advanced features include automatic date fields, elaborate report overlays, multilevel indexing and sorting, and even some relational functions as part of the reporting process.

USING A FILE MANAGEMENT SYSTEM

Planning the Records

In planning the records, the user must decide what fields will comprise each record. A *field* is an element of data which, when grouped together with other related fields associated with a given entity, forms a record. A customer file is likely to have the following fields: NAME, STREET-ADDRESS, CITY, STATE, ZIP CODE, and PHONE-NUMBER. In specifying the fields the user must first name each field, then specify its length in bytes, its type, any validity checks (programmed checks to ensure that the data entered in the field are legitimate) that are desired, and possibly its location on the screen (where data are to be entered into the field). Each field name must be unique. The user will find that different programs differ

TABLE 9–1
Description of Field Types

FIELD TYPE	DESCRIPTION
Numeric field	Numbers that can be used in calculations. Numeric fields can be of two types: integer fields and decimal fields. Integer fields have no decimal point and no numbers to the right of the decimal. Decimal fields usually require that the user specify the number of digits to the right of the decimal. "Money" fields can be set up by specifying exactly two digits to the right of the decimal.
Text field	Used for names, addresses, and short textual information. Numbers placed in text fields cannot be treated as values even though they are displayed as numbers.
Phone and ZIP code fields	These are specialized fields specially preprogrammed for phone numbers or ZIP codes; they are treated like text fields.
Calculated field	A field whose value is calculated from other numeric fields; treated like a numeric field.
Logical field	A small field whose value is binary: true (T) or false (F), zero (0) or one (1), yes (Y) or no (N).
Date field	A preprogrammed field for storage of dates. When dates are stored within them, can sort file in ascending order by the date field. Can also add or subtract "days" from date fields.
Time field	A preprogrammed field that is very similar to a date field, with the same features and functions.
Comment or memo field	An extraordinarily long text field that is used to hold explanatory textual information. In some systems, an ordinary text field can be used this way, by simply declaring its length to be extra-long.

in the maximum number of fields allowed per record, in the maximum number of records allowed in each file, in the maximum length of each field in bytes, and in the types of fields supported. If the user has yet to acquire a file management program, it is best to define these requirements ahead of actual purchase of the software so that the user can be certain of purchasing a program that meets or exceeds his or her requirements. The field types that may be included in many file management programs are defined in Table 9–1.

When deciding what fields to include in the record, the issue is one of relevance and economics. From an economic point-of-view, it is sometimes impossible to include everything because of the cost of collecting, entering, maintaining and storing the data. What fields to include depends on the type of questions the data are to answer. It thus becomes necessary to anticipate the questions (or "queries" as they are called) that will be addressed to the data base in order to determine what relevant fields to include. If the data base designer should omit certain questions and thereby certain fields, it is possible to add these fields later.

The user must "size" the length of each field to accommodate the largest entry that could conceivably be placed in the field. For most file management systems, the fields (and the records) are of fixed length, in accordance with the user's specified length for each field. (The record length is simply the sum of the lengths of the individual fields that make up the record.) This means that choosing overly large field lengths will result in a lot of wasted space (in the form of embedded blanks required to fill out the rest of the field) within each field, and consequently within each record and the entire file. Hence, for fixed-length fields, some degree of care must be exercised in choosing the length of each field. When all fields (and consequently records) are the same length in a file, the file is called a *flatfile*.

However, some file management systems support variable-length fields and variable-length records. These systems will, nevertheless, expect the user to specify the length of each field. End-of-field (end-of-record) markers are placed on the last character of each field (each record) so the system will know where each field (and each record) ends.

Validity checks are "ranges" over which certain values in numeric fields can legitimately vary. For example, the month number in a date field must be in the range one to twelve. A cash-and-carry store may not carry any single item over $1,000. Thus a legitimate range would be 0 to $1,000. The validity check would then test all dollar values entered for an item to see if the item price is less than 0 or greater than $1,000. If so, the user would be notified by means of an audible sound and a message would be displayed on the screen. The user would then be asked to reenter the data. Validity checks help reduce inadvertent data-entry errors.

Creating the Records

Creating the records involves entering the record-related information into the file management system. The file management system requires this information so that it can present the screens used for data entry (sometimes called "forms") to the user.

Some file management systems supply preprogrammed data-entry screens. For most of these systems, a separate line of the screen is used for each user-named field, as shown in Figure 9–13. Adjacent to each name is the user-specified length of the field, shown in inverse video, or beginning and ending with a colon (:).

Many file management systems allow users to design their own data input screens, as shown in Figure 9–14. This can be done by "painting" the screen—moving the cursor to the position the user desires for each field. Data entry screens are saved in the same file as the data, or in some cases in a different file. The data-entry screens may be used each time a record is to be displayed, added, deleted, or updated. It is possible to define different screens for different uses. For example, each report will require that a different screen be defined as we shall see. Thus a file may have several screens associated with it. A good rule-of-thumb to use in forms design is to make the form resemble the appearance of the hardcopy form the data is being taken from. Many programs support the design of forms which look on-screen like familiar preprinted forms.

```
NAME:                                           :
ADDRESS:                                              :
CITY, STATE:                                             :
ZIP:                :
BIRTH DATE
Day:    :
MONTH:    :
YEAR:      :
```

FIGURE 9–13

A Preprogrammed Data-Entry Screen

FIGURE 9–14

A Painted Data Entry Screen

NAME:

ADDRESS:

CITY, STATE:

ZIP:

BIRTH DATE

DAY MONTH YEAR

Entering, Inserting, or Appending Records

Entering records involves using the record-related information and/or the data-entry screens previously defined to enter the data associated with each record. The user informs (usually through menu selection) the file management system that records are to be added to an existing file. The system then opens the file and retrieves the record-related information, the data-entry screen(s), or both. In some cases the data-entry screens may be retrieved from a different file than the one containing the records. In either case, the user then begins entering data into the fields exhibited on the screen. Once all the fields associated with the record are specified, the program displays the data just entered and asks if the data are correct. A **No** response would permit the user to edit the data and make corrections. Once the user is satisfied that the field entries are correct, the user selects a "SAVE" function from a menu or function key and the record is saved on the user-specified drive under the appropriate filename. The program then displays an empty data-entry form to the user, indicating it is ready for the user to enter the next record.

Suppose that in examining the fields just entered, the user discovers an error in one or more of the fields and wishes to return to the field(s) to correct the error before saving the record. By use of the cursor arrow keys and the <Return> key, it is easy for the user to navigate between fields. A down arrow will move the cursor to the next field immediately below, an up arrow will move the cursor to the field immediately above the current field, and so forth. Some lengthy records may require several data-entry screens to logically locate and position all of the fields. When entering data, the software transfers the user to the next field once she has pressed <Return> or <Enter>, indicating that she wishes to proceed to the next field.

The actual insertion of data into the fields specified in the previous step should be consistent with practices which will enable the data to be accurately searched and sorted. Table 9–2 describes some of the rules regarding entry of information into each field of the record.

The records that were entered are added to the file when the record is saved, as described above. The record may be appended to the end of the file, which is the case if the file is a sequential file, or the record may be inserted in the middle of the file in accordance with some sorted order. Adding a record between existing records requires considerably more time because the system must first determine where within the existing records the new record must be inserted (which requires

TABLE 9–2

Rules Regarding Entry of Information into Fields

1. All data placed within text fields should be left-justified, that is, starting in the leftmost position of the field. The data should have no inadvertent embedded blanks. A name field should appear as |Jones, Jim Bob | if both first and last names are placed within the field. Notice that in this instance the last name appears first, flush with the left side of the field. An address field should appear as |1223 89th Street |. Notice that blanks are allowed to appear where they would naturally appear, and of course, blanks are used to fill out the rest of the field. However, a name field which appeared as | Jon es, Jim Bob| has several significant problems. First, the name is not left-justified. Second, the name has unnatural embedded blanks, such as the blank between *n* and *e* in *Jones* and the extra blanks between *Jim* and *Bob*. These blanks would prevent the field from being properly sorted or searched. Usually, NAME fields are broken up into FIRST and LAST name fields to enable searches to be conducted on the last name as the primary field.
2. All data placed within numeric fields should have no inadvertent embedded blanks. As an example, suppose the number $1234.56 were placed in its twelve-position field as |123 4.56 |. The embedded blank could be interpreted as a zero, which would be equivalent to $12304.56—an obvious mistake. The use of commas in numeric fields is also forbidden. For some systems, the data should also be right-justified, that is, stopping in the rightmost position of the field. For example, the dollar value $12345.67 would be placed in a twelve-position numeric decimal field as | 12345.67|. However, many file management programs will accept decimal numeric input anywhere within the field, so long as the decimal point is included in the data entry. Blanks in front of the number are treated as blanks, while blanks after the number may be treated as zeros.

a search) and then the system may have to physically move all records that logically are below the new record in the sorted order to make room for the new record.

Searching for Particular Records

The user informs the system through menu selection or use of a function key that he or she wishes to search for one or more records. The system will prompt the user for a filename. The user enters the filename and the system opens that file, thereby making it accessible. The system then requests a record key for use in finding and retrieving the appropriate records. As previously defined, a *key* is a field or other identifier that enables the system to search for and find the appropriate record. Several different keys may be possible. For example, the user may request a specific customer record by customer last name, as in NAME = "JONES." The system then retrieves all records whose last name is JONES. Finding the appropriate records is a process which may be sequential, direct, or indexed-sequential, as previously explained. Once the file management system has retrieved the appropriate record, that record is displayed to the user using the data-entry screen that was defined for the file.

Most file management systems provide key words for specifying simple and compound searching and sorting keys. For example, the simple query / LIST FOR PHONE = "806-????????"/ would produce four records if applied to the file shown in Figure 9–8. These records would be either displayed on the screen, or printed. The phrase LIST FOR is a key word recognized by the file management system, whereas PHONE is recognized by the file management system as a field name. The "question-mark" wild-card characters indicate that any character would match those positions in the PHONE field. On the other hand, the compound query / LIST FOR PHONE = "806-????????" AND YR = "44"/ would produce only one record—the one associated with Kirk Kennedy. The conjunction key words AND and OR are frequently used to connect simple query phrases into more sophisticated compound query phrases, as indicated above. Evidently, a *query* is a command issued to the file manager which initiates a search.

Sorting queries or commands might begin with the key word SORT rather than LIST FOR. For instance, consider the query SORT OLDFILE BY ZIP TO NEWFILE. In this instance it would be understood that OLDFILE is the name of the old file to be sorted and NEWFILE is the name of the new file to be created with the records sorted in ascending order by ZIP code.

Editing and Deleting Records

When a customer or client changes addresses, the customer/client file must be updated. This takes place as follows. The user informs the system through menu selection or use of a function key that he or she wishes to edit one or more records. The system will prompt the user for a filename. The user enters the filename and the system opens that file, thereby making it accessible. The system then requests a record key for use in retrieving the record to be edited, just as when a search is to be performed. In fact, the editing/updating function involves a retrieval process, just as a search function does.

Once the file management system has found and retrieved the appropriate record, that record is displayed to the user with the data-entry screen that was defined for the file. The user may then use the cursor arrow keys to move the cursor to the appropriate field that needs updating and make the correction—in this case the address, city, and state fields. Once the user is satisfied that the record is correct as edited, the Save function is selected from a menu or by use of a function key. The updated/edited record is saved on secondary storage, usually in the same location it was retrieved from, thereby overwriting the old, outdated record.

When deleting records, the user must select the Delete function. Deletion of records from a customer or client file is necessary when customers or clients indicate that they wish to be one no longer. The user will be prompted for a filename and record key. A search for the appropriate record is performed. Depending upon the system, that record may or may not be retrieved and displayed. It is best if the record is retrieved and displayed so the user can verify that the displayed record is the one to be deleted. The system might then prompt the user once again to verify that this is the record to be deleted. When the user responds affirmatively, the record will be marked as inactive, but not actually removed in most systems.

Physical removal of the inactive (deleted) record may be accomplished in several ways. The record may be overwritten when another record is added to the file, which will result in physical removal of the record; or the record may be physically removed by requesting a "compress" or "pack" action to be taken on the associated file. The sole purpose of compress or pack commands is to remove all of the inactive records in the file and reduce the file to only its active records so it is smaller and takes up less space on the secondary storage medium.

Sorting and Indexing Records

Record files can be sorted once the user specifies the field(s) on which the sort is to take place, and whether the sort is to be in ascending or descending

NUM	NAME	ADDRESS	CITY, STATE	ZIP	PHONE	BIRTH DATE DA	MO	YR
3	Ford, Floyd	85 Willow Lane	Happy, TX	77345	806-775-3421	01	01	38
6	Redmond, Rob	484 Canyon Lane	Logan, UT	90113	707-866-4321	07	09	38
1	Carter, Cari	9000 Mountain Rd	Salida, CO	88200	303-987-6789	10	08	40
4	Neuman, Nancy	8605 Ave. Q	Ultra, TX	43321	817-692-5390	01	12	50
5	Norris, Norbert	1003 Overton Lane	Aurora, CO	88651	303-754-3345	04	04	65
2	Fisher, Freda	4th & Quinton	Sundown, TX	79123	806-665-0000	31	10	65

FIGURE 9–15

"Client" File Sorted on Birth Date

order. A primary field or key must always be specified. To break ties, a secondary key is specified. When a tie occurs, then the secondary field is used to determine the correct sorted order for the pair of records. For large files a tertiary key may be necessary to break ties in both the primary and secondary keys.

Suppose you wished to sort the client file in Figure 9–9 in ascending order by birth date from oldest to youngest. You would begin with the birth year as the primary key, and then use the birth month as the secondary key and the birth day as the tertiary key. Doing so would produce a sorted file whose appearance is shown in Figure 9–15.

It should be apparent that without the use of the secondary key record 6 might have been placed in front of record 3, which would have been incorrect. It should be noted, however, that the date is usually placed in a single date field, allowing it to be properly sorted with a single primary key.

Generating Reports

The printing and displaying of reports is one of the most important tasks of any file management system. The user must first decide what file a report is to be printed from. Then the user must select the fields from which the report is to be printed. The arrangement of fields on the printed or displayed page must then be specified. Ordinarily, the fields are arranged in columns down the page.

For example, suppose that a report based on the client file in Figure 9–15 is desired. This report is to include only the client names together with their birth dates in ascending order of birth date. The report would appear as shown in Figure 9–16.

FIGURE 9–16

Birthday Report of "Client" File

CLIENT NAME	BIRTH DATE MONTH	DAY	YEAR
Ford, Floyd	01	01	38
Redmond, Rob	09	07	38
Carter, Cari	08	10	40
Neuman, Nancy	12	01	50
Norris, Norbert	04	04	65
Fisher, Freda	10	31	65

Focus Feature

USING A SPREADSHEET LIKE LOTUS 1-2-3 AS A FLATFILE MANAGER

Like most flatfile managers, 1-2-3 has the capability to save and retrieve data, to sort and search for data, and to generate data. In Chapter 8, a discussion of the file management capabilities of spreadsheets was presented; these are similar to those provided by file management systems. For example, integrated spreadsheets such as 1-2-3, Symphony, Framework, SuperCalc^3, and others have the capability to store and retrieve worksheets (as files), and to combine worksheets.

In this article, we discuss some of the other file-related capabilities of spreadsheets. Spreadsheets generally are capable of sorting, searching, forms management, and so forth. Generally, each row of cells on the worksheet may be thought of as a record, and each column of the worksheet can be thought of as a field. As with the genre of file and record management systems, integrated spreadsheets can only work with one file (one worksheet) at a time, although other disk-based files may be combined into the "current" one. Moreover, the records on each worksheet are identical in the sense of having the same fields, field-widths, field-types, etc.

Unlike most file management systems, most integrated spreadsheets read the currently active file entirely into memory. Certainly this is true of 1-2-3. This distinction has important implications. First, files are limited to the amount of primary storage available. Second, searches, sorts, and other types of file manipulation tend to execute much faster because no disk accesses are required. Thus, although files may be smaller than what would be realizable with a disk-based flatfile manager, most operations will go much faster with a spreadsheet like 1-2-3.

With the very large worksheets that are supportable by today's hardware, it is possible to have more than one "file" embedded in a single worksheet. In fact, 1-2-3 requires the user to define three files in conjunction with the search-related EXTRACT command: an input area, an output area, and a criteria area. 1-2-3 uses the keys defined in the criteria area to select records from the input area for display within the output area, as shown in Figure 9–17. The output area can then be incorporated into a printed report of only the selected records.

Although integrated spreadsheets like 1-2-3 provide many data base functions, they generally lack the power and flexibility of dedicated, robust file management systems. The report generation capabilities of dedicated file management programs exceed those of the typical integrated spreadsheet. On the other hand, the close integration with spreadsheet and graphics capabilities can be a

Notice that the order of the MONTH and DAY fields have been reversed as compared with their order in the client file in Figure 9–15. This is easily accomplished. The user must provide labels for each column, which has been done in Figure 9–16.

HARDWARE AND SOFTWARE REQUIREMENTS FOR FILE MANAGEMENT SYSTEMS

Hardware requirements of file management systems can be minimal and are more dependent upon the actual application to which the file management program is being used. Certainly a half-megabyte of RAM, two floppy disk drives each with 360K bytes of storage, a monochrome monitor, and a dot-matrix printer are minimally sufficient to support a vast array of simple file management applications.

Summary

File management programs have as their primary goal ease of use, combined with enough capabilities to handle simple file management situations in which not

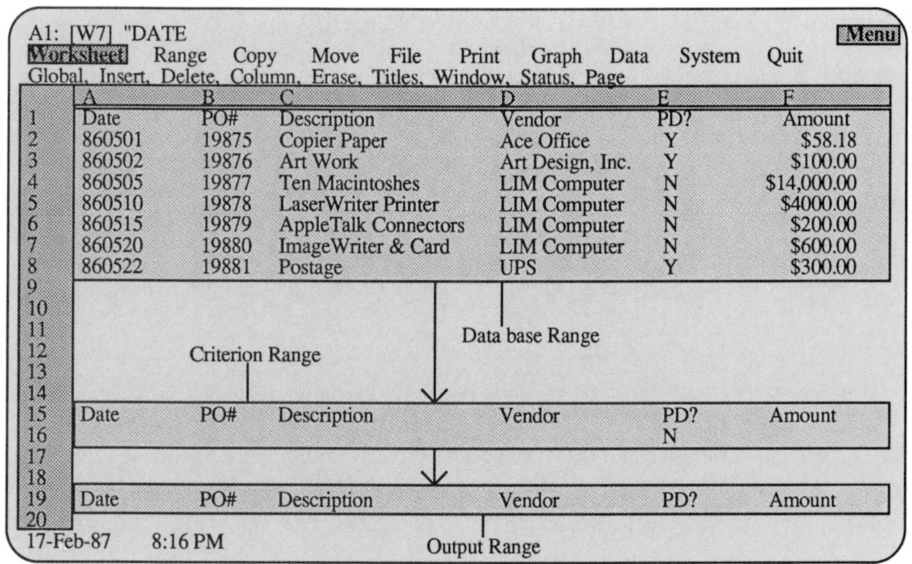

FIGURE 9–17

The Ranges Required to Perform a Search

significant advantage because users do not have to export/import data from/to the flatfile manager and the spreadsheet or graphics application.

The tutorial at the end of this chapter illustrates how 1-2-3 can be used as a flatfile manager, and describes the facilities it provides for this purpose.

more than one file need be open at one time and a single file is sufficient to specify all the necessary data associated with a particular application. File management programs are expected to maintain their ease of use while adding capabilities.[1,2] Some file managers are already capable of opening several files at once, even though little or no relational operations can be performed among the several files and no programming language is included.

One rather significant development in the flatfile management software category is the use of natural language interfaces. Natural language interfaces like HAL, which is available for Lotus 1-2-3 and Symphony, enable users to query and sort their data more easily.[1]

Until the full-blown data base management systems to be described in the next chapter become much simpler in their use, a significant market will remain for flatfile management systems. There are just too many applications for which the flatfile manager is quite sufficient. For these applications investing the additional cost of purchasing a more expensive data base management system and the additional time of learning a more complicated user interface just is not warranted. After all, why use an atom bomb if all you want to do is kill a fly? A checklist of functions and features of file management systems is provided at the end of the text. The next chapter, Chapter 10, focuses on data base management systems.

Key Terms

data base management system
direct search
export capability
field
file management system
flatfile manager
form
import capability
indexed-sequential search
key field
record
search keys
sequential search
sort keys

Self-Test

1. Describe how file management software and applications got their start.
2. Describe to what uses file management software is generally put.
3. Describe what features one can expect in file management software.
4. Describe what steps are involved in using a file manager.
5. Describe what hardware and software are required for the use of file managers.

Exercises

1. Discuss the advantages of index files over the alternative to index files. What is the alternative?
2. Discuss the advantages and disadvantages of record and file management systems.
3. Discuss the advantages and disadvantages of data base management systems.
4. What is meant by data redundancy? Is it more commonplace in data base management systems or file management systems? Is it desirable or undesirable? Why?
5. Define what is meant by a "record" for
   (a) a phone book
   (b) a dictionary
   (c) an encyclopedia

   For each of the above, define the "fields" within each record.
6. Characterize the features one can expect in a flatfile management program.
7. Research several flatfile management systems of interest to you and report on their features, user interface, capacities in number of records, length of each record, number of fields, length of each field, etc.

References

1. Mace, Scott. "File Management Software." *InfoWorld* 8, issue 36 (September 8, 1986): 29–30.
2. Mace, Scott. "Firms Hunger for Simpler Data Bases." *InfoWorld* 8, issue 36 (September 8, 1986): 30.

Additional Reading

Krajewski, Rich. "Database Types." *Byte* 9, no. 11 (October 1984) 137–47.

Krasnoff, Barbara, et al. "Flat-file Databases." *PC Magazine* 5, no. 13 (July 7, 1986) 187–212.

———. "Programmable Relational Databases." *PC Magazine* 5, no. 12 (June 24, 1986) 106–13.

Krasnoff, Barbara, and John Dickinson. "Project Database II." *PC Magazine* 5, no. 12 (June 24, 1986) 106–13.

Lima, Tony. "Rating File Managers for PC's and Compatibles," *InfoWorld* 8, issue 36 (September 8, 1986) 31–37.

Shapiro, Ezra. "Text Databases." *Byte* 9, no. 11 (October 1984): 147–55.

———. "Databases." *Byte* 9, no. 11 (October 1984) 135–37.

TUTORIAL

Lotus 1-2-3 File Management

In this tutorial you are going to create a flatfile that contains the name, address, city, state, ZIP code, phone number, and birth date of your friends or clients. In Lotus 1-2-3, fields are arranged in columns, and records in rows. Column widths may be adjusted as necessary to contain each field. Since all address fields and all name fields are exactly the same width, all Lotus "files" are flatfiles. Each row, except the first (in Figure 9–18), denotes exactly one record. The first row contains the field names. Each cell contains the field entry for that particular record. **At this time, create the flatfile shown in Figure 9–18.**

Setting up a file in Lotus 1-2-3 is no different from setting up an ordinary Lotus 1-2-3 worksheet. First type in the field names for the file. Position the cursor to A1 and type in **Name.** Move cursor to B1 (use the "–>" key to move one cell to the right) and type **Address.** Continue through row one until you have entered **Birth Date** in column G.

Next set up the column width of each column (column A through column G). Position cursor to cell A1. Type **/WCS16** (/ to invoke the menu, W to select Worksheet, C to select column option, S to select Set-Width option, and 16 to specify the cell column width). This key sequence sets column A to 16 characters width. Move cursor to B1. Type **/WCS17.** Move cursor to C1. Type **/WCS8.** Move cursor to D1. Type **/WCS3.** Move cursor to E1. Type / **WCS6.** Move cursor to F1. Type **/WCS13.** Move cursor to G1. Type **/WCS8.**

Now that you have specified the field names and column widths for each field, you are ready to key in the actual data. Position cursor at A2 and type **Carter, Cari** (last name first). Move cursor to B2 and type **'9000 Mountain Rd** (the single quotation ' is required in this case because the address begins with a number). The single quote means "left-justify" to Lotus. Move cursor to C1 and type **Salida.** Move cursor to D1 and type **CO.** Move cursor to E1 and type **'88200.** Move cursor to F1 and type **'303-987-6789,** remembering to type the ' first or else an error will occur. Move cursor to G1 and type **'40-08-10** (year-month-day). Position the cursor to A3 and type in the next record of data as shown in Figure 9–18 above. Remember to include a ' whenever a label field begins with a number instead of a letter, for example, in the ADDRESS and PHONE fields.

SORTING THE FIELD ON BIRTH DATE AND ZIP CODE

At this stage all the data shown in Figure 9–18 should be keyed in. Notice that the records are currently listed in alphabetical order. Suppose

(Continued)

Lotus 1-2-3 File Management (Continued)

	A	B	C	D	E	F	G
1	NAME	ADDRESS	CITY	ST	ZIP	PHONE	BIRTH DA
2	Carter, Cari	9000 Mountain Rd	Salida	CO	88200	303-987-6789	40-08-10
3	Fisher, Freda	4th & Quinton	Sundown	TX	79123	806-665-0000	65-10-31
4	Ford, Floyd	85 Willow Lane	Happy	TX	77345	806-775-3421	38-01-01
5	Kennedy, Kirk	122 Knobby Lane	Willoby	TX	76301	806-731-9888	44-07-23
6	Neuman, Nancy	8605 Ave. Q	Ultra	TX	43321	817-692-5390	50-12-01
7	Norris, Norbert	3004 15th St.	Texline	TX	79999	806-112-1134	65-04-04
8	Redmond, Rob	484 Canyon Lane	Logan	UT	90113	707-866-4321	38-09-07
9							
10							
11							
12							
13							
14							
15							
16							
17							
18							
19							
20							

FIGURE 9–18

A Lotus 1-2-3 Flatfile

instead that you want them listed in ascending order of birth date. The steps required to do this are listed below.

1. Make sure you are in the ready mode. If not, hit the <Esc> key until you get into the ready mode. Now type the "/" key.
2. Select **Data<Ret>Sort<Ret>,** where <**Ret**> is the return key. Recall that to select **Data,** you must first use the cursor arrow keys to position the highlight bar over the menu bar item **Data,** and then press <**Ret**>**.** The next submenu bar appears and you select **Sort** in exactly the same way.

3. Select **Data-Range<Ret>.** This option allows you to define the range of data to sort.
4. Type **A2..G8<Ret>** after the prompt `Enter Data-Range:.` Notice that the field names are not included in the range; only the data records are included.
5. Next, select the **Primary Key <Ret>.** Type **G1<Ret>** at the prompt `Primary sort key:.` Now, select the sort order ("A" for ascending and "D" for descending order). Since you want ascending order, you select **A<Ret>.**
6. Now, you must select the **Secondary Key<Ret>.** For the secondary key you will choose ascending order on the ZIP CODE field. Type **E1<Ret>** at the prompt `Secondary sort key:` and respond with **A<Ret>** to the prompt `Sort order (A or D).`
7. Select **Go<Ret>.** Immediately following this, the worksheet should appear as shown in Figure 9–19.
8. Your worksheet should now be in the ready mode.

SEARCHING AND EXTRACTING RECORDS FROM A FILE

Now, suppose you wanted to search/find or extract a particular record that meets criteria you have defined. Before you can proceed to find or extract a particular record, you first need to specify

1. *The input data range*—the records you want searched.
2. *The criteria range*—the criteria of your search. The first row of the criteria range should be the field names. The actual criteria are entered on the second row and subsequent rows if desired.
3. *The output range*—the range of cells into which the records that meet the criteria should be placed.

These then are the three areas of the worksheet required to perform an EXTRACT command: an input area, a criteria area, and an output area. As an example of how this works, suppose you wish to know which of your friends or clients live in Texas. These are the steps you need to take.

1. Bring the spreadsheet to the **ready** mode (it should already be in the **ready** mode.). Position the cursor at A1. Type the "/" key.

(Continued)

Lotus 1-2-3 File Management (Continued)

	A	B	C	D	E	F	G
1	NAME	ADDRESS	CITY	ST	ZIP	PHONE	BIRTH DA
2	Ford, Floyd	85 Willow Lane	Happy	TX	77345	806-775-3421	38-01-01
3	Redmond, Rob	484 Canyon Lane	Logan	UT	90113	707-866-4321	38-09-07
4	Carter, Cari	9000 Mountain Rd	Salida	CO	88200	303-987-6789	40-08-10
5	Kennedy, Kirk	122 Knobby Lane	Willoby	TX	76301	806-731-9888	44-07-23
6	Neuman, Nancy	8605 Ave. Q	Ultra	TX	43321	817-692-5390	50-12-01
7	Norris, Norbert	3004 15th St.	Texline	TX	79999	806-112-1134	65-04-04
8	Fisher, Freda	4th & Quinton	Sundown	TX	79123	806-665-0000	65-10-31
9							
10							
11							
12							
13							
14							
15							
16							
17							
18							
19							
20							

FIGURE 9–19

A Lotus 1-2-3 Flatfile Sorted on Birth Date

2. Select **Copy<Ret>**. Enter **A1..G1** at the prompt `Enter range to copy FROM:` . Next define your criteria area in response to the prompt `Enter range to copy TO:` **A10..G10<Ret>**. This step duplicates a copy of the field names into cells A10 to G10 for the criteria area, as shown in Figure 9–20 below.

3. Position the cursor at cell D11 (under the field name ST) and type **TX<Ret>**.

4. Type the "/" key again and select **Copy<Ret>**. Enter **A1..G1** at the

	A	B	C	D	E	F	G
10	NAME	ADDRESS	CITY	ST	ZIP	PHONE	BIRTH DA
11				TX			

FIGURE 9–20
Criteria Area

	A	B	C	D	E	F	G
15	NAME	ADDRESS	CITY	ST	ZIP	PHONE	BIRTH DA

FIGURE 9–21
Field Names for Output Area

prompt `Enter range to copy FROM:`. Next define your output area in response to the prompt `Enter range to copy TO:` **A15..G15<Ret>.** This duplicates a copy of the field names into cells A15 to G15 for the output area, as shown below in Figure 9–21.

5. Now type the "/" key and select **Data**<**Ret**> and then select **Query**<**Ret**>.
6. Select **Input**<**Ret**> to define the input range. Type **A1..G8**<**Ret**> at the prompt `Enter input range:`. The field names and all records are included.
7. Select **Criterion**<**Ret**> to define the criteria range. Enter **A10..G11** at the prompt `Enter Criterion range:`.
8. Select **Output**<**Ret**> to define the output range. Enter **A15..G15** in response to the prompt `Enter Output range:`.
9. Select **Find**<**Ret**> to invoke a search for records which match the criteria. If there is a record that matches your criteria, the first record that matches will be highlighted. Use <Down> or <Up> arrows to move to the next record or match. If no record or no more records match the criteria, a beep will sound. Press <**Ret**> to return to the query menu.
10. Select **Extract** <**Ret**> to extract records that meet your criteria to the output area. The extracted output is shown below in Figure 9–22.

Of course, you already know how to save, retrieve, and edit data files in Lotus 1-2-3, since this is the same as for any worksheet.

(Continued)

Lotus 1-2-3 File Management (Continued)

	A	B	C	D	E	F	G
15	NAME	ADDRESS	CITY	ST	ZIP	PHONE	BIRTH DA
16	Ford, Floyd	85 Willow Lane	Happy	TX	77345	806-775-3421	38-01-01
17	Kennedy, Kirk	122 Knobby Lane	Willoby	TX	76301	806-731-9888	44-07-23
18	Neuman, Nancy	8605 Ave. Q	Ultra	TX	43321	817-692-5390	50-12-01
19	Norris, Norbert	3004 15th St.	Texline	TX	79999	806-112-1134	65-04-04
20	Fisher, Freda	4th & Quinton	Sundown	TX	79123	806-665-0000	65-10-31

FIGURE 9–22
Extracted Output

EXERCISES

1. Build a file like the one above of all of your friends. If you don't know their birth dates, you may contrive this information. Addresses can usually be found in the phone book. Add the fields LIKES, DISLIKES. Sort the file in alphabetical order and print it. Perform an *extract* operation like the one above and print the extracted output. Describe what criteria you used.
2. Build a *contrived* file of course grades for all courses you may have heard of. Include in the file the following fields: COURSE NAME, NUMBER, INSTRUCTOR, and GRADE. Make the COURSE NAME field 20 character positions wide, the NUMBER field 5 character positions wide, the INSTRUCTOR field 15 character positions wide, and the GRADE field 1 or 2 character positions wide. Include at least 15 records and make the grades of 4 of these *A's*. Print the file. Now sort the file in alphabetic order on the COURSE NAME and print the file again. Now extract from the file all courses in which the grade was *A*. Finally, print just the extracted records.

DISK EXERCISES

1. Use the Lotus worksheet file FLATFILE.WK1 to perform the following. Identify the fields. Sort the file in alphabetical order on the NAME field. Print the sorted file.
2. Using the Lotus worksheet file FLATFILE.WK1, sort the file in ascending order on ZIPCODE. Print the sorted file.
3. Using the Lotus worksheet file FLTFILE1.WK1, extract all records whose STATE is CA. Print just the extracted portion of file; that is, print the extracted records.

CHAPTER

10

Data Base Management Systems

CHAPTER OUTLINE

Data Base Management Systems Defined 350

The History of Data Base Management Systems 352

Business and Personal Uses for a Data Base Management System 353

Software Concepts and Design Philosophies 353

FOCUS FEATURE Select, Project, and Join 354

Using a Data Base Management System 361

FOCUS FEATURE AI Meets DB 362

Hardware and Software Requirements for Data Base Management Systems 369

dBASE III AND dBASE III PLUS TUTORIAL 374

CHAPTER OBJECTIVES

In this chapter you will learn

1 what a DBMS is and how it differs from a file management system

2 how DBMSs are used

3 how to plan and create a data base

4 how to maintain and use a data base

5 what the relational operations are and how to use them

6 how to add, append, delete, sort, index, and search records in a DBMS

7 how to use dBASE III and dBASE III Plus

Information, that critical resource in the decision-making process, was once a rare commodity. In the past, companies that had effective information-gathering procedures had a decided advantage in the business world, because they had the knowledge necessary to assess economic trends, analyze a competitor's position, control production and personnel costs, and find the lowest-cost suppliers. Today, thanks in large part to the computerization of information collection and dissemination, many businesses are more threatened by an overload, rather than a shortage, of information.

A Data Base Management System (DBMS) is a powerful tool that can help a business or individual to organize and store the incoming tide of information, and to retrieve those portions relevant to current decisions and processes. Data base management systems have become essential tools in this information era and can be effectively employed in virtually every type of business.

This chapter studies the organization of data within a computer, looks at the historical basis for the development of data base management systems, and discovers their many applications in business, the professional world, and personal lives. The chapter considers the important features of DBMS programs and explains how they might be used effectively. At the end of the chapter is a guide to the use of one of the more popular and powerful DBMS packages for microcomputers, dBASE III Plus.

DATA BASE MANAGEMENT SYSTEMS DEFINED

Chapter 9 presented a brief overview of the hierarchy of secondary storage methods. The smallest entity of usable information is usually a field, which is composed of bytes. When several fields bear a logical relationship to each other, as with name, address, and department number of an employee, they are stored together as a record. Related records are, in turn, stored together as a file. The organization of information into files seems natural and intuitive, but it can lead to increased programming effort and a waste of precious storage media. For example, a company might keep its personnel records in a file containing employee names, addresses, employee numbers, and job classifications. Another file would be used for processing payroll, with almost all of the information from the personnel file plus wage rates, insurance plan selections, and the number and amounts of deductions. Still a third might be kept for recording information about each department in the firm, with the department name, department head, and employee names (see Figure 10–1).

Each of these files was designed to serve a separate application program, and unless extensive planning was done before their creation it is unlikely that the files share a common structure. If the firm develops information needs that were not originally planned for (e.g., a list of employees in accounting who earned more than $40,000), a new program must be written that extracts information from several files. This can be a costly and time-consuming undertaking.

A **data base** is a collection of logically related data elements organized in such a manner that several applications are supported. In a data base, all information pertaining to employees can be stored together, and the personnel, payroll, and departmental programs would extract their required information from a common

NAME	ADDRESS	SALARY	DEPT	SUPERVISOR
Brown, Buck	2000 Plano	35000	MKT	Smith, Sue
Smith, Sue	1200 East Way	65000	CEO	Smith, Sue
Jones, John	1 Jones Place	15000	MAN	Smith, Sue
Hart, Helen	800 Dip Road	25000	OPR	Smith, Sue
Moore, Mary	4563 15th St.	23000	FIN	Smith, Sue

FIGURE 10–1
An Employee File System

store of data. The software that controls the input, storage, and retrieval of information from the data base is known as a **data base management system.**

Data base management systems offer a number of advantages over application-specific file storage methods and file management systems:

1. Reduced **data redundancy.** In file-oriented storage methods, the same information is typically stored in several files, due to the complexity and inconvenience of dealing with multiple files. Data base systems can reduce or eliminate this redundancy. This saves precious memory and increases accuracy and reliability. An address field which requires changing need only be changed in one location rather than a half-dozen.
2. Greater **data integrity.** In conventional programming environments, if an employee's salary changes, updates to several files might be necessary. This introduces two problems: some files may be overlooked, or the information may be recorded differently in some files. Data base management systems simplify changing information and ensure that the information is the same for all applications. Because the information will be accessed by several users, the likelihood of catching errors is also increased.
3. Improved **data security.** In a file-based system, if a programmer or user is allowed access to a file to obtain the information from a given field, the entire contents of the file are available to him or her. Most data base management systems allow privacy locks to be placed on sensitive records or fields. Thus, a user may be allowed to view the number of deductions of an employee but cannot see the employee's wage rate without the proper authorization. Thus, protection levels can also be set that declare certain information to be read-only, eliminating alterations or updates on vital data. Other protection levels might prevent both read-only and update access to a field or record with a file. Protection levels are password-controlled.
4. **Data independence.** Information in a data base is stored with a unified structure, and the DBMS has its own language for retrieval. This frees the application programmer from having to know a great deal about the structure of stored information, and applications can be generated much more quickly.
5. Increased **flexibility.** A DBMS can allow information to be retrieved in ways that were not anticipated when the system was designed. Consider a data base that stores part numbers, supplier names and addresses, the cost of a part, and the component the part is used in. It might normally be used to answer questions such as "Show me all the supplier names and costs of components for product A." A DBMS can just as easily handle a question such as "Show me all the components that use part number 3452." Although planning the data base structure is still important (see the section on use of a DBMS), a DBMS can often handle almost any type of information request if the data elements are available. This ability to connect information in any logical manner is one of the principal benefits of a DBMS.

THE HISTORY OF DATA BASE MANAGEMENT SYSTEMS

Systems for the management of large sets of data have existed since the early 1960s. At that time (and even today) most business data processing organizations used COBOL (for COmmon Business Oriented Language). When data management needs became complex, many companies developed their own systems of file management. COBOL is a standardized language (the commands and data structures remain the same from machine to machine), so CODASYL (the Conference on Data Description Languages)—the committee responsible for the development and maintenance of COBOL—took note. They formed a special group known as the Data Base Task Group (DBTG) in an effort to standardize and make more available this new category of programs. Their final report, published in 1971,[1] paved the way for a great deal of research and development in data base management systems.

In 1970, E. F. Codd, in an article entitled "A Relational Model of Data for Large Shared Data Banks"[2] described a mathematically oriented approach to storing and connecting related data. This became known as the relational approach, and it revolutionized data base management theory. With the relational approach the storage requirements, types of record connections, and access times for information could all be defined with mathematical precision and systems could be optimized for performance or storage savings. Data base management systems using the relational approach did not begin to surface commercially until the late 1970s, however.

Data base management systems for microcomputers have no distinct origin nor initial product. Small file and record management systems began to appear on the market as soon as floppy disk storage devices became commonly available, and some of these reportedly employed the relational approach. In 1981 and 1982, two products were introduced that met with great commercial success, dBASE II from Ashton-Tate and Condor 20 from Condor Computer Corporation. These products had a great deal of power and flexibility and fostered an entire industry of data base software developers, resulting in the several hundred DBMS products available today.

Data base management systems for microcomputers are different from mainframe data base managers in at least one significant respect. The Data Manipulation Language (DML) for a mainframe DBMS (those commands and statements that add, retrieve, or update information in a data base) is designed to be used in a host language, usually COBOL. What this means is that an application program for the accounting or finance departments will be written in the normal manner in COBOL. When the application program needs data from the data base, special DML statements are embedded in the COBOL program. Some DBMS packages also have a **query language**, a group of commands that can access the data base without requiring a program. In the microcomputer environment, the user will not find DML commands that can be embedded in a host language. The data base in a microcomputer-based DBMS is entered, manipulated, and retrieved entirely through the data base management system—not external programs. To an individual trained on a mainframe DBMS, this might seem like a severe restriction. For most users, however, quite the converse is true. The microcomputer DBMS can often eliminate the need for some of the external programs and can put the power of easy data manipulation and retrieval in the hands of the end user, without reliance on data processing professionals.

BUSINESS AND PERSONAL USES FOR A DATA BASE MANAGEMENT SYSTEM

A glance through the annual index to any of the popular computer magazines is likely to turn up dozens of articles showing unique uses of data base management systems. They are used for everything from cataloguing cattle to indexing investments, from logging legal clients to arranging artwork. In fact, most businesses will find that a DBMS is their most versatile computer tool.

Data base management systems are commonly used to keep inventory and accounting information, two applications for which separate, dedicated packages exist. Although extra effort may be required to use a data base in this manner, it is often worthwhile for the flexibility that can be gained. For example, an inventory system can keep accurate accounts of supplier information but might not be able to tell you which suppliers for part #3854 are within a 50-mile radius, have at least 200,000 in stock, and will offer liberal credit terms. A data base system (assuming you record such information) can easily handle requests of this type. Likewise, an accounts receivable program can tell a doctor which patients are 30 or more days overdue in payment, but is unlikely to know which ones can be called to donate type AB blood.

A common use for a DBMS is to record information about clients and contacts. In addition to names, addresses, phone numbers, and business information, the names and birthdays of children, favorite foods, or golf handicap can be recorded. Churches can use a DBMS to keep track of parishioners, and political campaigns can use them for contribution records. Thus, a DBMS makes it possible to find a fourth for a golf match, locate which parishioners have not received a home visit this quarter, or identify political districts where contribution levels do not meet expectations.

Data base management systems are used by writers to keep track of characters or to store bibliographic material. They are used by several professional sports organizations to keep team and player statistics. A microcomputer system using dBASE II was used by the Los Angeles Police Department to help organize and record the activities of over 50,000 policemen and staff during the 1984 Summer Olympics.

SOFTWARE CONCEPTS AND DESIGN PHILOSOPHIES

Because of the large number of entrants in the DBMS market, there is bound to be great diversity in the type of products available. This section looks at the most significant category of DBMS software, the relational data base management system. It also considers three different methods of presentation, or user interfaces, and surveys the common features of most data base management system packages.

DBMS Categories

Among microcomputers, there are only two principal product categories for file or data base management: the file management system and the relational data

Focus Feature

SELECT, PROJECT, AND JOIN

Traditional (mainframe computer-oriented) thought in data base theory states that a DBMS meets the minimum qualifications as a relational DBMS if and only if it can perform the three fundamental operations of **relational algebra** (a structure for query languages). These operations are the Select, the Project, and the Join. These operations are known as **table construction operations,** since they can be used to extract data from an existing data base in order to create a new file. The user may see the response directly on the terminal, or he may view the newly created data base to find the answer to his query. For many mainframe DBMS packages, this table creation process is the only way of looking at the data in a data base.

In a **Select** operation, a horizontal (row-wise) subset of the table is extracted. Entire rows meeting a specified criterion are pulled from the data base. Figure 10–2a shows the result of the following query on a file called EMPLOYEE:

SELECT EMPLOYEE WHERE SALARY>30000 GIVING HIGH

The **Project** operator is used to display only certain columns in a table. To show all employee names, you might say

PROJECT EMPLOYEE OVER NAME GIVING NAMES

Figure 10–2b shows the effect of the above query when applied to the file EMPLOYEE, thereby creating the file NAMES. If the phrase GIVING NAMES is left off, the same information would be sent to the screen instead.

The Select and Project operators may be combined, using an intermediate file to store temporary results from the first operation, then performing the second operation on the temporary file. To find the names of the highly paid employees, you might say

SELECT EMPLOYEE WHERE SALARY>30000 GIVING HIGH
PROJECT HIGH OVER NAME GIVING HIGHNAME

Figure 10–2c shows the outcome of this query.

The **Join** operator will use a field or column name to compare two tables. Wherever a match occurs, all fields from both tables will be displayed (except the matching field, which will only be shown once). The Join is ordinarily used with either a Select, a Project, or both. If a firm kept an EMPLOYEE file with NAME, ADDRESS, and SALARY as fields, and a DEPARTMT file with NAME, DEPT, and SUPERVISOR as fields, the following query would give the information in both files for all employees (shown in Figure 10–2d).

JOIN EMPLOYEE AND DEPARTMT GIVING EMPLDEPT

Although these are powerful and versatile capabilities, a microcomputer DBMS is likely to give you the same query facility with less effort and without the need for intermediate files. For example, the Select-Project shown in Figure 10–2c might be handled with a simple

LIST NAME WHERE SALARY>30000

FIGURE 10–2a
SELECT

EMPLOYEE

NAME	ADDRESS	SALARY
Brown, Buck	2000 Plano	35000
Smith, Sue	1200 East Way	65000
Jones, John	1 Jones Place	15000
Hart, Helen	800 Dip Road	25000
Moore, Mary	4563 15th St.	23000

HIGH

NAME	ADDRESS	SALARY
Brown, Buck	2000 Plano	35000
Smith, Sue	1200 East Way	65000

EMPLOYEE

NAME	ADDRESS	SALARY
Brown, Buck	2000 Plano	35000
Smith, Sue	1200 East Way	65000
Jones, John	1 Jones Place	15000
Hart, Helen	800 Dip Road	25000
Moore, Mary	4563 15th St.	23000

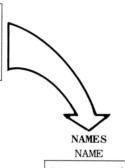

NAMES

NAME
Brown, Buck
Smith, Sue
Jones, John
Hart, Helen
Moore, Mary

FIGURE 10–2b
PROJECT

EMPLOYEE

NAME	ADDRESS	SALARY
Brown, Buck	2000 Plano	35000
Smith, Sue	1200 East Way	65000
Jones, John	1 Jones Place	15000
Hart, Helen	800 Dip Road	25000
Moore, Mary	4563 15th St.	23000

HIGH

NAME	ADDRESS	SALARY
Brown, Buck	2000 Plano	35000
Smith, Sue	1200 East Way	65000

HIGHNAME

NAME
Brown, Buck
Smith, Sue

FIGURE 10–2c
SELECT AND PROJECT

(Continued)

SELECT, PROJECT, AND JOIN (Continued)

FIGURE 10–2d
JOIN

EMPLOYEE

NAME	ADDRESS	SALARY
Brown, Buck	2000 Plano	35000
Smith, Sue	1200 East Way	65000
Jones, John	1 Jones Place	15000
Hart, Helen	800 Dip Road	25000
Moore, Mary	4563 15th St.	23000

DEPARTMT

NAME	DEPT	SUPERVISOR
Brown, Buck	MKT	Smith, Sue
Smith, Sue	CEO	Smith, Sue
Jones, John	MAN	Smith, Sue
Hart, Helen	OPR	Smith, Sue
Moore, Mary	FIN	Smith, Sue

EMPLDEPT

NAME	ADDRESS	SALARY	DEPT	SUPERVISOR
Brown, Buck	2000 Plano	35000	MKT	Smith, Sue
Smith, Sue	1200 East Way	65000	CEO	Smith, Sue
Jones, John	1 Jones Place	15000	MAN	Smith, Sue
Hart, Helen	800 Dip Road	25000	OPR	Smith, Sue
Moore, Mary	4563 15th St.	23000	FIN	Smith, Sue

base management system (RDBMS). File and record management systems were discussed in Chapter 9.

On mainframes and minicomputers there are two other types of DBMSs not prevalent among microcomputers: hierarchical DBMS and network DBMS. Both these types of DBMSs make extensive use of links and pointers to "relate" data in one file to data in another. As shown in Figure 10–3, the links and pointers are represented by arrows directed from one file to another. The links and pointers possess no loops in a hierarchical DBMS, whereas loops do exist among network DBMSs. The problem with all of the links and pointers is that they take up space. Furthermore, it frequently happens that a user wants to relate the data in the files a certain way that was not anticipated at the time the data base was created. Consequently, no links or pointers exist to permit the data to be related in such a way.

A **relational data base management system** is designed to manipulate information that may be stored in more than one file. A relational data base file is analogous to a two-dimensional table, complete with rows and columns, as shown

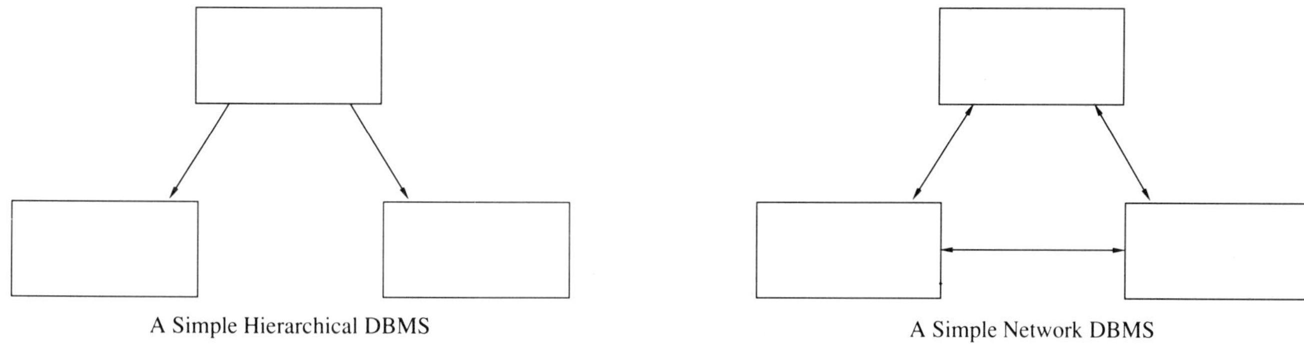

FIGURE 10–3
Hierarchical and Network DBMSs

in Figure 10–4. The rows (called *tuples* in RDBMS parlance) are similar to records in an ordinary file. The files in a relational DBMS are related through the use of the field names (called *attributes*) and by means of the techniques described in the article "Select, Project, and Join." There are no links or pointers. The columns (known as attributes) can be likened to fields. A table (known as a *relation*) contains the information that would normally be stored in a file, and indeed, microcomputer RDBMS programs will generally store each table in a separate file.

The User Interface

Microcomputer data base management systems can also be classified according to the method employed for presenting their features to the user. A DBMS is typically either **menu-driven, form-oriented**, or **command-driven.**

A menu-driven system is the easiest DBMS to use. In this type of system, data bases are created and accessed by selecting menu options. Whereas this type of user interface is most common on simple file managers, some very powerful relational data base management systems are menu-oriented. The major difficulty in these systems is that the user is limited to the selections offered in the menus and cannot customize a data acquisition system for a particular application. Each time the DBMS is used, a lengthy string of menu selections must be made to add, update, or retrieve information. In situations that demand complex data manipulation, the

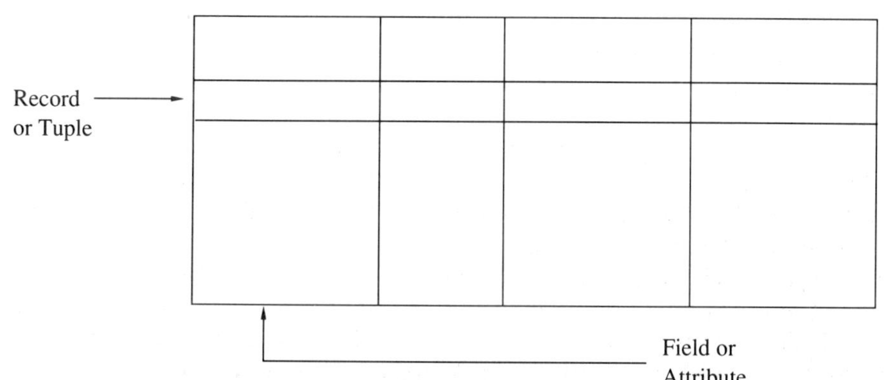

FIGURE 10–4
A Relational Table

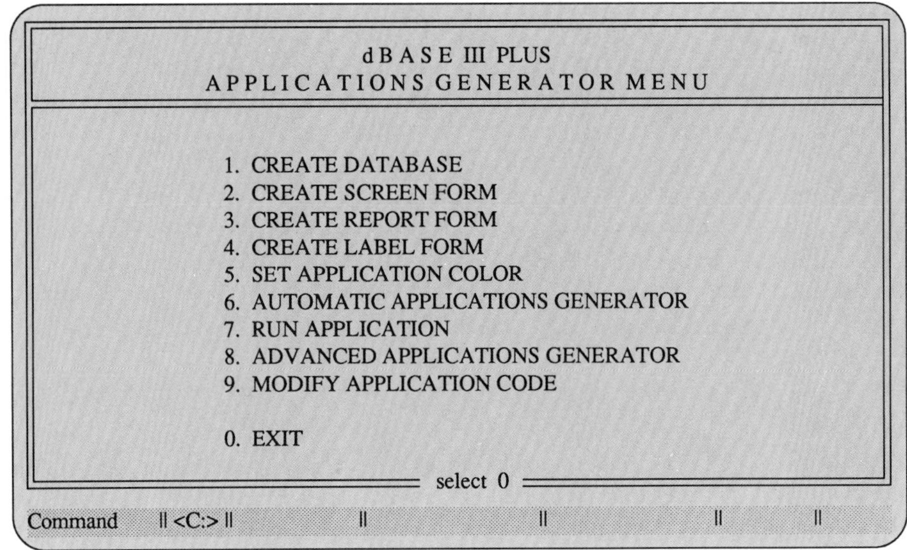

FIGURE 10–5
With the built-in "applications generator" in Ashton-Tate's new dBASE III Plus, users can easily create their own dBASE applications without programming.

menu-driven system is rarely adequate. Depicted in Figure 10–5 is the menu of the applications generator of dBASE III Plus.

A form-oriented (or screen-driven) DBMS uses forms or screens for all data manipulation activities. When creating a data base, the user is presented with a blank screen. Field names and any prompts or messages are placed wherever the user wants, creating a customized form like the one in Figure 10–6. Thus, the user specifies the location and width of each field. After the screen is completely specified, a series of questions is presented to the user concerning what type of data (character, numeric, etc.) is to go in each field location. Once the data base is defined, the custom form is used to input and print data. Most form-oriented DBMS programs will allow several different output forms to be tied to a single input form. Forms may be several screens long.

Forms are used in all types of data base management systems, mostly for input and printing of data. A form-oriented DBMS, however, will use forms for all of its operations, even retrieval. For example, to find an article written by Jones in a bibliographic data base, the user merely positions the cursor at the AUTHOR field, types in JONES, and presses <Return>. More works by Jones can be found by pressing a specially designated key that moves the user forward in the file. A form-oriented DBMS can be extremely easy to use but may not have the power to handle even moderately complex requests. If the bibliography file has separate fields for up to four authors (as would be necessary with many academic journals), finding all articles by Jones might involve four searches: Jones as first-listed author, Jones as second-listed author, etc.

In a command-driven DBMS the user often has menu prompts to guide the process of data base creation, and can create forms for outputting data to the printer. The distinguishing characteristic of the command-driven DBMS is that it also has a **procedural language** that can be used to customize the system. A procedural language gives a DBMS two significant advantages over either form-oriented or menu-driven data base management systems: (1) the user has virtually unlimited flexibility in the type of data requests that can be made, and (2) programs can be written in the procedural language to accomplish tasks that are out of the ordinary or to speed

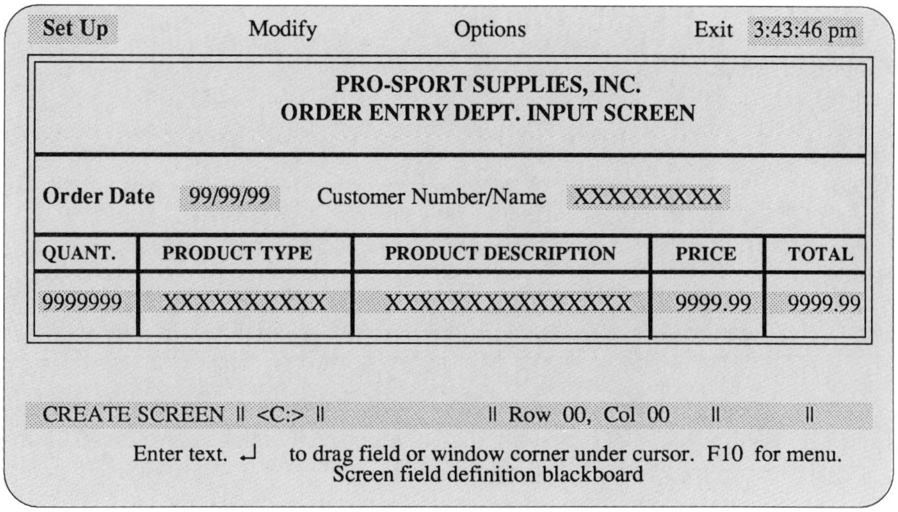

Set Up Modify Options Exit 3:43:46 pm

PRO-SPORT SUPPLIES, INC.
ORDER ENTRY DEPT. INPUT SCREEN

Order Date 99/99/99 Customer Number/Name XXXXXXXXX

QUANT.	PRODUCT TYPE	PRODUCT DESCRIPTION	PRICE	TOTAL
9999999	XXXXXXXXXX	XXXXXXXXXXXXXXX	9999.99	9999.99

CREATE SCREEN ‖ <C:> ‖ ‖ Row 00, Col 00 ‖ ‖

Enter text. ↵ to drag field or window corner under cursor. F10 for menu.
Screen field definition blackboard

FIGURE 10–6
Using the "screen painter" capability included in Ashton-Tate's dBASE III Plus, users can quickly design custom screens and forms for data entry and output without programming.

up the process of accessing data. If you keep a data base on clients, for example, and you ordinarily search for records by the client's last name, you might write a simple command file that opens your client data base, asks you for the name, and retrieves and displays the record for you (see Figure 10–7). This would eliminate many steps for simple searches. Procedural languages for some DBMS packages are quite extensive and have been used to write entire accounting systems.

For nonprogrammers, a command-driven DBMS may not be the best choice. Command-driven DBMSs have a tendency to be more difficult to use than menu-driven or form-oriented DBMS packages, even if they employ some menus and forms. For the firm or individual that anticipates extensive use of a DBMS or has complex data needs, a procedural language is almost a must. It should be stressed that the selection of a DBMS should not be based entirely, or even mostly, on the type of user interface, but rather on whether the features offered meet the user's needs. The next section explores some of the features that should be found in a good DBMS program.

DBMS Features

Regardless of the type of DBMS or the style of user interface, most packages have numerous features in common. The list below explains these features, provides a better feel for the capabilities of a DBMS, and helps a prospective buyer to evaluate whether a given feature is necessary for his or her data base needs.

Data dictionary. A data dictionary contains information about the field names, data type (character, number, date, etc.), and field size in bytes of each field in a data base. Most DBMS systems generate the data dictionary automatically when a data base is created, and they may store the data dictionary information either in a separate file or as the initial record in each data file itself.

Validation. A DBMS should have a method of ensuring that the user cannot input grossly erroneous data. Through a method called **range checking**, a field such as

FIGURE 10–7

Name Search Program (dBASE III PLUS)

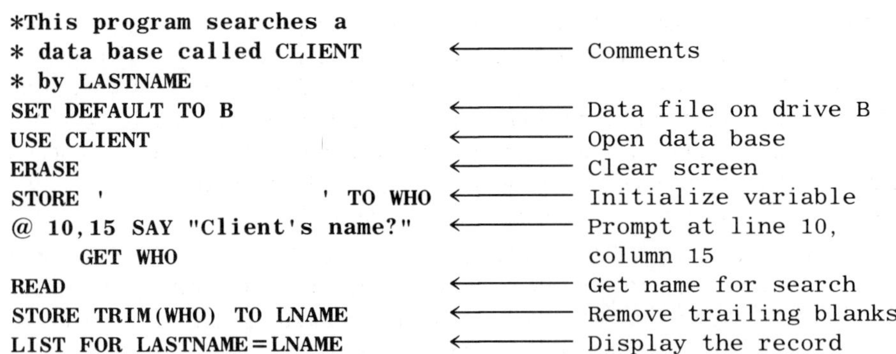

```
*This program searches a
* data base called CLIENT          <——— Comments
* by LASTNAME
SET DEFAULT TO B                   <——— Data file on drive B
USE CLIENT                         <——— Open data base
ERASE                              <——— Clear screen
STORE '                ' TO WHO    <——— Initialize variable
@ 10,15 SAY "Client's name?"       <——— Prompt at line 10,
    GET WHO                              column 15
READ                               <——— Get name for search
STORE TRIM(WHO) TO LNAME           <——— Remove trailing blanks
LIST FOR LASTNAME=LNAME            <——— Display the record
```

PURCHASE AMOUNT can be programmed to accept only values between $0.01 and $500.00 (or any range of amounts), and a field for EMPLOYEE NUMBER might accept four-digit numbers only. The acceptable ranges are provided by the user when the data base is created. The user might also be able to provide **default values** so that no entry need be made in a given field most of the time. For example, the user might declare the default for a field called TRANSACTION TYPE to be 1 (for a purchase) unless another number is entered.

Query capability. The search capability of a DBMS is one measure of its performance. A robust DBMS will allow complex queries using AND, OR, and NOT, the so-called *Boolean operators.* To find a marketing representative to send to her firm's Amazon office, a user might ask

LIST FOR DEPT = 'MKT' .AND. SEX = 'M' .AND. STATUS = 'Single'
.AND. (LANG = 'Spanish' .OR. LANG = 'Portuguese')

In addition to these operators, some DBMS packages allow a **substring search**, or a search for the occurrence of a string appearing anywhere within a field. This would be useful in a bibliographic data base to find all entries with a particular word anywhere in the title.

Index and sort. A DBMS will have the ability to sort records on any field, and may be able to sort a file on several fields. Sorting a file on the fields most commonly used for searching will greatly speed the search process. Indexes are another method of speeding up searches; but instead of physically rearranging the records in a file, a separate file is created that contains pointers to the exact location of each record on the disk, as explained in Chapter 9. When the user is searching for a record, the pointer will be read from the index and the program will go directly to the desired record without reading any of the intervening records. As new records are added to a file, the process of sorting or indexing must be repeated. The rewards can be handsome, however. dBASE III Plus will find any record in an indexed file (regardless of the file size) in under two seconds. Reading each record until the desired one is found might take considerably longer. Since most DBMS packages allow either sorting or indexing to speed up searches, the choice of whether to sort or index will be decided by the intended use. If a file is to be processed sequentially (i.e., record 1 first, then record 2, etc.), a sorted file will generally be faster. For random processing (e.g., find JONES, then find ADAMS), indexes will be faster.

Security. A DBMS will allow various kinds of protection for valuable or sensitive data. A field might be declared *read-only,* meaning that the entries may be looked at but not erased or altered (except by privileged users). Fields or records can also be protected from the view of unauthorized personnel, requiring a *password* before access is allowed. In a multiuser data base, **record locking** is an essential feature. With record locking, two or more users can be working in the same data base file but may not simultaneously access the same record. Without record locking, if two clerks were to simultaneously update the account balance of the same customer, the balance would only reflect one of the purchases.

Import and export capability. If information is already in the computer but not in the data base (for example, in a text or spreadsheet file), the DBMS should have the ability to convert it into a data base format. It should also be able to take data base records and store them in a way that is usable by these other programs. This can save the effort of reentering files.

Audit trail. An audit trail is a record of the transactions made with a data base. This is an advanced feature not found on most data base management systems, but it is important in multiuser business environments. When the data in records has been corrupted, an audit listing allows the user to trace backward to the last update and find the error. It will allow the user to correct the mistake without having to rebuild records or files from scratch.

Calculation. A DBMS is not a spreadsheet, and usually cannot perform complicated statistical analysis. It should, however, be able to provide totals and multiple levels of subtotals, either across a row (e.g., total all grades of a student) or by column (e.g., total all sales for a day). Some DBMS packages also have functions that find the minimum or maximum value in a row or column. If a DBMS has a procedural language, the user may be able to program almost any type of calculation.

Reporting. Virtually all DBMS packages have a built-in report generation feature for sending information to a printer or screen in a desired format. Most of these (even in a command-driven DBMS) will provide full-screen editing so the user can customize output formats to fit printed forms, such as invoices or shipping labels.

Capacity. A DBMS should be able to handle large jobs. Some systems, in an effort to achieve speed, limit the file size to whatever will fit in primary storage. The majority of DBMS packages will allow files to be limited only by the size of secondary storage, and some of these can even work with files that span several disks. Other important considerations include the number of fields that are allowed per file, the maximum size of each record, and the number of files that can be open simultaneously.

USING A DATA BASE MANAGEMENT SYSTEM

Data base management systems may seem a bit more complicated than other types of software, but for simple record keeping most programs can be learned in a very short time. It is the more sophisticated record management jobs that take considerable effort and may require some programming ability. Regardless of the complexity of the task or the type of package, using a DBMS will involve the following activities:

Planning the data base

Creating the data base

Focus Feature

AI MEETS DB

The handwriting was on the wall. It was only a matter of time before computers acquired the ability to think like human beings. You've no doubt heard of the computer programs that act as therapists; well, now we have data base management systems that respond to English—real English, not cryptic phrases that only a programmer could love. Perhaps it's not too late to make that career change you've been considering.

Actually, the situation may not be all that serious. One of the directions researchers in artificial intelligence (AI) have been pursuing is **natural language processing.** In natural language processing, the computer attempts to decipher commands that were entered without regard to syntax and structure. One of the first applications for natural language processors was in the user interface for data base management systems.

In 1984, four data base products were introduced that had natural language capability: CLOUT (for Conversational Language Option), a separate query interpreter for R:BASE 4000 from Micro Rim, SAVVY, and SALVO. Each of these programs comes with a basic vocabulary of words that they understand, and each allows the user to add new words to the list. Thus, a banker can define *rich* as meaning a person with an account balance over $1 million, and can ask his computer, "WHO IS RICH?"

Natural language processing can be very seductive, because it can provide an extraordinary amount of power to people with little or no programming aptitude. On the negative side, the processing may take a bit longer than if queries were made in a DBMS command language. To process a natural language query, these systems must break the sentence into words and search

Adding or appending records
Editing existing records
Sorting and indexing files
Searching for particular records
Generating reports

Planning the Data Base

Careful design of data base files and records is critical for proper performance. The amount of planning can affect the speed and ease of record retrieval, and a poorly designed data base may prove itself inadequate as the user's information needs grow. Designing of the data base should be done even before the DBMS is purchased, because it will give the user some picture of the type and capacity of the DBMS required. For complex data base needs, a data base professional or consultant should be contacted. For less ambitious tasks, several commonsense approaches will prove helpful.

One of the best techniques for designing a data base is to create files that mimic the manual office files they will replace. Most offices will, given adequate time, develop filing methods that are suited to their purposes, keeping data together that are logically related to each other and are grouped together to meet particular needs. In the example of Acme Freight Lines in Chapter 9, records of shippers and the locations they serviced were kept in the shipping department, while a list of customers and their addresses were kept elsewhere. This arrangement seems very natural. The shipping department has no need to keep customer addresses, since

through a file for the meaning of each word. When all words have been defined, the definitions are assembled and a small program is prepared with the correct syntax of the query written in the command language of the DBMS. This program is run to locate the appropriate records.

In addition to minor delays, natural language processors can get confused. Care must be taken when words are added to the program's vocabulary, in the same way that we might use certain words differently at different times. A baseball manager asking "WHO'S SLUGGING POORLY" might get the correct list of anyone with a slugging percentage below .100, if "POORLY" was so defined. To ask "WHO'S PITCHING POORLY" might bring up a list of pitchers with an earned run average below .100, certainly not poor in anyone's book. To ask "WHO'S ON FIRST" might create havoc.

Are computers getting smarter (in the human sense)? Perhaps. Then again, perhaps natural language processing is simply more bells and whistles to set one product apart from another. Users should experiment with different DBMS products before deciding if natural language is a must, or if they can wait for computers to display just a bit more intelligence. One reader of a popular computer magazine proclaimed he would believe computers are really intelligent only when he could give one a hundred dollars and tell it to meet him in Omaha.

they are probably given prepared invoices and shipping labels from the customer-order-processing department. The customer-order-processing department probably would rather not concern themselves with selecting shipping lines, either. The point here is that this method of filing, through it may not be perfect, has evolved over a period of time and is probably well suited to the information needs of the firm. The implication for file structures is simply this: use two files, one for shippers and their locations and another for customers and their addresses.

When manual systems are not available for studying, or when they have proved inadequate (hence, the need to use data base methods), the user must try to anticipate all possible uses for the data base, both now and in the future. The following guidelines will help the user in designing files:

1. Make a list of all the fields possibly needed for a particular application, such as preparing an invoice. Concentrate only on the invoicing task and do not try to design a data base for all company needs. To prepare an invoice, the user might want the customer's NAME and STREET address, CITY, STATE, ZIP, and the DATE. For each item purchased, the file must contain the ITEM number, the QUANTITY of purchase, the PRICE per item, SHIPPING and handling charges, and the TOTAL invoice amount. While making your list, record the data type (will it contain letters, dollar amounts, ordinary numbers?) and the *maximum* size of an entry in each field (plan for the largest case). Figure 10–8 illustrates how to do this.
2. Try to envision a transaction using these fields. Which items would be entered at each stage of the transaction? Group them accordingly. For example, normal procedures might go as follows: if an existing customer places an order, the clerk would write down the customer's name, the date, the item numbers, and

Field name →	NAME	STREET	CITY	STATE	ZIP	DATE
Data type →	char	char	char	char	num	system*
Field size →	25	25	20	2	9	6

Field name →	ITEM	QUANTITY	PRICE	SHIPPING	TOTAL
Data type →	num	num	dollar	calc**	calc
Field size →	4	6	10	6	11

***system** indicates that the user will not have to input a value; the computer will supply it.

****calc** fields will be derived from other values, e.g., TOTAL = QUANTITY × PRICE + SHIPPING. No space need be reserved for this field type.

FIGURE 10–8
Worksheet for Fields

quantities. Then the clerk would consult a customer file to get the customer's shipping address, and would consult a price-and-item file for the item price. This would suggest the data groupings in Figure 10–9.

3. If step 2 does not produce acceptable results, there is a more formal method of grouping fields into files. Determine which fields could possibly be used to uniquely identify other fields and rearrange the list so that the **determinant field** is grouped with those that it identifies. For any given NAME, for instance, there will be only one associated STREET, CITY, STATE, and ZIP. NAME is the determinant, therefore, of the other fields. It is easy to see that the converse is not true; for example, that STATE does not determine NAME, because many names may be associated with a given STATE. Sometimes two or more fields will combine to determine another field. For example, neither NAME, DATE, nor ITEM can determine quantity (several quantities can exist for the same customer, and an item might be bought by various customers in different quantities). Together, however, NAME, DATE, and ITEM are associated with only one value for QUANTITY. When identifying determinants, draw arrows from the determinants to the fields they identify, as in Figure 10–10.

   Note what happened when we grouped the fields by determinants. We found that for any ZIP, there is a unique CITY and STATE. This is a candidate for an alternative arrangement to that in Figure 10–9.

4. The next step is to look at transitive dependencies. A **transitive dependency** occurs when one field determines another, which in turn determines a third, all within the same file. The NAME field, for example, determines the ZIP field, which in turn can be used to determine the STATE and CITY fields. When

```
Group 1 – the transaction file
          NAME, DATE, ITEM, QUANTITY
Group 2 – the customer file
          NAME, STREET, CITY, STATE, ZIP
Group 3 – the item file
          ITEM, PRICE
```

FIGURE 10–9
Logical Groupings

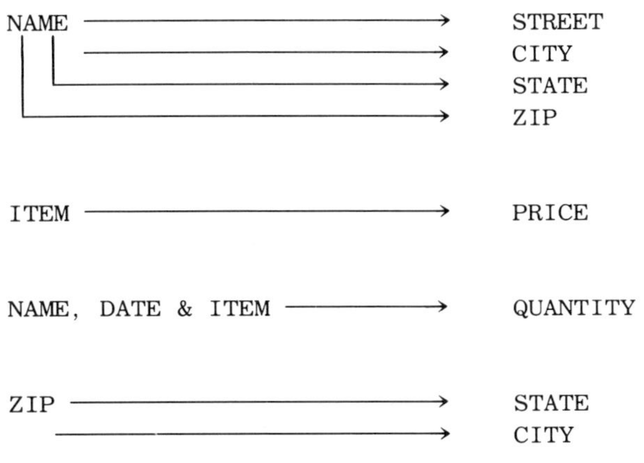

FIGURE 10–10
Fields Grouped by Determinants

FILE NAME	FIELDS
CUSTOMER	NAME, STREET, ZIP
TOWN	ZIP, CITY, STATE
ITEM	ITEM, PRICE
PURCHASE	NAME, DATE, ITEM, QUANTITY

FIGURE 10–11
Files without Transitive Dependency

transitive dependencies occur, it is considered best to break up a grouping of fields until no transitive dependencies result. The final groups are shown in Figure 10–11. Note that once a file is created containing ZIP, CITY, and STATE, we can eliminate CITY and STATE from the customer file. Retaining ZIP in the customer file allows us to associate the CUSTOMER file with the TOWN file, without either file having transitive dependencies within the file itself.

The user may not agree that separating ZIP, CITY, and STATE into their own file is the arrangement of files that will work best. If not, the three-file arrangement from Figure 10–9 may work just as well. However, the four-file arrangement has certain desirable properties. For one thing, it reduces the amount of entry required to create a new customer record. It may simplify the calculation of shipping charges, since most common carriers base their rate tables upon the ZIP code. The four-file arrangement generally requires less secondary storage. Last, but not least, it can be shown that the four-file arrangement will produce fewer problems as new records are added or old ones are deleted or updated (the proof for this, which is beyond the scope of this text, can be found in any thorough college-level data base textbook, under "normalization"). The four-file arrangement also follows some worthwhile advice for designing data bases: always make each file as simple (as few fields) as is practical.

Creating the Data Base

Once the user has determined the contents of each file, using the DBMS to create them is quite easy. The user selects or types in the option that says something like "Define data base" or "Create files." The user will be asked for the file name and the names of the fields and their size and data type. The user may also be asked for minimum, maximum, and default values for each field, and to indicate which fields will be indexed. Some DBMS packages will question the user about which other files may be connected to the current one, and whether any fields will require math, such as totaling.

A DBMS may allow the user to declare **aliases**, or alternative names for fields. This is a convenience feature. It allows the user to access a field by more than one name. When using aliases, caution should be taken to ensure that several fields do not share the same name or alias. Aliases are specified at the time the file is created, and some systems will let the user declare temporary aliases after the files have been created. If the user has given the same name to fields in two different files and these fields contain different types of information, declaring a temporary alias for one of the fields may be necessary before the two files can be used together.

If the DBMS is form-oriented, the process is slightly different. After providing the name for a file, the user will be presented with a mostly blank screen for designing forms. Forms are created by moving the cursor to a screen location of the user's choice, then entering a field name, as suggested in Chapter 9. After all fields are entered (users may also write text prompts or messages anywhere they choose), the DBMS will ask the user about each field until it has all of the information it requires (data type, size, minimum, maximum, etc.) for each field. This screen will be used for all data entry in the file and may also be used for retrieval of records from secondary storage. An illustration of one DBMS's screen painter capability appears in Figure 10–6. An illustration of how a menu-driven interface has been used in a DBMS to create files, add or edit data, and create reports appears in Figure 10–12.

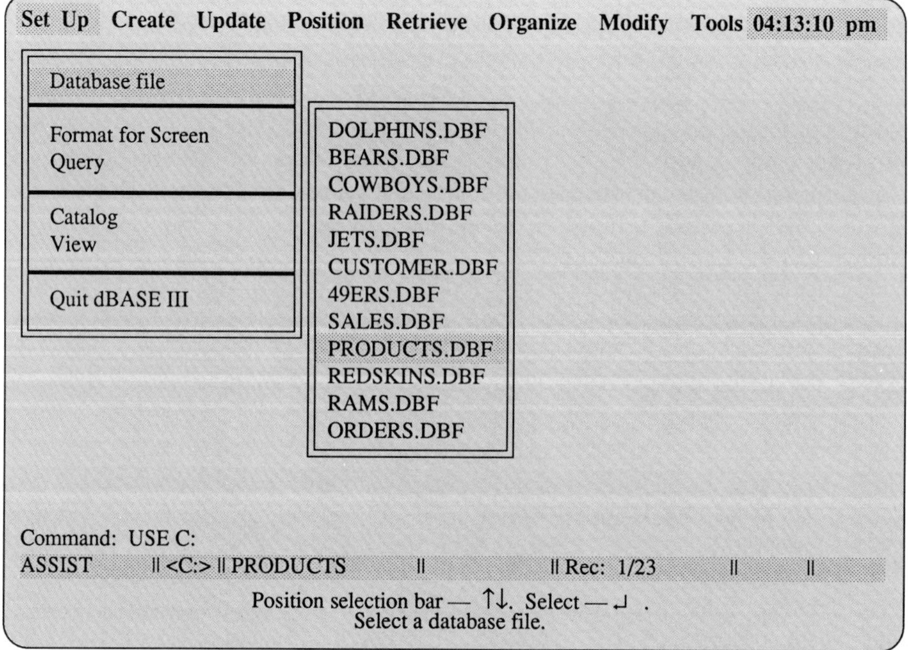

FIGURE 10–12

The Assistant in dBASE III Plus Features Pull-Down Menus. Users can accomplish day-to-day data management tasks; such as creating files, adding or editing data; without programming.

Adding or Appending Records

By entering APPEND or selecting the ADD RECORDS (or similar) option, you may enter new records into an existing data base. The DBMS will clear the screen before each new record is entered, and may present the user with the names of each field as a prompt for input. After the data has been entered in a field, pressing <Return> will usually get the user to the next field. When the last field of a record has been entered, pressing <Return> once more (or a specially designated key) will store the new record at the end of the file. The file will then be resorted or reindexed with the new entries. An illustration of how a record might be added is provided in the dBASE III Tutorial (Figure 10–17).

Editing Existing Records

If information was entered incorrectly, or if a value (such as a customer's balance due) changes over time, the user will need to alter existing records. Most DBMS packages provide a command or menu option to accomplish this. Upon invoking the command, the user may be prompted for a filename if it is not already apparent what file should be used. After entering information that enables the system to search for and retrieve the correct record to update, the system will display the record. The user can then move the cursor directly to the incorrect field and type in the correct value. Pressing <Return> twice will cause the updated record to be saved—literally written over the old record.

A powerful DBMS can perform updates on multiple records. To give all employees a 5% raise, the user might merely say

```
UPDATE EMPLOYEES
SALARY=SALARY * 1.05
```

Sorting and Indexing Files

After records have been entered, the data base files should be either sorted or indexed to improve system performance. As with the other procedures, sorting and indexing is done with a simple menu selection or command. The DBMS will ask which field is to be sorted and whether the sort will be in ascending or descending order. A new file will be created with the sorted information, so the user must ensure that sufficient space remains on the disk. Most systems will allow multilevel sorts. Our PURCHASE file (see Figure 10–11 above) could be sorted by NAME, by DATE within NAME, and by ITEM within DATE, as in Figure 10–13.

Searching for Particular Records

Data base management systems vary considerably in the ease and flexibility of their search facilities. In the least powerful programs, users are limited to finding records based upon a single indexed field. If the user's NAME field is indexed, he can search for "Jones" by selecting the search option and specifying the field and search value. Once the program has found the first record for Jones, it may present all records with Jones for NAME, or allow the user to see additional records by

FIGURE 10–13
A Multilevel Sort

NAME	DATE	ITEM	QUANTITY
ADAMS, BOB	10/04/88	3142	100
ADAMS, BOB	10/04/88	4127	5
ADAMS, BOB	10/07/88	3649	1000
ADAMS, BOB	10/08/88	1721	1
BARRETT, JIM	09/29/88	4141	200
.	.	.	.
.	.	.	.
.	.	.	.
ZOWALSKI, STAN	09/30/88	3943	50

pressing <Return> (most form-oriented DBMS packages display one record at a time).

Command-driven data base management systems will provide greater search flexibility at the expense of users having to learn the command language syntax. The style of the query will be different from package to package. If a user was to search a file called PERSONNEL to find names of employees in the marketing department earning over $30,000, she might use a query such as

```
SELECT PERSONNEL.NAME
FOR PERSONNEL.SALARY>30000
        AND PERSONNEL.DEPT=MKT                    (KnowledgeMan)
```

or

```
LIST FOR SALARY>30000 .AND. DEPT='MKT'            (dBASE III Plus)
```

or

```
SHOW MARKETING EMPLOYEES EARNING MORE THAN 30000   (Clout)
```

The names of the DBMS products used in the queries above are shown in the parentheses at the right. Some DBMS products enable complex queries to be built using pull-down menus. These queries may then be stored for later use. An example of this appears in Figure 10–14.

Generating Reports

Generating a report involves designing the appearance of the report, then specifying which records will be printed using the report. The first step, designing the report, is very similar to designing input forms in a form-oriented DBMS. The report may then be used by naming the file and designating which records are to be selected for printing. The report generator is of limited value for searching for records, but is a workhorse in a business environment. Many retailers use a report

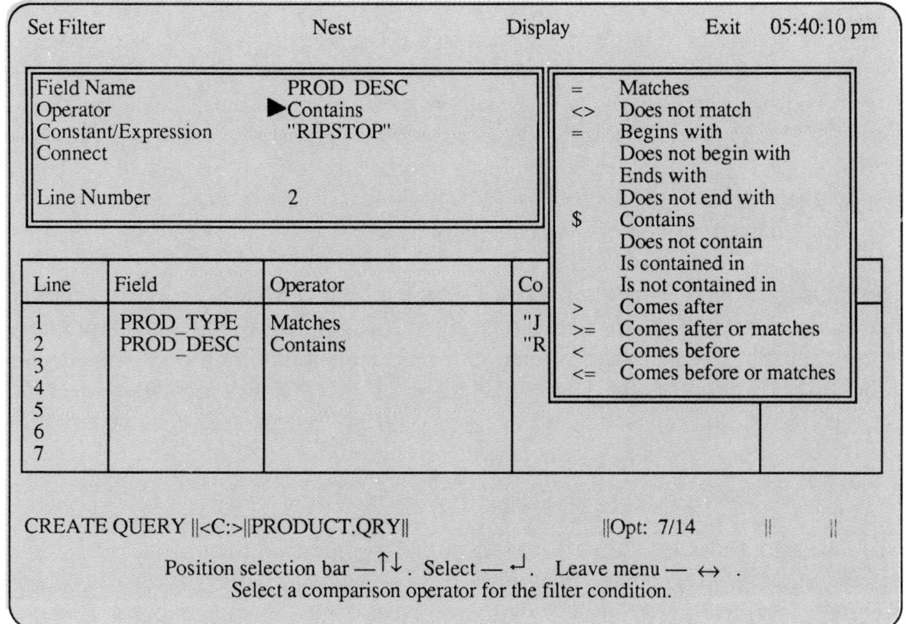

FIGURE 10–14

Ashton-Tate's dBASE III Plus Enables Users, Via the "Advanced Query System," to Create Complex Query Requests Through Simple Pull-down Menu Options.

form to print out a customer's receipt when a purchase is made, and reports may be customized to fit any printed form. Virtually all DBMS packages will provide prompts to help users through the report generation. They will prompt the user for the file(s) the report is to be printed from, the fields to be printed, the selection key, and so forth.

HARDWARE AND SOFTWARE REQUIREMENTS FOR DATA BASE MANAGEMENT SYSTEMS

Relational DBMS (RDBMS) programs can require 256K bytes of RAM, a 16-bit microprocessor, and a hard-disk drive. If one RDBMS needs only 128K bytes and another requires 256K, it does not necessarily mean that the program requiring more memory has more features. A DBMS that can work with multiple files will often set aside a portion of RAM for each file, to use as a buffer or work area. Programs that allow many files to be used simultaneously and want the speed gained from working mostly in RAM instead of on a disk will require a great deal of memory. Some of the largest DBMS packages have their own operating system and programming languages, occupying even more primary storage, if all the facilities of the DBMS reside in primary storage concurrently.

The speed and flexibility of these large programs is often equalled or surpassed by smaller DBMS packages that are efficiently written. Of greater concern to users should be the disk storage capability of their computer. Data base files can become extremely large in a business environment, and a hard disk is essential for business data base use, regardless of the DBMS's advertised requirements.

Data base management systems can save disk space by using a **variable record length.** If a name field has been created to hold names up to 30 characters long, a variable record length system would use only eight bytes to store "Ed Jones." A **fixed record length** system will use all 30 bytes, even though 22 will be blank. Variable record length systems sacrifice speed to gain disk space and may not perform acceptably with large files. For personal applications, users will need two floppy disk drives that store at least 360K bytes each.

Data base management systems need to be able to place data on the screen in any location and must be precisely configured to the video output of the user's particular computer. For this reason, a program that runs well on one computer may not run at all on another, even though both computers use the same operating system (recall the discussion in Chapter 4 on compatibility issues). An installation program provided with the DBMS may allow users to configure a DBMS package for their computer, but potential buyers are still advised to steer clear of any program that is not advertised for their specific computer configuration.

Summary

A data base is logically related data that is organized to serve several applications. A data base management system is the software that controls the entry, storage, and retrieval of the information in a data base.

Data base management systems provide security, data independence, data integrity, and flexibility that exceed conventional file management systems. Most important, they allow data from different files to be connected in many new ways, giving powerful data handling capability to nonprogrammers.

Data management programs for microcomputers generally come in two types: file managers (Chapter 9), capable of handling single-file operations, and relational data base management systems. Relational systems can work with several files simultaneously and often have their own language for customizing the system and dealing with complex tasks.

A DBMS may be used through menus, on-screen forms, or a command language. Each of these programs can perform suitably for small data needs, but complex tasks are best handled by a command-driven DBMS.

Important features of a DBMS include: input validation, query capability, import and export capability, indexing and sorting, calculations, and a report generator.

Seven operations are involved in the use of a DBMS: planning the data base, creating the files, adding records, editing records, sorting or indexing files, searching for records, and generating reports. Of all these activities, the planning stage is the most important and should be completed before any of the other operations are begun. Planning is so important, in fact, that prospective buyers are advised to plan their data bases before selecting packages, because the planning process will make them aware of which features will be necessary. Record lengths, file sizes, and the number of files that must be open and available at one time are all specific through planning. These parameters will have a significant impact upon the choice of a DBMS.

A DBMS often requires large amounts of primary memory (RAM), especially if it allows simultaneous use of many files and has a procedural language. More important is disk capacity. A data base for personal use may fit onto floppy disks, but most business applications will require a hard disk.

A concise tutorial on the use of dBASE III Plus is provided at the end of this chapter. dBASE III Plus is a popular DBMS program for use in microcomputers—hence, its choice as the vehicle of demonstration.

Key Terms

alias
command-driven
data base
data base management system
data independence
data integrity
data redundancy
data security
default value
determinant field
fixed record length
flexibility
form-oriented
join
menu-driven
natural language processing
procedural language
project
query language
range checking
record locking
relational algebra
relational data base management system
select
substring search
table construction operations
transitive dependency
variable record length

Self-Test

1. What is a DBMS, and how does it differ from a file management system?
2. Explain how DBMSs are used.
3. How does one plan and create a data base?
4. How does one maintain and use a data base?
5. What are the relational operations, and how does one use them?
6. How does one add, append, delete, sort, index, and search records in a DBMS?
7. Describe how DBMS software and applications got their start.
8. Describe to what uses DBMS software is generally put.
9. Describe what features one can generally expect in DBMS software.
10. Describe what steps are generally involved in using a DBMS.
11. Describe what hardware and software are required for use of DBMSs.

Exercises

1. List and explain the major differences between a file manager and a relational data base management system.
2. How might a data base management system's security features be used in a single-user environment?
3. List some of the major differences between mainframe and microcomputer-based data base management systems.
4. How does a user specify the search field in a form-oriented DBMS? What might be some of the advantages or disadvantages of this method?
5. Design the structure of a data base that an instructor might use to keep the records of a class. There are 30 students, who will receive eight grades each during the course of a semester. Show the data types and field sizes. How many files will be involved? If a Social Security Number field is included, should it be character or numeric?
6. Design an appropriate data base structure for the relationship of vendors to each item in the item file. Included with each item (in addition to ITEM and PRICE) are CURRENT INVENTORY, VENDOR1, VENDOR2, VENDOR3. Each item may be supplied by up to three vendors. Pertinent information associated with each vendor would include VENDOR NUMBER, VNAME, STREET ADDRESS, CITY, STATE, and ZIP CODE. Organize this

information to take advantage of the existing file structure depicted in Figure 10–11. In addition, management wants to retain pertinent information relating to purchase orders that are sent out; specifically, the following information would be sufficient to specify a purchase order: VNAME, VDATE, VITEM, VQUANTITY. Determine what files are required, and what fields within each file are essential.

7. In exercise 6 above, suppose that there are 10,000 inventory items and that the required field lengths for each item are as follows:

NAME	*length in bytes*
ITEM	10
PRICE	10
CURRENTINV	5
VENDOR1	8
VENDOR2	8
VENDOR3	8

   How much storage capacity is required to accommodate the ITEM file? Hint: determine the record size and multiply that by the number of records.

8. Rich Lifestyle is inventorying all personal property. Occasionally, he will "trade up" a piece of furniture and the vendor will bring out a new sofa, bed, or whatever in exchange for the old one (and some cash).

   When draperies are worn and carpets are soiled, Rich wishes to replace with the same decor. His proposed system will enable him to track down the vendor so that worn-out items may be replaced with new fabric, carpet, or whatever, in exactly the same pattern.

   Rich is also interested in maintaining repair and service records on each item of personal property. For each item, he wishes to retain the date of last service or repair, the nature of the repair or service, and the repair or service agency that did the work.

   The following fields are identified (numbers in parentheses are field lengths) for each item of personal property Rich wishes to record: number (4), name (25), date of purchase (6), vendor name (25), vendor street address (20), vendor city (20), vendor state (2), vendor ZIP (9), vendor phone (10), date of last service (repair) (8), nature of repair (20), service agency name (20), agency street address (20), agency city (20), agency state (2), agency ZIP (9), agency phone (10).

   Design a data base that is free of transitive dependencies. Group fields into files by use of logical groupings and determinants. For each file, show which field is the determinant field.

9. For exercise eight above, size the data base you designed if the number of items of furniture is 100 or less, the number of vendors is 50 or less, the number of agencies is 50 or less, and the number of repair or service records is estimated at 100 or less. How many different ZIP codes (maximum) would you expect? Why?

10. John Long is a direct marketing representative for several precious metal and gem wholesalers. He sells investment-grade metals and gems to clients located throughout the Southwest. He has nearly 1,000 investor clients that he works with and he deals directly with 200 different wholesalers. He vends 500 different investment products. He inventories nothing and serves only as a broker who finds the best buy for his clients and completes the sale. Design a data base appropriate for John's business. How large would you expect this data base to be? Assume all city, name, street, and description fields are 25 characters long. Assume the record for each product has a quality field 25 characters in length, a price field 10 characters in length, and a vendor number field 3 characters in length, in addition to a name field and description field. Not more than 300 zip codes are expected.

References

1. Data Base Task Group of CODASYL Programming Language Committee. *Report.* Association for Computing Machinery, April 1971.

2. Codd, E. F. "A Relational Model of Data for Large Shared Data Banks." *Communications of the ACM* 13, no. 6 (June 1970).

Additional Reading

Brooner, E. G. *Microcomputer Data-Base Management.* Indianapolis: Howard W. Sams & Co., 1982.

Byers, Robert A. *Everyman's Primer, Featuring dBASE II.* Reston, Va.: Reston Publishing, 1983.

Castro, Luis; Jay Hanson; and Tom Rettig. *Advanced Programmer's Guide Featuring dBASE III and dBASE II.* Culver City, Calif.: Ashton-Tate, 1985.

Date, C. J. *An Introduction to Database Systems.* Reading, Mass.: Addison-Wesley, 1982.

Date, C. J. *Database: A Primer.* Reading, Mass.: Addison-Wesley, 1983.

Freiling, Michael J. *Understanding Data Base Management.* Sherman Oaks, Calif.: Alfred Publishing, 1982.

Kroenke, David. *Database Processing.* 2nd Ed. Chicago: Science Research Associates, 1983.

Kruglinski, David. *Data Base Management Systems: A Guide to Microcomputer Software.* Berkeley, Calif.: Osborne/McGraw-Hill, 1983.

Martin, James. *Principles of Data-Base Management.* Englewood Cliffs, N.J.: Prentice-Hall, 1976.

Martin, James. *An End-User's Guide to Data Base.* Englewood Cliffs, N.J.: Prentice-Hall, 1981.

Martin, James. *Managing the Data Base Environment.* Englewood Cliffs, N.J.: Prentice-Hall, 1983.

Publications

The following popular computer magazines will frequently have general articles on data base concepts and use, as well as reviews of current product offerings.

Byte
InfoWor'd
PC
PC World
MAC World

TUTORIAL

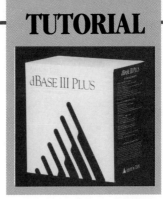

dBASE III and dBASE III Plus

In this tutorial, we will use dBASE III to create a simple bibliographic data base file, following the outline for use of a DBMS that was discussed earlier in the chapter. We will append records to it, edit some of those records, and sort and index the data base. We will not generate a report in the tutorial; students are encouraged to explore this, and other, commands that are beyond the scope of our brief tutorial. We will also look at some of the options available for searching through the data base.

To complete this exercise, you will need to place a copy of dBASE in disk drive A (the top or left drive on the computer) and a blank, formatted disk (or one with at least 20,000 bytes free) in disk drive B. Prompts or messages displayed by dBASE will be shown in computer print. Your response is shown in bold text. The <Control> key (to the left of the letter *A*) will be indicated by <**ctrl**> and the <Return> key will be shown as <**CR**>. The function keys for an IBM PC or compatible computer are shown as <**f1**>, <**f2**>, etc.

PLANNING THE DATA BASE

Planning a bibliography file is not terribly complex. Let's see, there needs to be a field for author, title, journal or publisher, place of publication (for books), publication date, page number, volume, and number. All we need to figure out is how big to make the fields. But wait—what about books with three or four authors? What happens when the article is one of a collection in a book of readings? What about editors? What do we do about the fields that will go unused (such as an editor field when we are dealing with a book that doesn't have one)?

Even with a simple data base, planning is important. One approach to our problem is to determine what types of reports will be generated from our data base, and what types of searches will be conducted for the information it contains. To be truly useful, our bibliographic data base should be able to generate reports that can be used by a word processor with minimal editing. It should also be able to accommodate the worst-case entry. Since dBASE III Plus will truncate information when we attempt to put more in a field than it was designed for, it would be a shame to enter a hundred references before we find an entry that will not fit. The logical approach would be to start searching through bibliographies. Find the longest title listed, the longest author name, the longest place of publication, etc.

The number of author fields is difficult to gauge. Academic journals will occasionally list five authors, but if we were to include five fields, we would have to search all five to find an article by Jones. This could prove cumbersome. Since dBASE III Plus uses fixed record lengths, there would be blanks in an output file for any unused author fields. These would have to be removed, either by a command program in dBASE III Plus or through editing with our word processor. Also, a lot of disk space will be used by the empty fields. The solution to this problem is to create a single, large author field. This will save us a great deal of space, because the likelihood of having five authors who all have long names is pretty remote.

Below in Table 10–1 is one structure for our bibliographic records that might accommodate almost any type of reference entry. The names for the fields must be ten characters or less in dBASE III Plus.

A few explanations are in order. The TITLE and JOURNAL fields are set to 120 bytes (academic journals, especially if they are proceedings of a conference, can easily take up three lines). The NOTES field, where we will make comments and annotations, can be up to 4,000 bytes long when using the dBASE III editor, or 512 kilobytes if a word processor is used for entering data. The NOTES field occupies 10 bytes because dBASE III Plus stores

TABLE 10–1

Field Definitions for Bibliographic Data Base

Field Name	Data Type	Field Size	Comment
AUTHOR	Character	60	This should work
TITLE	Character	120	For three-line titles
JOURNAL	Character	120	Conference proceedings
PUBLISHER	Character	30	For associations
EDITOR	Character	30	
DATE	Character	18	To write it out
VOLUME	Character	2	
NUMBER	Character	2	
PAGE	Character	9	Start and finish (1101–1023)
PLACE	Character	25	
CATALOG	Character	20	To find in the library
NOTES	Memo	10	

(*Continued*)

dBASE III and dBASE III Plus (Continued)

memo fields separately. Including the library's catalog number can prove useful when you need to find a book at another time. None of the fields will need to be numeric or date fields, because these declarations will restrict the type of entry we can make.

CREATING THE DATA BASE

Once the disks are in the correct drives, you are ready to begin. When you have booted up the system and are at the operating system level (the A> prompt), enter

dbase<**CR**>

Start with SYSTEM DISK #1 in drive A. Once you've entered **dbase**<**CR**>, you will see the red in-use light come on. Then dBASE will prompt you to remove SYSTEM DISK #1 and insert SYSTEM DISK #2 in the A drive and to press <Enter> after having done so. dBASE III will respond with a full screen of copyright information. Down in the lower left corner of the screen is a dot, or period. This is the dBASE prompt, letting you know that dBASE III Plus is awaiting your command. If you were an experienced user of dBASE III Plus, you might perform your data base functions entirely in the command language (as you had to do in dBASE II), without menus to aid your selection. Fortunately, dBASE III Plus has another mode of operation, and it is accessed by entering **ASSIST** <**CR**> (or depressing the function key <**f2**>). This will bring up the dBASE III Plus ASSISTANT to guide you through your work. The left and right arrow keys will move you between menu selections. The <Home> key on the PC keyboard will bring you back to the SET UP menu when you are deep inside the menu system. The display will appear as shown in Figure 10–15.

Before we create our data base, we are going to take a look around. At the top of the screen, you will find a list of the other menus available. At the

TABLE 10–2

User Entries Required to Create a File Using the dBASE ASSISTANT

Enter	Action
<right>	Brings the CREATE menu into use, placing the CREATE menu on screen
<CR>	Registers our selection

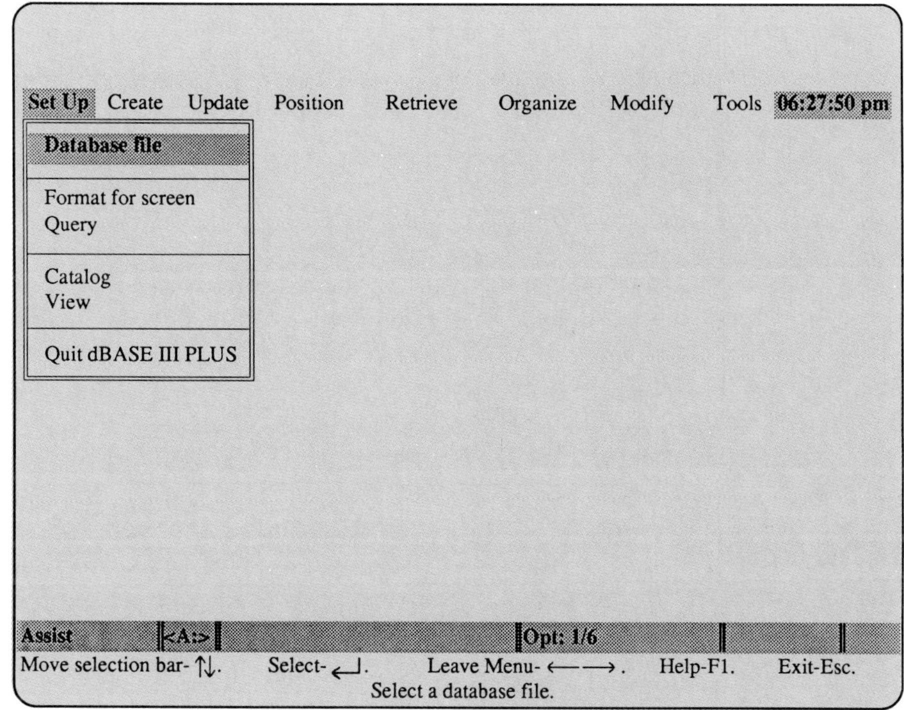

FIGURE 10–15

Opening Display of dBASE III Plus in Assistant

left side of the top line the words SET UP are highlighted with inverse video. Directly below this first line will be a pull-down menu for SET UP.

For the present, let's create our bibliographic data base by selecting CREATE and DATABASE FILE.

At this point, it is worth noting that if we had entered **CREATE<CR>** at the opening dot command, we would be in exactly the same place we are now. The dBASE III Plus ASSISTANT is an extremely helpful aid for the inexperienced dBASE user, but it is awkward and too slow for the average user, since it takes nearly two seconds for some pop-up menus to appear. Although you can move directly to the selection you want without waiting for help to arrive, you will also find that the major commands can be learned without too much effort, eliminating the need for the ASSISTANT after only a few sessions. For this tutorial, we will try commands both with and without the ASSISTANT. When in the assistant mode, our menu selections will be displayed on a command line at the bottom of the screen. This line will show us

(*Continued*)

dBASE III and dBASE III Plus (Continued)

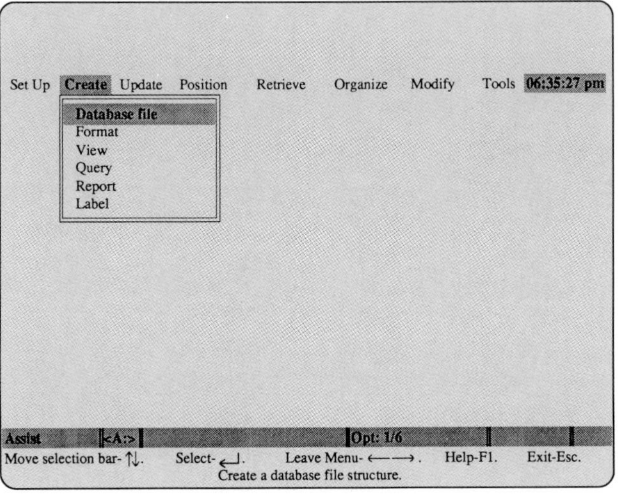

FIGURE 10–16a
The dBASE III Plus Display After Highlighting CREATE

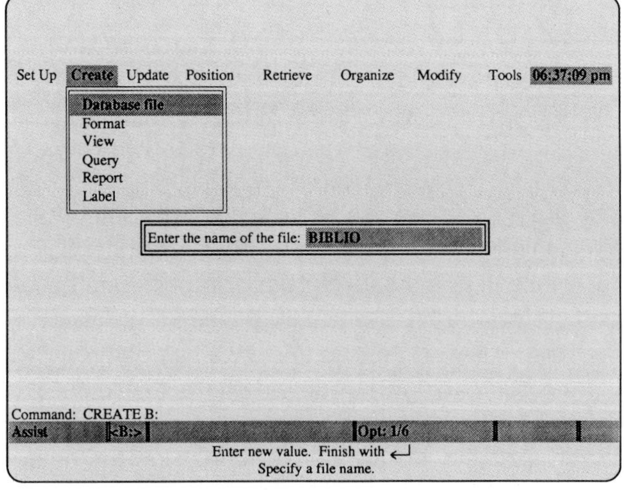

FIGURE 10–16b
The dBASE III Plus Display After Selecting CREATE By Pressing <Return> and Specifying Drive B: Again By Pressing <Return>

the syntax of the commands we are using, as if they were entered at a dot prompt without the ASSISTANT.

After CREATE has been selected, dBASE III Plus will ask for the drive and the name of the new file to create. Select **B:** and enter **BIBLIO**. The screen will now appear as shown in Figure 10–16c.

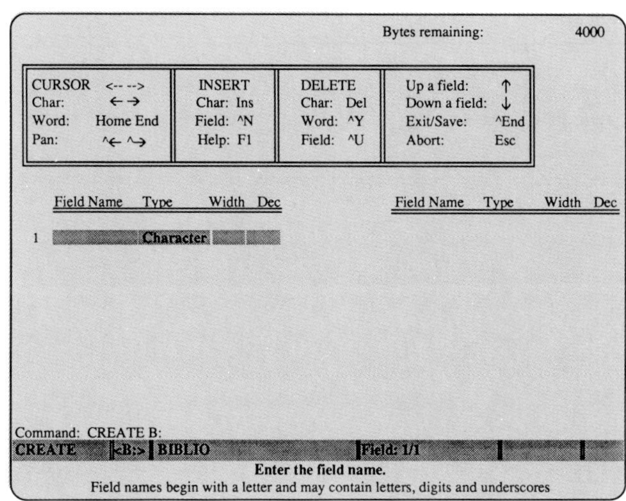

FIGURE 10–16c

The DBASE III Plus After Entering BIBLIO and Pressing <Return>

You are ready to enter the names, data types, and field sizes for your file. Refer to the list we made earlier. If you make a mistake in entry, refer to the top of the screen for information about how to move to the error and correct it. Each time you enter a new field, press <**CR**> and the cursor will automatically move you to the next entry point. At the top right of the screen, you will see the number of bytes remaining in a record (the total of those already entered is subtracted from the maximum record length) and the number of fields that have been defined. When all fields have been defined (field name, type, and width) and you are moved to a new line, press <**CR**> to terminate the create process.

ADDING RECORDS

dBASE III Plus should be asking you if you want to add records at this time. Enter **Y** to proceed. You are now in the append mode, and the screen will appear as shown in Figure 10–17.

The cursor is at the first field of our record. The record number is displayed at the bottom of the screen. APPEND is one of dBASE III Plus's full-screen editing modes, so we have the freedom to move around and correct our entries before they are stored in our data base file. For now, try entering

(*Continued*)

dBASE III and dBASE III Plus (Continued)

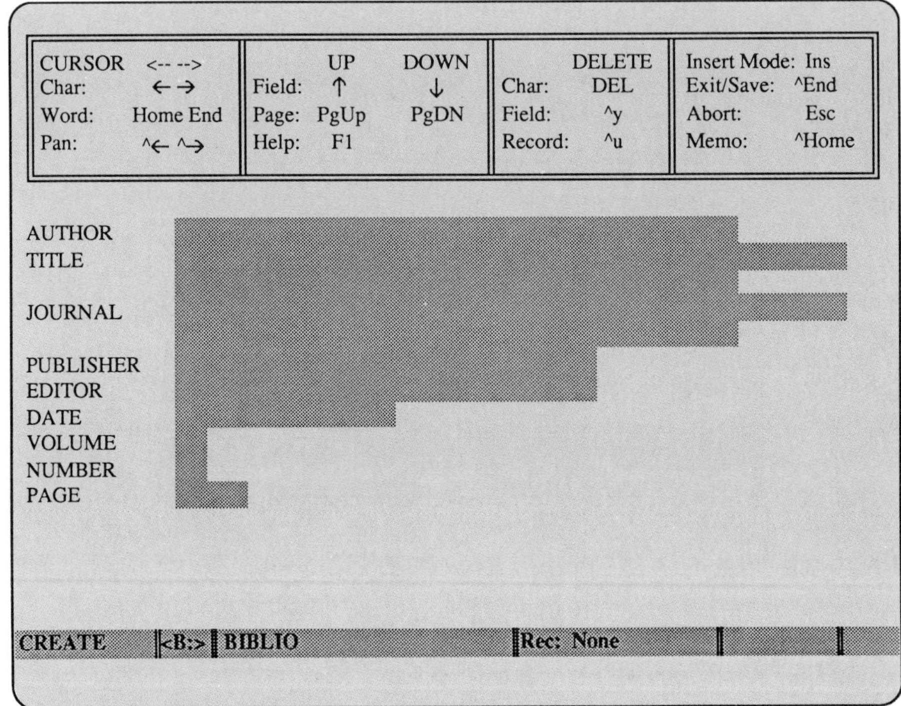

FIGURE 10–17

The APPEND Screen. The display is used to add (APPEND) records. The fields are shaded.

the record listed below. Remember to press <**CR**> at the end of each field entry. Don't worry about underlining or quotation marks, because we do not want these in our data base (we can add them later if we copy information into text files).

Naisbitt, John, *Megatrends,* Warner, New York, 1982.

Were you able to determine where everything went, and how to get past fields where no entry was made? When you got to the last field (NOTES) and pressed <CR>, the screen cleared and put you in the AUTHOR field of record number 2. Press <**CR**> to stop entering records. Voila, you are back at the main menu of the ASSISTANT.

For the present and subsequent sessions, you must USE a data base file (open it) before any further actions can be taken. Press <**CR**> at the SET UP option, then again when the cursor is over B:. The file we created, BIB-

LIO, will be highlighted. Press <CR>, then **N** when asked if indexed. Notice that we are entering our file name in the lower left area of the screen. This is dBASE III Plus's command line. It already has entered the word USE for us. Before moving on to enter more records, browse through some of the main menu options. Pressing <**f1**> calls in the help facility, and you are encouraged to become familiar with it, as well.

When you are ready to enter the remainder of the records, move the cursor to UPDATE on the top line. Press <**CR**> to select APPEND. You are now back to the record entry form, at record number 2. Enter the following records:

Le Carre, John, *The Little Drummer Girl,* Alfred A. Knopf, New York, 1983.

AAAS-NASA Symposium on the Physics of Solar Flares, *Proceedings of a Symposium Held at the Goddard Space Flight Center, Alamogordo, New Mexico, October 28–30, 1963,* ed. Wilmot N. Hess, Government Printing Office, Washington, 1964.

The Republic of Plato, ed. James Adam, Cambridge University Press, London, 1909.

National Society for the Study of Education, *Social Deviancy Among Youth,* Sixty-fifth Yearbook, Part I, University of Chicago Press, Chicago, 1966.

Conover, W. J., *Practical Nonparametric Statistics, 2nd Edition,* John Wiley & Sons, New York, 1980.

McWilliams, Peter A., *The Personal Computer Book,* Prelude Press, Los Angeles, 1982.

EDITING EXISTING RECORDS

Editing records can be accomplished in several ways within ASSIST. Briefly, they are as follows:

Use LOCATE to find the record, then enter EDIT. The LOCATE command is found under POSITION, while the EDIT command is under UPDATE.

Use UPDATE, then EDIT, then press the <PgUp> key or <PgDn> key until the record we want is found.

(*Continued*)

dBASE III and dBASE III Plus (Continued)

Use the REPLACE command (under UPDATE) to change the contents of a single field on a single record.

Select BROWSE under UPDATE to bring several records on the screen, then use the arrow keys to move to the field we will change.

These options do not exhaust the possible methods of changing the contents of a field. They are presented here to show a few things about the way dBASE III Plus operates. The first choice employs dBASE III Plus's record pointer. dBASE III Plus is always pointing to a current record, either the first one in the file or the last one accessed. If you enter EDIT, the edit operation is performed on the current record. The LOCATE command is used to position the record pointer to the record of interest, so that it may be viewed or edited. The second method shows that dBASE III Plus allows you to move backward or forward through a file while in the EDIT mode. The third method, REPLACE, can be used to change the contents of a record without having to move the pointer to it first. REPLACE is a very powerful command that can be used to change the contents of the same field in all records of a file, or just in selected records. These three methods can be complex in their use, so we leave it up to you to experiment with them. Through the ASSISTANT, you should be able to find your way through the maze of commands. As you select options, pay attention to the command line on the bottom of the screen, because it will show the commands that can be employed outside of the dBASE III Plus ASSISTANT.

At this time, move the cursor to UPDATE, and select BROWSE (<**down**><**down**><**down**><**CR**>). Your screen should appear as shown in Figure 10–18.

Experiment with moving around the screen in the browse mode, including using <**ctrl**><**right**> and <**ctrl**><**left**> to pan across the screen. Use the cursor arrow keys to move to the TITLE field in record 3, the AAAS-NASA publication. We will change the location in the JOURNAL field from Alamogordo, New Mexico to Greenbelt, Maryland. The easiest way to do this is to use the <**right**> arrow key until you are at the *A* in Alamogordo. Press <**Del**> until the city and state are eradicated, then press <**INS**> and enter **Greenbelt, Maryland.**

The remainder of this tutorial will be conducted without the ASSISTANT. Before we proceed, let's save the change we've just made. Press <**ctrl**><**End**>. Now to leave the ASSISTANT, press <**ESC**>. We have our dot back.

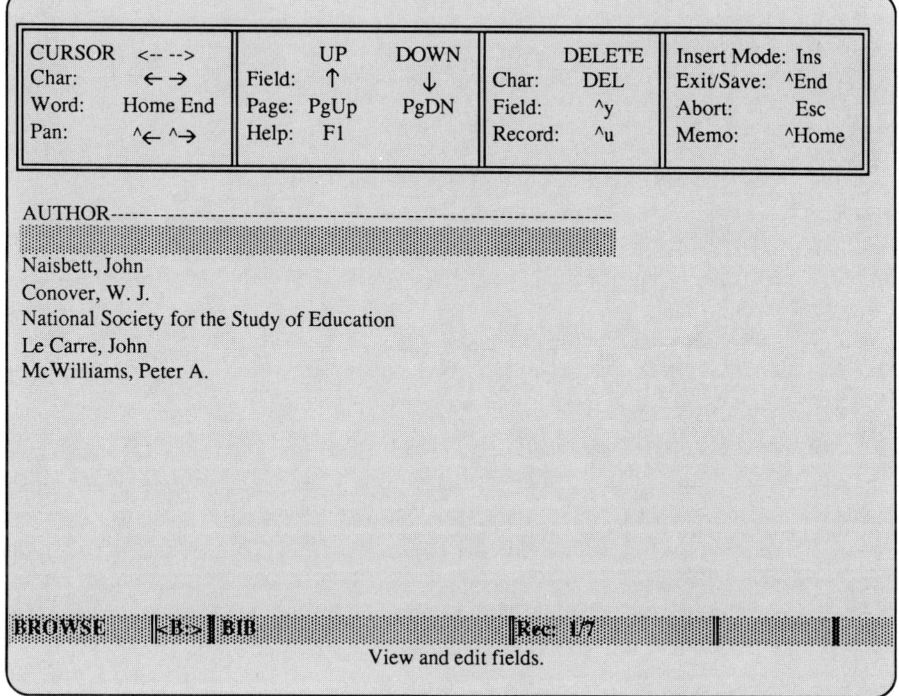

FIGURE 10–18
The BROWSE Screen

SORTING AND INDEXING THE FILE

dBASE III sorts a file by creating an external file to store the sorted output. Since a new file is created, you must ensure that enough space (equal to the size of the file) remains on the disk. The SORT command requires that we specify the field to sort on and the file to sort to. Enter

.SORT ON TITLE TO BIB<CR>

After a moment, dBASE III will inform us that the file has been sorted. To view titles in our sorted file, type

.USE BIB<CR>
.LIST TITLE<CR>]

(Continued)

dBASE III and dBASE III Plus (Continued)

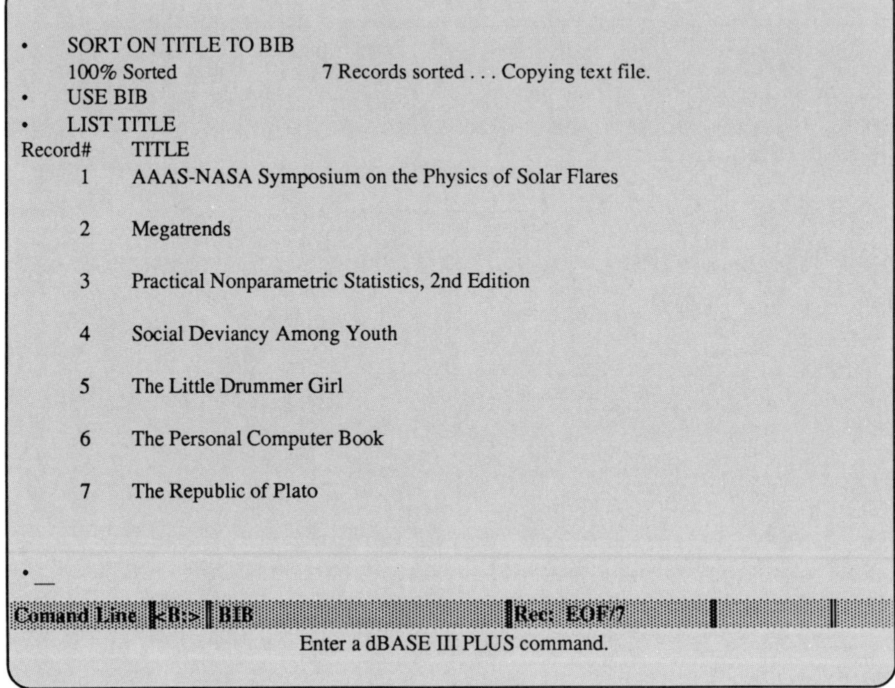

. SORT ON TITLE TO BIB
100% Sorted 7 Records sorted . . . Copying text file.
. USE BIB
. LIST TITLE
Record# TITLE
1 AAAS-NASA Symposium on the Physics of Solar Flares
2 Megatrends
3 Practical Nonparametric Statistics, 2nd Edition
4 Social Deviancy Among Youth
5 The Little Drummer Girl
6 The Personal Computer Book
7 The Republic of Plato
Comand Line <B:> BIB Rec: EOF/7
Enter a dBASE III PLUS command.

FIGURE 10–19
The Sorted File BIB (title field only)

The consequences of these commands are displayed in Figure 10–19.

Once the file has been sorted, the original file can be erased. Enter **.DIR B:<CR>** within dBASE after the dot prompt to see which files are on the disk in drive B. Notice the entry called BIBLIO.DBF. The .DBF file extension was provided by dBASE III. Files with this extension are dBASE data base files. Now enter **ERASE B:BIBLIO.DBF <CR>**.

To index the file, you must first select a field for indexing. dBASE will allow indexes on multiple fields, but this is generally not a good idea. If multiple indexes are in use, they will be automatically updated with each record addition, modification, or deletion, and this will slow the system down. Since the file is already sorted by the TITLE field, it would be superfluous to index that field as well. Let's index AUTHOR. Enter **.INDEX ON AUTHOR TO B:AUTHOR<CR>**. This command will create an index file based upon the AUTHOR field.

SEARCHING

Before we look for records in our data base, we will leave dBASE III and reenter, so that we know the steps to go through in subsequent sessions. Enter **.QUIT<CR>.**

If we enter **DIR B:** from the DOS prompt A>_, we will find that dBASE III has created a file called AUTHOR.NDX. The .NDX is the file extension for index files. Next, reenter dBASE, using the same two-disk procedure suggested at the beginning of this tutorial:

A> **DBASE<CR>**

Once you're into dBASE, and its "." prompt is displayed, enter the following:

.SET DEFAULT TO B<CR> (this eliminates the need to preface our file names with "B:")
.USE BIB INDEX AUTHOR<CR>

The last command opens two files. It opens our data base file (BIB.DBF), and it opens the index file we have just created (AUTHOR.NDX). Opening an index file at the time the data base file is opened allows you to use the index. You may have indexes on every field, if you wish, but you may desire to use them only one at a time.

In dBASE III, a number of methods can be used to search for data. We will experiment with all of them to search for our fifth record, *The Little Drummer Girl.* Afterwards, we will explain some of the differences between the methods. After each one, enter **.GO TOP<CR>** to reposition the record pointer at the beginning of the file.

1. 5<CR>DISPLAY<CR>
2. .LIST FOR 'Little' $ TITLE<CR>
3. .LOCATE FOR 'Little' $ TITLE<CR>
   .DISPLAY<CR>
4. .DISPLAY FOR 'Little' $ TITLE
5. .FIND Le Carre<CR> {doesn't work unless
   .DISPLAY<CR> BIB is indexed on TITLE}

With the first method, we must know the record number of our desired record before we can access it. This will be little-used in most applications,

(Continued)

dBASE III and dBASE III Plus (Continued)

but is very fast and easy if we can arrange our file so that the record number serves as the key. For example, we could assign our customer numbers in sequence, beginning with 1.

The second method uses the "$", which is the dBASE substring search function. The dollar sign is equivalent to the phrase "occurring anywhere within the field," so the entire statement is interpreted as LIST FOR 'Little' OCCURRING ANYWHERE WITHIN THE FIELD TITLE. This will help us find an individual in our AUTHOR field, regardless of the position of authorship. Note that we needed to put quotations around the string to search for. This is usually necessary when working with character data in dBASE III. dBASE III does not care if you use single or double quotation marks, but you must be consistent. Having both available allows you to search for contractions or possessive nouns, as in LIST FOR "Harrah's" $ TITLE.

The LOCATE command does not display the record. Rather, it moves the record pointer to the first record that matches the search value. DISPLAY is then used to show the record contents. This command is extremely useful for programs written in the dBASE III command language, but will not be used much in an interactive mode. LOCATE has two useful characteristics: it can be used on a field that is not indexed (as can LIST and DISPLAY), and it automatically moves the record pointer to the top of the file before the search begins if the option NEXT is not used.

DISPLAY operates very much like LIST, and can take the same optional statements. DISPLAY, however, can show values that are not stored in records, such as the date or computed values (e.g., DISPLAY SALARY – DEDUCTIONS). LIST is restricted to the contents of the fields that were declared when the file was created. Because of these differences, DISPLAY tends to be used more in dBASE III command language programs, while LIST is more often used at the dot prompt.

The FIND operation can operate only on indexed fields. It will allow extremely rapid location of the record of interest. The search value can be stated either with or without the quotation marks, and can be any portion of the field starting from the beginning. We could not use this command to search for Carre. The FIND command will not display the record for us, so we must use DISPLAY. It also finds only the first matched record. If more records contained "Le Carre," we could locate them in succession with repeated use of FIND NEXT. FIND (and SEEK, which operates virtually identically) is the principal method of locating records in large indexed files, since it operates so quickly.

FIGURE 10–20

dBASE III Program for Order Entry

```
SET DEFAULT TO B          :eliminates the need to preface
                           our filenames :with "B:"
CLEAR ALL                 :closes all files, releases all
                           memory variables :and SELECTS 1
SET TALK OFF              :eliminates on-screen prompts
SELECT 2                  :select work area 2
USE item INDEX item       :use file item in work area 2
SELECT 1                  :select work area 1
USE purchase              :use file purchase in work area 1
SET  RELATION TO item INTO item     :set relation between the two files
                          :on the key expression field item.
STORE 0 TO SUMALL         :initialize variable SUMALL to 0
STORE 0 TO SUMPART        :initialize variable SUMPART to 0
STORE 'Y' TO MORE         :initialize variable MORE to 'Y'
DO WHILE MORE='Y'         :do what follows until MORE <> 'Y'
     CLEAR                :clear screen
     APPEND BLANK         :append a blank record to file purchase
     REPLACE DATE WITH DATE( )      :set DATE field of purchase to the
                          :current date
     @ 10,0               :put cursor at line 10, column 0
     ? 'ORDER ENTRY'      :display 'ORDER ENTRY'
     ?                    :print two blank lines
     ?
     ? DATE
     @ 15,30 SAY 'NAME' GET name      :display NAME? at line 15,
                          :column 30, and wait at this position for
                          :READ statement.
     @ 16,30 SAY 'ITEM NUMBER?' GET item      :display ITEM NUMBER? and
                          :wait for READ statement.
     @ 17,30 SAY 'QUANTITY?' GET quantity   :display QUANTITY? and
                          :wait for READ statement.
     READ                 :read-in user-specified name, item and quantity.
                          :store in name, item and quantity fields of current
                          :record in file purchase.
     GO RECNO(  )         :let file item know which item this is.
     STORE QUANTITY*ITEM.PRICE TO SUMPART    :let SUMPART=QUANTITY*PRICE.
                          :this price is not in current work area, so
                          :need to preface.
     STORE SUMALL+SUMPART TO SUMALL   :accumulate the total to SUMALL.
     @ 20,30 SAY 'MORE?' GET MORE     :more? If 'Y', do above again.
     READ                 :read user-entered response into MORE.
ENDDO                     :this is the end of the DO WHILE loop.
DISP SUMALL               :print total on the screen.
```

(*Continued*)

dBASE III and dBASE III Plus (Continued)

MULTIPLE FILES

To close our tutorial, we will give you a taste of the power of the dBASE III command language when used for application development. At the same time, we will illustrate how two files can be used together within an application. When we analyzed the order entry and invoicing problem earlier in this chapter, it was determined that four files would be suitable: CUSTOMER, TOWN, ITEM, and PURCHASE. Figure 10–11 lists the fields that each of these files will contain, and Figure 10–8 shows the data types and field widths. In our example, we will assume that these files have already been created and are in use (our ITEM file contains all items in the inventory, and our TOWN file has all the ZIP codes, cities, and states of our customers). We will also assume that all fields in all files have been indexed.

For a simple order-entry transaction, the order clerk should have to enter as little information as possible to record the order, and should be able to tell the customer the amount of purchase over the phone. The program in Figure 10–20 shows the code for the order-entry portion of the complete system.

Before describing the program, we will first make some comments about the dBASE III procedural language. dBASE III can work with up to ten work areas. Each work area has a number, and only one file can be USEd in each work area. To switch work areas, use the command SELECT. Here are some examples. At the dBASE prompt . enter

```
.SELECT 1<CR>
.USE purchase<CR>
```

We selected work area 1, in which the file **purchase** is used. Now if you want to open (or USE) another file and still keep the **purchase** file open, you must select another work area:

```
.SELECT 2<CR>
.USE item INDEX item<CR>
```

The file **item** is opened at work area 2. Now work can be performed at work area 2. Any direct command is related to **item.** For example, **.LIST<CR>** will list the contents of file **item** on the screen. If you want to see information in the file **purchase,** you can type SELECT 1 to switch to work area 1, which contains a portion of **purchase.** Then the question that comes to mind is,

GRAPHICS FOR ANALYSIS, DESIGN, AND PERSUASION

Graphics is the hard or soft copy output of anything other than text or numbers. It serves two very important purposes: the improved comprehension of the system being analyzed or designed by analysts and designers, and the capacity to persuade or convince others regarding the validity of those designs and analyses. Thus, the larger purpose of graphics is visual appeal and comprehension. It makes eminently good sense, therefore, to combine graphics with color for added persuasion and professionalism in our presentations.

In what follows we present first the kinds of graphics that are customary in business settings, then the hardware required for graphics, and finally the illustrations of graphics output in various contexts. The hardware includes devices for soft copy output, such as displays and the video cards that drive them; as well as devices for hard copy output, such as printers and plotters.

Soft Copy Graphics

Line charts, bar charts, and pie charts make up the bulk of business graphics as the pictures on this page show. The "bars" in bar charts may be horizontal or vertical, they may be stacked (different color bars on top of each other), and they may be neatly arrayed behind each other, but still partially within view. Pies are always circular and are useful for showing how a budget was allocated amongst various departments or budget categories. Line charts or plots are appropriate for showing trends and variable variation over time.

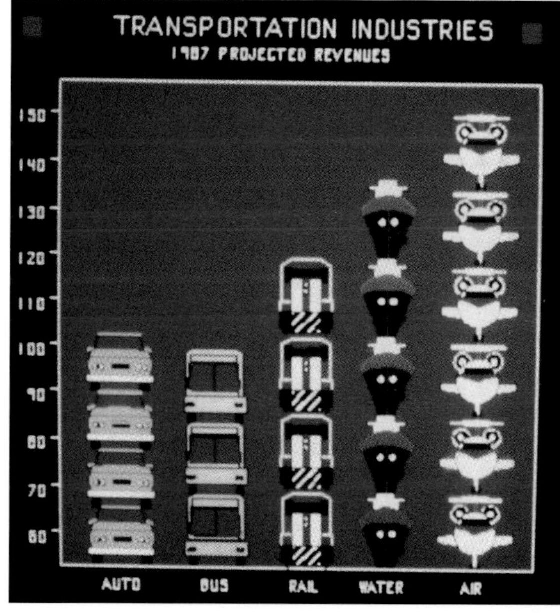

The bar chart in the photo to the left uses stacked icons, representative of the type of transportation mode depicted, to produce simple bars. Various types of software programs are available to enable PC users to produce such creative and colorful visual displays. *(Courtesy of Lotus Development Corporation)*

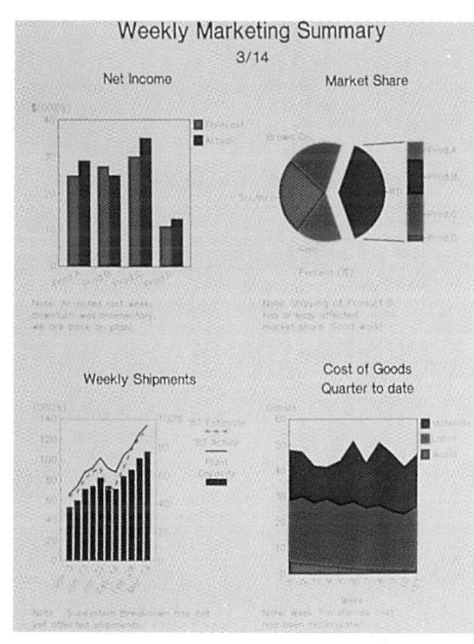

In the photo to the right, a page of varied graphics has been conveniently created. Note the use of the third dimension to create depth perception in the charts. The third dimension is easily and commonly applied in presentation graphics by computers, and does not require the talents of an artist. *(Courtesy of Lotus Development Corporation)*

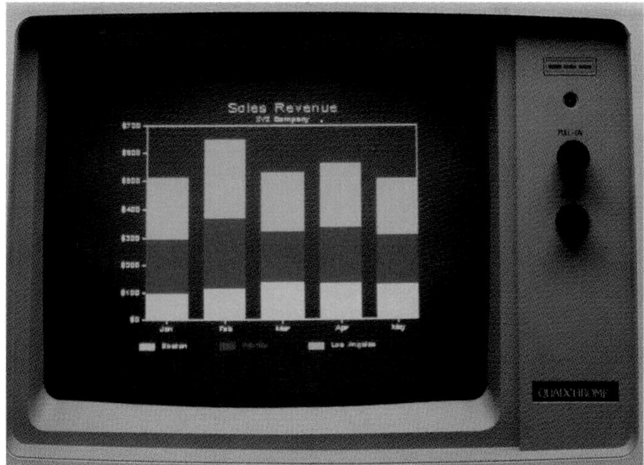

The CGA (Color Graphic Adapter) video card was introduced by IBM at about the same time that it introduced its PC in 1981. The card supported graphics at a very low level of resolution, with only four colors displayed, and text could not be mixed with graphics. *(Courtesy of Quadram)*

It quickly became apparent that the CGA standard had limitations, so the EGA (Enhanced Graphics Adapter) standard was developed by IBM. It and the PGC (Professional Graphics Controller) standard were introduced in late 1984 along with the IBM AT computer. The EGA card supported medium resolution with up to 16 colors displayed, and text could be mixed with graphics. The display in this photo is compatible with the EGA standard and is being driven by an EGA video card. Compare this display to the one in the previous picture. Hundreds of software packages now support the EGA standard. *(Courtesy of Quadram)*

A VGA (Very-high Resolution Graphics Adapter) card is required to drive this display. It is intended primarily for computer-aided design/computer-aided manufacturing applications, as these applications require very high resolution. *(Courtesy of Paradise Systems, Inc., a Western Digital Co.)*

As a result of the introduction of new PCs and new displays with their appropriate video controller cards, new standards for high-resolution monochrome and color graphics have been defined.

The monochrome display shown above has high enough resolution to support computer-aided-design applications. *(Courtesy of International Business Machines Corporation)*

This color display is being used to delineate a cutaway of the Earth's strata. Such a picture could be used by geologists, seismologists, and petroleum engineers. *(Courtesy of International Business Machines Corporation)*

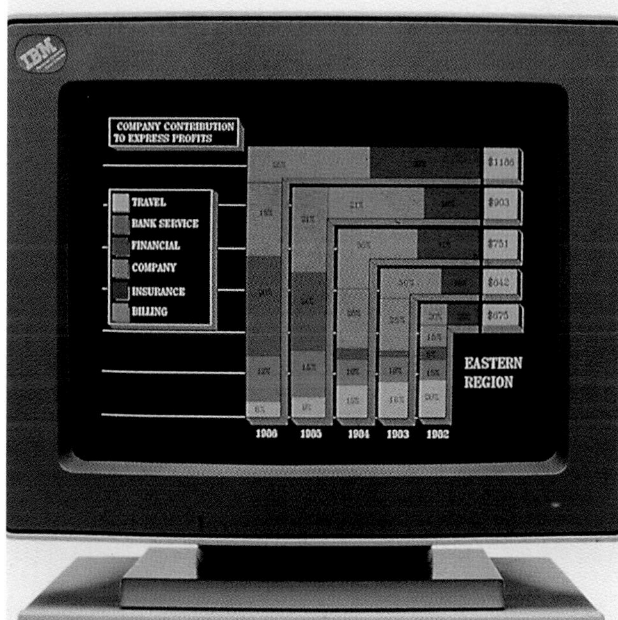

This 16-inch analog display supports very high resolution with up to 256 colors on-screen. Up to 51 lines of text can be displayed with 146 characters per line. *(Courtesy of International Business Machines Corporation)*

This color display shows a very high resolution with at least 16 colors being displayed. Ultimately, the capability exists to support resolution comparable to an engineering work station with 64 or more colors displayed. *(Courtesy of Apple Computer, Inc.)*

Hard Copy Graphics

The system depicted to the right can be driven by any PC to produce graphics on slides. The resolution of the system is twice that of an EGA display, and the number of colors displayed is 16, selected from a palette of 72 colors. Once the image is created, the recording time is approximately two minutes, the development time varies from one to two minutes, and the time to mount the slide is about one minute. Thus, in five minutes a slide can be produced once the image is created. *(Courtesy of Polaroid Corporation)*

Shown in the pictures below are examples of presentation graphics that can be produced. *(Courtesy of International Business Machines Corporation)*

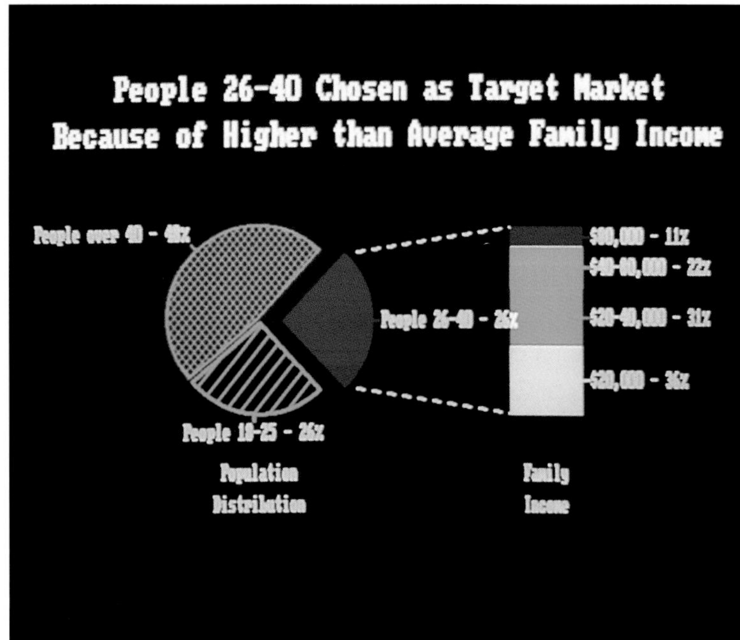

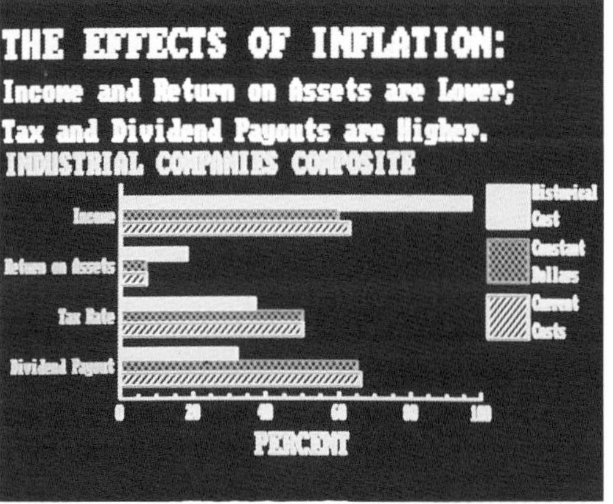

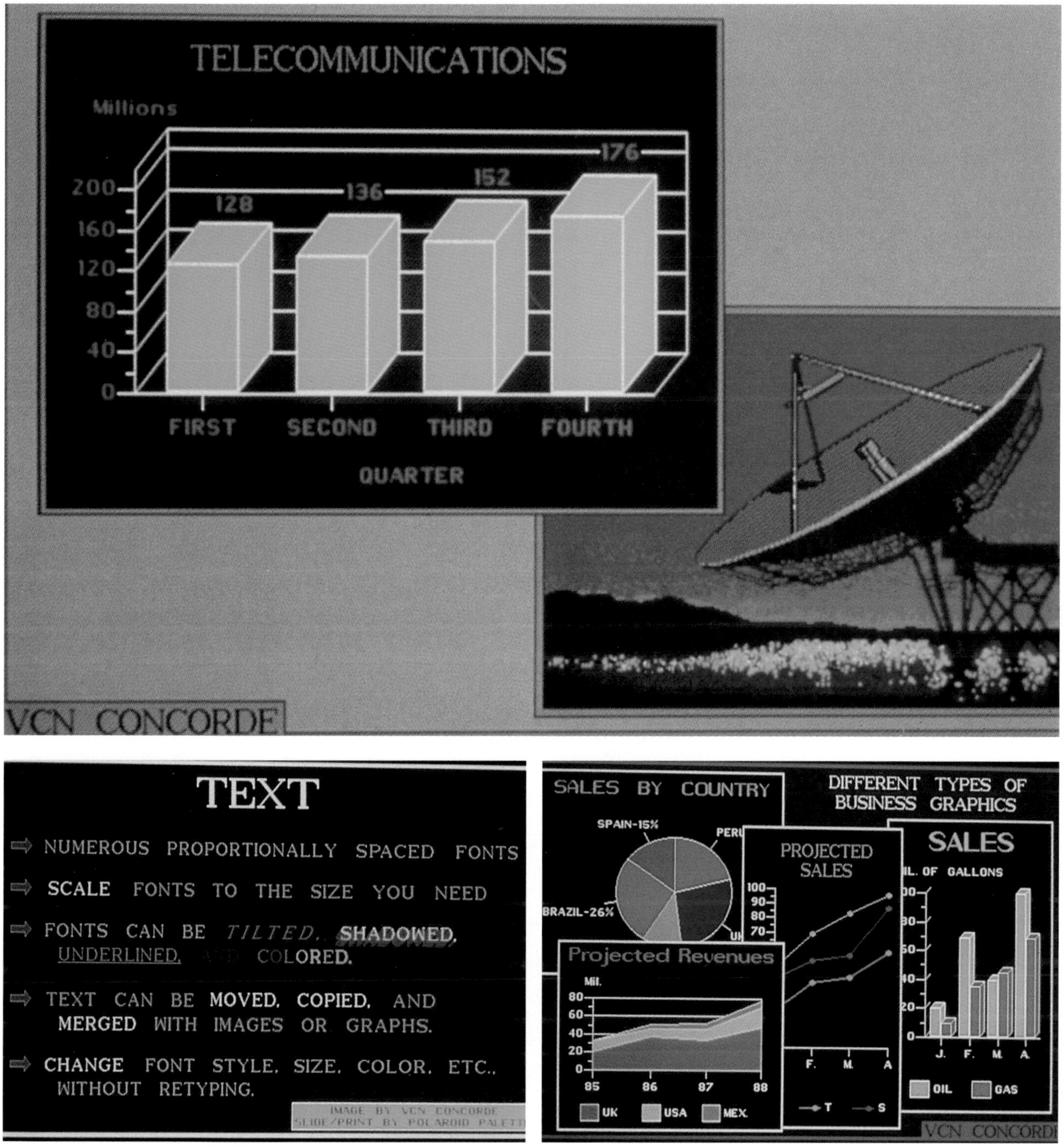

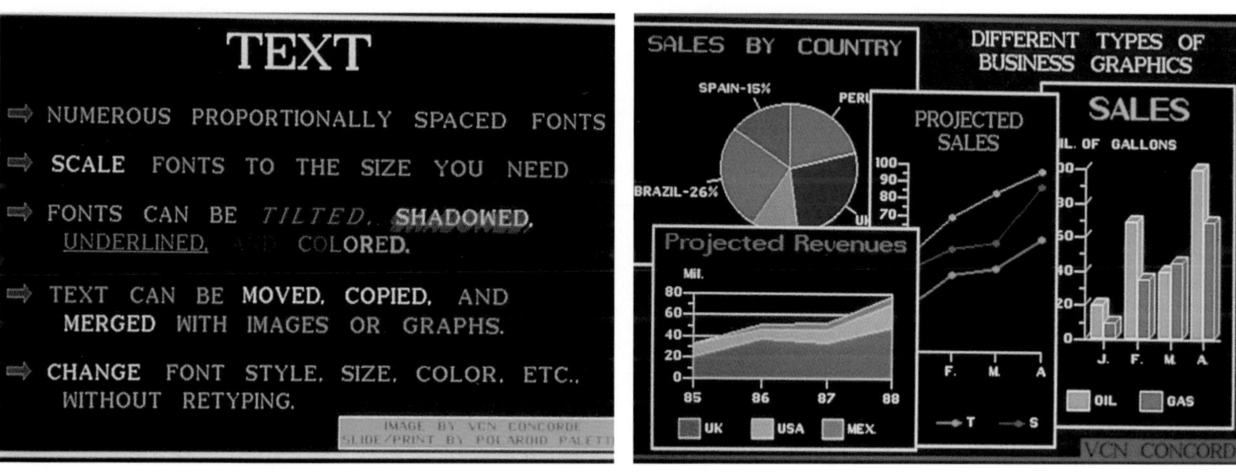

The graphical images depicted above are intended to be used in presentations. The computer generation of these very polished and persuasive facsimilies is fast and inexpensive by comparison to manual methods. And the microcomputer, along with its supporting software, provides a facility which makes revisions and editing a breeze. *(Courtesy of Polaroid Corporation)*

Plotters for Hard Copy Graphics

The plotter shown at right can produce colorful and informative high-quality charts and graphics on paper for reports and documents, or on overhead transparencies for visual aid presentations. *(Courtesy of Hewlett Packard Company)*

Computer-Aided Design/Computer-Aided Manufacturing (CAD/CAM)

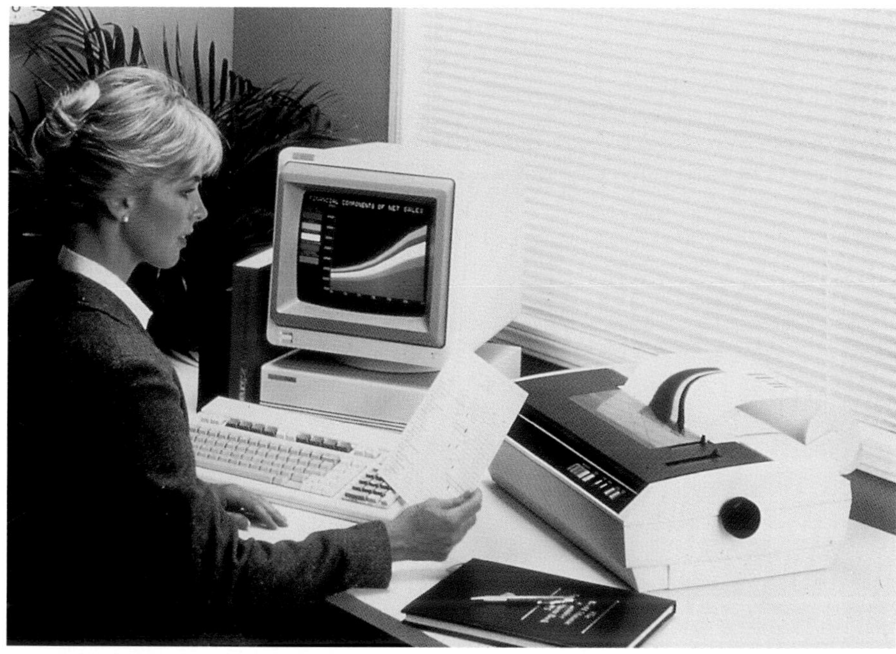

The increased capabilities of the PCs available today allow complex designs to be created with speed nearly equivalent to large minicomputer systems. A typical PC-CAD (computer-aided design) system includes: PC, graphics display, input devices, and drafting plotter. *(Courtesy of Hewlett Packard Company)*

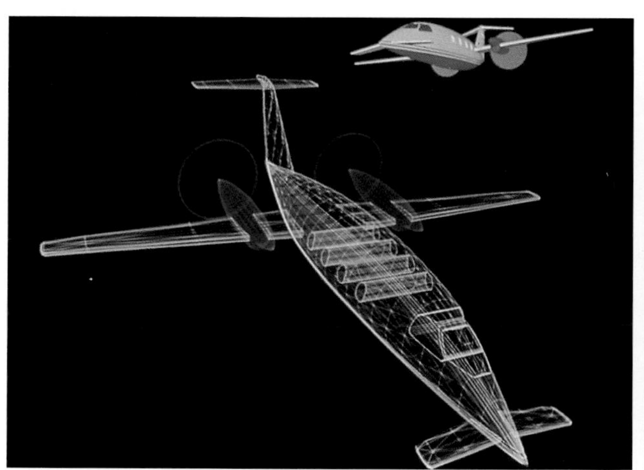

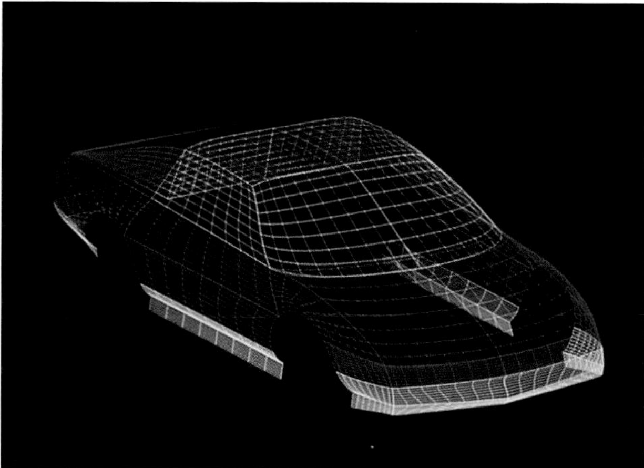

Graphics is a significant component of computer-aided design. Shown above is an automobile and an airplane being designed by computer, with the results of that design being graphically portrayed back to the user. *(Courtesy of Evans and Sutherland)*

Animated Simulation with Graphics

The capability to put the graphical image in motion, to animate the graphics, provides the designer with an improved understanding of the dynamical behavior of the system being designed. Graphical animation can reveal bottlenecks to a manufacturing supervisor before actual assembly takes place, and it can show potential congestion areas to a fast-food restaurant designer before the kitchen area layout plan is finalized. In the four photos that follow, a display screen was photographed as it dynamically depicted how the space shuttle would land at Edwards Air Force Base along with its pace plane. This is a simulation of the actual landing in which the computer animated the entire process. *(Courtesy of Evans and Sutherland)*

In this photo essay we have shown how graphics can be used advantageously to benefit business, engineering, and science. The pictures presented here portray the reality and persuasion of graphics, and suggest how graphics is used in these areas.

"How do we get information from work area 1 and still work within work area 2?" This can be done by simply typing the work area name before the field you want to see:

.DISP Purchase ->QUANTITY<CR>

This command will display the QUANTITY field of the current record in the **purchase** file.

dBASE III has a powerful command to set relations between two (or more) files. Suppose we wish to work in work area 1, and we want the pointer of the file **item** which is in work area 2 to be synchronized with the file **purchase;** that is, when we get an **item** name in the **purchase** file, we want the pointer of the file **item** to point to the same **item** record, so we can get the correct item price. This command is

.SET RELATION TO item INTO item<CR>

Note that the file which is related must be INDEXed on the key expression.

Now, the program code presented in Figure 10–20 can be read.

SUMMING UP

From our brief tutorial, it is apparent that dBASE is a large, complex program. Many options are available at almost every turn. For people who will develop systems in dBASE, most of these options are welcomed; they give dBASE applications a power and flexibility not found with most DBMS packages. For the novice, there appear to be far too many commands for the program to be learned easily. This is not quite true. dBASE III Plus can be worked with at several levels. Many users will never write a program in dBASE's command language, and will remain oblivious to many of the commands we have used in the tutorial (we've really only scratched the surface of the dBASE III Plus command language). These users will find that dBASE can be very manageable and quite serviceable by learning only six commands:

CREATE. to begin a new data base file

USE. to open an existing file

APPEND. to add records to the file

(Continued)

dBASE III and dBASE III Plus (Continued)

EDIT. for modifying previously entered records

LIST. for locating records

REPORT. to customize the appearance of the output

EXERCISES

1. CREATE a data base of your friends. Decide what fields you would want and then organize these into files. For example, you would most likely want a separate TOWN file consisting of ZIP, CITY, and STATE. And, you will need a FRIENDS file consisting of NAME, ADDRESS, ZIP, and whatever else you want to include. Add as many records as possible to your data base—at least ten to each file.
2. INDEX the data base you created in exercise 1 on the fields NAME, ADDRESS, etc. Use FIND to locate a record.
3. Try to code a simple program. Use the bibliographic data base you have already made to initiate the library book search system. That is, when you enter key words for search information (such as author's name, title, etc.), the screen will display the book's information in which you are interested. Screen-print these displays.

DISK EXERCISES*

1. Use the files ITEM.DBF and PURCHASE.DBF to produce a file called PURITEMS.DBF with the following attribute order: NAME, DATE, ITEM, QUANTITY, PRICE. Print the newly created file PURITEMS.DBF. What is this process called in the relational DBMS parlance? Note: See the article on "Select, Project, and Join," in addition to this tutorial, to see how to do this.
2. Use the CUSTOMER.DBF file to create another file called CUSTZIP.DBF containing the names, street addresses, and ZIP codes of only those customers living in ZIP codes 01122, 10022, and 98105. Print the newly created file CUSTZIP.DBF. Note: See the article on "Select, Project, and Join," in addition to this tutorial, to see how to do this.
3. Use the CUSTOMER.DBF file to create another file called NAMES.DBF containing the names of all customers in the CUSTOMER.DBF file. Print the newly created file NAMES.DBF. Note: See the article on "Select, Project, and Join," in addition to this tutorial, to see how to do this.
4. Use the file PURCHASE.DBF to produce a file called HIGHITEM.DBF containing just the names of those items in the PURCHASE.DBF file costing more than $1,000. Print the newly created file HIGHITEM.DBF.

*If you are using the student version of dBase III Plus, you must employ the files ITEM1.DBF, PURCHSE1.DBF, and CUSTMER1.DBF in place of ITEM.DBF, PURCHASE.DBF, and CUSTOMER.DBF in order to complete these disk exercises.

CHAPTER

11

Graphics Applications and Integrated Software Packages

CHAPTER OUTLINE

Graphics 392

Integrated Software Packages 402

A Definition of Integrated Software 403

Why Integrated Software? 403

Goals of Integrated Software Packages 404

Features of Integrated Software 405

Software Concepts and Design Philosophies 406

Advantages/Disadvantages of Integrated Software 407

All-in-one Integrated Software Packages 408

Integrating Environment Packages 409

Lotus 1-2-3 Graphics Tutorial 412

CHAPTER OBJECTIVES

In this chapter you will learn

1 why graphics is important and is always a component in integrated all-in-one programs

2 what the major uses and applications of graphics are

3 what devices are used for graphics input and output

4 what hardware is recommended to support graphics applications

5 what graphics editors are

6 what is meant by integrated software

7 what types of integrated software are available

8 who the major integrated software vendors are

9 what major functions or applications are included in integrated software

Business and professional people are always presenting or listening to "show-and-tell" seminars or "dog-and-pony" shows. This chapter describes a category of software that can greatly facilitate and expedite the creation of the visual content of these presentations. Like word processing, spreadsheets, and data base applications, graphics applications are another category of software that can significantly enhance the productivity of the professional. Graphics applications are available in two forms: packaged with other managerial productivity tools, and as stand-alone packages. This chapter describes both.

Yet another related category of software, integrated software packages, is described in this chapter. Almost all integrated software packages have some kind of graphics capability, as shall be seen. Most integrated software packages include word processing, a spreadsheet application, a data base application, and a communications function in addition to graphics. By the time the graphics application has been discussed, all of the major application components of integrated software packages, except possibly data communications, will have been covered. Therefore, this chapter shall digress a moment to discuss this important category of software. In addition, the chapter is accompanied by a graphics tutorial that uses Lotus 1-2-3.

The chapter begins with a discussion of graphics applications in general, and treats integrated software packages in the second half of the chapter.

GRAPHICS

In our contemporary graphics-driven society, large corporations, small businesses, government, and nonprofit institutions all rely on visual graphics to communicate essential information. Hence, graphics is an application of the microcomputer that is both pervasive and profound. We have chosen to discuss it here not only because it consistently gets included in integrated, all-in-one programs, but also because there are hundreds of stand-alone graphics programs that may be more capable than the limited graphics components included in some of the early integrated programs. In addition, much commercial art and advertising art is being created by use of microcomputers and graphics software.

Graphics Applications

The old adage that "a picture is worth a thousand words" (or a thousand numbers) has never been more true than the present. More so than ever before, managers and professionals are overwhelmed with more information than they can absorb. The role of graphics has never been more important or crucial, because graphical presentation can greatly speed the rate of comprehension of both text and data. In addition, studies show that retention of visual graphics is longer and more accurate. It is estimated[1] that in 1983 there were 557 million business slides presentations as compared to only 263 million in 1978. At the same time, in 1983 computers generated 16 million of those slides, whereas only 300,000 were generated in 1978. Although these are impressive numbers, they are not nearly as impressive as their graphic representation is, as shown in Figure 11–1.

The use of graphics software and hardware is becoming commonplace. With minimal software and hardware a user can prepare personalized greeting or Christ-

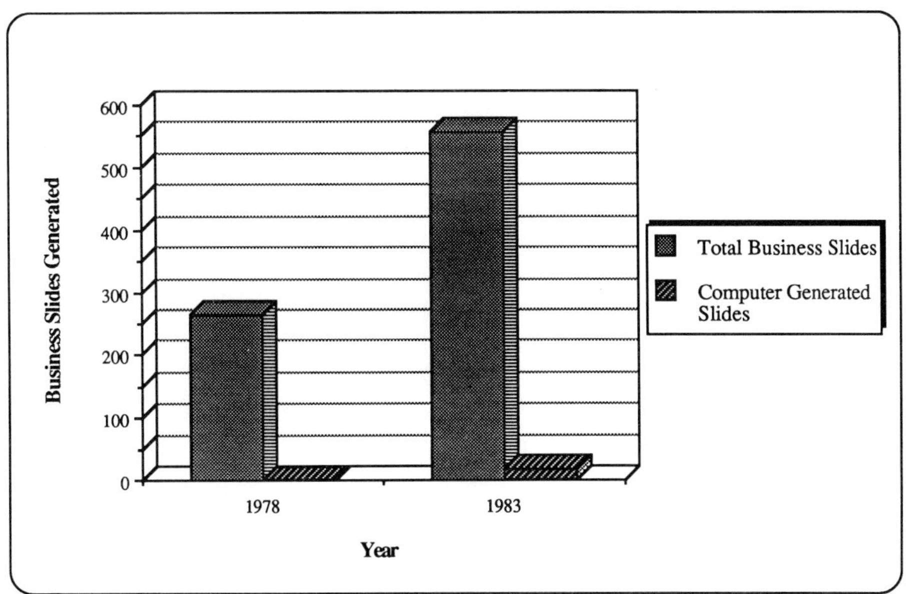

FIGURE 11–1

The Growth in Uses of Business Graphics

mas cards on a home computer. A church secretary can design attractive posters and signs for a variety of purposes. A professor can design attractive overheads for use in class. A copy shop can design professional calling cards, stationery, or art for advertising. There are myriad everyday uses of graphics. Because of the television set, we, as a society, have become accustomed to very professional-looking graphics. When the news is presented to us, when we watch a commercial, when we view a weather forecast, all are accompanied by professional graphics that computers can generate. Increasingly, a lot of these presentations are being done by the microcomputer. Without the use of graphics, any presentation—whether to one individual or to thousands—fails to meet our expectations, so accustomed have we become to the use of graphics.

Many other important classes of graphics can be generated by the microcomputer besides presentations. Several times already, we have mentioned the word *design.* Computer-aided design/computer-aided manufacturing (frequently referred to as **CAD/CAM**) has been an important application of mainframes and minicomputers for years. The motherboard in your microcomputer was designed using CAD software; your automobile was most likely designed using CAD software. The layout of the neighborhood you live in may have been designed by use of CAD software. Today, CAD software is available for the microcomputer. Table 11–1 summarizes some of the uses of graphics on the microcomputer that are commonplace today.

TABLE 11–1

Commonplace Uses of Microcomputer Graphics

1. Business and professional presentations, seminars, documents, and reports
2. Computer-aided design/computer-aided manufacturing (CAD/CAM)
3. Industrial/commercial art and advertising
4. Education and instruction
5. Graphics-driven user interfaces, as in Gem and Macintosh

In general, the goal of graphics is to enhance communication and comprehension within any particular usage.

Types of Charts and Graphs, and Their Uses

Typical of the graphical aids in use today are bar and stacked bar charts, pie charts, scatter plots, line graphs, and X-Y coordinate plots. Pie charts can be turned on their side, with one or more wedges exploded. Typical examples of all these types are shown in Figures 11–2a through 11–2c.

Users of bar, stacked bar, and pie charts should be careful to observe certain rules to ensure that these figures are correctly interpreted by others. One important rule is that the components of a single stacked bar or of a single pie should add up to 100% of the total, and should not be overlapping. For example, in a chart involving costs, manufacturing costs might include inventory costs, production costs, and distribution costs, yet all four of these are shown separately as parts of the "bar stack" representing costs, or the wedges of the cost pie. This would be misleading and might cause a reader to surmise that these costs are twice what they actually are, or that production costs are 25% of total costs when in fact they are 50% of total costs. Other rules for building acceptable charts are given in Table 11–2.

Analytic versus Presentation Graphics

The graphical aids depicted in Figures 11–2a through 11–2c may have as their intent either analysis by a single user or ultimate presentation before a much larger viewing audience. In the former case the graphics do not require the formality or

FIGURE 11–2a
A Typical Stacked Column Chart

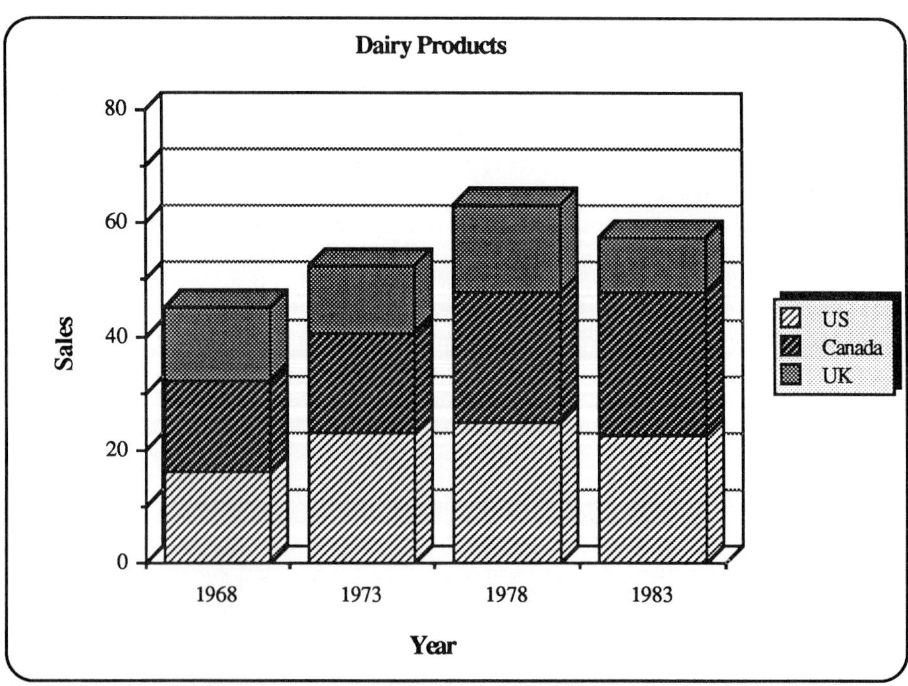

polish that would otherwise be appropriate. Analytic graphics should be easily and rapidly obtained, as can be provided when the graphics function is tightly integrated with the origin or source of the data: a spreadsheet or DBMS. In an analytic context, the user wishes to explore the consequences of several different policies or strategies and desires to comprehend the consequences of these alternative managerial actions as quickly as possible through the use of **analytic graphics**. This is an

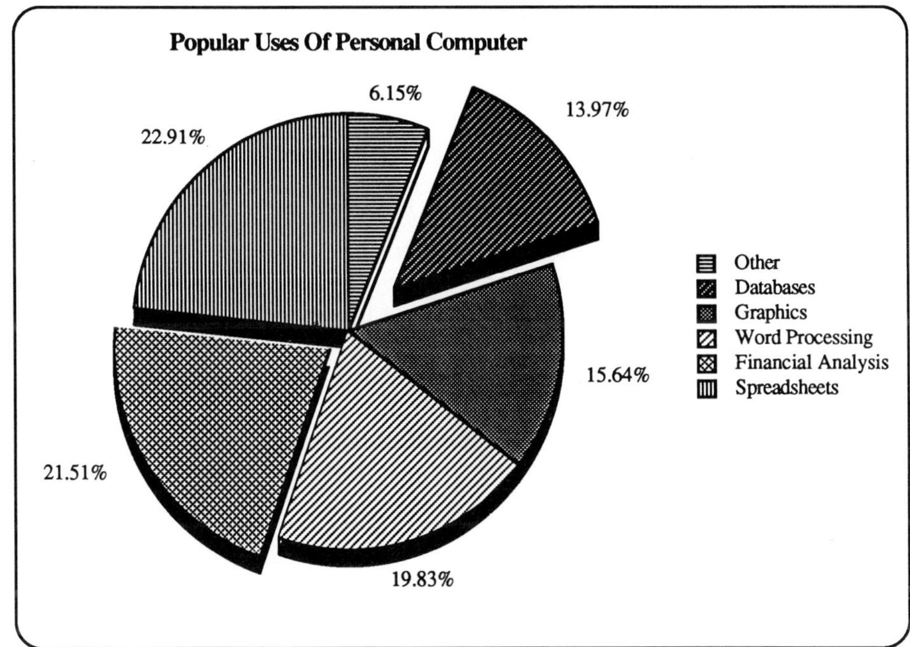

FIGURE 11–2b
A Typical Pie Chart with "Exploded" Sectors

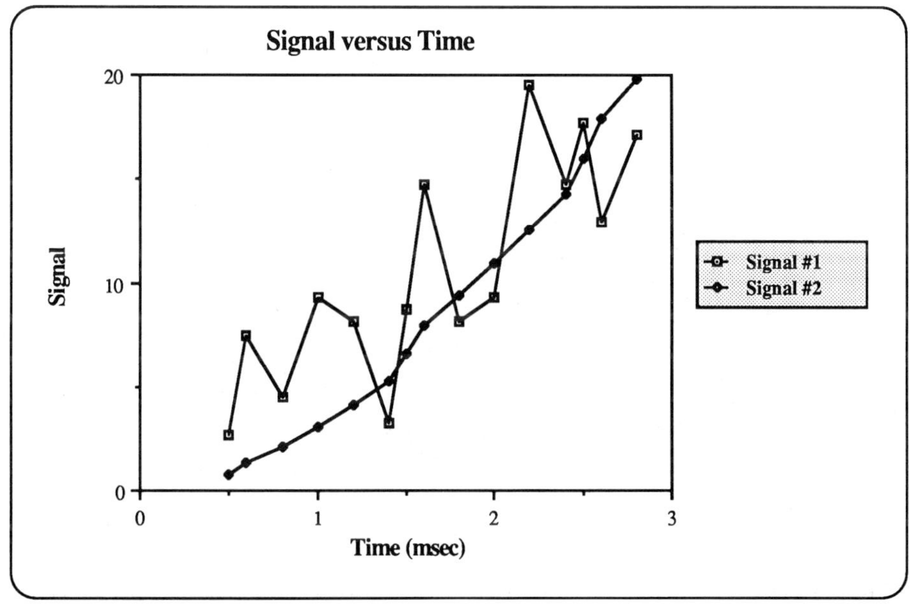

FIGURE 11–2c
A Typical Line Chart

TABLE 11–2
Rules Governing Formation of Bar Charts and Pie Charts

1. The components of bar stacks and wedge pies should be exclusive; that is, they should not be overlapping.
2. A succession of bars whose heights are to be compared should all represent the same commodity; that is, sales, profit, or costs. To represent a different commodity, a separate set of bars whose fill-in background is different can be superimposed on the first set.
3. Imposing too many sets of data on the same graph can be confusing.
4. When comparing two or more graphs, their scales must be the same.
5. Increasing the number of data points in a data set is likely to increase the accuracy of the resultant chart.

opportune occasion for the use of an all-in-one integrated program that will produce graphs almost as fast as the spreadsheet can perform a recalculation.

In **presentation graphics**, the user has ultimately settled on a few charts, graphs, or plots and requires a high degree of polish since the graphics are intended for viewing by others. The user is through with the analysis phase and does not require tight integration between the source of the data and its visual characterization. In this context, stand-alone graphics packages may be at least as appropriate as tightly integrated ones. Of primary importance is the capability to generate graphics of presentation quality. Stand-alone graphics packages should be able to accept ASCII or **.DIF files** as generated by spreadsheets and data base management systems. And they may accept manually inputted data as well. They usually contain **graphics editors**, which enable the user to add text and titles, color and shade in certain objects, label axes on a graph, rotate the image, enlarge or diminish the graph, and so on. Graphics editors will, hence, enable users to build that extra "punch" into the graphics that enhances communication of important concepts with greater persuasion and professionalism.

The use of color adds significantly to the appeal, attractiveness, and quality of the graph. Of importance is the resolution of the display and the number of colors that can be displayed at one time. In general, the higher the resolution and the greater the number of colors that can be displayed, the better the quality of the displayed graphics.

Graphics Software

Table 11–3 lists some of the stand-alone graphics packages together with the graphics capabilities of each. Several hundred such packages are available in the marketplace.

Stand-alone graphics software for general use by business and professional people can be classified into roughly five different categories, as suggested in Table 11–4. Calligraphy software is generally able to drive a "standard" dot-matrix printer in such a way as to produce very high quality print in a large variety of fonts and sizes. This software will also provide a variety of characters, icons, and symbols for dressing up a graph to enhance its assimilation by others.

Software for charting, plotting, or graphing is capable of producing the various bar charts, pie charts, line drawings, and plots. Limited calligraphy capabilities will also exist with this type of software for labeling axes on the graph, and for adding text within the graph or chart itself.

TABLE 11–3

Stand-alone Graphics Software Packages

NAME/ADDRESS	MAXIMUM COLORS	RESOLUTION*	COST
PC Paint Mouse Systems 2336H Walsh Ave. Santa Clara, CA 95051 (408) 988-0211	16 in 6 palettes	320 × 200	inexpensive (less than $100)
Lumena Time Arts Inc. 3436 Mendocino Ave. Santa Rosa, CA 95401 (707) 576-7722	16.7 million	512 × 481	very expensive (more than $5,000)
The Grafix Partner Brightbill-Roberts, Ltd. Suite 421 University Building 120 E. Washington St. Syracuse, NY 13202 (315) 474-3400	16 in 4 palettes	320 × 200	inexpensive
Imigit Plus Chorus Data Systems, Inc. P.O. Box 370 6 Continental Blvd. Merrimac, NH 03054 (800) 624-6787	256	512 × 512	moderately expensive (more than $500)
Artwork & Brushwork West End Film, Inc. 2121 Newport Pl., N.W. Washington, D.C. 20037 (202) 331-8078	256	512 × 480	expensive (more than $2,000)
Videogram Version 3.0 Softel Inc. 34½ St. Mark's Place New York, NY 10003 (212) 677-6599	64	640 × 350	inexpensive

*Measured in pixels. The first number is the number of rows of pixels, the second is the number of columns.

TABLE 11–4

Categories of Graphics Software

1. Software for calligraphy with supportive characters, symbols and icons. Examples: Fontasy, Fancy Font.
2. Software for charting, plotting, and graphing. Examples: Microsoft Chart, Lotus Freelance Plus, Harvard Presentation Graphics.
3. Software for freehand painting and drawing. Examples: MacDraw, MacPaint, PC Draw, PC Paint.
4. Combinations of the above with animation. Examples: Executive Picture Show from PC Software of San Diego, Show Partner from Brightbill-Roberts, PC Storyboard from IBM.
5. Software for specific computer-aided design. Examples: AUTOCAD.

Software for freehand painting and drawing is used in artwork applications: advertising, education, and entertainment mostly. Some more expensive graphics software packages will have all of the capabilities listed in categories one through three of Table 11–4. Categories 2 through 5 in Table 11–4 are likely to have graphics editors, icon libraries (collection of preformed images), and a variety of textures for backgrounds and fill-in.

Hardware Required for Graphics

Graphical applications impose particular needs upon the hardware used to display and print/plot the graphics. In general, for MS-DOS machines the user will need a color graphics adapter card and a color display if color is a requirement. IBM's extended graphics adapter (EGA) card is a considerable improvement over the older color graphics adapter card in that the EGA's 16 on-screen colors and near-monochrome 640 × 350 resolution are in themselves a great improvement over the 4 on-screen colors and 320 × 200 resolution that the older card offered. Newer and more powerful EGA standards are expected to offer more on-screen colors and even higher resolution. Many other color graphics adapter cards are available from manufacturers like Paradise, Hercules, and others. Each of these may have different specifications of on-screen colors displayed and resolution. It should be pointed out (for potential purchasers) that if the software is capable of supporting 64 colors and 640 × 350 resolution, but the hardware supports only 4 on-screen colors and 320 × 200 resolution, then the hardware limitation determines the ultimate performance of the two components. For this reason, the software, the adapter card, and the monitor should all be selected to provide the ultimate in matched performance and compatibility.

The Personal System/2 product line introduced by IBM in April of 1987 opens up new vistas in resolution and colors displayed. The IBM Personal System/2 Display Adapter 8514A, coupled with the IBM 8514 Color Display will provide a maximum of 1024 × 768 pixels of resolution with up to 256 colors displayed simultaneously, selected from a palette of 256,000. Support for combined text and graphics is also provided. And the 16-inch screen can hold up to 51 rows of text at a time, with each row containing up to 146 characters.

Input Devices In addition to the customary keyboard, other devices have been designed for the input of data into graphics applications. These devices include the mouse, the light pen, the touch screen, and the digitized pad among others. Some of these devices were described in Chapter 3.

Light pens are input devices that provide a way of drawing directly onto a screen. The light-sensing mechanism at the point of the pen, when aimed at the CRT, detects the electron beam and that creates the images on the screen. This beam scans horizontally across each row of pixels on the screen, repeating this process several times each second. The instant in time when the electron beam "hits" the light pen is detected. This instant is then used to determine the location of the pen, based upon where the beam would be located on the screen at that instant in time. The light pen can be pointed at anything on the screen (a menu, say) to make the user's selection. It can also draw lines on the screen. The light pen must respond only to the light of the electron beam, so the phosphor of the screen needs to be matched with the light pen sensor. Figure 11–3 depicts a typical light pen and CRT display.

FIGURE 11–3

A Light Pen and Associated CRT Display *(Courtesy of FTG Data Systems—Stanton, CA)*

A digitizer or writing tablet can be used to transfer complex drawings into computerized form. The position of the stylus, in terms of x and y coordinates, is used to steer the cursor. The tablet is a flat, rectangular slab of material upon which a stylus is moved. The wire mesh method is one way to detect the position of the stylus. A matrix of wires is embedded into the surface of the tablet. When the stylus is pressed against the surface, it causes the wires underneath to sense the position of the stylus and to transmit this to the computer. Other technologies for sensing the position of the stylus on the pad are also in use, but will not be discussed here. With a digitizer, the information contained in a map or a drawing of a landscape or printed circuit can be transferred to the computer simply by tracing the lines. Figure 11–4 shows a typical writing tablet.

Output Devices Output devices include the monitor, the printer, and a plotter. The monitor should be a color monitor with a resolution capability that matches the user's requirements and is compatible with both the color graphics adapter card used to drive the monitor and with the graphics software.

For printing, a dot-matrix printer with a graphics capability is the minimum requirement. Considered desirable would be either a laser printer or plotter.

The delineation of graphic images on microcomputer screens is accomplished by means of a **bit-mapped display**, as shown in Figure 11–5. Corresponding to each pixel (short for picture element) is one or more bits (0-1 devices which are the fundamental memory elements of primary storage). Images are generated on the display by turning certain pixels on or off, which is accomplished by setting the corresponding bit in primary storage to zero or one. There are literally thousands of pixels on any microcomputer display; the greater the number of pixels, the greater the resolution of the display and the finer the detail of the images exhibited. Stored in the computer primary storage area is the information necessary for determining which pixels should be lighted and which should be dark, to produce any desired image or character.

FIGURE 11–4

The Kurta IS/ONE Input System with Four Types of Pointing Devices. *(Photo courtesy of Kurta—Phoenix, AZ)*

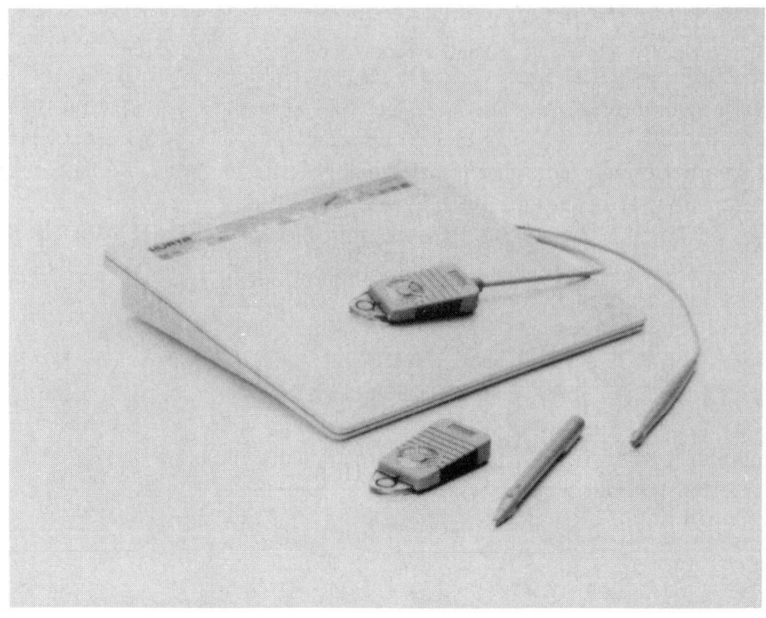

Most microcomputers use a type of display called a **raster-scan** display. In a raster scan display, an electron gun directs a beam of electrons toward the phosphor screen. By varying the voltage of the gun, the intensity with which electrons illuminate the phosphor can be controlled, allowing for dark areas by turning down the voltage and light areas by turning up the voltage. The beam of electrons is scanned from left to right across each row of pixels on the screen. When one row is completed, the beam begins the next row below, turning off the voltage as the gun makes its backward sweep. When the beam reaches the lower rightmost row of pixels, it returns to the upper leftmost row and repeats the scanning process all over again. This happens dozens of times in a single second—so often that the human eye is unable to detect it. A pixel whose corresponding bit value is 0 will thus be lighted by the beam, while a pixel whose bit value is 1 will be dark.

It should be noted, however, that the formation of characters on monochrome displays may occur in a slightly different way if the display is **text-mapped** rather than bit-mapped as just explained. Text-mapped displays consist of a matrix (rows and columns) of character positions. Each character position on the display is itself made up of a matrix of pixels called a **character box** (as in Figure 11–6). Stored in the computer's memory (ROM, usually) are the pixels within the character box that are to be lighted. When a particular character is to be displayed, a driver called a **character generator** goes to the area of memory where the pixels to be lighted for each character are stored and sends the pixel information to the display.

An advantage of this type of memory-mapped display is that less primary memory is required to store all of the pixel information for the display. Since the display effectively consists of a matrix of character boxes (usually 24 or 25 rows by 80 columns), only the character to be displayed in each box need be retained in primary memory. If there are 25 rows and 80 columns of characters, this would mean that 2,000 characters would have to be stored. Since the byte is the amount of storage required by each character, 2,000 bytes (16,000 bits—recall that there

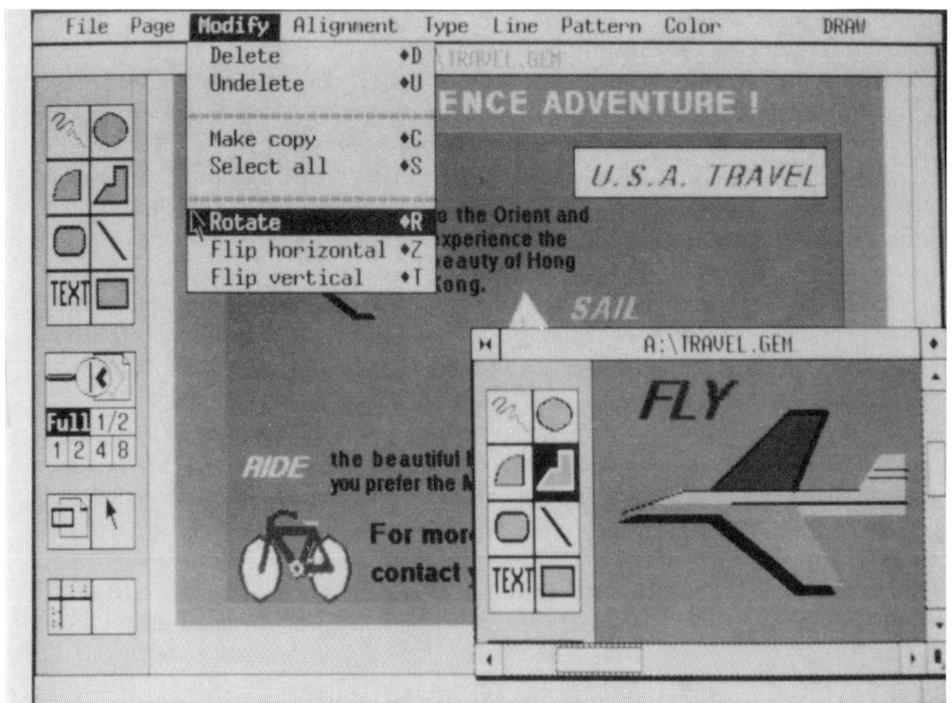

FIGURE 11–5

A Bit-Mapped Display Driven by Digital Research's GEM Draw Plus for the PC and Compatibles Note toolbox at left side of screen and pull-down menu along top. *(The above photo is copyright © 1987 Digital Research, Inc. All Rights Reserved. Used with Permission.)*

are 8 bits in a byte) would be required. By contrast, a monochrome bit-mapped display with 640 × 200 resolution requires 128,000 bits or 16,000 bytes of video RAM, assuming no half-intensity capability. (There are 640 times 200 pixels (128,000 pixels) and each requires one bit.)

A disadvantage to this type of (text-mapped) display driver is that the user is limited to the 256 characters whose character boxes are permanently encoded within the computer. This usually means that italics, different fonts, and pitch cannot be displayed, whereas all of these are possible with bit-mapped displays.

It is noteworthy that many displays, whether color or monochrome, can be bit-mapped or text-mapped. The Macintosh, Atari ST, and Commodore Amiga all use high-resolution bit-mapped displays, however. The IBM PC display can be either bit-mapped or text-mapped. The application software makes this determination. Some word processing programs written for the IBM PC drive the screen with a text-mapped driver, others use a bit-mapped driver, for example.

Plotters (see Figure 11–7) come in a variety of shapes, costs, and sizes. The distinguishing feature of a plotter which makes it different from a printer is its use of pens rather than a print wheel or print head. The most common form of plotter is the flatbed plotter, in which the platen (upon which all drawing takes place) is a flatbed. Pens move up and down on a screw-driven bar while the paper moves back and forth underneath it. Different pens are accessible to the pen driving mechanism, or can be manually changed. The pen driving mechanism lifts the pen off the page while moving the pen to a different location, when no line is required between the stopping and restarting positions.

This concludes our discussion of graphics, graphics applications, graphics software, and graphics hardware. We consider next integrated software packages.

FIGURE 11–6

A Character-Driven Display and Character Box

This is a character-driven display. There are limitations on the pitch and font that can be presented.

At right is a blow-up of a character box so you can see the pixels that make up the dot matrix character box.

Dot Matrix Character Box

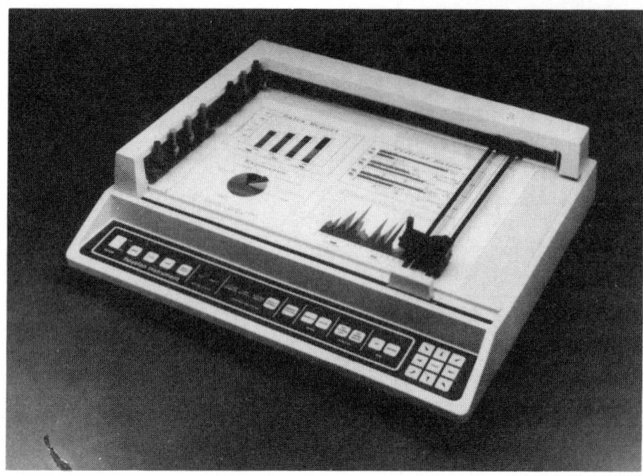

(a)

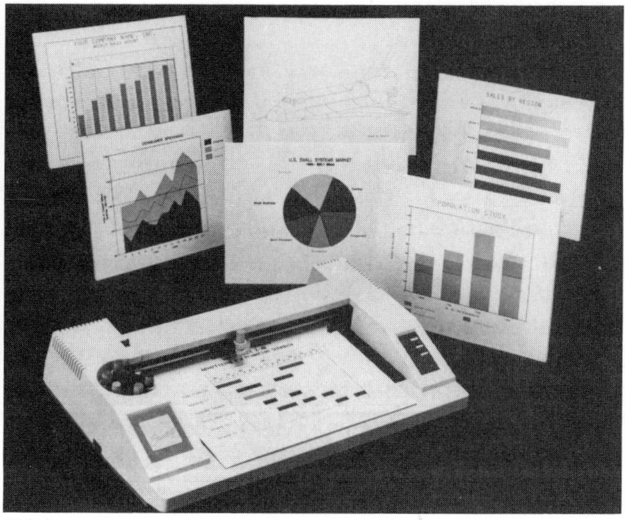

(b)

FIGURE 11–7

Some Common Forms of Microcomputer Plotters

(a) The eight-pen DMP-29 flatbed plotter from Houston Instrument features a maximum pen speed of 22 inches per second and an addressable resolution of .001 inch. (b) Enter Computer's Sheet-P Plotter.

INTEGRATED SOFTWARE PACKAGES

In 1980, Gib Hoxie and Brian Fischer, two researchers in a consulting firm, did a $1.5 million study to determine the information needs for the corporate manager. The results indicated that a microcomputer must be capable of handling five specific applications that a corporate manager performs: the writing of reports and memos; the storing, searching, and sorting of data; the analysis of information in an easy-to-understand graphic form; and the ability to communicate with other computers. With these basic needs defined, Hoxie and Fischer formed their own company, Context Management Systems, and developed a software product that included a word processor, a spreadsheet, a file manager, a business graphics package, and a telecommunications capability. In July 1982, Context MBA, the first commercially available integrated software package for personal computers, was introduced. This package, and many others based on the same concept, has given rise to a class of software known simply as integrated software packages. What are the goals of these packages, and how do they measure up to the individually packaged application software already considered? What are the advantages and disadvantages of integrated software? These are the issues to be addressed in this section of Chapter 11.

A DEFINITION OF INTEGRATED SOFTWARE

Following Chang,[2] **integrated software** shall be defined as any multi-application product that allows easy transfer of data between applications, lets the user accomplish complicated tasks over a short period of time and with a minimum of user interaction, and is easy to use. As will be seen, several different software categories fit this definition; these different categories are compared in this chapter.

WHY INTEGRATED SOFTWARE?

The motivation for integrated software derives from the way in which managers and professional people do their work. As in the previous applications, the ultimate objective is increased productivity. Imagine for the moment that you, as manager of a sales organization, expect your existing sales to grow by 10% during the next year. Your overhead costs will grow at an annual rate of 5%, but your variable costs will decrease by 7% during the year. Existing sales and cost data for all products are contained in your computerized data base. You want to move this data into your worksheet model where you can project it, interrelate it with other data, and perform what-if analyses on it. Then you want the worksheet data moved into the graphics component, where a bar chart can be prepared showing projections. You are also preparing a word processing document that describes the worksheet results and charts for different policies that you have tried. You want the worksheet models and their bar charts linked into the appropriate positions of the word processing document. Finally, you want to invoke the communications function to send the entire collection of files to the front office in Chicago, so that top management can evaluate your work.

As a further example, suppose you are manager of an advertising department and you must prepare the quarterly advertising report for the vice president of marketing. You've run your budget through your spreadsheet some thirty different ways, and found several promising budget plans. You wish to present these plans to your vice-president with words, numbers, and graphics so that they will be quickly comprehensible to him. He will then be able to make the final judgment regarding which plan to implement. You have two days to prepare and present the written report. These two examples are typical of the myriad situations in which integrated software can make a difference.

There are situations in which integrated software does not make sense, however. Suppose, for example, that you are writing a novel. A robust word processing package, spelling and style checkers, and a thesaurus are probably sufficient for such an undertaking.

GOALS OF INTEGRATED SOFTWARE PACKAGES

The goals of integrated software are compelling, and include the following: (1) the provision of the professional productivity tools—word processing, worksheets, and data base management; (2) file compatibility among the applications, allowing a spreadsheet file to be easily merged into a word processing document, for example; (3) a common set of user interface conventions; (4) the ability to depart one application, go to another, and return to the original application at the same point, with expediency; (5) the ability to make a change in one file and expect that change to appear in all documents into which that file was merged; and (6) overall lower cost as compared with the totaled cost of purchasing all applications separately. Each of these goals is treated in some detail in what follows.

Most integrated software packages either furnish the user with software specific to the needs of word processing, spreadsheets, data base management and graphics, or provide an environment in which these applications can be integrated, even though the vendors of these applications are different. As shall be seen, there are many instances in which the use of the microcomputer can benefit from integration of these specific applications along with graphics and communications. Such is the intent of the first goal mentioned above.

The ability to create a spreadsheet file and pass that file to a word processing document where it could be accompanied by appropriate explanatory material is intuitively appealing. Such is the sense of the second goal mentioned above. As previously explained in Chapter 7, this was accomplished before integrated software was available by means of a .DIF (Data Interchange File), as developed for Visicalc. Other programs, such as 1-2-3 and dBASE III, can also send and receive information in this format.[2] The process is not particularly convenient, however. The segment to be saved as a .DIF file must be marked and appropriate commands entered to indicate that the material is to be saved as a .DIF file. Next the user must exit the current application, load and enter the target application, whereupon the .DIF file is read into the appropriate place within the word processing document. But if the data imported into the word processing document from the .DIF file were not exactly what the user wanted, the whole process must be repeated again. A similar procedure must be followed in exporting data from a worksheet to a graphics program, or to a data base management system. In short, previously many programs met at the common ground of .DIF, but the process was not efficient.

With an integrated software package the whole process is carried out a lot more quickly and easily. First, users never have to exit one application and enter another, because all applications are open and running concurrently, or so the theory goes. **Concurrency** simply means that different applications function within the computer's memory at the same time.[3] The user can load word processing and spreadsheet applications into memory and switch instantaneously from one to the other with a single keystroke. This saves time because the process of saving the results from one application, leaving the application, starting up another application, importing the results from the previous application, and continuing with the next step in the process is time-consuming. Hence, the second and fourth goals mentioned above are related; they both have as their intent that of increasing the productivity of the user.

The third goal of integrated software as mentioned above is to provide a common set of user interface conventions. When the conventions for cursor control are different in every application, then the user is faced with learning and maintaining a proficiency in each of the conventions. For example, <Ctrl>KD saves a document in WordStar whereas /FS saves a worksheet on disk in Lotus 1-2-3. These differences seem minor until the need arises to master more independent applications, each with its own set of user interface conventions. Integrated software endeavors to provide a single common set of conventions regardless of the application being used.

The fifth goal relates to the way in which files are exported from a source task and imported into a receiving task. The files can either be linked or physically moved. In the former case, if the user changes something in the exported file, he can expect that change to be automatically reflected in all of the documents into which the file was linked. In the latter case, the change would not be reflected without going through the export/import process all over again. Theoretically, integrated software will let users link anything to anything else in all directions.[4] In practice, however, it may not be possible to link a word processing file into a data base file, say.

The sixth and last goal relates to cost. In general, users should be able to purchase an all-in-one integrated package (with the applications included) for less than it would cost to purchase the applications separately. Not all categories of integrated software are integrated all-in-one packages—just those that specifically include the application modules in the ultimate product, which is a single integrated program often called an **all-in-one program**.

FEATURES OF INTEGRATED SOFTWARE

In addition to some of the facets of integrated software already mentioned, one distinguishing feature of integrated software is its use of windows. **Windows** are partitions on the screen that allow the user to view several applications at once. In one window is shown a certain page of a word processing document. In another is shown a portion of a worksheet. In a third window is shown a graphic illustration of the data contained in the displayed portion of the worksheet (the spreadsheet window). Figure 11–8 shows the window concept as used in several integrated software packages. Windows can be moved, enlarged, and reduced, as well as opened and closed. The contents of windows can be scrolled, enabling viewing access to the entire document. In general, windows are overlapping so that one window partially covers one or more other windows, like pages on a desk. In fact, many integrated software packages exploit the desk analogy, referring to the computer display as a "desktop." The exception to this is the use of **tiling**, in which all windows are exactly sized to fit on the screen with no overlap. If one window is enlarged, the others are reduced.

Other devices frequently used in the user interfaces developed for integrated software are those of **pull-down menus**, **pull-up menus**, and **pop-up menus**. These are temporary "windows" that present the user with a set of selection alternatives that relate to a particular function. The user makes a selection by using the cursor to point to or highlight the desired option and then pressing <Return> or some other key. Once the selection is made, the menu disappears. Such usage is commonplace on Apple's Macintosh and on all-in-one integrated software packages discussed in this chapter.

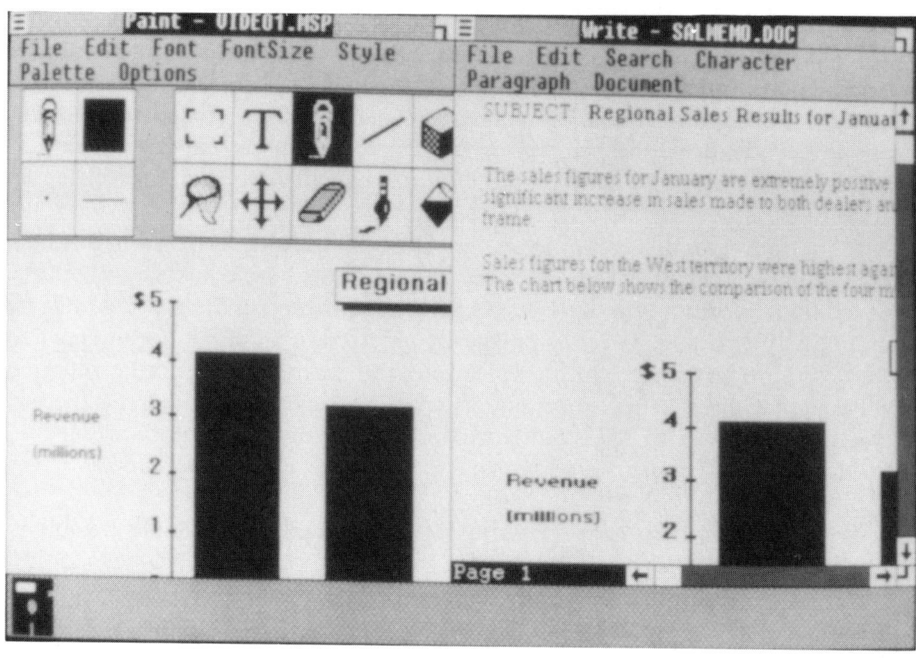

FIGURE 11–8

Windows as Produced by Microsoft's Windows

(Courtesy of Microsoft, Inc.)

Finally, concurrency in integrated software packages creates a **multitasking** capability, allowing the microcomputer to carry out more than one task at a time. Hence, in addition to consistent user-interface conventions, file sharing and compatibility, functional integration, and a window approach to display management, these packages may have the capacity for performing several tasks (applications) concurrently. A true multitasking capability would permit the content of two or more displayed windows to change concurrently. Hence, the graphic representation of a worksheet would be changed concurrently with the recalculation of the worksheet.

SOFTWARE CONCEPTS AND DESIGN PHILOSOPHIES

There are several ways in which commercially available integrated software can be classified. For our purposes we choose the following classification. Integrated software may be categorized into three types: product families, all-in-one programs (consisting of full-blown packages that provide an integrating environment and the applications software for each major application), and integrating environments. They differ from each other primarily in the degree of integration.

Product families are individually marketed software packages produced by the same vendor. The main advantage of product families is that all of the programs come from the same company, and thus are guaranteed to work together. User interface conventions are the same or similar. The major problems of family approaches are that concurrency is usually not supported and methods of file sharing are often one-way. For example, many of these systems do not have the ability to allow text created by a word processor to be used within other applications in the family. The Super, PFS, and Perfect programs are representative of this type of product, as listed in Table 11–5.

TABLE 11–5

List of Vendors Providing Family Products

Microsoft, Inc., (Multiplan and Word), 16011 N. E. 36th Way, Box 97017, Redmond, WA 98073–9717.
Perfect Software, Inc., (Perfect Series), 10001 Camelia St., Berkeley, CA 94710, (415) 527-2626.
Software Publishing Corp., (PFS Series), 1901 Landings Dr., Mountain View, CA 94043, (415) 962-8910.
Computer Associates, Inc, (Super Series), 2195 Fortune Drive, San Jose, CA 95131, (408) 942-1727.

The second and third categories of integrated software are the ones about which there has been most interest. In fact, it was the appearance of all-in-one packages that quickened the heartbeat of many a microcomputer journalist in this field. Hence, much has been written about integrated all-in-one packages in microcomputer literature. Listed in Table 11–6 are current products belonging to this category.

The **integrating environment software** packages listed in Table 11–7 below represent another software layer between the system software and the application software. These products do not include the software for the actual applications themselves, but nevertheless do provide an integrating environment for application software sold by independent vendors. For Microsoft's *Windows,* the independent software vendors must design their products to conform to the environment provided by Windows.

ADVANTAGES/DISADVANTAGES OF INTEGRATED SOFTWARE

The advantages of integrated software correspond with the goals and features of integrated software, and need no further elaboration. The disadvantages of the so-called all-in-one programs, however, require further explanation. First, the robustness of each application may not measure up to that offered by the independent application products. In some integrated packages, there is one well-supported, well-conceived application, with the other applications playing minor (supportive) roles in relation to the one major application. In other products there may be two adequate applications, but a third or fourth application included with the packages is weak and inappropriate for some contexts. For example, two popular integrated software products (Framework and Symphony) do not provide relational data base capabilities and have file sizes limited to the amount of memory available.

Second, the demands on the hardware are considerable and, as will be discussed later, require large amounts of primary memory and usually a hard disk. Future generations of microcomputers will be able to handle the demands imposed by the integrated software with ease. Certainly this is a situation in which the user is well advised to try before buying. See the system demonstrated before making that final purchase decision.

In fairness to the family series of integrated products, it is important to remark that they do not suffer from the shortcomings just alluded to, since they are not

TABLE 11–6

Full-Blown Integrated Software Vendors[4]

Alpha Software (Electric Desk), 12 New England Executive Park, Burlington, MA 01803, (617) 229-2924.
Arktronics (Jane), 113 S. 4th Avenue, Ann Arbor, MI 48104, (313) 769-7253.
Ashton-Tate (Framework), 10150 W. Jefferson Blvd., Culver City, CA 90231, (213) 204-5570.
Context Management Systems (Context and Corporate MBA), 23868 Hawthorne Blvd., Torrance, CA 90505, (213) 378-8277.
Cullinet (Golden Gate), 400 Blue Hill Dr., Westwood, MA 02090, (617) 329-7700.
Infomatics General (Answer series), 21031 Ventura Blvd., Woodland Hills, CA 91364, (213) 887-9040.
Innovative Software (Smart series), 9300 W. 110th St., Suite 380, Overland Park, KS 66210, (913) 383-1089.
Lotus Development Corp. (Symphony), 161 First St., Cambridge, MA 02142, (617) 492-7171.
Lotus Development Corp. (Jazz—for the Macintosh), 161 First St., Cambridge, MA 02142, (617) 492-7171.
Martin Marietta Data Systems (IT Software), Box 2392, Princeton, NJ 08540, (609) 799-7500.
Microsoft, Inc., (Excel), 16011 N. E. 36th Way, Box 97017, Redmond, WA 98073-9717, (206) 828-8080.
Migent, Inc. (Ability Plus), 865 Tahoe Blvd., Call Box 6, Incline Village, Nevada 89450–6062, (800) 633-3444
Mosaic Software (Integrated-7), 1972 Mass. Ave., Cambridge, MA 02140, (617) 491-2434.
Noumenon (Intuit), 512 Westline Dr., Alameda, CA 94501, (415) 521-2145.
Peachtree Software (Decision Manager), 3445 Peachtree Rd., NE, Atlanta, GA 30326, (404) 239-3000.
Schuchardt Software Systems (InteSoft), 515 Northgate Dr., San Rafael, CA 94903, (415) 492-9330.
Softrend (Aura), 2 Manor Pkwy, Salem, NH 03079, (603) 898-1777.
Software Products International (Open Access II), 10240 Sorrento Valley Rd., San Diego, CA 92121, (619) 450-1526.

tightly integrated systems. The fact that they are not tightly integrated, however, translates to some inconvenience in switching applications, and in transferral of files.

ALL-IN-ONE INTEGRATED SOFTWARE PACKAGES

The future for these packages appears uncertain even though the programs are easy to use now and are getting better. Creative Strategies, Inc., a market research company, estimates that the integrated software business will grow from essentially nothing in 1982 to $3.8 billion in 1987. Further refinements and improvements of

TABLE 11–7

List of Vendors Providing Integrating Environments[4]

Digital Research (Concurrent PC-DOS and GEM), Box 579/160 Central Ave., Pacific Grove, CA 93950, (408) 649-3896.

International Business Machines (Topview), Entry Systems Division, Boca Raton, Florida (discontinued).

Microsoft (Microsoft Windows), 16011 N. E. 36th Way, Box 97017, Redmond, WA 98073-9717, (206) 828-8080.

Quarterdeck Office Systems (Desqview), 150 Pico Blvd., Santa Monica, CA 90405

the systems in this category are expected, so that each function of the integrated package is as sophisticated as that of the individual packages. Finally, additional new types of applications may be integrated into these products as these new applications become more widely accepted in the marketplace.

Most of the all-in-one programs available today have one major application that is central to all the others. Suppose, for example, that all applications are performed in the context of the worksheet. All information must therefore be stored in "cells" of the worksheet. Hence, the word processing and data base management applications are performed within the context of the spreadsheet using the same rows and columns format. This decreases the flexibility and usefulness of the word processing and data base applications. Corporate MBA (Content Management Systems) and Symphony (Lotus Development Corp.) are both based on the spreadsheet application.

INTEGRATING ENVIRONMENT PACKAGES

Ecological integration, as provided for in such packages as Topview, Windows, and Desqview, can be accomplished essentially two ways. One, the operating system can be submerged or replaced; in the other, the package uses the operating system for essential functions including screen drivers, memory management, disk accesses, printer drivers, and so on. A short discussion of this class of software can also be found in Chapter 4 under the heading "Applications Environments."

Each of the packages listed in Table 11–7 works in a somewhat different way. For example, *Desqview* can be used to expedite switching from one application to another when these applications rely on the operating system directly. Desqview is designed for off-the-shelf programs and does not require specially written programs. *Topview* requires that the application software vendor revise its stand-alone products to work compatibly with the *Topview* environment. Windows stakes out middle ground between that of *Topview* and *Desqview* in that Windows can run existing stand-alone software (when that software uses the operating system for essential functions) and programs specially written for the environment it provides.

Hardware Required to Support Integrated Software

Integrated software constitutes one of the most demanding types of software, in terms of primary storage size and raw microprocessor processing speed, that has been considered thus far. In general, the user will want as much of both of these as the pocketbook can stand if there is a manifest need for integrated software of either the all-in-one variety or the integrating environments. Certainly the minimum requirement for primary storage capacity is 640K bytes.

Summary

Tremendous growth is taking place in business graphics, and this in turn is becoming an increasingly important function of the microcomputer. Graphics generators may be used in an analytic or presentation context. Analytic graphics should be performed using software in which the graphics application is tightly integrated with the application generating the data. Presentation graphics should be performed using software which permits the user to build a lot of appeal, polish, and persuasion into the final product. For presentation graphics, a color capability is desirable, as is a graphics editor which enables the user to add text, to add titles, and to enhance overall attractiveness.

Integrated software packages are products capable of supporting the major managerial/professional applications in a compatible, integrated way. Frequently, such applications are supported using a windowing and desktop metaphor as the user interface while operating concurrently with integrated productivity tasks. Integrated software may one day permit people to turn the computer on in the morning, leave it on all day, and never have to change the program loaded into primary storage.

Key Terms

all-in-one program
analytic graphics
bit-mapped display
CAD
CAM
character box
character generator
concurrency
.DIF file
graphics editor
integrated software
integrating environment software
multitasking
presentation graphics
product families
pull/down, pull/up, pop-up menus
raster-scan CRT
text-mapped display
tiling
windows

Self-Test

1. Why is graphics important in, and always a component of, integrated all-in-one programs?
2. What are the major uses and applications of graphics software?
3. What devices are used for graphics input and output?
4. What hardware is recommended to support graphics applications?
5. What are graphics editors?
6. What is meant by integrated software?
7. What types of integrated software are available?
8. What major functions or applications are included in integrated software?

Exercises

1. Explain why the use of graphics is important. What benefits accrue to the user of graphics?

2. Explain what is meant by analytic graphics. By presentation graphics. Distinguish between these, and identify categories of software appropriate for both.
3. Listed in Table 11–3 are several stand-alone graphics packages. Which would you choose if you needed resolution greater than 400 × 200 and a price lower than $600?
4. Research the literature concerning the stand-alone graphics packages available today, and describe generally their characteristics in relation to cost. What application contexts are appropriate for each category of stand-alone graphics software?
5. When selecting display adapter cards, color graphics software, and color monitor, what considerations are important?
6. List and briefly describe the use of devices that are employed for input to graphics applications.
7. List and briefly describe the use of devices for output of both hard and soft copy in conjunction with graphics applications.
8. Describe what is meant by a raster-scan display, and explain how this works with a light pen.
9. What five applications are usually included in an all-in-one integrated software package?
10. What major advantages do integrated software packages offer over separate application packages that are not family products? What are some disadvantages of integrated software packages?
11. Research one major commercial software product for each of the three integrated software categories, and write a concise report on the features of each such product. Use the tables provided in this chapter to select a product for each category, and search the popular literature (*Infoworld, Byte, PC: Magazine,* or *PC World*) for reviews of the products.
12. Research the graphics application in three all-in-one integrated programs. Describe the functions of each and build a comparative evaluation table like Table 11–3.
13. Research three stand-alone graphics applications and characterize their degree of usefulness. Which ones have graphics editors? Which have color capabilities? Which are able to input files from other programs?
14. How important is it that the graphics function be well integrated with the word processing function? Some word processors will not support the specific graphics characters that might be placed in a graphics file, so that merging such a file into a word processing document might present problems for the word processing print utility. In some instances the output of both hard copy and soft copy is dependent upon a special graphics driver and requires special hardware. How might this be handled in a printed document? How would this complicating feature be handled if communications of both the word processing document and the graphics file are necessary?

References

1. Wilcox, David L. "The Boom in Business Graphics." *PC World* (August 1984): 54–61.
2. Chang, Dash. "An Introduction to Integrated Software." *Byte* 8, no. 12 (December 1985).
3. Gordon, Phillip. "What is Integrated Software." *PC World* (October 1984).
4. Lu, Cary. "Integrated Software Bids for Center Stage." *High Technology* 4, no. 11 (November 1984).
5. Markoff, John. "Microsoft Does Windows." *Infoworld* 5, no. 47 (November 21, 1983): 32–33.

Additional Reading

Ewing, David P., and Geoffry T. LeBlond. *Using Symphony.* Indianapolis: Que Corporation, 1984.

"The Future of Integrated Software." *Business Computing* (January 1984).

"Integrated Spreadsheets." *PC Week* (September 11, 1984).

Lotus Books. *The Lotus Guide to Learning Symphony.* Reading, Mass.: Addison-Wesley Publishing Company, Inc., 1984.

TUTORIAL

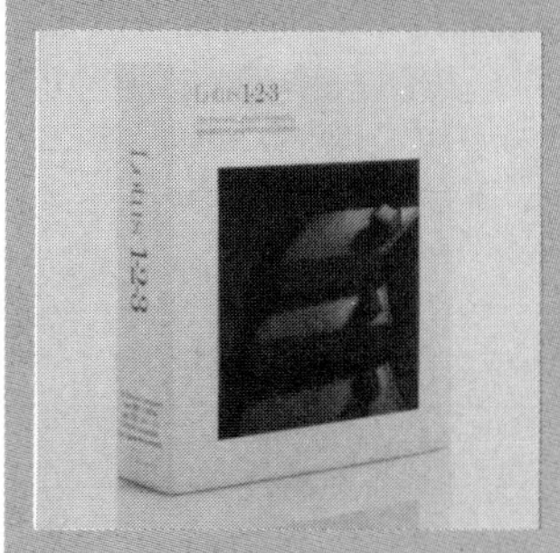

Lotus 1-2-3 Graphics

In this tutorial you are going to create bar and line charts. Creating a graph from your worksheet data is relatively easy in Lotus 1-2-3. First, you need to set up your worksheet as depicted in Table 11–8. Position the cursor to cell B1 and type **QTR 1.** Move the cursor to C1 **(→)** to move one cell to the right) and type **QTR 2** and so on through F1. Type in the text and values as shown in Table 11–8 except for cells B8 through F8 and B10 through F10. These cells contain formulas instead of labels or simple values. These formulas are given below.

```
B8=@SUM(B4..B6)  C8=@SUM(C4..C6)  D8=@SUM(D4..D6)  E8=@SUM(E4..E6)
F8=@SUM(F4..F6)  B10=+B2-B8       C10=+C2-C8       D10=+D2-D8
E10=+E2-E8       F10=+F2-F8
```

Note that in the formulas above, you are actually typing in only what appears to the right of the equal (=) signs. The cell coordinates into which the formula that appears to the right of each equal sign is to be entered is shown on the left of each equal sign.

Next, we set up the column width of column A. Position cursor to cell A1. Type **/WCS15** ("/" to invoke the menu, W to select Worksheet, C to select Column option, S to select Set-Width option, and 15 for the cell column width). This key sequence sets column A to 15 characters width. Columns B through F are wide enough for this example.

To get the dollar sign to show on the screen in Lotus, you need to format the values to currency format. Select **/RFC** and type **2** <**Ret**> at the first prompt and **B2..F10** <**Ret**> at the second prompt. (In the command sequence /RFC you are selecting Range, Format, and Currency. You can also do this with the menu bars, by positioning the highlight over Range followed

TABLE 11–8
Simple Balance Sheet

	A	B	C	D	E	F
1		QTR 1	QTR 2	QTR 3	QTR 4	TOTAL
2	INCOME	$176.91	$193.60	$222.88	$196.49	$789.88
3	EXPENSE					
4	Salaries	$43.10	$43.10	$43.10	$43.10	$172.40
5	Equipment	$89.12	$78.12	$13.50	$198.63	$379.37
6	Educational	$25.88	$21.53	$18.00	$20.01	$85.42
7						
8	TOTAL EXP.	$158.10	$142.75	$74.60	$261.74	$637.01
9						
10	BALANCE	$18.89	$50.85	$148.28	($65.25)	$152.69

by <Return>, positioning the highlight over Format followed by <Return>, and positioning the highlight over Currency followed by <Return>.) The two prompts are displayed for you below.

```
[Enter number of decimal places (0..15): 2<Ret>]
[Enter range to format: B2..F10<Ret>]
```

At this point your worksheet should look exactly the same as that in Table 11–8. If yours is not the same, then repeat the steps above. Be sure you are in the ready mode before you continue. With the worksheet correctly set up, it is time to plot a graph or two. Your final output on the screen should look similar to that of Figures 11–9 and 11–10. Figure 11–9 is a plot of expenses broken down into salary, equipment, and educational expenses for each

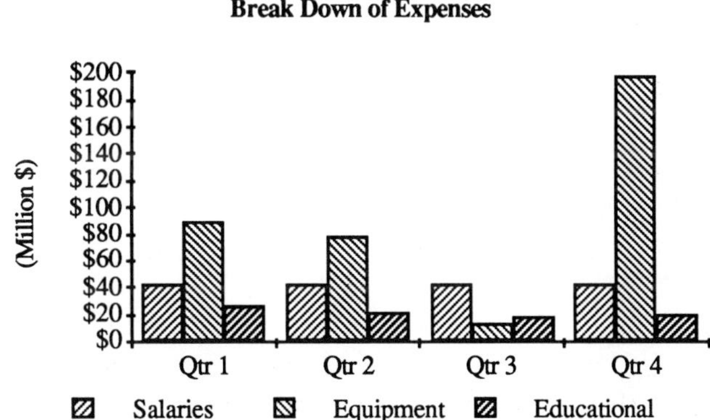

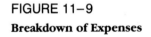

FIGURE 11–9
Breakdown of Expenses

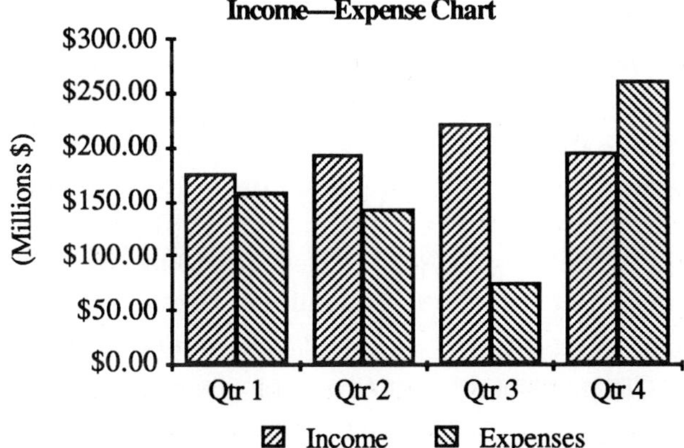

FIGURE 11–10
Income/Expense Chart

(Continued)

Lotus 1-2-3 Graphics (Continued)

quarter. Figure 11–10 is a plot of income and expenses for each quarter. Figure 11–9 will give you a good picture of where the expenses go and Figure 11–10 will give you a picture of how well the company is doing.

The steps presented below assume the user selects directives from the menu bars by highlighting the appropriate menu item (this is called "selecting") and then pressing <Return> which we are representing by <Ret>. The information provided in brackets is parenthetic material intended to show exactly how each prompt will be presented to you. Your response is shown in **bold** within these brackets.

Step 1. Select /**Graph**<**Ret**> to get into the Graphic menu.

2. Select **Type**<**Ret**> to define the type of chart you wish to create. Five chart types are available: Line Bar Xy Stacked-Bar Pie. Select **Bar**<**Ret**>.
3. Select **X**<**Ret**> to define the X-range or the category series and type **B1..E1**<**Ret**>. [Enter X axis range: **B1..E1**<**Ret**>]. In this case it is the four labels in cells B1 through E1.
4. Select **A**<**Ret**> to define the first value series or data range. Type **B4..E4**<**Ret**>. [Enter the first data range: **B4..E4**<**Ret**>].
5. Select **B**<**Ret**> to define the second value series or data range. Type **B5..E5**<**Ret**>. [Enter the second data range: **B5..E5**<**Ret**>].
6. Select **C**<**Ret**> to define the third value series or data range. Type **B6..E6**<**Ret**>. [Enter the third data range: **B6..E6**<**Ret**>]. Lotus allows up to six data ranges to be plotted simultaneously.
7. Select **Options**<**Ret**> to get into the option menu.
8. Select **Legend**<**Ret**> to specify the data range legends.
9. Select **A**<**Ret**> to define the legend for the first data range. Type **Salaries**<**Ret**> at the prompt. [Enter legend for A range: **Salaries**<**Ret**>]. Select **Legend**<**Ret**> and select **B**<**Ret**> and type **Equipment**<**Ret**> at the prompt. [Enter legend for B range: **Equipment**<**Ret**>]. Select **Legend**<**Ret**> and then select **C**<**Ret**> and type **Educational**<**Ret**> at the prompt. [Enter legend for C range: **Educational**<**Ret**>].
10. Select **Titles**<**Ret**> to specify graph title or axis title lines.

11. Select **First<Ret>** to specify first graph title line. Type **Break Down of Expenses<Ret>.** [Enter graph title to line: **Break Down of Expenses<Ret>**]. In this example a second line title for the graph is not required.
12. Repeat Step 10 and select **Y-Axis** this time to specify the Y axis title. Type **(Million $)<Ret>.** Enter Y axis title: **(Million $)<Ret>**]. In the example, an X axis title is unnecessary since the X category explains itself. Select **Quit<Ret>** to return to the Graphic Main menu.
13. At this point you have specified all the options and data you wish to plot and it is time to display the graph. Select **View<Ret>** to display it. Your chart should look similar to Figure 11–9.
14. Select **Save<Ret>** to generate a graph file. Type **CHART1<Ret>** at the prompt. [Enter graph file name: **CHART1<Ret>**]. This step is required if you need to print a graph later.
15. Select **Quit<Ret>** to get back to the ready mode. Select /**FS** and type **B:GRTUTOR<Ret>** at the prompt to save the worksheet. [Enter save file name: **GRTUTOR<Ret>**].

To plot Figure 11–10 you basically repeat Steps 1 through 13 and make appropriate changes to the title and data ranges, except in Step 6. You must select bar in Step 2. For this case, the input for Step 4, Step 5, and Step 6 should read:

4. Select **A<Ret>** to define the first value series or data range. Type **B2..E2<Ret>.** [Enter the first data range: **B2..E2<Ret>**].
5. Select **B<Ret>** to define the second value series or data range. Type **B8..E8<Ret>.** [Enter the second data range: **B8..E8<Ret>**].
6. Select **Reset<Ret>** and **C<Ret>** to cancel the C range. Select **Quit<Ret>** to get back to the Graphic Main menu.

After you have entered the appropriate steps, select **View<Ret>** to display the plot. It should look like the one in Figure 11–10. Select **Quit<Ret>** to get back to the ready mode. Enter /**GTL** and then **V** to display a line chart.

Changes on the worksheet will be reflected on the related graph if you depress the <f10> function key. As an example, move to cell B4 and enter

(Continued)

Lotus 1-2-3 Graphics (Continued)

FIGURE 11–11
PrintGraph Main Menu (Top Half)

```
Copyright 1985 Lotus Development Corp.  All Rights Reserved.  Release 2        MENU
Select graphs for printing
Image-Select  Settings  Go  Align  Page  Exit
=====================================================================================
GRAPH      IMAGE  OPTIONS                          HARDWARE  SETUP
IMAGES       Size                 Range  Colors      Graphs Directory:
SELECTED     Top        .395       X                   A:\
             Left       .750       A                 Fonts Directory:
             Width     6.500       B                   A:\
             Height    4.691       C                 Interface:
             Rotate     .000       D                   Parallel 1
                                   E                 Printer Type:
             Font                  F
               1  BLOCK1                             Paper  Size
               2  BLOCK2                               Width       8.500
                                                       Length     11.000

                                                    ACTION  OPTIONS
                                                       Pause: No   Eject: No
```

200<Ret>. Then press the <**f10**> function key and the new value will be reflected on the graph.

PRINTGRAPH

The Lotus 1-2-3 graph module does not allow you to print a graph directly. To print a graph created from Lotus 1-2-3, you first need to save the graph in "PIC" format, Quit Lotus 1-2-3, and use the PrintGraph application to print the graph. It is an inconvenience but it is not an overly complicated task. This part of the tutorial assumes that you have gone through Steps 1 to 14, or that there already exists a graph file with a PIC extension.

Step 1. In the ready mode, select /**Quit**<**Ret**> to quit Lotus 1-2-3 and type **Y** to get into the 1-2-3 Access System.

2. Select **PrintGraph** from the Lotus 1-2-3 Access System menu. You should see the following message:

```
        Insert PrintGraph Disk in Drive A
Press [RETURN] to continue or [ESCAPE] to quit.
```

Remove the Lotus System Disk from Drive A and insert the Print-

```
Copyright 1985 Lotus Development Corp.  All Rights Reserved.  Release 2        POINT
Select graphs for output

PICTURE      DATE        TIME      SIZE
-------------------------------------------------      [SPACE] turns mark on and off
CHART1       04-21-87    19:06     2423                [RETURN] selects marked pictures
CHART2       04-21-87    19:20     2863                [ESCAPE] exits, ignoring changes
LIM1         04-18-87    18:15     3834                [HOME] goes to beginning of list
LIM2         03-20-87    18:56     2543                [END] goes to end of list
                                                       [UP] and [DOWN] move cursor
                                                            List will scroll if cursor move
                                                            moved beyond to or bottom
                                                       [GRAPH] display selected picture
```

FIGURE 11–12
PrintGraph Image-Select Menu

Graph Disk (included in the Lotus 1-2-3 package) into Drive A. Type <**Ret**>.

3. Once in the PrintGraph main menu, your screen should look something like that shown in Figure 11–11.
4. Notice that Image-Select is initially highlighted. Select **Settings**<**Ret**> then **Hardware**<**Ret**> then **Graphs-Directory**<**Ret**> and type B: at the prompt. This sets the current disk directory/volume to drive B. Select **Quit**<Ret> and **Quit**<Ret> to get back into the main menu.
5. Now, from the PrintGraph main menu shown in Figure 11–11, select **Image-Select**<**Ret**>**.** Your display should appear like that shown in Figure 11–12. Move the cursor to highlight CHART1 (use the [UP] and [DOWN] arrow keys.) Type <**Ret**> to select the highlighted picture and return. You can select more than one picture by using the space bar and type <Ret> on the last one you want. If you wish to view the selected graph, press the <f10> function key. The <f10> function key is called the GRAPH key.
6. Select **Settings**<**Ret**> then **Hardware**<**Ret**> then **Printer**<**Ret**> and use the cursor keys in combination with the space bar and <Ret> key to select the graph output device. Select **Quit**<**Ret**> and **Quit**<**Ret**> to get back to main menu.
7. Make sure the printer is on and the paper aligned properly. Select

(Continued)

Lotus 1-2-3 Graphics (Continued)

Align<**Ret**> to let PrintGraph know that the printer is aligned to the top of the page. Next select **Go**<**Ret**> to commence printing.

8. Select **Exit**<**Ret**> and type **Y** to exit PrintGraph. This gets you back to the 1-2-3 Access System. Select **Exit** to end this session.

EXERCISES

1. What is the name of the Lotus module used to print graphs? What is the <f10> function key referred to, and what does it do? How many data ranges can be plotted simultaneously?
2. Does Lotus 1-2-3 Release 2 or earlier provide presentation-quality graphics, or is its graphics suitable for analysis only? Explain.

DISK EXERCISES

1. Use the file GRAPHIC.WK1 to construct a bar chart. Save the bar chart under the filename BAR1.PIC on your data disk. Plot the data ranges B1..E1, B4..E4, B5..E5, and B6..E6 on the bar chart. Label the X axis **Break Down of Expenses** and label the Y axis **(Thousand $).**
2. Use the file GRAPHIC.WK1 to construct a line chart. Save the line chart under the file name LIN1.PIC on your data disk. Plot the data ranges B1..E1, B4..E4, B5..E5, and B6..E6 on the bar chart. Label the X axis **Break Down of Expenses** and label the Y axis **(Thousand $).**
3. Use the file GRAPHIC.WK1 to construct another bar chart. Save this bar chart under the file BAR2.PIC on your data disk. Plot the data ranges B1..E1, B2..E2, B8..E8. Label the X axis and Y axis appropriately.
4. Use the file GRAPHIC.WK1 to construct another line chart. Save this bar chart under the file LIN2.PIC on your data disk. Plot the data ranges B1..E1, B2..E2, B8..E8. Label the X axis and Y axis appropriately.
5. Use the file GRAPHIC.WK1 to construct a pie chart. Use the cells B4..B6. Label the chart appropriately. Save the chart under the file name PIE.PIC on your data disk.
6. Print the file GRAPH1.PIC using PrintGraph.
7. Print the file you created called BAR1.PIC using PrintGraph.
8. Print the file you created called LIN1.PIC using PrintGraph.
9. Print the file you created called PIE.PIC using PrintGraph.

PART III

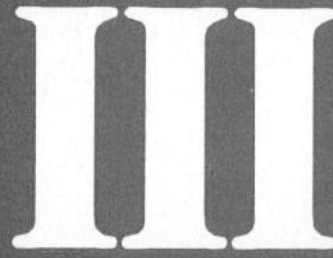

ADDITIONAL CONCEPTS AND APPLICATIONS

Part II of this book dealt with the managerial productivity applications: word processing, spreadsheets, file and data base management, and graphics. Included within Part III of this book are discussions of applications, concepts, and hardware that are equally as important as the productivity applications, although very different from them. This last part comprises Chapters 12 through 16.

Chapter 12 discusses four increasingly important categories of software for microcomputers—*desk organizers, project management, expert systems,* and *decision support systems*. What applications are served by each of these four software types, how each is used, why each is important, and what the future holds for each type are discussed.

Chapter 13 discusses one of the first applications to which microcomputers were put in small business: accounting systems and inventory systems. The chapter introduces the reader to *general ledger, accounts receivable, accounts payable,* and *inventory* packages.

Chapter 14 describes the benefits that can accrue from data communications. The types of data communications available are described as well.

Chapter 15 discusses local area networks. It has been said that 80% of data communications are local. Yet existing communication media (phone lines, principally) are not optimized to handle this communication efficiently. The need for a separate local communication network is described in this chapter.

Chapter 16 presents how to purchase microcomputer software and hardware. A method for competitive purchase of entire microcomputer systems is presented. The chapter describes such important issues as whether to make or buy software, vendor support, software maintenance, and capacity requirements planning.

Chapters 12 and 13 are primarily concerned with software. Chapters 14 and 15 deal with both hardware and software used in data communications and local area networks. Finally, Chapter 16 is concerned with purchase decisions of microcomputer hardware and software.

CHAPTER 12

Other Popular Software for Business and Personal Use

CHAPTER OUTLINE

Desk Organizers 423
Project Management Software 431
Expert Systems 440
Decision Support Systems (DSS) 446

CHAPTER OBJECTIVES

In this chapter you will learn

1 what desk organizers are and how they can be used
2 what components make up desk organizers
3 what project management packages do, and how they are used
4 what features to expect in project management packages
5 what the major categories of project management software are
6 what expert systems are, and what they can be used for
7 what decision support systems are
8 how decision support systems relate to spreadsheets
9 the anatomy of decision support systems

This chapter presents several important categories of microcomputer software for business and professional use. Each of the topics treated in this chapter could not be given exclusive consideration within a single chapter, but were nevertheless important enough to be worthy of being discussed as a major topic within this chapter. The topics include desk organizers like Borland's Sidekick, project management software, expert systems like Level Five's Insight, and decision support system generators like IFPS/Personal, Javelin, and MindSight.

Each of these categories of software have important business and professional applications. Desk organizers represent a recent development in productivity software, providing many of the functions of familiar desktop tools (calculators, appointment books, etc.) in a form that allows them to be accessed from within other programs. Project management software allows a firm to organize the events (milestones) of a project into a sequence that optimizes the use of resources, personnel, and money. Expert systems are intended to provide less sophisticated users access to the knowledge of the experts together with the experts' strategy for processing this knowledge. This knowledge can enable these users to perform their assignments and job descriptions like experts, even though they are neophytes. Decision support systems are models with more sophisticated features than spreadsheets. This chapter describes each of these categories in detail.

DESK ORGANIZERS

A glance at the desk of any business manager or clerical worker will reveal a wide assortment of tools that have become virtually indispensable to the organization of activities in a busy workplace. A calendar keeps notes on activities and goals for the day, as well as important meetings or events coming up. A calculator is kept handy for quick computations, as well as a scratch pad to jot down notes. A Rolodex™ or card file might be present to keep track of important phone numbers or client information. With the addition of a desktop computer, the typical businessperson's desk becomes, in a word, cluttered, and several software developers have seen this as an opportunity for the creation of a new category of software, the **desk organizer**.

Desk organizing software can remove a great deal of the clutter by allowing the computer to replicate most of these functions, and can prove to be a significant enhancement to productivity. Because a busy office worker's job often seems like a series of interruptions interspersed with occasional attention to primary responsibilities, a desk organizer allows the user to attend to the minor and major distractions of normal business activity without having to divert his eyes from the computer's CRT or his fingers from its keyboard.

More important, perhaps, is the ability of the desk organizer to improve upon the functionality of familiar desktop aids. Although a calendar can be consulted for important upcoming events, a desk organizer's calendar and appointment diary might be able to beep at the user when that important call needs to be made, display a friendly reminder when the boss's birthday is only two days away, or remind the user that it is time to attend an important meeting. Similarly, a Rolodex™ is handy for keeping names and addresses within reach, but a desk organizer's card file function often comes with most of the features of a file management system, allowing extensive notes and complex searches. It may even dial the number for the user once it has been found, through the computer's attached modem.

Background and Concepts of Desk Organizers

Desk organizers are part of a growing class of software that is **memory-resident**, that is, residing in memory even while other programs are being run. For this reason, desk organizers are referred to here as memory-resident programs. This type of software is usually loaded into memory before an application program (such as a word processor or spreadsheet) is used, often placed into memory by a program that is automatically executed upon system startup. Once in memory, it remains there until the computer is turned off, and can be invoked at any time by one or two specially designated keystrokes.

Memory-resident software takes advantage of the large amount of memory available on most 16- and 32-bit microcomputers. These programs select an area of memory that will not be used by either the operating system (which also remains in memory at all times), applications programs, or hardware devices (such as video display adapters). Once the program is loaded into this unused memory, it waits and listens to all signals (called "interrupts") that the user sends to the computer via a keyboard or other input device. When the user presses the right key combination (e.g., Ctrl-Alt for Borland's Sidekick program), the memory-resident program will spring to life. Normal processing of other programs will be suspended as the memory resident program takes control of the computer's microprocessor. When the user has finished his task with the memory-resident program, he is returned safely to his primary application program, precisely at the point he left it, without any disturbance of the data or files that were in use.

The development of desktop organizers can be traced to the user-friendly interface of the Apple Lisa computer (which, in turn, borrowed heavily from ideas developed by Xerox Corporation's Palo Alto Research Center in the early 1970s). The Lisa interface used the desktop metaphor to place an assortment of functions at the fingertips of users (like the Macintosh interface shown in Figure 12–1).

Although much of Lisa's acclaim (and criticism) concerned its use of graphic symbols, or "icons," many users were equally impressed with Lisa's ability to switch easily from function to function. The Lisa computer, introduced in 1983, was discontinued the following year, having been supplanted by the more affordable Macintosh. While retaining most of the innovative features of the Lisa, the Macintosh brought with it the ability to transfer data from one application to another by first marking it as a "note" and attaching the note to a "clipboard." After entering a new application, the note could be retrieved from the clipboard, allowing, for example, the information created by a data base management system to be incorporated into a word processing document.

The Lisa and Macintosh had these impressive capabilities because they were a part of the computer's operating systems, always present in memory. For IBM-compatible computers to offer similar capabilities a different approach had to be taken, because no such features were built into the operating systems. Early integrated programs could move information between different applications, but did not incorporate the assortment of handy desktop tools desired by users. Borland International, a software firm that had received notoriety for its Turbo Pascal programming language, pioneered the memory-resident program concept with the introduction of Sidekick (Figure 12–2), a desk organizer for the IBM PC. Sidekick created such a stir in the microcomputer world that it sold several hundred thousand copies and received *Infoworld* magazine's software Product of the Year award for 1984. As with any other successful software product, the market soon became filled with similar products, often surpassing the innovator in features.

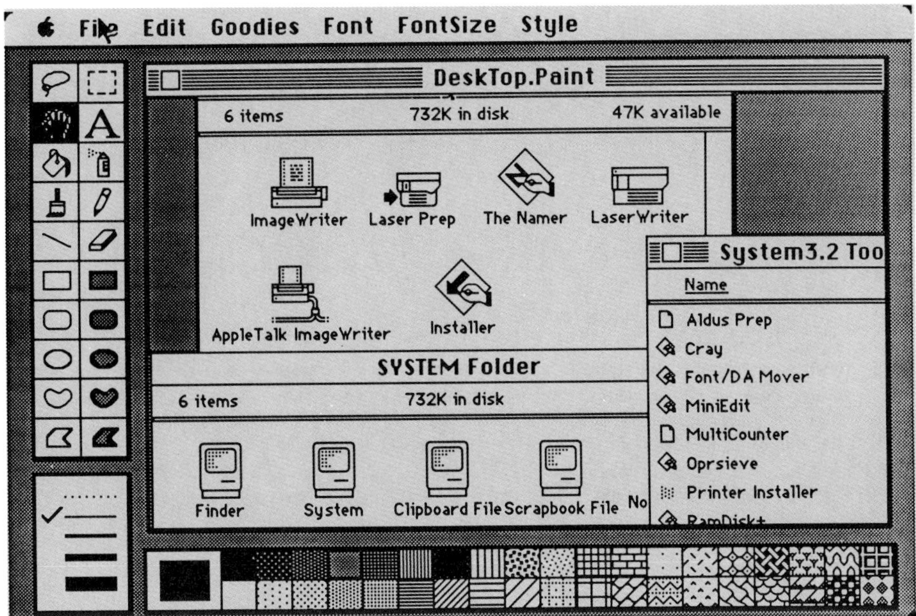

FIGURE 12–1

The Apple Macintosh Desktop

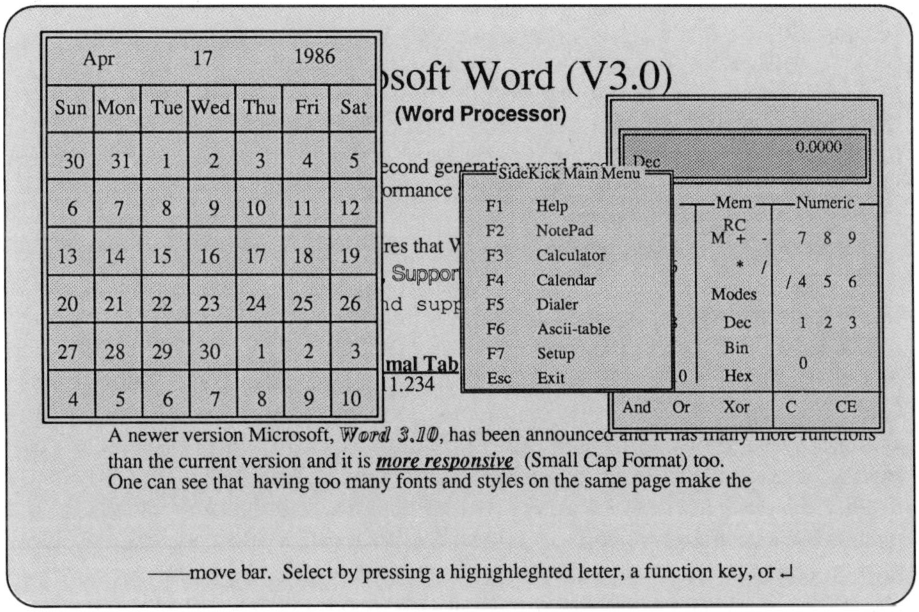

FIGURE 12–2

Sidekick (Borland International)

Desk Organizer Features

The number of features available in a desk organizer varies from a few to a dozen or more. Among the most commonly found are a notepad, card file, appointment book, calculator, data capture and transfer capability, a communications module, and access to operating system commands.

A desk organizer's **notepad** (or scratch pad) feature allows the user to record thoughts as they occur, even in the midst of working with a spreadsheet, a word

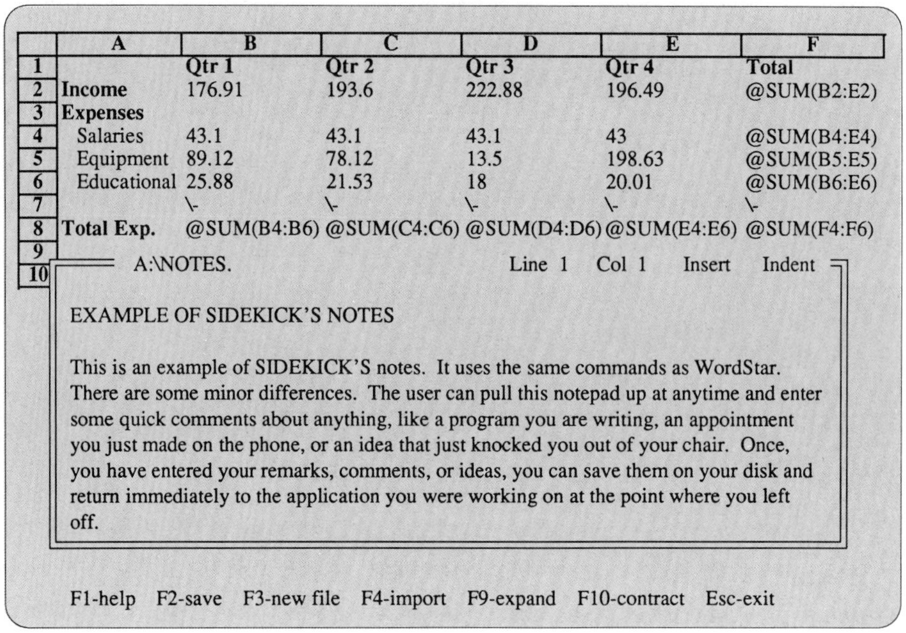

FIGURE 12–3
Sidekick's Notepad

	A	B	C	D	E	F
1		**Qtr 1**	**Qtr 2**	**Qtr 3**	**Qtr 4**	**Total**
2	**Income**	176.91	193.6	222.88	196.49	@SUM(B2:E2)
3	**Expenses**					
4	Salaries	43.1	43.1	43.1	43	@SUM(B4:E4)
5	Equipment	89.12	78.12	13.5	198.63	@SUM(B5:E5)
6	Educational	25.88	21.53	18	20.01	@SUM(B6:E6)
7		\-	\-	\-	\-	\-
8	**Total Exp.**	@SUM(B4:B6)	@SUM(C4:C6)	@SUM(D4:D6)	@SUM(E4:E6)	@SUM(F4:F6)
9						
10						

A:\NOTES. Line 1 Col 1 Insert Indent

EXAMPLE OF SIDEKICK'S NOTES

This is an example of SIDEKICK'S notes. It uses the same commands as WordStar. There are some minor differences. The user can pull this notepad up at anytime and enter some quick comments about anything, like a program you are writing, an appointment you just made on the phone, or an idea that just knocked you out of your chair. Once, you have entered your remarks, comments, or ideas, you can save them on your disk and return immediately to the application you were working on at the point where you left off.

F1-help F2-save F3-new file F4-import F9-expand F10-contract Esc-exit

processor, or other program. When invoked, the notepad function will overlay a portion of the screen with a blank work area for writing. Notes are then entered in the same fashion as with a word processor. When finished, the note is stored on the disk under a filename of the user's choosing and the work area disappears, leaving the underlying work undisturbed (Figure 12–3).

The editing features of a desk organizer's notepad can range from few to many, often rivaling word processing programs in their power. The note files created and saved by a desk organizer's notepad application can be read and edited by more powerful word processing programs. Most notepad features are intended only for simple recording or printing and users should rely upon a word processing program for extensive editing and formatting of the notes. Even with the very complete editing power available in some desk organizers, users will find that taking advantage of them may require learning an entire set of unfamiliar commands. There is also a limit to the size of the notes that can be recorded, because these are stored in memory until saved to disk. Desk organizers usually have a default file limitation of 4,000 to 7,000 bytes, but some desk organizers may allow this work area to be expanded to beyond 60,000 bytes.

Most desk organizer users find that they use the notepad more often than any other feature. When working with a large computer program or a worksheet that takes a long time to load into memory, the alternative to using a notepad requires exiting one program (after saving your current work), entering a word processor or editor to record the note, then returning to the primary application program. On a floppy-disk-based system, this will also require several disk swaps. The action of the notepad, by contrast, is swift and virtually without effort. The notepad allows comments about the spreadsheet or computer program to be recorded permanently so that the comments can later be incorporated into the documentation for the spreadsheet or computer program.

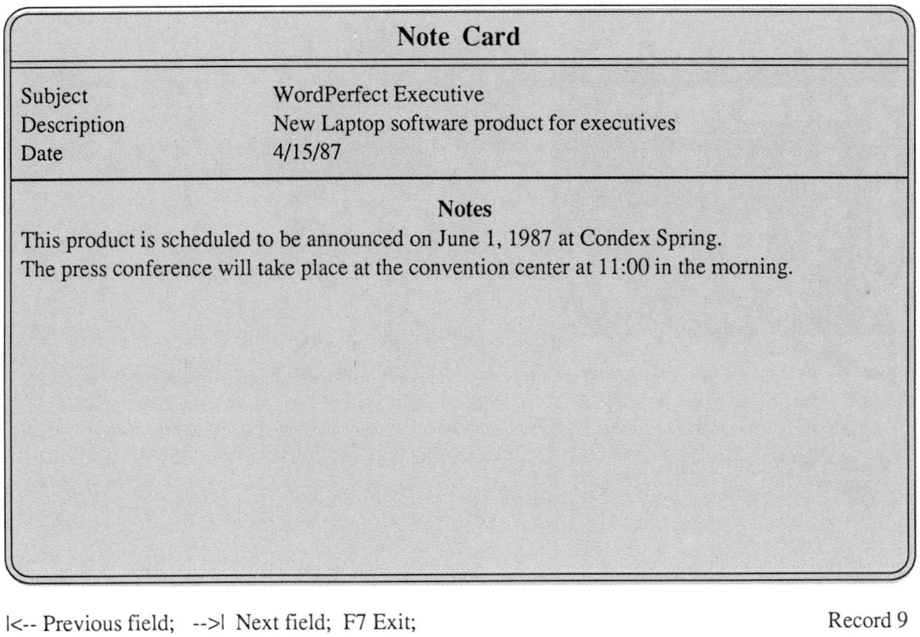

Note Card	
Subject	WordPerfect Executive
Description	New Laptop software product for executives
Date	4/15/87

Notes

This product is scheduled to be announced on June 1, 1987 at Condex Spring.
The press conference will take place at the convention center at 11:00 in the morning.

|<-- Previous field; -->| Next field; F7 Exit; Record 9

FIGURE 12–4

WordPerfect Library's Card File *(Courtesy of WordPerfect Corporation)*

A desk organizer's **card file** provides the same function as an address book or desktop Rolodex™. An entry area is provided for names, addresses, phone numbers, and a short note (Figure 12–4). The record cards are usually loaded from the disk into memory at the same time as the desk organizer. This places a limit on the number of cards (ordinarily 200 to 1,000), but greatly speeds up searches. It is also a great convenience if the user typically begins a computer session from a particular disk, because the records do not need to be stored on all the user's application disks. Although some card files have sophisticated search capabilities, desk organizers are not a substitute for file management systems except in the least demanding situations.

The **appointment book** (Figure 12–5) function of a desk organizer can be a tremendous aid to the businessperson whose time needs to be closely budgeted or who tends to forget appointments or events. As with the paper version, a desk organizer's appointment book can be used to enter meetings, remind the user of upcoming anniversaries and birthdays, or make a "to do" list for the day. Unlike the paper version, computer appointment books can also act as alarm clocks, signaling the user (with an audible beep or a message flashed on the screen) at predetermined times. Some appointment books will even allow the user to identify recurring events (for example, a business luncheon every Friday) so that the events need only be entered once. Of course, any appointment book can also serve as a calendar, and with a span of many years it is possible to find out on which day of the week a birthday falls in the year 2000.

A wide range of features are available in desk organizer **calculators**, sometimes rivaling expensive hand-held ones. Sidekick's calculator (Figure 12–6) performs decimal mathematics as well as operating on hexadecimal and binary numbers, including AND, OR, and XOR logic functions. PolyWindows DeskPlus, from Polytron, displays a "paper tape" record of calculator entries, allowing the user to

FIGURE 12–5
Appointment Book

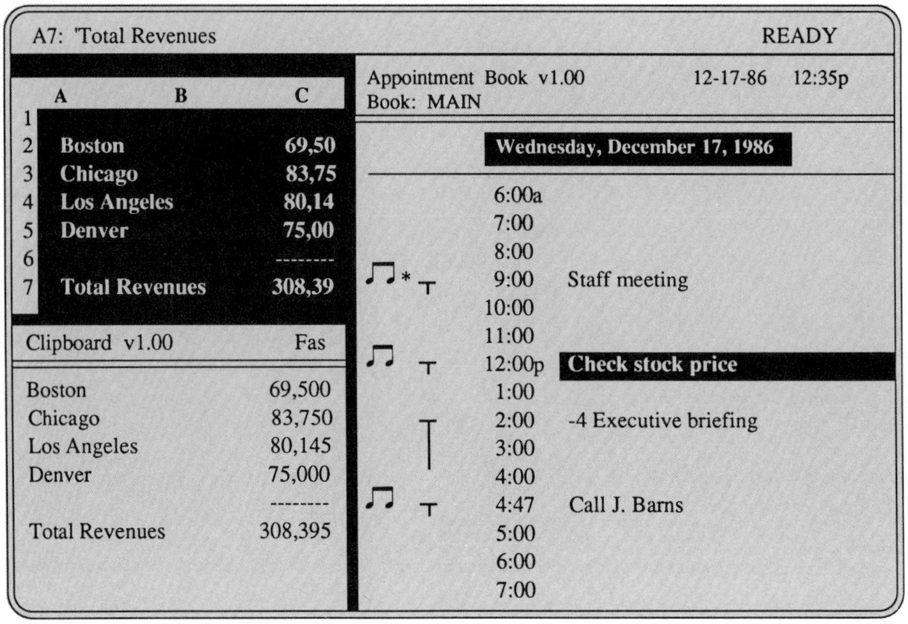

```
A7: 'Total Revenues                                              READY

    A        B          C      | Appointment Book v1.00     12-17-86   12:35p
1                              | Book: MAIN
2   Boston             69,50   |        Wednesday, December 17, 1986
3   Chicago            83,75   |
4   Los Angeles        80,14   |        6:00a
5   Denver             75,00   |        7:00
6                   --------   |        8:00
7   Total Revenues    308,39   |  *     9:00   Staff meeting
                               |       10:00
Clipboard v1.00          Fas   |       11:00
                               |       12:00p  Check stock price
Boston                69,500   |        1:00
Chicago               83,750   |        2:00   -4 Executive briefing
Los Angeles           80,145   |        3:00
Denver                75,000   |        4:00
                    --------   |        4:47   Call J. Barns
Total Revenues       308,395   |        5:00
                               |        6:00
                               |        7:00
```

search for mistakes. Bellesoft's Pop-Up DeskSet has two calculators, one designed for normal calculation, and one with features found only on financial calculators (present value, payment, etc.). Warner Software's The Desk Organizer has a programmable calculator that can accept up to twenty-six variables in its formulas. None of these programs are likely to completely replace the hand-held calculator, but they do offer two significant advantages: they can perform considerably faster than a hand-held calculator, and they don't get lost under a pile of paperwork.

A **data capture and transfer utility** can greatly simplify the transfer of information between applications programs. To move selected columns and rows from a spreadsheet's worksheet into a word processing document ordinarily requires saving the worksheet with a special format (or performing a "print to disk," writing the information to a disk file in exactly the form it would appear in print), then retrieving the file once inside the word processor. With several word processors, retrieval is impossible due to the unique nature of the program's storage method. A desk organizer may allow the user to mark any area of information displayed on the screen, store it in memory, move to the next application, and place the information back on-screen in the desired location, thereby making the information accessible to the new application. Some programs such as Sidekick allow the user to "cut" (store in memory or on disk) information, but cannot "paste" (place the information back on-screen).

The **communications module** of a desk organizer performs the same function as the automatic dialer of a telephone, dialing numbers through the user's modem device. Although this may not appear to save much effort, the desk organizer offers a few advantages. The desk organizer can hold hundreds of numbers in its memory, while the telephone's dialer is often limited to ten. A desk organizer can also search by name through its card file, saving the time required to look in a phone book. The user doesn't even need a card file with Borland's Sidekick, because it can be told to search through the entire screen display for a recognizable phone number.

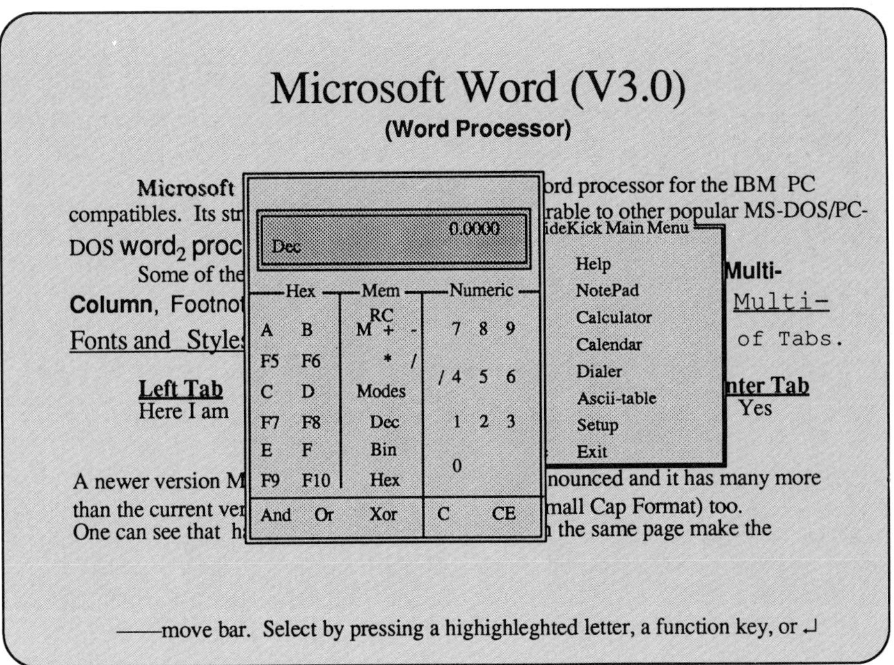

FIGURE 12–6
Sidekick Calculator

Sidekick's Macintosh version has modest terminal emulation capabilities, allowing it to act as a remote terminal for communicating with other computers.

Anyone who has worked with microcomputers for very long is likely to have encountered the following situation: after a lengthy session with a word processing or spreadsheet program, you are ready to save your efforts, but there is no room left on the disk, and no facility for deleting files without exiting the program (and losing your work). Perhaps you have forgotten to format the disk, and have none other available. Or, perhaps, you can't remember the name of the file you wanted to work on and must make an aggravating trip back to the operating system to view your directory. A desk organizer's access to **operating system commands** can prove useful in these situations. By allowing you to perform a few vital operating system activities (view or switch directories, format disks, erase or copy files, etc.) without exiting an applications program, a desk organizer can save the user from much frustration.

Other Desk Organizer Features

Some of the features listed above may not be found in all desk organizer programs. Other programs have features not included in the list. Several programs offer a keyboard enhancement feature (to store one or more commands on a selected key; discussed in Chapter 5). An ASCII table (a table of numeric codes associated with each character the computer can generate) is provided with some desk organizers, and is useful for programmers (Figure 12–7). The Desk Organizer from Warner Software has twenty-five standard business form letters that can be

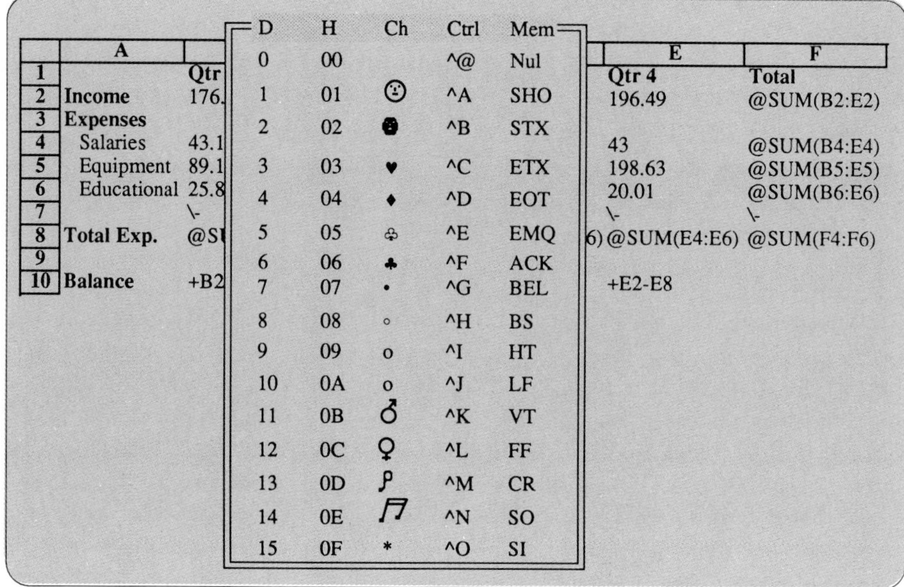

FIGURE 12–7
ASCII Table (Sidekick)

called up and filled in within seconds. In addition, most desk organizers have the capability to print all or part of the screen display (excluding special graphics characters) without saving the document to disk first.

More on Memory-Resident Utilities

Because of the decreasing cost of memory chips, more and more users have been encouraged to upgrade the internal storage capacity of their personal computers. This, in turn, has prompted software producers to generate a flood of programs that use that extra memory capacity. Memory-resident programs are now available that provide an assortment of useful, and even frivolous functions.

For word processing users, there are memory-resident spelling checkers that begin looking up words even before the typing is finished, and that will beep at the user if he completes a word they are unfamiliar with. A memory-resident thesaurus (available from several companies, including Borland) can find synonyms for the word nearest the cursor if called upon. And, of course, a keyboard enhancement program can cut laborious, repetitive tasks down to size. Keyboard enhancers provide a macro capability and enable key definitions to be changed.

Business users who are reclaiming a portion of their computer's cost by deducting it from their incomes at tax time should know that the Internal Revenue Service can now request a detailed log of the use of the equipment. A number of programs are available which record the times of day when a computer is in use, will obtain information on the purpose of the computing session, and will prepare usage logs in an IRS-acceptable format. Businessmen and writers who find that an outline processor (see Chapters 5 and 6) helps them organize their thoughts might be delighted by having the same capability from a memory-resident program (such as Ready! from Living Videotext, producers of Thinktank), able to be called from within any program.

For the less serious-minded (or perhaps to escape from too much seriousness), users can have their applications program suspended long enough for one or more jokes to appear on-screen (Chuckle Pops, from Enlighten Software). Are you tired of being overweight, trying to stop smoking, straining to find motivation, or needing some encouragement? A program entitled "Subliminal Suggestion and Self-Hypnosis Programs for Your Computer," from Greentree Publishers, can provide you with a steady stream of subliminal (below the threshold of consciousness) messages. You may select from Greentree's supplied phrases or design your own one- or two-line messages. During an eight-hour day at the computer, your message can be displayed tens of thousands of times, all unseen by the conscious mind but purportedly reaching the subconscious to positively alter your behavior.

The trend toward memory-resident utilities is likely to increase with the expanded capabilities of tomorrow's computers. These programs, moreover, have been remarkably well received by computer users (some would claim that you can become addicted to them). This may be merely a testimony to the enhancement of productivity that they afford, or to the typically low cost of the software (from $19.95 to $395, with most under $100). But it can present chaos within the computer if the user attempts to place too many programs in memory simultaneously.

Consider the user with a 640 K byte (main memory) IBM PC or compatible computer. After her operating system loads into memory (it uses slightly over 20K), she is ready for a word processing session. But first, she loads a few "necessary" programs into memory. A RAM disk and print spooler (see Chapters 3, 5, and 6) might occupy 160K and 64K, respectively. The spelling checker and thesaurus take up another 90K. Next in are the keyboard enhancer (45K), desk organizer (60K), and outline processor (128K). Finally, she attempts to load the word processor, but finds it will not fit in the remaining 73K (and she even left out the subliminal messages and the jokes).

A more likely scenario than the one above involves the user who appears to successfully load several programs into memory simultaneously, only to find out later that one program has overwritten a portion of another in memory. This is usually discovered after an hour or so of work, before anything has been saved to disk, and is signaled by the keyboard suddenly not responding to touch. The interactions between different memory-resident programs and even with well established applications programs are treacherous, baffling, and may never be resolved in the current generation of microcomputers, given the methods they employ to achieve "one-key" convenience. Some programs, moreover, may prohibit the use of memory-resident programs altogether. XyWrite, a popular word processor for the IBM PC and compatibles family, takes direct control of the signals from the keyboard (rather than letting the operating system do this). This control makes the word processor very fast, but does not allow a desk organizer to be used. Several other popular programs have employed similar tactics in order to gain a performance advantage.

It is worth noting that several memory-resident programs are available that manage the concurrent residence of the other memory-resident programs, to prevent one program from overwriting another. A list of selected vendors of desk organizer software is provided in Table 12–1.

PROJECT MANAGEMENT SOFTWARE

For many types of companies, business does not consist of a steady stream of repetitive tasks. Rather, each new client represents a new project requiring an

TABLE 12–1

Selected Vendors for Desk Organizer Software

Sidekick Borland International 4113 Scotts Valley Drive Scotts Valley, CA 95066	**PolyWindows Desk** Polytron Corp. P.O. Box 787 Hillsboro, OR 97123
The Desk Organizer Warner Software, Inc. 666 Fifth Avenue New York, NY 10103	**Spotlight** Software Arts 27 Mica Lane Wellesley, MA 02181
HOMEBASE Brown Bag Software 2155 S. Bascom Ave. Campbell, CA 95008	**WordPerfect Library** WordPerfect Corp. 288 W. Center Street Orem, UT 84057
Metro Lotus Dev. Corp. 55 Cambridge Pkwy. Cambridge, MA 02142	**Pop-Up DeskSet Plus** Popular Programs, Inc. (formerly Bellsoft) 2820 Northup Way Bellevue, WA 98004

individualized strategy for the utilization of part or all of the firm's resources. If only one project is undertaken at a time and each project is short-lived and uses few resources, the company may get by with minimal planning. When large amounts of time and resources are required, or when more than one project is under way, careful planning is required to ensure that the firm does not find itself habitually short of funds, personnel, and supplies, or repeatedly behind schedule.

Project management software will aid the managers of a business in preventing such difficulties by allowing them to develop a realistic plan for using the firm's time, money, and resources; and by aiding them in keeping track of how well the project is proceeding. Project management actually consists of two separate jobs: project planning and project control. **Project planning** is the development of a detailed plan for completing the project under consideration. Project planning software will answer questions concerning how much of each resource will be in use at each stage of the project, how much the total project will cost, and how much of that portion can be billed to the client. Project planning software can reveal time periods when personnel must wait for others to complete their jobs, provide dates when stages of the project will be completed, and provide helpful visual representations of the activities and resources involved in a project.

Project control (or project monitoring) allows the manager to see how a project is progressing in relation to the project plan. Ideally, project management should be able to determine, at any stage of a project, what percentage of the total project has been completed. If the project is running late or over budget, management should be able to obtain new estimates on the time and cost to complete the work. When unanticipated circumstances arise, the old project plan must be updated to reflect the new developments.

Only the more sophisticated offerings in project management software venture beyond project planning into project control. For most users, software that provides only a planning aid may be sufficient, since proper planning will go a long way toward more effective manual monitoring of a project, and since a plan can always be redrafted and compared with the original plan.

Using project management software can pay off handsomely. The cost of the software (between $49.50 and $2,500) can often be recovered from the first project on which it is used. Cost savings are gained through using personnel more efficiently, ensuring that resource shortages do not occur at critical times, reducing periods of inactivity, and helping develop better cost estimates. In addition to these benefits, firms that have good project planning methods will be able to complete more projects in less time, enhancing the firm's reputation and increasing its profits.

Project planning software can be used effectively in virtually any type of business, although it is most commonly associated with manufacturing and construction or architectural firms. In manufacturing, project planning is appropriate when considering new product development or when making changes in production facilities. In the construction industry, each structure is usually treated as a new project, with its own requirements on time, resources, and funds. Outside these industries, a computer software firm might use project planning software to coordinate all the activities involved in installing a new computer system or developing a new software product. A consumer goods maker can use project planning software in the development of a new advertising campaign or in the development of a new distribution system.

Project Planning Definitions

Every project consists of four elements that must be managed: activities, resources, costs, and time. An **activity** (sometimes called a "task") is a well-defined job with a clearly identifiable beginning and end that makes up a portion of the total project. Some programs allow an activity to be made up of many subtasks, while other project planning programs make no such distinction. In a large software development project, for example, we might identify the following major activities: (1) define the problem that will be addressed by the software; (2) perform a feasibility study for the software; (3) conduct analysis of the present system; (4) design the new system; (5) write, test, and debug the new software; (6) install the system and train users; and (7) monitor the system's success (see Figure 12–8). Each of these major activities may possess several subtasks or activities, and each must be accounted for in the development of the project plan.

1. Define problem to be addressed
2. Perform a feasibility study
   - 2.1 Assess user acceptance
   - 2.2 Assess managerial acceptance
   - 2.3 Assess economic impacts
   - 2.4 Assess organizational benefits
3. Conduct analyses
4. Design the new computerized system
   - 4.1 Perform preliminary design
   - 4.2 Perform functional design
   - 4.3 Perform detailed design
5. Write, test, and debug the software
   - 5.1 Code software
   - 5.2 Test software
   - 5.3 Debug software
6. Install system and train users
7. Monitor the system's success

FIGURE 12–8

Tasks in a Large Software Development Project

With every activity, there are associated **resources.** Resources for a task include the personnel involved (or a specific number of personnel hours), equipment materials that will be used, and money that must be budgeted. Identifying all of the resources of an activity is critical, since reliable estimates of true costs of a project are impossible without them. Unique, or limited, resources must also be identified, so that the program can apportion them properly between the tasks. For example, if Jim Smith is crucial to both the system design and program writing (tasks 4 and 5 in Figure 12–8), then he should be identified as a resource by name, rather than simply as "programmer/analyst," so that the project planning software will not require him to be working on two tasks simultaneously.

Any resource expended in a project has a cost. A project may, in fact, have several types of costs. For raw materials (building supplies or rented computer time, for example), there are **variable costs** (that is, they vary with the amount of the resource used). Other costs remain constant regardless of the level of output (such as rent or administrative expenses), and are known as **fixed costs.** All resources in a project must have a cost, although some programs allow the user to distinguish between those the client will be billed for and those he will not be billed for.

In addition to resources, each activity will require a certain amount of time, and the time required to complete an activity may depend upon numerous other factors. Performing the system analysis for our software project may require between 160 and 180 hours of a system analyst's time. This figure can be used to determine costs.

Apart from its significance in determining costs, time has another importance. Some tasks must wait to begin until others have been completed. If critical people that must be interviewed in the system analysis stage are taking vacations, or if the system analyst must divide his or her time between several projects, the entire project will be delayed, because the system design cannot begin until the analysis is complete. In some projects, certain tasks may not be able to begin until a specified date, placing still other constraints on the completion of the job.

During the course of a project, certain **milestones** (or **events**) will be reached. A milestone signifies a clearly identifiable point at which one or more related activities have been completed. A milestone is also an instant in time at which new activities are started. A milestone can serve as a reference point to determine the status of completion of a project. For example, many activities may be conducted during the system analysis stage of our project, but they will all terminate with the submission of a detailed system analysis report with diagrams of all pertinent data flows (see Figure 12–9). Since some of the system analysis activities can occur in any order, they cannot serve as an effective gauge of progress.

Using Project Management Software

Using project management software is a three-stage effort. First, all pertinent data about each activity must be entered. Then the program will analyze the data to find a solution to the problem of ordering the tasks properly. The user may then view the results through a variety of report formats. At each stage, there may be a need to revert to an earlier one. During the analysis stage, for example, the program may find that impossible precedent relationships have been entered (task C cannot begin until task B is complete, task B cannot begin until task A is complete, and task A cannot begin until task C is complete). In this case, the user must return to the activity entry stage and modify some of the task information. Or the user may

Activities	Milestones
Prepare for development	
Conduct programming	
Perform internal testing	
Finalize documentation and perform training	
Conduct acceptance testing	
Prepare development report	
	Submit developmental report
Install hardware, control software and communications	
Install new system	
Convert files	
Conduct system cutover	
Commence system operation	
Prepare implementation report	
	Submit implementation report

FIGURE 12–9

Project Milestones for Two Phases of a Major System Development Project

not be satisfied with the information provided at the report stage and will want to alter some of the task information.

Entering Activity Information

The first step in using project management software is to identify all of the activities or tasks involved in a project. For each task the user must provide information about the amount of time required for its completion, the number and type of resources that the task uses, and whether any tasks must precede it. Some programs also allow the user to enter task descriptions and notes.

Entering this information into the system is usually accomplished through a straightforward question-and-answer session. The Harvard Software series (Harvard Project Manager and Harvard Total Project Manager) uses a graphic display of boxes (representing activities) and lines (indicating precedent relationships) for entry. With each new activity entered, the screen is updated with a new box. To delete an activity, the user merely moves the cursor to an existing box, presses a few keys, and the screen is redrawn. These visual representations of the project make it much easier to see the sequence of events and identify and correct potential problem areas.

When all of the task information has been entered, other information may be asked for by the program, such as a start date for the project, cost figures for all of the resources, and, in more sophisticated programs, information on non-work dates (holidays) and resource or time constraints (such as, task C must conclude by August 12th).

Determining the Critical Path

Once all of the information has been entered, the project management program will begin its job of analyzing the data the user has provided. With most programs, this data analysis consists of ordering the tasks into the sequence that fulfills all of the time and resource constraints, preserves all precedent activity relationships, and is completed in the least amount of time.

In any large project, periods will occur when several tasks or activities will be conducted simultaneously. In building a house, for example, the electrical wiring may go in at the same time as the plumbing. Both must be completed, however, before final wall coverings can be installed. If the wiring is typically completed in three days while the plumbing takes two weeks, then the project completion time will be more affected by minor delays in the plumbing work than by similar delays in wiring. The time between the completion of a task and the beginning of the next dependent task (e.g., the time between the completion of the wiring and starting the walls) is known as **slack** (or "float"). Slack might be thought of as the longest time that an activity may be delayed without causing a delay in the overall project.

If several activities at a particular stage of a project have slack, then there must be at least one activity that has no slack—the activity or activities for which the next stage must wait. The series of connected activities with zero slack will determine the length of the overall project, and is known as the **critical path** (see Figure 12–10). A major job of project planning software is to find the critical path so that the project manager can see where delays might occur.

When the critical path has been found, all slack times are calculated. Some project management software will then try to arrange the activities with slack so that the utilization of resources is minimized. Assume, for example, that tasks J, K, and L in Figure 12–10 each required two workers with the same skills. By placing these jobs end to end, only two workers would be required, rather than the six needed by starting them at the same time. All three jobs would still be completed before task I, which lies along the critical path.

Minimizing the resources used at each stage can result in significant cost savings. Better project management software, however, will go beyond resource minimization to **resource leveling**, a method of smoothing out any large fluctuations in resource use during the life of a project. Requiring 60 people on a project one week, 12 the next week, and 125 the third week may produce the lowest total

FIGURE 12–10
Slack and the Critical Path

```
                    Days to Completion

             1          2         3           4          5
| 12345678901 | 23456 | 789012345678901234567 | 890123456789012345 |

      C           E          I      H                 N
| *********** | ***** | ******************** | ****************** |
      A           F       J                         O
| XXXX+++++++ | ***** | XXX+++++++++++++++++ | XXXXX+++++++++++++ |
      B           D        K
|             |       |                      |                    |
| XXXXXXXX+++ | X++++ | XXXX++++++++++++++++ |                    |
                  G          L
              | XXX++ | XXXXXXX+++++++++++++ |
                                M
                      | XXXXXXXX++++++++++++ |
   Legend:
      A-O = Project tasks     X = tasktime     * = critical
       |  = Milestones        + = slack          path
```

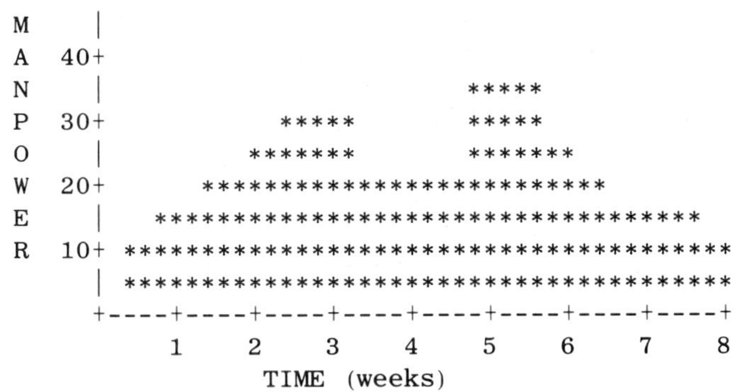

FIGURE 12–11

Project Manpower Use over Time

cost, but it may not be realistic. Experienced project directors often try to build up manpower gradually during the beginning of a project and cut back slowly at the end (see Figure 12–11). This makes the project much easier to staff and manage. Advanced project management software, such as Primavera and RMS-II, has these features.

During the analysis stage, the project management software may encounter difficulties with some of the data. Typically, all tasks must have a precedent activity except for the first task in a project. Suppose, however, that a task exists that could begin at any time, not depending upon any previous work, but must be completed before some other task can begin. Some project management software will force the user to select a precedent activity for the task, while others will compensate for it by creating "dummy" tasks (tasks with no resource or time requirements) to establish the necessary precedent relationship.

The precedent relationships themselves are usually limited to the finish-start type, in which one task must finish before another one begins. The most sophisticated programs will also allow finish-finish relationships, wherein one job cannot finish before another is complete, but both can be worked on simultaneously. It is not necessary, for example, for the pipeline trench to be entirely dug before the first section of pipe is laid. A flexible project management program can allow certain tasks to begin when another has reached a certain percentage stage of completion, and still others to begin on particular calendar dates (not triggered by other events).

Project Management Reports

After analysis has been completed, the user may view the results in a variety of formats. The most common reporting format is the **Gantt chart**, showing all the tasks of a project on a time line with the critical path highlighted in some manner (Figure 12–12). A Gantt chart (named after its developer, Henry Gantt) does not show interrelationships or dependencies between tasks, but will depict the starting and ending times of each activity. Virtually all project management programs will produce Gantt charts, although most require a printer for displaying them.

In order to see which tasks are dependent upon others, some programs produce either a CPM chart (for Critical Path Method) or a **PERT chart** (for Project Evaluation and Review Technique). In a CPM chart a box represents an activity and the lines only indicate preceding events, while a PERT chart shows activities as lines and uses boxes to denote the completion of activities or milestones (Figure 12–13).

FIGURE 12–12

A Gantt Chart (Super Project Plus) *(Courtesy of Computer Associates International)*

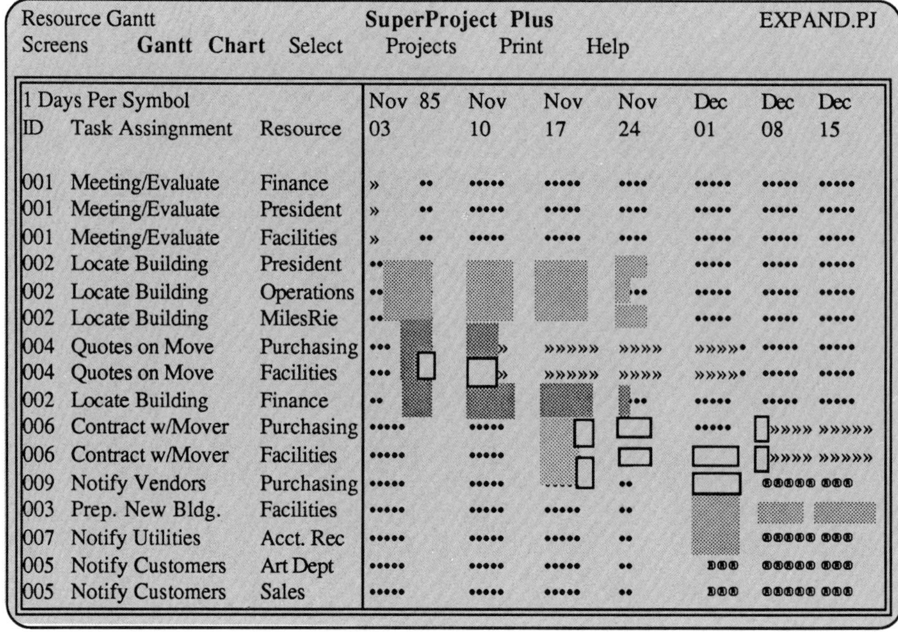

FIGURE 12–13

A PERT Chart (Super Project Plus) *(Courtesy of Computer Associates International)*

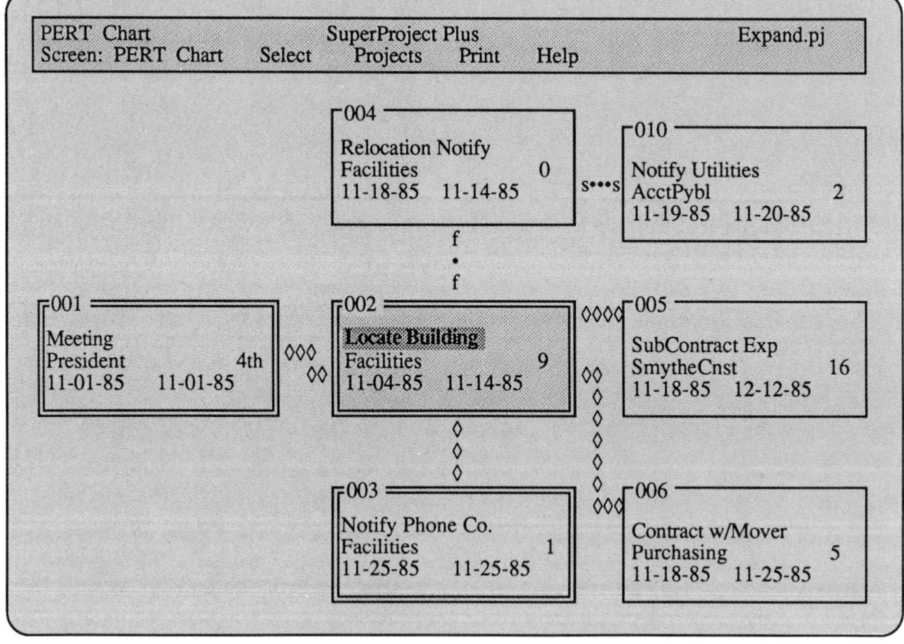

Although CPM and PERT charts look similar, the methods underlying them differ considerably, and they require different inputs and calculation methods. In CPM, the user supplies an estimated time for each activity. The program then calculates the earliest possible time that each activity can begin, as well as the latest it may begin without delaying the project. The difference between these times is the slack time. In PERT the user supplies not one, but three, times for each activity: the optimistic time, the pessimistic time, and the most likely time to complete. The program uses these times to calculate an expected time for each activity and can statistically determine the probability of completing the project on a given date.

In addition to a graphic depiction of the project activities, a project management program will provide a variety of useful reports. All programs will provide a listing of the project tasks, and most will offer a list of the resources that the project will require. A detailed project budget is provided by some programs, with costs broken down into many budgeting categories or even plotted against time. Still other programs offer a manpower use chart similar to that in Figure 12–11.

Types and Features of Project Management Software

Project management software can be grouped into three categories. The simplest type (which includes more than 75 percent of the products) focuses upon arranging the tasks in the proper order. This software will show which tasks must precede others and when periods of inactivity will arise. In addition, it will usually allow the calculation of a rough project budget, determined from the costs and amount of resources associated with each task. This simplest type of project management software does not offer much sophistication in the number and types of costs that can be affixed to a resource, or in the ability to determine work schedules for individuals. These programs will also not provide much assistance in tracking project progress after the initial plan has been completed. Most programs in this category work on the assumption that an unlimited supply of each required resource is available for each task. Although these might seem like severe limitations, they can still prove invaluable with the majority of small- to medium-sized projects.

The second category of project management software takes full account of limited personnel or other resources. These programs can also provide some type of project monitoring to determine the status of an ongoing project, and allow for updating a project master plan (rather than a complete redrafting).

The third category of project management software is distinguished by the ability to manage shared resources for several projects. A highway construction company may have half a dozen projects under way simultaneously. Heavy grading equipment will work for a limited time on one project and will be moved to another, not waiting for the first project to be completed. It may later return to the same project. Efficient utilization of resources requires as little idle time as possible for equipment and personnel, and only this third classification of project management software can allocate the same resources between multiple projects.

Beyond these simple classifications, each level of project management software offers an increasing flexibility in the constraints and costs that can be attributed to a project. For example, more sophisticated programs, such as Primavera Project Planner (Primavera Systems), will allow fixed costs to be divided into a number of cost categories (rent, utilities, administrative expenses, etc.) or allow multiple resource costs (normal labor rate and overtime, for example) to be accommodated. With a greater amount of data being allowed into the plan, these programs can also offer more types of project status and summary reports.

Project management software can also differ in subtle ways that may be important to prospective users. Some programs, for example, use a day as the smallest unit of time that may be assigned to an activity, whereas others will allow activity durations to be specified in hours or even minutes. A flexible project management program will adjust schedules to accommodate non-working days (holidays) or even special working hours requirements (on a round-the-clock project, for example, certain personnel may not be available after 5 P.M.).

A useful feature found in only a few programs is the ability to use libraries to store task and resource information. If a particular activity in building a house will always involve the same number of personnel, it can be stored in a library (or data base) of activities. Several subtasks, in fact, may always occur in the same order and use the same resources. A library of tasks and subtasks will greatly speed the entry of project data. Similarly, the costs associated with particular resources can also be stored for recall if they are not subject to rapid price fluctuations.

With increased sophistication of project management programs comes increased hardware requirements. The simplest of project managers can be used on a computer with as little as 64K of internal memory and a single disk drive. Project managers that handle multiple projects with shared resources, and offer libraries for storing task and cost information, usually require at least 512K and a hard-disk drive. A printer is necessary to obtain all of the reports, and because some programs use special graphics characters in their network charts, the printer may have to be IBM graphics character compatible. Some programs also allow the use of graphics plotters to produce their charts, but these are usually not required.

The number of project activities that the project management program can handle is ordinarily a function of the internal memory and disk storage capacity of the computer system. A typical project management program may be able to analyze projects with 100 activities in a floppy-disk-based computer system with 128K RAM, but will also analyze a 600-activity project in a 640K RAM system with a hard disk. The hardware requirements are the smallest in systems that require the least information to be input (and also provide the fewest output and analysis options). Provided in Table 12–2 is a list of selected vendors of project management software.

EXPERT SYSTEMS

Expert systems belong to a branch of science known as artificial intelligence. Perhaps no technology has created more excitement, aroused the interest and participation of more venture capitalists, and created more hope for an even brighter future for humankind than the technology known as **expert systems**. Listen to the platitudes being verbalized about this technology.[1]

> Expert systems will change the way businesses operate by altering the way people think about solving problems. . . . Expert systems will also help America solve its productivity problems. . . . chemical plants and nuclear reactors will soon be assisted by expert systems. . . . Skills that are now difficult to teach will become easy. . . .

In 1981 the government of Japan, having long realized the vast potential of expert systems and its mother discipline artificial intelligence, launched that country in what became known as the "Fifth-Generation Computer Project." The purpose of this project was to develop the fifth-generation computer. The fifth-generation computer is expected to handle the more demanding requirements of symbolic processing associated with artificial intelligence applications. Initially, the equivalent of $500 hundred million were to be spent on research. This led to competitive undertakings in this country, in Great Britain, and in Europe.

TABLE 12–2

Selected Vendors of Project Management Software

Primavera Project Planner Primavera Systems, Inc. 29 Bala Avenue Bala Cynwyd, PA 19004	**Micropert O, Version 3.2** Sheppard Software Company 4750 Clough Creek Road Redding, CA 96002
VisiSchedule VisiCorp 2895 Zanker Road San Jose, CA 95134	**Garland Pathfinder** Garland Publishing, Inc. 136 Madison Avenue New York, NY 10016
Plantrax Omicron Software 57 Executive Park South NE Atlanta, GA 30329	**MicroGANTT** Earth Data Corporation P.O. Box 13168 Richmond, VA 23225
RMS-II North America Mica, Inc. 11772 Sorrento Valley Road San Diego, CA 92121	**Microtrak** SofTrak Systems P.O. Box 22156 AMF Salt Lake City, UT 84122
Harvard Total Project Manager Harvard Software, inc. Software Park Harvard, MA 01451	**Milestone** Digital Marketing Corporation 2363 Boulevard Circle, #8 Walnut Creek, CA 94595
SuperProject Plus Computer Associates 2195 Fortune Drive San Jose, CA 95131	**Microsoft Project** Microsoft, Inc. 16011 NE 36th Way Redmond, WA 98073-9717

Just what are expert systems, why is the interest in them so intense, and what do they have to do with microcomputers for business? An expert system is a collection of computer programs that

1. is able to "reason" like an expert
2. is able to solve unstructured problems after the fashion of an expert
3. is able to acquire and retain the knowledge of an expert
4. can advise, analyze, categorize, communicate, consult, design, diagnose, explain, explore, forecast, justify, learn, manage, monitor, plan, present, retrieve, schedule, test and tutor
5. enables
   (a) the expertise of several experts to be fused
   (b) expertise to be distributed
   (c) expertise to be preserved and enhanced

History of Expert Systems

A history of the development of expert systems is shown in Figure 12–14, together with one possible scenario of its future.

Some of the classic historical applications of expert systems which are reported in the literature as shining success examples of the use of this technology include

Medical diagnosis and therapy (MYCIN)

Personal finance (TAXADVISOR)

Chess

FIGURE 12–14[1,2]
Expert Systems Milestones

1950	First scientific paper delivered on the subject.
1965	First expert system created.
1975	Sophisticated knowledge engineering tools developed.
1982	Industry and university collaborations lead to development expert systems. Emergence of hardware tools and development environments.
1985	Hardware and software prices begin to edge down. Over one dozen software packages are placed in the market place.
1987	Limited commercial expert system applications emerge. The use of the small computer for this type of application becomes commonplace.
1988	Sophisticated expert system applications are developed for business and professional use.
1990	Medical diagnosis systems are made available for use in homes and on small computers.
1992	Applications blossom in every area of business and the professions.

Mineral prospecting (PROSPECTOR)
Computer configuration (XCON)
Engineering structural analysis (SACON)
Electronics analysis (SOPHIE)
Symbolic mathematics (MATHLAB)

Most of these applications were developed on mainframe computers using abundant resources, brilliant programmers, and narrow problem domains. The fact that these applications were successful does not ensure that just any knowledge area we might choose can be successfully codified into an expert system on a microcomputer. The requirements for such success usually include a willing expert, narrow problem domains, lots of agreement as to what is known about the problem, and lots of patience and luck. As the technology develops, more sophistication will be built into the expert system shells, enabling the chances for a successful implementation to be greatly improved. **Expert system shells** are the basic software systems within which expert systems are built and used; they include everything except the knowledge base, as explained in the next section.

Expert Systems and Knowledge Bases

One of the most fundamental components of any expert system is its knowledge base. A **knowledge base** is a collection of rules and procedures that prescribe how information is to be transformed into action. It is the capability to represent knowledge within a computer that makes the expert system so powerful. Hayes-Roth[2] suggests the advantages associated with computerized knowledge representation are many and substantial, as listed in Table 12–3. It has been stated[3] that the knowledge in people's heads is at least an order of magnitude greater than what has ever been written down. If this knowledge can be codified and incorporated into the memory banks of the computer, Hayes-Roth suggests (Table 12–3) that new knowledge can be inferred from it; and moreover that this knowledge can be distributed to anyone who desires it.

TABLE 12–3

Why Computerized Knowledge Representation[2]

Knowledge is a scarce resource whose refinement and reproduction conserves or creates wealth.
The transmission of knowledge from human expert to trainee requires years of education.
Extracting knowledge from humans and putting it in computable forms can greatly reduce the costs of knowledge reproduction and exploitation.
The evolution of human culture into ever more sophisticated and complex forms requires a mechanism for preservation and codification of perishable knowledge.
Computerized knowledge representation permits artificial inferencing and reasoning to take place.
Computerized knowledge representation permits solutions to important problems which defy solution by other methods.
Computerized knowledge representation enables you to combine and apply routinely the expertise of many specialists.

Structure of Expert Systems

Depicted in Figure 12–15 is the overall structure of an expert system. Commercially available expert system shells consist of all the components shown in Figure 12–15 except the knowledge base. The knowledge base must be developed by the user for the particular application being considered. As previously mentioned, a knowledge base is a collection of rules, facts, and heuristics which are used by an expert in making intelligent decisions. The content of the knowledge base is problem-specific and must be provided by a consenting expert.

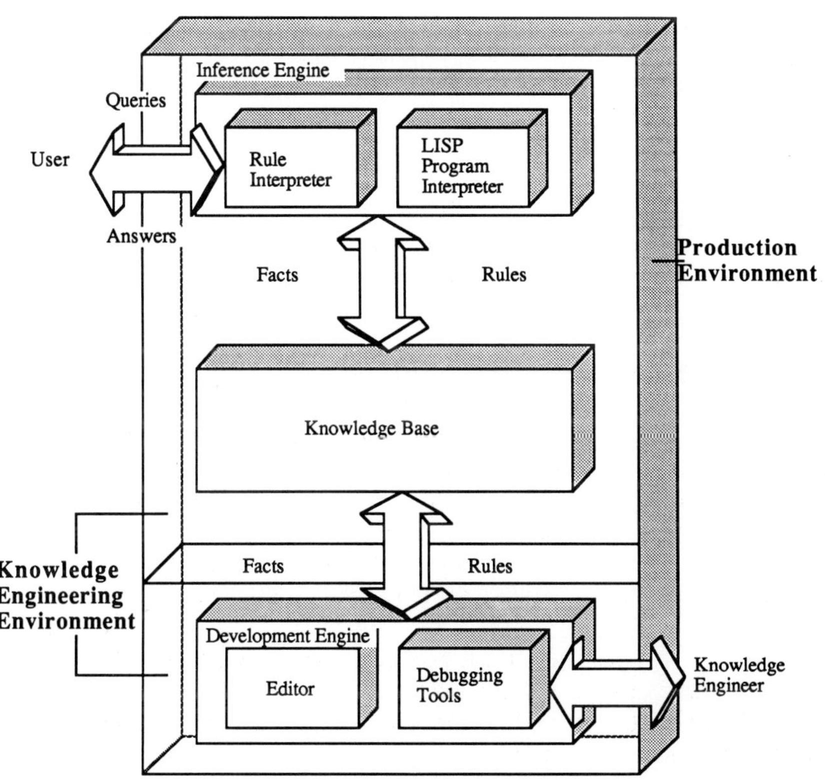

FIGURE 12–15

Structure of Expert Systems

Whereas the knowledge base is the component that provides the substance for reasoning, the actual reasoning process itself is carried out in the inference engine. The **inference engine** is capable of using the knowledge contained in the knowledge base to infer new knowledge. The inference engine uses a reasoning procedure similar to that actually employed by the experts in the subject area.

In addition to the inference engine or reasoner, the expert system shell will contain a knowledge acquisition engine. The **knowledge acquisition engine** facilitates the acquisition of knowledge and usually contains an editor for entering and editing the knowledge and debugging tools.

As shown in Figure 12–15, expert system shells are generally expected to consist of

artificial intelligence language
rule parser (compiler or interpreter)
data structures
justification and explanation system
user interface (natural language)
knowledge acquisition (development) engine
inference engine

Building Expert Systems

Before an expert system can be used, it must first be fabricated. This usually involves purchase of an expert system shell. A list of features to check for is provided in the checklist at the end of this book. It is particularly important that the shell be capable of representing the knowledge in a way consistent with the way the knowledge is structured in the expert's mind, and that the shell be capable of processing the knowledge in a fashion analogous to that employed by the expert.

Once the expert system shell is acquired, the actual process of building the knowledge base begins. Currently, the most popular form of knowledge representation is the use of rules together with facts and heuristics. Table 12–4 depicts some "typical" rules and associated "facts," as would be appropriate in football and cooking. Thus fabrication of the knowledge base involves entering rules, facts, and

TABLE 12–4

Some "Typical" Rules in Football and Cooking, and Associated Facts

Football	IF down = fourth AND needed-first-down-yardage>3 THEN play = punt. IF down = third AND needed-first-down-yardage>10 THEN play = pass.
Cooking	IF oven-timer = buzzing AND dinner-rolls-in-oven = light brown THEN action = remove-dinner-rolls-and-serve. IF oven-timer = isn't-buzzing AND dinner-rolls-in-oven = dark brown THEN action = remove-dinner-rolls-and-discard.

Note that each rule consists of a conditional part that begins with "IF" and ends with "THEN" and a conclusion part that begins with "THEN" and ends with a "." Naturally, one would not expect to find cooking rules in the same knowledge base with football rules. For the football rule base, the facts are the values assumed by the attributes "down" and the "needed-first-down-yardage," which for the first rule are "fourth" and ">3," respectively.

TABLE 12–5

Expert System Development Requirements[5]

SIZE OF SYSTEM	NUMBER OF RULES	DEVELOPMENT TIME	COST
Small	50–450	¼–½ person/yr	$40,000–$60,000
Large	500–3,000	1–3 person/yrs	$0.5 million–$1 million
Very large	10,000	3–5 person/yrs	$2–$5 million

heuristics into the knowledge base. Each new rule added to the rule base must be tested for consistency and accuracy as it interacts with the rules already entered into the knowledge base. This usually results in editing existing rules so that they interact appropriately with the newly added rule. In order for new knowledge (new facts) to be generated, the rules are chained together in either a forward or backward fashion to produce a new result. All potential interaction chains must be tested for validity in light of the results produced. Where necessary, rules must be edited and then retested. Hence, the process of generating a knowledge base is tedious and time-consuming. Table 12–5 provides a rough estimate of development times taken in relation to number of rules that make up the knowledge base.

Displays Produced by Expert System Shells

Shown in Figures 12–16 and 12–17 are typical displays produced by an expert system shell known as Nexpert (listed in Table 12–6). In Figure 12–16 a rule is being added to the rule base. One enters the rule using the rule editor and then moves the cursor to the up arrow to indicate that the rule is to be added to the rule base.

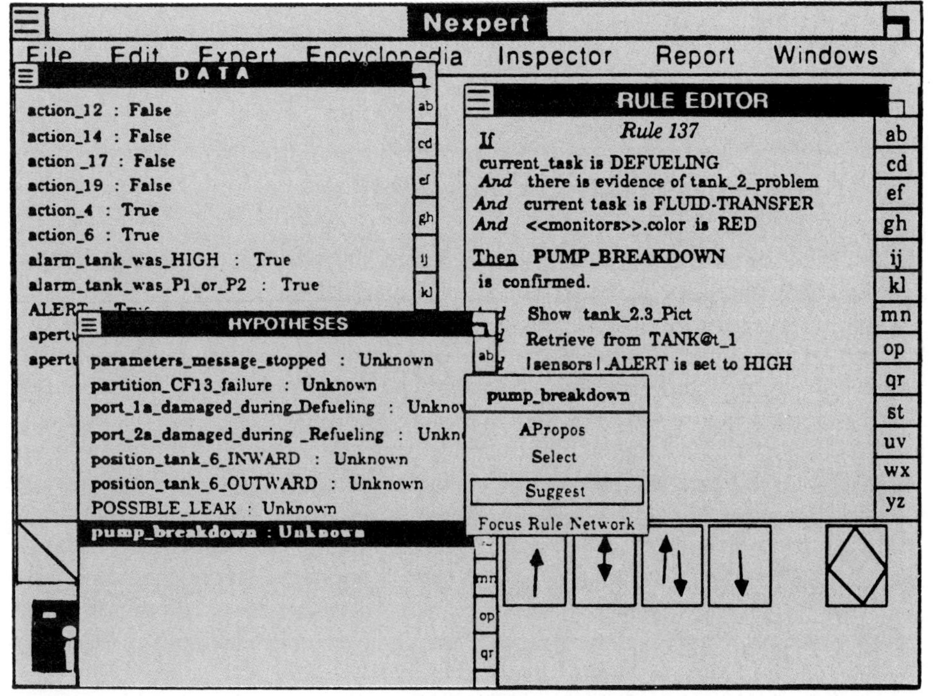

FIGURE 12–16

Nexpert Display Showing Rule Editor on Right and Current Attribute Values on Left

FIGURE 12–17

Sample Tree Generated Using Nexpert

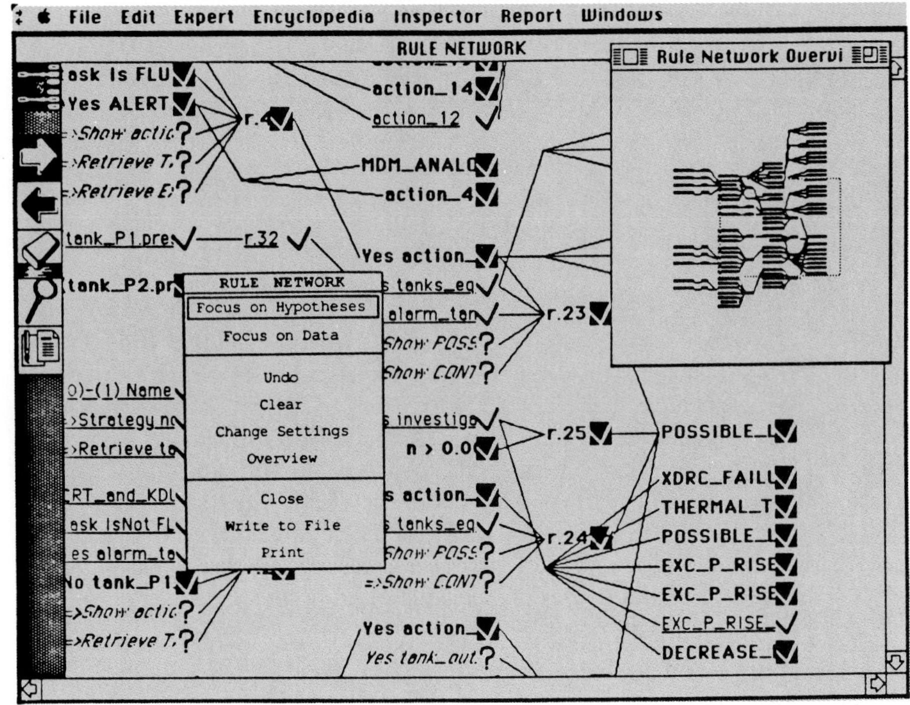

In Figure 12–17 is shown the network or tree of rules that have been chained together with the results that such chaining has produced.

Current Vendors of Expert System Shells

Listed in Table 12–6 are many of the vendors of expert systems shells for microcomputers.

DECISION SUPPORT SYSTEMS (DSS)

The economic environment in which every corporate and business entity is embedded is characterized by so much complexity that managerial decision making without some form of planning model would be like blindly throwing darts in a penny arcade. Since the mid-70s, a class of software known as **decision support systems** (or more properly, **decision support system generators**) has been used to develop corporate planning models for use by top and middle management within organizations. Originally, this class of software was available only on mainframes. More recently this software has migrated to minicomputers and microcomputers, where its impact has been even more significant. Decisions which traditionally had been based on experience and hunches have more recently been based on models and data developed by use of decision support system generators. Table 12–7 lists some of the myriad applications of decision support systems in the corporate world. Today, practically every corporate executive uses planning models to facilitate and improve the quality of decisions.

TABLE 12–6

List of Vendors of Expert Systems for Microcomputers

INSIGHT
Level 5 Research
4980 S-A1A
Melbourne Beach, Fl 32951
(305) 676-5810

Advice Language/X (AL/X)
J. Reiter, S. Barth, & A. Paterson
University of Edinburgh

ES/P ADVISOR
Expert Systems International
U.S. Office: 1150 First Avenue
King of Prussia, PA 19406
(215) 337-2300

NEXPERT
Neuron Data, Inc.
44 High Street
Palo Alto, CA 94301

Expert/Ease
Expert Software International, Ltd
c/o Jeffrey Perrone & Assoc.
3685 17th Street
San Francisco, CA 94114
(415) 431-9562

Knowledge Engineering System (KES)
Software A & E
1500 Wilson Blvd., Suite 800
Arlington, VA 22209
(703) 276-7910

TIMM
General Research Corporation
P.O. Box 6770
Santa Barbara, CA 93160
(805) 964-7724

Automated Reasoning Tool (ART)
Inference Corporation
5300 West Century Blvd., 5th Flr
Los Angeles, CA 90045
(213) 417-7997

Knowledge Engineering Environment (KEE)
Intellicorp
707 Laurel Street
Menlo Park, CA 94025
(415) 323-8300

M.1
Teknowledge Inc.
525 University Avenue
Palo Alto, CA 94301
(415) 327-6640

Personal Consultant
Texas Instruments
P.O. Box 809063
Dallas, TX 75380-9063
1-800-527-3500

SeRIES-PC
SRI International
Advanced Computer Science Dept.
333 Ravenswood Avenue
Menlo Park, CA 94025
(415) 859-2464

EXPERT
Weiss & Kulikowski
Dept. of Computer Sci.
Rutgers University
New Brunswick, NJ 08903

OPS5
Dept. of Computer Science
Carnegie-Mellon University
Pittsburgh, PA 15213

OPS5e
Verac, Inc.
10975 Torreyana
Suite 300
San Diego, CA 92121

S.1
Teknowledge, Inc.
525 University Avenue
Palo Alto, CA 94301
(415) 327-6640

LOOPS
Xerox Palo Alto Research Centers
3333 Coyote Hill Road
Palo Alto, CA 94304
(415) 494-4000

Decision support systems are designed to support and enhance decision making activities. In this regard they resemble spreadsheets, but they offer sophistication and features that exceed what is available in spreadsheets. For example, they facilitate what-if analyses by allowing the user to perform a great many executions of the model at one time. They contain a modeling language that permits the user to employ descriptive variable names rather than cell coordinates, and the language is able to interpret and execute equations involving these variables. They support **goal-seeking**—the ability to establish targets for certain "output" or goal variables, and to have the program find what inputs are required to achieve the

TABLE 12–7
Applications of Decision Support Systems

Balance sheet projections	Marketing planning
Cash flow analysis	Market share analysis
Cash management	Merger/acquisition analysis
Cost projections	New venture analyses
Financial analyses	Price projections
Financial forecasting	Profit planning
Financial information systems	Pro forma financial reports
Industry forecasts	Risk analysis
Investment analysis	Sales forecasts
Long-term forecasts	Short-term forecasts
	Supply forecasts

outputs. And, they may support optimization analyses, enabling the modeler to perform "what's-best" analyses.

There are significant advantages to the use of the microcomputer to perform such analyses as opposed to mainframes or minis. There is an added dimension of user friendliness. Cost is significantly less, in that a mainframe package might cost $50,000 whereas a similar microcomputer package offered by the same vendor might cost only $500. And, models can be constructed by the manager rather than by an analyst. The principal objective of decision support systems is to provide managers with a clear picture of the organization's current state and to simulate its future state under various environmental and managerial assumptions. Models are likely to have a much more significant impact upon decision making when they are developed, used, and maintained by the decisionmakers themselves, rather than by an analyst whose modeling initiative is ultimately written up in a report that rests on the manager's desk.

It is expected that decision support systems will facilitate decision making in three major areas. The first is financial manangement. At the highest level of the corporate entity, the decisions are fundamentally financial in content and character, as suggested in Figure 12–18. At the next highest level the decisions are of a marketing or operational nature. Operational decisions are primarily of a production or distribution nature and generally have as their goal that of reducing costs while maintaining the quality and availability of the product or service. Production decisions are driven by forecasts. As Table 12–7 suggests, decision support systems are greatly used in these three areas: finance, marketing, and operations.

Anatomy of Decision Support System Generators

Decision support system generators are like expert system shells in that they provide the necessary modeling environment but contain no problem-specific "knowledge" or, more appropriately, models and data. Figure 12–19 depicts the components (the architecture) of a typical decision support system generator.[4]

The decision support system generator (DSSG) is installed without particularized and appropriate data and models in the data base and model base. It is the user's task to develop models appropriate for the decision of interest and to enter relevant data. Once developed, the DSSG is a decision support system and can be used to perform a variety of analyses relating to the decision at hand.

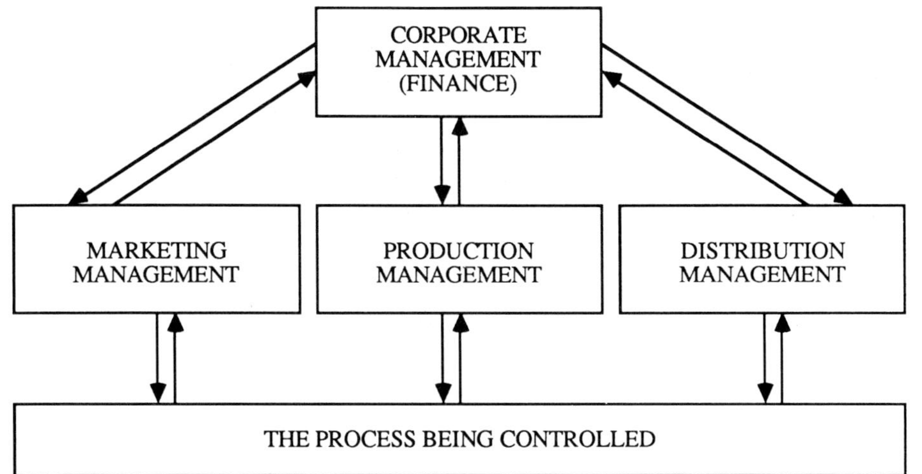

FIGURE 12–18
Management Hierarchy of Corporations

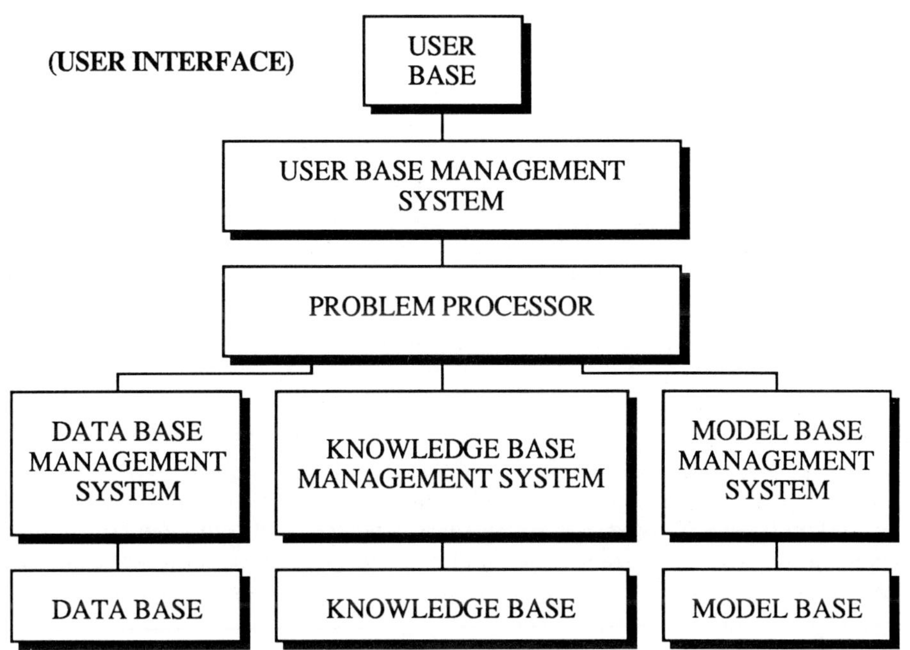

FIGURE 12–19
Decision Support System Generator Architecture[4]

Software Features of Decision Support System Generators

The following software features have generally become the accepted standard among decision support system generators.

User Interface The user interface guides the user through the maze of model building. A very strong trend in DSSG design is for the user interface to be as close to a normal human-to-human conversation as possible.

TABLE 12–8

Selected List of Vendors of Decision Support System Generators

IFPS/Personal
Execucom Systems, Inc.
3410 Far West Blvd.
Austin, Texas 78731
An analytic modeling tool designed to help the user explore alternatives. Price: $1,500

MindSight
Execucom Systems, Inc.
3410 Far West Blvd.
Austin, Texas 78731
Similar to **IFPS/Personal,** but available for the Macintosh.

Javelin
Javelin Software Corporation
One Kendall Square, Building 200
Cambridge, Massachusetts 02139
An analytic modeling tool that provides a spreadsheet and ten other perspectives of the user's model. Supports the exploration of alternatives (what-if analysis). Price: $199

Expert Choice
Decision Support Software, Inc.
1300 Vincent Place
McLean, Va. 22101
Designed to structure complex problems into manageable forms. Facilitates goal-oriented decision making. Price: $500

Decision Aide
Kepner-Tregoe, Inc.
Research Road
P.O. Box 704
Princeton, N.J. 08542
Provides a framework for making management choices by producing a management-type report to document the decision or recommendation. Price: $250

TM/1
Sinper Corp.
14 W. 40th St.
New York, N.Y. 10018
A support system designed for multidimensional table management applications with a coherent data base as its operational core. Price: less than $1,500

Data Base Management Subsystem The principal component of the data base management subsystem is to fulfill requests for data storage, retrieval, and update. It should have a significant report generator component that is able to format and print a variety of reports.

Model Base Management Subsystem The model base management subsystem must facilitate the creation, storage, retrieval, modification, deletion, and execution of models. The model base management subsystem must be capable of working through the problem processor and data base management subsystem to extract whatever data is required by the model and to store whatever data is generated by the model during its execution. Reporting of the results may be shared with the data base management subsystem.

Data Communications Capability The capability to extract relevant accounting, production, and demand data from other data bases, particularly mainframe data bases, is a very desirable feature that is not always available. If the decision support system is to provide timely, reliable, and accurate information, its data sources must likewise be timely and accurate. Hence, there is a real need for being able to tie into the corporate data base and to extract critical data items from it whenever users invoke the decision support system for the purpose of obtaining supportive information.

Graphics As was the case for spreadsheets, DSSGs need a closely integrated graphics capability. Such a capability might be a part of the report generation facility within the data base management subsystem, and it might be integrated within the model base management subsystem as well, so the user can graphically perceive how the model is dynamically behaving as the execution of the model progresses.

Vendors of Decision Support System Generators

Provided in Table 12–8 is an abridged list of vendors of varied forms of decision support software.

SUMMARY

Desk Organizers Desk organizer programs belong to a category of software known as memory-resident programs. They are loaded into a computer's memory before other applications programs and remain there until the computer is turned off. Thus, it is possible to call upon the features of a desk organizer from within a spreadsheet, word processing, or data base program. This aspect of desk organizers can save considerable time and effort. More than a mere convenience, desk organizer software can even make previously impossible data sharing between applications programs quite easy.

A wide variety of tools are present in most desk organizer software, including electronic equivalents of a notepad, card file, calculator, and appointment book, as well as data transfer and communications capability and access to operating system commands.

Other memory-resident programs are available to perform functions as diverse as checking spelling, saving keystroke sequences for later recall, or providing jokes at the press of a key. Standards do not yet exist which can warrant that no interaction will occur between two or more memory-resident programs, or even between one memory-resident program and certain applications programs, so the user is advised to exercise caution.

Project Management Software Project management software can enable a manager to organize the activities involved in a project into a sequence that is the most efficient in using the firm's time, resources, and money. This can often result in significant savings for the firm and can aid in ensuring that the project is completed by the required due date.

Using project management software begins with the entry of information about all activities in a project. Relevant dates, estimated completion times, materials and other resources used, and the costs of those resources are all entered. Project management software then assembles an appropriate network of activities for the project and finds the critical path: the sequence of activities that determine the entire length of the project. Once this path is found, the program can determine how much slack exists for noncritical activities.

Project management software can be classified into those programs that only find the critical path and order the activities, those that provide extensive facilities for managing resources and monitoring project progress, and those that can manage multiple projects with shared resources. With each step up in category, there is an accompanying increase in the amount of information about the project that is provided by the program.

Expert Systems Expert systems were examined in this chapter and it was found that many expert system shells are currently available in the microcomputer marketplace. In the future it is expected that a great many particularized expert systems will appear in such areas as medical diagnosis, personal and household finance, child rearing, and hundreds of other areas. These systems will use the expert system shells that are available in the microcomputer marketplace. The synergism between the microcomputer and the expert system is such that it enables each to enhance the usefulness and importance of the other. Literally hundreds of applications will blossom in the next few years, and the use of expert systems in conjunction with microcomputers may turn out to be one of the most important generic uses to which the microcomputer has ever been put. Such is the motivation for including a discussion of it here.

Decision Support System Generators Decision support system generators are a class of commercially available software which is used to build models (decision support systems) of decision situations of interest to managers. Unlike expert systems, decision support systems are not advice-giving systems. They do not perform diagnoses and they do not make decisions for the decision maker. Rather, they provide information about the outcomes (results) that are likely if a certain policy, program, or plan is pursued. They help decision makers make a rational choice or selection from among a set of alternative plans or policies. They help the decision maker to better understand the structure and behavior of the "system" he or she is endeavoring to manage. The goal is significantly improved quality of decision making. In this regard, decision support systems offer assistance in the same way that a worksheet model offers support and assistance to the decision maker. But the sophistication, features, and capabilities of decision support system generators exceed that available in spreadsheet programs.

Key Terms

activity
appointment book (electronic)
calculator (electronic)
card file (electronic)
critical path
data capture and transfer utility
decision support system
decision support system generator
events
expert system
expert system shell
fixed costs
Gantt chart
goal-seeking
inference engine
knowledge acquisition engine
knowledge base
memory-resident software
milestones
notepad (electronic)
PERT chart
project control
project management
project planning

resource leveling

resources

slack

variable costs

Self-Test

1. What are desk organizers, and how are they used?
2. What components make up desk organizers?
3. What do project management packages do, and how are they used?
4. What features do project management packages generally have?
5. What are the major categories of project management software?
6. What are expert systems, and what can they be used for?
7. What are decision support systems?
8. How do decision support systems relate to spreadsheets?
9. Delineate the anatomy of decision support systems.

Exercises

Desk Organizers

1. Describe why desk organizers are also called memory-resident utilities. What functions are included in most desk organizers? What are some of the more exotic features that are sometimes included?
2. What advantages are provided by desktop organizer software that may not be possible with other software, or with the manual counterparts of the desk organizer's features?
3. What are the dangers inherent in the lack of standards for memory-resident programs?
4. Are the current problems with memory-resident programs likely to increase or decrease as IBM PC and compatible computers move from a program work area of 640K to several megabytes?
5. What desk organizer or memory-resident program features would be most valuable to you? Are there any functions that should be offered in a memory-resident form that are not currently?
6. How does the use of desktop organizers and memory-resident utilities compare with operating systems (such as the Macintosh's Finder or Digital Research's GEM on the Atari 520 ST) that offer similar features? Does one approach offer advantages in flexibility, ease of use, or integration over the other?

Project Management Software

1. For which types of projects might the lowest level of project management software be effectively used? What types of firms are likely to require project management software that can handle multiple projects with shared resources?
2. Investigate some of the programs listed at the end of the project management software section and list their capabilities as regards the number of activities per project, types of costs that can be tracked, and forms of output that they provide.
3. What are the advantages of having a PERT chart of activities rather than simply a Gantt chart? What advantages does a Gantt chart provide over an ordinary PERT chart?
4. List some of the ways that resource and task libraries can make a project management system both easier to use and capable of providing better results. Are they more useful when managing multiple projects?
5. An assumption of the analysis stage of project management software is that all but the first activity must have precedent activities. Does this assumption closely resemble real life, or do some projects include activities that have no well-defined beginning or end, and that can occur at any stage of a project life? Cite examples.

6. Look again at Figure 12–12. In the text, it was suggested that combining activities J, K, and L would lessen the number of workers required at that stage of the project. If activity M also required the same two workers, the cost of two additional personnel could be saved by stacking activity M at the end of task L, even though it would delay the project by one day. This might be an acceptable tradeoff for a project director, but because it violates the critical path, project management software will not allow it. Should project management software be able to identify such potential resource-saving possibilities? How would they be identified?
7. Some large computer project management software offers simulation of a project. The idea behind the simulations is that some of the tasks will be completed ahead of schedule and others behind schedule. Using calculations based upon the optimistic, pessimistic, and most likely times provided for PERT analysis, each activities' completion times will vary over a limited range during repeated project calculations. What is found is that the critical path may change when noncritical activities exceed their most likely time, or when critical activities come in ahead of schedule. What types of information would be obtained from this type of simulation capability if it were offered in microcomputer project management software?

Expert Systems

1. Find an expert system shell of interest to you and characterize its features using the checklist in the appendix at the end of the text.
2. Explain why computerized knowledge representation is so important.
3. Describe the process of building an expert system.

Decision Support Systems

1. What is the relationship of a decision support system generator to a decision support system?
2. How do decision support system generators differ from spreadsheet programs?
3. How do decision support system generators differ from expert system shells?
4. From the list of selected DSSG vendors, pick one and write to them for further information. Write a two-page or less description of the DSSG. Describe what types of decisions the DSSG supports. Characterize the features of the DSSG.
5. Develop a taxonomy of DSSG types.

References

1. Harmon, Paul, and David King. *Expert Systems: Artificial Intelligence in Business.* New York: John Wiley and Sons, Inc., 1985.
2. Hayes-Roth, Frederick; Donald Waterman; and Douglas Lenat, ed. *Building Expert Systems.* Reading, Mass.: Addison-Wesley, 1984.
3. Forrester, Jay W. "Keynote Address to the 1975 National Computer Conference." 1975.
4. Minch, Robert P. *Decision Support Systems for Management Science Models.* PhD Dissertation, Texas Tech University, 1983.
5. Negoita, Constantin Virgil. *Expert Systems and Fuzzy Systems.* Menlo Park, Calif.: The Benjamin/Cummings Publishing Company, Inc., 1985.

Additional Reading

Dauphinais, Bill, and Leonard Darnell, "Project Management: One Step at a Time." *PC World* 2, no. 10, (Sept. 1984): 240–50.

Davis, Randall, and Douglas B. Lenat. *Knowledge-Based Systems in Artificial Intelligence.* New York: McGraw-Hill International Book Company, 1982.

Dunn, Robert J. "Expandable Expertise for Everyday Users." *Infoworld* 7, issue 39 (September 30, 1985).

Edwards, Ken, ed., "Project Management with the PO." *PC* 3, nos. 21, 22, and 23—a three article series (Oct. 30–Nov. 27), 1984.
Forsyth, Richard. *Expert Systems: Principles and Case Studies.* London: Chapman and Hall, Ltd., 1984.
Michie, Donald, ed. *Expert Systems in the Micro Electronic Age.* Edinburgh, Great Britain: Edinburgh University Press, 1979.
Naylor, Chris. *Build Your Own Expert System.* New York: Halsted Press, 1985.
Reitman, Walter, ed., *Artificial Intelligence Applications for Business.* Norwood, N.J.: Ablex Publishing Corporation, 1984.

CHAPTER

13

Integrated Accounting and Inventory Systems

CHAPTER OUTLINE

Accounting Systems Defined 457

A History of Accounting Systems 459

Business and Personal Uses of Accounting Systems 459

Software Concepts and Design Philosophies 460

Microcomputer Systems Accounting Software Vendors 460

General Ledger: The Heart of an Integrated Accounting System 461

Accounts Receivable Systems 467

FOCUS FEATURE Selecting and Installing an Accounting System 470

Accounts Payable Systems 479

FOCUS FEATURE Home Accounting Software Packages 482

Inventory Management Systems 486

Hardware and Software Requirements for Accounting 487

CHAPTER OBJECTIVES

In this chapter you will learn

1 the important concepts of accounting software
2 the important functions and features of (a) general ledger packages; (b) accounts receivable packages; (c) accounts payable packages; (d) inventory packages
3 "standard" reports produced by these packages
4 what kind(s) of accounting software is useful in various environments
5 how to select and install an accounting system
6 what home accounting software packages can do for you

This chapter describes one of the most common uses of microcomputers in small business: accounting and inventory systems. The chapter first provides an overview and background of integrated accounting systems, what they consist of, what they can do for users, and how to use them. Accounting systems for large mainframe and minicomputers have been in existence for some time. Accounting systems are defined, a history of their development is briefly outlined, and the uses of accounting systems are detailed. As has been the case for many of the software systems described in this textbook, the goal of accounting systems is *information-gathering*.

The chapter next provides a detailed look at accounts receivable and accounts payable packages. The accounts receivable and payable packages are among the most popular of the accounting models mentioned in Chapter 13. In one sense these programs are opposites. Given the time value of money, the goal of the former is to get paid for services rendered or products provided as soon as possible. On the other hand, the goal of the latter is to postpone payment for goods or services as long as possible, while still conforming to the terms negotiated with the vendor. In the accounting systems literature the term *accounts receivable* may be abbreviated with the short form A/R, *accounts payable* with A/P, and *general ledger* with G/L. Each section of this chapter describes the general procedure each package uses; the main files each package is responsible for; the various menus, screens, and inputs each package expects from the user; and the major reports each package produces. The housekeeping chores each program is expected to provide are also included in the respective sections.

Chapter 13 also briefly treats inventory systems, including invoicing customers, calculating reorder quantities, transmitting purchase orders, and providing reports which enable merchandise managers to better manage their inventory from a buying as well as a merchandising point of view.

Finally, the hardware and software requirements of accounting systems are presented.

ACCOUNTING SYSTEMS DEFINED

Accounting systems are software packages designed to assist users with the accounting-related aspects of running a business. This amounts to keeping books on expenditures and disbursements by category and amount, and producing a great variety of accounting-related documents such as invoices, statements, purchase orders, payroll checks, checks to vendors, etc. To accomplish these many and varied functions, accounting systems tend to be modular, but the modules are integrated so the files produced by one can be read by another. Typical of the modules that make up an accounting system are those listed and defined in Table 13–1.

Many businesses and concerns do not need all the modules listed in Table 13–1. For example, the payables of a company which provides services to the community may be very small—small enough to fit an entire year's worth of purchases into a manila folder. When this is the case, there is usually no need for an accounts payable package. Many service-oriented professions—including medicine, dentistry, insurance, law, architecture, accounting, and so forth—have far fewer payables than receivables. In many instances, these firms need only an accounts receivable package. This is especially true when these concerns are small (consisting of a half-dozen employees or less). Hence, accounts receivable packages can, like most of the other modules, operate in a stand-alone fashion.

TABLE 13–1
Accounting Modules Defined

Accounts Receivable. This is the most widely used module and is responsible for tracking the customers in terms of their purchases and payments. The module is able to generate instruments to induce payment by the customers—statements, and in some cases, invoices. The general motive behind these modules is to induce early payment for products provided or services rendered. The capability for aging of customer accounts is generally included in these packages.

Accounts Payable. This package is responsible for tracking vendors in terms of products and services purchased from them, and amounts owed to them. In addition to a variety of reports, these packages are capable of printing checks. The general motive of these packages is cash management. Given the time value of money, these packages are able to determine when a particular bill should be paid.

General Ledger. This package is able to accept files produced by the other packages, and to attribute or "post" the transactions recorded in those files to the appropriate accounts within the general ledger. The general ledger package is generally capable of producing the usual financial instruments: the balance sheet, the profit-and-loss statement, and the general ledger report.

Payroll. The payroll package is responsible for tracking employees within the firm in terms of hours worked, salary due, deductions required, etc. The package is capable of printing payroll checks and associated personnel reports.

Inventory. These packages will track the inventory levels of any and all items carried for sale. A great variety of reports are produced to help the inventory manager replenish depleted inventory and promote the sale of existing inventory.

Consider the situation faced by a moderate-sized accounting firm consisting of a dozen or more employees and hundreds of clients and customers. Such a concern would require an accounts receivable application and a payroll application. To merge these, a general ledger is required. As a general rule, whenever two or more area-specific accounting applications are required, a general ledger application is also required so that the financial instruments will reflect all the transaction activity of the firm.

Figure 13–1 shows the basic structural relationship that exists between the general ledger package and the other modules. Clearly, the other modules provide inputs to the general ledger package. In some instances there is interaction between the area-specific packages themselves. An inventory system might need access to

FIGURE 13–1
Relationships among Accounting Modules

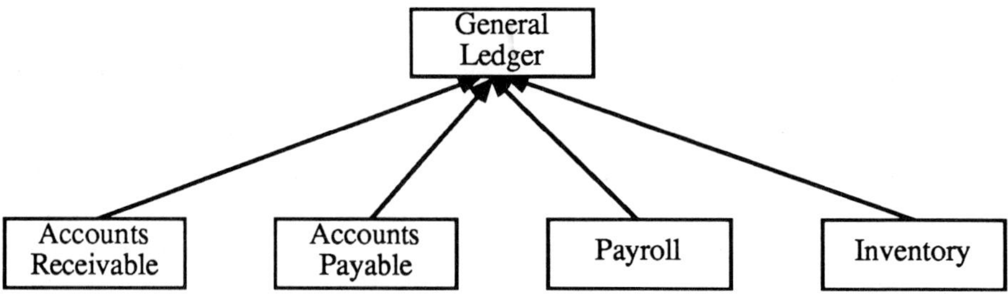

the customer data base file, which is generally regarded in the domain of the accounts receivable package.

Integrated accounting packages have several advantages over accounting packages which are not integrated. For one, transaction information needs to be entered only once. With packages that are not integrated, the information may need to be entered two or more times. Second, integrated systems generally retain the information in only one location instead of several (that file being available to all of the modules). If an error occurs in a record, only one location needs to be changed, not several.

A HISTORY OF ACCOUNTING SYSTEMS

Microcomputers were used for accounting applications well before the use of spreadsheets and data base management systems was commonplace. The widespread availability of accounting software for the earliest of microcomputers, like the Apple and the Radio Shack TRS-80, was in part responsible for the rapid growth in sales of these machines; it enabled small businesses to own their own computerized accounting systems. These systems permitted these businesses to automate their general ledger, receivables, payables, inventory, invoicing, and payroll. The result was increased accuracy, greatly improved productivity, and better information for management control. Demand for these systems greatly increased as it was perceived that the microcomputer would allow small businesses to automate their accounting functions for a fraction of the cost formerly associated with using a minicomputer for the same purpose. In the mid-to-late 1970s, computing systems sufficient to handle the accounting functions of small businesses cost from $30,000 on up. After 1985, the same computing power could be purchased for roughly $3,000.

BUSINESS AND PERSONAL USES OF ACCOUNTING SYSTEMS

Within which sectors of the business community is demand for microcomputer accounting systems likely to be greatest? As previously mentioned, small business is the area of commerce that can benefit the most from microcomputer accounting systems. Large organizations use accounting systems on their mainframe computers to assist with the accounting functions. Or, they might retain the services of a service bureau for this purpose. Occasionally, a department within a large organization can benefit from the use of a microcomputer general ledger package for tracking their budgetary accounts, but spreadsheets are more popular for this purpose.

Consider the service-oriented professions mentioned previously. A doctor's office can make expeditious use of an accounts receivable package with a customer master file that is enlarged to accommodate medical records. Similar statements can be made about attorneys, accountants, and architects. In many of these service-oriented professions, there is little in the way of payables, inventory, or personnel that requires computer-assisted accounting support. More will be said about accounts receivable packages in a subsequent section.

SOFTWARE CONCEPTS AND DESIGN PHILOSOPHIES

Most accounting systems use the double-entry method of bookkeeping. This does not mean that every number has to be entered twice. What these systems do is the following. For each transaction, one general ledger account is debited and another is credited. Consider what happens when an item is purchased and paid for later when the invoice arrives. The dollar amount of this sales transaction would be subtracted from the general ledger inventory account and added to the general ledger accounts receivable account. Hence the inventory account would be debited and the accounts receivable account would be credited. When payment for this purchase is received, this would result in another transaction that would debit accounts receivable and credit cash. Clearly, a set (chart) of accounts must be maintained. This collection of accounts is called the **general ledger**. The accrual of each transaction into the appropriate general ledger account(s) is called **posting** to the general ledger.

Transactions in an integrated accounting system are stored in files on secondary storage devices. Once a month (or possibly more often) the transaction files created by the area-specific modules are opened by the general ledger module and the dollar amounts of each transaction are credited to or debited from the appropriate accounts in the general ledger. These transactions are then saved in the general ledger transaction register (file). Following the update of the accounts, the accounts and their values are also saved. The individual area-specific transaction files are then cleared so they are ready to accept another month (or other period) of transaction activity. This process is called **closing**.

Integrated accounting systems are usually modular in the sense that a separate collection of programs makes up each module. The modules are integrated, meaning that the secondary storage files are accessible by the various modules that make up the integrated set. The accounts receivable transaction file would be created by the A/R module and then read and cleared by the G/L module at posting, for example. Figure 13–2 delineates a simplified file/program structure for integrated accounting systems.

The reports (also listed in the checklist in the appendix at the end of the book) generally produced by each accounting module are listed in Table 13–2 below. Also shown in Table 13–2 is the periodicity of these reports (whether they are needed daily, weekly, monthly, or quarterly), together with a brief description of how the report is used.

MICROCOMPUTER SYSTEMS ACCOUNTING SOFTWARE VENDORS

Listed in Table 13–3 are the suppliers of some of the major integrated accounting systems software for microcomputers. It should be noted, however, that there are literally hundreds of vendors of accounting systems software for microcomputers.

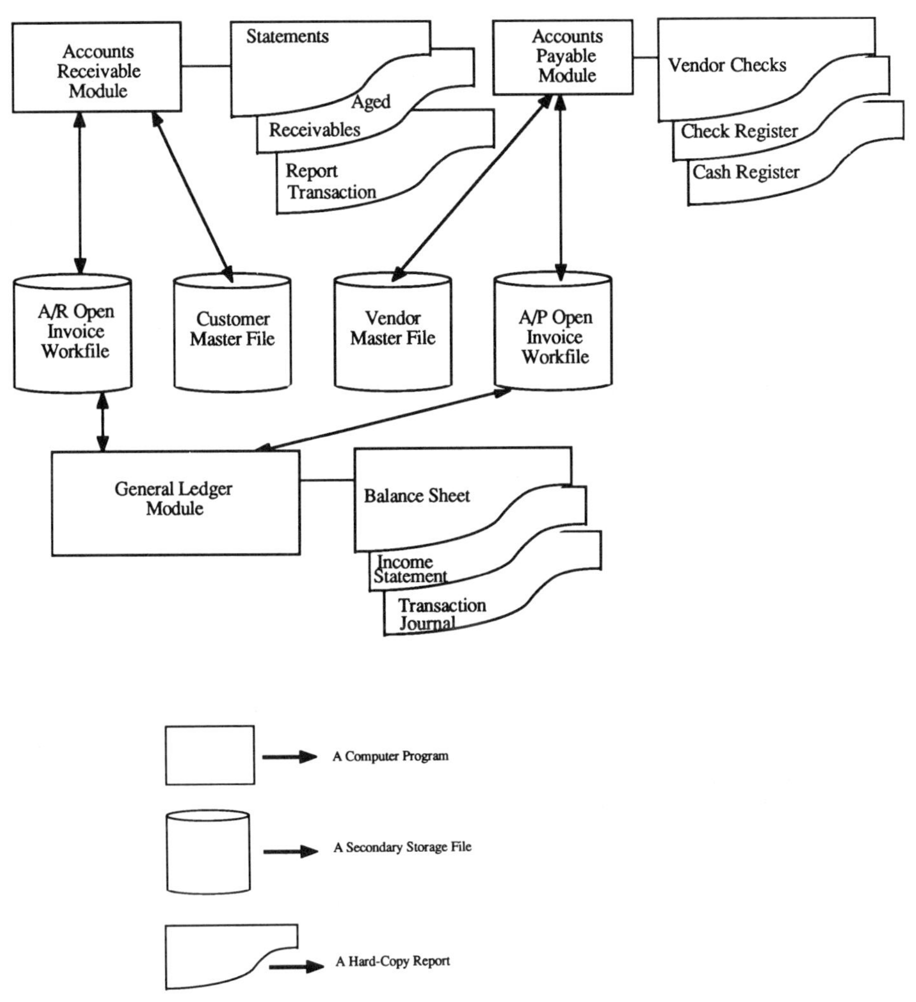

FIGURE 13–2

File/Program Structure of Accounting Systems

GENERAL LEDGER: THE HEART OF AN INTEGRATED ACCOUNTING SYSTEM

Before delving into more detailed discussions of integrated accounting modules, let us digress to describe the general ledger module.

First, a chart of accounts must be defined to the general ledger system by the user before the package can be used. The **chart of accounts** is nothing more than a file consisting of account numbers, account names, and a set of values for each account. When the chart of accounts is being set up, the general ledger module will usually want to know how many periods of activity to carry, and whether budget amounts are to be included. For example, if the accounting period is one month, and two years of accounting activity are required so this year may be compared with last, then this information must be entered into the system when the chart of accounts is set up. The firm's accountant is usually called in to assist with this. Setting up the chart of accounts is one of the most important activities in the implementation of a general ledger system. The accounts defined here will largely

TABLE 13–2

Reports Produced by the Accounting Modules

Accounts Receivable

Past due report, monthly, to determine how old a bill is

Invoice preview, biweekly, to preview before printing invoices

Statements, monthly, to inform customer as to status of account

Customer invoices, at point of sale, to provide a record of sale

Transaction register, at posting, to provide an audit trail of transactions posted

Mailing labels, monthly, for mailing

Trial balance, monthly, as a test on the overall balance of accounts

Customer account details, monthly, a printout of customer data

Accounts Payable

Complete vendor file, monthly, vendor details

Checks, monthly, to pay vendors

Check register, monthly, list of checks written

Open vendor invoice report, monthly, list of unpaid vendor invoices

Accounts payable aging report, monthly, to age unpaid bills

Cash requirements report, weekly, to determine cash requirements

General Ledger

Balance sheet, monthly, corporate financial position

Profit and loss statement, monthly, corporate business activity

General ledger, monthly, transaction register

Chart of accounts, on demand, a list of the corporate accounts

Payroll

Checks, monthly, to pay employees

Payroll register, monthly, list of payroll checks

Monthly summary

Unemployment tax report, monthly

The 941A report information, monthly

The W-2 forms, yearly, statement of earnings and taxes withheld

Inventory

Low stock report, weekly, list of low-inventory items

Over stock report, monthly, list of overstocked items

Joint stock requirements report, monthly or on demand, a list of all items furnished by a particular vendor

Purchase orders, on demand, to replenish overstocked items

Next receivers report, upon receipt of shipment, list of ordered items not yet received

determine the appearance of the balance sheet and income statement to be defined later. Listed in Table 13–4 are typical categories for the accounts that make up a chart of accounts.

Once a month (or whatever accounting period is used) the batched entries in all transaction journals are posted to the general ledger. When this happens, the books (journal files) are closed and a new period of accounting begins. At that time

TABLE 13–3

Accounting Systems Software Vendors for Microcomputers

American Business Systems	Micro Architect
BPI Systems, Inc.	Microcomputer Consultants
Certiflex Systems	Microdata
Computer Associates	Microsource
Computer Products International	North American Software
Cybernetics/MBS	Open Systems, Inc.
Computer Systems Design	Peachtree Software
Cromemco	Prodigy Systems
Designer Software	Radio Shack
Great Plains Software	Small Business Systems Group
International MicroSystems	Structured Systems Group
Layered, Inc.	Systems Plus

TABLE 13–4

List of "Typical" Accounts in the Chart of Accounts

ASSETS	
10000	Cash on hand
10010	Cash in bank
10100	Marketable securities
11000	Accounts receivable
11010	Notes receivable
11020	Interest receivable
12000	Merchandise inventory
12040	Finished goods inventory
12060	Work-in-process inventory
12080	Raw materials inventory
12090	Supplies inventory
12100	Prepaid insurance
13000	Prepaid rent
13010	Advances to suppliers
13040	Investment in securities
13050	Land
13060	Buildings
13070	Equipment
13080	Furniture and fixtures
13090	Accumulated depreciation
13100	Leasehold
13110	Organization costs
13120	Patents
LIABILITIES	
21000	Accounts payable
25000	Notes payable
25050	Payroll taxes payable
26000	Withheld income taxes
27000	Interest payable
28000	Income taxes payable
29000	Advances to customers
30000	Rent received in advance
31000	Mortgage payable
32000	Bonds payable
33000	Debenture bonds
34000	Convertible bonds
35000	Deferred income taxes
OWNER'S EQUITY	
50000	Common stock
51000	Preferred stock
52000	Retained earnings
53000	Treasury shares
INCOME	
60000	Product sales
60010	Service revenue
EXPENSES	
70000	Rent expenses
70010	Salaries expense
70020	Electricity and water expense
70030	Raw material expense
70040	Depreciation
70050	Packaging and distribution
70060	Marketing and promotion

TABLE 13–5

Steps in the Execution of General Ledger Modules

1. Inputs are entered manually and taken from summary files prepared by other packages—accounts receivable, for instance.
2. A balanced journal entry report is printed, showing all manual entries to the transaction register file.
3. The summary file data is thereafter merged with the manually prepared journal entry file.
4. The general ledger trial balance report is printed following the merge and carefully reviewed.
5. Corrections are entered and printed in another journal entry report. At this point the current transaction register report is prepared and printed.
6. The current transaction register is then used to update the consolidated transaction register file, and a new consolidated transaction register report is printed showing year-to-date summary totals, formatted to match the company chart of accounts.
7. The printing of detail ledgers by account number then takes place.
8. Using the consolidated transaction register file, the general ledger package then produces an income statement and a balance sheet.

the usual financial instruments—the balance sheet and the income (profit and loss) statement—are printed.

The steps typically used in a general ledger package are listed in Table 13–5.

Shown in Figure 13–3 is a typical system flowchart for a general ledger module. Rectangular blocks represent program submodules that do processing. Trapezoids represent manual inputs from the keyboard. Blocks that look like a piece of torn computer paper represent hard-copy output. The parallelograms with curved vertical lines are secondary storage files. Not shown in Figure 13–3 is the logic necessary to create and update the chart of accounts.

Figures 13–4, 13–5, 13–6, and 13–7 illustrate the four most important reports produced by the general ledger module. Depicted in Figure 13–4 is the balance sheet for a small firm.

The **balance sheet** lists the major categories of the firm's assets and liabilities and sums these. Its appearance is highly dependent upon the appearance of the chart of accounts. Its purpose is to enable an assessment of the financial condition of the firm. In general, assets are expected to exactly equal liabilities, to the penny. Many general ledger reports permit the comparison of this year's activity with the same period last year. One purpose of balance sheets is to permit lending institutions to assess the financial viability and loan worthiness of the firm at times when the firm is seeking additional capital for its operations.

The **profit and loss statement** (Figure 13–5) of a firm does not reflect the financial position of the firm so much as it reflects the sales and cost performance for the period in question and for the year-to-date. Sales, cost of goods sold, expenses, and gross and net profits are shown by major category. As for the balance sheet, the appearance of this report is heavily influenced by the accounts listed in the chart of accounts. Budgets in each category are prepared ahead of time by the manager and entered into the computer. The profit and loss report will then display the actual amount, the budgeted amount, and the ratio for each account category. In addition, the income statement (profit and loss statement) may show actual year-to-date totals in relation to account totals for the same period last year.

For all but the smallest of firms, the transactions are entered and maintained in category-specific transaction files which, when printed, are called journals. For

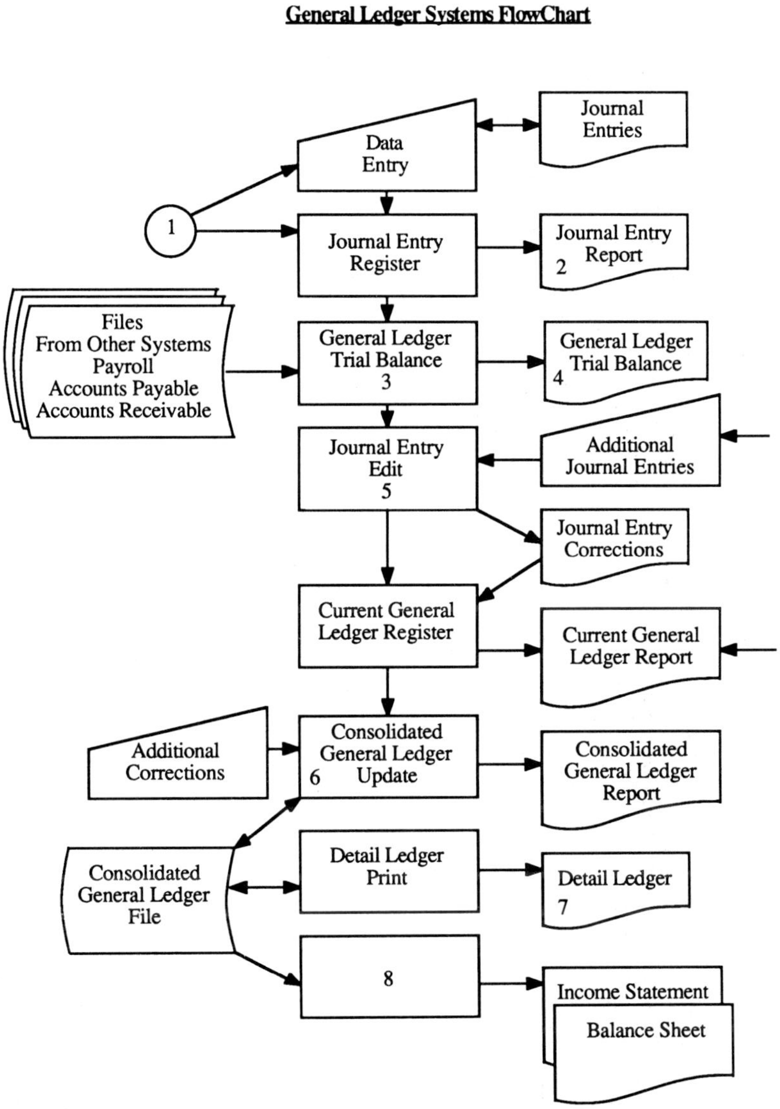

General Ledger Systems FlowChart

FIGURE 13–3

General Ledger Module Flowchart

example, a sales journal records customer invoices, a cash receipts journal records customer receipts, a cash disbursements journal records checks written, and so forth. At posting, the records in these files are used to credit and debit the appropriate general ledger accounts, after which the files are generally erased or compressed to make room for the next period's entries. A hard copy of the journal entries is retained as an audit trail.

The **transaction journal** (Figure 13–6) is the listing of all transactions posted to the general ledger and stored in its master transaction file. These transactions may have been entered manually or passed to the general ledger package from one of the other modules. As previously mentioned, for each transaction that is entered or passed, one general ledger account gets debited and one account gets credited. The general ledger software is able to determine which accounts to debit or credit based on the "code" of the transaction being entered or passed.

FIGURE 13–4

Typical Balance Sheet Report *(Used with Express Permission of Layered, Inc.)*

National Athletic Distributors Inc.

Balance Sheet as of 12/31/87

Boston Division

ASSETS				
Cash	2,204,488.38			
Petty Cash	1,500.00			
Certificates of Depos				
Accounts Receivable	487,642.49			
Allowance-Doubtful Acct.	-9,325.00			
Prepaid Expenses	8,100.00			
Inventory-ActiveWear	58,335.65			
Inventory-Sporting Goods	-1,185,074.35			
Employee Advances	8,500.00			
Total Current Assets		$ 1,574,167.17		
Furniture & Fixtures	55,000.00			
Automobile	52,500.00			
Leasehold Improvement	5,000.00			
Computer	20,000.00			
Accumulated Depreciation	-23,780.00			
Total Fixed Assets		$ 108,720.00		
Total Assets				$ 1,682,887.17
LIABILITIES & EQUITY				
Notes Payable	10,000.00			
Accounts Payable	172,167.96			
Taxes Payable	2,000.00			
Commissions Payable	21,843.96			
Sales Tax Payable	14,559.14			
Freight Payable	4,607.25			
Payroll Taxes Payable	857.80			
Total Current Liab.		$ 226,036.11		
Long Term Notes Payable	65,000.00			
Total Liabilities			$ 291,036.11	
Capital Stock	25,000.00			
Retained Earnings	136,098.40			
Net Income (Loss)	1,230,752.66			
Total Equity			$ 1,391,851.06	
Total Liability & Equit				$ 1,682,887.17

Page 1

The master file list (Figure 13–7) simply lists all accounts in the chart of accounts, indicating the account name, the account type, whether the account is a master or a subaccount, and the current value of the account. This value can be compared with a budgeted amount and with a year-to-date total.

A typical general ledger opening menu might appear as shown in Figure 13–8 below. Here the user enters the number corresponding to the desired selection. It is a good idea to have the **BUILD CHART OF ACCOUNTS** selection password protected, to control access to this selection and prevent unauthorized users from doing irreparable damage to the accounting files. In fact, several levels of password protection are desirable, in which the first level allows access to the accounting system and the highest level allows access to the chart of accounts.

FIGURE 13–5

Typical Profit and Loss Statement

LIM Manufacturing, Inc.
123 Africa Drive
Huntington, AL 87878

For Year Ending December 31, 1986

			Percent of Net Sales
Net Sales		$112,760	
Cost of Goods Sold		$85,300	75.60
Gross Margin		$27,460	24.30
Operating Expenses:			
Selling	$6,540		5.70
General & Administrative*	$9,400		8.30
Total Operating Expenses		$15,940	14.10
Earnings before Interest & Taxes		$11,520	10.20
Interest Charges:			
Interest on Bank Notes	$850		0.70
Interest on Mortgage Bonds	$2,310		2.00
Total Interest Charges		$3,160	2.80
Earnings Before Taxes		$8,360	7.40
Federal & State Income Taxes(@48%)		$4,013	3.50
Net Income		**$4,347**	3.80
Dividends Paid on Common Stock		$2,800	2.40
Earnings Retained		**$1,547**	1.30

*Includes $150 in annual lease payments.

FIGURE 13–6

Transaction Journal

LIM Electronics, Inc.
123 Alfonso Drive
San Pedro, Texas 12345

Date: August 2, 1987 **General Journal**

Date	Account #	Description	Debit	Credit
03/01/87		Japanese Electronics, Inc.		
	A100	Account Receivable	500.00	
	A200	Sales		500.00
03/02/87		Elma Computer, Inc.		
	A100	Account Receivable	8000.00	
	A200	Sales		8000.00
03/03/87		Elcorado Real Estate		
	A111	Rent	1000.00	
	A300	Cash		1000.00
03/15/87		Sure Fire Electronics, Inc.		
	A300	Cash	2000.00	
	A201	Sales Discount	100.00	
	A100	Account Receivable		2100.00
			11600.00	11600.00

ACCOUNTS RECEIVABLE SYSTEMS

It is interesting and insightful to consider how bookkeepers handled a sales transaction before computers were available. Although procedures varied from bookkeeper to bookkeeper, the following scenario is typical. The sale was first

FIGURE 13–7

Master File List (A portion only)

Account Number	Sub-Account	Account Name	Account Type	Report Type	Normal Balance	Total Level	Extra Lines	Sales Account	Special Report	This Month
10000	50	**Assets**	1	2	1	8	2			
11000	50	Current Assets	3	2	1	6	1			
11100	50	Cash	3	2	1	5	0			
11110	0	Revenue Bank	0	2	1	2	0		X	2000.30
11150	0	Petty Cash	0	2	1	2	0		X	50.80
11199	50	Total	2	2	1	5	1			
11400	50	Accounts Receivable	3	2	1	5	0			
11410	0	Finished Goods Sales Receivable	0	2	1	0	0		X	19990.00
11412	0	Consulting Fees Receivable	0	2	1	0	0		X	2000.00
11413	0	Allow for Doubtful Accounts	0	2	3	0	0		X	-150.00
11414	0	Employee Receivales	0	2	1	0	0		X	2500.00
11415	0	Other Accounts Receivable	0	2	1	1	0		X	500.00
11499	50	Total	2	2	1	3	1			
11500	50	Inventory — Finished Goods	3	2	1	4	0			
11510	0	Finished Goods	0	2	1	2	0		X	300000.00
11511	0	Raw Materials	0	2	1	2	0		X	10000.50
11512	0	Other Inventory	0	2	1	2	0		X	545.00
11599	50	Total	2	2	1	4	1			
11600	50	Prepaid Expense	3	2	1	5	0			
11610	0	Prepaid Insurance	0	2	1	0	0		X	906.00
11611	0	Prepaid Taxes	0	2	2	0	0		X	70.00
11612	0	Prepaid Rent	0	2	1	0	0		X	800.00
11615	0	Other Prepaid Expenses	0	2	1	0	0		X	300.00
11699	50	Total	2	2	1	4	1			
11999	50	Total Current Assets	2	2	1	5	7			

FIGURE 13–8

General Ledger Opening Menu

```
GENERAL LEDGER MENU

BUILD CHART OF ACCOUNTS        (1)
BUILD SPECIAL JOURNALS         (2)
UPDATE GENERAL JOURNALS        (3)
UPDATE SPECIAL JOURNALS        (4)
REPORTS                        (5)
RETURN TO MAIN MENU            (6)

SELECTION ?__
```

entered into a sales ledger and into a customer transaction file organized by customer. Cash receipts were recorded in a cash ledger and in the customer transaction ledger to balance out open invoices. At the end of each month the columns in all the ledgers were totaled, these total amounts were posted to appropriate accounts in the general ledger, and statements were manually prepared for each customer. This labor-intensive activity was time-consuming, hard work, and the opportunities for introducing inadvertent errors were considerable.

From this discussion the inputs to the accounts receivable system, whether manual or computerized, are apparent. They are the sales transaction, the cash receipt, and the data on each customer. The sales transaction may be initiated through a purchase order or through an outright (on-site) purchase of goods or services. The cash receipt is simply an entry in the cash journal designating the receipt of some form of payment and may not be accompanied by an actual receipt returned to the customer. Data on the customer probably included the shipping and billing addresses, the credit limit, and the amount of credit used up.

Accounts Receivable System Objectives

Listed in Table 13–6 are the objectives of any accounts receivable application.

Accounts Receivable Concepts and Design Philosophies

Accounts receivable packages are the primary tool for collecting funds owed by customers and for maintaining customer accounts. They are basically an information system for keeping customers apprised of their accounts with a business establishment. As such they must be capable of producing reports which, when transmitted to the customer, will encourage payment to the business firm.

The **customer statement** is the primary instrument used for this purpose; it is mailed out monthly to serve as a gentle reminder of the status of the customer's account with the firm.

The **customer invoice** is an equally important document, used for collection purposes, and is usually transmitted to the customer at the time of sale. Again, its purpose is to encourage payment, usually at the time of sale or service. Not all accounts receivable packages are capable of printing invoices, but all of them can print statements. Some accounts receivable packages are intended for use with a separate invoicing and billing package, hence do not themselves have the capability of printing invoices. A displayed customer invoice appears in Figure 13–9.

There can be no doubt that an invoice transmitted at the time of sale or service is an excellent inducement to early payment. Consider, for a moment, the needs of a plumbing contractor who does short-notice plumbing repairs. Suppose that you decide to avail yourself of the services of this plumber on a date that is early in the month. If this plumber uses an accounts receivable package without any invoicing capability, you won't receive a document requesting payment until the statement arrives at the end of the month. If the "terms" of the statement are "net 30," you have thirty more days before you must pay your bill. In total you have managed to postpone payment for nearly sixty days. By now you're probably saying, "Hey, what's this plumber's name?" The perspective from the plumber's point of view is not as bright; the longer payment is postponed, the less likely it is to be collectible at all. Hence, an invoicing capability can be a very important enhancement to the total accounts receivable function.

TABLE 13–6

Objectives of Accounts Receivable Systems

1. To maintain customer accounts
2. To induce customers to pay
3. To track invoices through to payment
4. To age unpaid invoices
5. To age unpaid customer accounts
6. To print sales analysis reports

Still another report capable of inducing payment from the customer is the **past-due notice.** Past-due notices may be sent out when any payment is more than fifteen days overdue. Consequently, a slow-paying customer receives two letters a month: the monthly statement at the beginning of the month, and the past-due notice after the fifteenth of the month. Although not all accounts receivable packages are capable of producing past-due notices, some accounts receivable packages

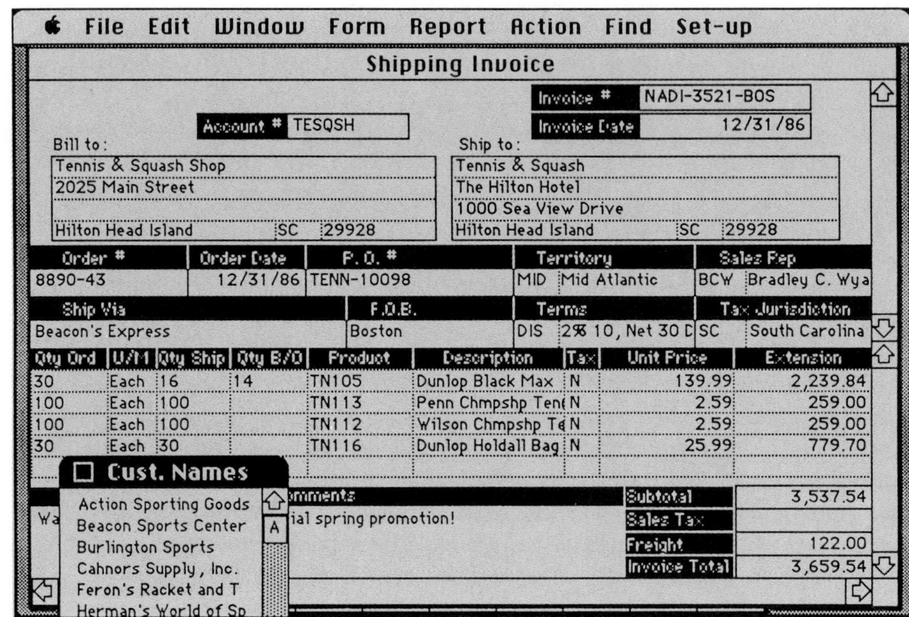

FIGURE 13–9

Shipping Invoice *(Used with the Express Permission of Layered, Inc.)*

Focus Feature

SELECTING AND INSTALLING AN ACCOUNTING SYSTEM

SELECTION

Accounting systems software differ drastically in their features and capabilities. At the same time, the accounting system needs of different business organizations differ substantially. It behooves the potential buyer/user, therefore, to weigh his or her needs carefully and assess package appropriateness in view of those needs. A precise methodology for doing this is presented in Chapter 16.

Each accounting package offers its own set of features in design philosophy, reports provided, and so forth. Some of these may be appropriate for your business. Others may be superfluous or even counterproductive. For example, if you run an auto parts store, you can hardly afford to use an inventory accounting system that forces you to record the location of every item in the store, in addition to its price, stock number, and quantity. Every time an oil filter, tune-up kit, or auto polish was moved, this would have to be recorded as a transaction. However, if you're operating a television appliance store or other store that stocks relatively high-priced goods, then location information might be expedient.

As a further example, consider the needs of a cash-and-carry retailer as compared with the needs of the law

will even print a letter (of appropriate severity, depending upon how late the payment is) to accompany the past-due notice.

Organizations which manage their receivables poorly incur higher operating costs resulting from the mailing of additional notices. They also lose revenues from forgoing the interest-earning potential of deferred payments, and from the larger percentage of uncollectable accounts.

Essentially three approaches are used in managing receivable accounts. These are called **balance-only**, **balance-forward**, and **open-item** systems. Balance-only accounts receivable systems are the simplest in concept and require the least amount of computer storage, because records on each transaction are not retained—only totals. Balance-only systems are used by some credit card agencies and department stores who maintain huge customer master files and therefore must minimize the amount of information carried on each customer. Past-due amounts carry an interest charge, but are not aged or supported.

Balance-forward accounts receivable packages provide considerably more detail on customer statements (Figure 13–10) than do balance-only systems. They are used by industries that serve commercial customers (as opposed to private individuals). Unpaid past-due balances are carried forward and segregated by age: thirty, sixty, and ninety days and over.

The most popular (and most complex) accounts receivable systems are called open-item accounts receivable systems. These carry purchase details along on successive statements until an invoice (purchase) is paid in full. The end result is a complete accounting of customer activity for all invoices that are either unpaid or being contested. Discounting is often used to encourage advance payment and interest charges are occasionally tacked onto late payments. An open-item statement is shown in Figure 13–11.

Some accounts receivable packages allow the user to designate which statement type a particular customer is to receive, be it open-item or balance-forward,

---

office down the street. While the law office might be able to make good use of an elegant accounts receivable package that sends out invoices and statements, there may be no use for these instruments in the cash-and-carry operation.

INSTALLATION

The process of installing and implementing an accounting system is discussed in detail in Chapter 16. The process also involves training the users of the system and testing the system to ascertain its proper functionality. All this takes time, and is at least as expensive as the software itself. There are too many instances in which the purchasers of microcomputer systems did not budget monies for maintenance and training and were sadly disillusioned when they realized how much the total installation and training expenses would cost. It is usually a good idea to bring on-line just one application area at a time (such as payroll, followed by accounts receivable and then accounts payable, perhaps). The idea is to fully test each application and to be convinced it is entirely operative before going on to another.

FIGURE 13–10
Balance-Forward Statement

LIM Electronics, Inc.
123 Alfonso Drive
San Pedro, Texas 12345

Edison, Albert
P. O. Box 114
Lubbock, Texas 79401

Acct. No.	Date
A123	August 15,1987

$______________Amount Remitted

Payment Due Due By August 31, 1987
Please Detach And Return With Your Payment

Date	Invoice No.	Description	Charges	Payment	Balance
		Balance Forward			$198.90
08/01/87	A110	Charge	$100.99		299.89
08/05/87	A115	Charge	200.00	-100.00	399.89
08/12/87	A118	Overdue Charge	5.00		414.89

Current	30 Day	60 Days	90 Days	Amount Due
				$414.89

and are thus capable of producing both statement types. Also, some accounts receivable packages permit codes to be assigned to each customer designating whether that customer is to receive invoices only, statements only, both invoices and statements, or neither.

Procedural and Structural Overview

The procedure used by any accounts receivable system differs depending on the package. One consideration is whether the accounts receivable system is to handle customer orders and print invoices. If it does not, then it may be interfaced to a customer order processing and invoicing package that does. Or, it may be intended for cash-and-carry retailers who do not require an invoicing capability. In what follows, order processing and invoicing is assumed to be part of the accounts receivable module, and a system based upon this assumption will be described.

Table 13–7 lists the major steps and activities found in most accounts receivable systems. Figure 13–12 exhibits the major files and processing functions required of accounts receivable systems. Files are shown as squares with double horizontal lines through them, whereas reports are rectangles with perforated edges.

In what follows, these three major categories of activity are discussed. This discussion is based upon Table 13–7 and Figure 13–12. It should be pointed out that posting (the transferring of transaction file data into the master files, usually followed by the deletion of most of the records in the transaction files and their subsequent compression) is not necessarily a daily activity. On the other hand, this may not be a monthly activity either, because the transaction files might get too large. Therefore, posting and its attendant activities are listed separately.

Daily Activities For the most part, daily activities consist of data entry and editing of three types of data: customer orders (including credit and debit memos), cash receipts, and adding customers to the customer file. Once entered, an audit list for each data type is printed and checked. Any errors which may have been detected are then edited out of the records that were created. These activities are the most labor-intensive of the accounts receivable system.

FIGURE 13–11
Open-item Statement

Statement

LIM Electronics, Inc.
123 Alfonso Drive
San Pedro, Texas 12345

Statement Date: 08/31/87

Account Number: PETCOM

St. Peterson Computer, Inc.
123 Japanese Land
Doncaster, S. Yorkshire, England

Invoice	Date	Terms or Ref	Code	Debits	Credits	Balance
A100	05/01/87	OC Reconcil	9		200.00	-200.00
A101	05/08/87	Net 10	0	100.00		-100.00
A112	05/15/87	Net 10	0	500.00		400.00
A115	05/30/87	Check #1023	5		400.00	0.00
A123	06/15/87	Net 10	0	345.50		345.50
A125	06/30/87	Net 10	0	154.50		500.00
A130	07/15/87	Net 10	0	500.00		1000.00
A131	07/30/87	Check #1123	5		500.00	500.00
				1600.00	1100.00	

Code

0 — Sale	5 — Payment		
1 — Freight	6 — Credit		
2 — Tax	7 — Return	**Credit:**	**$500.00**
3 — Service	8 — Discount		
4 — Misc. DB	9 — Misc. CR		

The entering of data for these two major categories of information is facilitated by means of data entry screens. Some typical data entry screens are exhibited in Figure 13–13.

Accounts Receivable Data Entry

Shown in Figure 13–13 is a typical data entry screen for accounts receivable transaction entry. Data entry fields are indicated as underscores.

Posting The next major phase is called posting. This task is accomplished almost entirely by computer and does not require much user interaction. Since it is a time-consuming task that also erases the contents of certain intermediate files (specifically, the order and cash receipts transaction files), posting may not be performed daily. As previously mentioned, posting refers to taking the contents of existing transaction files and entering their aggregate results into master files in which the data is saved in a categorized aggregate form. For example, each order record in the order transaction file would be reformatted into a record for the open invoice transaction file. Each such record in the invoice file would contain sufficient information to specify a line item on the invoice. These records would be batched by invoice number. The data contained in the order transaction file and the cash receipts transaction file are aggregated, summarized, and placed within the invoice master file, the sales history master file, the customer master file, and the general ledger file.

TABLE 13–7

Typical Steps and Activities Within the Accounts Receivable System

DAILY

1. Enter customer orders/purchases into order transaction file
2. Enter credit and debit memos into order transaction file
3. Print an audit list of entered orders/memos
4. Edit newly entered orders/purchases/memos
5. Enter cash receipts into cash receipts transaction file
6. Print an audit list of entered cash receipts
7. Edit newly entered cash receipts
8. Maintain customer file
9. Print transaction journals

WHEN POSTING OCCURS

1. Print invoices
2. Print appropriate reports
3. Post transactions

PERIODICALLY

1. Maintain customer file
2. Print customer master list

MONTHLY

1. Print statements
2. Print reports
3. End-of-month activities

Posting to the general ledger file is accomplished by use of general ledger account numbers. In some accounts receivable systems, every transaction that gets entered must be accompanied by the appropriate general ledger account number. In most systems, however, the appropriate account numbers are automatically known and posting takes place to these account numbers without user assistance. At this point certain reports would be printed, such as the invoices and probably some analysis reports needed by management.

End-of-month Activities The final phase of any accounts receivable system is the monthly activities. This would include printing the statements and the analysis reports (the sales history report, the cash receipts report, and the aging report). The statement and report printing activity can be a time-consuming task. To facilitate this activity, it is recommended that a spooling capability be used so that the microcomputer can continue to be accessed by a user even though printing is taking place. Spooling permits the computer to print and do something else concurrently, such as supporting a user who is interacting with a program.

Reports

The major reports produced by accounts receivable packages were listed earlier in this chapter. This section briefly describes the functions of some of these

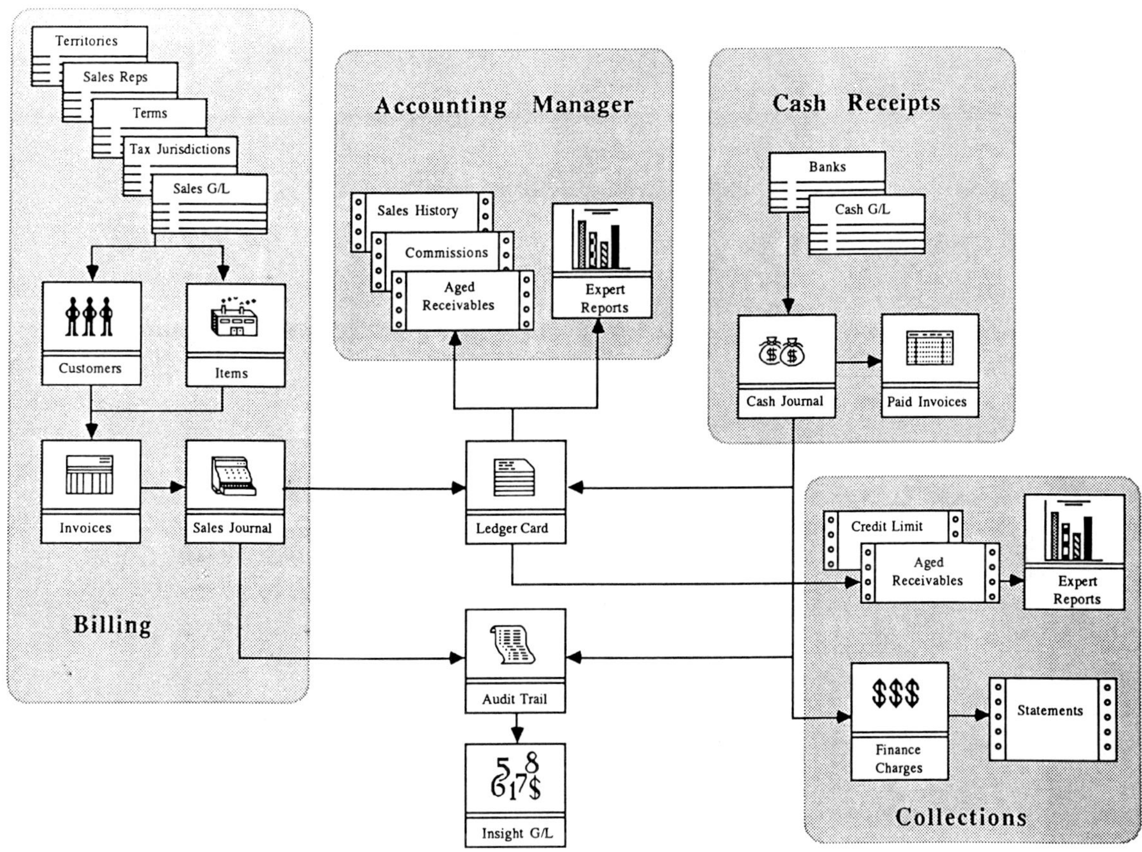

FIGURE 13–12

Accounts Receivable Process Flow *(Used with Express Permission of Layered, Inc.)*

reports. Much has already been said about the invoice and the statement, so those "reports" will not be discussed here; this section instead discusses the transaction journals, the detailed aging report, the past-due reports, and the sales-by-salesperson report.

Transaction Journals Transaction journals list all transactions entered between posting periods, and serve as instruments for controlling the accuracy and integrity of the data entry operation; they also provide a permanent audit trail of transaction activity. They should be printed at the end of each business day, as part of the end-of-day procedures. The cash receipts journal would show one line for each transaction entered. For each check received, the check number should be recorded, the amount of funds received should be shown, and the invoice to which the check was applied should be exhibited. For the order transaction journal, each record should show the invoice number; the tax, freight, and miscellaneous charges; and the invoice total amount. Records should be organized by customer and printed in ascending order from earliest to most recent, with total sales amount computed and net amount owed exhibited. Figure 13–14 illustrates a page of an order transaction journal.

Detailed Aging Report The detailed aging report should also be organized by customer. The report shows how much each customer owes by age cat-

FIGURE 13–13

Data Entry Screen for Entering Customer Orders

Name: International Computer, Inc.________________ **Cust. No.:** **12345**
Address: 123 Ipoh Street, Suite 1000 ________________
City: San Pedro ______**State:** TX _ **Zipcode:** **78901_**

Ship to:

Name: ________________
Address: ________________
City:______________**State:** ___**Zipcode:** ________

Date: 8/1/87______ **Salesperson:** J. C. Smith______

Description	Stock #	Quantity	Unit Price	Total
Widget — Type A Small	10000	100	8.50	850.00
Widget — Type A Larger	10001	100	9.25	925.00
Widget — Type B Small	10002	100	9.75	975.00
Spark Plug	10100	500	0.50	250.00
Spark Plug Cable	10101	500	4.00	2000.00
Ignition Coil	10200	50	30.00	1500.00
			Subtotal:	6500.00
			Taxes:	373.75
			Grand Total:	6873.75
				========

FIGURE 13–14

A Typical Page in the Order Transaction Journal

LIM Electronics, Inc.
123 Alfonso Drive
San Pedro, Texas 12345

Date: August 31, 1987 **Order Transaction Journal**

Date	Account #	Description	Debit	Credit
04/01/87		Acron Brick		
	A100	Account Receivable	500.00	
	A200	Sales		500.00
04/02/87		Falms Trees and Shrubs		
	A100	Account Receivable	8000.00	
	A200	Sales		8000.00
04/03/87		Hedge Brockerage		
	A111	Rent	1000.00	
	A300	Cash		1000.00
04/15/87		Plus Electronics, Inc.		
	A300	Cash	2000.00	
	A201	Sales Discount	100.00	
	A100	Account Receivable		2100.00
			11600.00	11600.00
			=========	=========

egory: current, 1–30 days, 31–60 days, over 60 days, and the total. Invoice numbers and due dates may be listed, as is the customer's phone number. This report should be printed once a month following the statement run, and is used for credit and collections purposes. A detailed aging report is shown in Figure 13–15.

Past-due Reports The past-due report should be requested at least weekly and is used for early detection of slow-paying customers. Managerial responses to

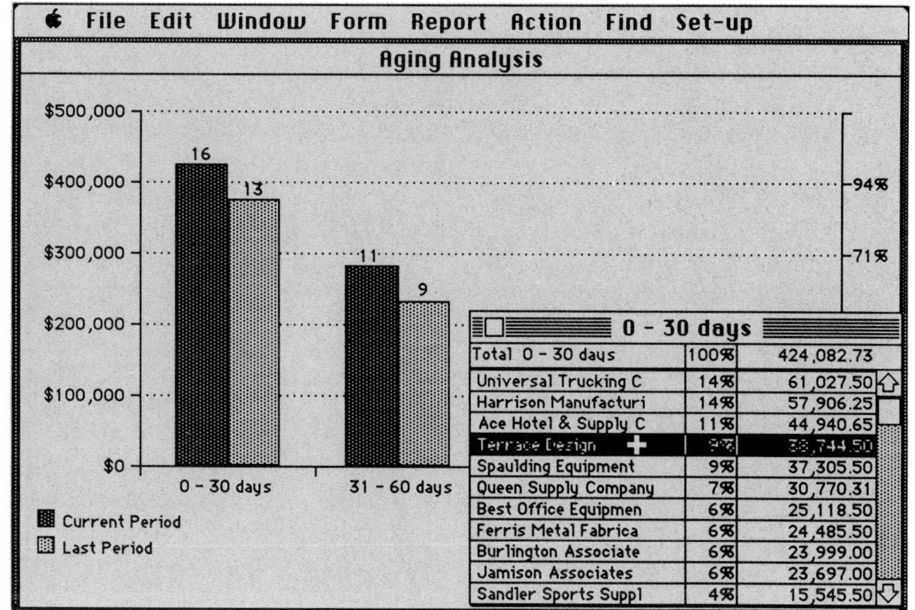

FIGURE 13–15

Aging Analysis *(Used with Express Permission of Layered, Inc.)*

LIM Electronics, Inc.
Past Due Report
July 31, 1987

Cust.#	Cust. Name/ Telephone #	Total Due	Current	31to 60	61 to 90	Over 90
1000	Japanese Electronics, Inc. (216) 756-8900	**2000.00**	1500.00	500.00		
1010	Modern Electronics, Inc. (512) 123-3452	1500.00	1500.00			
1020	British Computers, Co. (756) 567-1111	5500.95	2500.95	1500.00	1000.00	500.00
1030	Auckland Enterprise (908) 111-7867	8900.00	6000.00	2000.00	900.00	
1040	Tom Jack Corp. (809) 124-1567	450.00	250.00	200.00		
1050	American Pie, Inc. (512) 342-1232	3000.00	2800.00	200.00		
1060	Suzie's (314) 432-8900	305.95	305.95			

FIGURE 13–16

A Typical Past-due Report

this report include calling the customer, cutting off any further extension of credit to the customer, alerting salespeople to contact their slow-paying customers, and so forth. An example past-due report is shown in Figure 13–16.

Past-due Notices Past-due notices should be sent out mid-month to remind slow-paying clients and customers of their indebtedness to the agency or firm. Past-due notices display no transaction details, only the amount due. Not all accounts receivable packages have the capability to print past-due notices and not all business concerns have a need for such a capability.

Sales-by-salesperson Report The sales-by-salesperson report is usually produced weekly, as a hard-copy record of the past week's sales activity for each salesperson. The report serves the needs of management and the salespeople as well, because it will show how the salesperson is doing in relation to his or her quota, who the best customers were, and so on. In fact, customers are usually listed according to dollar volume, with those whose dollar-volume purchases were highest first.

Accounts Receivable Features

There are dozens of specialized features that accounts receivable packages may or may not have. Table 13–8 lists some of these. Users must make their own judgments as to how essential each feature is. For example, most users could do without the ability to define their own aging periods, because thirty days, sixty days, ninety days, etc. are entirely acceptable. However, few users could do without the capability to print mailing labels for mailing of invoices and statements. (Some systems will even print mailing labels in ZIP code order. This enables users to avail themselves of bulk mail rates, resulting in substantial savings on postage.) And most users would appreciate the capability to calculate and add on sales tax and interest charges.

Some of the other features listed can be functional for some types of businesses. For example, if a customer calls with a question regarding his or her statement, it would be nice if the operator could "call up" the customer's account on the screen, verify all payments and invoices, and thereby resolve the problem. An on-line customer inquiry capability would support such a requirement. In addition, late payments on invoices may not include interest charges. These small residual amounts may linger on for months. At some point, there must be a decision regarding the cost of printing and mailing additional notices versus the benefit of col-

TABLE 13—8

Some Features of Accounts Receivable Packages

Features
Accumulates revenues by store
Accumulates cost of sales
Allows user-defined aging periods
Calculates and applies finance charges
Calculates payment due date based on terms of payment
Calculates and adds on sales tax, when appropriate
Checks customer credit against a preassigned limit
Deletes old or uncollectible invoices
Interfaces with general ledger
Interfaces with customer order processing
Prints detailed writeoff report on uncollectible accounts
Prints mailing list labels (in ZIP code order)
Prints past-due notices
Provides on-line customer inquiry

lecting the interest charge. It becomes clear that further attempts to collect the residual are not worth the effort. At that point a deleted invoice capability would remove all such invoices, which are smaller than a preset amount or older than a preset date, and produce a printed report that can be used for tax purposes in writing off such collectibles.

ACCOUNTS PAYABLE SYSTEMS

If you keep a checkbook you have, in effect, manually operated an **accounts payable system.** Once a month or so, you look over your stack of bills, consider your cash position, decide which ones to pay given your cash available, write out checks to the firms you selected, and mail the checks. At the same time you will update your check register, which shows what checks you have written, for what amount, and to whom, and how much cash is remaining in your bank account. As shall be seen, that is exactly what an automated accounts payable system does—that and a whole lot more. So you already have a good feel for how an accounts payable system works.

It is interesting to contrast the operation of accounts receivable systems with accounts payable systems. Accounts payable systems operate in a way that is analogous to accounts receivable systems. For example, one of the driving inputs of accounts payable systems is the vendor invoices, just as customer orders (and hence, invoices) were a driving input for accounts receivable systems. In fact, for the accounts payable application, vendors assume the role that customers held within the accounts receivable application. In addition to vendor invoices, the package is concerned with cash disbursements and must be capable of printing checks. In accounts payable packages, the printing of checks is analogous to the printing of statements in accounts receivable packages.

Accounts Payable System Objectives

Listed in Table 13–9 are some objectives of accounts payable packages.

Procedural Overview

Table 13–10 details the major processing steps in any accounts payable activity. The accounts payable process flow is shown in Figure 13–17.

TABLE 13–9
Accounts Payable Objectives

1. To determine when to pay
2. To determine what amount to pay
3. To provide management with a way of allocating available cash
4. To evaluate vendors on the basis of total cost of goods produced
5. To reconcile vendor invoices with purchase orders
6. To manage cash flow

TABLE 13–10

Accounts Payable Processing Steps

DAILY

1. Enter approved vendor invoices
2. Print audit list for editing purposes
3. Edit newly entered vendor invoice records
4. Enter manually written check vouchers
5. Print audit list for editing purposes
6. Edit newly entered check voucher records
7. At end of each day, print vendor invoice and check voucher transaction journals

POSTING

1. Post transactions to the general ledger, vendor, and other files

WEEKLY

1. Determine which vouchers to pay
2. Print checks and a check register
3. Maintain vendor master file as necessary

MONTHLY

1. Produce reports:
   (a) open voucher report
   (b) accounts payable aging report
   (c) cash requirements report
2. At the end of each month, prepare the general ledger transfer file and post to the general ledger

Daily Activities The daily data entry into the accounts payable system begins with a careful consideration of each vendor invoice, in which each invoice is linked to a purchase order transmitted by the firm to the vendor. Only approved vendor invoices are entered into the accounts payable system.

At the end of each data entry session, an audit list of the recently entered transactions should be printed out. As in an accounts receivable system, this listing should be used for editing and accuracy purposes. The next session should commence with the editing of the previously entered transactions. At the end of each business day, the transaction journals should be printed. Each line will correspond to a record in the respective file. For the vendor invoice transaction file, each line will show the gross amount due, the payment due date, the discount, the discount amount, and the interest charge if there is one. The transaction files may be used for accuracy and editing purposes, but they also serve as an audit trail (a permanent record of transaction activity for that day).

In addition to vendor invoices, there are periodic expenses which are not invoiced, such as rent. Some accounts payable systems can be configured so that all such periodic, noninvoiced expenses are stored in a file and (once a month) transferred into the vendor transaction file, whereupon payment can take place.

Each vendor who submits an invoice for payment will specify the terms of payment. For example, a vendor may provide a discount if the invoice is paid by a certain date; a penalty, service, or interest charge may be tacked on if the payment

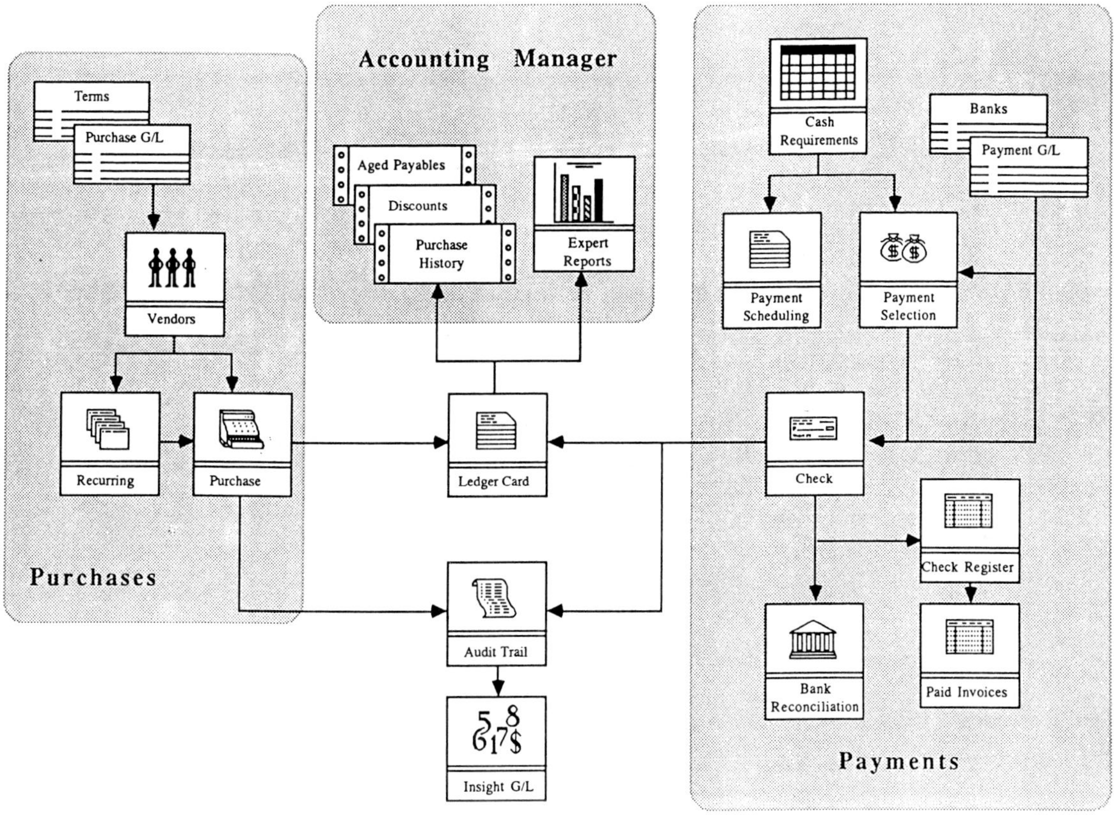

FIGURE 13–17

Accounts Payable Process Flow *(Used with Express Permission of Layered, Inc.)*

is not received by a second specified date. Typical invoice terms might be 2% 10, net 30, and 1½% interest charge on late payments. This would be interpreted as a 2% discount if paid within ten days, net amount is due if paid after the tenth day but before the thirty-first day, and a 1½% interest surcharge per month on late payments more than thirty-one days late. Given these terms, one task of the accounts payable system is to help the firm's buyer to decide when to pay each bill.

Posting Posting will generally occur once every other day or so, but should not take place until the operator is absolutely certain that the newly entered records are error-free. As in an accounts receivable package, accounts payable posting involves debiting and crediting appropriate accounts in the general ledger master file. Accounts payable posting also involves making changes to the vendor master file, and adjusting records within other files as necessary.

Weekly Activities Once a week, the list of outstanding invoices should be reviewed, and decisions made as to which ones will be paid this time around. This may be performed by an operator using a keyboard and display, or by computer, in which each vendor invoice cutoff date (entered at the time the invoice itself was entered) is compared against the current date and those that match or are exceeded are automatically paid. Check vouchers for the selected vendors should be printed,

Focus Feature

HOME ACCOUNTING SOFTWARE PACKAGES

Accounting software for the home is becoming increasingly popular among professionals who do much work out of the home. These packages facilitate keeping a home budget, tracking payables by category, keeping your checkbook, and even provide counsel on where to invest your money for the greatest return. The goal of these packages is to help you control your finances by tracking how you save and spend your money.

One such program, called *Dollars and Sense* (Tronix Publishing Inc., 8295 S. La Cienega Blvd., Inglewood, CA 90301), divides your finances into accounts and transactions categories. Three categories of accounts are supplied: household accounts, business accounts, and tax preparation accounts. Each set of accounts is divided into smaller accounts for personal checking, cash, receivables, inventory, IRA payments, and savings. This program will track your cash flow into and out of the accounts. The account data that you enter is stored on a month-by-month basis and from this data, tabular reports and bar charts can be produced. It allows you to define your own accounts, to enter, edit, and print transactions, to modify checking account data, to reconcile bank statements, to prepare financial statements, to write checks, and to backup your accounting files.[1] Of major interest is that this program will print your checks for you once each month (on specially prepared check forms) and will tell you how you have spent your money.

Another program, called *Your Personal Net Worth* (Scarborough Systems, Inc., 25 N. Broadway, Tarrytown, NY 10591), will also print your checks for you and print out a check register. Like *Dollars and Sense,* the program is a prescription for disciplined household financial rec-

along with mailing labels (or envelopes), and mailed. Each check printed should be accompanied by a stub that reports the vendor invoice number being paid. This review process may occur less often than once a week if desired.

Monthly Activities Once each month, the analysis reports should be printed, including the open voucher report, the accounts payable aging report, and the cash requirements report.

Data Entry Screens

Typical screens for data entry are shown in Figures 13–18 and 13–19. Figure 13–18 depicts the fields and data required to enter a vendor invoice. Figure 13–19 illustrates the screen for editing records in the accounts payable journal.

Reports

Listed in Table 13–11 are typical reports produced by many accounts payable packages. Space will not permit discussion of all of these; however, the major ones are described in what follows.

Vendor List The vendor list report lists each vendor by name, and includes vendor ID, address, phone, year-to-date purchases from the vendor, year-to-date

ord keeping. The program is very easy to use and is well organized. It is designed to help you set up a budget, monitor your income and expenses, organize a household inventory, record stock transactions, create a balance sheet of personal assets and liabilities, expedite tax preparation, reconcile bank accounts, handle loan setup and payment, and give you a sense of your overall net worth.[2] The program walks you through an abridged version of *Sylvia Porter's New Money Book for the 80s* and thereby teaches you the rudiments of money management.

Still another program, which is very similar in form to *Your Personal Net Worth* yet even more robust, is Andrew Tobias's *Managing Your Money* (Micro Education Corporation of America, 285 Riverside Avenue, Westport, CT 06880). This program integrates home accounting, investment and financial planning, and tax planning into a single package. There are seven major components: insurance planning, budgeting and checkbook maintenance, investment portfolio management, income-tax estimator, financial calculator, reminder of important dates, and a net-worth calculator.[3] This last function is in fact a composite of all the previous six functions.

In each of the above-cited cases a new kind of integrated software package has emerged—one combining home accounting with financial and tax planning and a graphics capability to boot. However, there are dozens of less sophisticated check register programs that will do nothing more than keep your checkbook if that is all you need.

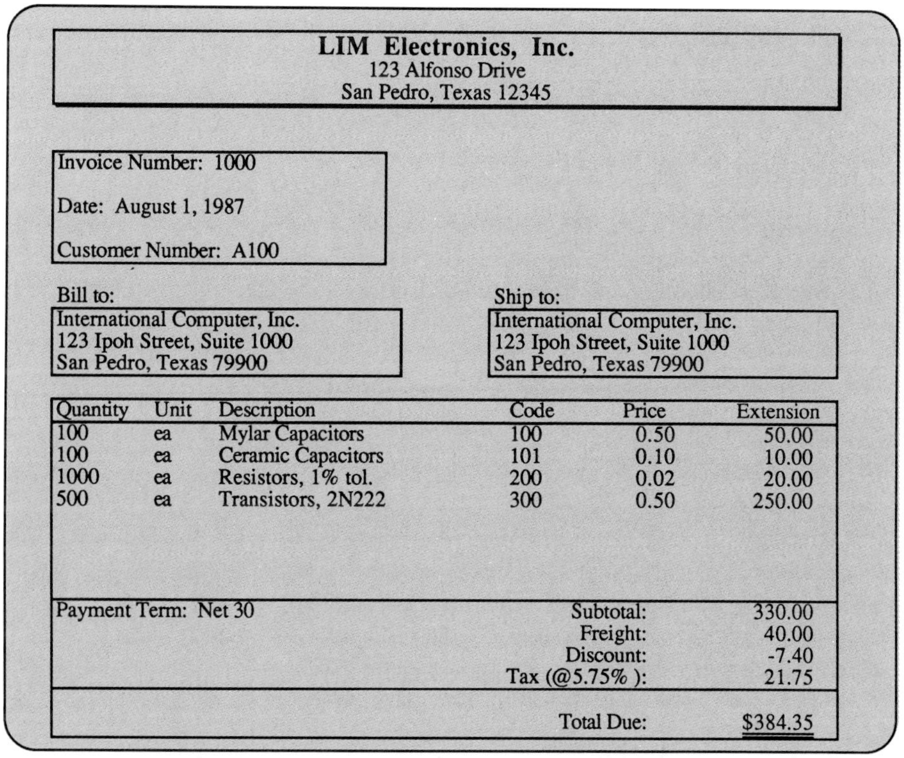

LIM Electronics, Inc.
123 Alfonso Drive
San Pedro, Texas 12345

Invoice Number: 1000

Date: August 1, 1987

Customer Number: A100

Bill to:	Ship to:
International Computer, Inc. 123 Ipoh Street, Suite 1000 San Pedro, Texas 79900	International Computer, Inc. 123 Ipoh Street, Suite 1000 San Pedro, Texas 79900

Quantity	Unit	Description	Code	Price	Extension
100	ea	Mylar Capacitors	100	0.50	50.00
100	ea	Ceramic Capacitors	101	0.10	10.00
1000	ea	Resistors, 1% tol.	200	0.02	20.00
500	ea	Transistors, 2N222	300	0.50	250.00

Payment Term: Net 30		
	Subtotal:	330.00
	Freight:	40.00
	Discount:	-7.40
	Tax (@5.75%):	21.75
	Total Due:	$384.35

FIGURE 13–18

Data Entry Screen for Entering Vendor Invoices

FIGURE 13–19

Data Entry Screen for Editing Records in the Accounts Payable Application

Data Entry Screen For Accounts Payable Transactions
Enter Vendor Number Or Press Enter To Exit

Vendor Number: ______________

Voucher/Check Number: ______________

Date: ____________ General Ledger Account: __________

Gross Amount: ____________ Debit Memo: __________

Discount %: ________ Clearance (Y or N): _____

payments to the vendor, current balance owed to the vendor, and the date, number, and amount of the last check. A typical report is shown in Figure 13–20.

Cash Requirements Report The cash requirements report lists all unpaid vendor invoices chronologically by due date and accumulates the amount owed in the rightmost column, as shown in Figure 13–21.

Check and Stub The check voucher and stub is the most important report produced by the accounts payable system. The stub lists invoice numbers and due dates so the vendor knows what invoices are being paid by the check. Figure 13–22 depicts a typical check and stub.

Check Register The check register shows what checks have been written, the date of writing, the associated invoices that were paid, the payee, and the check amount. Also provided is the total amount (in number of checks and dollars) of the checks that were written.

Accounts Payable Features

Listed in Table 13–12 are features which may or may not be provided by a specific accounts payable system. Some of these are considered desirable in almost any context or business environment. For example, the capability to enter checks

TABLE 13–11

Accounts Payable Reports

Accounts payable aging report	Vendor list
Cash requirements	Vendor analysis
General ledger distribution	Transaction register
Invoice register	Pre-check writing
Check register	Check and stub
Open item/unpaid	Manual check register
Debit/credit memo list	Journal/batch proof
Bank reconciliation	Mailing labels
History file	Monthly cash summaries

File Edit Windows Forms Reports Actions Find Set-ups

Vendor Information Card

Account #	S1000	Balance	9,230.20	Expense G/L #	Ratio
Name	Sir Speedy Inc.			50120-100-100	50.00 %
Address	120 Congress Street			50120-200-100	25.00 %
				50120-300-100	25.00 %
City	Boston				
State	MA	Zip Code	02120		
Contact	Ms. Karen Carlson			Open Item	☒
Telephone	617/291-2010			Liability G/L #	20200-000-000
Terms	2%10, Net 30 Days			Standard Product	Printing

This is historical information. It cannot be changed.

Total	Current	31-60 Days	61-90 Days	Over 90
9,230.20	6,394.20	2,836.00		

	Purchases	Discounts Taken	Discounts Lost	Service Charges
Month to Date	5,209.35		80.49	
Year to Date	75,286.45	804.72	701.01	280.40
Last Year				

	Date	Amount		Date	Amount	Opened
Last Purchase	8/12/86	5,209.35	Last Payment	7/28/86	3,290.50	2/11/86

FIGURE 13–20

A Typical Record in the Vendor File *(Used with the Express Permission of Layered, Inc.)*

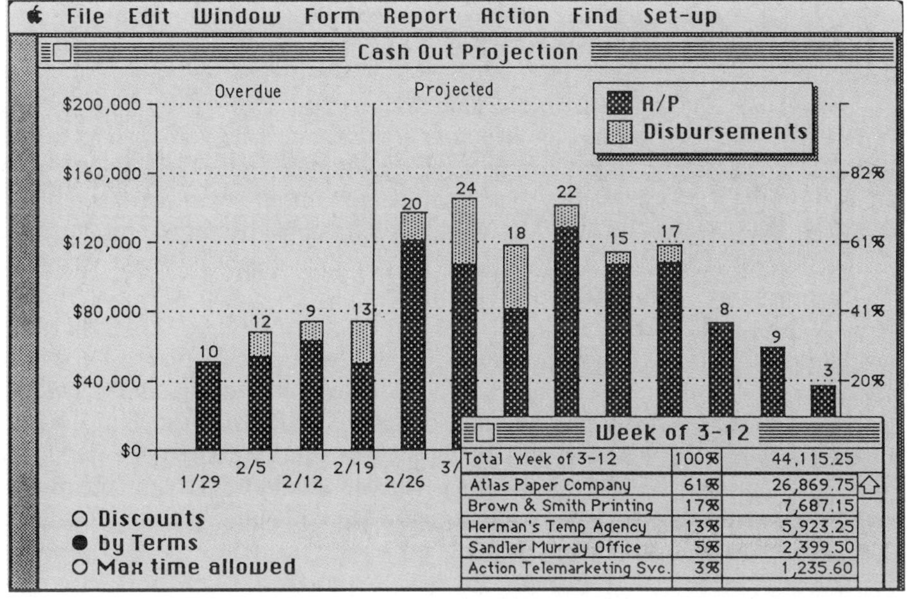

FIGURE 13–21

A Typical Page of the Cash Requirements Report *(Used with Express Permission of Layered, Inc.)*

that were manually written is a must in any small business. In addition, most businesses can benefit from the capability to accommodate multiple bank accounts and to handle multiple cost centers. Moreover, some of the features listed in Table 13–12 are standard with almost any accounts payable system. For example, most would be integrated with the general ledger package if that package was vended by the same software company that vends the accounts payable package.

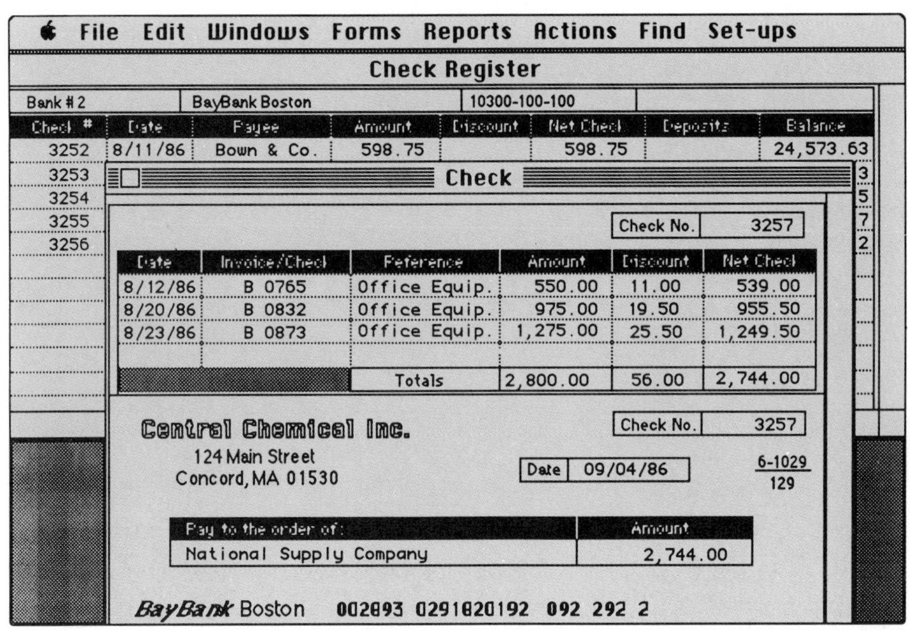

FIGURE 13–22

A Typical Vendor Check and Stub *(Used with Express Permission of Layered, Inc.)*

INVENTORY MANAGEMENT SYSTEMS

Inventory is goods with an economic value that are stored for later use or for sale. The purposes of carrying inventory are to create sales and to support the manufacturing of goods. In fact, inventory systems are often classified according to whether they are sales inventory systems or manufacturing inventory systems.

Unfortunately, inventory brings with it certain costs that, in the profit-maximizing interests of the company, should be minimized subject to meeting the requirements that established a need for the inventory to begin with. Such is the intent of **inventory systems.** One such cost is the opportunity cost associated with having capital tied up in inventory when it could otherwise be placed in a bank where it would earn interest. Other costs include the cost of storing the inventory, the cost of pilferage, shrinkage, and of obsolescence or decay. On an annual basis, the inventory cost may easily run as much as 30 percent or more of the purchase cost of the inventory. Ideally, an inventory manager would want to arrange things so that the delivery truck pulls up to his dock just a few minutes before the customer walks in the door to purchase the product that was just delivered. This is never possible in practice.

Inventory systems for microcomputers are of two basic types: systems for maintaining and monitoring sales inventory for wholesalers and retailers, and systems for maintaining inventory of manufacturing items in which demand for these items is dependent upon demand for the parent product.

Sales Inventory Systems

Sales inventory systems may be further broken down into two types: systems for retailers and systems for wholesalers. Wholesaler systems must be capable of

TABLE 13–12
Accounts Payable Features

Actuarial basis	Finance charges added
Aging by due date	Manual payments (checks)
Aging by invoice date	Multiple bank accounts
All vendor payments	Multiple cost centers
Audit trails	One-time vendors
Auto general ledger integration	Payments by due date
Automatic checks	Partial payments
Automatic discounts	Selected vendors
Batch processing	Trail payment run
Cash basis	Number of aging periods
Credit/debit memos	Recurring transaction dump

adjusting computerized records of stock-on-hand based upon customer order or invoice data and data on received shipments. There is a need for sophisticated scheduling, and ordering capabilities. Frequently, wholesalers use price discounting based upon volume of the order. Pricing based upon other considerations may also need to be accommodated. Inventory software packages for wholesale operations must be robust in the areas of ordering, pricing, delivery scheduling, and discounting.

Retail inventory systems usually must accept point-of-sale detail rather than customer orders or invoices. These systems require less sophistication in pricing and scheduling as compared with wholesale inventory systems.

Inventory Systems for Manufacturers

The need here is to determine the raw material requirements based upon finished product demand which is known or has been forecast. The raw material items that are used to assemble the finished product are said to have their demand *dependent* on the demand of the finished product.

As an example of a dependent demand situation, consider a small manufacturing firm which makes chairs. Each chair consists of a seat, backrest, and four legs. These are the items. If there is a demand for fifty chairs, then fifty seats are needed, as are fifty backrests and two hundred legs (assuming all legs are exactly the same). Clearly the demand for seats, backrests, and legs is dependent upon the demand for chairs. Inventory systems for dependent demand items are usually called material requirements planning systems, or MRP systems for short.

HARDWARE AND SOFTWARE REQUIREMENTS FOR ACCOUNTING

Desirable hardware for accounting applications will, as a minimal requirement, include a system with 512K of main memory, two floppy-disk drives, an 80-column by 24- or 25-line screen, and a detachable keyboard. A hard or fixed disk is very desirable, because it greatly speeds the processing and allows for file sizes that might exceed the capacity of a single floppy diskette. A general ledger system which took an hour and fifteen minutes for posting on a floppy computer system took only twelve minutes on a hard-disk system. This is because of the input/output-intensive nature of all accounting applications. We say programs are input/output intensive when there is much reading and writing of records to and from secondary storage. The access time and data transfer rate of fixed disks (see Chapter 3) is faster by roughly an order of magnitude as compared with floppy diskettes.

Summary

This chapter has presented an overview of integrated accounting systems. Such systems may consist of an accounts receivable module, an accounts payable module, a payroll module, an invoicing/billing module, and an inventory module, all unified by a general ledger module. In fact, a general ledger module is usually required only when two or more area-specific modules are required. For the service-related professions—doctors, dentists, attorneys, accountants, architects—the application of greatest need is an accounts receivable module to track patients, customers, and clients. In such professions there are usually very few vendors, items of inventory, or employees that require tracking.

The heart of any integrated, multiarea accounting system is its general ledger package. The purpose of this module is to consolidate all of the transactions entered into the area-specific modules along with any manual entries that may not have been reported elsewhere, to debit and credit the appropriate accounts associated with each transaction, and to produce (print) the pro forma financial statements: the balance sheet and the income statement. These reports serve as information to support the highest levels of decision making within the firm.

The automation of two important accounting functions—receivables and payables—are described in this chapter. The judicious management of a firm's receivables and payables makes an important contribution to the overall profitability of a firm. Three types of accounts receivable systems were described: balance-only, balance-forward, and open-item. Emphasis was focused on the last two types. The major differences among these types are in the quantity of information retained on each invoice. Some accounts receivable systems permit the operator to designate some accounts as balance-forward accounts and others as open-item accounts. In addition, the issue of whether the accounts receivable system prints invoices or not was addressed. Some businesses can make expedient use of an automated invoicing capability while others cannot. Again there are accounts receivable systems that let the operator designate whether a particular customer is to receive invoices or not.

The inputs to the accounts receivable system are the customer orders or purchases, the cash receipts, and data on the customers themselves. The outputs are the statements, the transaction journals, and the analysis reports (including the sales analysis report, the past-due report, and the aged receivables report).

Accounts payable systems determine which vendor invoices will be paid when, based upon the terms of payment specified by the vendor and the cash available. These systems are used to manage cash flow, since they are able to project the cash requirements of the firm.

The inputs to the accounts payable system are the vendor invoices, data on the vendors themselves, and manually prepared checks. The outputs received from the accounts payable system are the vendor checks, the transaction journals, and the analysis reports (including the cash requirements report, the aged payables report, and the check register).

Key Terms

accounting systems
accounts payable module
accounts receivable module
balance-forward statement
balance-only statement
balance sheet
chart of accounts
closing
customer invoice
customer statement
general ledger module
installation
inventory systems
open-item statement
payroll
posting
profit and loss statement

Self-Test

1. List the important functions and features of
   (a) general ledger packages
   (b) accounts receivable packages
   (c) accounts payable packages
   (d) inventory packages
2. List the "standard" reports produced by the packages listed in Self-Test exercise 1 above.
3. What kind(s) of accounting software is likely to be useful in the following environments:
   (a) a doctor's office
   (b) a cash-and-carry retailer
   (c) a wholesaler
   (d) a small manufacturing operation
   (e) the home
4. How does one select and install an accounting system?
5. What can home accounting software packages do for you?

Exercises

1. Choose three accounting packages from the list of vendors in Table 13–2 above and obtain their descriptive brochures. Compare the various modules with respect to size (capacity), using the checklist on accounting systems in the appendix at the end of this book.
2. Discuss the importance of the chart of accounts within the framework of the general ledger system.
3. A small business is considering automating its accounts receivable, accounts payable, general ledger, and inventory systems. Which of these applications should be brought on-line first? Why? Should the applications be implemented sequentially or simultaneously? Why? If sequentially, what order of implementation would you recommend?
4. Compare three accounts receivable packages using the checklist in the appendix at the end of the book.
5. Compare three accounts payable packages using the checklist in the appendix at the end of the book.
6. Compare three general ledger packages using the checklist in the appendix at the end of the book.
7. Compare three inventory packages using the checklist in the appendix at the end of the book.
8. Compare three payroll packages using the checklist in the appendix at the end of the book.
9. Briefly describe the main purpose or objective behind each of the following packages:
   (a) accounts receivable

(b) accounts payable
(c) payroll
(d) inventory
(e) general ledger

10. Describe the general ledger application with regard to when it is likely to be needed, what purposes it serves, what reports it produces, and so forth.
11. Discuss the separate functions of the balance sheet and the income statement.
12. Discuss the objectives of an accounts receivable system.
13. Discuss the objectives of an accounts payable system.
14. Describe the process flow of an accounts receivable system.
15. Describe the process flow of an accounts payable system.
16. What are the major files in any accounts receivable system? Design a typical record within each accounts receivable file.
17. What are the major files in any accounts payable system? Design a typical record within each accounts payable file.
18. Go to your nearest microcomputer store and collect literature on the accounts receivable systems they have for sale. Prepare a table comparing these systems with respect to capacities and features.
19. Do what exercise 18 suggests for accounts payable systems.
20. Discuss what you believe are the most important features of an accounts receivable system for a small firm of attorneys. Assuming that the firm consists of two or less attorneys, do you think such a firm would need an accounts payable system?
21. Consider the needs of a fresh produce wholesaler. The wholesaler buys produce from the grower and sells the produce to the retailer. Would such a firm need an accounts receivable package? An accounts payable package? What specific features of each would you consider essential?
22. Discuss the differences among the three types of accounts receivable systems described: balance-only, balance-forward, and open-item.
23. Discuss the importance of each of the accounts receivable reports. What additional reports can you think of that might be desirable?
24. Discuss the significance of each of the accounts payable reports. What additional reports can you think of that might be desirable?
25. Discuss the specialized features of certain accounts receivable systems with a small business manager. Determine which of these features would be especially valuable and important to him or her.
26. Discuss the specialized features of certain accounts payable systems with a small business manager. Determine which of these features would be especially valuable and important to him or her.

References

1. Crabb, Don. "*Dollars and Sense:* Money Manager has Good Performance, Some Problems." *Infoworld* 6, issue 32 (August 6, 1984): 60–61.
2. "*Your Personal Net Worth.*" *PC World* (March 1985): 165–67.
3. Freedman, Eric. "How to Be Your Own Best Financial Advisor." *PC: The Independent Guide to IBM Personal Computers* 3, no. 17 (September 4, 1984): 279–314.

Additional Reading

Best, Peter J. *Small Business Computer Systems.* Sydney: Prentice-Hall of Australia Pty Ltd, 1980.

Eliason, A. L., and K. D. Kitts. *Business Computer Systems and Applications,* 2nd ed. Chicago: Science Research Associates, Inc., 1979.

Guttman, Michael K. "How to Choose an Accounting Package." *PC World* 2, no. 11 (October 1984): 56–72.

Haueisen, William D., and James L. Camp. *Business Systems for Microcomputers: Concept, Design, and Implementation.* Englewood Cliffs, N.J.: Prentice-Hall, 1982.

Klooster, Dale H., and Warren W. Allen. *Integrated Accounting on Microcomputers.* Cincinnati, Oh.: Southwestern Publishing Co., 1983.

"Micros Revolutionize American Industry." *PC Week* 2, no. 22 (June 4, 1985): 47–64.

Poole, Lon, et al. *Accounts Payable and Accounts Receivable.* Berkeley, Calif.: Osborne/McGraw Hill, 1979.

Poole, Lon, et al. *General Ledger.* Berkeley, Calif.: Osborne/McGraw Hill, 1979.

Price Waterhouse Report. "Inventory Control for Retailers." *PC: The Independent Guide to IBM Personal Computers* 3, no. 15 (August 7, 1984): 213–26.

Warren, Carl, and Merl Miller. *From the Counter to the Bottom Line.* Dubuque, Iowa: Dilithium Press, 1979.

CHAPTER

14

Data Communications

CHAPTER OUTLINE

Why Communicate? 493
Types of Data Communication 493
FOCUS FEATURE Working for the Home Office 494
FOCUS FEATURE Are You Secure? 496
The Components of Data Communications 499

CHAPTER OBJECTIVES

In this chapter you will learn

1 why data communication is so important
2 the types of data communication that take place
3 the components of data communication systems
4 what information utilities are
5 what bulletin board systems are available
6 what interfaces and ports are required for data communication
7 how a modem works and what it does

Despite the dramatic changes of the past decade that have resulted from the widespread use of computers, most experts agree that the computer's impact on our lives is still in its infant stages. Many of the changes that the future portends will come as a result of the advances in, and increased use of, **data communications**, the electronic transmission of data from one device to another.

This chapter looks at some of the principles of data communications, examines the hardware and software required for data transmission to occur, and explores some of the exciting uses for data communication in our business, professional, and personal lives. It also takes a brief look at the role this rapidly growing area will play in our futures.

WHY COMMUNICATE?

For some users, data communications represents an inexpensive and convenient method of rapidly transmitting information from one location to another. With data communications, a newspaper reporter can submit an article on a Washington meeting to a Los Angeles newspaper within minutes; a salesperson can check on stock availability, enter an order, and obtain an invoice number and shipping schedule, all before leaving the client's office; a businessperson can send an urgent letter to an office in another city within minutes, using either personally owned facilities or the services of a carrier or even the local post office; or a consumer in Nashville can purchase a new camera from a computer shopping service in New York and have it billed to a charge card without even leaving the living room.

For many businesses, data communications is not merely convenient, it has become an indispensable part of their daily operating procedures. Whenever information is collected at several locations and must be accessed quickly by other users, data communications becomes essential. In a bank with branch facilities, for example, data communications allows a customer's account to be immediately updated by a transaction occurring anywhere within the system. Among other things, this prevents a dishonest customer from making the rounds of all the branch banks, withdrawing the full amount of his or her savings account from each.

Data communications can cut the costs of doing business. To send a document between offices in different cities can cost $12 to $30 via overnight mail services. The same file can be transferred over data communications lines within the hour at a cost of only $3 or $4. Companies also gain from not having to key the document in at the receiving end. Publishers save thousands of dollars by accepting an author's output directly into their computer, where it can be electronically typeset. Rekeying information is expensive not only due to labor costs, but because of the key-in entry errors that will need detection and correction by the author or the editor.

TYPES OF DATA COMMUNICATIONS

Data communications can take many forms. In a **wide area network**, two or more computers converse with each other over distances so large that they preclude the direct connection of the devices and must rely upon the services of an outside enterprise (such as the telephone company) for a portion of the transmission task. In a **local area network**, computers are physically close enough to one another that information is transmitted over user-owned transmission media. A **remote processing** system is one in which all computing jobs are performed on centrally located equipment, but computer users are geographically dispersed. At an even more restricted level, data communications occurs between the central processing unit of a computer and a peripheral device, such as a printer.

Wide Area Networks

Wide area networks (see Figure 14–1) are employed in situations where information processing takes place on a local level at a number of locations, but the results of some of the processing must be shared with other locations. Most major city police departments, for example, perform their own computer processing locally, but are connected to other police departments and centralized crime information bureaus through a wide area network. A major corporation with manufacturing facilities around the country or around the globe might use a wide area network to transmit important business data back and forth between locations. Hospitals are often connected to other hospitals or to the Center for Disease Control in Atlanta.

Wide area networks are principally for firms and agencies with a frequent need to communicate large amounts of data. Because they cannot afford the possible delays (while waiting for available transmission lines), low transmission rates, and unreliability (in number of transmission errors) of the lowest-cost media (voice-

Focus Feature

WORKING FOR THE HOME OFFICE

One of the more interesting (or disturbing, depending upon your point of view) prospects made possible by data communications is the ability to perform almost any type of office work at home, having the results of the work electronically transmitted to the office computer. Called **telecommuting,** this has become an accepted alternative to daily trips to the office. Computer programmers, writers, secretaries, and even financial analysts have been performing office functions at home for years. No concrete data is available to determine how many workers telecommute, but it is reasonable to estimate that the number is still below 1 percent of the labor force. Labor trend analysts, however, point out that the number is rising dramatically each year, and some futurists predict that by the turn of the century, that number will exceed 50 percent of the white-collar labor force.

Working from the home can appear very attractive to many office workers. Telecommuting allows an office worker with young children to use the evening hours or quiet portions of the day to get a lot of work accomplished. Persons with introverted personalities may find that they are more productive or creative when removed from the anxieties of the office. For individuals with certain handicaps, telecommuting can remove many of the physical barriers to a successful career. And all enjoy saving the expense and time required by getting to work and maintaining the appropriate business attire.

Many employers are equally enthusiastic about having employees telecommute. Some report significant productivity increases and reduced costs resulting from a diminished need for office space and supplies.

Telecommuting is not for everyone, however. Workers who were, at first, enthusiastic have occasionally returned to the office because they miss the social inter-

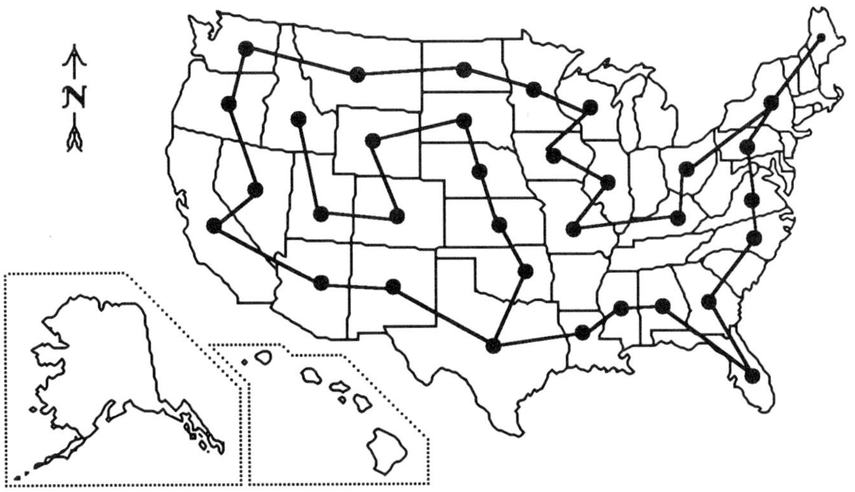

FIGURE 14–1
A Wide Area Network

grade telephone lines), these organizations will use **leased lines.** By paying a premium rate to a communications company, a leased line user is guaranteed constant transmission line availability, a higher transmission rate, and a specified maximum level of transmission errors.

The transmission lines for wide area networks are owned and operated by a variety of communications companies. Companies that offer a wide range of communications services are known as **common carriers.** AT&T is the best known and

action found there. Others have found that their work effectiveness is partly dependent upon those informal communication channels (office banter). Some workers find the level of distraction in the home to be much higher than at work. Individuals who are intensely interested in moving up the career ladder might find that the adage, "Out of sight, out of mind" applies to the home worker, because they may receive less recognition than equally talented workers in the office. Some telecommuters find that lack of contact and recognition hampers their own self-esteem, and their output suffers accordingly.

The social and business impact of significant increases in telecommuting are unclear. While some sociologists view widespread telecommuting as having potential for aiding in the restoration of the American family, others warn that it is more likely to further isolate us from our neighbors and may have disastrous consequences. Labor leaders have expressed the view that home workers will be unfairly used by their employers, and are lobbying vigorously to have government controls imposed on the types of work that can be performed in the home (several states have for decades had statutes prohibiting piecework in the home, and the legality of applying these statutes to telecommuting is being hotly debated).

In short, telecommuting offers the potential of being either a blessing or a burden for office workers. The social implications of this volatile issue will be a hot topic for researchers during the next several years. At this point, only one thing seems certain: that the number of telecommuters will rise rapidly each year until at least the end of the decade. Perhaps the automated office of the future will be a very small one, indeed.

most widely used of these companies. Communications companies that offer a restricted number of services, such as long distance service only, are known as **specialized common carriers.** Other companies, known as **value added carriers,** may not have their own transmission facilities, but provide a number of specialized services for the transmission of computerized data.

Value added carriers use their own computers in the transmission process to provide a number of valuable services. If an IBM computer in Milwaukee needs to send information to a DEC computer in Portland, a value added carrier's computer may provide the translation service that allows these incompatible machines to converse normally. Because most land-based transmission lines are very slow, value added carriers offer a more efficient transmission method called **packet switching.** In a packet switching system (Figure 14–2) such as GTE Telenet and Tymnet, data to be sent between major cities is collected by the communication company's computer until it is in a large enough bundle, or packet, to send. It is then sent in a rapid burst of data to the next city, using high-speed microwave or satellite communications. At the receiving end, another computer collects the packet and retransmits it over ordinary communications lines to its original destination. By working in this mode, much more information can be sent over existing channels and, because an individual transmission requires so much less time, the cost to the user is often much lower.

Focus Feature

ARE YOU SECURE?

November, 1983—Ronald Austin, a nineteen-year-old physics major at UCLA, is arrested for alleged malicious tampering with several hundred research and defense accounts residing in computers all over the world that are connected by the Department of Defense's Advanced Research Projects Agency Network (ARPAnet). The cost of restoring damaged files and reprogramming systems is estimated at $200,000.

August, 1984—Informants make headlines by describing the ease and frequency of abuses to the nation's largest on-line credit source, TRW Information Services. Although TRW denies security breaches, others respond that access codes can be obtained from any of thousands of subscribers, can be used to snoop anyone's personal credit history, and have been used to manufacture false ones for a fee.

July, 1984—The FBI seizes the IBM PCs, Apple IIs and Commodore 64s of four youths, aged thirteen to sixteen, who allegedly broke into computers at NASA's Marshall Space Flight Center in Huntsville, Alabama. No charges were filed.

1978—Stanley Mark Rifkin, a computer consultant for a firm that had installed computers for Security Pacific National Bank in Los Angeles, had the bank electronically transfer $10.2 million to a Swiss bank account, to be used two days later to purchase $8 million in Russian diamonds. Rifkin was caught when he returned to the U.S. and told his attorney what he had done. His attorney called the FBI.

Stories about computer crime are becoming so commonplace nowadays that even large crimes are being relegated to the back pages of the newspapers, and by the estimate of most law enforcement officials, the number of unreported crimes is several times the number that make it into print. Refuting the claims of some that the media has blown the problem all out of proportion, the American Bar Association, in a June 1984 report, showed that more than 25 percent of 283 responding Fortune 500 companies have had "verifiable losses due to computer crime."

Local Area Networks

A local area network (LAN) is used to connect computers within a small region. Because of their proximity, computers within a LAN (see Figure 14–3) are often directly connected by transmission wires or are serviced by short-range broadcasting equipment. In a large corporate office, a LAN might connect several mainframe and minicomputers, dozens of personal computers, and hundreds of computer terminals. The LAN offers rapid communications capability and enables a user in one location to access the programs and files of a computer elsewhere within the system. The specialized hardware and software considerations of local area networks are the topic of Chapter 15.

Remote Processing Systems

The category of data communications that is, perhaps, most familiar to the average mainframe computer user is remote processing (Figure 14–4). In a remote processing system, one computer handles the processing chores for a number of remotely located users. Users provide input for the central computer through a computer terminal or a microcomputer that **emulates** (functions like) a terminal, and typically receive output through the same device.

There is no doubt that computer crime has been made easier by the proliferation of home computers and telecommunications equipment. The amount of the losses can be staggering, too; the average annual loss reported by the ABA survey respondents ranged from $2 million to more than $10 million. Even when no money has been taken, malicious destruction of business, research, and defense information costs tens of millions of dollars annually and could pose a serious threat to national security.

For some, the solution to the problem lies in adequate legal penalties for computer criminals. Computer crime is a relatively new phenomenon, and few state and federal statutes have been devised that clearly define and prescribe penalties for theft or destruction with a computer. Others question whether stiffer laws will have much effect on certain types of computer crime. They note that the electronic funds transfer (EFT) systems of some large banks transmit billions of dollars daily, and the theft of a few million dollars might go unnoticed for as long as thirty days (note: EFT systems are usually more difficult to break into because they use leased lines and cannot be dialed up).

Veteran system programmers generally lay the blame on lax security procedures and inadequate planning on the part of corporate computer operators. They explain that with good programming and enforced security measures, most computer thieves can be thwarted, but these measures can be expensive. The computer security consulting industry is presently experiencing rapid growth.

Although not adequate to stop all intruders, some new, sophisticated modems are helping some companies fight computer crime. When the company's computers are dialed, these new modems will hang up, check your authorization, and dial you back. Many companies are finding that this is an inexpensive solution to many of their problems.

FIGURE 14–2
A Packet Switching System

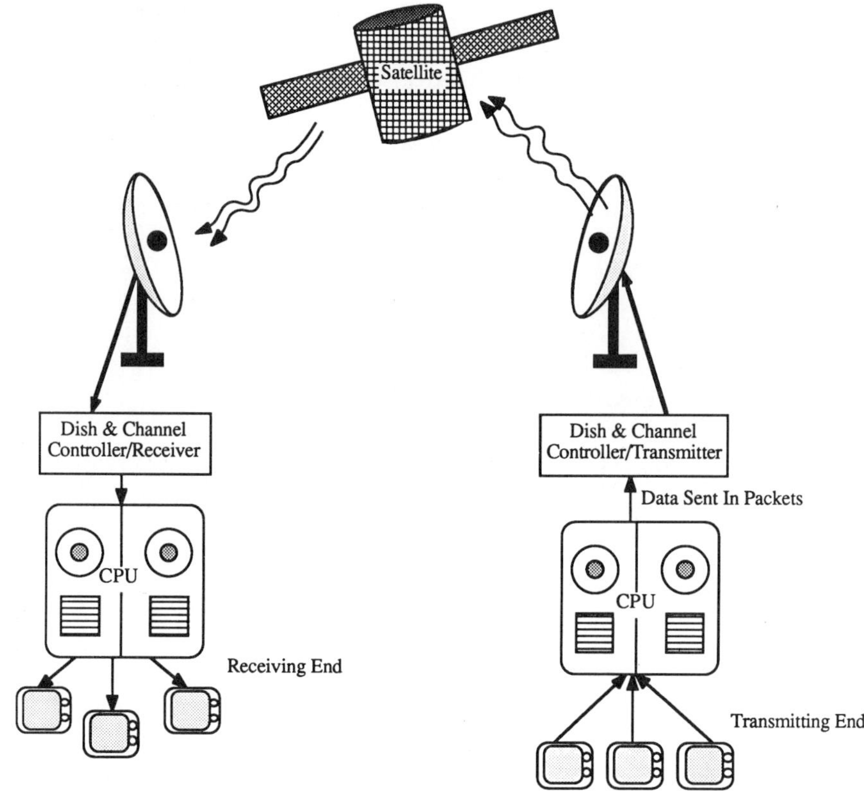

The uses for remote processing systems are myriad. The automatic teller machines (ATMs) of a bank are actually special function terminals in constant contact with the main computer facilities of the financial institution. An airline reservation system consists of many remote terminals connected through phone lines to a large host computer. Many colleges and universities alleviate computer-room congestion by allowing students with terminals or microcomputers to dial the campus computers by phone and work from their homes.

An increasingly important use for remote processing is for accessing information made available through information services and public access electronic bulletin boards. With a microcomputer or terminal, some inexpensive communi-

FIGURE 14–3
A Local Area Network

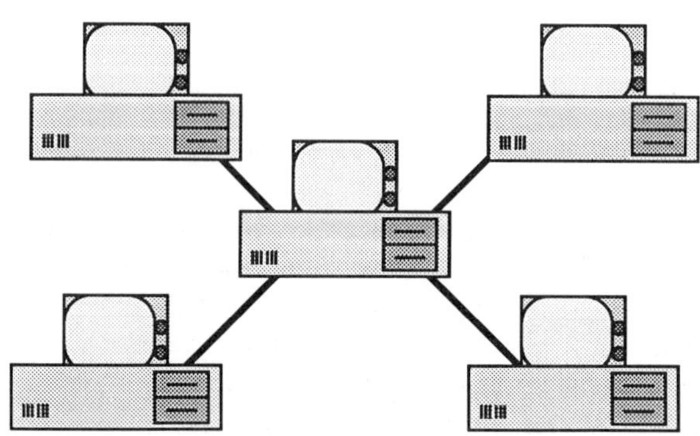

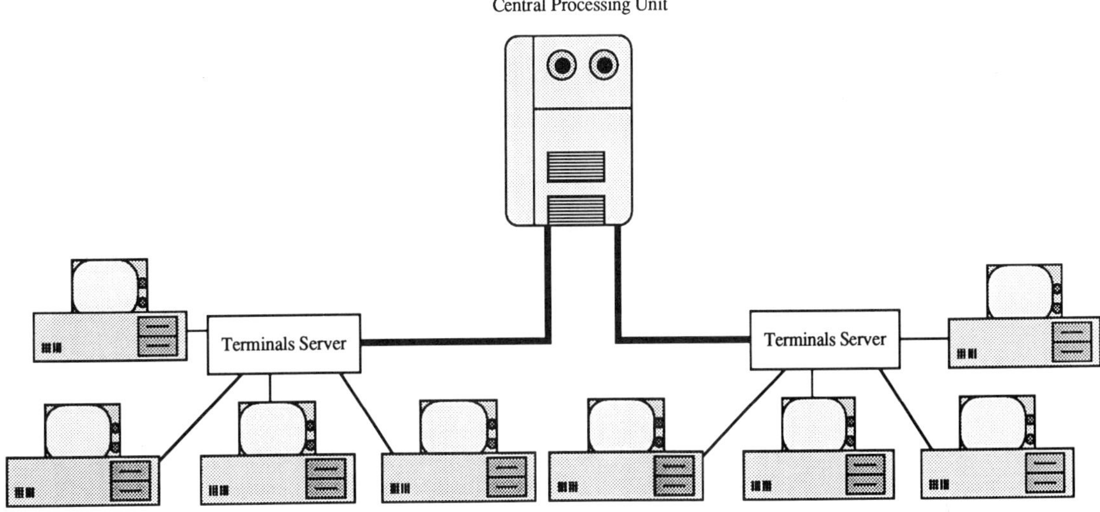

FIGURE 14–4
A Remote Processing System

cations equipment, and appropriate software, anyone can avail themselves of a world of knowledge on virtually any subject. Up-to-the-minute stock quotations, world news, help with a particularly sticky hardware or software problem, computerized banking services, government statistics, psychological counseling, or even a chat with a friend in Missoula, Montana are all available through these services, occasionally at no cost other than the price of a phone call. A special section that appears later in this chapter will describe, in more detail, some of the information and bulletin board services available.

Peripheral Communications

Even the individual user of the microcomputer (with no desire to converse with other computers) may require an understanding of at least some of the fundamentals of data communications in order to derive the greatest benefit from his or her computer equipment. Computers use data communications to transmit information between the various components of a system (Figure 14–5). Although the typical user will never need to worry about how the microprocessor speaks to the memory chips or the monitor, it might be necessary to learn about channels, media, and protocol (discussed below) before a printer or external disk drive can be connected.

THE COMPONENTS OF DATA COMMUNICATIONS

Any transmission of electronic data is comprised of at least four elements: the sending or transmitting device, the receiving device, the **channel** over which communication occurs, and the message that is transmitted, as depicted in Figure 14–6.

An understanding of data communications begins with a look at data transmission within a computer and the devices required for communication to the outside world. Inside the central processing unit (CPU) all data for processing is

FIGURE 14–5
Peripheral Communications

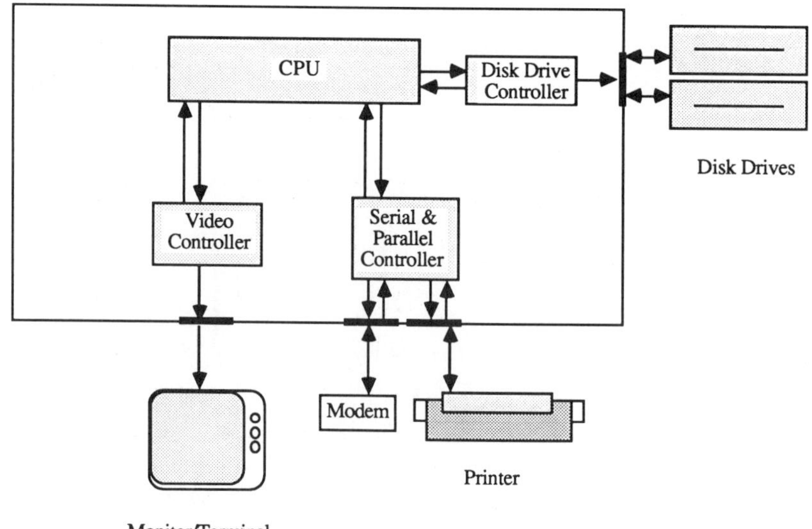

kept in a standard format that is convenient for the microprocessor to perform its calculations. It does not matter whether the information originated from a keyboard or a disk drive, nor does it matter if it is destined for another computer across the country or for the video screen a few inches away.

Ports and Interfaces

As discussed in Chapter 3, all data enters and leaves the CPU of a computer through a **port**, a data entry or exit point. In a typical configuration, a computer will have ports for devices such as keyboards, video displays, printers, disk drives, speakers, or internal clocks. The CPU transforms the information according to the instructions it has been given and sends the results out through the same or other ports.

In order for the CPU to maintain a single internal data format while communicating with a number of very different devices, each port will have an **interface device** attached. It is the job of the interface to repackage the information sent from

FIGURE 14–6
Data Communications Components

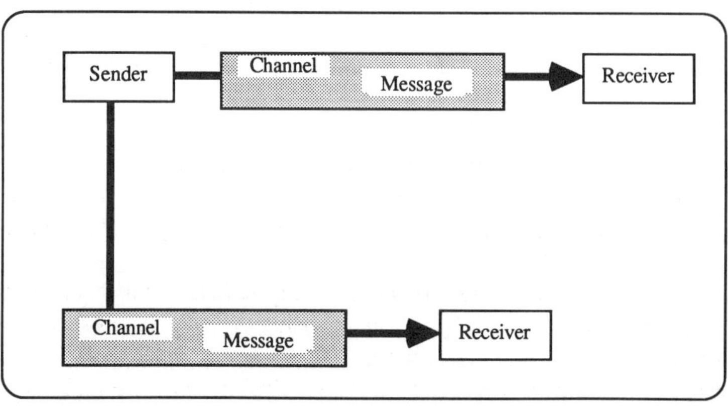

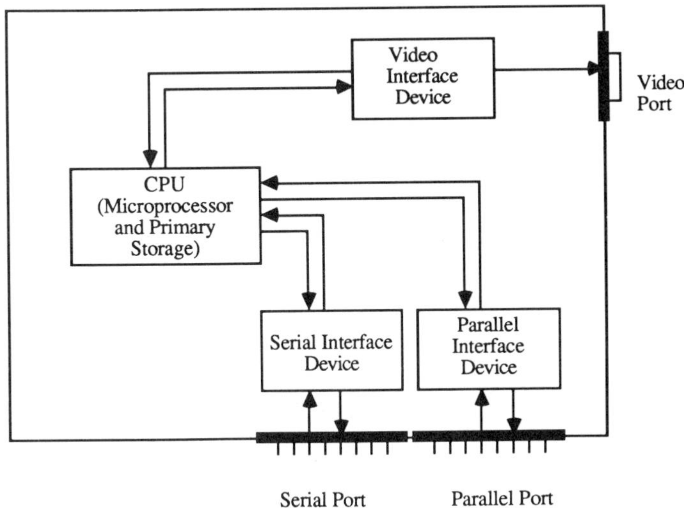

FIGURE 14–7
The CPU and Interface Devices

the CPU into a format that is usable by the device attached to the interface. A video adapter, for example, is an interface device that transforms information sent by the CPU into the format necessary for display on a video screen. Likewise, a floppy disk controller must translate the CPU's data format into a format for storage on a disk. Two special types of interface devices, the serial interface and the parallel interface, are designed to allow the computer to communicate with the outside world. Shown in Figure 14–7 is the typical configuration between a CPU and interface devices.

Serial and Parallel Interfaces When communicating to external devices, the CPU transmits the data byte by byte. In **parallel transmission**, all eight bits in the byte are sent at the same time, traveling toward their destination over parallel lines. In a **serial transmission**, a single line carries the eight data bits, one after the other, in series. Therefore, a parallel transmission should, theoretically, be considerably faster than a serial one. For this reason, most computers relay information to and from disk drives over parallel lines (flat ribbon cable). A well-designed serial interface, however, can achieve speeds that equal those of the best parallel devices (Apple's Macintosh uses a special serial interface for communicating with an external disk drive).

In practice, the selection between serial and parallel communications will normally be determined by the type of device the user is communicating with and the distance a transmission must travel. Telephone lines consist of two wires between any two connecting points, and that is not enough wires to support parallel transmission. Therefore, computers converse with one another through the serial interface when using telephone lines. Many scientific instruments will operate only through a parallel device. Printers, on the other hand, are available for both serial and parallel transmissions. Serial printers are more complicated to manufacture (extra circuitry is required) and to install, and often cost more than the same model in a parallel version. As mentioned in Chapter 3, printers usually have parallel interfaces.

Parallel communications are limited to short distances. Even though all eight data bits are transmitted simultaneously, they do not reach their destination together because the wires will not have uniform electrical properties (impedance) over their entire length. The amount of difference in the arrival time of the eight bits

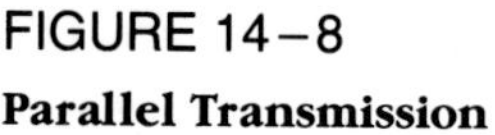

FIGURE 14–8
Parallel Transmission

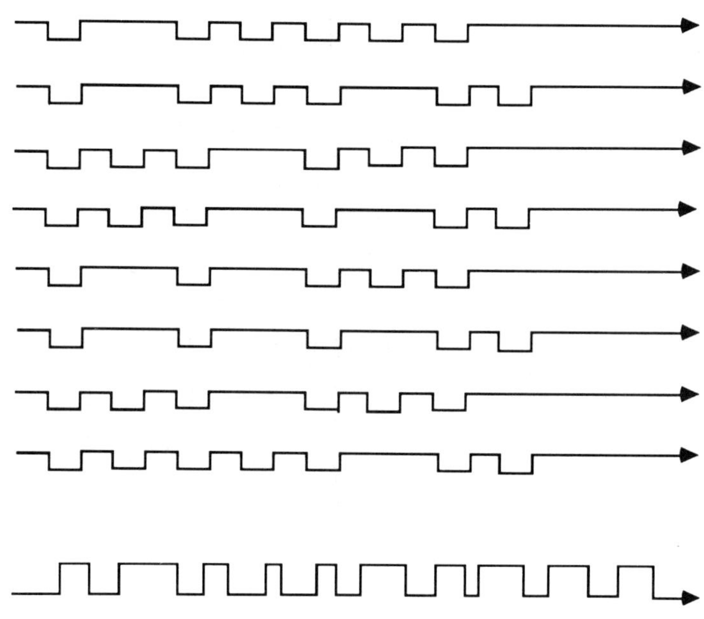

FIGURE 14–9
Serial Transmission

will vary with the distance traveled and factors such as bends or kinks in the wires (Figure 14–8). To ensure that all eight bits have been received before the first bit of the next byte arrives, a ninth signal, called a **pulse**, is sent between each byte.

Because a serial transmission sends all of the data bits over a single line, there is no possibility for a bit to race ahead of a previously transmitted bit, yet serial transmissions also use special signals to signify the beginning and ending of each byte. Figure 14–9 depicts serial transmission.

Communication Channels

The term **channel** describes the complete system for connecting two devices for communication. It includes the interfaces at the sending and/or receiving ends, the media over which the message is transmitted, and any other devices necessary to make the communication link. In **telecommunications** (communicating over telephone lines) an important part of the communications channel is the **modem**, short for modulator/demodulator.

A modem is a **transducer**, a device for changing one form of energy into another, just as a stereo speaker transforms electrical signals into acoustical energy. During the **modulation** process, a modem converts the computer's digital signal (used for internal operation and peripheral communication) into an analog signal (see Figure 14–10) that can be sent over telephone lines. At the receiving end, another modem **demodulates** the signal, returning it to its digital form for use by the receiving device. Figure 14–11 depicts the complete telecommunications system involving a digital signal that is sent out through the serial communications port of the transmitting computer, and that is modulated by a modem into an analog signal where it is sent over telephone lines. At the receiving end it is demodulated by a modem back to a digital signal before entering the serial communications port of the receiving computer.

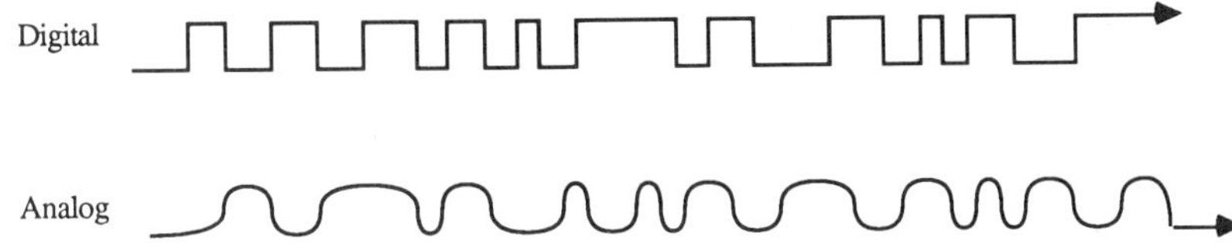

FIGURE 14–10
Digital and Analog Signals

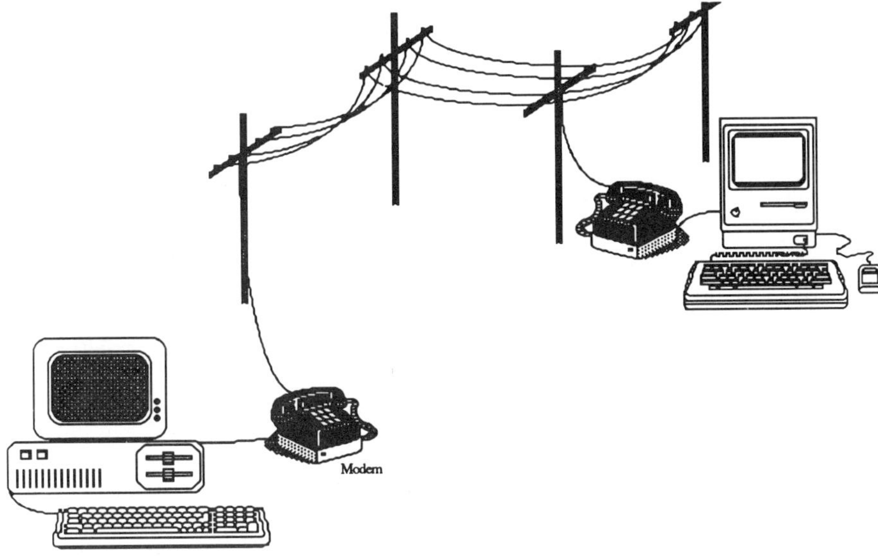

FIGURE 14–11
Telecommunications

Modems for Microcomputers Modems for microcomputers are available from a large number of manufacturers, ranging in price from $35 to over $1,000. A modem's price and suitability depends upon its transmission rate, its type, the number of features it offers, and whether or not communications software comes with the purchase.

A modem's transmission rate is measured in **bits per second** (bps), with 300 bps, 1,200 bps, 2,400 bps, 4,800 bps, and 9,600 bps being the most popular modem speeds. Because each byte may be packed with start and stop bits or other control signals, a good rule of thumb states that 10 bps translates to approximately one character per second (cps). A 1,200-bps modem, therefore, transmits information at about 120 characters per second, requiring less than 20 seconds to fill a computer's screen with a full 2,000 characters. Transmission rates for telecommunications have an upper limit because error rates go up with increased speed. Because of varying long distance quality and atmospheric or terrain factors, even 2,400-bps communication is occasionally unsuccessful. Veteran users of data communications will tell you that communication quality (and the potential transmission rate) can change from day to day between two cities, and will even vary with different locations within the same city. Even though 2,400-bps modems are available (and 4,800-bps modems will be coming out soon) these may already be breaching the upper limits of intercity transmission speed.

FIGURE 14–12

An External Modem The Hayes 2400 bps external modem. *(Courtesy of Hayes Microcomputer Products, Inc.)*

An external modem comes in its own housing, designed to sit near the computer. External modems, furthermore, may be classified as either **direct-connect** or **acoustic coupler** modems (Figure 14–12). Direct-connect modems are inserted into the signal path leading from the wall's phone jack to the telephone handset (most are connected at the telephone end, although some modems attach to the wall jack and others are placed between the phone's base unit and its handset). When signals arrive at the modem, they are routed either to the computer or the telephone, depending upon whether it is a data or voice communication. An acoustic coupler modem is connected between the phone and the computer by placing the telephone's handset into specially formed cups. These modems listen for the audible signals of data transmission and cannot be used with many of the newer style phones. Acoustic coupler modems, once very popular, are not very reliable at high transmission rates (they are usually limited to 300 bps) and have been dropped from the product lines of many modem manufacturers. There are still quite a few of them around, however, and an economy-minded shopper should find them very inexpensive (under $100).

An internal modem (Figure 14–13) has all of its circuitry mounted on a card which is placed in an open expansion slot of the computer. Internal modems generally cost $50 to $150 less than comparable external modems, because they do not require a separate box and will not have as many lights and switches. On certain computers (IBM compatibles, for example), they offer further savings because they connect directly to the CPU, eliminating the need to purchase a separate serial interface. Internal modems are made for only a few popular brands of computers, but may fit other compatible brands.

Although all modems allow a user to dial up other computers, some of them will allow that user's computer to be dialed up by others. To call another computer, the user's modem is placed in an **originate mode.** To receive calls, it must also have

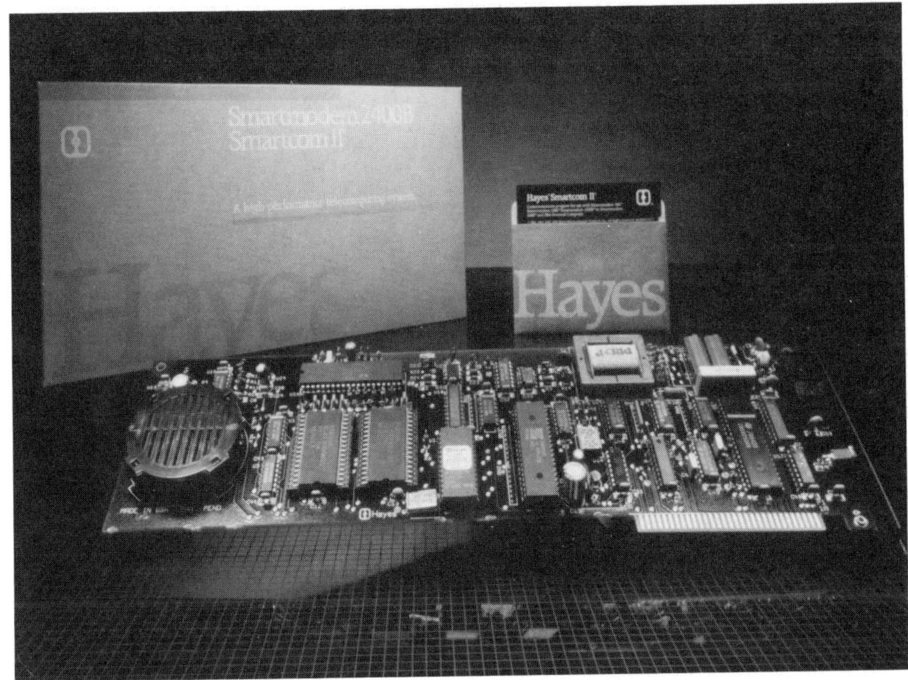

FIGURE 14–13

An Internal Modem The Hayes 2400 bps internal modem. *(Courtesy of Hayes Microcomputer Products, Inc.)*

an **answer mode.** A more sophisticated modem will automatically determine whether it should be in the originate or answer mode, and can even dial the telephone numbers and hang up the phone line at the conclusion of the conversation.

A survey of modems will show a wide range of products and features available. High-speed modems (up to 38,000 bps) for short-range transmissions are available. Modems that originate only (for terminals) or answer only (for speaking to those terminals) can also be obtained. These modems are likely to be found only in large businesses, because of their high price tags. Modems for microcomputers should be capable of both originate and answer modes. When two microcomputers are communicating via phone lines, the modem associated with one of them must be in the answer mode and the modem for the other in the originate mode. It doesn't matter which is which, only that both not be set in the same mode.

Before concluding this discussion of modems, it should be noted that there must be a certain amount of agreement between the modems on the sending and receiving ends before communication can take place. They must both operate at the same transmission rate, and they should both be using the same communications standards (an agreement on the types of signals used for transmitting. Most, though not all, modems follow the Bell 103 or Bell 212A standards for 300 and 1,200 bps, respectively).

Transmission Direction Another aspect of the communications channel is the direction of the transmissions. In **simplex** communication (Figure 14–14), the data is transmitted in one direction only, from the sender to the receiver. Simplex communication is rarely used nowadays. **Half-duplex** communication (Figure 14–14) allows transmission in both directions, but not simultaneously. The sending device transmits a message, then receives data back, in much the same manner that police communicate over a two-way radio. Transmission that takes

FIGURE 14–14
Transmission Directions

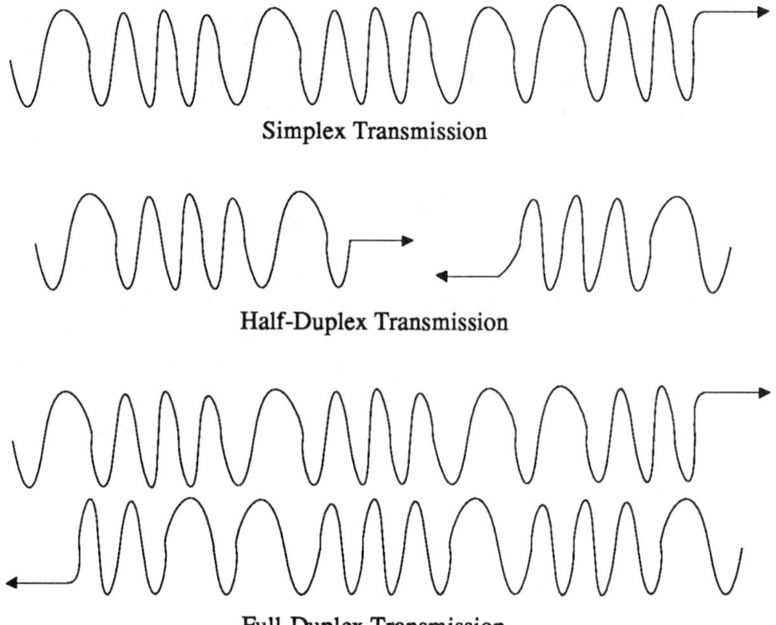

place in both directions at the same time is known as **full-duplex** (Figure 14–14). A user is unlikely to notice any difference in operating characteristics between half-duplex and full-duplex. The sender and receiver must, however, agree on which mode will be used. Remote users of large computers can set their modems to accommodate the directional desires of the host computer's modem. Most newer modems either have a switch to select the direction or operate in full-duplex mode, using communication software to emulate half-duplex transmission.

Other Transmission Media Telephone lines are, by far, the most convenient and least expensive means of transmitting electronic data between distant computers. Telephone lines extend into nearly every home and place of business in the United States, and few companies could afford the expense of establishing their own data transmission lines between New York and Los Angeles offices. Telephone lines are not the only means of transmitting data, however, and they do place some severe restrictions on transmission speed. For local area networks, coaxial cable (the thick wire that brings cable TV to your house) and fiber optics provide far greater speeds and enhanced reliability than ordinary telephone lines. These are discussed more fully in Chapter 15.

Some of the intercity data communications are in the heavens. Land-based telephone lines carry only a portion of voice communications in the United States, because the combination of microwave and satellite transmissions has shouldered most of the burden. Several companies, including RCA (the Americom system), Western Union (Westar), and Satellite Business Systems (formed by IBM and Aetna Life) own telecommunications satellites, and many more will be launched in the next several years. Recent advances in communications allow even relatively small companies to have satellite "earth stations," leasing time on commercial satellites and bypassing the majority of land-based communications equipment.

As it turns out, an increasing portion of intercity data communications is returning to the land. This is because of the increased usage of fiber-optics cable. Fiber-optics cable consists of thousands of tiny strands of fiber. Each strand can handle up to 6,000 low-speed, concurrent data links (phone calls).

The Data Communications Message

The final essential component of data communications is the message that is transmitted. Although almost any information that can be stored in a computer can be transmitted to another device, there must be agreement between the sender and the receiver upon the form that the message will take during transmission and upon the signals that will be used to control and direct the transmission. Either or both of these two elements, packing the data for transmission and control signals, are required for transmitting data over common transmission media. The system of control signals used to direct the transmission is known as **protocol**, a set of rules or standards for orderly data communication.

Synchronous and Asynchronous Communication Not all data transmission uses protocol. In **synchronous** communication, the sending and receiving devices "synchronize" internal clocks when a "beginning of transmission" signal is sent over the line. From that point on, data is sent in large, uniform-sized blocks, and both parties observe the clock to determine when the transmission is finished. Synchronous communication requires relatively expensive transmission equipment, and is mostly found in remote processing situations with an IBM mainframe computer as the host processor. The principal advantage of synchronous communication is its rapid transmission rate. It has limited use for long-range transmission over common phone lines, and can result in the loss of large blocks of data if the equipment and transmission media are less than perfect. Most data communication over phone lines is **asynchronous**, or not time-synchronized (this is often called start-stop communication).

"Packing" Data and the ASCII Standard A distinguishing characteristic of asynchronous communication is that each byte to be transmitted must be "packed," or surrounded with additional bits, to ensure that it is accurately received. The additional bits come in three forms: **start bits**, **stop bits**, and **parity bits**. The start and stop bits merely declare that the beginning or end of a byte has been reached. Start bits are always 0, while stop bits are 1. A series of bytes sent in a typical asynchronous transmission is depicted in Figure 14–15.

The combination of start bits, stop bits, and parity bits helps to detect any transmission errors due to data dropouts or garbling. If the receiver detects stop bits before it has received a full byte of data, it can (if protocol is being employed) tell the sender to transmit the last byte again. When parity bits are used, they also protect against faulty transmissions. In a parity system, a bit is transmitted after the byte so that the sum of the 1 bits will always be even (in an even parity scheme) or odd (for odd parity). For example, the transmission depicted in Figure 14–15 uses an even parity method, that is, each byte with its parity sums to an even number of 1 bits. If the receiver found a byte and corresponding parity bit whose 1 bits summed to an odd number, it would request retransmission.

A packed byte for asynchronous communication, therefore, typically involves ten bits. Obviously, the sender and receiver must agree upon the number of start

FIGURE 14–15
Asynchronous Transmission

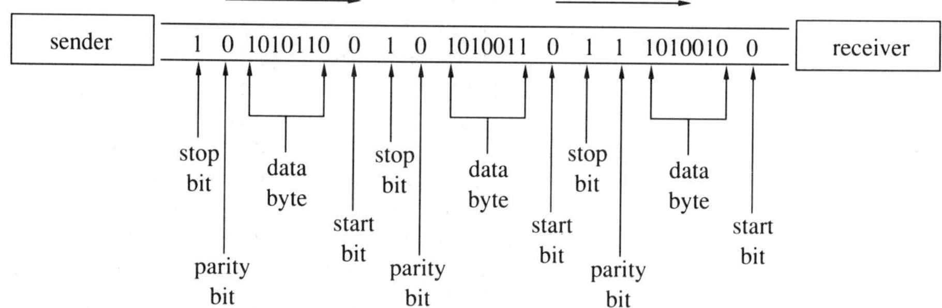

and stop bits and whether parity will be employed (and the type of parity). One host computer (receiver) may require a start bit, eight data bits, no parity, and one stop bit, while another uses one start bit, seven data bits, a parity bit, and one stop bit. Information utilities provide the correct communication settings for their subscribers, and these can be found in a number of popular communication books (see the listing at the end of this chapter).

Surprising to many is that the number of bits in each portion of transmitted data can vary. We learned in Chapter 2 that a byte is comprised of eight bits, each having a value of zero or one. That is true of data within a computer, and equally true for data that will be transmitted to the outside, although the code or format of the data may be different. The format that is always used in asynchronous transmission is called the American Standard Code for Information Interchange, or **ASCII** for short. ASCII codes are seven-bit codes, originally. With only seven bits, 128 different combinations of ones and zeros (2^7) can be represented. This is enough to represent all of the letters in the alphabet, in both lower- and uppercase, the digits zero through nine, an assortment of punctuation symbols, special symbols (such as $, #, + @, &, and %), and still have quite a few unused values. The ASCII assignment of values is shown in Figure 14–16.

Within the computer, all eight bits may be required by a binary coding method (non-ASCII), or the eighth bit may simply be used to store video display information for an otherwise normal ASCII byte. In an IBM PC, decimal values above 127 (the ASCII table starts at 0) are used for special graphics symbols and foreign language characters. What happens to this eighth bit during data transmission? If the eighth bit is a parity bit, it is discarded once parity has been checked and found to be satisfactory. If the eighth bit is part of the code itself, then the user must specify "no parity" as part of the pretransmission preparation, and the bit will be retained and interpreted as part of the code. If the file to be transmitted is stored in binary code (as is the case with a program's object code), it must first be converted to ASCII before it can be sent. Conversion to ASCII (if it can be done) is accomplished either by the operating system or utility programs.

Protocol Observant readers will have noticed that the first thirty-one values of the ASCII table in Figure 14–16 contain some strange codes. Many of these are special symbols reserved for data communications protocols. In a protocol transmission system, the sending and receiving devices will carry on an active conversation during, simultaneous to, but independent of, the message that must be transmitted. The subject of the conversation is the progress of the message transmission. With a protocol system, one computer can tell another that it has received all the

Decimal	Binary	ASCII	Decimal	Binary	ASCII	Decimal	Binary	ASCII
000	00000000	NUL	043	00101011	+	086	01010110	V
001	00000001	SOH	044	00101100	,	087	01010111	W
002	00000010	STX	045	00101101	-	088	01011000	X
003	00000011	ETX	046	00101110	.	089	01011001	Y
004	00000100	EOT	047	00101111	/	090	01011010	Z
005	00000101	ENQ	048	00110000	0	091	01011011	[
006	00000110	ACK	049	00110001	1	092	01011100	\
007	00000111	BEL	050	00110010	2	093	01011101	]
008	00001000	BS	051	00110011	3	094	01011110	^
009	00001001	HT	052	00110100	4	095	01011111	_
010	00001010	LF	053	00110101	5	096	01100000	'
011	00001011	VT	054	00110110	6	097	01100001	a
012	00001100	FF	055	00110111	7	098	01100010	b
013	00001101	CR	056	00111000	8	099	01100011	c
014	00001110	SO	057	00111001	9	100	01100100	d
015	00001111	SI	058	00111010	:	101	01100101	e
016	00010000	DLE	059	00111011	;	102	01100110	f
017	00010001	DC1	060	00111100	<	103	01100111	g
018	00010010	DC2	061	00111101	=	104	01101000	h
019	00010011	DC3	062	00111110	>	105	01101001	i
020	00010100	DC4	063	00111111	?	106	01101010	j
021	00010101	NAK	064	01000000	@	107	01101011	k
022	00010110	SYN	065	01000001	A	108	01101100	l
023	00010111	ETB	066	01000010	B	109	01101101	m
024	00011000	CAN	067	01000011	C	110	01101110	n
025	00011001	EM	068	01000100	D	111	01101111	o
026	00011010	SUB	069	01000101	E	112	01110000	p
027	00011011	ESC	070	01000110	F	113	01110001	q
028	00011100	FS	071	01000111	G	114	01110010	r
029	00011101	GS	072	01001000	H	115	01110011	s
030	00011110	RS	073	01001001	I	116	01110100	t
031	00011111	US	074	01001010	J	117	01110101	u
032	00100000		075	01001011	K	118	01110110	v
033	00100001	!	076	01001100	L	119	01110111	w
034	00100010	"	077	01001101	M	120	01111000	x
035	00100011	#	078	01001110	N	121	01111001	y
036	00100100	$	079	01001111	O	122	01111010	z
037	00100101	%	080	01010000	P	123	01111011	{
038	00100110	&	081	01010001	Q	124	01111100	:
039	00100111	'	082	01010010	R	125	01111101	}
040	00101000	(	083	01010011	S	126	01111110	~
041	00101001	)	084	01010100	T	127	01111111	DEL
042	00101010	*	085	01010101	U			

FIGURE 14–16

ASCII Values

information it can handle, and to stop transmitting until it has a chance to store or print the data it has already received. Or, if data has not come across clearly, the receiver can request that it be sent again. In short, protocol helps ensure smoother transmissions.

Several protocol systems have become fairly standard for asynchronous communication: X-ON/X-OFF (decimal values 17 and 19 in the ASCII table), EXT/ACK (for end of text/acknowledge), XMODEM (a popular system for electronic bulletin boards), and KERMIT (a university-developed protocol for file transfers) are among the most commonly found.

Communications Software

Communications software was not included in the discussion of data communications components because not all transmissions require it. Two computers can be directly connected by running a cable from the serial interface of one to the serial interface of the other. Long-distance data communications is even possible without software, by transmitting at a low enough rate (300 bps) and manually entering protocol signals (a Control-Q, for example, will generate the X-ON signal to start sending data). With most data communication terminals, all the settings required for transmission are controlled by setting hardware switches. Microcomputer users, however, will need a software program to control communications with information utilities, bulletin board systems, and other microcomputers.

Communications software programs are available from a variety of sources. A few modem manufacturers include the software when their hardware is purchased. Most computer users groups and information utilities can provide members with a free public domain communications program, usually one that employs the XMODEM protocol. Communications programs can also be purchased, at anywhere between a few dollars and several hundred dollars.

The most important feature of a communications program (some would argue it is the *only* important one) is ease of use. The lengthy discussion of communication components pointed out a number of parameters upon which agreement must exist between the sender and receiver before communication can take place. Both devices must be operating at the same transmission rate, use the same number of start bits, stop bits, and data length. They must agree on whether or not parity bits will be included, and, if so, what type of parity (even or odd). Finally, they must use the same protocol signals to control the transmission. A communications program, therefore, should make it easy to enter all the correct values for these parameters before the beginning of the actual transmission. Since different information systems are likely to use different values for these settings, the program should have a method of storing all the settings in one or more files so the user does not have to reenter them each time he or she uses the program. If the user has logged onto a system and does not have the correct settings (he will know by the unreadable gibberish on his screen), the software should allow him to change settings without making him hang up the line and dial again.

When a computer is equipped with a modem that can dial numbers, the software should allow the keyboard to be used for dialing. When using a packet switching network or a long-distance company such as MCI or Sprint, phone numbers and access codes can be as long as fifty digits, and may require the user to wait for a dial tone somewhere in the middle of dialing. Better communications programs allow users to store this long sequence of numbers and pauses along with the communications settings. Users can then dial a number and have their computers correctly configured very easily, often with a single keystroke.

Since information utilities or campus computers can get quite crowded, many programs can be set to keep trying until they get through, at which time they will beep to notify the user. One step beyond this is the capability of storing an entire set of commands to be executed at a designated time. With this feature, it is possible to have the computer work while the user sleeps. If there is a file that must be transferred to someone else (called **uploading** a file), or a program on a bulletin board that the user wants (receiving files is called, appropriately, **downloading**), she can leave her computer on and go to bed. At two or three in the morning, when the lines are not quite so congested, the computer will dial the number until the connection is made, supply the proper codes to gain access to the system, give the appropriate commands to send or receive the desired file(s), and hang up when the transmission is completed.

All of the features listed in the preceding paragraphs are convenience features. They are not necessary for data communication, but they can make the experience a lot more enjoyable. Most commercial programs make extensive use of menus and prompts to allow easy setup (see Figure 14–17). Some of the programs load into an unused area of the computer's memory, and can be recalled (to change settings on the fly) with a single key.

Other features are more necessity than convenience. In order to download files, for instance, a communications program must have a method of capturing data until it can be stored. Programs vary in their method of handling this, but most will reserve areas of memory for use as **capture buffers**, places to hold incoming data until it is stored on disk. A good communications program will also allow the user to send incoming information directly to the printer, and will let the print function be toggled on and off with a special key or command. **Terminal emulation**, the ability to use the command sequences of another terminal, can be important in remote processing situations. In order to use the full-screen editor or receive graphics information from some DEC computers, the user's computer or terminal must be able to emulate a DEC VT100 terminal. Some communications programs provide a variety of terminal emulation modes, with the terminals most frequently emulated being the DEC VT100 and VT52, Lier-Siegler ADM3A, TeleVideo 925 and 950, and the IBM 3270 and 3278.

Information Utilities and Bulletin Board Systems

The principal reason most individuals purchase modems and communications software is to gain access to the thousands of information utilities and bulletin board systems available across the country. They can provide entertainment, companionship, advice, or the daily news. They can provide information on everything from up-to-the-minute stock prices to a description of the payload on the next space shuttle launching. They can be a horrendous drain on the pocketbook, or save thousands of dollars on the cost of an ill-informed decision or costly information search. And they have made late-night information addicts out of a sizable portion of the American population.

Information Utilities An **information utility** is a data base, a collection of data bases, or an on-line news service which makes its information available to dial-up users, usually for a fee. By the end of 1984, there were over 3,000 on-line data bases, more than 2,000 of them offered by the nearly 400 commercial services. The remaining data bases and news services are provided by government agencies, universities, medical associations, labor unions, and other nonprofit organizations.

The commercial data bases search through hundreds or even thousands of periodicals, newspapers, books, and other published sources for information on a particular subject. They will store the information as either an index to the original

FIGURE 14–17

Configuration Menu of a Popular Communications Program (Microphone™ on a Macintosh) (a) A communication settings display. (b) A terminal settings display. (c) A file transfer settings display.

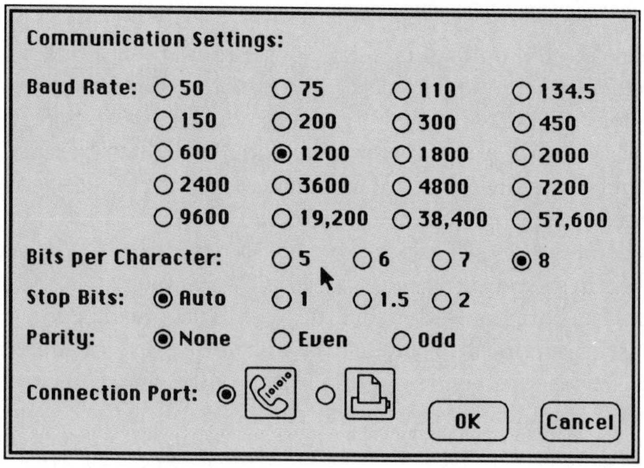

Communication Settings:

Baud Rate: ○ 50 ○ 75 ○ 110 ○ 134.5
○ 150 ○ 200 ○ 300 ○ 450
○ 600 ◉ 1200 ○ 1800 ○ 2000
○ 2400 ○ 3600 ○ 4800 ○ 7200
○ 9600 ○ 19,200 ○ 38,400 ○ 57,600

Bits per Character: ○ 5 ○ 6 ○ 7 ◉ 8

Stop Bits: ◉ Auto ○ 1 ○ 1.5 ○ 2

Parity: ◉ None ○ Even ○ Odd

Connection Port: ◉ ○

OK Cancel

(a)

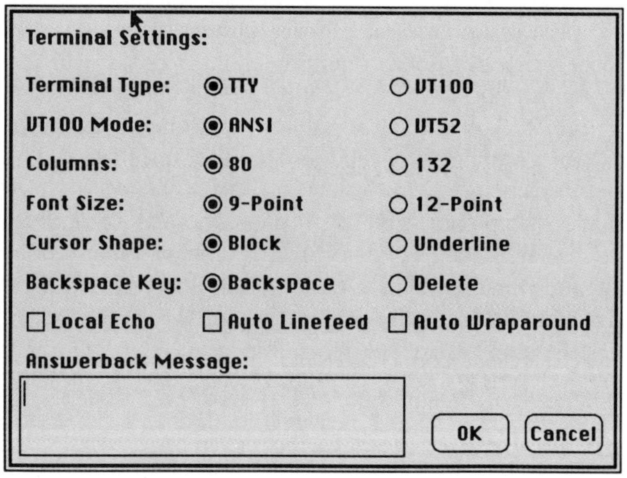

Terminal Settings:

Terminal Type: ◉ TTY ○ VT100

VT100 Mode: ◉ ANSI ○ VT52

Columns: ◉ 80 ○ 132

Font Size: ◉ 9-Point ○ 12-Point

Cursor Shape: ◉ Block ○ Underline

Backspace Key: ◉ Backspace ○ Delete

☐ Local Echo ☐ Auto Linefeed ☐ Auto Wraparound

Answerback Message:

OK Cancel

(b)

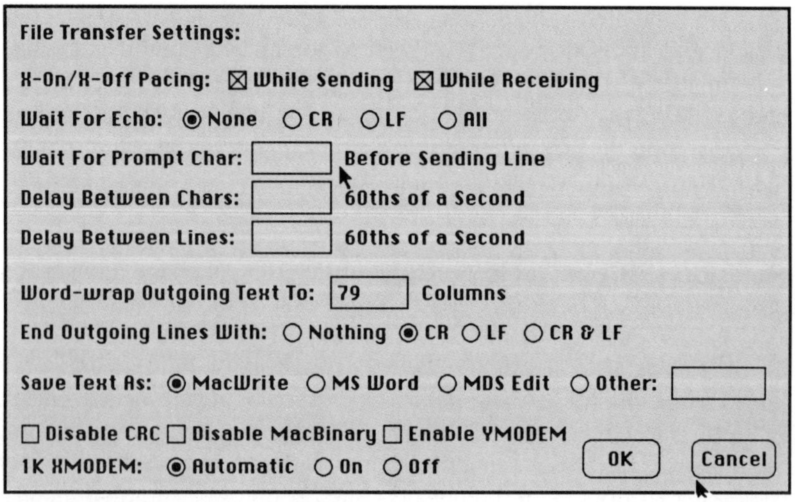

File Transfer Settings:

X-On/X-Off Pacing: ☒ While Sending ☒ While Receiving

Wait For Echo: ◉ None ○ CR ○ LF ○ All

Wait For Prompt Char: [ ] Before Sending Line

Delay Between Chars: [ ] 60ths of a Second

Delay Between Lines: [ ] 60ths of a Second

Word-wrap Outgoing Text To: [79] Columns

End Outgoing Lines With: ○ Nothing ◉ CR ○ LF ○ CR & LF

Save Text As: ◉ MacWrite ○ MS Word ○ MDS Edit ○ Other: [ ]

☐ Disable CRC ☐ Disable MacBinary ☐ Enable YMODEM

1K XMODEM: ◉ Automatic ○ On ○ Off

OK Cancel

(c)

TABLE 14–1

Types of Information Available from On-line Data Bases*

Agriculture	Graphics
Artificial intelligence	Hardware
Biomedical information	Market intelligence
Books	Nuclear energy
Business forecasts	Office automation
Chemicals	Patents
Citations	Periodicals
Cold weather	Physics
Computer-assisted instruction	Price forecasts
Defense contracts	Public policy
Education	Scientific leaders
Electronic publishing	Software
Engineering	Technology transfer
Environment	Testing
Fiber optics	Translation
Foreign computer science	

*From "The On-Line Search," by Suzana Lisanti. *BYTE* (December 1984).

source, an abstract (summarized contents), or may even contain the full text of the articles. Abstract and index data bases use restricted vocabularies (ranging from under a thousand words to over 8,000) to ensure that information is stored in a consistent manner and can be searched with predictable results. Information is available to serve almost any type of information need, from the latest poultry farming techniques (available through AGRICOLA, a service of the National Agricultural Laboratory) to sunset and moonrise times for any date or location in the world (from the U.S. Naval Observatory).

For some professions, these services are so valuable that they border on essential. Physicians use on-line services to search through hundreds of medical journals for information on a particular disease or procedure. Attorneys and law clerks can accomplish, in minutes, the legal research that formerly required several days. Government contractors can save small fortunes by reviewing the information found in on-line data bases (including all Department of Defense contract awards). Table 14–1 lists a few of the many categories of information available.

Business users also have a number of information services that carry only business news or financial information. Among the more important are

Nexis. This service carries the full text of over a hundred business magazines and journals and several general publications. It also carries abstracts and indexes to several major newspapers (including the *New York Times*). Users can read the text at their terminals (very slow) or have Nexis print the desired information and send it to them (for a fee, of course).

Dow Jones News/Retrieval. Carries the full text of the *Wall Street Journal* and *Barron's,* as well as a summarized news wire service and stock prices. Users can search for all news on an industry or a specific company.

ABI/Inform. This service indexes every article found in 300 business journals and publications, and selectively indexes another 300. Each indexed article is also abstracted.

Predicasts F&S Indexes. Twelve hundred U.S. and international business publications are indexed, making this an important source of information for businesses with overseas operations.

Bulletin Board Systems **Bulletin board systems** are a means of electronically connecting users that share the same interests. They do not collect and store information for resale. In fact, most bulletin boards are free (except for certain services, and, of course, the cost of the phone call). Since a bulletin board system can be established by anyone with a modem that has an answer mode, there is no accurate census of the number available. Most estimates run into the thousands.

A bulletin board system offers a forum for sounding off, seeking advice, conducting electronic conversations with old friends or new acquaintances (or leaving messages for them), playing games, or downloading shareware. There are bulletin boards for games players, religious bulletin boards, bulletin boards for writers, and bulletin boards for almost all of the different microcomputer types. In fact, bulletin boards exist for almost every area of major interest to microcomputer users.

Some of the most informative bulletin board systems are operated by computer users groups. If a user is having problems getting a software program to run properly, it is likely that another person has also encountered the problem and a search through a users group's bulletin board might show several potential solutions. If not, the user could leave a request for help and a message describing the problem. With an active system, the user will probably collect several responses over the span of a few days. Some users groups, such as the Boston Computer Society (12,000 members), the IBM PC Users Group (5,000), and the First Osborne Group (15,000) offer considerable expertise acquired from years of use, almost all of it available on the bulletin boards run by the groups. In addition, these boards also allow members to download the considerable body of public domain (free)

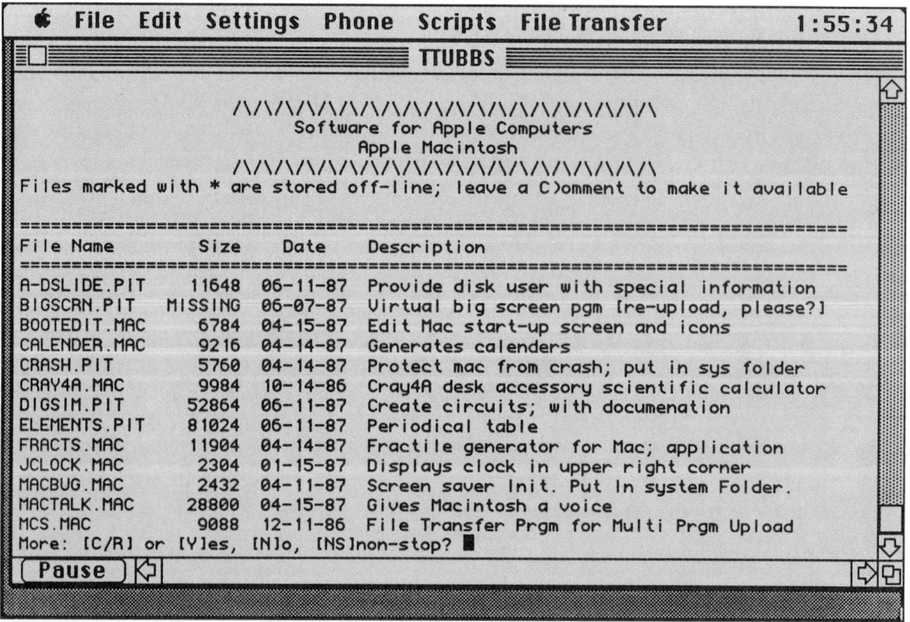

FIGURE 14–18
Conversing with a User's Group Bulletin Board System

software that is available on the bulletin board(s). Exhibited in Figure 14–18 is a dialog between a user and a bulletin board.

Major On-line Services Offering the services of both information utilities and bulletin boards are the major on-line services. CompuServe Information Service and The Source (acquired by Reader's Digest in 1980) are the best-known ones, but many others offer similar services. Table 14–2 lists the major on-line networks. These services can offer a startling number of features for both the home and professional user (Table 14–3 shows a small selection of services offered by CompuServe). The major systems typically do not perform the same function as the on-line data bases—that of collecting and summarizing information. Instead, they are information vendors, or brokers, purchasing access to on-line data bases and reselling them. Both the on-line data base company and the information broker find that this increases the use of their respective services.

An interesting trend is the number of companies that use these services to receive consumer feedback or provide information to product owners. Several computer hardware and software companies began this practice in the early 1980s and now a wide assortment of companies are monitoring the services.

Using On-line Information Systems Using one of the major on-line services requires a 300-bps, 1,200-bps, or 2,400-bps modem, a communications program, and a telephone line. Most systems allow nonsubscribers to dial up (using the phone numbers in Table 14–2) and view a portion of their menus and receive information on becoming a subscriber (most of it will be mailed). Alternatively, users may write the companies and receive the same information.

After paying a registration fee, users are given an access code (member number) that allows them to use the system. Registration fees range from free (these systems have a minimum monthly charge of $15 to $50 instead) to $100. In addition, some systems require the purchase of a starter kit with special software required by the system ($30 to $80). The major on-line services frequently change their registration fees, and offer limited time discounts or other sales incentives such as

TABLE 14–2
Major On-line Services

SERVICE	LOCATION	ACCESS
BRS After Dark	New York, NY	(800) 833-4707 (800) 553-5566 (NY)
CompuServe	Columbus, OH	(800) 848-8199 (614) 457-0802 (OH)
Delphi	Cambridge, MA	(800) 544-4005 (617) 491-3393 (MA)
Dow Jones News/Retrieval	Princeton, NJ	(800) 257-5114 (609) 452-2000 (NJ)
Knowledge Index	Palo Alto, CA	(800) 227-1960 (800) 982-5838 (CA)
NewsNet	Bryn Mawr, PA	(800) 345-1301 (215) 527-8030 (PA)
Nexis	Dayton, OH	(800) 227-4908
The Source	McLean, VA	(800) 336-3366 (703) 734-7500 (VA)

a free connect-time hour for new subscribers. Modem manufacturers also make arrangements with on-line services to offer free starter kits or registration fees with a modem purchase.

TABLE 14–3

A Small Sample of CompuServe Services

Home and Personal Services

AP Videotex—News, weather, and politics

Shop-at-home (over 50,000 products are sold at mail-order discounts of 10 to 40 percent)

Banking services

Special Interest Groups (SIGs)—CompuServe has groups for educators, musicians, poets, and golfers, as well as for owners of any major computer or software product.

Games—There are dozens you can play on-line, including trivia, adventure, and children's games

Communications—
- Electronic mail (you send messages addressed by user ID numbers and can check for your own messages)
- User directory
- Several advice columns
- National bulletin board (send your messages to all users who care to read them)

Education—
- The World Book and Academic America encyclopedias (complete, except for pictures)
- Instructional programs on everything from auto repair to gourmet cooking
- Guide to colleges and universities

Entertainment and travel
- Movie reviews
- Travel guides (including the Mobil Travel Guide, with hotel and restaurant ratings for 1,600 cities)
- Airline reservation systems (all U.S. carriers, most international ones; sold through travel agents)
- Hollywood hotline (on-line gossip column)
- EMI flight planning service for private pilots

Astrological forecasts and biorhythms

Intelligence tests and human sexuality assessments

Humor (including a fun one called the National Satirist)

Personal Computing Services

Newsletters from major hardware and software companies

The Micro Advisor (Q & A with experts)

Public domain software (downloadable)

On-line software purchase

Business and Professional Services

Stock quotations

On-line stock trading (handled through a discount broker)

Standard & Poor's business information reports

Value Line Financial Reports

Business news (the *Washington Post* business section, the Business Information Wire, and Commodity News Service)

Rapaport Diamond Brokerage

Several economic forecasting services

Home financial management programs

Access to dozens of on-line business data bases

FINTOL—a collection of programs for financial analysis

Once the user is ready to begin, there is a connect-time fee for using the system. All the major systems offer several rates. The rates vary with the type of services used, the transmission rate, and the time of day. Standard service is similar to the assortment of public channels available on cable television. Premium services are like the no-commercials movie channels that TV viewers pay an extra fee for. Most of the personal and home services are available at standard rates, ranging from $6/hr. late at night to $72/hr. during peak hours. Most of the business and financial services (especially access to data bases) are charged at premium rates, ranging from about $20/hr. to over $500/hr. Nexis users pay for each data base search (in addition to standard service rates) rather than by the hour. Dow Jones News/Retrieval charges by the minute (13 cents to $1.20/min., depending upon the time of day and the type of service). Stock prices are charged on a per-quotation basis (2 cents to 5 cents). Rates for 300-bps users are normally less than for 1,200- or 2,400-bps users. All of these fees can be charged to a Visa or MasterCard number.

It should be clear to the reader that using these services can create a considerable drain on the pocketbook. Many services are so large that users spend their first several on-line hours just becoming familiar with the selections available. Conducting searches through the data bases requires additional time to learn the appropriate keywords to try and the procedures used to search. For this reason, several information services and independent software publishers have developed communications programs that simplify and speed up information retrieval. Programs like Telehelp allow users to familiarize themselves with the major information systems without being connected to them. They can also let users program searches in advance. Then the program handles the dialing and searching, usually saving considerable on-line time. The Dow Jones Spreadsheet Link even allows the user to download financial information directly into the formats used by Multiplan, Lotus 1-2-3, and VisiCalc. For frequent users of information services, these products will pay for themselves in very little time.

Summary

Data communications, the electronic transmission of information from one device to another, is a complex topic, but it holds exciting prospects for the future. Individuals, businesses, and professions of all types can use data communications to enhance their productivity and save costs.

There are four major categories of data communication. Wide area networks are used to connect computers that are separated by great distance. They transmit their information with the aid of a common carrier or with packet switching systems that offer greater speeds and potential cost savings. Different computers that are close enough to each other can be connected with a local area network, or LAN. LANs are the subject of Chapter 15. When a terminal, or a computer acting as a terminal, is using the processing capability of a distant computer, this is called remote processing. Remote processing is the common operational mode for many businesses, such as banks. **Peripheral communications** are short-distance communications that do not require complex software or communications equipment. A computer's CPU speaks to disk drives, printers, and, sometimes, a directly connected computer using peripheral communications.

In order for data communications to exist, four components must be present: a sender, a receiver, a communications channel, and the message itself. The sender directs all communications from the CPU out a port. Ports for communicating across the country look the same to the CPU as its own disk drive ports.

Packaging the data as it comes out of a port is an interface device, an essential portion of the communications channel. The parallel interface is used primarily for peripheral communications. It sends out all eight bits of a data byte simultaneously over parallel lines. The serial interface sends the bits one after another over the same transmission line. All telecommunication, or data communication over telephone lines, employs serial communication. Telecommunications also requires a modem, a device for converting the data from a digital signal into an analog one that can be transmitted. Modems vary widely in features, speeds, and prices. Data transmissions are conducted using telephone lines, coaxial cable, fiber optics, microwaves, and satellite broadcasts.

To ensure accurate transmission of information, two methods are generally employed. In synchronous communications, the sender and receiver mark the end of a message by the amount of time that has elapsed. Most telecommunications use asynchronous, or start-stop, transmission. In an asynchronous transmission, data bytes must be "packed" with a variety of appended bits, such as start bits, stop bits, and parity bits. Protocol, a set of rules for ordinary data transmission, is the control signals used to coordinate the transmission.

Software packages are available, usually at a reasonable cost or free, to set all the parameters for communication. The principal feature of a communications software program is its ease of use, since communications settings are complex and will differ from system to system. Other useful features include the ability to upload and download files, a printer toggle key, terminal emulation, and automatic dialing from a stored file of phone numbers and terminal settings.

With the proper equipment and software, users can connect to a large number of information utilities, bulletin boards, and major on-line services. Information utilities scan hundreds of sources for information on selected subjects, and allow users to access it in abstracted or full-text form. Information utilities are becoming increasingly important for some occupations, such as medicine and law. Bulletin boards allow users with similar interests to communicate electronically. Bulletin boards operated by computer users groups can offer a wealth of free information and help, and bulletin boards exist for most other interests, as well. Major on-line services can provide all of the features of both information utilities and bulletin boards, as well as unique services like computer shopping, airline reservations, and stock quotations. These services can be expensive to use, however.

Key Terms

acoustic coupler
answer mode
ASCII
asynchronous
bps
bulletin board system
capture buffers
channel
common carrier
data communications
demodulation
direct-connect
downloading
full-duplex
half-duplex
information utility
interface device
leased line
local area network
modem
modulation
originate mode
packet switching network
parallel transmission
parity bit
peripheral communication

port
protocol
pulse signal
remote processing
serial transmission
simplex
specialized common carrier
start bit
stop bit
synchronous
telecommunications
telecommuting
terminal emulation
transducer
uploading
value added carrier
wide area network

Self-Test

1. Why is data communication so important?
2. What types of data communication are there?
3. What are the components of data communication systems?
4. What are information utilities?
5. What bulletin board systems are available?
6. What interfaces and ports are required for data communication?
7. How does a modem work, and what does it do?

Exercises

1. Identify the form of communication that is most likely to be employed in the following situations:
   (a) grocery store automatic checkers (bar code readers)
   (b) wiring money via Western Union
   (c) dialing from your PC to a friend's across town
   (d) operating a computer club's bulletin board
2. Discuss the reasons for the development of ASCII. What other standards are available?
3. Communications software can emulate half-duplex transmission with a full-duplex modem. Why is the converse not possible?
4. Develop a list of the signals employed by the X-ON/X-OFF, EXT/ACK, XMODEM, and KERMIT protocols. What are their ASCII equivalents (how can they be reproduced without communications software)?
5. Describe the major differences between popular communications software packages such as Smartcom and Crosstalk III.
6. Why is parity used?
7. Make a list of the equipment and software required to connect to a major on-line service such as Dow Jones News/Retrieval or The Source. What communications parameters must be set for each system?
8. Make a list of the information utilities that carry news or articles that would be of interest to professionals in your college major subject area.
9. Why would a user or firm select synchronous communication rather than asynchronous? Why not?
10. Publishers were mentioned in the text as one type of user that can save considerable money by having work submitted through telecommunications. What other industries have gained significant cost savings this way?
11. As a businessperson, would you prefer abstracted or full-text data base information utilities? Why?

12. CompuServe provides each subscriber with 128K bytes of secondary storage on the CompuServe computers. What uses might this have?
13. Major on-line services advise customers never to use their real names in messages. Why?
14. A few ethical questions:
    (a) In a well-publicized case, Los Angeles bulletin board operator Tom Tcimpidis was arrested and had his equipment seized because stolen telephone credit card numbers were placed by anonymous individuals (a relatively common occurrence) on his free, unattended board. Tcimpidis maintains he was not aware of them. Should system operators be held responsible for the way their services are used by irresponsible individuals?
    (b) Major on-line services offer message service that is protected from the view of unauthorized persons. Some are used to transmit sensitive business information to agents in the field. Should system operators have the right to view the contents of these protected files? Should the U.S. government have this right? Why or why not?
    (c) Bulletin board systems frequently carry information on how to break the copy protection schemes of popular software packages, ostensibly so that users may know how to make backup copies or transfer the program to a hard disk. Is this illegal? Should it be?
15. Describe a communications system that might connect two individual computer owners. What equipment must each have? Which user should be in originate or answer mode? What protocol might they select (do they even need protocol)? What software should each have (must it be the same program)? What types of information could they communicate?

Additional Reading

Glossbrenner, Alfred. *The Complete Handbook of Personal Computer Communications.* New York: St. Martin's Press, 1983.

CHAPTER

15

Local Area Networks

CHAPTER OUTLINE

LANs Defined and Depicted 522

Advantages/Functions of Local Area Networks 522

Local Area Network Topologies 524

FOCUS FEATURE Multiuser Systems 526

Local Area Network Media 526

Local Area Network Architectures 528

Specialized Nodes 535

Software Considerations 537

CHAPTER OBJECTIVES

In this chapter you will learn

1 what local area networks are
2 why local area networks are important
3 LAN topologies
4 LAN media
5 LAN architectures
6 the role software plays in a LAN

In his book *Megatrends,*[1] Naisbitt suggests that networks are one of the megatrends characterizing our age. This chapter is about local area networks, or LANs as they are frequently called. It has been said[2] that 80 percent of all communications take place within local environments. Local area networks are concerned with local communication primarily of data, but voice and video communication are also possible. It is the need for data communication in local environments (offices, buildings) that is the driving force behind this technology. In this context existing communication network technologies—principally the phone network—are not optimized for data communication in local environments. Consequently, there is a need for a separate network dedicated to serve primarily the needs of data communication. Local area networks are more than just wires or cables required to connect the machines of the automated office, as will be seen.

This chapter delves a bit further into the technology of data communications (initially discussed in the previous chapter) by describing LANs in light of their function, capabilities, and inner workings (how LANs put it on the line). Along the way some of the language of LANs is introduced, and some of the principal products in the marketplace are characterized.

LANs DEFINED AND DEPICTED

LANs are intra-organizational, user-owned and operated communication networks that offer reliable high-speed communications channels optimized for connecting information processing equipment in a limited geographic area, such as an office, a building, or campus.[2] They are expected to provide superior approaches to resource sharing and information dissemination, as discussed in the next section. In addition, LANs are capable of interconnecting a variety of office machines—from intelligent printers and copiers to building security and energy-management systems, to work stations, word processors, personal computers, terminals, and mainframes. Each machine is referred to as a **node** on the network that is able to communicate with any other node. Depicted in Figure 15–1 is a typical LAN for an office environment.

ADVANTAGES/FUNCTIONS OF LOCAL AREA NETWORKS

LANs can serve to enhance the productivity and efficiency of the office in a variety of ways. One of those ways is through the use of resource sharing. LANs will permit several users to share expensive resources, such as a high-speed laser printer, a hard disk, or a software package.

Aside from the obvious economics of sharing an expensive resource, additional benefits can accrue from the sharing of a secondary storage medium. Such sharing permits many users to access a common data base. These users can contribute to a central data base, which permits the data from several users to be joined, selected, merged, and projected in ways that will produce new and improved insights into the performance of the organization.

Thus, LANs are one very viable means of achieving a multiuser capability. Many situations exist in which such a capability is a requirement. For example,

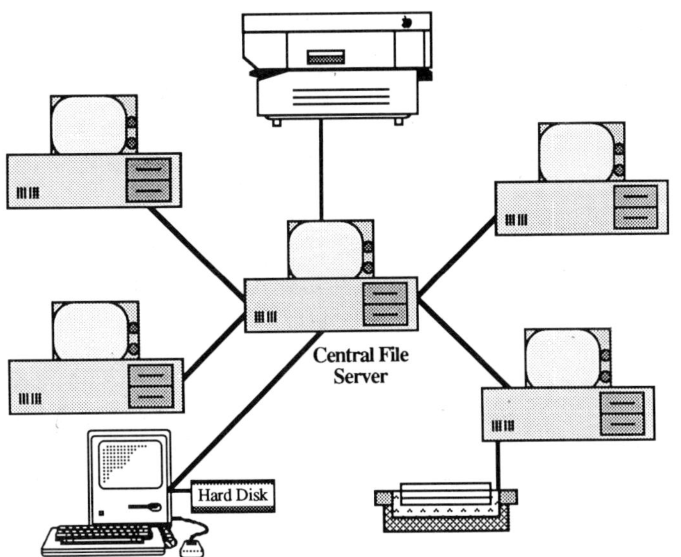

FIGURE 15–1
A "Typical" Small Local Area Network

suppose that an accounting application is to be brought on line and automated. Currently, it takes several individuals to enter the journal entries into a single set of books. With a multiuser system using LANs, this can be easily achieved. Each user has his or her own computer through which the accounting books (resident on a centralized data base such as a hard disk) can be simultaneously accessed and updated.

One of the trends in data processing over the last ten years has been to distribute the computing capability. Originally, all computing resources were located at a centralized data center. Users had to go to the data center to use the computer. Gradually, time sharing came into being. Users stayed at their work stations and interacted with the centralized mainframe computer by means of a terminal, modem, and phone line (or possibly, a direct connect line). Eventually, organizations owned their own minicomputers, which were networked into the mainframe by means of a dedicated high-speed line. This was the beginning of what is called **distributed computing.** Today, in large organizations, three levels of computing can take place: a microcomputer on the end-user's desktop; the organizational minicomputer at the organization or department level; and a mainframe computer at the centralized data center. LANs are the infrastructure (cables, wires, controllers, software) necessary to connect all these computers. Without this infrastructure, the data and knowledge bases on these machines would be highly fragmented.

Other functions and advantages of LANs require consideration. One of these is the use of electronic mail. **Electronic mail** is the term used to describe the capability of sending messages electronically to other users of the network. The messages are stored on a secondary storage medium and forwarded to their destination when the destination user requests them. This has its advantages over playing "telephone tag" with correspondents who are always on the go, and away from the phone. It does, however, depend on the disciplined use of the electronic mail service, lest the messages go unnoticed.

Another function of LANs is often referred to as **electronic phone.** Suppose the person you wish to "chat" with is also on-line (using the system at the same time you are). You can then type messages to him and receive messages from him in a concurrent fashion. The advantage here is the ability to send him some document you are working on, so he can interact with you about it. You don't have to phone him, and he can see what you are doing, without your having to send him hard copy by messenger or ordinary mail.

LANs provide for limited communication compatibility among diverse machines and manufacturers. The capability to pass an ASCII file from an IBM PC to an Apple IIe may be supported, for example. However, one cannot expect a machine language program that runs on an IBM PC and is transferred from the IBM to an Apple to run on the Apple. Nevertheless, LANs permit a great number and variety of machines to exchange large quantities of data at high speeds.

LANs can be expected to provide better overall performance than previous short-haul communications technologies in the sense that data rates are higher, error rates are lower, and failures are fewer. LAN transmission speeds vary from as little as 100K bits per second (bps) to as high as 30M (30 million) bps or more.[2] At 30M bps, the entire contents of this book could be transferred in less than a second. Moreover, LANs provide for a higher level of simplicity, flexibility, and ease of use than was formerly possible. Their simplicity makes them not only easy to use but also easy to maintain and inexpensive to purchase.

In short, LANs offer much greater speed and efficiency to the information nets within an organization. They permit computer resource sharing, they support a multiuser capability among small single-user computers, and they reduce the fragmentation of data and knowledge bases on distributed computing systems. In general, LANs provide for superior cost/performance as compared to what was previously available. This is not to say that every organization should have one. Some organizations may be able to share printers and files by simply passing diskettes around among the PC users. LANs are appropriate whenever the features afforded by LANs cannot be obtained at comparable or lesser cost by some other means.

LOCAL AREA NETWORK TOPOLOGIES

Figure 15–2 depicts some common forms of structuring or arranging networks, conventionally referred to by communications technologists as the **topology** (i.e., the geometry or physical shape) of the network. Specifically, three topologies are in use: the star, the ring, and the bus. Each is discussed in turn.

The star topology was commonly used in time-sharing systems that were popular among mainframe and minicomputer users during the 1970s. They permitted many terminals to be connected into a centralized computer system. One difficulty with such a configuration is the single point of failure that resides at the central computer system. When the centralized node is down, the entire network is down.

Ring topologies have met with some usefulness in networking mainframes and minicomputers. One difficulty ring topologies have is this: the failure of any node on the network may bring the entire network down. This is especially true when each node plays an active role in data transmission. Ring topologies frequently use a method of channel access that employs the use of a token. A **token** is an electronic device for sending or carrying a message consisting of data from one node to another. Only one token is available in the network; and before any node

FIGURE 15–2

Some Common Network Topologies

Ring

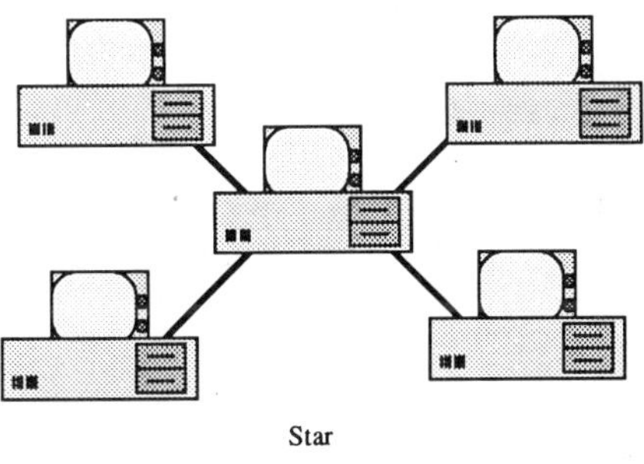

Star

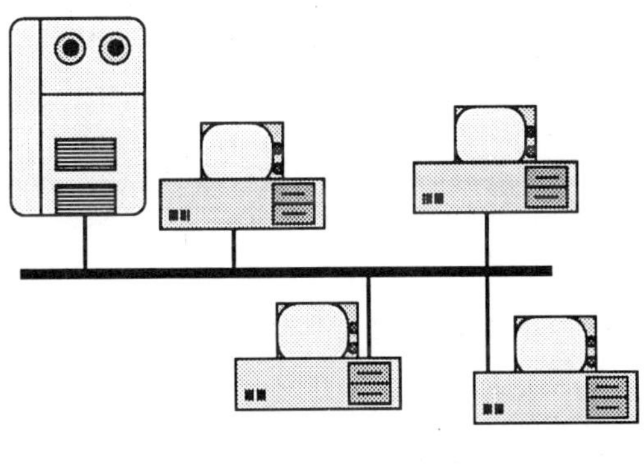

Bus

can transmit to any other node, it must first gain control of the token. In this somewhat crude way, the possibility of two or more nodes transmitting at the same time (and consequently garbling each other's messages as they are transmitted within the channel) is eliminated.

By far the topology of greatest use in LANs is the bus topology (and the closely allied branching tree). These topologies differ from the star and ring topologies in that the nodes are connected by multipoint links rather than point-to-point links. Bus and tree topologies appear to have advantages over the star and ring topologies in that the failure of a single node does not result in the entire network being down. Moreover, adding a node can be easily accomplished without disturbing the rest of the network. Hence, an entire "wing" or "building" of additional nodes can be added while the existing network continues in full swing.

LOCAL AREA NETWORK MEDIA

The media typically used as the connecting infrastructure of the networks is usually of two types: bounded and unbounded. The following types of bounded media are commonplace: twisted-pair wire, coaxial cable, and fiber optics, as shown in Figure 15–4. Least expensive of these is twisted-pair wire at a few cents per foot, whereas coaxial cable costs a few dollars per foot and fiber optics costs up to $10

Focus Feature

MULTIUSER SYSTEMS

In a **networked single-user system,** each user has his or her own single-user computer and operating system. Data or programs stored on other computers can be accessed by other users through the network hardware and software (see Figure 15-3). There may be some severe limitations to this arrangement, however, and they should be thoroughly explored before the need for such a system arises. The network's command structure for accessing records stored on another computer may be difficult to use; there may be restrictions on the simultaneous use of a file or a record within a file; accessing data on another computer may interfere with the operations of the other user; and the cost of networking equipment can sometimes exceed the cost of the computers themselves. In other environments networking can be a low-cost, efficient, and highly desirable means of implementing multiuser systems, and is often the only choice available when single-user systems have entrenched themselves within an organization before the need to link them was recognized.

File server systems are a form of networking, but are simpler in design than the systems described above. In a file server system, single-user systems are not linked to each other, but to a central large secondary storage device. Several vendors offer systems with a high-capacity hard disk, an intelligent microprocessor as a controller, and the necessary software. With this type of system each user's computer thinks that it has a hard disk of its very own, and is unaware of other users on the system. The file server hardware and software will control access to the data stored on the disk, creating short delays for one user while another accesses the same data, or denying access to protected data in other users' files. File server systems can be an excellent method of allowing data sharing between computers, or of expanding the secondary storage capacity of several machines. They also have their limitations, however. They are expensive; they can only work with computers running under the same operating system; they can measurably slow the performance of multiple users accessing the disk concurrently; they are only available for use with certain operating systems; and they may not work at all with certain applications programs.

Network star topology with multiprocessors and time-sharing systems consist of hardware and operating systems that are designed to be used by several individuals simultaneously. As shown in Figure 15–1, they can offer considerable cost benefits over the previous two alternatives, even with a small number of users. In general, as the number of users increases, so does the cost advantages of multiuser systems.

In a **network star topology with multiprocessors,** the central computer has a separate microprocessor for each user, plus one or more microprocessors that control the interaction between users and centrally stored data. Some multiprocessor operating systems are *proprietary;* that is, developed by the hardware manufacturer for use on their own equipment only. Other systems, like XENIX™, are offered by independent software houses for use on a variety of computers. The principle advantage of multiprocessor systems is that each work station is supported by its own microprocessor. Unless several users simultaneously attempt to access the disk, there is likely to be no noticeable performance degradation as more users are added to the system.

With a multiprocessor operating system from an independent software house, one computer will serve as the master processor. To add users, a hardware board with its own processor will be inserted into an expansion slot, and a terminal for the new user will connect to the

a foot.[3] Hook-ins (taps or tie-ins to the line) are also more expensive for coaxial and fiber optics cable, as indicated in Figure 15–4. Most of the currently available LANs use either twisted-pair wire or coaxial cable. The twisted-pair wire is similar in form to what the phone company uses, whereas coaxial cable is the media used by the CATV (community antenna TV) cable utilities.

Coaxial cable is considered to have superior performance as compared to twisted-pair wire. Twisted-pair wire generally has very limited capacity, and this translates to slow data rates. And the error rates for twisted-pair wire are generally

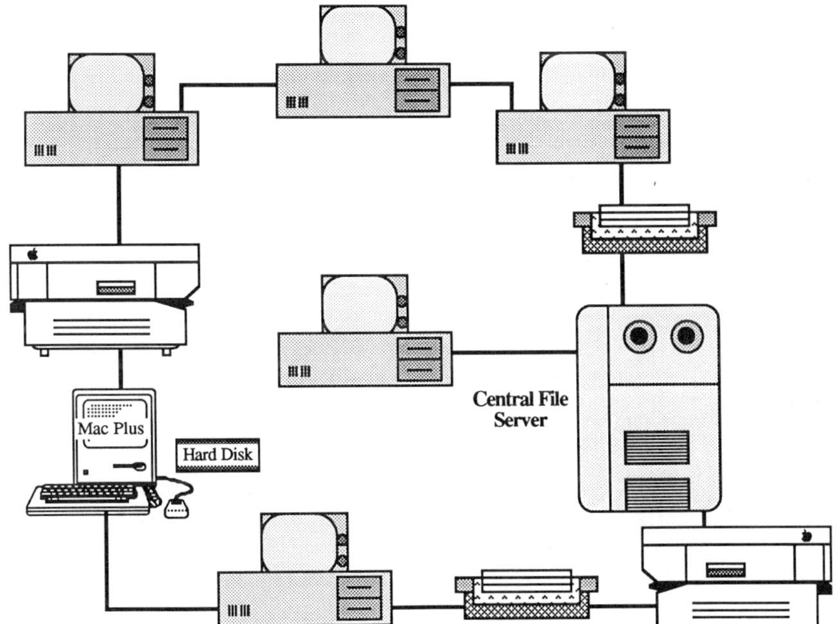

FIGURE 15–3

Networked, File Server, and Multiuser Systems

serial port on the board. These systems are usually limited to no more than six or eight simultaneous users. In a proprietary multiprocessor system, expansion restrictions may not be as severe.

In a **time-sharing system,** one microprocessor serves all the users on a system. These systems take advantage of the fact that the majority of a computer's time is usually spent waiting for input from a user. Even with a 100-word-per-minute typist, the typical microprocessor can execute thousands of instructions between each keystroke. In a time-sharing system, the microprocessor will alternate between the keystrokes of several users. The method of handling the cycling between users will vary, but in most microcomputer time-sharing systems there is a considerable reduction in the system's speed as each new user comes on line. With a fast microprocessor and a large amount of primary memory, the time-sharing system can perform more than adequately, and is the least expensive of all the multiuser configurations.

FIGURE 15–4
Some Common Network Media

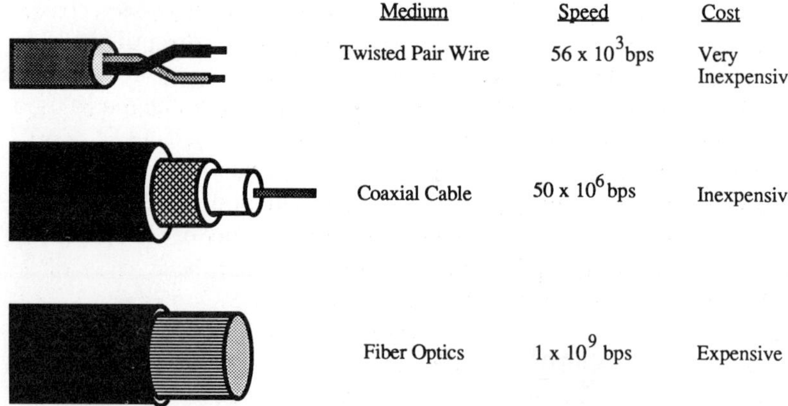

higher as compared to coaxial cable. Of the three major LAN architectures to be considered in this chapter, only one of them uses twisted-pair wire. The other two generally use coaxial cable, as shall be seen.

Medium
Speed
Cost
Twisted Pair Wire
56×10^3bps
Very Inexpensive
Coaxial Cable
50×10^6bps
Inexpensive
Fiber Optics
1×10^9 bps
Expensive

Unbounded media simply use the "air waves," because messages are broadcast in the same way that radio and television signals are broadcast. There are three basic signal types: radio, microwaves, and infrared. The advantage of this approach is that no physical medium has to be interlaced through the crawl spaces and ceilings of the building. Although this can be an advantage, the possibility of interference is greater and data transmissions could be garbled or jammed.

LOCAL AREA NETWORK ARCHITECTURES

Essentially three basic network architectures are characteristic of local area networks. They are referred to as the **PBX exchange LANs**, **broadband LANs**, and **baseband LANs**. Each of these is discussed in what follows and commercially available LANs for each category are presented. The advantages and disadvantages of each type are also discussed in this section.

The PBX Exchange

The basic idea here is to replace the phone company's private branch exchange (PBX) switch with a new computer-controlled PBX switch. Originally, the PBX exchange was used as a means of switching telephone calls within a business site, and from the site to outside lines. Today, these PBX exchanges are still being used by the phone company, only now they must serve the needs of both voice and data.

Since the PBX uses a computer-controlled electromechanical switch, it suffers from all of the shortcomings associated therewith, including slow speed, limited capacity, and long setup times (the time required to set up the channel between the originating node and the destination node, which can be longer than the time needed to send the message). The newer PBXs are capable of faster switching and more efficient allocation of available circuits.

Limitations continue to persist in the PBX exchange LAN technologies. These limitations stem from the media used (twisted-pair wire), the switching techniques employed, and the dual roles of transmitting both voice and data over the same wires. Many PBX exchange technologies do not support the capacity for receiving or transmitting data from several different sources at one time. Previously (Chapter 11), managers were envisioned as wanting to do several different tasks concurrently, such as writing a report and including within it spreadsheet data and graphics, and finally mailing it electronically to a destination. Add to this the need for monitoring incoming electronic mail, glancing at the Dow Jones ticker tape, and the user has a requirement for receiving and transmitting data from/to several different sources at once. This requirement is usually not supported by existing PBX exchange LAN technology. Nevertheless, the PBX exchange architecture is rather widely used and appropriate for many organizations. Commercially available LANs in this category are listed in Table 15–1.

AT&T Dimension
Datapoint
ITT System 3100
NEC Electra IMS
Northern Telecom
Rolm

TABLE 15–1

Commercially Available PBX Exchange LANs

Broadband LANs

Broadband LANs use coaxial cable with a bus topology. The total capacity (or bandwidth, as it is often called) is divided into a number of smaller channels, as shown in Figure 15–5. Such division allows for many nodes to communicate at the same time. This is called **frequency division multiplexing**, a term used to describe how multiple signals are transmitted simultaneously through the same medium. All signals are transmitted as analog signals, so digital data must be converted by use of modems on both ends. As with the long-haul communications described in Chapter 14, broadband LANs require a modem at each node for the purpose of converting digital signals to analog, and vice versa.

The bandwidth of coaxial cable, as indicated in Figure 15–5, is 300 to 400 MHz—enough to support the simultaneous transmission of 50 to 66 ordinary television channels, each television signal requiring 6 MHz of bandwidth. (One hertz (Hz) is one wave or cycle passing through the channel every second. One millihertz (MHz) is one million such waves passing every second). This supports very high data transmission rates and very low error rates—one error in every 10^8 or 10^{11}

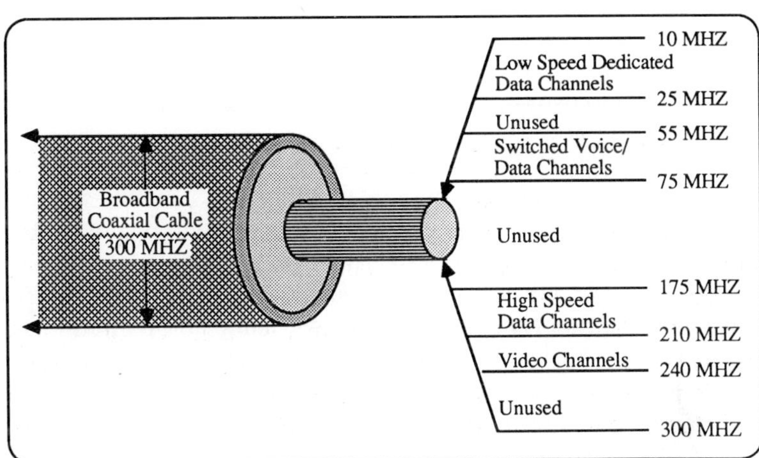

FIGURE 15–5

Channel Divisions on Broadband LANs

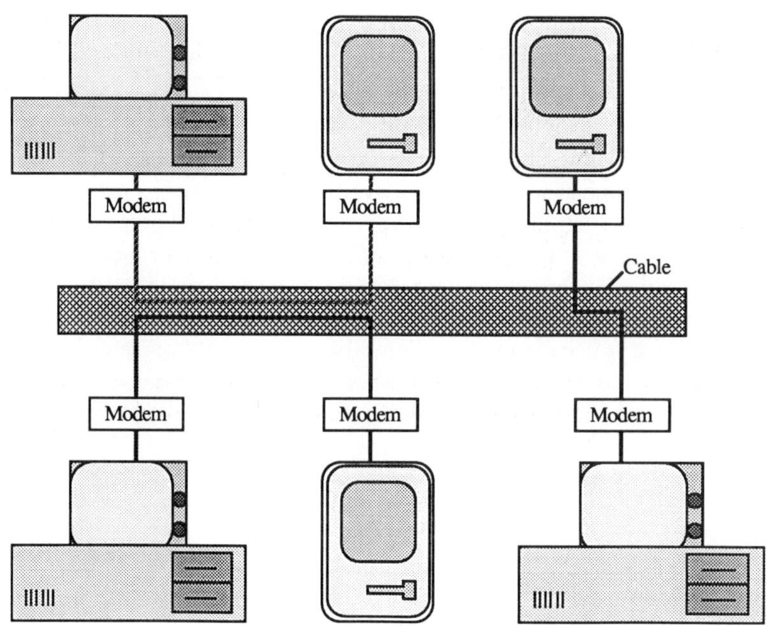

FIGURE 15–6
Broadband LANs
Broadband LANs divide the channel into smaller frequency bands. Each pair of communicating computers must be tuned to the appropriate frequency. Modems are required because signals are analog.

bits. The subdivided channels, as indicated in Figure 15–6, can have varying capacities so that a variety of applications can be supported. For example, broadband LANs can support simultaneous transmission of voice, video (television), and data on the same medium in analog form.

In broadband LANs, transmitted signals must travel in one direction very similar to the way radio waves travel from their transmitter to a receiver. To support two-way communication, separate send and receive channels must be established to allow for a two-way exchange. This can be accomplished in two ways. One way is to use a single cable and to divide its bandwidth roughly in half, using one half to send messages and the other half to receive messages. For example, the range from 10 to 110 MHz can be dedicated to sending messages, while the range 175 to 310 MHz is used for receiving (and the range 110 to 175 MHz is a buffer). At the end of each cable is a device called a Central Retransmission Facility, or CRF, whose function is to turn sending frequencies around so they become receiving messages. Only one cable is required, and each node requires only one tap into the cable. Single-cable broadband LANs are somewhat less expensive (as compared with the next approach to two-way communication with broadband LANs). The CRF, however, is a single point of failure. Since the total bandwidth must be divided between sending and receiving frequencies, less than half the total bandwidth of the cable is available for the transmission of information.

The second approach to two-way communication on a broadband system is to use two cables, one to send information and another to receive information. At the end, the cable just loops on itself, so a CRF is not needed. Furthermore, with such a setup the entire bandwidth of the cable is available for transmission, allowing more than twice the bandwidth capacity for network nodes, as compared to single-cable systems. However, twice as much cable and twice as many cable taps will be required.

A sample frequency allocation scheme for a dual-cable broadband LAN is shown in Table 15–2. Clearly, a variety of communication requirements can be

TABLE 15–2

Sample Frequency Allocation Scheme for Dual-Cable Broadband LANs[2]

FREQUENCY RANGE	DESCRIPTION	TYPICAL HARDWARE
10–15 MHz	48 dedicated point-to-point channels, each set at a fixed frequency, supporting up to 9,600 bps	1 fixed-frequency modem per user, each device conforming to RS232-C
15–25 MHz	32 dedicated point-to-point channels, each set at a fixed frequency, supporting up to 64,000 bps	1 fixed-frequency modem per user, each device conforming to RS449
25–55 MHz	Unused/reserved	
55–75 MHz	128 switched, point-to-point channels, supporting data rates up to 9,600 bps	1 variable-frequency modem per device, conforming to RS232-C, plus 1 data switch for the 128 channels
75–175 MHz	Unused/reserved	
175–210 MHz	High-speed data communication (10,000,000 bps)	
210–240 MHz	5 standard CATV video channels	
240–300 MHz	Unused/reserved	

met, including different data rates. For example, the broadband LAN can support over 100 point-to-point connections (node pairs) in only 20 MHz, each transmitting at data rates of up to 9,600 bps. This type of service might be allocated to the 55- to 75-MHz regime of the total 300-MHz bandwidth, as suggested in Table 15–2.

Although most of the total bandwidth (nearly two thirds) is unused or reserved, there is still tremendous capacity. The 10 to 15 MHz band and the 15 to 25 MHz band would support up to 80 users connected into a centralized computer, such as a mainframe. All communication would have to take place through the centralized computer in a star topology. The centralized computer could address mail to each user on the basis of the frequency assigned to the user's node. Each node communicates with the centralized computer on a point-to-point basis via the assigned frequency bandwidth.

The next band, 55 to 75 MHz, closely resembles a PBX exchange LAN. Each modem must be of the variable-frequency (frequency-agile) type, so it can be set to any of several different frequencies. The communication frequency can be established manually or automatically. In either case the node pairs wishing to communicate have their frequency-agile modems tuned to the appropriate frequency, at which time communication between the node pair can take place. The allocation of frequencies is accomplished by means of a switch, which gives this band many of the characteristics of a star configuration with a central node that can be a central point of failure.

The next usable band, 175 to 210 MHz, functions in a way identical to a baseband LAN. Subsequent discussion of baseband LANs in general will apply to this sub-band as well.

The last usable band, 210 to 240 MHz, supports the simultaneous transmission of five television channels.

With all the versatility and diversity of broadband LANs (the capability to emulate the other types of LANs, for example), one would expect such a complicated system to be expensive. Such is the case. There is an economy, however, in that users are able to employ one (dual) coaxial cable for all their communication needs.

Baseband LANs

Baseband LANs are rapidly becoming the most popular form of LAN for networking microcomputers in a business or professional context. The media used is almost always coaxial cable and the topology is usually bus, but ring and star topologies are also possible. Baseband LANs do not divide the capacity of the communication channel into many subchannels (each with its own frequency range), as in broadband LANs. As shown in Figure 15–7, all nodes communicate over the same channel by taking turns in the same way that a classroom full of students would conduct a discussion forum. Each student waits until no one else is talking before addressing the rest of the class. The listening students all hear what the student who is talking says, even if what is being said is not intended for all to hear. Occasionally, two or more students might start talking at once. This will be detected, and those students who were talking will back off and wait a random interval of time before attempting to voice their concern again. Each time a student wishes to

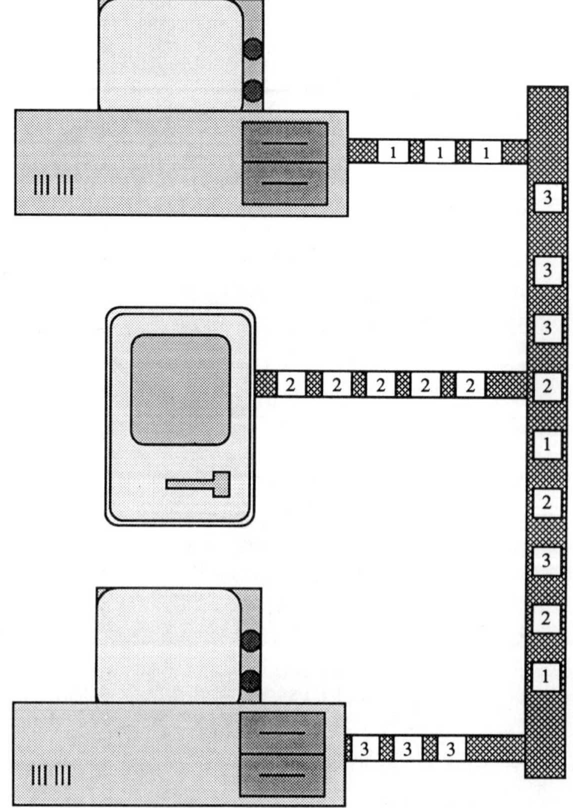

FIGURE 15–7

Baseband LANs Baseband LANs place messages in packets which are separated from each other in time. Packets are broadcast over the entire bandwidth of the channel. No modems are required.

talk, the student listens to see if anyone is talking; if such is the case, the student waits until the air is clear before starting to talk.

All baseband transmissions are digital rather than analog, as in broadband and (in some cases) the PBX exchange LANs.[2] Of all the LANs considered so far, baseband LANs come the closest to being a natural extension of the microcomputer's internal I/O bus.

In baseband transmissions, all messages are packetized in a form similar to that used by the packet switching networks discussed in Chapter 14. The packets are digital transmissions ranging from 64 bytes to 1,518 bytes in length. The transmission rate is very high, usually around 1,000,000 bps, but can be up to 10,000,000 bps and higher. These high transmission speeds are made possible by the very wide bandwidth of the undivided communication channel. Figure 15–8 depicts the packet format for baseband LANs.

As indicated in Figure 15–8, the packet consists of a preamble, a destination address, a source address, a type field, a data field, and a frame-check field. The preamble is always 8 bytes long, and its purpose is to synchronize the receiving nodes and put them in a listening mode. Next comes the destination address, which is 6 bytes long. The destination can be one, several, or all of the nodes on the network. This is followed by the source address, which is a 6-byte field that identifies the address of the node sending the packet. Then the type field (two bytes long) permits information coming from different network architectures to be placed on the channel and processed appropriately when received by the destination node. The data field can be any size from 46 bytes to 1,500 bytes long, and contains the actual data being transmitted. Last, the frame-check field (four bytes long) is used to check the accuracy of the information contained in each transmitted packet.

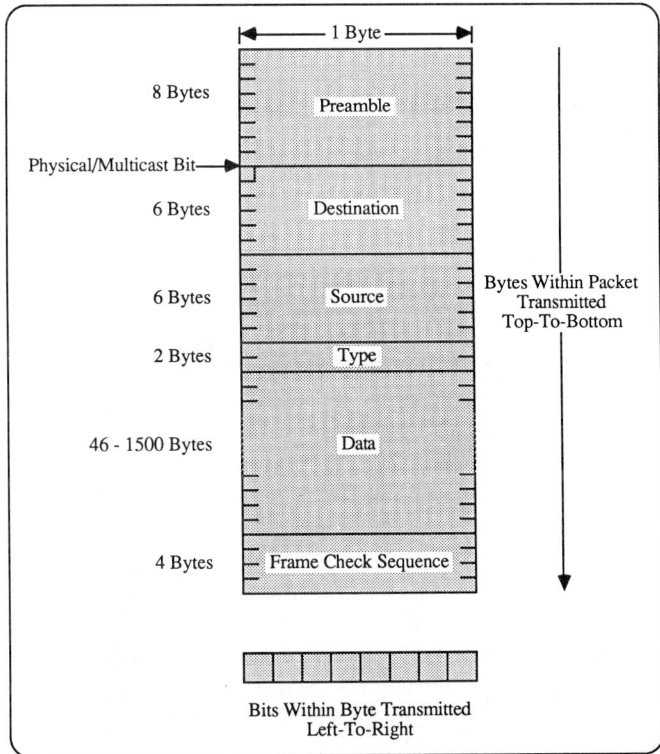

FIGURE 15–8

Packet Format for Baseband LANs

FIGURE 15–9

Basic Hardware Components of Baseband LANs

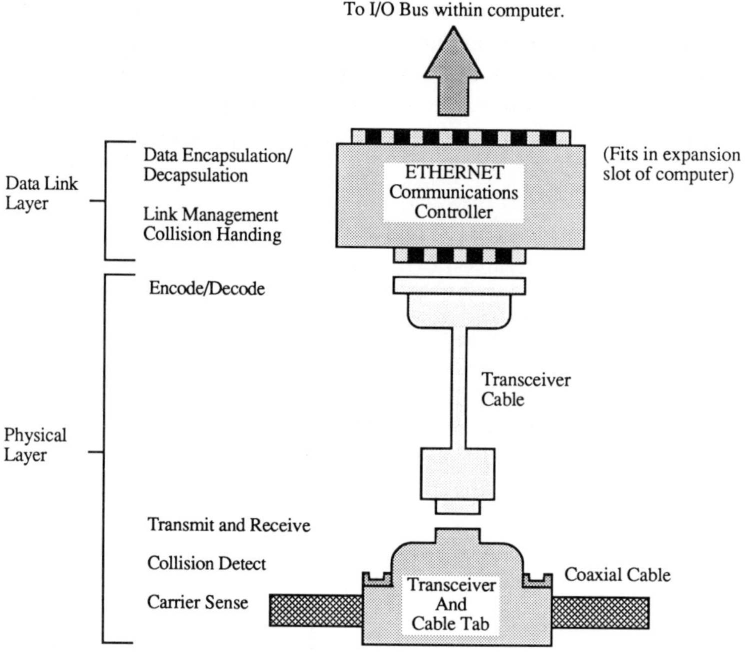

In addition to the coaxial cable, several other rather standard components make up the baseband LAN hardware, as shown in Figure 15–9. The tap into the cable itself is accomplished by means of a device called a **transceiver.** The transceiver listens to the line to determine when it is free to receive a message. The transceiver is also responsible for transmitting the messages that come down to it from the controller card, which is either placed in one of the expansion slots of the microcomputer or connected to one of its external ports. Furthermore, the transceiver is responsible for receiving all packets placed on the line and for detecting packet collisions when they occur.

The controller card is responsible for the data encapsulation and decapsulation of the packets placed on and received from the coaxial cable and transceiver. Each controller card is also responsible for channel control. In this sense the channel control is distributed among all the nodes in the network. For example, if the transceiver indicates that a transmission is in progress, the controller card will defer the transmission of any data it has received for transmission on the channel until the transceiver indicates that the channel is idle.

Baseband LANs use a contention and (packet) collision avoidance technique that works very much like the classroom analogy described above. The access protocol is called **CSMA/CD**, an abbreviation for Carrier Sense Multiple Access/Collision Detect. This access protocol works as follows. Each node (specifically, the controller card and transceiver) listens to the line to ascertain if messages are being transmitted. A node that has a requirement for transmitting a message waits until the channel is idle. The message is preceded by a preamble, which places all other nodes in a listening mode and synchronizes their clock mechanisms. Then the message to be transmitted is packetized by the controller card, sent to the transceiver, and placed on the line. Each listening node checks the destination address to ascertain if the message is intended for it. If not, the message is discarded. The destination node will retain the packet, check it for accuracy, and send it up for processing by its node.

Occasionally, it happens that two nodes try to transmit at the same instant in time. This is called a **collision**, and it is detected by the transmitting nodes from the presence of extraordinarily high energy levels on the line. Each transmitting node continues to "jam" the channel for a short period of time, then backs off, waits a random interval of time, and then tries to transmit again. Listed in Table 15–3 are selected vendors of baseband LANs.

AST-PCnet II
Corvus Omnishare
Corvus Novell
Davong Multilink
Davong Novell
Fox 10-NE
Nestar PLAN 3000
Nestar PLAN 4000
Novell NetWare/S
Novell Netware/X
Orchid PCnet
Quadnet VI
Quadnet IX
Tecmar
TeleVideo PM/16
3Com Native/XT
UBI Net/One
XComp X-Net

TABLE 15–3

Some Typical Baseband LANs for the IBM PC and Compatibles

SPECIALIZED NODES

In addition to the usual microcomputer, numerous specialty nodes exist that facilitate sharing of resources or permit connection to other networks of like or different architectures. Shown in Figure 15–10 are several LAN configurations. Specialized nodes are used throughout.

One such node is the repeater. The **repeater** allows different segments of a baseband LAN to be connected.

Another oft-used specialized node is the server. There are many types of servers, which are themselves a form of microcomputer with a dedicated function. One such server is the disk server. **Disk servers** enable many nodes to access a hard disk. This is usually accomplished by partitioning the hard disk into segments, each of which logically acts like a dedicated hard disk. References to the hard-disk segment are by means of a drive letter, following the standard conventions established by the DOS. Files contained in separately partitioned segments of the hard disk are not necessarily "public," and therefore accessible to all the users, unless they reside in a designated public partition. By use of the DOS-provided COPY utility, however, it is possible to copy a file from one partition to another. The integrity of public partitions is the most difficult to maintain. One way around this is to declare all such files as read-only files.

A closely related server is the file server. The **file server** enables many nodes to access common secondary storage devices, on which are placed files that are accessible by all of the nodes (assuming security permits such access). File servers are more sophisticated and efficient than disk servers, for several reasons. It is not necessary to partition the disk into segments, for example. The hardware required for a file server is practically identical to that of a disk server, but the software is much more complex and versatile. Rather than having the server appear to network nodes as additional disks, users access the data contained on the hard disk via individual files.

Printer servers enable printing resources to be shared by the users of the network. Sometimes printer servers are combined with file or disk servers into one central unit.

Routing servers enable nodes of like architecture to communicate over long-haul network connections.

Gateway servers permit nodes on networks of different architecture to communicate. Gateways will translate protocols to permit communications between the two different architectures.

Servers can be classified in several ways—according to function, as indicated above, but also according to how they interact with the operating system. Some servers are **dedicated**, in the sense that the host computer is completely taken over

FIGURE 15–10

Some Typical Baseband LANs

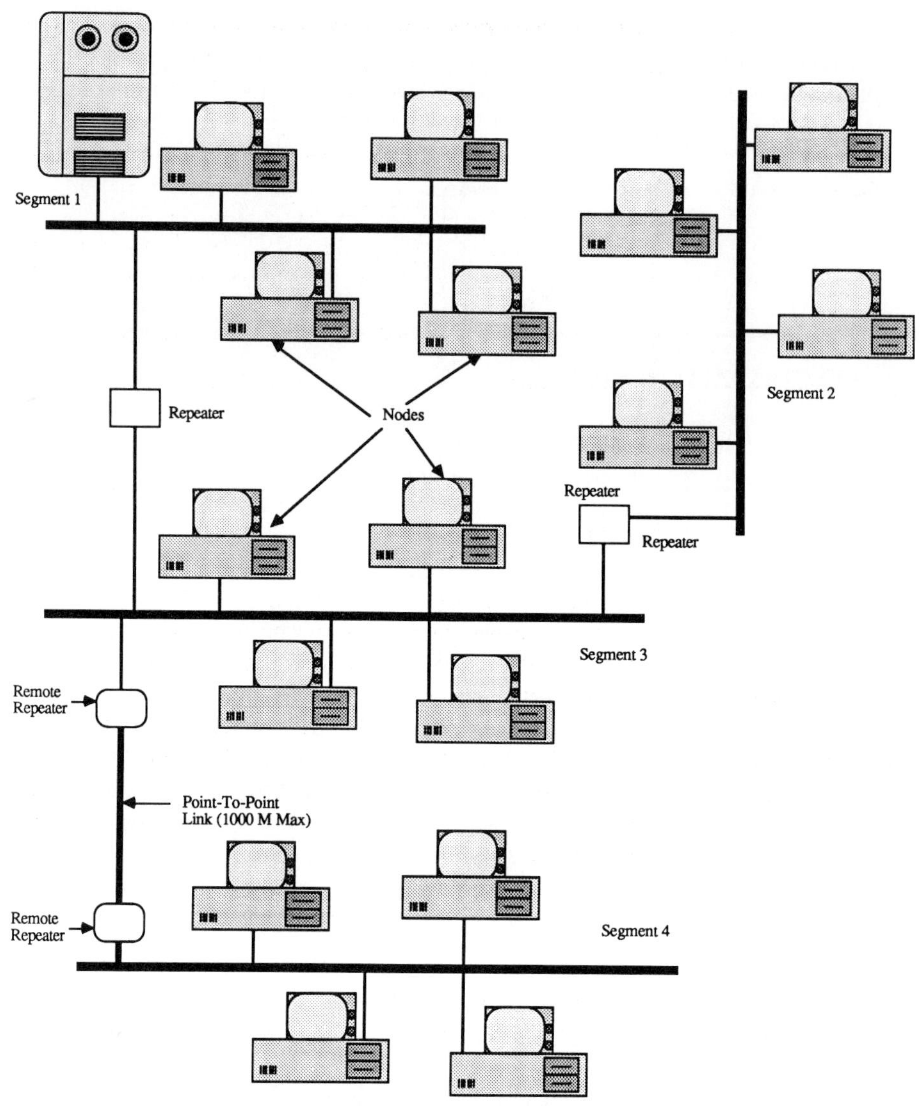

and is not user-accessible. Several dedicated servers may reside on the network. Other servers may not be dedicated, and therefore the host computer can be used for other activities. Usually, these activities are slowed demonstrably by the occasional need to service the network. The file or disk server node is usually the most powerful machine on the network, and will always contain a hard disk. Dedicated servers, by their very nature, permit one less user to be supported for the same number of nodes. However, they will provide faster access to shared files and are an excellent choice for applications subject to heavy disk use.

In addition, servers may be central or **distributed,**[4] depending on whether one or several machines are used to service the network. In one popular LAN for the IBM PC—Orchid Technology's PC NET—every node is a nondedicated server. When service of the network is required by a particular node, the user's program on that node is interrupted and processing of the program is temporarily halted or slowed. This is an example of a distributed file server.

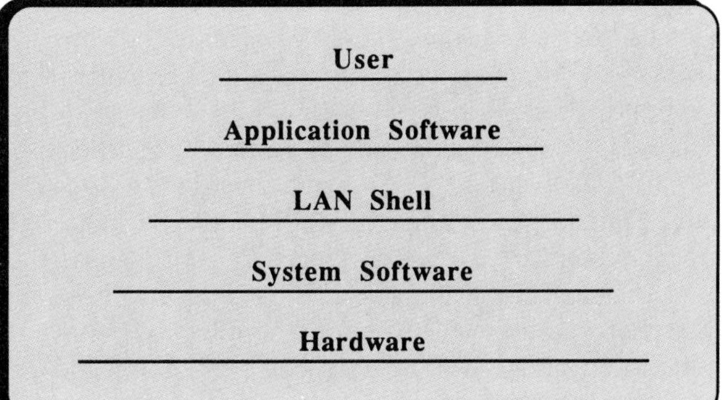

FIGURE 15–11
The LAN Shell in Relation to Other Software

SOFTWARE CONSIDERATIONS

The LAN software resides as a **shell** (or layer; see Figure 15–11) between the applications software and the stand-alone system software, as shown in Figure 15–11. In actuality, the LAN software becomes an integral part of the system software. User-issued commands are first processed by the LAN shell. If the command is a LAN command, it is processed by the shell; on the other hand, if the command is an ordinary system command, it is sent to the resident DOS for processing.

The first and foremost important purchase consideration of a LAN is the software that drives it. The software is the greatest single determinant of the features and performance of the LAN—more so than the topology, the media, the architecture, and most certainly the advertised data transmission rate in bits per second. This is because the software will be the determinant of such important issues as

1. Whether files can actually be shared on the secondary storage devices that are common to all users (nodes), or just space on the storage device itself (is shared). In the latter case the file has to be copied from one user's workspace to another's.
2. What security is available to protect access by some nodes and users in confidential portions of the data base, such as sensitive salary data or company-proprietary information.
3. Whether print spooling is supported for a commonly shared printer, or whether printer use has to be manually coordinated by the users.
4. Whether file locking is supported to prevent one user from changing a file while it is being used by another.
5. Whether record locking is supported to prevent one user from changing a record (within a file) while it is being used by another (a more desirable feature than 4, above).

LAN software must support one or more file servers so that individual files can be shared. Novell's NetWare provides a near-mainframe capability for file sharing and file protection. A file designated as "nonsharable read/write" (the default designation) is capable of being opened and accessed by only one user and program at a time. Once the user gains control of a nonsharable file, the user can read from or write to the file. Access to the file by any other user during this time is denied. True file locking in this sense is a rarity among LAN software, because most software packages use the PC-DOS or MS-DOS approach of placing a flag in the directory to designate the file as open. If a particular program being used by some node on the network does not look for the flag and deny access to opened files, then the file could accidentally be ruined by another user.

The shell should be compatible with most of the PC-DOS and MS-DOS software. WordStar, 1-2-3, and dBASE III should be supported, for example, as should any other software the user regularly uses or plans to use on the system.

The shell should not disturb or change DOS in any way. In fact, PC-DOS is booted first, in the usual way, and then the LAN software is booted. The shell sits immediately above DOS and processes all commands, as in Figure 15–11. Local commands are sent down for processing by DOS, whereas commands involving network servers are handled exclusively by the shell. Hence, DOS is allowed to do all local processing while the shell handles all network processing.

The network shell should provide extensive security. Four levels of security should be supported: logon/password, trustee, directory, and file. The logon/password is required for access to the network. Once logged on, the user's trustee level determines whether that user can read, write, open, create, or delete files; search the directory; or modify file attribute flags. Directory rights determine which directories can be seen, and file rights determine which files can be opened and accessed. Without the shell, the data on the formatted hard disk should not be accessible from PC-DOS.

The shell software should support dynamic volume allocation. The size of any volume on the hard disk (a volume being effectively a "logical" disk with its own subdirectory) should vary with the cumulative size of all files copied to it. As files are added, changed in size, or erased, the size of the volume should vary accordingly.

The shell should support a sophisticated print-spooling capability that permits all print files to be written to the hard disk and then spooled out to the printer according to some priority. Spooler options include printing a banner before each job, printing multiple copies of a document, changing paper during printing, checking to see which print jobs are pending in the print queue, reorganizing the queue, redirecting a file to a different printer, and so forth.

As suggested in References 3 and 5, the potential purchaser is well advised to examine the driving software that comes with the LAN before looking at anything else, including media, topology, architecture, and overall transmission speed. This is just as true of LANs as it is of microcomputers themselves.

Summary

Organizations that exchange diskettes in order to share files, data, and hardware may improve their data handling by installing a LAN. Organizations that find their data base is very fragmented and unaccessible by most of the users who require such access should benefit from the installation of a LAN. Organizations which require a lot of intra-organizational communication will benefit from the use of a LAN to support such network-related applications as electronic mail, electronic phone, and electronic community bulletin board services. It is in fact possible to create all the power and capability of a mainframe or minicomputer with LANs using microcomputer technology. However, this concept runs counter to the mentality that created the microcomputer revolution in the first place: namely, giving each user personal (and private) computing power that is under that user's total control.

This chapter defined LANs and explained what potentially desirable features and applications LANs can support. It mentioned that LANs support sharing of resources and files, that LANs create a multiuser capability, and that LANs support distributed computing. It showed how some multiuser computer systems are effectively network-in-a-box computers, giving each user a processor board with RAM. And it described some of the network-related applications of LANs, such as electronic mail and electronic phone (chatting).

The chapter also introduced some jargon and terminology of LANs, such as topology, transmission speed, media, channel allocation/control, and LAN architecture. Three basic topologies were mentioned: the ring, the star, and the bus. Three bounded media types were described: twisted-pair wire, coaxial cable, and fiber optics. Three methods for channel allocation and control were briefly discussed: token passing, CSMA, and CSMA/CD. And three basic LAN architectures were presented: the PBX exchange, the broadband LAN, and the baseband LAN.

One of the more popular baseband LAN configurations is the Ethernet and the Ether series. Ethernet uses coaxial cable with a bus topology which permits up to 1,024 nodes to be tapped into the network. Ethernet has enough power and capability to network an entire campus of buildings.

This chapter also discussed the importance of software in view of the overall performance of the LAN. It presented a commercially available LAN software package that is considered the state of the art. It is software that is the determinant of how hard disks are shared, what file security is available, and whether print spooling is supported.

In the appendix at the end of this book is provided a checklist for evaluating alternative LAN configurations.

Key Terms

collision
CSMA/CD
dedicated server
disk server
distributed server
file server
frequency division multiplexing
gateway server
node
routing server
token
topology
transceiver

Self-Test

1. What are local area networks?
2. Why are local area networks important?
3. What are LAN topologies, and what topologies are available?
4. What LAN media are frequently used?
5. What three LAN architectures are described, and which of these supports Ethernet?
6. What role does software play within any LAN?

Exercises

1. List what you believe are the important criteria for deciding among LAN alternatives.
2. Distinguish between the three LAN architectures, characterizing each with regard to
   (a) raw transmission speed
   (b) typical media used
   (c) typical topology employed

(d) flexibility and versatility
(e) method of channel allocation and control
(f) cost

3. Discuss the contents of each packet on the baseband LAN. Why is the information packetized? What is the purpose of the preamble?
4. What are some of the major considerations in servers for microcomputers? Under what circumstances would a dedicated server be better than a nondedicated one? Under what circumstances would a bona fide file server be required over a disk server?
5. How important to the efficiency of the LAN is the speed of transmission in bits per second?
6. What are the network-related applications of LANs, and how do they work? What benefits do such applications provide over more conventional communication approaches, and why are the LAN approaches advantageous?
7. Describe the principal design concepts (architecture, topology, media) for an Ethernet.
8. Discuss in some detail the capabilities/features/advantages afforded by LANs. Why are LANs needed (as compared to what is conventionally available)? What are some applications of LANs?
9. Describe the process of transmission and reception of a packet on the Ethernet. How are collisions handled?

Case

As a consultant, you have been asked how a small business can expand its stand-alone personal computer to accommodate its accounting functions. Currently, it takes two clerks to post to two different sets of books on the accountant's computer. Although the books are kept separate, there is a need for their being merged at the end of each period for tax purposes. The company wishes to use its existing PC, which it currently uses for spreadsheets and word processing for about six hours each day. Management wishes to parameterize its spreadsheets with accounting data. What conceptual system would you recommend? How many work stations would you include? What category of server do you think is appropriate; that is, disk or file, dedicated or nondedicated, distributed or centralized, etc.? What components would be required? How should the manager of this business proceed?

References

1. Naisbitt, John. *Megatrends: Ten New Directions Transforming Our Lives.* New York: Warner Books, 1982.
2. *Introduction to Local Area Networks.* Waltham, Mass.: Digital Equipment Corporation, 1982.
3. Derfler, Frank J. Jr. "The Lay of the LANs." *PC: An Independent Guide to IBM Personal Computers* 4, no. 3 (February 5, 1985): 116–25.
4. Goldhaber, Nat, and Winn L. Rosch. "Networks at Your Service." *PC: An Independent Guide to IBM Personal Computers* 4, no. 3 (February 5, 1985): 125–30.
5. Shoch, John F. *Design and Performance of Local Computer Networks.* August 1979.

Additional Reading

Cowart, Robert, and Peter Feldmann. "Benchmarks for Network Ratings." *PC: An Independent Guide to IBM Personal Computers* 4, no. 3 (February 5, 1985): 152–68.

Cowart, Robert, and Steve Rosenthal. "The Novell Solution." *PC: An Independent Guide to IBM Personal Computers* 4, No. 3 (February 5, 1985): 131–35.

Derfler, Frank Jr., and William Stallings. *A Manager's Guide to Local Area Networks.* Englewood Cliffs, N.J.: Prentice-Hall, 1983.

Dickinson, John. "LAN Speed Trials." *PC: An Independent Guide to IBM Personal Computers* 4, No. 3 (February 5, 1985): 168–78.

Fritz, James S., Charles F. Kaldenbach, and Louis M. Progar. *Local Area Networks: Selection Guidelines.* Englewood Cliffs, N.J.: Prentice-Hall, 1985.

Haugdahl, J. Scott. "Local-Area Networks for the IBM PC." *Byte* 9, No. 13 (December 1984): 147–79.

Mier, Edwin E. "The Evolution of a Standard Ethernet." *Byte* 9, No. 13 (December 1984): 131–47.

"Network Survey: Battle of the Network Stars." *PC: An Independent Guide to IBM Personal Computers* 4, No. 3 (February 5, 1985): 178–272.

"The Organizational LAN." *PC World* (February 1985): 72–107.

Sammons & Associates, "An Inside Look at IBM's LAN." *PC: An Independent Guide to IBM Personal Computers* 4, No. 3 (February 5, 1985): 136–43.

"Six Leading LANs." *PC World* (February 1985): 108–215.

CHAPTER

16

Microcomputer Purchase Considerations

CHAPTER OUTLINE

Software Purchase Considerations 543
FOCUS FEATURE About Custom Software Development Projects 544
FOCUS FEATURE Of Vendor Support 550
System Purchase Considerations 555
FOCUS FEATURE Capacity Requirements Planning 556

CHAPTER OBJECTIVES

In this chapter you will learn

1 a formal methodology for purchasing microcomputer systems
2 what an RFP is
3 a methodology for choosing the right software package
4 why custom development of software from scratch to satisfy a particular application does not make sense today
5 what capacity requirements planning is, and what role it plays in the system procurement process
6 how to grade vendor proposals (for computer systems)
7 how to do an after-tax, net-present-value analysis of cost of a microcomputer system
8 how to select a microcomputer system, considering the cost and grade of the proposed computer system

Microcomputer purchases must be directed by a strategy that is exactly opposite to that conventionally used in making major purchase decisions. Traditionally consumers purchase their stereo and then their records. Unfortunately such an approach does not work with microcomputers, in the sense that one should not purchase the computer and then the software. The wiser approach is to decide upon software based on a careful consideration of the applications to be computerized and then to determine what hardware systems will run the software.

The problem relates to the fact that not all software runs on just any machine. Suppose you visited a friend who demonstrated the latest integrated software package to you. You've shopped and considered the alternatives and are convinced that his choice was the correct one. Now the problem is reduced to finding a microcomputer that the selected software package will run on, given that microcomputers all have different capabilities and run different software packages.

A related problem is that of capacity planning. **Capacity requirements planning** refers to how many work stations are required to support the target application(s) and to how much memory (primary and secondary storage) is required to support the applications to be computerized. It also refers to how much printing capacity is required. Capacity planning issues are addressed in one of the articles in this chapter. They are extremely important in any microcomputer purchase decision.

In addition to software purchases, this chapter presents a methodology for procurement or purchase of entire computer systems. The methodology begins with a needs analysis, continues with a consideration of what software is available to satisfy the identified need(s), suggests how to evaluate software that would satisfy those needs, and so forth. These then are the topics to be addressed in this chapter, which integrates all the issues relating to microcomputer software and system procurement.

SOFTWARE PURCHASE CONSIDERATIONS

An issue of increasing importance today is that of how to purchase software. Such procurement may involve outright purchase or development of the software. When purchasing software one needs to know where to go to shop software, how to evaluate the software, and how to implement the software once it is purchased. Such is the subject of this section.

Why is software procurement an important enough issue to warrant its being formally treated here? There are several considerations. First, most hardware systems do not come with bundled applications software, even though they do include the systems software. The applications software must be purchased separately from the purchase of the hardware.

Second, there are literally tens of thousands of applications software packages to choose from. If a particular application must be supported, then the user is usually faced with a choice of buying the software or developing it. For the most part, developing your own software makes about as much sense as developing your own hardware. There are exceptions, of course. In some instances a third option is possible in that a user can pay a use or subscription fee for the privilege of using an application software package that is made available by an information utility or service bureau, as discussed in Chapter 14.

Make versus Buy Decisions

For the major applications (word processing, spreadsheets, and data base management), most of us would never think of developing such software from scratch. After all, it is estimated that the cost of developing software may run from ten to one hundred times (or more) that of purchasing a package intended for the same application. For lesser applications, however, the situation may not be so black and white.

If cost alone isn't enough to discourage most users from developing their own packages, consider this. The lead time to purchase (time required to obtain) a software package is usually a matter of hours, or at most, a few days. Usually the time required amounts to no more than driving to the local software retailer, making the purchase, and then returning home or to the office. The software may also be purchased from a mail-order house, in which case the delivery time may be overnight, or at most a few days.

By contrast, consider the lead times associated with development of the software. Studies suggest that for most software projects, the lead time for development of a major software package is at least a year.

Moreover, the issue of software maintenance must be addressed within the

Focus Feature

ABOUT CUSTOM SOFTWARE DEVELOPMENT PROJECTS

In those rarest of instances in which an application is so unique and unusual that there is no software suitable for the task, then the manager may be faced with a software development project. Once the decision to develop the software is made, all sorts of options must be addressed. Will the software be developed with in-house expertise, or will an outside agency be used? If an outside agency is used, what contractual arrangements are necessary to protect both parties? How will the manager decide among the various outside software development agencies available?

Assume for the moment that management has decided to go with an outside agency. We recommend that a request for proposal approach be used to decide among the various software houses that are willing to bid on the project, exactly as described in another section of this chapter. It is best if the software can be procured through a fixed-price contract with the outside agency selected as the winner of the bidding competition. A **fixed-price contract** is one which requires the software development agency to deliver a specified software product for a fixed price. It is understood that any embellishments will cost the firm funding the project extra. Such an arrangement works well when the firm initiating the project has a well-defined and -specified software system. This is delineated in the **procurement specifications,** which are a part of the fixed-price contract and the essence of the request for proposal.

Some issues that must be addressed in the context of the contract with the outside software vendor include training and implementation, warranties, deliverables, and rights to the software. We shall delve into the issue of training and implementation in a later section of this chapter. Will the vendor warrant the software as capable of performing up to its specifications? What deliverables will be required of the vendor when the software is ultimately developed? For example, will the vendor be required to furnish the source code, or will object code be sufficient? (**Source code** refers to the high-level language statements that comprise the program developed by the vendor, whereas **object code** refers to the machine-language instructions that were generated when the source code was translated by the compiler so the program could be executed by the computer; see Chapter 4.)

Second, who owns the rights to the developed software—the vendor or the firm funding the development? Normally, the funding firm owns the rights unless other-context of the make-versus-buy decision. Suppose that you, as an employee of a small firm, decided that developing your own payroll and tax program made judicious sense. You would then retain the services of a programmer to develop the software for you. Custom programming typically costs $35/hr. To write a payroll and tax program may take anywhere from 50 to 1,000 hours or more to write, depending upon its level of sophistication. Nevertheless, you would be able to control exactly what it did, and you could make changes to it whenever such changes were warranted. It would, in fact, be custom-tailored to your specific application (for that reason, such software is often called "custom software").

Payroll and tax programs contain rules and formulas that depend heavily upon Internal Revenue Service (IRS) stipulations. For example, withholding schedules, depreciation formulas, tax credits, depletion allowances, and such are frequently changed by the IRS. If you maintain your own payroll and tax software, then you must rehire that programmer to update your own software each time the rules get changed. If you purchased your payroll and tax software from a software house, and pay a yearly update fee, then you will find that the cost of the updated software is many times less than the cost of maintaining your own software, probably by a factor of ten.

wise specifically stated in the contract. By **rights** we refer to the rights of copyright ownership. This includes, among other things, the right to sell and distribute the program. In view of the technical and legal details of the contract between the funding firm and outside vendor, it is recommended that the manager(s) soliciting the software development project seek legal counsel if no template for the contractual arrangements suitable to both parties is available.

In some cases, the make-or-buy decision is not absolute. For example, it frequently happens in many specialization areas that a particular package is purchased and then modified so as to tailor it to the specific needs of the application. For mainline applications like word processing and spreadsheets, this almost never happens, but for accounting applications, revision or modification of existing software is frequent.

In order to effect these modifications, it is necessary for the vendor doing the modifications to have access to the source code. Without the source code, substantial modification of a program is almost impossible and most certainly not economical. In addition the vendor must have good documentation of the program's structural contents. Today, it is rare that a program is supplied with source code and good programming documentation. For these reasons, it is recommended that whenever possible and financially expedient, the application user or manager should contract with the software vendor who originally developed the software to do the modifications.

There are several other reasons why this is advantageous. First, the software vendor who developed the software in the first place is going to be well acquainted with the structure and form of the software. You won't be paying someone just to get acquainted with the software so they can render the modifications. Second, the developing software vendor is going to understand the features and structure of the software and how to retain these in view of your specific requirements. Third, once the software is modified and installed, if there is a problem, only one agency is responsible for the integrity of the software and hence the mitigation of the problem. When you contract with a separate software vendor to do the modifications and a problem surfaces later, then the question of who is responsible for correcting the problem arises. It may turn out that each vendor will point an accusing finger at the other.

Finally, in view of the high cost of software development and the long development lead times, it is rare that a developed package will have the polish that a purchased one would have. Polish can be assessed by the quality of the documentation, the quality of the printed or displayed reports, the provision of help screens and menus, the security provisions, and the error traps. Time and money simply do not permit much capability to be incorporated in these areas. As a result, packaged software will generally have a much higher degree of polish and sophistication associated with it, as compared with custom software.

A Methodology for Selecting Software

Now that the issue of developing versus buying software has been resolved, this discussion presents a method for selecting software. The basic steps are listed and briefly described in Table 16–1.

Worthy of mention is that a separate application package is not needed for each and every application the user has in mind. As explained in Chapter 11, several applications can be supported by a single all-in-one program. Nevertheless, it is expedient that the user go through all of the steps listed above for each of the applications that are perceived as required. In what follows each of these steps is described in greater detail.

TABLE 16–1
Ten Simple Steps to Software Acquisition/Installation

1. Define the application to be computerized. What are the inputs, the outputs? What makes your requirements different from those of other users, if the application is commonplace?
2. Develop a list of the software available to support the application. To do this you have to know where to shop for software.
3. Gather information about available packages. One source of information about microcomputer software is the trade literature, which frequently reviews new software.
4. Narrow the list of possible choices down to less than a half-dozen. For example, there are about two hundred major word processing programs. A thorough scrutiny of all these would be impractical.
5. Obtain hands-on demonstrations of the few remaining packages. If the candidate programs are readily available at your local retailer, ask the dealer to demonstrate them to you and give you an opportunity to test them yourself.
6. Of those that remain, perform a final detailed evaluation. If possible, read the operations manuals. Check the features to see if they match your requirements. Observe the outputs and reports to ascertain if they will be functional in your application.
7. Make a decision. Decide which of the programs will provide all of the desired features at the lowest cost. Costs must include all the potential costs associated with purchase, modification, installation, training, and updating.
8. Purchase the package. The issue here is one of who to purchase the package from, a local retailer or a mail-order house. The tradeoffs are obviously cost versus service.
9. Learn to use the package. After following the vendor's installation instructions, you are ready to begin learning how to use the package. Many packages provide a tutorial to facilitate such training.
10. Implement the package within the context of the intended application. Use the package to create the records and files that you intended.

Define the Application to be Computerized Suppose you, like so many other microcomputer users, are in the market for a word processing package. However, your application is different from theirs in that you want to be able to support scientific symbols—particularly those used in mathematics and statistics. Clearly, you have defined a requirement that will result in your making a choice that may be quite different from the word processing package choices of your acquaintances.

As a part of this step, you will want to carefully delineate the format of the reports your application is to produce, especially if the application is accounting-related. And you will want to specify the capacity requirements of your application. For example, if you have a requirement for a word processor that will support the preparation of large, multiple-file documents, then a word processor designed primarily to support the production of letters and memos may not provide the features necessary to support the heavier word processing activity.

Develop a List of Available Software There are at least eight major sources of information about microcomputer software: the microcomputer trade literature, microcomputer software directories, software search bureaus, computer stores, user groups, turnkey system suppliers, mail-order discount houses, and the software manufacturers themselves.

The utility of the microcomputer trade literature and directories has been discussed in Chapter 2. Certainly they are the best place for one to start becoming acquainted with the microcomputer software base. More will be said about this information resource later.

Computer stores will stock the trade literature and will provide access to the software itself. Ultimately, the user will want to see demonstrations of those packages of greatest interest, as discussed in what follows. Computer retailers are usually accommodating in this regard.

For detailed information about a software package that is not provided in any of the literature, contact the software manufacturer directly.

In major metropolitan areas, user groups exist for just about every category of microcomputer. The groups will generally seek to educate their memberships regarding the software available and its usage on a microcomputer. To find out about user groups in your area, inquire at your local computer retailer.

Gather Information about Available Packages Reviews of major applications software frequently appear in such periodicals as *Infoworld, PC: An Independent Guide to the IBM Personal Computer, PC World, Byte,* and many others. In addition to the advertising found in these periodicals, the reviews are a good source of information about software. Another source of important information about existing programs is Datapro's *Directory of Microcomputer Software.* Once again, evaluations of the software are published based upon user responses to questionnaires sent out by Datapro. Hence, in this material the software is reviewed and evaluated by users. The presentation is in the form of two-dimensional tables, which enable a side-by-side comparison of user satisfaction with various aspects of all packages.

It is important to point out that reviews are often flawed, superficial, overly critical, and inconsistent. Almost never is all the software available for a given application reviewed by the same reviewer or set of reviewers. As you read a review, reflect on the following questions: does this review suggest that the reviewer is qualified to make the judgments about the package that is presented? Are the findings backed up with substantive tests and evaluations? Is the review superficial in the sense that the reviewer passes the package off with some laudatory remarks but provides no depth, no comparative evaluations, and little content? Is the review overly critical in the sense that the reviewer finds fault with almost every facet of the program and backs these harsh pronouncements up with little or no substance? To be on the safe side, consult the findings of several reviews for packages that are of particular interest to you.

Software manufacturers may be very helpful in providing technical information not available elsewhere. For example, you might have a requirement for a high-level language that will support large amounts of in-memory data. Such a requirement is typical in scientific computing. Many languages have a 64K-byte data-segment limitation which makes them unsuitable for such applications. However, some do not. (For your information, Microsoft FORTRAN and Microsoft Quick Basic 4.0 do not, but Microsoft's MS-DOS BASIC interpreter does.) This type of technical detail may not be supplied with any literature that you have seen, and the salespeople at the local computer emporium may not know the answer. In such cases you must call or write the software manufacturer.

Narrow the List of Possible Choices Down One criterion available to owners of microcomputers who have not yet defined all their applications is this: "Does the package run on my computer?" If it doesn't, there is little use in giving the package any further consideration unless you are willing to exchange computers.

Obtain Hands-on Demonstrations A pleasure visit to the computer store is essential at this point in your evaluation. Before you buy any package, it is appropriate first of all to have that package demonstrated to you and, if possible, to actually test the package using some tests you might have developed beforehand. For example, if the package is a word processing package, bring along a page of text and try entering, editing, saving, and retrieving the textual material. The program should not contain any surprises for you. Its user interface should be acceptable in view of your level of computer literacy. Are the basic features of the program seemingly clean, fast, and efficient when executed? In short, this is your opportunity to verify what you have no doubt read about in the reviews and other literature pertaining to the software being examined.

Glossbrenner[1] gives us the following list of items to consider during the demonstration. First, what hardware is required to support the package? Must additional graphics boards, RAM cards, or peripherals be purchased in connection with the software package? These may not be visible, so be sure to ask the salesperson. Does the software require expanded-capacity floppies, a RAM disk, or a hard disk?

Second, can you actually begin using the program without reading the instructions? Most programs are not quite this obvious in their use; however, some are. This is a benchmark of the program's user-friendliness. It has been said that a program should be designed so that you could use it even if you hadn't used it for six weeks and you lost the manual a month ago. To what extent is the program icon- or menu-driven? As observed in Chapter 11, pop-up, pull-up, and pull-down menus are becoming increasingly popular. These operate via a menu bar at the top or bottom of the screen. Such programs are usually both menu- and command-driven. And the commands are obvious, concise representations of the menu's items. As you test the program, ask yourself, "Are the prompts and commands easy to understand?"

In Reference 1 are suggested several tests to put a program through its paces, including deliberately trying to cause the program to fail. For example, you might enter an invalid response to a prompt just to see how it responds. If a number is expected, enter a letter. If a letter is expected, enter a number. When the program prompts you for a filename, enter an invalid one just to see how it responds. Is the program "blown away" by these invalid responses, or does it "hang the machine," so that you have to reboot and start over? Or does the program trap your error and provide a graceful remedy, perhaps by suggesting why your response was invalid and thereafter letting you reenter your response? For example, if the program requests a filename, and you commit an error in typing in the filename, it should inform you that the filename you entered was not found. It should give you an opportunity at this point to examine the directory of the diskette and to reenter the filename. Glossbrenner[1] suggests doing a disk access with no disk in the drive to see how the program reacts. This will cause many programs to revert to the operating system level.

Perform a Final Evaluation In a subsequent section a grading system based upon the attributes of the software, the weights you attribute to them, and the grade you assign to them is proposed for the evaluation of computer systems and hardware. That scheme is equally appropriate in the evaluation of software. To use it, simply develop a list of attributes you consider desirable, assign weights to those attributes, and then grade each package you are considering in each of the attribute areas, as shown in Figure 16–1. The grade you actually assign to each package in each attribute area will be influenced by your impressions of the package derived from the demonstration and hands-on examination described above.

Table 16–2 (on page 552) illustrates how this method of grading software is carried out in practice. Notice that the weights attributed to each attribute are assigned in such a way as to reflect the relative importance of the associated attribute. The grade assigned to each package is a number between zero and one. The overall grade calculated for each package is determined by multiplying the attribute weight by the corresponding package attribute grade and summing all of the resulting products. The resulting overall grade will always be a number between zero and one, with one being perfection and zero designating no worth.

Make a Decision Your final decision will want to relate cost to performance or grade, as shown in Table 16–2. In the previous step, a grade for each product

FIGURE 16–1

A Method for Grading Software

	Weight	**Package 1**	**Package 2**	**Package 3**
Ease of learning				
Editing features				
Formatting features				
Printing features				
File handling features				
Ability to interface w/other programs				
Speed				
Vendor Support				

being considered for a single application was arrived at. In this step, you will want to determine the overall cost of each package. The cost must include not only the purchase price but also the cost of any additional hardware that may be required, the cost of any additional software that may be required, and the cost of changing your way of doing business (if there are tangible costs in this area).

Once the costs for each alternative software product are computed, these must be related to the grade of the product by simply computing performance/cost ratios for each alternative. These ratios are computed by simply dividing the grade of the software package by its cost. The highest of these is the most obvious selection. However, there can be nonquantitative, intangible considerations that can lead to selecting a product other than the one with the highest performance/cost ratio.

Purchase the Package The issue here is who to purchase the package from. For example, you can purchase software from the local computer retailer or you can purchase the same package from a national mail-order house and save 20 to 30 percent off the retail price. If you purchase the package from your neighbor-

Focus Feature

OF VENDOR SUPPORT

FIGURE 16–2

Two Typical Software Warranties

WARRANTY 1

________ MAKES NO WARRANTIES, EITHER EXPRESSED OR IMPLIED, AS TO THE QUALITY, PERFORMANCE OR MERCHANTABILITY OF THIS PROGRAM, NOR AS TO THE FITNESS FOR ANY PARTICULAR PURPOSE OR PARTICULAR RESULTS OBTAINED THROUGH USING THE PROGRAM. YOU ACCEPT THIS PROGRAM "AS IS" AND ASSUME ALL RISK OF DEFECTS AND ALL COSTS OF SERVICING, REPAIRS AND CORRECTIONS.

________WILL NOT BE LIABLE FOR ANY DIRECT, INCIDENTAL, OR CONSEQUENTIAL DAMAGES RESULTING FROM THE USE OF THE PROGRAM, EVEN IF ________ HAS BEEN ADVISED OF THE POSSIBILITY OF SUCH DAMAGES....

One attribute of particular interest to the potential purchaser is the level of vendor support that comes with the package. Here are some of the facets for judging the level of vendor support.[1] First, does the software come with a customer registration card or form in the documentation? By registering your software, the firm has a way of informing you when updates are available and ready. Second, is there a definitive policy for replacing damaged disks, especially if the programs are copy-protected? Usually, you can expect the software vendor to require that you return the damaged original disk(s) and pay a fee of $10 to $25 to cover their handling and diskette costs. Third, does the vendor have some kind of policy regarding program updates? When the vendor releases a new version of the software, it is under no obligation to inform its registered customers. However, by doing so, it is possible for the firm to realize additional revenues from the sale of the upgrade at a reduced price. Finally, does the software vendor offer a customer support hotline? The customer should be leary of any soft-

hood computer retailer, you can expect to pay more, but you will also receive a much higher level of service and support. For many people there are decided advantages to developing a good rapport with the neighborhood computer retailer. When problems arise, someone is close by to resolve your difficulties and answer your questions. It is not fair, however, to expect your computer retailer to answer questions about a package that you have purchased (or are going to purchase) from a mail-order house at a discount. If you have decided to purchase the product from a local retailer, then you are faced with a choice of which retailer, since dozens of retailers may be within a short drive of your campus or metropolitan residence. You will make your decision on the basis of the level of support and service offered by the dealer. Issues of concern here relate to whether the dealer will provide some instruction in the use of the package and if so, at what price; whether the dealer is willing to install the software for you; whether the dealer is willing to take the time to answer your questions; and whether the dealer will take back the software should you, for any reason, find it unsatisfactory. To find out about issues like this you will have to talk with the dealer in person, and with former patrons of the dealer.

WARRANTY 2

_________warrants for a period of one hundred (100) days from the date of purchase that, under normal use, the material of the magnetic disks and the manuals will not prove defective; that the Software program will prove to operate substantially in accordance with what is described in the manuals and in advertising for the software; that the programs are properly encoded on the disks; and that the user manuals are substantially complete and contain all essential information necessary for the use of the software. If during the one hundred (100) day period the software does not meet the above warranty, it may be returned to the dealer for replacement without charge or for a refund at the dealer's option.

EXCEPT FOR THE LIMITED WARRANTY DESCRIBED ABOVE, THERE ARE NO OTHER WARRANTIES, EITHER EXPRESS OR IMPLIED, PROVIDED WITH THIS PROGRAM. THESE INCLUDE, BUT ARE NOT LIMITED TO, IMPLIED WARRANTIES OF MERCHANTABILITY OR FITNESS FOR A PARTICULAR PURPOSE, AND ALL SUCH WARRANTIES ARE EXPRESSLY DISCLAIMED.

ware vendor who does not either publish its number or provide a hotline number. Some vendors provide a toll-free hotline number. The purchaser should also examine the vendor's warranty. Most software vendors supply a disclaimer of warranty which releases them of any indemnification or liability. The disclaimer reads something like this: "This software is not warranted for any particular application or purpose . . . while ________believes this to be a high-quality product, the purchaser must assume all risks of using the software." Figure 16–2 exhibits two possible warranties. It is impossible for software companies to anticipate all of the possible ways in which the software might be used. Given the complexities of these programs, and the wide variety of uses to which they will be put by tens of thousands of users, it is easy to discern why software vendors judiciously include such disclaimers in their software warranties.

TABLE 16–2

A Software Grading Illustration for a Word Processing Application

ATTRIBUTE	WEIGHT	PACKAGE 1	PACKAGE 2	PACKAGE 3
Ease of learning	.14	.7	.8	.9
Editing features	.15	.6	.7	.6
Formatting features	.13	.8	.5	.3
Printing features	.14	.9	.8	.7
File handling features	.15	.6	.8	.9
Ability to interface with other programs	.15	.5	.6	1.
Speed	.14	.7	.8	.9
OVERALL GRADE		.681	.716	.764
COST		$135	$395	$350
PERFORMANCE/COST		.00504	.00181	.00218

Learn to Use the Package Before you can begin to use a package, you must first install it. This involves running an install program that comes with the package. The install program is going to ask you what brand of computer, what brand of display, and what brand of printer you have. It will then patch this information into the modules that make up the package. Effectively, the device drivers associated with the brand-specific devices you designated will be used by the modules for display, for printing, for disk accesses, and the like. This will allow the package to make optimal use of the hardware you are running the package on. The install programs are straightforward in their use and require no user sophistication or training in order to be used.

Most major applications today are relatively easy to learn, even if difficult to master. **On-line tutorials** (software provided on diskette that teaches you how to use another software package) are frequently becoming commonplace, and context-sensitive help screens are also provided. Your first task is just learning how to navigate within the package. Once you've mastered that, you will want to learn how to create, retrieve, and save files. There are also many helpful books that enable you to learn the package. And last but not least, there is the operation manual that comes with the package itself. You should have judged it readable in content before making the final decision to purchase the package.

Implement the Package Generally implementation is regarded as involving installation, training, and testing of the system. However, since we have already discussed the issues of installation and training, we are going to be concerned here with bringing into service one or more applications software packages and testing those packages for a period until you have absolute confidence in their integrity, accuracy, and appropriateness. This is called **conversion**: from an old system of doing things to a newer one. Conversion is a relatively straightforward process when a single user brings into regular usage a single application software module, such as a word processing module. On the other hand, for accounting systems conversion is one of the most difficult stages in the technological evolution of an organization. This is because the test-related aspects of it require that users run the old and the new systems in parallel for a period of time until the new system has been vindicated. This is true not only of accounting systems but of decision support systems as well. In general, these are complicated situations involving an office full of users who ultimately wish to bring on line a whole spectrum of applications. Some good advice can be applied within this context.

First, when several applications are to be "automated," keep the situation simple by working with just one application at a time. Install the associated applications software, train yourself, your staff, or both, and begin using the package. For example, suppose you are implementing a new accounting system consisting of accounts receivable, accounts payable, general ledger, and inventory. Then the best approach is to convert one application at a time, completing the conversion before beginning another.

Figure 16–3 depicts several ways in which conversion can be accomplished. As indicated, these ways are labeled "crash conversion," "parallel conversion," and "pilot conversion." Crash conversion involves a total termination of the old system

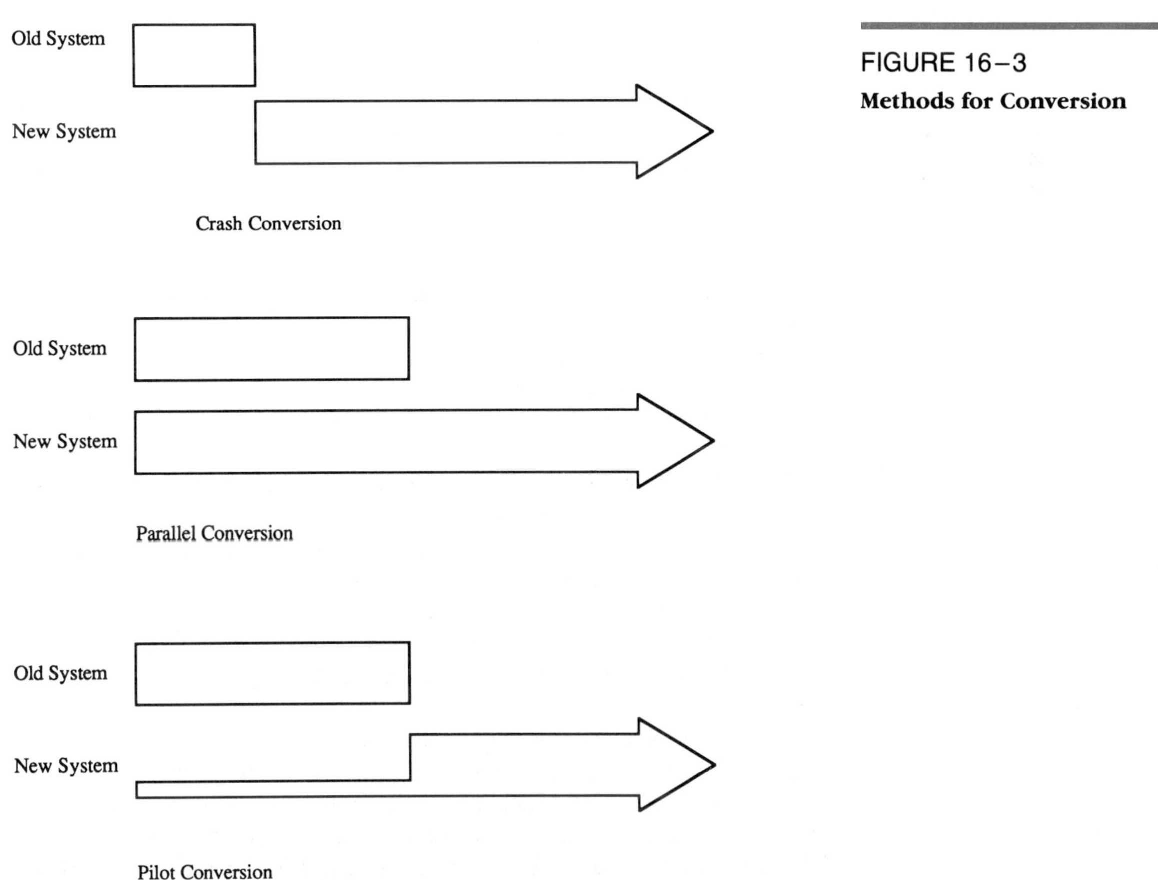

FIGURE 16–3
Methods for Conversion

of operation and immediate initiation of the new one. There is no period of testing and integrity checking. Although this entails little or no implementation costs, it is not necessarily the least expensive. Consider the costs that might be sustained if the new accounting system is losing records, or fails to invoice your customers properly.

Parallel and pilot conversion involve checking the new system against the old one for whatever length of time is necessary to ascertain that the new system is working properly.

Pilot conversion is clearly advantageous over parallel conversion because it involves less effort. Yet if it is administered properly, it can be just as effective as parallel conversion. In the early stages of the conversion, bring on-line to the new system just a portion of the total operation. Use that portion to test and debug the new system. Only that portion is duplicated in the old system, which is running in parallel with the new. This is far less work than trying to run the entire operation on both systems in parallel.

Of Protection and Piracy

Since microcomputers support the capability to copy files from one disk to another for backup and organizational purposes, it is very easy to use these utilities to make unauthorized copies of original diskettes of application packages. Typical single-user license agreements do not permit or condone this kind of copying. A typical single-user license agreement is shown in Figure 16–4. Many software vendors "try" to protect their programs from illicit and unauthorized copying by users who have not purchased the program. This has led, in turn, to the practice by "hackers" of seeking to break these copy protection schemes. Hackers will find and publish on community bulletin boards the patches necessary to override the protection schemes that some software vendors have incorporated into their programs.

A copy protection scheme has a very simple purpose: to prevent unauthorized use of the software by unlicensed users. These schemes may permit backups to be prepared, but the backups will not be executable. The backups can only be used to reconstruct the original manufacturer diskette, should that diskette become unusable. Once the backup is copied back onto the original, the original becomes an executable diskette again.

Copy protection schemes impose some moderate inconveniences. First, copy-protected software cannot be entirely executed from a hard disk, or if it is, the original manufacturer diskette must reside in a designated floppy disk drive (such as drive A). Operation of the program is slowed by the need to occasionally do a disk access on drive A to make certain that the manufacturer's diskette is there. With pure floppy-disk-based systems, the user may be required to do disk swaps whenever the copy-protected software wishes to check the diskette in drive A to make certain it is a legitimate copy. The interests of productivity are not well served by such activities.

The top-selling programs for microcomputers are also the most copied programs. For this reason, some personal computer columnists like Jerry Pournelle (*Byte Magazine*) and John C. Dvorak (formerly with *Infoworld* and now with *PC Magazine*) will suggest that one secret of software success is the lack of copy protection (Dvorak avows that this is one of the most important components of success.[2]) Whereas the absence of software copy protection may encourage the proliferation and exposure of the software, it does little to prevent users from

Software License Agreement

LICENSE. _________owns the enclosed software program ("Program") and all copyrights and other rights and interest in such Program. _________grants you a non-exclusive license to use the enclosed Program subject to the terms and restrictions below.

RESTRICTIONS ON USE: You may use the Program only on a single workstation or computer. You may not use the Program on more than one computer nor with multiple terminals or multiple computers in a network without a separate license for each computer or terminal. You may modify the Program or merge it into any other program but all such portions remain subject to the restrictions of this license.

RESTRICTIONS ON COPYING: The Program and documentation are copyrighted and may only be copied as permitted by this license. You may copy the machine-readable form of the Program only for back-up or archive purposes, provided that no more than three (3) copies are in existence at any one time without prior written consent from _________. You must maintain a record of the number and location of all such copies. You must include the _________copyright notice on any copy modification or merged portion. You may not copy, in whole or in part, any documentation which is provided in printed form with the Program.

RESTRICTIONS ON TRANSFER: You may physically transfer the Program from one of your own computers to another of your computers provided that the Program is used on only one computer at a time. You may not transfer the Program electronically over a network. You may not distribute copies of the Program or documentation to others. You may transfer this license together with all originals, copies, modifications, and merged portions of the Program and documentation, provided that the person to whom you transfer agrees to be bound by the terms of this license and notifies _________in writing. YOU MAY NOT USE, COPY, PRINT, OR TRANSFER THE PROGRAM OR DOCUMENTATION, EXCEPT AS EXPLICITLY ALLOWED BY THIS LICENSE.

TERM: This license continues in effect until terminated. You may terminate this license only by destroying all originals, copies, modifications, and merged portions of the Program and documentation, in any form. The license will also terminate if you fail to comply with any term or condition of this license. You agree upon such termination to destroy the Program and documentation together with all copies, modifications, and merged portions in any form.

FIGURE 16–4

A Typical Single-user License Agreement

purloining copies of the software for their serious business or professional use. For these people the software procurement methodology is simple: go find a friend who has the unprotected version of the package and make a copy of it. This is piracy (a federal offense) and it is punishable by imprisonment and/or fines amounting to thousands of dollars. It is appropriate to point out that such individuals compromise the interests of their friend in that it is the friend who is at risk, especially if that friend is a registered licensee. Most software packages have imbedded and encrypted serial numbers within them, and if the copied software package makes its way back to the software company for whatever reason, it is the friend who will be liable. The illegitimacy of the software package would be traceable to the friend because the serial number embedded in the software would be the same as the serial number on the friend's registration card.

SYSTEM PURCHASE CONSIDERATIONS

Whenever initial procurement expenditures are expected to exceed $5,000, it is good advice to use a formal procedure for procurement of microcomputer hardware and/or software. The formal strategy to be presented here is focused

Focus Feature

CAPACITY REQUIREMENTS PLANNING

Capacity requirements planning is concerned with a determination of the requirements in terms of capacity for the proposed system. For example, how many work stations are required? Must these work stations be connected? How much primary storage is needed for each work station? How much secondary storage is needed, and in what form? We begin with a consideration of work stations.

WORK STATION REQUIREMENTS

The number of work stations needed is usually determined on the basis of the number of users whose applications are to be computerized. Assume that accounting applications are to be computerized; and suppose that two clerks currently do all data entry into the accounting books manually, and that they spend all of their time daily doing nothing else. If it is proposed to automate the accounting functions of this organization, then two work stations would be required. (The automation of the accounting functions may not produce such gains in productivity that one of the two clerks could now do the job that two were doing manually.) If the manager wishes to make periodic inquiries into the accounting data base without disturbing the posting clerks, then a third work station must be added.

This scenario seems straightforward enough, but how many work stations should be included in the system if the data entry clerks are busy only 60 percent of the time under the manual system? These deliberations result in the analyst's having to give a thorough consideration to the typing speeds of the two clerks and to the number of characters that must be entered each business day.

Table 16–3 illustrates a technique for rough calculation based upon certain assumed typing speeds for the data entry clerks in an accounting organization. Suppose, for example, that 30 payroll entries must be keyed every day, one for each hourly employee, and that 200 purchase orders are received daily. Fifty percent of these involve new customers whose names and addresses must be entered into the customer master file. Each payroll entry requires exactly 138 characters to be entered. Each purchase order requires an average of 120 characters to be entered if the customer already has an account with the firm. If the customer does not have an account, a new account must be set up, which involves entering the customer's record into the customer master file. Each new customer record requires 165 characters on average.

Each data entry clerk is assumed to have a 75 percent productivity factor. This allowance compensates for coffee breaks and corrections to data entry errors. This would mean that out of each eight-hour day, six of those hours are actually productive. An average of 4,000 characters per hour conservatively estimates the productivity of the data entry clerks. How much time is required to get all of the data entered? To calculate this, the total daily data entry requirement in characters is determined, as shown in Table 16–3. The character requirement for payroll is clearly 138 × 30, or 4,140. The character requirement for purchase orders involving existing customers is 120 × 100, or 12,000. The character requirement for purchase orders involving new customers is (120 + 165) × 100, or 28,500. The sum total is 44,640. This number divided by 4,000 characters per hour yields the total daily requirement in hours: 44,460/4000 = 11.16 hours required. This just about fills up the productive time available to two data entry clerks in any given day. Hence, there is a clear requirement for two work stations now, and there must be potential for future expansion as the company grows.

PRIMARY STORAGE REQUIREMENTS

The capacity requirements for primary storage must be addressed on a per work station basis. For each work station, there must be a determination of the applications to be implemented. The application with the largest primary storage requirement is the one that becomes the determinant of how much primary storage is required at that work station. This assumes that only one application will be placed in primary storage at one time.

Work stations that require a RAM disk must have this requirement added to the primary storage requirement to determine the total bytes of random access memory required.

At least as important as the actual primary storage requirement is the potential maximum primary storage upgrade possible. A microcomputer with 256K bytes primary storage may not be sufficient for some applications,

TASK/ ACTIVITY	CHARACTERS/ RECORD	NUMBER OF RECORDS	CHARACTERS TOTAL
Hourly payroll	138	30	4,140
p.o. old customers	120	100	12,000
p.o. new customers	285	100	28,500
TOTAL			44,640

ALLOWANCE FOR NONPRODUCTIVE TIME: 25%
ACTUAL TIME AVAILABLE: (1 to .25) * 8 hrs/day = 6 hrs/day
ESTIMATED DATA ENTRY SPEED IN CHARACTERS/HR: 4,000
NUMBER OF DAILY HOURS REQUIRED TO ENTER DATA: 44,640/4000 = 11.16
NUMBER OF WORK STATIONS REQUIRED: 11.16/6 = 1.86, or 2

TABLE 16–3
Work Station Requirements Analysis

but if there is the potential of upgrading this to 640K or more bytes, the buyer need not be wary. Most microcomputers have this kind of capability, which lessens the criticality of the capacity requirements for primary storage. Of greater concern, then, is the maximum primary storage possible. In general this will be different from the address space, as discussed in Chapter 3.

SECONDARY STORAGE REQUIREMENTS

Capacity planning for secondary storage must begin with a consideration of the applications to be computerized, just as for work stations and primary storage. Based upon a consideration of these applications, there must first be an assessment of the types of secondary storage required: floppy disks, hard disks, RAM disks, cartridge tape, etc. In what follows we shall consider the type of secondary storage first before treating the actual capacity requirements for the type of secondary storage medium chosen.

RAM disks are a productivity advantage for any application in the sense that they will greatly speed up the disk-related processing activities of the application. However, they must not be regarded as permanent storage at this time. Therefore, some other form of secondary storage must be included in addition to RAM disks. The most conventional form of secondary storage is the floppy disk, be it 3½ inches, 5¼ inches, or 8 inches in diameter. The breadth of applications supportable by the floppy disk is broad indeed, and almost all packaged software for sale is placed on this medium. For this reason, at least one floppy disk is a necessity for all applications today. With the possible exception of cartridge tape, it is the slowest form of secondary storage available in transfer rate and access time.

If the decision is to use a pure floppy system without a hard disk, then the user must ascertain whether there is sufficient on-line storage to accommodate the most demanding of the proposed applications. If the decision is to use a floppy disk in conjunction with a hard disk, then the sizing question is different altogether. With a hard disk the capacity requirements of all the applications must be on-line (and resident on the hard disk) at the same time. This is especially true if the hard disk is nonremovable, which it usually is. Therefore, the hard disk must be capable of accommodating all the capacity requirements of all the applications at the same time. One particularly strong indication of a need for a hard disk is when the size of any one file exceeds the capacity of the floppy and the associated software is unable to split the file across several floppies. For such applications, a hard disk is an outright necessity.

Consider the capacity sizing question for a pure floppy system. Thanks to the removable nature of the floppy media, sufficient storage to accommodate only

(Continued)

one application at a time is required, namely, the application currently being executed on the work station. When one application is finished and another must be started, the user simply removes the diskettes associated with the former application and inserts the diskettes associated with the application to be executed next. Thus, as previously stated, the capacity sizing issue becomes one of determining the secondary storage capacity requirements of each ultimate application and sizing the secondary storage around the most demanding of these applications. It is important to point out that each application is supported by system software, application software, and required data files. In general, space must be allocated for all of these components on the secondary storage floppies.

For example, suppose that the accounts receivable merge/update program is one of the intended applications. At the end of each month, this application is run to merge the accumulated receivables detail (the file of receivables transactions that have accumulated since the previous month) into the master file of consolidated receivables, while simultaneously updating the customer file. Assume each record in the accumulated receivables file or the master file of receivables is 150 bytes in length. Assume that each customer record in the customer master file is 200 bytes in length. Assume further that never more than 500 transactions have occurred within any given month, that the list of existing and potential customers is not expected to exceed 600, and that, based on experience, the consolidated receivables will not exceed 1,500 records. Then it is possible to compute the required length in bytes of all the on-line files. To this must be added the length in bytes required for the application program and those components of the system software, which in general are required to be on-line. Suppose that the application program requires 57,000 bytes and the system software 24,000 bytes. Table 16–4 shows the required calculations for this single application.

It should be apparent that this application could be accommodated with dual floppy systems that store 360K bytes or more per disk. Such a configuration would provide ample room for expansion, should the need arise. Of course, applications that use variable-length records cannot be sized in this way.

Now suppose that, in addition to this program, other programs have been sized in a similar way. The

TABLE 16–4

Secondary Storage Requirements for an Accounts Receivable Application (Update/Merge)

FILE/ COMPONENT	BYTES/ RECORD	# RECORDS	BYTES TOTAL
Accumulated transaction file	150	500	75,000
Consolidated receivables file	150	1500	225,000
Customer master file	200	600	120,000
Application program			57,000
System software			24,000
TOTAL			501,000

TABLE 16–5

Applications to be Computerized and their Capacity Requirements

NAME	CAPACITY REQD. IN BYTES
Accts. receivable (update/merge)	501,000
Accts. receivable (print statements)	487,000
Payroll	195,000
Customer invoicing and order processing	556,000
Spreadsheet (Lotus 1-2-3)	480,000
General ledger	195,000
Accts. payable (update/merge)	325,000
Accts. payable (print statements)	286,000
Word processing	125,000

results are shown in Table 16–5. From the numbers given here, it should be clear that the customer invoicing and order processing application is the most demanding, and the one around which the floppy system should be sized. It is also apparent that a dual floppy system in which each disk has a capacity of 360K bytes or more would be able to accommodate any of the listed applications.

As another example, consider an inventory application robust enough to support 10,000 items of inventory. The files required to support this application are an item (inventory) file, a customer master file (the same one as required by the accounts receivable application above), a vendor master file, and a general ledger file. Each inventory item requires a 200-byte record, each vendor record is 100 bytes long, and each general ledger record is 150 bytes long. There are 300 vendors and 1,000 accounts in the general ledger. Table 16–6 shows the results of analysis like that shown in Table 16–4.

Several points regarding the analysis in Table 16–6 are worthy of mention. First, this application, like inventory applications in general, is much more demanding in terms of secondary storage than any we've looked at. In fact, the total storage requirement is so large that it requires seven on-line floppy disk drives if each has a total capacity of only 360K bytes. If a floppy system were to be used in conjunction with such an application, one would clearly want floppy-disk drives with much larger capacity than a mere 360K bytes. Second, there is a single file with a capacity requirement of two million bytes. If a floppy system were to be used to accommodate this application and the drive capacities of the proposed hardware are less than two million bytes each, then it would be necessary to check the documentation of the application program to see if multiple disk files can be accommodated by the software. If so, then this very demanding application could still be implemented on a microcomputer system with floppy disks only. However, performance would be slow and lots of manual disk swaps would be involved in maintaining files. A much better secondary storage arrangement could be configured through the use of a hard disk. A hard disk in this context would eliminate the manual disk swaps required. This, along with the much faster access times and transfer rates of hard disks, would greatly speed the processing of the inventory system and all disk-intensive applications.

What about the capacity requirements of a hard disk to support all of the applications listed in Tables 16–5 and 16–6? Since the hard disk is generally not removable, the capacity requirements of all applications must be simultaneously supported, if those applications are to use the hard disk. If we add up the capacity requirements of all applications listed in Tables 16–5 and 16–6, we obtain some idea as to the capacity requirements of the hard disk. The total is 5,540,000 bytes. This could easily be accommodated by a 20-megabyte hard drive. In this regard it is desirable to have the capacity of the hard drive exceed the proposed capacity of the planned applications by 60 to 100 percent or more, to allow for future growth in the capacity requirements of the applications.

TABLE 16–6

Secondary Storage Requirements for an Inventory Application

FILE/ COMPONENT	BYTES/ RECORD	# RECORDS	BYTES TOTAL
Item (inventory) file	200	10,000	2,000,000
Vendor master file	100	300	30,000
Customer master file	200	600	120,000
General ledger file	150	1,000	150,000
Application program			66,000
System software			24,000
TOTAL			2,390,000

TABLE 16–7
Work Station Requirements Analysis

Formation of a selection committee

- ☐ End users of the anticipated system should be included.
- ☐ Experts in microcomputer systems must be included.
- ☐ Determine the application(s) to be computerized.

The feasibility study

- ☐ Evaluate the cost-effectiveness of the proposed system(s).
- ☐ Evaluate the probable impact on the organization.
- ☐ Evaluate the economic impact.
- ☐ Perform capacity requirements planning to determine generally what software and hardware is needed.

Preparation of the Request for Proposal

- ☐ Prepare the RFP. Specify the capacity requirements in terms of the volume of transactions, number and length of fields in each record, and number of records total in each file as accurately as possible.
- ☐ Contact vendors, and transmit the RFP to them.
- ☐ Await their responses.

Evaluation of the proposals and selection

- ☐ Evaluate the hardware.
- ☐ Evaluate the software.
- ☐ Evaluate the vendor.

upon a **request for proposal,** or RFP. Retail computer stores are accustomed to writing proposals and will usually prepare one in response to an RFP at no expense to the customer. A formal procedure for microcomputer system procurement is outlined in Table 16–7.

Some remarks about the strategy outlined in Table 16–7 are necessary. The inclusion of users and experts on the procurement selection committee should be obviously desirable. If there are no resident experts in the organization, then management might wish to solicit the services of a consultant at that point. It is incumbent upon the members of this committee to decide upon the applications to be computerized, the extent to which these applications should be integrated, and to delineate any special requirements that might affect the configuration of the ultimate system as well as the final selection process.

The selection committee should conduct a feasibility study to determine the impact of the system under consideration on the organization. The study should consider the economic as well as the social and behavioral effects which the proposed computer system is likely to have. In general the selection committee will be interested in the extent to which the proposed system will be used and accepted by the rest of the organization. In the past when microcomputers were just beginning to penetrate organizations, the equipment was purchased and installed, but the intended users were reluctant or unwilling to use the new equipment. The feasibility study should include a needs analysis to ascertain that all the requirements of the target users will be accommodated by the system. The capacity requirements planning material presented in the focus feature on the previous four pages provides an analysis format that will enable the selection committee to determine the hardware requirements.

On the basis of the previous analyses, the selection committee is in a position to prepare the RFP. A prototypical format for the RFP is shown in Table 16–8, and the accompanying cover letter is exhibited in Table 16–9. The RFP should contain as much detail as would be appropriate for the vendor to adequately assess the requirements, and to "design" a system suitable for the needs of the organization originating the RFP.

The RFP format presented in Table 16–8 addresses three broad areas of concern: an introduction, software/hardware requirements, and vendor qualifications. The introduction describes the requesting organization to the vendor. Cur-

TABLE 16–8

Sample Request for Proposal (RFP) Format

Introduction

A. Description of the organization
B. Summary EDP requirements, present and future
C. Current EDP equipment
D. Groundrules for the selection process
E. Applications to be implemented

Computer and system requirements

A. Software requirements
   1. Operating system capabilities: multiprogramming, virtual memory, multitasking, multiuser, etc.
   2. Languages required (COBOL, BASIC, etc.)
   3. Utility packages
   4. Special features
   5. Applications software
B. Hardware features requirements
   1. CPU speed, word length, etc.
   2. Types of I/O equipment
   3. Primary storage capacity
   4. Secondary storage capacity
   5. Number of work stations (keyboards and displays)
C. Expandability of the system
D. Support required
   1. Backup facilities
   2. Availability of test time
   3. Availability of designers and programmers
E. Time constraints
   1. Delivery date for hardware and software
   2. Minimum throughput capacity

Vendor qualifications

A. Years in business
B. References/clientele

TABLE 16–9

Cover Letter for Request for Proposal

Dear

Our organization is presently giving serious consideration to the procurement of a new computer system. Our initial plans call for the installation of this machine within the next six months, with near-immediate implementation of four application packages. The four applications required include: payroll, general ledger, accounts payable, and invoicing and accounts receivable. A fifth application, inventory management, is scheduled for implementation in the spring of 199X.

We are currently in the process of system selection and are scheduling initial presentations from several vendors. With this in mind we have included a copy of a Request for Proposal. If you feel that your organization can provide the system attributes we require, then we would welcome listening to a one-hour presentation. This presentation will be attended by members of a consulting organization that we have retained for assistance in the selection process.

Within a week or two of these initial presentations, we hope to have narrowed our choice down to the two or three vendors who appear to have met our requirements best. Then we will begin a more extensive screening of the remaining vendors to determine which system best meets our needs. At that point more extensive requirements descriptions will be made available to the remaining vendors.

The enclosed Request for Proposal is divided into three sections. The first consists of a brief description of our organization, the system we require, and the automatic data processing capabilities we now have available. The second section details our requirements for a new system, along with some options we would find desirable. The second part also provides a brief narrative description of the applications we will require to have implemented within the next year. You will note that these packages are to be part of the system proposed. We have also indicated our time constraints for having this system in-house and installed, and we have indicated what support we feel is necessary. The third part is your opportunity to detail your qualifications for this procurement award.

If you have any further questions concerning this Request for Proposal, or wish to schedule a presentation with us, please call.

Cordially yours,

rent Electronic Data Processing (EDP) equipment should be described to the vendor if there is a need for interfacing the new equipment with existing equipment, which there often is. The vendor will also want to know the groundrules of the selection process, as well as generally what applications are to be computerized. All of these topics should be presented in the introduction.

The software/hardware requirements section describes the known software and hardware requirements. These do not have to be delineated in the detail suggested by the RFP format in Table 16–8, but some indication as to the operating system(s) desired, what languages and utilities are required, and what applications software is necessary would be very desirable. The RFP should also describe the number of work stations desired, whether these should be connected into a multiuser system, and what processing speed is required.

Under the computer and system requirements section of the RFP, it is important that the vendor characterize the expandability of the system. For example, does the system have expansion slots, which will allow additional users or hardware to be brought on-line at a later date? Or, does the system have an expansion port through which an expansion unit could be interfaced if necessary?

Then the RFP should describe the support required of the vendor, in the form of backup equipment, training, custom programming, end-user testing of the system, and so forth. The time constraints required of the vendor should also be delineated with regard to when the system should be in-house and up and running, and when the applications should be on-line.

The last section of the RFP requests vendors to describe their qualifications with regard to years in business, number of installations, and to provide a list of recent customers and clientele.

The selection committee should contact the vendors to determine their interest in bidding on this procurement solicitation. Interested vendors should then be transmitted the RFP with the understanding that a response will be forthcoming from the vendor within a reasonable period of time.

Once the proposals have been received, the selection committee's next job is to grade the proposals. Proposal grading is usually done by assigning a grade (between zero and one or between zero and ten) to each of the major attributes of the proposed system and its vendor. Listed in Table 16–10 are some major attributes upon which the proposals should be graded. Each attribute should be assigned a weight. Suggested weights are shown in Table 16–10.

Weight Determination

The weights are chosen so that their sum at any given level and within any given category is equal to one. Choosing the weights in this fashion will cause the ultimate grade of the proposal to fall within the same range as used for the grades assigned to each attribute. For example, suppose the grade range used for all attributes is zero to one, with one being perfection. Then the ultimate proposal grade will also fall within this range. A grade of zero would mean that the proposal has absolutely no worth, while a grade of one would be absolute perfection. The overall grade thus provides those who are considering it an assessment of how close to "perfect" the proposed system actually is. In addition to choosing the weights so their sum within any given category and level is one, the user must assign weights to reflect his/her subjective assessment as to the relative importance of the attribute. In that sense the weights assigned above are for demonstration purposes only. The user will want to adjust these to properly reflect his or her concerns. The weights in the far right column of Table 16–10 are found by multiplying the category weights for all categories that apply to the attribute. Thus for "languages" the category weights are .3, .5, and .3, respectively, which when multiplied together yield .045.

Grading Vendor Proposals

Grading vendor proposals is a three-step process. The first step involves assigning grades to each of the attributes. The grade for each attribute is assigned a number on a scale of zero to one (or ten), with zero representing no worth and one (ten) representing absolute perfection. It is best to do this in a comparative way so that grades assigned for each proposal appear side-by-side in a row. Next, the user computes the product of each attribute weight as shown in the last column of Table 16–10 with the grade assigned to that attribute. The resulting products are summed to arrive at the ultimate proposal grade. Table 16–11 shows exactly how this works.

TABLE 16–10
A List of Attributes and Associated Weights for Grading Vendor Proposals

		WEIGHT		ATTRIBUTE WEIGHT
Software	.3			
Systems software		.5		
utilities			.2	.03
languages			.3	.045
DOS			.5	.075
Applications software		.5		
application 1			.1	.015
application 2			.1	.015
⋮				
application 3			.8	.12
Hardware	.2			
Processor(s)		.5		
raw throughput power			.3	.03
software base			.7	.07
Secondary storage		.25		.05
Printer		.25		
paper feed mechanism			.2	.01
speed			.3	.015
quality of print			.5	.025
Upgrading Potential	.2			
Additional work stations		.3		.06
Additional memory		.3		.06
Software upgrade capability		.4		.08
Time Considerations	.1			
Equipment delivery date		.5		.05
Application on-line by		.5		.05
Manufacturer/Vendor	.2			
After-sale service		.5		.1
Option to buy		.2		.04
Reputation of manufacturer		.3		.06

After-Tax, Net-Present-Value Analysis of Proposed Cost

Present-value analysis has as its goal that of mapping all costs associated with microcomputer procurement to a specific point in time, namely, the present. This permits different payment schedules for different (or the same) systems to be compared. For example, one proposed computer system may cost $2,000 down and $300 per month for the next five years. Another comparable computer system may cost nothing down and $375 per month for the next five years. This latter computer system may also be purchased outright for $15,000. Which of these two

	ATTRIBUTE WEIGHT	PROPOSAL 1	PROPOSAL 2	PROPOSAL 3
Software				
Systems software				
utilities	.03	* .8 = .024		
languages	.045	* .7 = .0315		
DOS	.075	* .9 = .0675		
Applications software				
application 1	.015	* .7 = .0105		
application 2	.015	* .9 = .0135		
⋮				
application 3	.12	* .3 = .036		
Hardware				
Processor(s)				
raw throughout power	.03	* .5 = .015		
software base	.07	* .1 = .07		
Secondary storage	.05	* .7 = .035		
Printer				
paper feed mechanism	.01	* .8 = .008		
speed	.015	* .7 = .0105		
quality of print	.025	* .5 = .0125		
Upgrading potential				
Additional work stations	.06	* .9 = .054		
Additional memory	.06	* .8 = .048		
Software upgrade capability	.08	* .7 = .056		
Time Considerations				
Equipment delivery date	.05	* .5 = .025		
Application on-line by	.05	* .5 = .025		
Manufacturer/Vendor				
After-sale service	.1	* .8 = .08		
Option to buy	.04	* .7 = .028		
Reputation of manufacturer	.06	* .6 = .036		
TOTALS		.686		

TABLE 16–11
Computation of Overall Grade for Three Competing Proposals

systems is the least expensive? If the latter computer system is the least expensive, which of the two proposed purchase arrangements would be the least expensive?

To answer such questions, it is necessary to give consideration to the after-tax aspects of the purchase, as well as its present-value aspects. The tax effects of a microcomputer purchase will lessen the actual cost of the computer because of tax savings that will accrue. For example, a microcomputer purchased outright for $2,000 and used in conjunction with one's business can be depreciated over roughly five years. (Since there are frequent changes in IRS depreciation rules, the assumed depreciation period may change.) In what follows the combined effects of present-value and after-tax analysis are considered, in order to determine the real cost of a microcomputer purchase.

Net-present-value analyses require an estimate as to the cost of capital for the purchasing firm or individual. The cost of capital is essentially the interest rate at which money could be borrowed by that firm or individual. Essentially two formulas are used. One is the present-value-of-an-annuity (PVA) formula, given as follows:

$$PVA = A(1 - (1 + R)^{-N})/R$$

where A is the annuity amount, R is the interest rate or cost of capital, and N is the number of pay periods. For example, suppose that you must choose between paying \$100 monthly for 60 months for a five-year computer maintenance agreement, or paying an outright amount of \$4,600. On the surface it may seem best to pay the \$4,600 since that is less than \$100 × 60, or \$6,000. Your cost of capital is 12% a year, or 1% a month. However, to render a fair comparison, it is necessary to map all 59 future payments in the amount of \$100 back to the present. To do this we use the annuity formula above, in which A = 100, N = 60, and R = 0.01. Making payments in the amount of \$100 each month is analogous to paying an annuity in the same amount each month. The value of this formula in our case is the following:

$$PVA = 100(1 - (1 + 0.01)^{-60})/0.01 = \$4,495.50$$

Thus the present value of a \$100-a-month payment for 60 months is \$4,496 to the nearest dollar. Hence, it would still be better to pay the \$100 a month than to pay the \$4,600 outright, assuming a 12% cost of capital.

The other formula is the simplest present-worth formula, given by the following:

$$PV = FW(1 + R)^{-N}$$

Here PV is the present value, FW is the future worth, R is the interest rate or cost of capital, and N is the number of periods. Suppose that three years from now, you expect to save \$3,000 in taxes from the purchase of a microcomputer in the present. What is the present worth of the future tax savings, assuming the cost of capital is 12% a year? We can find out by using the present-worth formula with FW = 3,000, R = 0.12, and N = 3. The result is the following:

$$PV = 3000(1 + 0.12)^{-3} = \$2,135.34$$

Thus the present worth of the \$3,000 in future tax savings is \$2,135 to the nearest dollar. These formulas will enable us to do all relevant calculations in the present-value analysis. Of course, a microcomputer would greatly ease the task of calculation.

Table 16–12 shows the present-value, after-tax effects of a microcomputer purchase in which the computer system is bought outright for \$11,000 with an assumed cost of capital of 8%. According to existing IRS rules (which will be changed by the time this is printed), the equipment can be depreciated over a period of five years using the Accelerated Cost Recovery System (ACRS) method of depreciation. This method calls for 15% depreciation in the first year, 22% in the second year, and 21% in the third, fourth, and fifth years. The purchaser is assumed to be in a 27% tax bracket and has decided to purchase the maintenance agreement at \$100 a month. It should be apparent that the annuity formula was applied to determine the present value of the variable costs: the maintenance contract costing \$100 a month. The present-worth formula was applied to map the future worth of all tax savings back to the present. For example, the present value of the \$948 future tax savings in year four is computed as follows:

$$PV = 948(1 + 0.08)^{-4} = \$697$$

The tax saving column is computed by summing the depreciation and maintenance columns and multiplying this amount by 0.27 (27% tax bracket).

TABLE 16–12

Present-value, After-tax Analysis of Microcomputer Purchase

Assume the following:

Cost of capital	8%
Tax rate	27%
Equipment life	5 years
Depreciation	ACRS (15%, 22%, 21%, 21%, 21%)

NET PRESENT VALUE

Total Outflow	Fixed costs: $11,000	$11,000
	Variable costs: $100/mo	4,932
	Total Flow Out:	$15,932

	YEAR	DEPREC.	MAINT.	TAX SAVING	NPV
Tax Effects	1	$1,650	$1,200	$770	$713
	2	2,450	1,200	985	844
	3	2,310	1,200	948	753
	4	2,310	1,200	948	697
	5	2,310	1,200	948	645
	Total tax savings:				$3,652

Net-present-value, after-tax cost: $15,932 − $3,652 = $12,280

Note: All calculations have been rounded to the nearest dollar.

Suppose the computer system described above could be leased for $400 per month with a lease period of three years. At the end of the 36-month lease, the computer system can be purchased from the lessor for 20% of its original cost. Would it be more advantageous (from a present-value, after-tax point of view) to lease the system or to purchase it outright, assuming a 8% cost of capital and a 27% tax rate? Table 16–13 presents the five-year calculations for this method of financing. The calculations assume the equipment can be depreciated over five years using the ACRS method, just as for new equipment.

Relating the After-Tax, Present-Value Cost to the Grade

Once the present-value, after-tax cost of all the alternative proposals has been computed, it is possible to relate the cost to the proposal grade. This is done by means of a scatter plot, as shown in Figure 16–5. Notice that the horizontal axis is the present-value, after-tax cost whereas the vertical axis is the grade on a scale of zero to one or ten, depending on how the attribute grades were assigned.

Each number shown in Figure 16–5 above corresponds to a proposal. Each numbered proposal is positioned in the chart on the basis of its grade and its cost. Proposals worthy of further consideration are generally those that are on the efficiency frontier. It should be clear, for example, that proposal 4 would be preferred to proposal 5 because both have roughly the same grade or performance, but proposal 5 is much more costly.

TABLE 16–13

Present-value, After-tax Analysis of Microcomputer Lease-Purchase

Assume the following:

Cost of capital	8%
Tax rate	27%
Equipment life	5 years
Depreciation	ACRS (15%, 22%, 21%, 21%, 21%)

NET PRESENT VALUE

Total Outflow	Fixed costs: 0.2 * $11,000 = $2,200	$ 1,746
	Variable costs: $400/mo for 36 mos	12,765
	Variable costs: $100/mo	4,932
	Total Flow Out:	$19,443

	YEAR	DEPREC.	LEASE EXPENSE	MAINT.	TAX SAVING	NPV
	1		$4,800	$1,200	$1,620	$1,500
	2		4,800	1,200	1,620	1,389
Tax	3		4,800	1,200	1,620	1,286
Effects	4	$330		1,200	413	304
	5	484		1,200	455	310

Total tax savings: $4,789

Net-present-value, after-tax cost: $19,443 − $4,789 = $14,654

Note: All calculations have been rounded to the nearest dollar.

FIGURE 16–5

Plot for Relating Proposal Cost to Grade

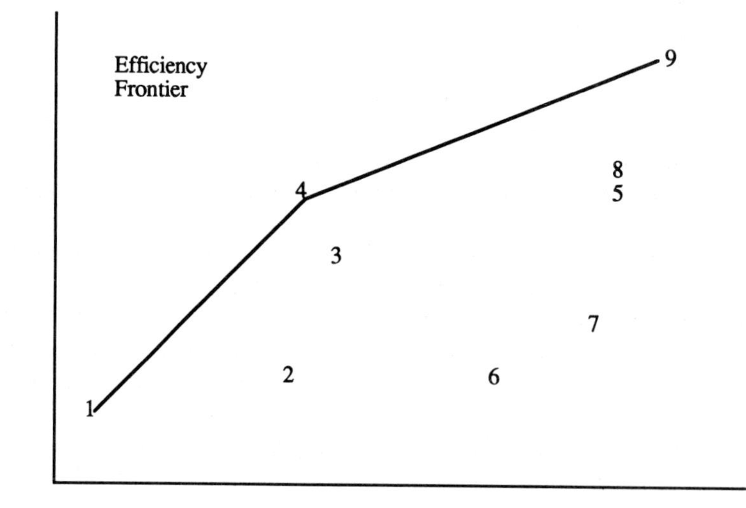

Summary

This chapter has provided methodologies for acquisition of software and for microcomputer systems procurement.

The chapter has addressed several important issues relating to acquisition of software. First, the issue of buying versus building from scratch was considered.

Almost none of the professional applications discussed in this book should be developed from scratch, unless the intent is to produce a marketable product. Too many excellent products are already available in each of the major software categories to justify a user developing his own word processing program from scratch, for example. Applications like word processing, spreadsheets, and data base management are generally quite homogenous. Hence, the existing base of generic software will usually satisfy these needs. Such is less true in the accounting application area. Much accounting software begins with a generic product which is then modified to meet the specific needs of the organization. The production application area is for the most part quite heterogenous and a good amount of the software in this area is custom software, in the sense of having been developed from scratch.

Next, the chapter presented a methodology for acquisition of software. That methodology consists of the following steps:

1. DEFINE the application to be computerized.
2. Develop a LIST of what software is available to support the application.
3. GATHER information about available packages.
4. NARROW the list of possible choices down to less than a half-dozen.
5. Obtain a hands-on DEMOnstration of the package.
6. EVALUATE in detail those that remain.
7. DECIDE—make a decision.
8. PURCHASE the package.
9. Learn to USE the package.
10. IMPLEMENT the package within the context of the intended application.

The chapter also provides a discussion of protection and piracy.

The system and software procurement methodologies are based upon an assessment of needs. For system procurement, the needs assessment is the basis for capacity requirements planning, the next step in that methodology. Capacity planning relates to the size and speed of various components that make up the computer system. The chapter specifically illustrated the use of capacity planning to sizing of primary and secondary storage and to a determination of how many work stations are required. Capacity planning applies to a determination of printer requirements as well.

Having generally determined what the capacity requirements are, the chapter suggested the use of a Request for Proposal to present these requirements to prospective vendors. It is expected that these vendors would then respond with a formal proposal. Each proposal would be graded using a weighting scheme. The present-value, after-tax cost of each proposed system is also determined using the methods presented in the chapter. Then the cost is related to the grade by means of a scatter plot, which enables the number of viable proposals to be reduced to two or three, eliminating the others. An ultimate determination is then made and the selected system is procured.

Key Terms

capacity requirements planning
conversion
fixed-price contract
object code
on-line tutorials
present-value analysis
procurement specifications
request for proposal
rights
source code

Self-Test

1. Briefly describe the methodology for procurement of microcomputer systems.
2. What is an RFP?
3. What are the steps for choosing the right software package?
4. Why does custom development of software from scratch to satisfy a general application not make sense today?
5. What is capacity requirements planning, and what role does it play in the system procurement process?
6. Describe the process of grading vendor proposals.
7. What is the purpose of an after-tax, net-present-value analysis?
8. Describe the process of selecting a microcomputer system, considering the cost and grade of the proposed computer system.

Exercises

1. A particular computer system costs $12,000 for the hardware and $4,000 for the software. The maintenance contract runs $100 per month. The purchaser plans to keep the system for five years. Assume the purchaser is in a 28% income tax bracket and the discount rate is 8% per year. No tax credit is allowed on the system, but it is depreciated in the same fashion as the examples. What is the after-tax present value cost of the equipment? (Use the ACRS method with the following percentages: 15%, 22%, 21%, 21%, 21%).

2. The same purchaser mentioned in exercise 1 above could avail himself of a service bureau. The purchaser's output and data-entry requirements are the following.

   (a) The data entry requirements are

Payroll	50,000 characters/month
General ledger	200,000 characters/month
Inventory	200,000 characters/month
Invoicing/order entry	250,000 characters/month

   Assume the data entry clerk can type 100 characters/minute when doing data entry.

   (b) The output requirements are

Payroll	3,000 lines/month
General ledger	10,000 lines/month
Inventory	10,000 lines/month
Invoicing	10,000 lines/month

   Assume the printer operates at 100 lines/minute.

   (c) The average CPU usage/month is estimated at 0.5 hour.

   The service bureau's charges are the following:

   (a) Initial outlay of $3,000 for printer and terminal.
   (b) Usage charges per CPU hour run $300 and connect charges run $7.00 for each hour logged on.
   (c) The maintenance contract on the hardware runs $40/month.
   (d) The monthly phone bill for this use is $50/month.

   Determine the total monthly variable costs. Calculate the present-value, after-tax cost of the service bureau for a 5-year usage period.

3. Assume in exercise 1 above that the $16,000 system can be leased for $550.00/mo., which includes the maintenance contract. The lease is for a period of 3 years. At the end of this time the system can be purchased for 10% of its initial cost. Calculate the after-tax, present-value cost of this strategy.

4. Assume in exercise 1 above that the purchaser has decided to borrow the money to purchase the system outright. Only 80% of the original cost can be loaned. The annual rate of interest on this loan is 16%. The loan is for a period of 5 years (60 months). What is the monthly principal and interest payment? Calculate the after-tax, present-value cost of this strategy.
5. Write and run a computer program to perform the calculations in exercises 2 through 4 above.
6. Discuss the subjective considerations that must be factored into any service bureau, buy outright, buy on time, or lease decision.
7. A client of yours plans to bring on line the following applications:

   (a) payroll

   (b) accounts receivable

   (c) general ledger

   (d) accounts payable

   He currently has 25 employees working for him. Last year 4,000 transactions were entered by his bookkeeper and 450 accounts were listed in his chart of accounts. He would like to keep two years of transactions on line at one time. Each payroll record is 200 bytes long, whereas each record for the other three applications is 100 bytes long. How much primary and secondary storage would you recommend?
8. An auto parts store plans to computerize its order-entry/invoicing/inventory/purchase order system. It has 20,000 separate items of inventory and 500 suppliers. The firm needs three display terminals, one for each of two sales clerks and one for the buyer. How much primary and secondary storage would be required? What hardware would you recommend to support this multiuser operation?
9. A small real-estate office consists of a realtor who wishes to use spreadsheets, real estate software, and data base management systems, and a secretary who needs word processing support. What specific questions need to be asked to decide what hardware is required to support these applications?
10. An office of attorneys is concerned about the following:

    (a) production of legal documents in a timely and efficient way

    (b) billing of clients in accordance with time spent on the case

    There are five attorneys in the office and two secretaries. What system would you envision as appropriate for this situation?
11. A doctor's office consists of two medical doctors, a receptionist, an insurance clerk, and a nurse. The doctors are concerned about timely payment of bills. Instead of a monthly statement of services rendered and charges assessed, they would prefer to present each patient with an up-to-date invoice upon departure and to request payment at that time. What configuration would you recommend? Is software currently available to support this? Describe how such a system might differ from conventional medical billing software.
12. Describe how the software procurement steps must be modified for purchasers who are considering integrated software packages only.
13. List the primary reasons why buying packaged software makes far more sense than developing custom software.
14. What are the major contractual considerations when software is to be developed by an outside vendor?
15. List the major attributes to be considered when evaluating word processing software. Refer to the chapter(s) on word processing if necessary.
16. List the major attributes to be considered when evaluating spreadsheet software. Refer to the chapter(s) on spreadsheets if necessary.

17. List the major attributes to be considered when evaluating data base management software. Refer to the chapter(s) on data base management systems if necessary.
18. Describe what tests you would apply in the hands-on examination of word processing software.
19. Describe what tests you would apply in the hands-on examination of spreadsheet software.
20. Describe what tests you would apply in the hands-on examination of data base management software.
21. List some major considerations in evaluating dealer support and service.
22. List some major considerations in evaluating vendor support and service.
23. Deciding which software package to purchase for a given application involves a consideration of the grade or quality of the software in relation to its overall cost. What are the major components of the cost of the software?
24. What three facets or activities are generally involved in implementation? To which of these does *conversion* generally refer?
25. What are the considerations relating to the decision to purchase a software package from a local dealer as opposed to purchasing from a mail-order house?
26. Describe what is involved in installing a software package.
27. What learning aids are included in most major software packages to assist you in learning to use the program?
28. Describe three methods for conversion. Which of these is the most efficient in view of the goals and costs of the conversion process? Which is the least desirable?
29. What is the purpose of copy protection?
30. Three different application software programs are being considered by a potential purchaser for a word processing application. The weights associated with each attribute and the grades assigned to each attribute have been determined and are shown in the table below. Compute the overall grade for each package and determine its performance/cost ratio. On this basis, which package should be purchased?

ATTRIBUTE	WEIGHT	PACKAGE 1	PACKAGE 2	PACKAGE 3
Ease of learning	.15	.7	.9	.9
Editing features	.14	.2	.7	.1
Formatting features	.14	.5	.9	.3
Printing features	.13	.7	.3	.8
File handling features	.15	.6	.8	.9
Ability to interface with other programs	.14	.9	.6	.8
Speed	.15	.6	.9	.3
OVERALL GRADE				
COST		$275	$395	$450
PERFORMANCE/COST				

31. Three different application software programs are being considered by a potential purchaser for a spreadsheet application. The weights associated with each attribute and the grades assigned to each attribute have been determined and are shown in the table on the top of page 573. Compute the overall grade for each package and determine its performance/cost ratio. On this basis, which package should be purchased?

ATTRIBUTE	WEIGHT	PACKAGE 1	PACKAGE 2	PACKAGE 3
Ease of learning	.15	.9	.5	.5
Editing features	.14	.6	.3	.6
Formatting features	.14	.7	.9	.7
Printing features	.13	.3	.8	.2
File handling features	.15	.5	.7	.4
Ability to interface with other programs	.14	.5	.6	.6
Speed	.15	.7	.3	.5
OVERALL GRADE				
COST		$200	$165	$333
PERFORMANCE/COST				

32. Three different application software programs are being considered by a potential purchaser for a data base application. The weights associated with each attribute and the grades assigned to each attribute have been determined and are shown in the table below. Compute the overall grade for each package and determine its performance/cost ratio. On this basis, which package should be purchased?

ATTRIBUTE	WEIGHT	PACKAGE 1	PACKAGE 2	PACKAGE 3
Ease of learning	.15	.3	.4	.8
Editing features	.14	.4	.8	.4
Formatting features	.14	.8	.7	.9
Printing features	.13	.5	.4	.6
File handling features	.15	.7	.6	.7
Ability to interface with other programs	.14	.9	.7	.9
Speed	.15	.3	.8	.2
OVERALL GRADE				
COST		$600	$125	$225
PERFORMANCE/COST				

References

1. Glossbrenner, Alfred. *How to Buy Software.* New York: St. Martin's Press, 1984.
2. Dvorak, John C. "Formula for Software Success." *Infoworld* 6, issue 50 (December 31, 1984).

Additional Reading

Datapro Directory of Microcomputer Software. Datapro Research Corporation, Delran, New Jersey 08075, 1984.

Checklist

The reader should use this checklist to comparison shop for hardware and software. A methodology for grading hardware and software based upon this checklist has been described in Chapter 16.

CHAPTERS 1 AND 2

Since no specific hardware components or software applications were considered in these chapters, no checklist is possible or necessary.

CHAPTER 3: HARDWARE FOR SMALL COMPUTERS

The following checklist is broken down into five basic categories—central processing unit, keyboard, secondary storage, printer, and display. A (y/n) notation after a feature indicates the response should be either yes or no.

Central Processing Unit

Vendor name ____________________

Vendor reputation ____________________

Product reliability ____________________

Microprocessor used ____________________

- Clock speed (Mhz) ____________________
- Number of data lines ____________________
- Number of address lines ____________________
- Instructions/second ____________________

RAM (Total bytes) ______
Maximum RAM configuration ______
ROM (Total bytes) ______
Serial interface (y/n) ______
Parallel interface (y/n) ______
Sound generator (y/n) ______
Potential for expansion ______

Display

Vendor name ______
Vendor reputation ______
Product reliability ______
Resolution in pixels ______
Size of character box (e.g., 8× 8) ______
Color (RGB or monochromatic) ______
If color, number of colors displayed and associated resolution ______
Smooth scrolling (y/n) ______
Tilt (y/n) ______
Swivel (y/n) ______
Brightness control (y/n) ______
Number of columns in text mode ______
Number of rows in text mode ______
Normal or reverse video selectable (y/n) ______
Non-glare screen (y/n) ______
Characterize its graphics capability ______
Compatible with CPU (y/n) ______
Crisp and distortion-free (y/n) ______

Keyboard

Any detectable key bounce (y/n) ______
Detachable (y/n) ______
Separate numeric keypad (y/n) ______
Auto-rollover (y/n) ______
Auto-repeat (y/n) ______
Audible key click (y/n) ______
Type ahead (y/n) ______
Separate cursor control keys (y/n) ______
IBM Selectric typewriter layout (y/n) ______
Programmable function keys (y/n) ______
Mouse-controlled cursor (y/n) ______

Printer

Vendor name ______

Vendor reputation ______

Product reliability ______

Printer type (dot-matrix, daisy-wheel, thimble, etc.) ______

Speed in characters/second ______

Graphics capability ______

Paper-feed type (friction-feed, tractor-feed, etc.) ______

If dot-matrix, size of character-box (e.g., 7×9) ______

Subscript/superscript capability (y/n) ______

KSR or RO ______

Maximum number of print columns ______

Choice of print fonts (y/n) ______

Multiple pass capability (y/n) ______

Print buffer size (minimum 2K—preferably 16K or more) ______

Parallel or serial interface ______

Bidirectional (y/n) ______

Logic-seeking (y/n) ______

Width of carriage ______

Print quality ______

Duty cycle ______

Secondary Storage

FLOPPIES

Reliability of disk drives ______

Number of disk drives ______

Average access time of disk drives ______

Capacity of disk drives (in Kbytes) ______

Format compatibility (list major machines) ______

HARD DRIVES

Reliability of disk drives ______

Number of disk drives ______

Average access time of disk drives ______

Capacity of disk drives (in Kbytes) ______

Support multiple users (y/n) ______

If so, is there individual file security (y/n) ______

Nature of backup ______

CHAPTER 4: SYSTEM SOFTWARE AND OPERATING SYSTEMS

High-level Languages

Structured programming support (y/n) __________

Object-oriented programming support (y/n) __________

Compiler or interpreter __________

Speed of compilation __________

Supports separate compilation (y/n) __________

Supports Intel 8087 and 80287 coprocessors (y/n) __________

Supports binary coded decimal (y/n) __________

Supports program chaining (y/n) __________

Maximum program size in bytes __________

Has built-in editor (y/n) __________

Supports overlays (y/n) __________

Speed of object code __________

Object code format (machine or P-code) __________

Maximum data segment size in bytes __________

CHAPTERS 5 AND 6: WORD PROCESSING CONCEPTS AND MECHANICS

Overall Orientation

Disk-based (y/n) __________

Memory-based (y/n) __________

Copy-protected (y/n) __________

Display Features

SCREEN-FORMATTED

SCREEN DRIVER

Text mode __________

Graphics mode __________

CURSOR MOVEMENT AND CONTROL

Arrow keys __________

Mouse __________

Editing Features

Command- or menu-driven __________

Insert and overwrite modes __________

Word wrap (y/n) __________

Right justification (y/n) __________

Search and replace (y/n) __________

Text movement ______

Block move (y/n) ______

Block copy (y/n) ______

Block delete (y/n) ______

Block write to disk (y/n) ______

File insertion from disk (y/n) ______

Column block operations (y/n) ______

Reformatting (y/n) ______

Case change (y/n) ______

Hyphenation help (y/n) ______

Programmability (y/n) ______

Undo command (y/n) ______

Windows (y/n) ______

Automatic-save during editing (y/n) ______

Multiple files open at one time (y/n) ______

Formatting Features

Adjustable margins (y/n) ______

Centering (y/n) ______

Indentations (y/n) ______

Adjustable line spacing (y/n) ______

Page numbers and headings (y/n) ______

Adjustable character width (10 or 12 characters/inch) (y/n) ______

Headers and footers (y/n) ______

Multiple line headers and footers (y/n) ______

Superscripts and subscripts (y/n) ______

Page breaks (y/n) ______

Printing Features

Editing during print (background printing) (y/n) ______

Print queues (y/n) ______

Printing to a disk file (y/n) ______

Printing in columns (y/n) ______

Chain printing (y/n) ______

Utilities

List processors (mail merge) available (y/n) ______

Spelling checker (y/n) ______

Style checker (y/n) ______

Grammar checker (y/n) ______

Outline processor (y/n) ______

On-line thesaurus (y/n) ______

Drivers

What screen drivers are available? ______

What printer drivers are available? ______

CHAPTERS 7 AND 8: SPREADSHEET CONCEPTS AND MECHANICS

Overall Orientation

Size of spreadsheet ______

Capability to link worksheets (y/n) ______

Supports three-dimensional worksheets (y/n) ______

Disk-based (y/n) ______

Memory-based (y/n) ______

Display Features

Windowing capability (y/n) ______

Displays cell contents of all visible cells (y/n) ______

Editing Features

Supports commenting of cell formulas (y/n) ______

Assessment of Speed

Recalculation speed ______

Retrieval speed ______

Save worksheet speed ______

Formatting Features

Money representation (y/n) ______

Date representation (y/n) ______

General representation (y/n) ______

Label or ASCII cells ______

Exponential representation (y/n) ______

Data Import/Export

ASCII ______

DIF ______

DBF ______

SDF ______

PFS ______

SYLK ______

WKS ______

User-defined ______

Drivers

What screen drivers are available? ______

What printer drivers are available? ______

Graphics

Supports analytic graphics (y/n) ______

Supports high-quality presentation graphics (y/n) ______

CHAPTER 9: RECORD AND FILE MANAGEMENT SYSTEMS

File Structure Limits

Number of fields per record ______

Maximum record size in bytes ______

Number of records per file ______

Maximum field size in bytes ______

Data (Field) Types

Money field (y/n) ______

Date field (y/n) ______

Zipcode field (y/n) ______

Phone number field (y/n) ______

Logical field (y/n) ______

Data Entry and Editing

Range testing (y/n) ______

Default values (y/n) ______

Requires specific values (y/n) ______

Lookup to external data tables (y/n) ______

Double-entry verification (y/n) ______

Required fields (y/n) ______

Must-fill field (y/n) ______

Forced uppercase (y/n) ______

Date conversions (y/n) ______

Automatic-incrementing fields (y/n) ______

Unique fields (y/n) ______

Automatic data entry ______

Data Import/Export

ASCII ______

DIF ______

DBF ______

SDF ______

PFS ______

SYLK ______

WKS ______

User-defined ______

Data Manipulation

Indexing (y/n) ______

Number of index files maximum ______

Can respecify indexed fields (y/n) ______

Sorting (y/n) ______

Number of sort fields maximum ______

Maximum number of open files ______

Table merging (join) (y/n) ______

Maximum number of tables merged ______

Command Strategy

Menu type ______

- Vertical bar (y/n) ______
- Horizontal bar (y/n) ______
- Pull-down windows (y/n) ______
- Pop-up windows (y/n) ______

Menu selection Function keys ______

- Point and shoot (y/n)
- Specified single key (y/n) ______

Support Materials

On-screen tutorial (y/n) ______

Manual tutorial/sample files (y/n) ______

On-line help (y/n) ______

Input Facilities

Preprogrammed data-entry screens (y/n) ______

Painted data-entry screens (y/n) ______

User-defined data-entry screens (y/n) ______

Number of screens per file (y/n) ______

Drivers

What screen drivers are available? ______

What printer drivers are available? ______

CHAPTER 10: DATA BASE MANAGEMENT SYSTEMS

File Structure Limits

Number of fields per record ______________________

Record size ______________________

Records per data file ______________________

Records per data base ______________________

Field size ______________________

Data Types and Sizes

Character? ______________________

Numeric? ______________________

Integer? ______________________

Floating Point? ______________________

Money? ______________________

Logical? ______________________

Date? ______________________

Time? ______________________

Long text? ______________________

Speed as Determined by Time(s) in Seconds

Sort data file by last name ______________________

Index records ______________________

Retrieve and display records without index ______________________

Execute entire report ______________________

Sort data file by salary ______________________

Data Entry and Editing

Range testing (y/n) ______________________

Default values (y/n) ______________________

Require specific values (y/n) ______________________

Lookup to external data table (y/n) ______________________

Double-entry verification (y/n) ______________________

Required fields (y/n) ______________________

Must-fill field (y/n) ______________________

Forced uppercase (y/n) ______________________

Date conversions (y/n) ______________________

Automatic-incrementing fields (y/n) ______________________

Unique fields (y/n) ______________________

Automatic data entry (y/n) ______________________

Calculated fields on entry screen (y/n) ______________________

Carryover data from previous record (y/n) ______________________

Data Import/Export

Error processing ______

ASCII ______

DIF ______

DBF ______

PFS ______

SDF ______

SYLK ______

WKS ______

User-defined ______

Indexing ______

Data Manipulation

Number of index files ______

Compound indexes (y/n) ______

Index values must be unique ______

Can respecify indexed field(s) (y/n) ______

Can respecify file definition (y/n) ______

Sorting (y/n) ______

Number of sort fields ______

Ascending order (y/n) ______

Descending order (y/n) ______

Maximum number of open files ______

Multiple record deletions and updates (y/n) ______

Math updates (y/n) ______

Text updates (y/n) ______

Table merging (y/n) ______

Maximum number of tables merged ______

Command Strategy

Static menus ______

- Function keys (y/n) ______
- Ctrl or Alt key combinations (y/n) ______
- Point to Command, press "Enter" (y/n) ______
- Specified single key (y/n) ______

Dynamic menus ______

- Function keys (y/n) ______
- Ctrl or Alt key combinations (y/n) ______
- Point to command, press "Enter" (y/n) ______
- Specified single key (y/n) ______

Typed commands ______

Whole words (y/n) ______

Abbreviations (y/n) ______

Mouse/other input device ______

Disk Requirements

Floppy disk (y/n) ______

Hard disk (y/n) ______

KBytes occupied by program files ______

Number of distribution diskettes ______

Total ______

Number required to run program ______

Copy-protected (y/n) ______

Support Material

On-line help (y/n) ______

Reference documentation (y/n) ______

On-screen tutorial (y/n) ______

Paper tutorial (y/n) ______

Audiotape tutorial (y/n) ______

Videotape tutorial (y/n) ______

Input Facilities

Screen definition ______

Painting (y/n) ______

Coordinate specification (y/n) ______

Automatic (y/n) ______

Programming (y/n) ______

Number of screens per file ______

Number of files per screen ______

Output Facilities

Report generation ______

Prompt messages for fields (y/n) ______

Arithmetic functions (y/n) ______

Aggregate functions (y/n) ______

Statistical functions (y/n) ______

Multiple file reports (y/n) ______

Predefined mailing labels (y/n) ______

Report definition method ______

Painting (y/n) ______

Form layout (y/n) ______

Automatic (y/n) ______

Programming (y/n) ______

Stored report definitions (y/n) ______

Headers ______

Footers ______

Printer setup facility ______

Output reports to: ______

Printer ______

Screen ______

Disk file ______

Query language ______

Multiple file access (y/n) ______

Stored queries (y/n) ______

Boolean expressions (y/n) ______

Phonetic searches (y/n) ______

Global searches (y/n) ______

Miscellaneous

DOS 2.0 directory support (y/n) ______

Change default directory (y/n) ______

Access from another directory (y/n) ______

Macros (y/n) ______

Customize keyboard (y/n) ______

Customize color screen (y/n) ______

User-access security provisions (y/n) ______

Data encryption (y/n) ______

Drivers

What screen drivers are available? ______

What printer drivers are available? ______

CHAPTER 11: GRAPHICS APPLICATIONS AND INTEGRATED SOFTWARE PACKAGES

Graphics Software Checklist

Type of graphics software (Table 11.4) ______

Analytic/presentation/both ______

Graphics editor available (y/n) ______

Types of Charts/Graphs Supported

Bar (y/n) ______

Stacked bar (y/n) ______

Pie (y/n) ______

Exploded pie (y/n) ______________________

3-D (y/n) ______________________

Line (y/n) ______________________

Organization (y/n) ______________________

Gantt (y/n) ______________________

Scatter (y/n) ______________________

Chart Features

Number of fonts ______________________

Number of data ranges ______________________

Number of type sizes ______________________

Free positioning of chart on page (y/n) ______________________

Free positioning of labels, titles (y/n) ______________________

Presentation Features

Picture library (y/n) ______________________

Slide-show feature (y/n) ______________________

Signs and banners (y/n) ______________________

Data Formats That Can Be Imported

1-2-3 files (y/n) ______________________

DIF files (y/n) ______________________

ASCII files (y/n) ______________________

SuperCalc files (y/n) ______________________

Image files created by spreadsheets (y/n) ______________________

Display Graphics Card Compatibility

Hercules monochrome card (y/n) ______________________

IBM standard color/graphics card (y/n) ______________________

IBM EGA color/graphics card (y/n) ______________________

Other color graphics card supported (y/n) ______________________

Input Devices Supported

Light pens (y/n) ______________________

Mouse (y/n) ______________________

Digitizer (y/n) ______________________

CHAPTER 12: OTHER POPULAR SOFTWARE FOR BUSINESS AND PROFESSIONAL USE

Desk Organizer Checklist

General Characteristics

Memory used (minimum/maximum) ______________________

Can redefine colors (y/n) ______________________

Moveable windows (y/n) ______

Expandable windows (y/n) ______

Allows removal of features already loaded (y/n) ______

On-line help available (y/n) ______

ASCII table (y/n) ______

Keyboard macro-enhancer (y/n) ______

Copy-protected (y/n) ______

Data capture and transfer facility (y/n) ______

Price ______

Notepad

File size limit ______

Word wrap (y/n) ______

Prints files or window only ______

Can merge files (y/n) ______

Supports block moves (y/n) ______

Produces ASCII only as well as own internal file type (y/n) ______

Can work on multiple documents (y/n) ______

Calculator

Number of digits displayed ______

Shows or prints calculator "tape" record (y/n) ______

Supports financial functions (PV, FV, PMT, etc.) (y/n) ______

Supports statistical functions (STD, VAR, CORR, etc.) (y/n) ______

Supports trigonometric functions (SIN, COS, TAN, etc.) (y/n) ______

Binary/hexidecimal math supported (y/n) ______

Exponential/scientific notation supported (y/n) ______

Can insert result in work (y/n) ______

Appointment Book/Calendar/Clock

Can print or display calendar for any month/day/year (y/n) ______

Programmable alarm clock (y/n) ______

Number of alarms allowed ______

Displays time (y/n) ______

Time interval for appointment book entries (15 min.–1 hr.) ______

Prints appointment book entries (y/n) __________

Allows single entry of repeating events (y/n) __________

Card File

Maximum characters per card __________

Variable or fixed card size __________

Maximum number of cards __________

Allows multiple decks of cards (y/n) __________

Prints cards (y/n) __________

Search any field (y/n) __________

Exchange data with major data base programs (y/n) __________

Communications Module

Auto-phone dialer (y/n) __________

Terminal emulation (y/n, and type of terminal) __________

File transfer capability (y/n) __________

DOS Functions

Directory display (y/n) __________

Copy files (y/n) __________

Format disks (y/n) __________

Change hard disk directories (y/n) __________

Project Management Software Checklist

General Characteristics

Memory required __________

Number of disk drives required __________

Hard disk required (y/n) __________

Has on-line help (y/n) __________

Includes tutorial (y/n) __________

Technical support available (y/n) __________

Copy-protected (y/n) __________

Capacities

Number of projects that can be managed simultaneously __________

Number of tasks per project __________

Maximum dollar amount handled __________

Scheduling unit (hours, days, weeks, etc.) __________

Number of levels of subtasks __________

Number of tasks displayed simultaneously __________

Number of resource categories __________

Can allocate scarce resources to tasks __________

System Inputs

Task descriptions allowed (# of characters) __________

Can get task information from libraries (y/n) __________

Can get resource information from libraries (y/n) __________

Insertion/deletion of tasks (y/n) __________

Allows readjustment of dependencies (y/n) __________

Allows multiple billing rates (y/n) __________

Allows fractions of a resource to be allocated (y/n) __________

Processing

Provides resource-leveling (y/n) __________

Allows gradual manpower buildup and cutback (y/n) __________

Shows critical path onscreen (y/n) __________

Shows slack (y/n) __________

Shows percentage of activities completed (y/n) __________

Allows comparison of progress with original plan (y/n) __________

Uses Critical Path Method (y/n) __________

Uses PERT method (y/n) __________

Can incorporate inflation factor into long-term projects (y/n) __________

Outputs

Produces project plan/activities list (y/n) __________

Produces Gantt chart (y/n) __________

Produces network chart (y/n) __________

Produces PERT chart (y/n) __________

Produces resource list (y/n) __________

Produces manpower use chart (y/n) __________

Produces calendar schedule (y/n) __________

Produces funding schedule (y/n) __________

Provides cost breakdown by budget category (y/n) __________

Knowledge Base

Supports rules (y/n) __________

Supports frames (y/n) __________

Supports "variable rules" (y/n) __________

Supports "examples" (y/n) __________

Accommodates uncertainty (y/n) __________

  Accepts uncertainty factors (y/n) __________

  Accepts probabilities (y/n) __________

Inferencing/reasoning Capability

Backward-chaining algorithm (y/n) __________

Forward-chaining algorithm (y/n) __________

Depth-first search (y/n) __________

Breadth-first search (y/n) __________

Procedural control (y/n) __________

Decision tree algorithm (y/n) __________

Explanation/justification Capability

Can provide answers to "why" requests (y/n) __________

Can provide answers to "how" requests (y/n) __________

User Interface

Provides LISP environment (y/n) __________

Provides PROLOG environment (y/n) __________

Knowledge-base editor (y/n) __________

Case facilities (y/n) __________

Graphic display __________

  Windowing capability (y/n) __________

  Displays rule tree (y/n) __________

Environmental Interface

Accepts inputs from sensors (y/n) __________

Can be linked with other languages and procedures (y/n) __________

Can retrieve inputs from other data bases (y/n) __________

CHAPTER 13: INTEGRATED ACCOUNTING AND INVENTORY SYSTEMS

Accounting Software Checklist

Accounts Receivable: Potential Capabilities

Interfaced to general ledger package (y/n) __________

Interfaced to order entry and sales analysis packages (y/n) __________

Accumulation of revenue and expense by profit center (y/n) __________

Aging reports (aging of accounts) (y/n) __________

Invoice preview (y/n) __________

Prints statements (y/n) __________

Prints customer invoices (y/n) __________

Prints general ledger journal (y/n) __________

Prints account labels for mailing (y/n) __________

Prints trial balance (y/n) __________

Prints customer account details (y/n) __________

Prints trial balance report (y/n) __________

Allows user to define aging periods (y/n) __________

Create, edit, add, delete records in customer file (y/n) __________

Capability to define fields and field widths in customer file (y/n) __________

Accounts Receivable: Capacity

Maximum number of customers in customer file __________

Maximum number of open invoices in invoice file __________

Maximum length of customer record __________

Accounts Payable: Potential Capabilities

Create, edit, add, delete records in vendor file? __________

Prints complete vendor file (y/n) __________

Prints checks (y/n) __________

Prints check register (y/n) __________

Prints open vendor invoice report (y/n) __________

Prints accounts payable aging report (y/n) __________

Prints cash requirements report (y/n) __________

Accounts Payable: Capacity

Maximum number of vendors in vendor file __________

Maximum number of invoices in vendor invoice file ______

Maximum number of checks per month ______

Maximum days invoices unpaid ______

General Ledger: Potential Capabilities

User-defined chart of accounts (y/n) ______

Interfaced with other accounting programs (y/n) ______

Automatic "Out of Balance" detection (y/n) ______

User-defined accounting periods (y/n) ______

Interfaces well with your business (y/n) ______

Prints balance sheet (y/n) ______

Prints profit and loss statement (y/n) ______

Prints general ledger (y/n) ______

Prints chart of accounts (y/n) ______

Chart of accounts password protected (y/n) ______

Permits budgets to be defined for each account (y/n) ______

Allows account balances to be compared with budgeted amount (y/n) ______

Allows account balances to be compared with balances this time last year (y/n) ______

Prints trial balance report (y/n) ______

Displays "Running Balance" and "Transaction Count" during entry (y/n) ______

General Ledger: Capacity

Maximum accounts in the chart of accounts ______

Maximum number of year-to-date transactions ______

Payroll: Potential Capabilities

Add, change or delete records in the employee file ______

Print the employee file (y/n) ______

Can change or update the tax information files (y/n) ______

At the end of a pay period: ______

- Calculates pay (y/n) ______
- Prints checks (y/n) ______
- Prints payroll register (y/n) ______

At the end of a month: ______

- Prints the monthly summary (y/n) ______

Prints the unemployment tax report (y/n) ________

Prepares a G/L transfer file (y/n) ________

At the end of a quarter: ________

Prints the 941A report information (y/n) ________

At the end of a year: ________

Prints the W-2 forms (y/n) ________

Payroll: Capacity

Maximum number of employees in the employee file ________

Inventory: Potential Capabilities

Add, change, or delete records in the inventory file (y/n) ________

Prints the inventory file (y/n) ________

Is able to calculate reorder quantities and to determine when a purchase order should go out (y/n) ________

Prints the following reports ________

Low stock report (y/n) ________

Over stock report (y/n) ________

Joint stock replenishment report (y/n) ________

Purchase orders (y/n) ________

Next receiver's report (y/n) ________

Inventory Systems Checklist

Sales Inventory Systems

Interfaces with accounting software (y/n) ________

Versatility of forecasting methods ________

Is able to do joint stock replenishment (y/n) ________

Facilitates vendor analysis (y/n) ________

Reports are useful and adequate (y/n) ________

Facilities for forecasting (y/n) ________

Computes economic order quantity (y/n) ________

Computes holding costs (y/n) ________

Computes ordering costs (y/n) ________

Add, change, or delete records in the inventory file ________

Prints the inventory file (y/n) ________

Is able to calculate reorder quantities and to determine when a purchase order should go out (y/n) __________

Capacity

Maximum number of items (records) in inventory file __________

Maximum number of fields per item __________

Maximum length of each inventory record __________

Interfaces with accounting software (y/n) __________

CHAPTER 14: DATA COMMUNICATIONS

Modems

Internal/external __________

Auto-answer (y/n) __________

Auto-hangup (y/n) __________

Auto-dial (y/n) __________

What sense lights? __________

Speed (in bps) __________

Answer/originate toggle (y/n) __________

Communications Software

Saves communication parameters in fields (y/n) __________

Printer on/off toggle (y/n) __________

Upload/download facilities (y/n) __________

Terminal emulation of what terminals? __________

On-line adjustment of communication parameters (y/n) __________

Auto-dial/auto-log-on (y/n) __________

Host mode/terminal mode capability (y/n) __________

CHAPTER 15: LOCAL AREA NETWORKS

Local Area Network Components Checklist

The following checklist is broken down into two basic categories—hardware and software. This list can be used to evaluate various LAN alternatives being considered. All such evaluation should be preceded by a well-defined set of capabilities and attributes that the local area network is expected to achieve. Once these are defined, it is easy to assign weights to each of the items in the checklist below and to then evaluate each LAN alternative accordingly. A formal methodology for grading alternative designs is provided in Chapter 16. The following list should be used separately for each LAN alternative that is to be considered.

Hardware

Cost per node ______

Number of nodes per segment ______

Number of servers per segment ______

Compatible with existing small computer(s) (y/n) ______

Transmission medium ______

Topology ______

Ease of installation ______

Ease of maintenance ______

Reliability ______

Shared peripherals available ______

- Serial printers (y/n) ______
- Parallel printers (y/n) ______
- Plotters (y/n) ______
- Tape cartridge backup (y/n) ______
- Other mass storage (y/n) ______
- Modems (y/n) ______
- IBM 3270/3278 protocols (y/n) ______

Software

Degree of compatibility with existing software base ______

Server(s) dedicated or nondedicated ______

Server(s) distributed or central ______

Server(s) "disk" or "file" ______

Security provisions ______

- File protection (y/n) ______
- Record protection (y/n) ______
- Log-in ID ______

Efficiency of usage of hard disk ______

Print spooling facilities ______

Processing speed ______

Electronic mail capability (y/n) ______

Electronic phone capability (y/n) ______

Community bulletin board support (y/n) ______

Store and foreward voice (y/n) ______

Utilities (y/n) ______

RAM Disk (y/n) ______

CHAPTER 16: PROCUREMENT CONSIDERATIONS

Since no specific hardware components or software applications were considered in this chapter, no checklist is possible or necessary.

Glossary

Absolute cell referencing Cell coordinates so designated remain unchanged when a formula is copied.

Access time The time required to position the read/write head over the disk track and sector containing the data.

Accounting systems Software packages designed to assist users with the accounting-related aspects of running a business.

Accounts payable module This module is used to track vendors' products, services purchased, and amounts owed to vendors.

Accounts receivable module In accounting systems, this module is used to track customers' purchases and to induce early payment.

Acoustic coupler The type of modem that connects between the phone and the computer by placing the telephone handset into specially formed cups.

Active area In a spreadsheet, the rectangle beginning with row 1, column 1, and extending as far down and to the right as the last cell with an entry.

Active cell In a spreadsheet, the intersection of a row and a column where the cursor is currently residing.

Activity In project management, a well-defined task with a clearly identifiable beginning and end that makes up a portion of the total project.

Address lines One of the four types of busses found on the motherboard that is used to pass addresses from the microprocessor to primary storage.

Address space The number of available storage locations (bytes of primary storage).

Algebraic operator A binary operator that includes the following: "^", "*", "/", "+", "−", and "=".

Alias In DBMS, the term for alternative names for fields. These allow the user to access a field by more than one name.

All-in-one program A program that contains multiple applications including word processing, spreadsheet, file management, graphics, and communications.

Analytic graphics Graphics designed to be easily and quickly obtained, which are tightly integrated with the origin of the data.

Answer mode A mode used by a modem to receive calls.

Application software The set of programmed instructions designed to perform a specific application through use of the system software and hardware.

Appointment book (electronic) The part of the desk organizer that keeps a record of appointments.

Arguments In spreadsheets, the values used within functions.

ASCII codes American Standard Code for Information Interchange, an established standard of codes representing each letter and number.

Assembler The translator for assembly language that converts assembly language to machine code.

Assembly language A language having a mnemonic equivalent for each instruction in a microprocessor's instruction set.

Asynchronous Data communications over the phone that are not time-synchronized. Also referred to as start-stop communications.

Audit trail A record of the transactions made with a data base. Permits tracing backward to the last update to find the errors.

Auto-repeat On keyboards, this feature causes the character associated with the key to be repeated across the screen when the key is held down for longer than half of a second.

Background printing The capability of the word processing program to send text to the printer for printing while the user edits text files with the word processor in the foreground.

Backup An identical copy or duplicate of some application program or data set contained on a floppy diskette.

Balance-forward statement Customer statements in which full transaction details since the last statement are shown with the balance carried forward.

Balance sheet A document that lists the major categories of the firm's assets and liabilities and sums these.

Bar cursor A cursor that is more than one character wide.

BASIC Beginners All-purpose Symbolic Instruction Code—the most widely used high-level microcomputer language.

Batch processing The ability to process a sequence of operating system command statements stored in a text file.

BDOS This is a Basic Disk Operating System, which contains a number of routines that are used by the CCP or are called directly from applications programs.

Binary operator An operator that relates a constant, variable, or expression on its left with a constant, variable, or expression on its right; hence, two operands.

BIOS This is a Basic Input/Output System, which contains all of the necessary functions to control the activities of the microprocessor, as well as all of the other hardware.

Bit A binary digit (the smallest unit of memory); an on/off device.

Bit-mapped display This feature delineates graphic images on microcomputer screens and contains pixels that correspond to one or more bits.

Block move This feature allows the user to move a block of text from one place in a document to another.

Boilerplate Text that has been carefully prepared and saved to be pulled from the library into a document at a later date.

Booting The process of loading the operating system.

Border In spreadsheets, the highlighted horizontal and vertical bars along the top and left-hand sides of the display.

Bps Bits per second.

Buffer A reserved area of RAM used for input/output to a disk or printer.

Bulletin board system A means of electronically connecting users that share the same interests.

Byte Composed of eight bits, the amount of storage space required to accommodate a single character.

CAD Computer-aided design.

Calculator (electronic) One of the many components in a desk organizer which provides all the features of a hand-held calculator.

CAM Computer-aided manufacturing.

Capacity requirements planning This refers to how many work stations, the amount of memory, and the printing capacity required to support the target applications.

Card file (electronic) The part of a desk organizer that provides the same function as an address book or desktop Rolodex.

CD-ROM Compact Disk-Read Only Memory, a revolutionary type of secondary storage allowing for data to be read from but not written onto.

Channel The complete system for connecting two devices for communication.

Character box A matrix of pixels that make up a character.

Character generator Used in text-mapped displays to send the pixels to be lighted for each character to the display.

Chart of accounts A set of accounts indicating the account number and the account name.

Chip A silicon surface containing thousands of solid-state devices sandwiched in plastic. The microprocessor and RAM are chips.

Circular reference In spreadsheets, this occurs when two or more cells contain formulas that depend upon each other to compute their values.

Closing In accounting systems, once a month the transaction files are opened by the general ledger and the amounts of each transaction are credited to and debited from the appropriate accounts.

Collision Occurs when two nodes on a baseband local area network try to transmit at the same instant in time.

Column width In spreadsheets, the width of the column, measured in number of characters.

Command console processor (CCP) This interprets the user's commands and directs processing to the appropriate routines within the BIOS and is loaded into primary storage at bootup; part of the operating system.

Common carrier Companies that offer a wide range of communications services, such as AT&T.

Communications software Software that allows a microcomputer to emulate a terminal when talking to other computers and to transmit or receive files to/from those computers.

Compiler This program converts the entire source code program to object code before any of it is run.

Concurrency The feature of different applications functioning in the computer's memory at the same time.

Contents format In spreadsheets, this prints/exhibits the formulas and screen-formatting information of each cell.

Control panel In spreadsheets, an area outside of the worksheet window that contains several special lines including the status line, the entry/menu line, and the prompt line.

Conversion The process of bringing into service one or more applications software packages and testing those packages for a period.

CP/M Control Program/Microcomputer; an operating system for 8-bit microcomputers.

CPU The Central Processing Unit which consists of two subcomponents: the microprocessor and the primary storage.

Critical path In project management, the series of connected activities with zero slack which will determine the length of the overall project.

CRT The Cathode Ray Tube or display screen that is used to communicate information from the computer to the user.

CSMA/CD A local area network access protocol called Carrier Sense Multiple Access/Collision Detect.

Cursor An indicator on the display screen that lets users know where they are on the screen. It may be a highlighted underline, box or arrow, a solid block or a blinking block.

Customer invoice In accounting systems, this is used for collection purposes and is usually transmitted to the customer at the time of sale.

Customer statement In accounts receivable systems, the primary instrument used to encourage payment; is mailed out monthly.

Daisy-wheel printer A type of printer that derives its name from the print element it uses that has the appearance of a daisy with "petals" on it.

Data base A collection of logically related data elements (files) organized in such a manner that several applications are supported.

Data base management system Also referred to as DBMS, is the software that controls the input, storage, and retrieval of information from the data base.

Data communications The electronic transmission of data from one device to another.

Data compression program The program is used when disk space is limited, to store a file in a more compact form.

Data independence Information in a data base is stored with a unified structure, and is free of transitive dependencies.

Data processing The translation of raw data into information.

Data protection programs Programs that can encode or otherwise protect a file so that persons without the proper password may not access or view it.

Data redundancy In file-oriented storage methods, the same information is typically stored in a number of files.

Data security The capacity within data base management systems to password-protect sensitive records or fields.

Date and time utilities Programs that work with a computer's internal clock circuit to record information about when a file was created or modified.

Decision structure This tests a condition (in programming) using an If statement.

Decision support system This is a system that supports and enhances decision-making activities. It offers sophistication and features that exceed what is available in spreadsheets.

Decision support system generator This provides the necessary modeling environment but contains no problem-specific "knowledge" or models and data.

Dedicated server A computer node on a network that is completely taken over and is not user-accessible.

Dedicated word processor Computers that were designed solely for textual processing.

Default value When these values are provided, no entry need be made in a given field as the program will use a built-in value.

Demodulation In data communications, the process of returning an analog signal to its digital form for use by a receiving device.

Dependent variable Variables that have their values determined from formulas involving cell references that can be traced back to the independent variables.

Determinant field The field that determines other fields in a file.

Device allocation programs These are used to control the input and output channels on a computer.

Device driver Computer programs which direct the hardware in specific tasks, such as turning on a floppy disk drive.

Device status programs These programs display the current device assignments.

Dif file Data Interchange Format, a popular spreadsheet storage method.

Digitizer A method of data entry used to transfer complex drawings into computerized form.

Direct-connect A type of modem that is connected directly into the phone line.

Directive A command by which the user communicates with the system software and hence the computer itself.

Direct search A method of retrieving a record from a file where the user must specify a computer-assigned record number.

Disk buffer A buffer filled with information to be recorded on a disk.

Disk format designators These control a disk drive to read and write disks in the format of another computer.

Disk formatter This will magnetically arrange a new disk into a track and sector layout arrangement that the operating system can read.

Disk server This feature enables many network nodes to access a hard disk.

Display format This creates an image on paper that duplicates the screen display.

Distributed server This server is characterized by every network node having a nondedicated server.

DOS Disk Operating System, the operating system.

Dot matrix A matrix of dots that can be turned on or off and that is used to form characters on printers and displays.

Dot matrix character box Each character on a display is formed by use of this box that consists of nine or more rows and seven or more columns of dots.

Downloading The process of receiving files during data communications.

DSS Decision Support System.

Editing This function involves moving the cursor to the location of the error and overwriting it with corrected text and/or inserting the correct text.

Electronic mail The sending of messages from one workstation to another electronically.

Electronic spreadsheet A computerized calculator designed to solve almost any type of mathematical problem where the data can be arranged into rows and columns.

Entry area The area where all data, formulas, and commands are entered.

Events In project management, a clearly identifiable point at which one or more related activities have been completed.

Expert system This system is intended to provide less sophisticated users access to the knowledge of the experts together with the experts' strategy for processing this knowledge.

Expert system shell The basic software systems within which expert systems are built and used and where there is everything except the knowledge base.

External port An external connection point through which data may be imported or exported.

Extracting from a worksheet Saving portions of a worksheet is one way of breaking up a large worksheet into smaller modules.

Field An element of data which, when grouped together with other related fields associated with a given entity, forms a record.

File A collection of records with each record being specified by a row or line.

File management system Software for data management where only one file may be open at a time.

File server This component enables many network nodes to access common secondary storage devices.

File transfer programs Programs that make copies of files from one disk to another or on the same disk.

Filter Program modules (in UNIX) that transform the data in the pipe.

Fixed costs Costs that remain constant regardless of the level of output.

Fixed-price contract A contract which requires the software agency to deliver a specified software product for a fixed price.

Fixed record length A feature where all records are the exact same length in the file.

Flatfile Any file whose records are all of the exact same length.

Floating-point coprocessor A chip designed to do hardware floating-point arithmetic (fractions and decimal numbers).

Form A preprogrammed screen or printed report.

Form-oriented Also referred to as a screen-driven system, this feature uses forms or screens for all data manipulation activities.

Formula This uses cell names or coordinates to perform an action much like an algebraic formula uses variable names.

Forward reference In spreadsheets, when cells derive part of their values from areas that follow them in the calculation order.

Frequency division multiplexing This feature describes how multiple signals are transmitted simultaneously through the same medium.

Friction-feed In a printer, the process where paper is drawn through by pressing it between rollers and utilizing the friction that exists between them.

Full-duplex Transmission that takes place in both directions at the same time.

Function A pre-defined process or calculation, used in spreadsheets and DBMSs.

Gantt chart In project management, this chart shows all the tasks of a project on a time line with the critical path highlighted.

Gateway server This component permits nodes on networks of different architecture to communicate.

General ledger module This module maintains the basic corporate ledger accounts and prints *pro forma* financial statements.

Goal-seeking The ability to establish targets for certain "output" or goal variables, and to have the DSS program find what inputs are required to achieve the outputs.

Graphics editor This feature enables the user to add text, color, and shade-in certain objects, label axes on a graph, rotate the image, enlarge or diminish the graph, and so on.

Half-duplex Transmission that takes place in both directions, but not simultaneously.

Handshaking The means by which two data transmission devices get prepared to send and receive data between themselves.

Hardcopy The printed output off a computer.

Hardware The physical equipment used in the microcomputer system.

Icon Small picture representing the thing about which some action is to be taken.

Independent variable Variables which are not dependent on any other values contained in the worksheet.

Indexed sequential search A method of retrieving records from a file where one or more index files are maintained in addition to the original file.

Inference engine Provides the actual reasoning process and is capable of using the knowledge contained in the knowledge base to infer new knowledge.

Information Facts that have implications for action.

Information utility A data base or collection of data bases, or an on-line news service, which makes its information available to dial-up users (usually for a fee).

Insert mode The mode in which new text is entered at the location of the cursor, and any previously entered material is moved to the right.

Installation The process of training the users of the system, testing the system to ascertain its proper functionality, and bringing the system on-line.

Installing a printer A process that ensures the codes from a program being used can be understood by the printer.

Integrated software Any multi-application product that allows easy transfer of data between applications, and supports a common set of user interface conventions.

Integrating environment software This software represents a software layer between the system software and the application software.

Interface device A device that repackages the information sent from the CPU into a format that is usable by the device attached to the interface.

Interpretive prompting Once the first letter of a command has been entered, the remainder of the command will be written for you in the entry area.

Inventory system This module will track the inventory levels of any and all items carried for sale.

Join A relational table operation in which two files are joined together.

Joystick An electromechanical device used for input into the computer.

Justified Text that is spread so that both left and right margins are straight.

Key A field with a specified value or range used for searching and sorting.

Key definition program This program allows the user to write command sequences, long strings, or even entire paragraphs and store them in memory for rapid recall.

Knowledge acquisition engine This feature facilitates the acquisition of knowledge and usually contains an editor for entering and editing the knowledge and debugging tools.

Knowledge base A collection of rules and procedures that prescribe how information is to be transformed into action.

Label Text that identifies a cell. This can be used in place of the ordinary cell designations in some spreadsheet programs.

Leased line Leasing telecommunication lines from common carriers.

Left margin The blank columns on the far left side of the page.

Library Indexed collections of text files saved on a floppy or hard disk.

Light pen An input device that provides a way of drawing directly onto a screen.

Line The number of spaces of text that can be displayed horizontally on the screen or printed on a page.

Line length The number of spaces of text from the left margin to the right margin.

Line spacing The number of lines printed per inch.

List processor Sometimes referred to as a print merge program, this can combine the form letter and the mailing list to produce an unlimited number of "personalized" documents.

Local area network User-owned and operated networks used in local environments.

Logical operator The operators AND, OR or NOT which may be used within the logical function IF.

Macro A sequence of keystrokes or commands that is saved so it can be played back when needed.

Macro languages Allow the user to create and assign a name to a stored sequence of commands (macro).

Mainframe computer A large computer that is fast, has a great deal of storage, is expensive and requires special wiring, air conditioning, and a data processing staff.

Margins The blank columns at the left or right of the page and the blank lines at the top or bottom of the page.

Memory resident software Software that resides in memory even while other programs are being run.

Menu An on-screen listing of available commands. Some programs use menus as reminders of the keys that access the various commands.

Menu line A line or lines used to display the major options (commands) available to the user.

Microcomputer Any computer whose processor is entirely contained on one chip called a *microprocessor.*

Microprocessor A processor on a single integrated circuit or chip that performs all arithmetic and logical operations and is responsible for overall system control.

Microprocessor family Chips that share a common core of instructions are said to be in this family.

Milestones In project management, an event at which one or more related activities have been completed.

Mnemonic A memory aid that enables directives to the computer to be more easily remembered by users.

Modem A device that allows text and data to be transmitted to other computers via the phone lines.

Modulation The process of using a modem to convert the computer's digital signal into an analog signal that can be sent over telephone lines.

Modula-2 A language introduced in the early 80s in an effort to correct some of Pascal's shortcomings.

Mouse A small device that the user rolls on a table top to control movement of the cursor on the screen.

Multitasking Allows the computer to carry out more than one task at a time.

Multiuser Simultaneous access by several users to the same computer or the same data.

Nanosecond 10 to the minus 9 (10^{-9}) seconds.

Natural language processing The computer attempts to decipher commands that were entered without regard to syntax and structure.

Node The point on a network where a computer or terminal is connected.

Notepad (electronic) Part of the desk organizer that allows the user to record thoughts as they occur.

Object code This refers to the machine-language instructions that were generated when the source code was translated by the compiler.

Office automation The term used to describe an office in which managerial access to information is more or less automated.

On-line tutorials Software on a diskette that helps instruct the user in how to use another software package.

Open-item statement This feature carries purchase details along on successive statements until an invoice is paid in full.

Operating system A collection of related computer programs used to supervise and direct the tasks and operations engaged in by the hardware.

Operator Usually binary, any of the operations represented by +, −, /, *, ^, (), >, >=, =, <=, <, <>.

Originate mode A mode used by the modem to call another computer.

Orphan When the first line of a paragraph prints at the bottom of a page.

Overwrite mode This mode allows the typist to replace text at the cursor with the new entry.

Packet-switching network Data to be sent between major cities is collected and transmitted in bundles or packets.

Page break A horizontal line across the screen that indicates where the page ends and another begins.

Page length The total number of lines on the page. For an eleven-inch paper at six lines per inch, there are 66 lines.

Page offset The blank spaces on the lefthand side of the page to the left of the left margin.

Pagination The determination of where page breaks occur.

Parallel port The port through which a byte is sent over eight send wires, usually from computer to printer.

Parallel transmission This type of transmission utilizes eight wires to send signals and additional wires for handshaking and control; used to connect peripherals.

Parity bit In asynchronous (serial) transmission, a special bit transmitted after a byte so that the sum of the bits will always be even or odd.

Pattern recognition The recognition of a signature, handwritten characters, or voice recognition.

Payroll An accounting module that is responsible for tracking employees within the firm in terms of hours worked, salary due, deductions required, etc.

Peripheral A hardware computer component that is exterior to the system unit.

Peripheral communication Short distance communications that do not require complex software or communications equipment.

Pert chart This type of chart shows activities as lines and uses nodes to denote the completion of activities or milestones.

Picosecond 10 to the minus 12 (10^{-12}) seconds.

Pipe The UNIX name for a channel through which data flows.

Posting The accrual of each transaction into the appropriate account.

Presentation graphics Graphics that require a high degree of polish since the graphics are intended for presentation or viewing by others.

Present-value analysis A type of analysis where cash payments to be made in the future are discounted back to the present in order to reflect the time value of money.

Primary storage Storage that is part of the central processing unit and consists of RAM and ROM.

Printed circuit board The motherboard or planar board in which all integrated circuits are attached.

Print queue The queuing or chaining of a number of document files that are to be printed in a specific order.

Print queue managers Also called print spoolers, these can send files to the printer while the computer is being used for other jobs.

Procedural language In a DBMS, this type of language provides significant advantages over either form-oriented or menu-driven DBMS.

Procedure Modules that perform the actual processing and make up the program body in Pascal programs.

Procurement specifications Detailed descriptions of what a computer system is expected to do.

Product families Individually marketed software packages produced by the same vendor that will work together.

Profit and loss statement The business statement that reflects the sales and cost performance of the firm for the period in question or for the year to date.

Program debuggers These features are used to display and alter the contents of a disk program file.

Project Any undertaking which can be broken down into smaller tasks or activities.

Project control Also referred to as project monitoring, this process allows the manager to see how a project is progressing in relation to the project plan.

Project management Project planning and project control.

Project planning The development of a detailed plan for completing the project under consideration.

Prompt area The area used to display messages while you are making menu selections or entering commands.

Protocol The convention by which sending and receiving devices will converse to control the message that must be transmitted.

Pull/down, pull/up, pop-up menus Temporary "windows" that present the user with a set of selection alternatives that relate to a particular function. Once the selection is made, the menu disappears.

Pulse signal In parallel transmission of an eight-bit byte, a pulse is sent between each byte to ensure that all eight bits have been received before the first bit of the next byte arrives.

Query language A group of commands that can access the data base without requiring a program.

RAM Random Access Memory.

Ram disk emulators Sets aside a portion of the user's available RAM to be used as if it were another disk drive.

Range Any rectangular area of the worksheet.

Range checking Prevents the entry of grossly erroneous data into a field by only accepting values in a certain range.

Raster-scan crt A cathode ray tube that is irradiated by means of an electron gun that scans rows left to right.

Record All the information associated with a single entity whose data is a component in a file.

Record-locking Two or more users can be working in the same data base file but may not simultaneously access the same record.

Relational data base management system A type of system designed to manipulate information that may be stored n more than one file by means of the relational algebra.

Relational operator A binary operator which uses any of the following: >, >=, =, <=, <.

Relative cell referencing When the copy command is used to copy formulas, cell references in the formulas are adjusted so they have the same relative position to the cell into which they are copied.

Remote processing All computing jobs are performed on centrally located equipment, but computer users are geographically dispersed.

Request for proposal A document transmitted to computer vendors describing the computer system desired and the application to be performed on it.

Resources The personnel, equipment, or money needed to complete a project.

RGB Red, Green and Blue (the primary colors); a type of color monitor.

Right margin The blank column on the far right side of the page.

Routing server This enables nodes of like architecture to communicate over long-haul network connections.

Scanner A device for inputting a paper image into a computer.

Scrolling The movement of text or data across a computer screen—either up, down, left, or right.

Search Finding the appropriate word, phrase, or record.

Search programs Programs that can scan through files for key words supplied by the user, then display or print any records in which the key words are present.

Search and replace A search for a particular word or phrase followed by replacement of the word or phrase.

Secondary storage Permanent (nonvolatile) storage. The two basic types of secondary storage are the hard disk and the floppy disk.

Select One of three fundamental operations of relational algebra.

Sequence structure Statements are executed in sequence or in the order of their appearance, or one after the other.

Sequential search This type of search allows for a record-by-record check on any field.

Serial transmission In this type of transmission data transmitted is sent out serially in bits, with one bit following the other sequentially.

Shell An additional layer of system software that processes additional commands.

Simplex Data that is transmitted in one direction only.

Slack The longest time that an activity may be delayed without causing a delay in the overall project.

Small computer Another term for a microcomputer.

Softcopy Displayed output.

Software The programmed instructions necessary to drive the hardware in those tasks the user wants done.

Sort To arrange data or text in virtually any conceivable manner.

Sort programs Programs available to arrange data or text in virtually any conceivable manner.

Source code This refers to the high-level language statements that comprise the program developed by the vendor.

Space A character position within a line filled with nothing.

Specialized common carrier Communications companies that offer a restricted number of services.

Spreadsheet merging The process of pulling in one worksheet and then loading another worksheet file.

Start bit This feature declares the beginning of a byte transmitted. The start bit is always a zero.

Status line This feature shows the name of the document being worked on and the location of the cursor within the document.

Stop bit This declares the end of a byte transmitted and is always a one.

Structured programming A complicated procedure that is broken into successively smaller portions which take the form of the loop, the decision, or the sequence structure.

Substring search A search for the occurrence of a string appearing anywhere within a field.

Supercomputer A very large computer with a great deal of memory that is used for scientific data processing.

Synchronized windows A feature represented by both windows scrolling together.

Synchronous communications A type of communication where the sending and receiving devices synchronize internal clocks when a beginning of transmission signal is sent over the line.

Systems software The housekeeping or host software that interfaces directly with the hardware and with the user or applications software.

System unit Consists of CPU and secondary storage, primary storage, and disk drives.

Telecommunications The type of communication that occurs over telephone lines.

Telecommuting The ability to perform almost any type of office work at home and transmitting the results to the office electronically.

Template A worksheet model devoid of problem specific data.

Terminal An unintelligent device consisting of a keyboard and display or print mechanism.

Terminal emulation The ability to use the command sequences of another terminal.

Text-mapped display Displays consisting of a matrix of character positions.

Tiling A feature where all windows on a screen are sized exactly to fit on the screen with no overlap.

Token An electronic device for sending or carrying a message consisting of data from one node to another.

Topology The geometry or physical shape of the network.

Touch screen A type of input device that requires the use of the finger to point to some object on the screen.

Track balls An electromechanical device for input to the computer.

Tractor-feed A process of paper-feeding where sprockets are used to mesh with the perforations on the edges of the fanfold paper to pull the paper through the print-platen.

Transceiver In baseband LAN's, the tap into the cable to transmit information is accomplished by this device.

Transfer rate The rate per second that bits can be transferred between secondary and primary storage.

Transitive dependency This occurs when one field determines another, which in turn determines another, all within the same file.

Type-ahead The storing of keystrokes on a keyboard buffer when the processor is busy doing something else.

Uploading In data communications, the sending of a file.

User interface The various ways in which system software and applications software may interact with users.

User prompts These are prompts from the computer that elicit more information from the user.

Utilities Programs that may perform functions as diverse as recovering files from a damaged disk.

Validation This is the process of submitting the worksheet model for scrutiny by others closely associated with the project.

Value A simple number or character data (comments, titles, or even necessary data elements).

Value-added carrier Companies that provide a number of specialized services for the transmission of computerized data.

Variable costs Costs that vary with the amount of resources used or output.

Variable record length This feature uses only the number of bytes required for the data regardless of the specified length.

Verification This is the process of performing a manual recalculation for comparison with the computerized spreadsheet calculations.

Voice recognition The recognition by the computer of voice commands.

Wait state A period of time in which the microprocessor waits on primary storage.

Wide area network Two or more computers conversing with each other over distances.

Widow When the last line of a paragraph prints at the top of a page.

Windows Partitions on the screen that allow the user to view several applications simultaneously.

Word-length The number of bits processed internally.

Word processing The entry, manipulation, storage, and retrieval of written communication.

Word wrap The feature characterized by the action that when the right margin is reached, the cursor and any word that will not fit automatically go onto the next line.

Worksheet The grid area that will be used for the building of calculations and displaying the results.

Worksheet window The area where the results of all entries will be displayed on the worksheet.

Write-protect notch When this is covered, data cannot be written onto the diskette.

Index

ABI/Inform, 513
Ability Plus, 408
Absolute cell referencing, 253
Accelerator cards, 58
Access time, 63
Accounting applications, 17, 34
Accounting systems, 457
Accounts payable (A/P), 457–458
Accounts payable systems, 479–484
Accounts receivable (A/R), 457–458
Accounts receivable systems, 467–479
Acoustic coupler modem, 504
Active area, 228
Active cell, 219, 243
Activity, 433
Adam, James, 381
Adding records (DBMS), 367
Address bus, 57
Address lines, 60
Address space, 59
Advice Language/X, 447
Aktronics, 408
Alberta-Hallam, Teresa, 23
Aldus Pagemaker, 180–181
Algebraic expressions, 263
Alias, 366
Allen, Warren W., 491
All-in-one program, 405
Alpha Software, 408
Alvernaz, Bil., 24
Amdek, 29
American Business Systems, 463
Analog signals, 528–532
Analytic graphics, 395
Answer mode, 504
Answer Series, 408
APPEND (dBASE III Plus), 379–380
Apple 1, 9
Apple Computer Inc., 6, 80
Applications environment, 89, 101–102
Applications software, 15, 27, 34
Appointment book (electronic), 427
Arguments (of a function), 261
Artwork and Brushwork, 397
ASCII codes, 32, 508–509
Assembly language, 102
ASSIST (dBASE III Plus), 376
AST Research, Inc., 58
Asynchronous communication, 507
Attribute, 357
Audit trail (DBMS), 361
Aura, 408
Austin, Ronald, 496
AUTOEXEC.BAT, 121
The Automated Office, 25
Automated Reasoning Tool (ART), 447
Automatic save, 143
Auto-repeat, 75

Background printing, 176
Background tasking, 99
Backup, 51
Balance-forward statement, 471
Balance-only statement, 471
Balance sheet, 464
Banahan, Mike, 115
Baseband LAN, 532–535
BASIC, 103
Basic Disk Operating System (BDOS), 90
Basic Input/Output System (BIOS), 90
Batch file, 121
Batch processors, 111
Bernoulli box, 66
Berst, Jesse, 24
Bidirectional print, 79
Bit, 31
Bit-mapped display, 399
Bits per second (bps), 503
Block manipulation, 163
Block operations, 143
Boilerplate, 167
Boolean operators, 360
Booting, 30, 60
Bootstrap program, 38
Border, 243
Borders, 218
Borland International, 332, 430
Bottom margin, 161
BPI Systems, Inc., 463
Bps (bits per second), 503
Bricklin, Dan, 219
Briefcase computer, 37
Broadband LAN, 529–532
Brooner, E. G., 373
Brown Bag Software, 432
Brown, Jerald R., 24
BRS After Dark, 515
Bulletin Board Systems, 514
Bunnell, David, 86
Bus, 57
Business Software, 25
Bus topology, 525
Byers, Robert A., 373
Byte, 21, 25, 30

C, 106
CAD/CAM, 393
Calculated field, 334
Calculation (DBMS), 361
Calculator (desk organizer), 427
Camp, James L., 491

Canning, Richard G., 86
Capacity requirements planning, 543
Capture buffer, 511
Card file (electronic), 427
Cartridge tape, 70
Cash requirements report, 484
Castro, Luis, 373
CATV, 527
CD-ROM disks, 66
Central processing unit, 27, 30
Central retransmission facility, 530
Certiflex Systems, 463
CGA display, 74
Chang, Dash, 411
Channel, 499, 502
Character box, 400, 402
Character generator, 400
Character width, 141
Chart of accounts, 461
Check register, 484
Check and stub, 484
Chip, 30
Circular references, 227
Clark, Thomas D., 24
Clock rate, 68
Close, Kenneth S., 277
Closing, 460
Coaxial cable, 526–528
COBOL, 352
Coburn, Edward J., 23
CODASYL, 352
Codd, E. F., 352, 373
Coffron, James W., 24
Cohen, J. A., 23
Color display, 72
Column insertion (1-2-3), 290
COMMAND.COM, 90, 116
Command-driven interface, 44
Comma-Separated Values (CSV), 269
Comment field, 334
Commodore Business Machines, Inc., 10
Commodore Pet, 9–10
Common carriers, 495
Communications module (desk organizer), 428
Communications software, 33
Compaq Computer Corporation, 35, 36, 73
CompuServe, 515
Computer Associates, 463
Computer Associates, Inc., 407, 441
Computer Decisions, 21, 25
Computer Products International, 463
Computer Systems Design, 363
Computer Systems News, 21
Concurrency, 404
Connolly, Edward S., 86
Conover, W. J., 381
Console Command Processor (CCP), 90
Contents format (spreadsheet), 258
Context Management Systems, 408
Context MBA, 408–409
Control bus, 57
Control panel (spreadsheet), 243
Conversion, 553
Cook, Curtis R., 24
COPY (DOS command), 41, 120–121
Copying formulas (1-2-3), 298
COPY (1-2-3), 249
Cordata Computer Corporation, 36
Cortesi, David E., 86
Coward, Robert, 540
CP/M, 39, 95
CPU, 27
Crabb, Don, 490
Crash conversion, 553–554
Cray Research, Inc., 8
Cray II Supercomputer, 8
CREATE (dBASE III Plus), 377
Critical path, 436
Cromemco, 463
CRT, 27, 30
CSMA/CD, 534
Cullinet, 408
Cummings, Bryan, 24
Cursor, 44, 75
Cursor anchoring (spreadsheet), 245
Cursor movement, 142
Cursor pointing (spreadsheet), 245
Curtin, Dennis P., 23
Customer invoice, 469
Customer statement, 469
Cybernetics/MBS, 463

Dahmke, Mark, 115
Daisy-wheel printers, 75
Darnell, Leonard, 454
Data base, 12, 350
Data base management systems, 14, 16, 34, 320
Data bus, 57
Data capture and transfer utility, 428
Data communications, 493
Data compression programs, 111
Data dictionary, 358
Data files, 32
Data independence, 351
Data input (flatfile), 330
Data integrity, 351
Data Interchange Format (DIF), 269
Datamation, 21, 25
Data processing, 5
Datapro Research Corporation, 23
Data protection programs, 111
Data redundancy, 329, 351
Data security, 351
Date, C.J., 373
DATE (DOS command), 41
Date field, 334
Date stamp, 39
Date and time utilities, 111
Davis, Frederic E., 24
dBASE III Plus, 358, 359, 366, 369, 374–390
Decision Aide, 450
Decision Manager, 408
Decision Support Software, Inc., 450
Decision support system generators, 446
Decision support systems, 446
DEC VAX11–780 minicomputer, 7
Dedicated server, 535
Dedicated word processors, 130–131
Default settings, 47
Default values (DBMS), 360
DELETE (1-2-3), 250
Deleting records, 330, 338
Delphi, 515
Demodulation, 502
Dependent variables, 232
Derfler, Frank, 540
Designer Software, 463
Desk organizer, 423
Desktop computer, 6, 34
Desktop Computing, 21, 25
Desqview, 409
DEST Corporation, 151
Detached keyboards, 152
Detailed aging report, 475
Determinant field, 364
Device allocation programs, 110
Device drivers, 32
Device status programs, 110
Dickinson, John, 342, 540
DIF files, 396, 404
Digital Equipment Corporation, 7, 137
Digital Marketing Corporation, 441
Digital Research, Inc., 401, 409
Digital signals, 532–533
Digitizer, 399–400
DIR (DOS command), 40, 95
Direct-connect modem, 504
Directives, 33
Direct search, 331–332
Disk access method controllers, 111
Disk-based word processor, 139
Disk buffer, 69
DISKCOPY (DOS command), 119
Disk format, 93
Disk format designators, 110
Disk formatter, 110
Disk recovery programs, 110
Disk server, 535
Display format (spreadsheet), 258
Displays, 71
DisplayWrite 3, 183
Distributed computing, 523
Distributed server, 536
Dollars and Sense, 482
Dologite, D. G., 23
DOS, 38
Dot-matrix character box, 71
Dow Jones News/Retrieval, 513, 515
Downloading a file, 511
DSSG, 448
Duaphinais, Bill, 454

Dunn, Robert J., 455
Duty cycle, 78
Dvorak, John, 554, 573

Earth Data Corporation, 441
EDIT (dBASE III Plus), 382
Editing during print, 142
Editing features, 142
Editing records, 338
Editing records (DBMS), 367
Editing the worksheet (1-2-3), 298
Edwards, Ken, 454
EGA display, 74
Electric Desk, 408
Electronic mail, 12, 523
Electronic phone, 523
Electronic spreadsheet, 218
Eliason, A. L., 491
Embedded-command word processor, 137
ENIAC, 11
Enter Computer, 402
Entry area, 244
ERASE (DOS command), 41
ES/P ADVISOR, 447
Ettlin, Walter, 115
Event, 434
Ewing, David Paul, 277, 411
Excel, 218
Execucom Systems Corporation, 231, 450
Expanded memory cards, 58
Expansion slots, 57
EXPERT, 447
Expert Choice, 450
Expert Software International, Ltd., 447
Expert system, 17
Expert system shells, 442
Expert Systems International, 447
Expert/Ease, 447
Export capability, 332
Export capability (DBMS), 361
EXT/ACK, 509
Extracting (spreadsheet), 269

Feldmann, Peter, 540
Fiber optics, 527–528
Field, 321
File comparison programs, 110
File handling, 142
File management system, 320
File restructure capability, 333
File server system, 526
File transfer programs, 110
Filter, 97
Financial modeling programs, 230
Finkel, LeRoy, 24
Fischer, Brian, 402
Fixed costs, 434
Fixed-price contract, 544
Fixed record length, 370
Flatfile, 335
Flatfile manager, 321
Flexibility (DBMS), 351
Floating-point coprocessor, 69
Floppy disks, 61
Footers, 142
Footnote programs, 145
Form, 335
FORMAT, 116–118
Formula, 219
Forrester, Jay, 454
Forsyth, Richard, 455
FORTH, 108
Forward reference, 227
Frankston, Robert, 219
Freedman, Eric, 490
Freiling, Michael J., 373
Frequency division multiplexing, 529
Friction-feed, 75
Friedman, Daniel, 10
Fritz, James S., 541
FTG Data Systems, 399
Full-duplex, 506
Function, 219
Fylstra, Dan, 219

Gantt chart, 437–438
Garland Pathfinder, 441
Garland Publishing, Inc., 441
Gateway server, 535
GEM Draw, 401
General ledger (G/L), 457–458, 460
General Research Corporation, 447
Generating reports, 339
Generating reports (DBMS), 368
Gigabyte, 66
Glossbrenner, Alfred, 520, 548–549, 573
Goal seeking, 230, 447
Golden Gate, 408
Goldhaber, Nat, 540
Goldstein, Larry Joel, 23
Gordon, Phillip, 411
GOTO key (1-2-3), 291
The Grafix Partner, 397
Grammar checkers, 144–145
Graphics editors, 396
Grauer, Robert T., 23
Great Plains Software, 463
Grigonis, Richard, 18–19, 23
Grogono, Peter, 115
Guttman, Michael K., 491

Half-duplex, 505
Hallam, James, 23
Hallam, Stephen F., 23
Hand-held computer, 37
Handshaking, 82
Hansen, Bob, 24
Hanson, Jay, 373
Hard copy, 27
Hard-disk backup programs, 110
Hard-disk controller cards, 58
Hard disks, 63
Hardware, 8
Harmon, Paul, 454
Harvard Software, Inc., 441
Harvard Total Project Manager, 441
Hatch, Richard A., 24
Haueisen, William D., 491
Haugdahl, J. Scott, 541
Hayes Microcomputer Products, Inc., 58
Hayes-Roth, Frederick, 454
Head crash, 64
Headers, 142
Headings, 141
Heiser, Dick, 23
Help facility, 111
Help menus, 136
Hercules Computer Technology, 58
Hess, Wilmot N., 381
Hiding cells, 266
Hierarchical DBMS, 357
Hierarchy of operators, 260
Hogan, Thom, 115
Holt, Jack A., 277
HOMEBASE, 432
Home computer, 6
Horizontal window (spreadsheet), 254
Horrock, David, 86
Houston Instruments, Inc., 402
Hoxie, Gib, 402
Hyphenation, 180, 182

IBM Personal System/2 Model 50, 6
IBM Writing Assistant, 183
Icon, 100
Icon-driven interface, 44
Ideassociates, Inc., 58
IFPS/Personal, 450
Imigit Plus, 397
Import capability, 332
Import capability (DBMS), 361
Indenting, 141
Independent variables, 232
Indexed-sequential search, 331–332
Indexing files (DBMS), 367
Indexing records, 338
Index and sort (DBMS), 360
Inference Corporation, 447
Inference engine, 443
Informatics General, 408
Information Storage, Inc., 67
Information utility, 511
Infoworld, 21, 25
Innovative Software, 408
Input/Output cards, 58
INSERT (1-2-3), 250
Insert mode, 142
INSIGHT, 447
Installable device drivers, 98
Installation, 471
Installation program, 149
Instruction set, 92
Integrated-7, 408

Integrated software, 403
Integrating environment software, 407
Intel Corp., 58, 59, 60
Intellicorp, 447
Interface device, 500
Internal RAM buffers, 79
International Business Machines Corp., 6, 7, 36, 57, 130, 409
International MicroSystems, 463
Interpretive prompting, 248
InteSoft, 408
Intuit, 408
Inventory, 458, 486
Inventory management systems, 486–487
Inventory systems, 486
Isshiki, Koichiro R., 23
IT Software, 408

Jane, 408
Javelin, 272, 450
Javelin Software Corporation, 450
Jazz, 408
Jobs, Steve, 9
Johnston, Randolph, 23
Join operator, 354
Joystick, 79
Justification, 180, 182

Kepner-Tregoe, Inc., 450
KERMIT, 510
Kernighan, Brian, 115
Kerning, 180, 182
Keyboards, 74
Key definitions programs, 110
Key field, 324
King, David, 454
Kitts, K. D., 491
Klooster, Dale H., 491
Knowledge acquisition engine, 444
Knowledge base, 442
Knowledge Engineering Environment (KEE), 447
Knowledge Engineering System (KES), 447
Knowledge Index, 515
Koala Technologies, 141
Krajewski, Rich, 342
Krasnoff, Barbara, 342
Kroenke, David, 373
Kruglinski, David, 373
Kurta, 400

Label, 218
Label entry formats (1-2-3), 288
LaFore, Robert, 115
Language translators, 89,102–110
LAN shell, 537
Laptop computer, 37
Layered, Inc., 463
Leading, 180, 182
Leased line, 495
LeBlond, Geoffrey, 277, 411
Le Carre, John, 381
Left margin, 161
Lenat, Douglas B., 454
Letterspacing, 181, 182
Level 5 Research, 447
Leventhal, Lance A., 23
Lewis, Theodore G., 24
Libraries, 167
Lieberman, Philip, 86
Light pen, 398
Lima, Tony, 342
Line, 160
Linespacing, 141
LIST (dBASE III Plus), 383, 385
List processing, 132–133
Local Area Network, 494, 497, 522–540
Local area network cards, 58
Logical field, 334
Logical operators, 263
Logic-seeking, 79
LOOPS, 447
Lotus Development Corp., 408, 432
Lotus 1-2-3, 220, 222, 243, 244, 246–247, 251, 262–264, 278–311, 343–348, 412–418
Lotus 1-2-3 access system, 282
Lu, Cary, 411
Lumena, 397

M.1, 447
Mace, Scott, 342
Macintosh desktop, 100
Macintosh Plus, 6
Macros (spreadsheets), 266
Macros (word processing), 167, 170
MacWorld, 21
MacWrite, 172, 183, 187
Madron, Thomas, 24
Mainframe computer, 7
Major on-line services, 515
Managing Your Money, 482
Manual recalculation, 227
Margins, 141
Markoff, John, 411
Martin, James, 373
Martin Marietta Data Systems, 408
Maxtor Corporation, 64
McGlynn, Daniel R., 24
McLeod, Raymond, Jr., 24
McNichols, Charles W., 24
McWilliams, Peter A., 24, 381
Memory-based word processor, 139
Memory map, 30
Memory resident utilities, 422, 430–432
Menu-driven interface, 44
Menu line (1-2-3), 244
Menu types, 136
Merge printing, 177
Merging (spreadsheets), 269
Message, 507–510
Metro, 432
Michie, Donald, 455
Micro Architect, 463
Microcomputer Consultants, 463
Microdata, 463
MicroGANTT, 441
Microjustification, 79
Micro-to-mainframe Link Cards, 58
Micropert O. Version 3.2, 441
Microprocessor, 6, 30, 58
Microsoft Excel, 218, 223, 254, 258, 271, 312–318
Microsoft, Inc., 407–409, 441
Microsoft Multiplan, 270
Microsoft Project, 441
Microsoft Windows, 406
Microsoft Word, 136, 138, 173, 183, 184
Microsource, 463
Microtek, 140
Microtek Lab, Inc., 81
Microtrak, 441
Mier, Edwin E., 541
Migent, Inc., 408
Milestone, 441
Milestones, 434
Miller, Merl, 491
Minch, Robert, 454
MindSight, 231, 450
Minicomputer, 6
Mini-Micro Systems, 25
MITS Altair, 10
Mnemonics, 136
Modem, 37, 502
Modem cards, 58
Modulation, 502
Mosaic Software, 408
Motherboard, 56
Motorola Corporation, 60
Mountain Computer, Inc., 65, 70
Mouse Systems Corporation, 28, 140, 397
MOVE (1-2-3), 249
MS-DOS, 38, 88, 96–98, 116–125
MS-DOS tutorial, 116
MTBF (Mean Time Between Failures), 78
MTTR (Mean Time To Repair), 78
Multifunction cards, 58
Multimate, 147, 150, 183, 186
Multimate Advantage, 183, 185
Multiplan, 220, 244, 271
Multiple-copy printing, 142
Multiple-file printing, 142
Multiple type fonts, 79
Multitasking Operating systems, 95
Multiuser systems, 95

Naisbitt, John, 380, 520, 540
Nanosecond, 17
Natural language processing, 362
Natural recalculation order, 227
Naylor, Chris, 455
NEC Home Electronics, 37, 72
NEC Information Systems, Inc., 80

Negoita, Constantin Virgil, 454
Network DBMS, 357
Networked single-user system, 526
Network star topology with
multiprocessors, 526
Neuron Data, Inc., 447
NewsNet, 515
Nexis, 513, 515
NEXPERT, 447
Node, 520
North America Mica, Inc., 441
North American Software, 463
Norton, Peter, 24
Notepad (electronic), 425
Noumenon, 408
Novation, Inc., 58
Novell netware, 537
Novogrodsky, Seth, 24
Numeric field, 334

Object code, 544
O'Brien, James A., 24
The Office, 25
Office automation, 12
Omicron Software, 441
On-line thesauruses, 171
On-line tutorials, 552
Open Access II, 408
Open-item statement, 471
Open Systems, Inc., 463
Operating system, 32
Operating systems, 88, 89–101
Operating system version number, 92
OPS5, 447
OPS5e, 447
Optical character recognition, 151
Optical disk storage, 65
Orchid Technology, Inc., 58
Originate mode, 504
Orphans, 174
Osborne, Adam, 24, 86
Outline processors, 171
Overlays, 112
Overwrite mode, 142

Packet format, 533
Packet switching, 496
Packet switching network, 498
Page breaks (word processing), 140, 142
Page composition, 180
Page length, 161
Page offset, 172
Page-oriented word processor, 142
Pagination, 174
Palm rest, 152
Paradise, 58
Parallel conversion, 554
Parallel interface, 501
Parallel port, 82
Parallel transmission, 501
Parity bit, 507

Pascal, 105
Past-due notice, 470, 477
Past-due report, 476
Pattern recognition, 81
Payroll, 458
PBX exchange LAN, 528–529
PC Magazine, 21, 25
PC NET (Orchid), 536
PC Paint, 397
PC Tech Journal, 21, 25
PC Technologies Inc., 58
PC Week, 25
PC World, 21, 25
PC Write, 186
Peachtree Software, 408, 463
Peltu, Malcolm, 86
Perfect Software, Inc., 407
Peripheral communications, 499, 517
Peripherals, 27
Personal computer, 6
Personal Computer Age, 25
Personal Computer Support Group, 58
Personal Computing, 21, 25
Personal Consultant, 447
PERT chart, 437
PFS:Professional Write, 183
PFS:Write, 183
PGA display, 74
Phone field, 334
Pica, 181
PICK operating system, 88
Picoseconds, 17
Pilot conversion, 554
Pipe, 97
Pixel, 71, 399
Planar board, 56
Plantrax, 441
Plotters, 401
Plus Development Corporation, 65
Pocket computer, 37
Point, 181
Point-size, 180, 182
Pollack, Lawrence, 24
Polytron Corp., 432
PolyWindows Desk, 432
Poole, Lon, 491
Popular Computing, 25
Popular Programs, Inc., 432
Pop-Up DeskSet Plus, 432
Pop-up menus, 405
Port, 27, 500
Porter, Leslie R., 23
Posting, 460, 473–474
Pournelle, Jerry, 554
Power bus, 57
Predicasts F&S Indexes, 514
Presentation graphics, 396
Present value analysis, 564
Primary storage, 30
Primavera Project Planner, 441
Primavera Systems, Inc., 441

Print queue managers, 111
Print queues, 176
Printed circuit board, 30, 56
Printed circuit card, 56
Printers, 75
Printer server, 535
PRINTGRAPH (1-2-3), 416–417
Printing the worksheet, 257–259, 268,
303–306
Procedural language, 358
Procurement specifications, 544
Prodigy Systems, 463
Product families, 406
Profit and loss statement, 464
Program debuggers, 111
Program files, 32
Project control, 432
Project management software, 432
Project operator, 354
Project planning, 432
Promotheus Products, Inc., 58
Prompt area (10203), 244
Proportional spacing, 79
Protected mode, 99
Protecting cells, 266
Protocol, 507, 508–510
Pull-down menus, 405
Pulse signal, 502
Purdon, Jack, 24

QMS, Inc., 80
Quadram Corp., 29, 58
Quarterdeck Office Systems, 409
Qubie Distributing, 58
Query capability (DBMS), 360
Query-driven interface, 44
Query language, 352
QWERTY keyboard, 75

Radio Shack, 463
Radio Shack Advertising, 9, 35
RAM access time, 68
RAM disk emulators, 110
RAM disks, 65
RAM (random-access memory), 59
Randal Davis, 454
Random Access memory, 30
Range checking (DBMS), 359
Raster-scan display, 400
Record, 321
Record locking, 361
References, 233
Reflex, 332
Registers, 59
Reitman, Walter, 455
Relation, 357
Relational algebra, 354
Relational data base management system,
356
Relational operators, 263
Relative cell referencing, 253

Remote processing, 494, 497
Removable Magnetic Disk Storage, 65
RENAME (DOS command), 41
Repeater, 535
REPORT (dBASE III Plus), 390
Request for Proposal (RFP), 559–560
Resource leveling, 436
Resources, 432
Rettig, Tom, 373
Reverse line-feed, 79
RFP (request for proposal), 559–560
RGB monitor, 72
Rifkin, Stanley Mark, 496
Right margin, 161
Rights, 545
Ring topology, 524–525
Ritchie, Dennis, 115
RMS-II, 441
Roberts, Ed, 10
Rollover, 74
ROM (read-only memory), 59
Rosch, Winn L., 540
Ross, Steven C., 277
Rotational delay, 63
Routing server, 535
Row insertion (1-2-3), 290
Rutter, Andy, 115

S.1, 447
Sales-by-salesperson report, 478
Sargent, Murray III, 24
Scanners, 81
Schuchardt Software Systems, 408
Screen-driven interface, 44
Screen-formatted word processor, 137
Scrolling, 159
Seagate Corporation, 64
Search keys, 331
Search programs, 110
Searching for records, 331
Searching for records (DBMS), 367
Search and replace, 142
Search and replace options, 143
Secondary storage, 27, 31
Security, 360
Security (DBMS), 360
Select operator, 354
Sequential search, 331–332
Serial interface, 501
Serial port, 82
Serial transmission, 501
SeRIES-PC, 447
Shapiro, Ezra, 342
Shaw, Donald R., 24
Shell, 97
Sheppard Software Company, 441
Shoch, John F., 540
Shoemaker, Richard L., 24
Shrayer, Mark, 130
Sidekick, 429–430
Sideways (Funk Software), 236–237
Sigel, Hillel, 24
Silver, Gerald A., 86
Simplex, 505
Single-user systems, 94
Sinper Corp., 450
Slack, 436
Small Business Computers, 21
Small Business Systems Group, 463
Small Systems World, 25
Smart series, 408
Soft copy, 27
Softrend, 408
SoftTrak Systems, 441
Software A & E, 447
Software Arts, 432
Software license agreement, 555
Software News, 25
Software piracy, 554–555
Software Products International, 408
Software Publishing Corp, 407
Software warranties, 550–551
Solgerg, Gregory, 115
Sondar, Norman E., 24
Sony Corporation of America, 67
Sordillo, Donald A., 24
Sorting files (DBMS), 367
Sorting records, 331, 338
Sort keys, 331
Sort programs, 110
The Source, 515
Source code, 544
Space, 160
Specialized common carriers, 496
Spelling checkers, 143–145, 170
Spotlight, 432
Spreadsheet functions, 261–263
Spreadsheet internal operations, 225–226
Spreadsheet operators, 260
Spreadsheets, 14, 15–16, 34
Spreadsheet speed, 226
SRI International, 447
Stafford, Irvin, 23
Start bit(s), 507
Star topology, 524–525
Status line, 243
Status lines (word processing), 140
STB Systems Inc., 58
Stiegler, Mark, 24
Stop bit(s), 507
Structured programming, 104–105
Structured Systems Group, 463
Style checkers, 144–145
Style sheets, 172
Subscripts, 142
Substring search, 360
Sullivan, David R., 24
SuperCalc, 220
SuperCalc³, 252, 262
SuperCalc4, 274
Supercomputer, 8
SuperProject Plus, 441
Superscripts, 142
Swapping, 112
Sweet-P Plotter, 402
Symphony, 408
Synchronized window (spreadsheet), 254
Synchronous communication, 507
System diskette, 38
System software, 88
Systems Plus, 463
Systems software, 27, 32
System tracks generators, 110
System unit, 56

Table construction operations, 354
TECMAR Inc., 58
Teknowledge, Inc., 447
Telecommunications, 502
Telecommuting, 494
Template, 222
Templates, 265, 266
Terminal, 27
Terminal emulation, 511
Texas Instruments, 447
Text field, 334
Text files, 32
Text-mapped display, 400
Text movement, 142
Tiling, 405
TIME (DOS command), 41
Time field, 334
Time-sharing system, 527
Time stamp, 39
TIMM, 447
TM/1, 450
Today's Office, 25
Toggle, 162
Token, 524
Top margin, 160
Topology, 524
Touch screens, 81
Track ball, 79
Tracking, 180, 182
Tractor-feed, 75
Traister, Robert J., 86
Transaction journal, 465, 475
Transceiver, 534
Transfer rate, 63
Transitive dependency, 364
Transportable computer, 34
TRS-80 Model 1, 9
Tuple, 357
Tutor (1-2-3), 279
Twisted pair wire, 526
Type-ahead, 75
TYPE (DOS command), 41

UCSD p-system, 88
UNIX operating system, 88, 96
Updating records, 330
Uploading a file, 511
USE (dBASE III Plus), 380

User interface, 33
User interface (DBMS), 357
Utilities, 33
Utility programs, 89,110

Validation, 234
Validation (DBMS), 359
Value, 218
Value-added carriers, 496
Variable costs, 434
Variable record length, 370
Veit, Stanley S., 86
Vendor list, 482
Verac, Inc., 447
Verification, 234
Vertical window (spreadsheet), 254
Video attributes, 93
Video cards, 58
Videogram Version 3.0, 397
Virtual memory, 111
VisiCalc, 219
VisiCorp, 441
VisiSchedule, 441
Voice recognition, 152

Wait state, 68
Waite, Mitchell, 115
Warm boot, 38
Warner Software, Inc. 432
Warren, Carl, 491
Waterman, Donald, 454
Weiss & Kulikowski, 447
Wide area network, 493, 494–496
Widows, 174
Wilcox, David L., 411
Wilkenson, Barry, 86
Windows, 405
Wolff, Terris B., 24
WordPerfect, 137, 149, 183, 184, 185, 202–215
WordPerfect Corp., 432
WordPerfect Library, 432
WordPerfect tutorial, 202
Word processing, 5, 14, 34, 129
Word-processing display features, 139
Word processor, 6
Word-wrap, 142
WordStar, 136, 138, 147, 149, 150, 173, 191–201
WordStar tutorial, 191
Worksheet, 217
Worksheet navigation (1–2-3), 286
Worksheet window, 243
Work station, 6
WORMs, 66
Wozniak, Steve, 9
Write-protect notch, 49
Writing tablet, 399–400

X-ON/X-OFF, 509
Xenix compatibility, 99
Xerox Palo Alto Research Centers, 447
XMODEM, 510
XyWrite III, 183

Your Personal Net Worth, 482

Zenith Data Systems, 37
Zip code field, 334

Trademarks (continued)

SideKick is a registered trademark of Borland International, Inc.
SuperCalc3, SuperCalc4, and SuperProject Plus are registered trademarks of Computer Associates International.
The Source is a service mark of Source Telecomputing Corporation, a subsidiary of The Reader's Digest Association, Inc.
TRS–80 is a registered trademark of the Radio Shack Division of Tandy Corporation.
UNIX is a registered trademark of AT&T Bell Laboratories.
WordPerfect is a registered trademark of WordPerfect Corporation.
WordStar is a registered trademark of MicroPro International Corporation.

Photo Credits

Contents **ix** Courtesy of West Publishing Company; **x** *(top)* Courtesy of Radio Shack Advertising; **x** *(bottom)* Courtesy of Plus Development Corporation; **xi** *(top)* Courtesy of Digital Research Corporation; **xi** *(bottom)* Courtesy of Zenith Data Systems; **xii** Tom Tracy Photography; **xiii** Courtesy of Microsoft Corporation; **xiv** Courtesy of Lotus Development Corporation; **xv** Courtesy of Borland International; **xvi** Courtesy of Ashton-Tate; **xvii** *(top)* Courtesy of Polaroid Corporation; **xvii** *(bottom)* Courtesy of Microsoft Corporation; **xviii** Used with express permission of Layered, Inc.; **xix** *(top)* Courtesy of Hayes Corporation; **xix** *(bottom)* Courtesy of Jit Fu Lim; **xx** Courtesy of ComputerLand

Part openers **2** Courtesy of International Business Machines Corporation; **126** Courtesy of Apple Computer, Inc.; **420** Courtesy of International Business Machines Corporation

Tutorials **191** Courtesy of MicroPro International Corporation; **202** Courtesy of WordPerfect Corporation; **278** Courtesy of Lotus Development Corporation; **312** Courtesy of Microsoft Corporation; **343** Courtesy of Lotus Development Corporation; **374** Courtesy of Ashton-Tate; **412** Courtesy of Lotus Development Corporation